Dearest Simon,

I almost forgot this!

Lots of love

Mia xx

TOTTENHAM HOTSPUR

ILLUSTRATED HISTORY 1882–1995

AUDERE·EST·FACERE

TOTTENHAM HOTSPUR

THE OFFICIAL

ILLUSTRATED HISTORY 1882–1995

PHIL SOAR · PREFACE BY GARY MABBUTT · FOREWORD BY ALAN SUGAR

HAMLYN

ACKNOWLEDGEMENTS
The statistics for the first two editions were prepared by
Ray Spiller, Chairman of the Association of Football
Statisticians, with the late Morely Farror and Alex Wilson.
The statistics for the years from 1985–1995 were prepared by
Andy Porter.

Original design by Brian Thomas,
additional design by Leigh Jones.

Additional text and contributions from Pat Collins, Jonathan
Culverhouse, Martin Tyler and Richard Widdows.

Editors: Peter Arnold and Adam Ward
Picture Research: Maria Gibbs
Production Controller: Nicky Connell

EDITORS' NOTE
The editors would like to thank John Fennelly for his
assistance in helping Gary Mabbutt put his thoughts about
Spurs into words so skillfully, to Martin Oliver for his
assistance with the new documentary photography for this
edition, to John Moulding, Ashley Weller and Andy Porter for
their co-operation at various stages of the book's production.

First published in Great Britain by Hamlyn Publishing in 1982
under the title *And the Spurs Go Marching On . . .*

This edition published in 1995 by Hamlyn an imprint of Reed
Consumer Books Limited, Michelin House, 81 Fulham Road,
London SW3 6RB and Auckland, Melbourne, Singapore and
Toronto

ISBN 0 600 58706 1

A CIP catalogue record for this book is available
from the British Library

PHOTOGRAPHIC ACKNOWLEDGEMENTS
All pictures by Action Images / Tottenham Football Club except the following:

Action Images 185 top, 185 centre, 185 bottom, 195 top, 197 bottom, 199 top left, 200, 201, 202 bottom,
207 bottom left, 208 top, 209 top, 213 top, 214, 215 top, 215 centre, 216 top, 217 top, 221 top, 221 centre, 221 bottom, 223 top, 225 top, 228 top, 228 bottom; Mick Alexander / Sportsimage 131 top, 133,
137, 145, 151, 155, 175; David Allen 25, 34; Allsport 6, 160, 223 bottom, 225 bottom, 226, 227 top;
Danny Blanchflower 73, 76, 77, 78, 79, 82, 83; Hedley Bull 10, 14; Carleton Photographic Services 131
bottom; Central Press 61, 89, 92, 93, 134, 169; Colorsport 42, 43, 117, 128, 157, 159, 183 top, 217 bottom, 219 centre, 219 bottom, 219 top, 224, 227 bottom; Fox Photos 63, 64, 65, 75, 98; Ray Green 70,
71, 121, 125, 156; Hulton Deutsch Collection 20, 27, 36, 37, 39, 40, 41, 44, 45, 47, 50, 51, 53, 54, 56,
57, 58, 172; Keystone 67, 92; Mark Leech 143; Marshall Cavendish 162; Popperfoto 69, 84, 85, 96, 97,
100, 102, 103, 104, 105; Professional Sport 151 bottom; Press Association 104, 105, 119; Sport &
General 80, 105, 114, 115; Sunday Times Newspaper 186 top; Syndication International 87, 94, 95, 100,
103, 108, 110, 111, 112, 116, 122, 126, 134, 135, 136; Bob Thomas 155; Tottenham Hotspur F.C. 8,
174, 178.

STW 9, 10, 12 top, 17, 18, 19, 20, 21, 22, 23, 24, 26, 28, 29, 30, 31, 32, 33, 35, 38, 39, 45, 47, 48, 49,
59, 60, 66, 80, 89, 90, 91, 93, 94, 95, 107, 138, 140, 141, 144, 146, 147, 148, 149, 152, 153, 171, 172

Contents

Preface
by Gary Mabbutt

Tradition plays its part in making any Club great and there is no doubt that Tottenham Hotspur possesses that vital quality in abundance. Money, success, influence . . . they are all obviously important but it is tradition that makes a Club something special.

There will always be an exceptional aura about White Hart Lane that lives on despite the stadium developments of recent years. Indeed, the current new look to our famous ground has retained the unique atmosphere and I still receive a special 'buzz' whenever I drive through those black and gold gates.

I still recall how arriving here sent a shiver down my spine when I transferred from Bristol Rovers back in the summer of 1982. I had just turned 21 when I was invited up to London for pre-season training – the majestic presence of the place struck me from the beginning.

And then there was the dressing room! Not the ambience nor the fixtures and fittings - this time it was the quality of the players, with so many household names that I was quite staggered. Spurs had just retained the FA Cup and were regulars in European competition at the time. The team, led by Steve Perryman, reflected that success and ambition: Glenn Hoddle, Ossie Ardiles, Steve Archibald, Ray Clemence, Garth Crooks, Graham Roberts, Tony Galvin, Ricky Villa . . . there was quality and strength in depth in every department.

No wonder then that I was to adopt a utility role and play in just about every outfield position before settling in midfield and then moving back to central defence. And how apt, playing in that company, that my Spurs debut should come at Wembley! It was the Club's Centenary season, and since then, there have been many glorious years. Throughout them all, that distinctive sense of tradition has perpetually shone through.

The history of the Club is so important to everyone at White Hart Lane, and I quickly became aware of Spurs' proud past. When I arrived, there had already been seven FA Cup triumphs, plus the glorious 'Double' of 1961 (the year of my birth). Spurs were the first non-League side to win the Cup; the first British club to win a major European competition; the first to win the League Cup twice; the first English club to play in three major European Finals . . . the list of 'firsts' goes on and on, making you feel both honoured and under pressure from the moment that you signed!

From a personal point of view, I have achieved many milestones and as I have reached each of them I have looked back with pride. Playing in Europe - and helping Spurs lift the UEFA Cup in my second season - made me reflect back on those famous 'Euro Nights' at White Hart Lane and we've certainly had a few more since! I was only a baby when we won the European Cup Winners' Cup in 1963 but the individuals in Bill Nicholson's great side were known throughout the country in the years that followed and will long be revered and remembered. It was humbling to follow in the footsteps of such greats as Danny Blanchflower, John White, Dave Mackay and so many others and even more incredible when you look through the pages of this book and appreciate the great names associated with the Club since those early days more than a century ago.

It was the same when I was appointed captain in 1987. I felt immense pride when I considered the marvellous Spurs captains who had gone before me. And when I led the side to that record eighth FA Cup win of 1991, I was so aware of my predecessors who had climbed those Wembley steps in a Spurs kit to claim that same elusive prize. And yes, before the letters arrive, I *am* aware that our first two FA Cup Final wins were not at Wembley!

Our Wembley win over Nottingham Forest was all the more rewarding for the fact that we had lost 2-3 to Coventry City just four years before when I had scored at both ends in yet another final that had gone to extra time. So to play such an important part in our winner over Forest, when the unfortunate Des Walker conceded an own goal as I challenged for the ball, went a long way towards helping me forget that Coventry agony. I also felt so sorry for my England team mate Des because I obviously knew exactly how he felt.

Since then there has unfortunately been a great deal of trauma and uncertainty off the field that has seized the spotlight in this corner of North London. But Chairman Alan Sugar has steadied the ship, bringing in manager Gerry Francis to give us fresh impetus and optimism.

So having started this preface with the word 'tradition,' I now conclude with 'optimism.' We again have a team packed with internationals and the ability to succeed. As with all Spurs fans, my dream is the Championship, the ultimate accolade to ability, consistency, courage, stamina . . . plus a bit of good fortune.

This book represents the 'Ghost of Seasons Past.' The present and future promise just as much . . . and more.

Foreword

by Alan Sugar

As Chairman of Tottenham Hotspur I am delighted at this opportunity to play even a cameo role in the compilation of this important work because of my immense pride in this great club.

Such historical productions are important because clubs such as Spurs have almost an immeasurable history and that journey through time has helped shape the club into the institution that we have today.

As with all aspects of life, we can understand the present that much more by appreciating the past and the pages that follow are our tribute to those who have gone before and played a part, no matter how small, in giving the name Tottenham Hotspur the international perspective that it currently enjoys.

Of course there is another aspect of this book – to highlight the success that has marked our history and to unashamedly wallow in the memories of cups and goals, great games and great players. We have so much to be proud of and true Spurs fans can enjoy this nostalgia in the certain knowledge that I am determined that such glories will again be re-visited before too long.

Tradition is the quality that emanates from this book and so few clubs can claim that title. We have it in abundance at White Hart Lane and our fortunes are followed in the hearts of so many who are unable, for so many reasons, to actually watch our games.

We appreciate that we have an immense family of loyal supporters throughout the world and once this club is in your blood you never change. As a youngster, I still remember with clarity my father bringing me to watch Spurs at White Hart Lane and from that moment this was my club.

All my family and friends were Spurs fans and I am delighted to say that that passion continues today.

And this club continues to belong to everyone because, as I have said before, I see myself as a trustee of an institution that is not set in bricks and mortar but in the hearts and souls of all those who share my devotion.

True, it must also be a business because without that logic, attention and application, it could all tragically cease to be. But at 3pm on a cold winter's afternoon there is an intangible wisp of enchantment that settles on us all – and I could not now live without it.

Enjoy these pages. This is the story of our club. A club built on the dreams of little boys under a gas lamp in the High Road just outside our main gates.

Inevitably so much has changed and even now we continue the work to make our stadium second to none and a fitting home to lead us into the next century. Our optimism burns as brightly as ever – and may that never be extinguished.

Alan Sugar.
White Hart Lane.
June, 1995.

Early Days

If you have been watching Tottenham Hotspur play on some sunny September afternoon and are leaving White Hart Lane, pause a while. Instead of heading for your car, or for White Hart Lane station, turn left outside the ground and walk south down the High Road towards the City. Not far, just until you reach the traffic light on the corner of Park Lane. Stop there, and try to imagine that scene as it was one hundred years ago. Imagine, if you can, a group of perhaps a dozen or so boys in their early teens gathered there. Of course, in those days it would have been a delicate gas-lit lamp and not the sturdy traffic signal that we see today. Underneath it were not badly dressed boys, for they all came from relatively good homes around Northumberland Park. Not poorly educated boys either, for nearly all of them attended either St John's School (a local Scottish

Presbyterian institution run by a Mr Cameron) or Tottenham Grammar School, now part of The Somerset Comprehensive School on White Hart Lane.

In the way of boys of all nationalities and ages, they would have answered to two nick-names – the 'Northumberland Pups' or the 'Saints' (after their school). The local rivals, who were soon to resent their pretensions in running a formal football club, were the 'High Road Cads', sons of shopkeepers on the main street, and 'Barkers' Bulldogs', from a rival school apparently run by a Mr Barker.

The Pups had probably been playing cricket down by the River Lea on Captain Delano's farm. He was the uncle of two of the boys under that lamp-post – the Thompson brothers – and he didn't mind them and many of their friends playing cricket on his land. If he, or any of their parents, were aware of the name they

The earliest picture of a Spurs team, probably taken before the club's first ever competitive match, a London Cup tie against St Albans on Saturday 17 October 1885. The team was (back row l to r) W. C. Tyrell, F. Lovis, Jack Jull, John Ripsher (President), Hedley Bull (who kept this print), Sam Casey and (front row l to r) T. W. Bumberry, R. Amos, Bobby Buckle, Billy Mason, Billy Harston and Frank Cottrell. The team is wearing its new blue and white strip, after Blackburn Rovers.

TOTTENHAM HOTSPUR FOOTBALL CLUB.

(ESTABLISHED 1880.)

PROGRAMME

OF FIRST GRAND

ANNUAL ATHLETIC MEETING

(Under A. A. A. Laws), held in the Grounds of

BRUCE CASTLE, TOTTENHAM,

ON SATURDAY, JUNE 13, 1891,

During Loan and Industrial Exhibition,

Commencing at 3.30 p.m.

OFFICIALS.

Referee (Pink Rosette)—HARRY LOOMAN, Esq. (Hon. Sec. S.C.C.C.A.)

Judges (Blue & White)—A. E. MARTIN, Esq., H. W. MILES, Esq. (Finchley Harriers), H. V. STARBUCK, Esq., J. TURNBULL, Esq., and S. A. MORRIS, Esq. (Tower A.C.)

Clerks of the Course (Red)—Messrs. A. E. BROADBERRY, R. BUCKLE, T. W. BUMBERRY, H. D. CASEY, J. M. DEXTER, F. DEXTER, H. GODDARD, J. C. JULL, W. MASON, A. S. PETTER, E. RUDSTON, H. R. STEPHENS, and F. S. WALFORD.

Starter (White)—F. J. MACKIE, Esq. (Tower A.C.)

Timekeeper (Yellow)—H. H. COOPER, Esq. (Tower A.C.)

Handicappers—Open Events—HARRY LOOMAN, Esq. (S.C.C.C.A.) Members Events—Messrs H. GODDARD (Tower A.C.) and F. G. HATTON.

Sports Committee—Messrs R. BUCKLE, T. W. BUMBERRY, H. D. CASEY, J. C. JULL, F. J. MACKIE, H. R. STEPHENS.

Hon. Sec. Club (Badge)—Mr. R. BUCKLE, White Cottage, White Hart Lane, Tottenham.

Hon. Sec. Sports (Shield)—Mr. F. G. HATTON, 3, Richmond Villas, Park Lane, Tottenham.

PRICE TWOPENCE.

PRINTED BY E. H. CRUSHA, "HERALD" OFFICE, TOTTENHAM.

gave themselves, the Hotspur Cricket Club no doubt they were amused by such airs and graces. September is the time that the cricket season comes to an end, so discussion no doubt turned to what to do during the winter. And in such simple fashion was born one of Britain and the world's greatest soccer clubs.

The boys decided to form a football club to be called, naturally enough, the Hotspur Football Club, and to play to association rather than rugby rules. Despite the fact that the Football Association had been in existence nearly 20 years, there was still no single set of soccer rules, though this was to be rectified within months at the first formal meeting of the four national associations. The date of formation of the Hotspur Football Club is usually given as 5 September 1882, the day

ABOVE: The first pro-gramme known to have been issued by the club, for an athletic meeting in 1891. Note that the date of establishment is given as 1880, almost certainly when the cricket club came into being but two years before football was adopted. RIGHT: Hedley Bull's membership card, dated 17 September 1887. Note that the annual subscription was 7s 6d (37p) and that the club gave its ground as the Marshes. The cards were coloured navy blue and this is thought to be the oldest existing memento of the club.

that subscriptions to the new club were first received. That day was actually a Tuesday.

There were, appropriately, just 11 founder members – E. Beaven, Bobby Buckle (the club's first captain), Fred Dexter, Stuart Leaman (the first goalkeeper), E. Wall, the brothers Anderson (J. and T.), the brothers Casey (L. and Ham who was sometimes nicknamed Sam) and the brothers Thompson (Jack and Peter), whose uncle loaned them that cricket pitch. Another eight members were to join during the year and, as all wanted to play, this was thought more than enough for the time being.

How exact are the date and details of the club's foundation cannot now be determined, but the basic facts were related as late as the mid-twentieth century by Charlie Denyer, who joined the club soon afterwards, and by L. R. Casey, the club's first treasurer. Casey's father had provided the club's first set of goalposts, symbolically painted blue and white, and it was an older Casey brother who had given the club its first ball and had, apparently, been the man responsible for suggesting the name Hotspur for the cricket club.

Harry Hotspur, immortalized in numerous history books and by Shakespeare in Richard II and Henry IV Part I, was the teenage son of the Earl of Northumberland. Sir Henry Percy, to give Hotspur his correct title, died leading rebel forces against the usurper King Henry IV at the battle of Shrewsbury in 1403. Henry IV had come to power just four years before by deposing Richard II, whom he later had killed in Pontefract Castle. The Northumberland family are better known as the Percys, the lords of the Scottish border who dominated northeast England for centuries as if it were their personal kingdom. From their great castles at Alnwick and Warkworth they controlled the main route to Scotland and were arguably the most powerful family in the land after the crown. They came to own lands in North London and part of that area later became known as Northumberland Park.

One of the football club's earliest bases, the YMCA, was called Percy House and they were to use the Northumberland Arms intermittently as a changing room for several years. The lives of the club's founders, then, were regularly touched by the history of the Percys, so what better name for their creation than Hotspur, a name so redolent of youth and glory. We have cause to be grateful to brother Casey for his suggestion. Along with the likes of Sheffield Wednesday and Nottingham Forest, Tottenham Hotspur is one of those romantic names which breaks up the dull litany of Citys, Towns and Uniteds on a Saturday evening.

EARLY MATCHES

The Hotspurs' first serious game was apparently against neighbours Latymer, but it was not until the following season, 1883–84, that their fixtures could really be described as at all formal. By this time they had asked a John Ripsher to place the club on a more permanent footing. Mr Ripsher was a prominent local figure both at All Hallows Parish Church and at the YMCA. Several of the team attended his bible classes and he had helped earlier with the cricket club. Such church connections

ABOVE LEFT: The site of what was once Captain Delano's farm, where the young Hotspurs started playing cricket in 1880. The ground is still marshy and the River Lea is beyond the tree-lined bank in the right distance.

ABOVE: This traffic light, which has replaced the street lamp on the corner of the High Road and Park Lane, now marks the site where the Hotspurs are reputed to have decided to form a soccer club. In the distance are the Red House, their headquarters from 1886 to 1891 and now adorned with a cockerel, and the White Hart pub, from whch the ground draws its name.

were not rare at the time; Everton and Southampton sprang from similar origins. Ripsher used the YMCA as the team's first base and, at what could be called the club's first Annual General Meeting in August 1883, 21 boys turned up.

Among the first rules were that all club members should attend scripture classes at All Hallows Church on Wednesdays, and that a rota should be established to determine which boys should carry the goalposts on Saturdays.

They had carried on playing soccer close to where they played cricket, on some marshy ground between the Great Eastern Railway and the River Lea, and the stationmaster at Northumberland Park allowed them to keep the posts in the station during the week. No doubt the players of the time were pleased that there was no crossbar to carry, only a tape. The Marshes (as the area has always been called locally) were already the home of two other clubs; University College Hospital played rugby there, while Park FC (later to be absorbed by Hotspur) played soccer.

The organiser of that first AGM was a clerk in Edmonton County Court named Jim Randall. He had joined the Hotspurs from local rivals the Radicals and was elected the new captain with Billy Harston as his deputy. Harston had an amazing career with the club. He partnered Bobby Buckle on the left wing for ten years, remained behind the scenes afterwards as assistant secretary and, over sixty years after being elected vice-captain, was still to be seen at home games as press box steward.

The Hotspurs did not stay at the YMCA long. During one scratch game in the basement of the building, a YMCA councillor investigating the noise was hit in the face by a ball, while other minutes mention the propensity of some boys to 'play cards and sample the mulberries at the end of the garden'. Having been ejected from Percy House, the club moved briefly to Dorset Villas and then on to the Red House in the High Road, which was used as headquarters for six years (1886–91). By remarkable chance this building, adjacent to the present ground, was later purchased by the club and is now used as their administrative offices with the address 748 High Road; truly a return to their roots. They did not actually get changed at the Red House, which was nearly a mile away from their pitch, but hired rooms in pubs closer to the Marshes, usually the Milford, the Park, or the Northumberland Arms.

The first game the club completed which was actually recorded anywhere was that match against Latymer. Playing on Saturday 6 January 1883, our young heroes lost 8–1! Matters improved and, over the next two seasons, 1883–84 and 1884–85, the Hotspurs were reported to have played 47 games, of which they won 27 and drew 4. One must treat these reports with caution, however, for it is impossible to gauge the quality of the opposition or even if they were playing first elevens. By this time it appears that only four of the founding fathers, Bobby Buckle, Fred Dexter, Sam Casey and Stuart Leaman, were still regular members of the first team.

Particular interest was always taken in that local derby against Latymer. It was the Spurs v Arsenal clash of its day and the history of

TOP: A picture of the whole club, also taken before the game with the City business house club St Albans in 1885. Back row, left to right, L. Brown, T. Wood, T. W. Bumberry, John Anderson, John Ripsher, Ham, known as Sam, Casey (the first secretary); middle row, left to right, R. Amos, W. Tyrell, Frank Lovis, Jack Jull, H. E. Goshawk, H. Hillyer, Stuart Leaman (the club's first goalkeeper), A. Bayne, Jim Randall, organizer of the first AGM and club captain; bottom row, left to right, Jack Thompson Jnr, Billy Randall (Jim's brother), Bobby Buckle (the first captain), G. Burt, G. Bush, P. J. Moss, Billy Mason, Billy Harston, the deputy captain and still press box steward as late as 1946, Frank Cottrell and Hedley Bull. Though the club's badge was supposed to be a large 'H', close examination shows that, at this stage, it was a Maltese Cross. This photograph was taken on the banks of the River Lea and, if the photographer had turned round, he would have seen the view below.

BOTTOM LEFT: Displaced in time by a century. There is nothing remaining to suggest that football was ever organized on the Marshes, but it is probable that the Hotspurs played where the allotments are today. White Hart Lane is about a mile in the distance and Alexandra Palace, where a joint ground with Arsenal was proposed in the mid-1970s, is over to the far left.

Mr. H Bull
159 Birkbeck Rd
Tottenham

+ TOTTENHAM + HOTSPUR + F.C. +

R. BUCKLE,	H. D. CASEY,
WHITE COTTAGE	SHERWOOD LODGE,
WHITE HART LANE, TOTTENHAM.	PARK, TOTTENHAM.

Date as Post Mark.

Dear Sir, v. *Coldstream Guards*
(replayed Cup Tie)
You have been chosen to play in the above Match on Saturday
next, at *Park*

Should you be unable to play, please advise us at once.

Yours faithfully,

R. BUCKLE, | Joint Hon. Secs.
H. D. CASEY,

DRESSING ROOM

In the club's early days, players were informed that they had been selected by postcard. This one was sent to Hedley Bull on 11 November 1891 and asked him to turn out at Park (meaning the Northumberland Park ground) at 3pm on the following Saturday, 14 November. Their opponents were Coldstream Guards in a replayed Luton Charity Cup match, which Spurs went on to win 7–2. As can be seen from the printed card, Bobby Buckle and Sam Casey were still running the club, nearly 10 years after they had founded it.

contests between the two clubs makes delightful reading. On 27 December 1883, Latymer turned up with only five players, though two arrived later. At the end of the match the teams could not agree on the score (Hotspur said it was 2–0 in their favour) and it remained unprinted in the *Tottenham Weekly Herald*, though that paper did remark that Latymer had suffered much verbal abuse from Hotspur supporters. Next time round the *Herald* got even more irate, pointing out that the club captains had submitted completely contradictory reports and that the paper would not print any more until they sorted things out. Then, as now, local papers relied on the clubs to give accurate reports of what transpired. Latymer attempted to overcome these various hurdles the next season by playing with twelve men, until the ruse was discovered at half-time. They tried the same thing in a reserve match soon afterwards but the Hotspurs had got wise to such ungentlemanly conduct by their neighbours and the fixture with the Edmonton club was dropped.

At the end of the 1884–85 season came another significant change. Sam Casey, the secretary, had been receiving mail addressed to another club called London Hotspur. As a result the Hotspurs decided to change their name to Tottenham Hotspur and distinguish themselves from this other side – which presumably soon passed out of existence after its brief appearance on the stage of football

history. At the same time the club decided to change its strip from all blue to blue and white. This was the result of a visit to Kennington Oval to see the 1885 Cup final. Blackburn Rovers, in their familiar blue and white, won the Cup for the second consecutive year by beating Glasgow's Queen's Park 2–0, and so impressed the Tottenham lads that the latter paid their own tribute. In case anyone should mistake them for the Rovers, the Tottenham shirts had a large 'H' near the left shoulder, though on the very first team picture, taken in October 1885, the badge appears to be a Maltese cross. For a few seasons in the 1890s the team bedecked itself in red shirts and navy blue shorts, even changing for a time to the then Wolves strip of chocolate and gold. It was not until 1900, after playing Preston North End in the Cup, that the Preston colours of white shirts and navy blue shorts were adopted and they have remained the same to this day.

A CHANGE OF HOME

Despite their relative success, life for the club was nothing if not impermanent. The marshland between the River Lea and the railway was public ground and the club had no more right to play there than a dozen kids who happened to turn up with a ball made from old rags. Fights over who could use a marked out pitch were not uncommon. The club had no control over any spectators who turned up, nor could it charge them anything. As the side became more established things did become a little easier – they were recognised as the best in the district and no longer had to fight for their pitch – but matters could not be said to be satisfactory.

P. J. Moss, who played for the club around this period, wrote about the last season on the Marshes in *The Football News* in 1900: 'In some of the games, with absolutely no gate money, it is no exaggeration to say that 4,000 spectators surrounded the field. They were not always considerate of the feelings of visiting teams and I well remember some East End Cup ties in which the visitors were pelted with mud, rotten turnips and other vegetable refuse.'

In 1888 Bobby Buckle, Sam Casey and Jack Jull (the club's best player, who had appeared whenever he was home from school right from the earliest days) found a pitch for hire just off Northumberland Park (which is actually a street running off the High Road, not a patch of open ground). It was an area shared by Foxes FC and was used for tennis in summer. The rent was £17 per annum. The first match there was reported to be a reserve game versus Stratford St John's early in September 1888 and the takings were a heady 17 shillings (85 pence). At the time there was much muttering locally about the club overreaching itself and getting 'too big for its boots' and it must be remembered that this really still was a group of ex-schoolfriends, few out of their teens, playing friendly matches every Saturday. In essence it was not so different from thousands of weekend pub teams around the country today.

In their later years on the Marshes, Spurs had begun to entertain some not undistinguished guests. In October 1885 they played their first ever competitive match in the first round of the London Cup. A crowd estimated at 400 saw them beat St Albans (not the

current side of that name but a club based in the City of London) though the second round was something of a let-down as they crashed 8–0 to mighty Casuals at Wandsworth. Still, even to play the Casuals was something – in 1894 that club was to reach the final of the first ever Amateur Cup. The following season Spurs also entered the East End Cup and reached their first final, where they played another side to scale the heights of amateur football in later years, the Caledonians. The final was decided on the Marshes on Saturday 16 April 1887, but Tottenham were to lose by the only goal of the game, a low shot which skidded through their goalkeeper's legs. Hotspur were to find Cup finals rather easier in years to come.

THE ARRIVAL OF ARSENAL

One last game on the Marshes must be mentioned, Spurs first ever against Royal Arsenal. The game took place on 19 November 1887 and Spurs were leading 2–1 when the game was abandoned 15 minutes from time. Apparently Arsenal had turned up late, scored an early goal, defended for the rest of the match and were saved by the fall of darkness. Nonetheless, it was an auspicious start for Spurs in what was to become one of the greatest of all derby fixtures.

The first season at Northumberland Park proved a great success and the club even made a profit of £6. On Saturday 13 October 1888 the Old Etonians had come to Tottenham in the first round of the London Senior Cup, winning 8–2 with five of their goals scored by Arthur Dunn, a great Corinthian who was to give his name to the annual Public Schools Cup. The significance of the fixture could only be seen retrospectively. Just six years earlier Old Etonians had won the FA Cup. For nearly two decades it was felt that they may have been the last Southern side ever to do so – but who could then have believed that

THE WEEKLY HERALD, FRIDAY, April 30, 1886.

ANNUAL DINNER OF THE TOTTENHAM HOTSPUR FOOTBALL CLUB.

The first annual dinner of the above Club was held at the Milford Tavern, Park-lane, Tottenham, on Tuesday, the 20th inst., when 40 members and friends sat down to an excellent repast provided by the host (Mr Reeves), who deserves great praise for the perfect arrangement of all the details. John Ripsher, Esq., president, occupied the chair, and J. H. Thompson, Esq., one of the vice-presidents, the vice-chair.

After the cloth was cleared the chairman gave the usual loyal toasts, which were received with great enthusiasm, followed by Mr A. E. Broadberry giving the well-known song "Football." The Chairman then gave the Army, Navy and Reserve Forces, to which Mr S. H. Casey responded in a few well-chosen words, after which Mr A. Kemp sang "Too Late," which created a great impression, and in response to an encore gave a comic song "Right before the Missus too." The Chairman in rising to propose the toast of the evening "Success to the Tottenham Hotspur Football Club," said that football was now running a close race with cricket as the national pastime of this country, and it had been proved that football was played in England nearly 600 years ago. Many rulers had endeavoured to stop the playing of the game, notably Queen Elizabeth and King James let for various reasons, but football had survived through all, and he would as an instance point out to Lancashire where it is estimated that 100,000 people are either players or spectators at football every Saturday afternoon. He (the chairman) believed that the abuses to which football was subjected had entirely disappeared under the present scientific mode of playing the game, and he therefore called upon the gentlemen present to rise and drink "Success to the Tottenham Hotspur Football Club." The toast was drunk with three times three. Mr W. Mason, hon. sec., in responding, gave a sketch of the Club's career this season. He said that taking everything into consideration they had had a very successful season, much more so than they anticipated, for the fixtures were much stronger than those of previous seasons. They entered for the London Association Challenge Cup and had, to their surprise, succeeded in getting through the first round defeating their opponents (St. Albans) by 3 goals, the score being 5 to 2, but in the second round they were drawn against a club, viz. the Casuals, which proved too strong for them and were defeated by 8 goals to nil. With regard to the other matches they had been very successful, they had played 37, won 24, lost 11 and drawn 2; won 111 goals and lost 53. (Cheers.) There were 20 matches scratched mainly in consequence of the severe weather, otherwise their results most probably would have been better. Mr Mason also said that they had played 8 local matches and had only lost one, and that a 2nd xi fixture which was played with 4 men short, and he therefore thought that they had a right title of the first local club (cheers), but he was not certain they had played every local club, he was sure that they would not refuse to play any other should they think fit to challenge them. He said he had nothing further to say, but hoped the Club would still be more prosperous in their engagements next season. (Cheers.) Mr F. C. Hobbs now gave a song entitled "The Old Brigade," which was heartily received, and as an encore, gave "The Powder Monkey."

The Vice-Chairman (J. H. Thompson, Esq.), after referring in a few touching remarks to the high estimation in which Mr Ripsher was held by everyone in the Club, proposed "The President of the Club" which was drunk with musical honours. Mr Ripsher, in response to the toast, said it was five years ago that he was asked to fill the post of President, and he might say that during the whole of that time he had been always courteously treated by every member of the Club, and he hoped that the time was far distant when his connection with the Club would cease.

The toast of "The Vice-Presidents" was next proposed by Mr J. Jull, and drunk with musical honours, and responded to by J. H. Thompson, Esq., who said it gave him great pleasure to fill the post as a Vice-President of The Tottenham Hotspur Football Club, and he would be pleased to do anything in his power to further their success.

Mr Mason now read letters of regret which he had received from the other Vice-Presidents, viz. Joseph Howard, Esq., J.P., M.P., John Robson, Esq., and W. A. H. de Pape, Esq., who were unable to be present.

The Chairman next proposed "The Visitors," which was responded to by Mr F. C. Hobbs in a very humorous speech.

In giving the last toast of the evening, viz. "The Host," the Chairman took occasion to thank Mr Reeves for the perfect manner in which everything was carried out, and hoped, that although this was their first dinner, it would not be the last.

A long list of songs followed, and a most enjoyable evening was brought to a close by singing "The National Anthem" and "Auld Lang Syne."

LEFT: The Herald's report of the club's first annual dinner, held at the Milford Tavern on Tuesday 20 April 1886.
FAR LEFT: The Milford Tavern on the corner of Park Lane and Somerford Grove as it appears today. The annual dinner would have been held in the upstairs rooms, which were also often hired by the club as changing facilities before their games on the Marshes in the 1880s. The Tottenham that we know today was not the Tottenham of the club's founders. As late as the 1870s a traveller wrote: 'Tottenham has many outlying farms and much of the land is under plough . . . flowers are grown for the London market in the numerous nurseries.' It was, indeed, one of those nurseries (Beckwith's) which was to become White Hart Lane. The population of the area was much smaller. In 1881 there were only 23,000 people living in Edmonton, but the next twenty years saw new housing throughout North London, and Edmonton had grown to 62,000 by the time Spurs won the Cup in 1901.

Spurs would emulate this achievement within a dozen seasons?

In 1889 the club joined the Football Association as a full member. Crowds were increasing (reaching 3,000 for another appearance by the Casuals in the London Senior Cup in 1893) and the team was taking on more and more of what we would now call a professional appearance. Bobby Buckle resigned as secretary in the same year, leaving only Jack Jull of the early club members still playing. Jull had been a fixture at right-back from 1883 and was club captain for many years, also becoming the first Spurs player to win representative honours when he was selected for Middlesex in 1889. He died aged only 53 on 22 December 1920 and the *Weekly Herald* carried a glowing obituary, by chance alongside the first instalment of their 'History of Tottenham Hotspur'. Sam Casey remained as assistant secretary, and Bobby Buckle and Jack Thompson Jnr (his father, Jack Snr, had helped the club in its early days) were still on the committee.

PROFESSIONALISM ARRIVES

Obviously by this stage the club was looking for something better. It could continue arranging friendlies for ever, but the players were more ambitious. There were, nonetheless, obstacles. Soundings had already been made by the same Royal Arsenal who had come to the Marshes in 1887 about setting up a Southern League, with the implication that at least some of the teams would be professional. In 1892 a meeting of interested clubs had been held and 12 sides were provisionally elected. Spurs had tried to join but came bottom of the poll with only one vote, presumably their own. As it happened, nothing came of this meeting anyway. Most of the senior sides had been scared away by the intransigent attitude of the London FA, which made it quite clear that it would suspend any member club which embraced professionalism in any form.

This was a problem which was to continue for some years, finally reaching its bitter conclusion with the founding of the Amateur Football Alliance by the London, Middlesex and Surrey FAs in 1907. Arsenal had decided to ignore the threats and joined the Football League in 1893. Other senior clubs (and Spurs were, at the time, only in the second rather than first rank of these) faced worsening problems. They were experiencing the same difficulties as had the major Northern and Midland clubs before the formation of the Football League – namely that repetitive friendlies were not very attractive to crowds and that games had to be cancelled or rearranged at short notice when opponents found themselves engaged in the later stages of numerous cup competitions. At the same time, lack of organised fixture lists and unpredictable crowds meant that they were unable to sign the very best players, who went to Football League clubs. Spurs solved this problem, albeit temporarily, by joining the newly founded Southern Alliance with Erith, Slough, Windsor and Eton, Polytechnic, Old St Stephen's and Upton Park (not the current West Ham). They lost only three games in this league in its only season, and reached the fourth round of the London Senior Cup before losing again to old rivals Casuals. All in all, a satisfactory season, if one which consisted largely of marking time.

The same year saw the comical incident which led to the club becoming professional. It became known, melodramatically, as 'The Affair of Payne's Boots'. The gentleman in question was one Ernie Payne, a left-winger who had not played for Fulham's first team for some time when, at the beginning of the 1893–94 season, Spurs offered him a game. At the time both clubs were amateur and, if a player could not get a game with one club, he was perfectly free to move where he could. For some reason, however, Payne's move to Spurs was not appreciated by some at the Half Moon (where Fulham then played) and, on the morning of his first game for Spurs (21 October 1893), he found his kit had disappeared. Spurs thus had to kit him out. As they had no spare boots which fitted he was given ten shillings to buy a pair. Fulham heard about this and presumably still annoyed by the incident, complained to the London FA that Spurs were guilty of poaching and professionalism. A week later Spurs were found guilty of paying inducements to Payne, though they were found not guilty of poaching the player.

Payne returned the ten shillings to the club and it was argued, not unconvincingly, that if a club official, rather than Payne himself, had run out to buy the boots then the charge would not have held water. At the end of the day Spurs were suspended for a fortnight, and Payne for one week – actually rather a light

The 'Spurs have got through the first round of the qualifying stage of the English Cup, but victory was only achieved after a very hard struggle. The attendance was the largest the 'Spurs have had this season, over 2,000 persons being present.

The local team was the same that beat the Casuals with the exception that Julian played instead of Dickie. Jull, contrary to anticipations, filled his old position at back, and Monk kept goal. Elliott and Burrows were absent, the former thinking it better to go over to Notts Forest, whilst the latter aided the Arsenal Reserves. Elliott's re-instatement apparently, was of little good. Stanley Briggs looked like an old warrior with his head bound up.

West Herts were handicapped by the absence of two or three of their prominent men, including Weeler, but their eleven included footers of considerable ability. Their team was as follows: S. King (goal); L. S. Lidderdale and J. R. Paul (backs); J. Penney, F. C. Robins and G. E. Green (halfbacks); H. R. L. Wright, S. C. Hobbs, J. O. Anderson, S. S. Taylor and R. M. Strout (forwards.)

Play was commenced very punctually, Mr Bisiker tootling the whistle at half past three exactly. West Herts forwards showed pretty combination. Julian having fouled, the ball was sent into the net without touching any body and directly after Monk was called upon to save, which he did, although at the expense of a corner. Goodall cleared and in turn either goal was visited. The locals attacked, and Payne was conspicuous for tricky play. After the Herts forwards had again been stopped, Hunter gave to Cubberley who put in a clinker but Lidderdale mullified. Jull brought up the visiting forwards and Payne had a chance of scoring. Instead, he shot yards over.

'Spurs were pressing. Archie Cubberley was tricking the Herts defence again and again, and sending in some fine shots. Taylor, by a splendid effort put the home citadel in danger but his shot was too feeble to get past Monk. Anderson also kicked over. Eccles transferred play to the other end. Payne secured and passed to Hunter who headed the ball into the net amidst great cheers.

'Spurs attacked almost continuously from now to half time. It was only occasionally that the Herts forwards could get away. King was a tower of strength to his side. Frequently had he to use his fists in expelling the sphere from the goal mouth, and right well did he acquit himself. Eccles, Payne, Cubberley and Goodall each shot but they found King invulnerable. At last the latter got the ball by the custodian and so was able to place his team two on.

Upon the sphere being set in motion, Welham had to repulse an attack of West Herts, and then the 'Spurs again gave their opponents defence a warm time of it. There was only one team in it now, the locals doing pretty well as they liked, except that they could not get the pilule past King. At half-time no more goals had been scored.

Having had four-fifths of the game with the slope against them it was naturally expected that the 'Spurs would be the superior lot in the second half. But how often does the unexpected happen. Whether they had been dosed with some wonderful physic during the interval, I can't say, but, West Herts now played with the utmost vigour. A corner was obtained directly after the restart, and Wright directed the ball into the net, cheers from the visitors supporters—of whom, by the bye, there were several—greeting such a successful re-commencement. Herts again looked dangerous but the home defence interposed with success. Julian shot across to Payne, who sent in a clinker, King stopped and fell to the ground with the ball. A general scuttle ensued at the goal mouth, the poor custodian remaining on the ground; at last he got the sphere away, being loudly cheered. It was more like a bit of Rugby.

West Herts again pressed. Strout passed to the right wing, and Hobbs headed a second goal for his side, thus making the scores equal. All was now suspense, and excitement ran very high. The visitors still hung round the home goal, and Monk and Jull in turn saved. Then Cubberley relieved, and Hunter tried King without effect. Roused by the cheers of their supporters the home forwards showed better combination. The sphere reaching Goodall from Cubberley, he balked the West Herts defence. King ran out to meet him, but was not in time and Donald was able to score a third point with an easy shot.

Thundering were the cheers that followed. Directly after the locals all but scored again. West Herts were not dismayed and getting up placed Monk's charge in jeopardy. Shephard just managed to clear. Hands against 'Spurs was followed by Payne sending in a splendid centre which Goodall should have—but did not—converted into a goal. Eccles tried his luck, and it appeared that the ball went under the cross-bar, but the referee ruled otherwise. The visitors, although trying hard, failed to equalise and so the 'Spurs won by 3 goals to 2.

RIGHT: White Hart Lane was ready for use in September 1899 and the opening first team match was a friendly against Notts County on the evening of Monday 4 September. County, who were fifth in the First Division the previous season, were well beaten, 4–1. The ground had no official name at the time and the report carefully avoids mentioning a title. The substitute goalkeeper who so impressed everyone, Walter Bull, was later to join Spurs.

OPPOSITE: The critical decision to go professional, made on Monday 16 December 1895. The committee obviously tried to stage-manage the meeting and push the proposal through. Several of the players opposed the move, expecting to find themselves without a first team place if it succeeded. They were quite right; within three months only Stanley Briggs (the club captain and its best player, who refused to come to the meeting) and Ernie Payne remained in the side. The other nine were all new professionals.

THE WEEKLY HERALD, FRIDAY September 8 1899.

A Knock for Notts.

THE LAMBS LOSE.

Fresh from their splendid victory over Derby County in the League, Notts County came South to give the Spurs their first game on the new ground on Monday evening. They altered their team in one or two respects, the most interesting of the changes being to substitute Montgomery, the old Spurs' back, for Prescott. The Spurs gave Morris a run in place of Stormont, but otherwise the eleven was the same as against Millwall. To add some semblance of dignity to the opening proceedings, Mr. C. D. Roberts, the chairman of directors (in the absence of Col. H. F. Bowles, M.P., who had been invited to perform the function) set the ball rolling.

In spite of the warmth, the first half was very spiritedly contested, and the play was decidedly interesting. In former days it used to be reckoned that League clubs, when playing exhibition matches in the South, always kept a bit up their sleeves. Other times have brought other methods, and, now if League teams want to win they have to go their hardest and then are frequently unsuccessful. Notts were in no mood to be beaten. They went at it hammer and tongs until the interval, and so did the Spurs. The visiting forwards were very smart with the ball, and they had a hard and vigorous style. The Spurs played a somewhat closer game, and exhibited an excellent understanding, with the result that they also were frequently on the offensive. In fact the play was of a very spicy character, the ball travelling backwards and forwards with great rapidity, and oft-times either goal was in danger.

A sharp bit of play by the Notts' left wing afforded McCairns a chance to score, but he aimed too wide. Almost directly after, Smith and Pratt initiated an attack from which Kirwan nearly scored. The ex-Everton man was conspicuous in these early stages, and one shot from him was only stopped by Suter throwing himself on to the ground. In the mere matter of exchanges the teams could, perhaps, cry quits, but some twenty minutes from the start Notts obtained a goal, the shot going off Tait into the net. With a little luck they would have quickly scored again. Fletcher or was it McCairns—seemed to have the goal at his mercy, but Clawley rushed out and interrupted his kick. Smith got a chance to equalise, and lifted the ball too high. However, the Spurs had not very long to wait before drawing level. Smith and Pratt worked the ball prettily into the Notts' quarters, and the former shot it across the goal-mouth. Kirwan sent it back again into the centre, and Pratt rushing in kicked it through. Thus, at half-time the scores were one all.

Notts County had the misfortune to lose the services of Suter, their goalkeeper, when the second half was fifteen minutes old. Copeland, in trying to head the ball through, caught him with his foot under the heart, and he was led off. In the first half he also had been stretched out, but this was a mere temporary matter. Bull fell back into goal, and a right good custodian he made. But the enforced change threw the team out of shape, and the Spurs had by far the most of the subsequent play. Before

Suter left the Spurs succeeded in taking the lead. The goal was first jeopardised by Cameron, who, after running past the opposition, kicked the ball a trifle too far from him so that the goalkeeper reached it first, and Copeland, who struck the post, but the latter made no mistake when he was left with another opening, after Suter had cleared from Pratt.

The Notts defence, as deranged, failed to hold the Spurs' forwards, who played in brilliant style. Copeland registered a third goal from a pass by Cameron, and before the finish he also converted a centre from Kirwan. In addition to these successes Cameron twice put the ball through from offside positions. These reverses could not be put down to the account of Bull. He saved any number of shots, difficult ones, too, and was just the man for the place in such an emergency. The Notts' forwards did their best to make headway, but four men cannot do so much as five, and the home backs were able to save Clawley from any serious trouble. The final score was:—

SPURS 4, NOTTS 1.

The hour and a half's play at Millwall apparently had an excellent effect in knitting the Spurs together. The combination of the forwards was greatly improved, and they seemed to have got into thorough working order.

The front line was sound in every part. Pratt is not a showy player, but we are thinking the Spurs will have a warm right wing. His weight is an important factor, and in this game it was respected. Tom Smith was very speedy, and he could easily leave Lewis behind. One run of his in the second half roused the spectators to a high witch of excitement. Copeland was a capital pivot, and was in amongst the goals. Cameron and Kirwan's play is all that could be desired. The Spurs' manager is a footballer of the first rank.

Of the half-backs, Morris was continually to the front, both in the matter of tackling and feeding. McNaught and Jones were likewise up to the mark, and the backs and goalkeeper performed satisfactorily, without doing anything exceptional. By the way Mr. Brettell considers that Tait was the best left back in the League last season. We do not suppose Woolwich would have been so badly beaten but for the mishap to Suter, who is a goalkeeper of ability. Bull played a clever game at half-back, and when he fell back the line was considerably weakened. Our old friend Montgomery, with his partner, performed well in the first half, but we did not seem to see so much of them afterwards.

The turf had a greatly improved appearance, and except for one of two places where it was loose, played well. The Notts team, we are told, had a flattering opinion of the ground. There were about 5,000 people present, and the takings at the gate amounted to £115.

Tottenham Hotspur:—Clawley; Erentz and Tait; Jones, McNaught and Morris; Smith, Pratt, Copeland, Cameron and Kirwan.

Notts County:—Suter; Lewis and Montgomery; Ball, Bull and Lowe; Hadley, Macconachie, McCairns, Fletcher and Chalmers. Referee: C. D. Crisp.

---

punishment. G. Wagstaffe Simmons, later vice-chairman of the club, wrote that: '. . . the London FA issued a series of findings that staggered the football world . . . in their naked absurdity . . .' Bobby Buckle was rather more relaxed about it. He told Julian Holland some sixty years later that the committee of the time never had any doubts that the club would be suspended and were just unlucky to be caught breaking the extremely strict rules of the time.

But out of disaster can come strength, and so it was with Tottenham Hotspur. The Payne affair had drawn attention to the club and they were popular opponents everywhere; for instance, over 6,000 turned up to see them at Southampton St Mary's a month or so later. The committee had also begun to seriously doubt the wisdom of remaining within the control of the London FA, given its almost fanatic obsession with professionalism. This attitude is a difficult one to convey today, perhaps the only comparable modern example being the Rugby Union's censure on anyone who has ever played rugby league. It might also be recalled that Corinthians, the premier amateur club of the day who were twice chosen en bloc (in 1894 and 1895) to represent the *senior* England side in a full international, had an article in their constitution stating that they could not enter any organised competition of any kind.

Spurs, though without any conspicuous competitive success, had clearly exhausted the possibilities open to them as an amateur club. The move towards change was helped by the election of a new president in 1894. John Oliver, a carpet manufacturer in the City who was able to offer his players jobs, had been responsible for founding the Southern Alliance. He must have seen the potential that Spurs presented and was soon dragging them, some kicking and screaming, towards professionalism. It was a course that had already been adopted in the south by Woolwich Arsenal, Millwall Athletic and Luton Town.

He quickly erected the first stand at Northumberland Park and though it fell down in a gale soon afterwards it was a move in the right direction. By autumn 1895 the critical decision had been made and the club voted to go professional on Monday 16 December 1895. Only one member, a Mr Roynan, voted against, though there was much dissension at the meeting and a fair number of fans apparently transferred their allegiance to the still amateur London Caledonians over in Tufnell Park. Stanley Briggs, probably the club's best player at the time, was also against and refused to attend the meeting at The Eagle. He was the only amateur to continue playing for the side on a regular basis after professionals had been added to the staff.

AMATEUR CUP FROLICS

Tottenham had been having a successful time on the field. The previous season they reached the fourth qualifying round (roughly equivalent to the last 64) of the FA Cup and the second round of the Amateur Cup. Spurs' career in the Amateur Cup was short but not without incident. They had been invited, along with 80 other sides, to institute the competition in 1893 and their first game was in the second round (having got a bye in the first). That was on 11 November 1893, when Vampires were beaten 3–1 at Northumberland Park. Unfortunately Spurs were unable to play Clapham Rovers, 1880 FA Cup winners, in the next round because of their suspension after the Payne's Boots affair.

The next season saw a strange juxtaposition of events. On 13 October 1894 Spurs played West Herts in their first ever FA Cup match, winning 3–2. A week later, they were contesting the Amateur Cup and crushed Old Harrovians 7–0. One Peter Hunter scored in both games. The next two rounds of the Amateur Cup also saw impressive results; 6-1 against City Ramblers and 8–0 away at Romford. The fourth qualifying round was tougher – 1–1 and 3–3 draws against London Welsh (not the rugby club) followed by a 4–2 win at the Spotted Dog, at the time the home of the Upton Park club. By this time Peter Hunter had scored nine goals in the competition. Nottingham club Beeston were the next to go down, 2–0 at home, in the first round proper. The second goal, the last ever scored by Spurs in the Amateur Cup, was Hunter's tenth in the competition.

On 16 March 1895 Spurs entertained Amateur Cup holders Old Carthusians at Northumberland Park in the next round and crashed 5–0 before a massive 5,000 crowd. The Carthusians line-up had five full England internationals, including the immortal centre-forward G. O. Smith and the Walters brothers, A.M. and P.M. Full-back partners for many years, they were inevitably nicknamed Morning and Afternoon. Carthusians remain one of only two clubs ever to win both the FA and Amateur Cups. Spurs also progressed well that year in the FA Cup, reaching the fourth qualifying round before losing a replay to Luton Town.

The next season, 1895–96, Spurs were allowed to go through to the first round proper of the Amateur Cup, where they were drawn against Chesham. The game was never played, for as the *Weekly Herald* plaintively commented on 20 December 1895: 'Had not the Spurs adopted professionalism last week they would have had to play Chesham after Christmas. The Spurs are now drawn against Stoke in the first round of the English Cup (the name commonly used for the FA Cup at the time) on 1 February. The Spurs have certainly had no luck in the draws this season . . . it is not likely any effort will be made to induce Stoke to come to Tottenham to play their tie.' How different from the 1981 competition, when Spurs won the Cup after leaving London just once in nine matches.

Tottenham's first game as a professional club was actually against the old enemy, the Casuals, on 21 December and they won 3–1. No declared professionals were allowed to play against amateur teams like the Casuals.

THE WEEKLY HERALD,
FRIDAY December 20, 1895.

The team selected by the North Middlesex League against West Norwood, on Boxing Day, is as follows:—Hale, (Barnet); Searle, (Noel Park), Toon, (Barnet); Hilton (Highgate Town), Vanderpump (Enfield), McLeod (Hornsey United); Shepherd (St. James), Hollyman (Noel Park), Crickmer (Wood Green), Stokes (Edmonton Minerva), and Speedy (Novocastrians.)

Edmonton Minerva (R) journeyed to Walthamstow to fulfill their league engagement with St. Gabriel's. Minerva sustained defeat by 3 goals to nil. [The report was received mid-day yesterday, which compelled us to cut it down. All reports should be sent in EARLY in the week.]

THE 'SPURS AND PROFESSIONALISM.

Every other matter, locally, so far as football is concerned, pales before the adoption of professionalism by the 'Spurs. For some weeks past the necessity of adopting this course has become more and more apparent, and for two or three reasons. One reason is in regard to the quality of the team. Those who have been present at the last two or three matches must have been struck with the fact that the 'Spurs have no good men to fall back on in case of accident to the ordinary players, and the result is that we have had bad displays, which are a source of much grumbling on the part of the spectators. I am not altogether an advocate of professionalism, as I think it tends to make sport a business; but under existing circumstances and conditions, I don't know that the 'Spurs had any option if they wished to maintain the prestige of the club.

The question was decided on Monday night. The club room at the Eagle was crowded with an excited gathering. Mr J. Oliver, the president, occupied the chair, and among those present were most of the committee, and several of the players, namely Pryor, Jull, Collins, Shepherd, Hunter, and Almond. Stanley Briggs was not there. The meeting quickly came to business, Mr Buckle proposing the adoption of a recommendation by the committee that the time had now arrived when professionalism should be adopted. The committee, it appeared, had met on Tuesday, and after full consideration of the matter, unanimously resolved to make the recommendation. Mr Buckle pointed out the difficulty that was now experienced in raising a good team when men were injured, and declared that unless the course suggested by the committee were agreed upon, their gates would dwindle down to one-half of what they were at present. Ralph Bullock seconded, and the Chairman and Mr J. H. Thompson, Senr., and others spoke in favour, all of them agreeing that the club could not ascend any higher in the ladder of fame if it remained an amateur organization. The Chairman said that unless the resolution were carried, he should at once resign the presidency of the club.

A considerable number of questions were asked, and once or twice the meeting became very excited. An opinion was expressed by one member, Mr Roynan, that the matter should not have been sprung upon them as it had been, and he proceeded to allude to the secrecy that had been observed. Despite of this, he said, he had it from one of those "in the know" what the meeting was to be about. This statement was the cause of considerable uproar, as the Chairman demanded to know the name of the person divulging the secret, a demand in which he was supported by a majority of the gathering. Mr Roynan, however, refused to give the name, and the Chairman then went so far as to order him to leave the room, but Mr Roynan did not obey.

One person wanted to know if a company were to be formed, and the reply was in the negative. Other questions put were as to the club's financial position, and whether the books had been called for. It appears that the club is in debt to the extent of £65, including £60 due upon the grand stand, but it was mentioned that hitherto a large number of matches had been played away. Regarding the other matter, the club's books had been called for, but not until after the notices for the meeting were issued. Another point was as to whether the players were favourable to the change. Mr Buckle said most of them were supporting the proposal.

At last the question was put to the vote, and the resolution was heartily carried, only one hand being held up against. Several abstained from voting.

ARCHIE CUBBERLEY'S BENEFIT.

The proposal to play a benefit match for Archie Cubberley has taken practical effect, and all the preliminary arrangements have been decided, as will be seen from the following letter from Mr F. J. Golding, who is interesting himself a great deal in the matter:—

SIR,—A meeting of local junior football club secretaries was held at the Spotted Dog, Church-road, Tottenham, on Monday evening last, when the [illegible] were duly passed and [illegible] local press.

the leading clubs in the land in friendlies (Notts County beat them 5–1, mighty Aston Villa, unarguably the best of them all, won 3–1 on 11 April 1896) but Spurs clearly needed the stimulus of competition. In July 1896 they applied to join the Southern League, created by Millwall Athletic's persistence two years earlier, and were elected straight to the First Division. A month earlier they had applied to join the Football League, where they were resoundingly rejected, coming bottom in a poll of ten clubs with just two votes. The actual voting was Blackpool 19, Walsall 16, Gainsborough 15, Burslem Port Vale 10, Luton 10, Crewe 4, Fairfield 3, Glossop 3, Macclesfield 2 and Tottenham 2.

THE SOUTHERN LEAGUE

Because of Spurs' dramatic rise to fame at the turn of the century, it is often assumed that the club was a great success in the Southern League days. It is true that they never finished lower than seventh during their twelve-year stint, but generally there were no more than half a dozen good sides in the League at any one time (usually Southampton, Portsmouth, Fulham, Millwall, the two Bristols and Tottenham themselves). Apart from their Championship season of 1899–1900, with virtually the same team that won the Cup a year later, Spurs never looked like winning the Southern League. When they applied for membership of the Football League in 1908 they had finished only seventh in the Southern League, behind QPR, Plymouth, Millwall, Crystal Palace, Swindon and Bristol Rovers and could thus count themselves fortunate to be elected. None of the sides above them applied and, even then, Spurs finished fifth out of six in the first ballot.

During their Southern League career Spurs regularly fielded senior sides in other competitions – notably the Western League – and their first team fixture list was invariably crowded. An important Western League match one week might see most first team players involved, whereas the following Saturday might throw up a Cup tie and either a Southern League or a rearranged Western League match. In this case the Western League side would effectively be the second team. Other leagues, such as the United or Thames and Medway, were less important and, although they were always recorded as first-class fixtures, the reserve side must often have deputised. For this reason it is very difficult to chart the exact record of the Spurs senior team in these years. In 1899–1900 they supposedly played 67 senior fixtures, winning 49 and scoring over 200 goals (thought to be a record in a single season by a genuinely senior club) but it is simply not possible that Spurs were represented in all of these games by their best side. The League tables from these years are all included in the appendices, as are all games which could have been senior matches, but readers should beware of interpreting their standard absolutely literally.

ABOVE: The two men who ran Tottenham Hotspur for almost half a century; secretary Arthur Turner (left), whose arrival spelt the end of the Cameron era, and Charles Roberts, who was chairman from 1898 until his death in 1943. It was Roberts who decided in 1898 that the club must become a limited company and needed a better ground. RIGHT: Roberts proposed the formation of a company at a meeting in the Red Lion pub on the High Road on 2 March 1898. This picture, taken 83 years later before the 1981 FA Cup final, is a good indication of how close the club has always been to its locality and how its roots have remained on the High Road throughout its history.

The first competitive game as a professional club was that tie at Stoke on 1 February. It was not a memorable start – Stoke won 5–0.

The new professionals were paid between 15 and 25 shillings per week (75p to £1.25) and, amazingly enough, three months into 1896 only two of the side which had played for the club in December 1895 remained in the team. They were Ernie Payne, of boots fame, and Stanley Briggs, the tough centre-half who had joined the club in 1890. The founding fathers by now had virtually no influence on the club's direction, despite it being only thirteen years old. John Ripsher had become the patron and even John Oliver remained on the committee only until 1898 before fading from the scene.

Having turned professional Spurs had no formal fixture list and they took to entertaining

1901

John Cameron • Southern League champions • Percy Park or White Hart Lane • Charles Roberts • The First FA Cup • Joining the League • Promotion and Relegation • Sick as a Parrot

There have been, perhaps, no more than a dozen great sides in English soccer history. Tottenham has produced at least two of these – the 1960–61 Double team, arguably the greatest of them all, and the 1901 Cup winners, who so astounded their contemporaries. For the origins of that earlier side, one has to go back a couple of years into the nineteenth century. Like 1908 and 1958, the year from mid-1898 is one of the most critical in Tottenham's proud history. The team performed only moderately on the pitch and at the next AGM the club declared a loss of over £500 but, firstly, the club turned itself into a limited company, secondly it moved to White Hart Lane and thirdly, and most importantly, it began its first, brief, flowering with the appointment of John Cameron as manager. It was, incidentally, also the season in which the club won its first ever trophy – the reserves heading the London League.

The first of these key events was formalised on Wednesday 2 March 1898 at the Red Lion in the High Road. Though the team was moderately successful on the field, attendances were not really up to expectations and the club was sliding slowly into the red. The club had plenty of time to consider off-the-field matters at the time as the ground had been closed and several players censured on 21 February after a mini-riot during a game against Luton. Spectators had invaded the pitch and assaulted three of the Luton team!

One Charles D. Roberts was a figure known in the northern home counties for fund raising via events like military tattoos. He had also, apparently, once been a baseball pitcher with the Brooklyn Dodgers in New York. He was

Sandy Brown (shaking hands on edge of goal area) has just equalized from a John Kirwan (on far side of field) free-kick in the 1901 Cup final against Sheffield United at Crystal Palace. His 25th minute header was his 13th goal of the competition that season and he went on to make it a record 15 in all. Sheffield United goalkeeper Billy Foulke, about to pick the ball out of the net, was the largest man ever to play first-class football. At this time he weighed around 21 stone.

approached by Spurs, probably with a view to organising a fund-raising event at Northumberland Park. Once he got involved, however, it became apparent to him that the club needed far more cash than a mere tattoo could raise and he recommended turning Tottenham Hotspur into a limited company as a means of both raising money and protecting the committee from taking personal risks. It was around this time that the major clubs in the land were doing the same thing. The major advantage of this step was that it encouraged clubs to take risks and invest in the game, without the individuals in charge having to fear that they would become personally responsible for the club's debts and failures.

Roberts' proposal was accepted by the members, 8,000 shares of £1 apiece were issued and subscriptions were invited. A new board of directors was appointed – consisting of Charles Roberts (who remained a director until his death in July 1943), John Oliver (who resigned in November 1898), Bobby Buckle (who remained on the board until 1900, the last link with the original Spurs), Jack Thompson (another original Hotspur, nephew

of Captain Delano, who resigned in 1899) and Ralph Bullock (who resigned on leaving the country in 1902). One can only speculate as to why four of the five original directors resigned so quickly – but Charles Roberts was apparently not noted for having a shy, retiring personality. To the evident surprise of the directors, the share issue did not go well. Twelve months later a mere 296 applications had been received for only 1,558 of the shares. This left over three-quarters of the shares unsold.

But while money may not have been coming in through shareholdings, it was beginning to accumulate through the gate. On 29 April 1899 Northumberland Park saw its greatest ever attendance – 14,000 for the game against Woolwich Arsenal. That was at least twice as many as could see the game in comfort (there were still very few banked terraces on English football grounds) and dozens of people climbed onto the roof of the refreshment bar. It couldn't stand the weight, collapsed and there were some minor injuries.

That accident, fortunately not serious, persuaded the directors that they should find better accommodation. They struck lucky, for just a few yards from where the club had been founded, and where the heart of its support had always been, was an undeveloped plot called Beckwith's Nursery. The only buildings on it were greenhouses and nursery sheds used for growing plants. The land had been bought by Charrington's Brewery as it was adjacent to their White Hart public house on the High Road. They were thinking of building some rows of terraces on the site, partially to provide custom for the pub.

The landlord of the pub had spread around a rumour that a football club was interested in taking the land, because his previous pub had been near the Millwall ground and had been worth a fortune to him. He was therefore extremely keen to attract another club to the open space behind his premises. Having heard the rumour, and discovered the landlord was basically flying a kite, Charles Roberts and Bobby Buckle then approached Charringtons. After considerable debate the brewers agreed to Spurs leasing the ground – asking only that the club guarantee 1,000 spectators at first team matches and 500 at reserve games.

In return, Tottenham have served only Charrington beers ever since. The stands (rather flimsy structures) were moved from Northumberland Park and the new stadium had undercover accommodation for 2,500 seated ticket holders. The ground was formally opened on Monday 4 September 1899 when Spurs beat the country's oldest professional club, Notts County, 4–1 in a friendly and 5,000 people paid a total of £115 to watch.

This was not actually the first game on the pitch. There had already been three 'Whites versus Stripes' trials and a game for schoolboy hopefuls. All four matches had been open for the public. Though before the First World War it was generally referred to as 'The High Road Ground', it has been known as White Hart Lane ever since – despite the fact that its address is 748 High Road and it is some distance from White Hart Lane itself. The White Hart Ground would no doubt be a better name but the club, having initially preferred Percy Park, were happy to accept any name popularly bestowed upon their new 30,000 capacity stadium. Within a decade improvements had taken the capacity up to

ABOVE: The crowd at Crystal Palace surrounds the grandstand as the Tottenham players go up to be presented to Sir Redvers Buller at the end of the game. The Cup was not, of course, being presented. Note the packed banks behind the stand.
LEFT: More of the hemmed-in crowd, no doubt all hoping to see Spurs become the first non-League club to lift the FA Cup. Although the Cup final was held at Crystal Palace between 1895 and 1914, the ground had no terracing in the sense it is understood today. Spectators gathered on the slopes of what was effectively a natural amphitheatre and, needless to say, few got a good view of proceedings.
BELOW LEFT: Fans from the banked seats invade the pitch at the end of the game. The old pitch markings with a penalty line and the two arcs drawn six yards from the goal-posts were changed a year later.

OPPOSITE: A series of cigarette cards issued by Ogden's at the time of the 1901 Cup final victory. They are shown here full size and were printed black and white. The players are (top) David Copeland and Harry Erentz; (middle) John Kirwan, George Clawley, Tom Morris, John Cameron, Jack Jones; (bottom) Alex Brown, Alex Tait, Edward Hughes and Tom Smith. The reversed card is that of Jim McNaught, who lost his place to Edward Hughes after being injured against Preston (by courtesy of David Allen Esq).

BELOW: What they all took home from Bolton, an FA Cup winners medal. This is actually John Cameron's; his name is engraved on the front.

40,000, easily large enough for all but FA Cup semi-finals.

In 1901, Roberts bought the freehold of the ground from Charringtons for £8,900 and, at the same time, purchased land and houses behind the northern end (then called the Edmonton goal) for another £2,600. To finance this he organised another share issue, but this proved no more successful than the last, raising only £2,000. Roberts borrowed the balance of the money and Charringtons helped him out by turning £6,500 of the purchase price into a long-term mortgage to be paid back over several years.

The game against Notts County was the first of the 1899–1900 season, the year that John Cameron's great team gelled. Cameron had joined the club in that critical autumn of 1898. A native of Ayr, he had played for his home town club and then for mighty Queen's Park, where he had won a Scottish cap against Ireland. He had moved to Liverpool, where he worked for Cunard and played for Everton as an amateur. It was not until Spurs asked him to come to London that he had ever been paid for playing football. He was a classic Scottish inside-forward in all except build, being a slim six-footer. As well as playing, he soon became secretary-manager and this remarkable man also took on the administration of the newly formed and ill-fated Players' Union. Within two years of his, and the club's, arrival at White Hart Lane together they had won both the Southern League and the FA Cup.

THE FIRST GREAT SIDE

What was truly remarkable about the 1901 Cup winning side was that none of the eleven had played for the club for more than four seasons and only four could recall playing at Northumberland Park just two seasons before the FA Cup win. How John Cameron got them to play as a team so quickly remains something of a mystery, if a massive compliment to his footballing genius.

The old-timer of the side was Jack Jones, who had joined the club in 1897, was captain of the Cup winning team and won 16 Welsh caps in all. A strong left-half, he formed the critical left-wing triangle with Kirwan and Copeland which was to create so many of Spurs' vital goals in the Cup run. Spurs were his sixth club – he had already played for Rhuddlan, Bootle, Stockton, Grimsby and Sheffield United. Harry 'Tiger' Erentz had been signed from Newton Heath (later to become Manchester United) at the same time as Cameron in 1898. A Scotsman, born in Dundee, he was the heaviest (13 stone) and toughest member of the side, a fierce tackling right-back who followed an elder brother on to Spurs' books. The fourth player from the pre-1899 era was Thomas Smith, who had also joined the club in 1898. Born in Maryport, he had played for Preston before moving south. Essentially a simple right-winger, his great strengths were his pace (he was a cup winning sprinter) and the accuracy of his crosses.

In 1899 Cameron was to add six more of his great side. George Clawley, born in the Potteries, came from Southampton to keep goal and he was to feature in a quite remarkable incident in the 1901 final itself. He broke a leg during his first season at White Hart Lane, but recovered in time to regain his place for the Cup run. Sandy Tait, the left-back, was perhaps the best of all Cameron's signings. He hailed from the famous village of Glenbuck, bordering Ayrshire and Lanarkshire and later noted for its junior team, the Glenbuck Cherrypickers, which brought on such names as Bill Shankly. Tait originally played for Motherwell, moving to Spurs via Preston.

Tom Morris, the right-half, had the distinction of being born in Grantham, which made him special in being born further south than any of the other ten and hence closest to Tottenham itself. The hard man of the team, he was signed from the Lincolnshire club Gainsborough Trinity, which had a brief spell in the League between 1896 and 1912. Edward Hughes was the surprise member. Standing only 5ft 6in, he took over the centre-half spot when team captain Jim McNaught was injured in the 1900–01 first round tie against Preston. He played so well that McNaught never regained his place. Another Welshman, Hughes had been a colleague of Cameron at Everton and eventually won 14 Welsh caps, the last in 1907.

Cameron showed a distinct liking for players with a similar background to himself and his inside-left, Davie Copeland, was even born in the same town, Ayr. He was the quiet one of the team, having had a fairly undistinguished career with Ayr Parkhouse and Walsall Town Swifts. Outside Copeland, Cameron added John Kirwan, a genuinely tricky winger who had also played with his new manager at Everton. Copeland and Kirwan, who won 16 Irish caps, developed a critical understanding on the left flank, often aided by Cameron holding back behind them to play as a scheming midfield man.

There was only one gap in this remarkable team, and this was not to be filled until the beginning of the 1900–01 season when Alexander 'Sandy' Brown joined the team as centre-forward from Portsmouth. Like the other 'Sandy', Alexander Tait, Brown was born

Winner's Medal   *Reverse*

24

THE ENGLISH CUP.

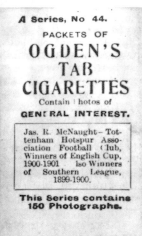

A Series, No 44.

PACKETS OF

OGDEN'S
TAB
CIGARETTES

Contain Photos of
GENERAL INTEREST.

Jas. R. McNaught – Tottenham Hotspur Association Football Club, Winners of English Cup, 1900-1901 Also Winners of Southern League, 1899-1900.

This Series contains 150 Photographs.

in Glenbuck. He had played for St Bernard's in Edinburgh before joining Preston, like Tait and Smith. He had gone to Portsmouth the season before and, so far in his career, had done little to suggest that he was suddenly to become one of the most talked about centre-forwards of all time and one whose record of 15 goals in one season's FA Cup competition still stands. His career with Spurs was quite astonishing. Despite his fame he played for the club for just twelve months – moving on to Middlesbrough in the autumn of 1901 before winning his one Scottish cap.

He was an excellent header of the ball and Cameron had clearly decided that he needed a target for the accurate crosses of Smith and Kirwan. Despite being a great trier Brown was never really skilful enough (a fact fully appreciated by the newspapers of the time,

if not by opposition defences) and Cameron was either remarkably perspicacious or remarkably lucky to fit him in at that particular time. Brown's brief flowering was astounding: he was to score in every round of the competition, the first man known to do so, and netted four in the semi-final. Given the run of the ball and the confidence of success, he had an excellent shot and was a fine header of the ball. And yet he was a relatively easy player to 'find out' and hence to mark out of a game. He did not have the all-round range of skills that a great centre-forward needs, nor the genuine speed. Spurs' relative decline after 1901 was in large part because Cameron never again had a player on song like Brown to convert the team's neat approach play into goals. Vivian Woodward, Brown's successor, was a great

player, but was arguably not a great centre-forward, as Brown certainly had been for that one amazing year.

The coincidences in the team Cameron built are too glaring to be ignored. Five were Scots, four of them coming from Ayrshire and its Lanarkshire borders. Two were Welsh, one Irish and, of the three Englishmen, none was born within 100 miles of White Hart Lane. Three had played for Preston, three for Everton. Thus despite being brought together quickly, then, the team members did find much that was familiar at Tottenham and John Cameron was there, on the field and off, to build a remarkable side.

The club had already had its first taste of real Cup success in 1898–99, although only four of the 1901 team were playing at the time. In all Tottenham played 10 games in the competition that year, eventually defeating Wolverton, Clapton (after a replay), Luton (after two replays), Newton Heath (1–1 at home then a 5–3 win in Manchester) and mighty Sunderland (League Champions in 1892, 1893 and 1895) 2–1 at home before

12,371 fans. In the quarter-finals, however, they had to travel to Stoke and the Potters, just as they did in Spurs' first professional game, had little trouble eliminating them – this time 4–1. The following season Spurs were allowed to go through to the competition proper without contesting the qualifying rounds, but had the misfortune to be drawn away at Deepdale and went out 1–0 at their first hurdle. Imagine their concern, then, when in 1900–01 they were yet again drawn against Preston in the first round, albeit at home.

By that time, at least, Spurs did have the confidence of having won a major competition. In the 1899–1900 Southern League they won 20 and drew 4 of their 28 games, scoring 67 goals and finishing three points clear of Portsmouth. All in all they won 49 of their 67 first team matches, losing only 10. After the financial loss of the previous year the club made a profit – if only £71 18s 8p (£71.94). Even the reserves did well, finishing second in the London League, and the club was dubbed 'The Flower of the South' by the London newspapers. Support was beginning to grow

fast, and the mood of the district is well summed up by a verse originally printed in the *Tottenham Herald* and repeated by Julian Holland in his book *Spurs*:

> What care I of things South African,
> Or whether the Boers will fight,
> Or that France has ceased to know the way,
> Between what is wrong and right?
> I care not for things political,
> Or which party's out or in,
> The only thing I trouble about,
> Is will Tottenham Hotspurs win?

Note that the club was still popularly referred to as Hotspurs at the time.

The references to South Africa related to the Boer War, then at its height. The local ardour cooled a little as the 1900–01 season got under way. By November Tottenham were well down the field, quite unable to reproduce the understanding of the previous season. But from then onwards things began to improve, too late to assist in the League, where they finished a mediocre fifth out of fifteen, but just in time for the Cup, which started as late as Saturday 9 February that year, delayed because of Queen Victoria's death. Like many sides before and since, Spurs were unquestionably helped by having only the Cup to think about for the second half of the season.

THE 1901 CUP RUN

Spurs did not start well in their Cup tie against Preston. Perhaps it was the blue and white stripes they had agreed to wear because of the colour clash (it was not until 1924–25 that the away side changed automatically). After 28 minutes a long shot by the Lancastrian full-back McMahon left Clawley unsighted and Preston, 1–0 up, retreated back into defence for the rest of the game. The tactic almost paid off. Peter McBride in the Preston goal was excellent while Sandy Brown, in his first Cup tie for Spurs, could barely do a thing right. The man Brown had replaced, Tom Pratt, had been transferred to Preston and was having by far the better game. Who could have guessed then what was to happen in the next three months ? In the 82nd minute Kirwan broke clear and centred for Brown to throw himself at the ball and thus score what was, by all accounts, a remarkable goal. No doubt the 18,000 crowd would, by that time, have regarded any goal as remarkable. So the final score was 1–1 and the tie had to be replayed at Deepdale on Wednesday 13 February, where the home side were clear favourites. Surprisingly, large numbers of fans travelled from London, paying 21/9 (£1.09) return for the privilege. Spurs made two changes. Hughes came in at centre-half for the injured McNaught and Jack Jones returned at left-half in place of Stormont, taking over as captain from McNaught. The team was to remain unchanged throughout the rest of the Cup run.

The Lancastrian home crowd of 6,000 was soon disappointed. In quick succession Cameron and Brown (twice) scored for Spurs and the game was effectively over by half-time. In the second half Brown completed his hat-trick and Preston's two goals from Becton and Pratt, against his old club, were academic.

The Tottenham team with the Southern League Championship Shield at the end of the 1899–1900 season. The Shield is held by Jack Jones, the Welsh club captain.

ABOVE: The Cup itself was photographed at the King's Hall in Holborn during the celebration banquet. This was the first time that a club had been known to put coloured ribbons on the trophy. At the end of the banquet they were taken home by Mrs Morton Cadman, wife of one of the directors, and she took them with her to the 1921 Cup final and placed the very same ribbons on the new FA Cup two decades later.

ABOVE RIGHT: The 1901 board with their first national trophy; (back row) J. Hawley, T. Deacock, Morton Cadman, Ralph Bullock; (seated) John Cameron and Charles Roberts. Cameron was the club's second secretary-manager, taking over from Frank Brettell in 1899. Brettell had taken on the job when the club became a limited company in March 1898.

Tottenham's reward for beating Proud Preston was an even tougher tie – against Cup holders Bury. The Lancashire club, known as The Shakers, was proof that, even in football, every dog has its day. Bury's day was around the turn of the century. At Crystal Palace in 1900 they had beaten Southern League Southampton 4–0 and, in the 1903 final, were to go two better by beating Derby County 6–0 for what remains the record Cup final victory. Bury had been drawn away in every round of their 1900 Cup run and had won their first round tie in 1901 away again, 1–0 at The Wednesday. No wonder, then, that 21,000 people turned up at White Hart Lane on Saturday 23 February. As they had against Preston, Tottenham started nervously and, within just two minutes, they were a goal down. For half an hour it looked as if Bury would overrun the home side but then a cross from Smith reached Brown and his shot beat keeper Thompson easily; 1–1 at half-time and Spurs had a chance. The second half saw just one goal, a rerun of the first with Smith centring for Brown to score his sixth goal of the competition so far. Spurs were into the quarter-finals of the FA Cup for only the second time in their history.

Tottenham were relatively lucky in the next draw – away to Southern League Reading on 23 March 1901. All the other six sides in the quarter-finals – including the West Midlands quartet of Small Heath (Birmingham), Villa, Wolves and West Brom – were in the Football League. Reading were a modest Southern League side, at the time ninth in the table, but they had home advantage and were known as a tough, hard-tackling team.

It is usually the case that the team which wins the FA Cup has one critical moment which can be ascribed to good fortune rather than skill – an incident on which their success is later seen to turn. In Spurs' case, this occurred in the last few minutes of their match at Reading. The score at the time was 1–1. For the third consecutive tie, Spurs had gone behind in the first half – this time to a 20-yard shot by Evans – and John Kirwan had

equalised in the second half. Then, in the dying minutes, a Reading shot dropped over Clawley's head and Sandy Tait dashed in to fist it behind just before it crossed the line. There does not seem to have been much doubt in the minds of anyone who saw the incident that it was a penalty. But the referee was unsighted and the linesman, who was consulted, had apparently not seen anything and a goal-kick was given. The 14,417 crowd, then the largest Elm Park had ever seen, was not well pleased and the officials were abused right up to the final whistle. Spurs fans, who had paid 3 shillings (15p) for a cheap-day return, were no doubt mightily relieved. It was an incident which, in retrospect, might not only have altered the course of 1901 for Spurs, but could have changed the club's whole history.

The teams met again at White Hart Lane on Thursday 28 March before a crowd of 12,000. This time things were completely different. Copeland and Brown (from another Smith cross) had scored by half-time and Brown got another (his eighth of the competition) early in the second half; 3–0 to Spurs and they were in the semi-finals for the first time ever.

The draw for the semi-final had already been made and Spurs were to meet West Bromwich. The West Brom directors had been at the replay and immediately approached the Tottenham board to suggest Villa Park as a semi-final venue, despite it being only three miles down the road from The Hawthorns. Surprisingly Tottenham had no objections, perhaps because they would be guaranteed the receipts from a massive crowd there, and the match was set for Easter Monday. At the time clubs could make their own arrangements with the FA's approval, which was forthcoming.

Spurs could not play on the Saturday as their Southern League opponents, Bristol City, refused to let them cancel that day's match, nor would the Southern League let Spurs put out a reserve team. City were annoyed because Spurs had sent a reserve team for the Western League fixture at Bristol on 27 March, before the first team played Reading, and the West Countrymen stood to lose part of a second large gate within two weeks if they again faced the reserves. As a result, the first team played against City, won 1–0, and went up to Birmingham for what is, as far as is known, the only semi-final initially scheduled for a Monday afternoon.

The game itself, on Monday 8 April, proved a massive anti-climax. Albion, though bottom of the First Division of the Football League, were favourites but Spurs, playing as well as the club had ever done in its history, were to win easily 4–0. As *The Sporting Life* said at the time, with considerable understatement: '. . . it is very difficult to single out any particular Spurs player for praise, but possibly Tottenham will regard Brown as the hero of the match. It really must be said that the centre-forward made the most of his opportunities . . .' In fact Sandy Brown scored all four goals, two with his head and two with his feet, one from 30 yards. This is an astonishing semi-final performance by any standards – and as far as can be ascertained from the records Brown remained the only man to score four goals at this stage until Fred Tilson did so for Manchester City in 1934.

Oddly all the goals came in the second half. Yet again it was the service Sandy Brown received from wingers Kirwan and Smith that broke Albion – the pattern of the previous games was sustained and Cameron's tactical planning had proved itself against yet another major side.

Because of the delayed start to the competition, the final followed just twelve days later, on Saturday 20 April at Crystal Palace. The enthusiasm and excitement were probably unprecedented before a Cup final. The reasons are not hard to find. Tottenham stood on the verge of a threefold triumph – that of becoming the first southern club since 1882, the first London professional side, and the first non-Football League club since that body was created to win the FA Cup. It is certainly true that clubs like Wanderers, Old Etonians and Clapham Rovers were London, or at least Home Counties, based, but their organization and support were as far removed from those of Spurs as the Isle of Man League is from the German Bundesliga.

Tottenham was the first London club with a widespread support and with working-class origins to reach an FA Cup final, then unquestionably the event in the football calendar. They were not, incidentally, the first professional southern club to reach the final – Southampton had done that the year before only to lose 4–0 to Bury. After knocking out Preston, Bury and West Bromwich, London really believed that this could be Tottenham's year, and turned up in their tens of thousands to see it happen. Estimates of the size of the crowd vary, but the papers the following day gave it as 114,815 and this is not likely to be an over-estimate.

This was the first game in football history which attracted a crowd of over 100,000 and it remains the third largest crowd ever for a football match in England – the two higher attendances being for the 1913 and 1923 Cup finals. The press of bodies was so great that the Spurs team could not get in through the players' gate, so director Ralph Bullock took them round to the official entrance. Here, in an incident so beautifully symbolic of its era and of many of the attitudes behind the Football Association, the team were told they couldn't come in because they hadn't got the right tickets. Bullock, to his credit, did manage to persuade the officials concerned that their

The 1921 Cup winners banquet was also held at the King's Hall in Holborn and the 1901 side was invited. All attended except goalkeeper George Clawley, who had died the year before, and the two sides were photographed together.

BELOW: After Spurs' Cup win John Cameron became something of a celebrity; among other writing assignments he was commissioned to produce one of the first, if not the first, guide on how to play the game. Not all of the illustrations were entirely convincing; the two featured here are entitled 'Centring from the left wing' and 'Shooting with the instep'.

attitude was a little short-sighted, but one wonders what significance was placed on the incident by the Tottenham players. It also begs the question of what those same officials thought the huge crowd of 114,815 people had turned up to see.

Their opponents were Sheffield United, though most of the crowd would have turned up just the same if it had been Penzance United. The Blades had won the League Championship in 1898, the FA Cup in 1899 and had beaten Sunderland, Everton, Wolves and Villa (all First Division clubs) on their way to the final. It was their semi-final defeat of the

great Aston Villa which had made United favourites for the Cup, though they were only 14th in the League. They had a remarkably talented team. In goal was Billy Foulke, 6ft 2in and even then weighing 21 stone, the biggest man ever to play professional football. In the centre were Tom Morren, one of only two men to win both FA and Amateur Cup winners medals, and the incomparable Ernest 'Nudger' Needham. The forward line was equally famed – Bennett, Field (the only one of the 22 players born in London or anywhere near it), Headley, Lipsham and Fred Priest, who became one of only half a dozen men to score three goals in FA Cup finals and the first to score two in a final and still finish on the losing side.

ASSOCIATION FOOTBALL

AND HOW TO PLAY IT

By **John Cameron**

SECRETARY
PLAYERS' UNION

PRICE

1/=

Net

WITH
NUMEROUS
ILLUSTRATIONS

"HEALTH & STRENGTH," Ltd.
12, BURLEIGH STREET, STRAND, LONDON, W.C.

On form, history and individual flair United certainly deserved to be favourites. Jack Jones and Nudger Needham tossed just as the guest of honour, Redvers Buller, took his seat to, according to the papers, great public support. Buller has found lasting fame in the history books by failing to win a single Boer War battle but could do little harm at Crystal Palace. Needham won the toss and, sensibly enough, chose to play with the sun and wind at his back. Kicking off at 3.30 p.m. Spurs again started nervously, and after 12 minutes Fred Priest shot past Clawley from 20 yards. This was not so disheartening for the Londoners crowded on the shallow banks – Spurs had now conceded the first goal in four of their five ties, in each case early on in the game.

It took the inevitable Sandy Brown only 13 minutes to equalise. John Kirwan took a free-kick on the left, up went Brown for the header and Foulke could only pick the ball out of the net. The game was following the script of Tottenham's well rehearsed earlier ties. There was no further score at half-time but, six minutes after the restart, Brown popped up again for his 14th goal of the competition. Jones to Kirwan, Kirwan to Brown, an interchange of passes with John Cameron and Brown was away to finish the move with a rasping, high shot off the crossbar – 2–1 to the Londoners and the crowd went berserk.

Those who saw Jack Allen score the 'over-the-line' goal for Newcastle against Arsenal in the 1932 final will argue that it was the most contentious ever conceded in an FA Cup final. They are wrong. One minute after Spurs had gone ahead thirty-one years before, Sheffield United 'scored' the goal that never was. So certain was everyone concerned, and everyone watching, that the ball had never gone over the line, that it has never been decided to whom the goal should be credited. And the ultimate irony was that the referee, Derby-based Mr Kingscott, became the first (but by no means the last) official ever to be caught out by the camera; the game was the first ever to be filmed and the producers, realising they were sitting on a gold mine, rushed out prints of the incident the following week. The moving pictures, which still survive, support the view that the ball never went over the line, or even went within a foot of it.

What happened was that Bert Lipsham, on the United left, got in a shot that Clawley could not hold. As the ball bounced in front of the goalkeeper, William Bennett rushed in but could only force it off Clawley behind the goal-line. Clawley appealed for a goal-kick, Bennett for a corner (a view which the linesman supported) and the referee gave a goal. For a time no-one could understand why, but Mr Kingscott eventually explained that he thought the ball had gone over the line when Clawley fumbled Lipsham's shot. The referee refused to consult his linesman, who clearly disagreed with the decision, and the goal stood. If it was any consolation to Tottenham, the fates were perhaps only taking back what they had so generously given earlier at Reading. After this the game was played in a slightly unreal atmosphere, Sheffield having the better of the play but neither side coming near to scoring, and the game ended at 5.12 p.m. as a 2–2 draw. It was not until 1913 that extra time was allowed if the scores were level after 90 minutes, so the teams shook hands and left the pitch contemplating a replay.

THE EMPTY REPLAY

The teams met again the following Saturday, 27 April 1901, at Burnden Park, Bolton. Yet again, the officials of the Football Association had failed to distinguish themselves with the arrangements for the replay, the first in a Cup final for fifteen years. They had originally proposed Goodison Park as the venue (the scene of the 1894 final) but Liverpool had protested as they were playing Nottingham Forest at Anfield, just a mile away, on the same day. Quite why the FA could not have chosen one of the Birmingham (Villa were away) or Nottingham grounds, quite convenient for both clubs, remains something of a mystery. Bolton was also patently a bad choice as the main railway station was being rebuilt and the Lancashire and Yorkshire Railway did not want hordes of soccer supporters invading the town. As a result they refused to offer cheap-day return tickets and the paying gate was only 20,740, easily the smallest at a Cup final this century (though pre-paid tickets and some Bolton season ticket holders probably pushed the figure over 30,000). Sad and sorry tales were told for years afterwards of pie salesmen having to throw away their uneaten wares, the expected exodus from London and Sheffield never having materialised. Spurs own receipts from the match were only £400. Eighty years later, the final and its replay eventually grossed over

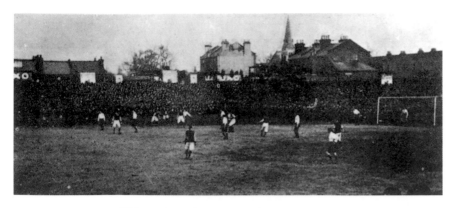

ABOVE TOP: A packed crowd watches the first half of the second round FA Cup tie between Spurs and Aston Villa at White Hart Lane on Saturday 20 February 1904. At half-time, with Villa leading 1–0, the crowd, which had been allowed to sit round the edge of the pitch (note that the corner flag has almost disappeared), invaded the pitch causing referee Jack Howcroft to abandon the match. The Herald reported that gates had been broken down (or possibly inadvertently left open) and that there were far too many people inside the ground. The FA fined Spurs £350 and ordered a replay at Villa Park the following Thursday. Spurs went on to win this game (ABOVE) 1–0 but were knocked out by The Wednesday in the next round.

£1,500,000, a sum unthinkable in 1901, to be shared between the FA, the FA pool, Spurs and Manchester City.

It was a cold day, with occasional showers and a strong wind. This, combined with what one newspaperman called '. . . a peculiar ground, sloping from the centre to the touch lines . . .' made for a rather scrappy game. The teams were unchanged, Sheffield again displaying their nine internationals opposed to Tottenham's four. Five minutes before the interval Tottenham yet again went behind, for the fifth time in their Cup run, when an unchallenged Fred Priest banged the ball home. Only three players (in 1970, 1989 and 1990) have since scored two goals in a Cup final and ended with a losers medal as reward.

It took Tottenham until the 55th minute to equalise, via a John Cameron snap shot, and from this point onwards the Spurs midfield took control. Tom Smith scored a clever second after another Cameron shot had been blocked and the inevitable Sandy Brown back-headed a third from either a Cameron or Kirwan (the newspaper reports differ) corner with ten minutes left. It was his 15th goal in the 1900–01 FA Cup, scored in only five rounds (rather than the six today) and established a record that will surely never be beaten. It was also the last Cup goal he was to score for Spurs. Kirwan, for his part, grabbed the ball at the end of the game, took it home and kept it until his death.

The trophy was presented to Jack Jones by Lord Arthur Fitzgerald Kinnaird, the President of the FA. Appropriately for it was he, as captain of Old Etonians in 1882, who had been the last man to receive the Cup on behalf of a southern side. When he did so, standing on his head in front of the pavilion at The Oval in celebration, Tottenham Hotspur FC had not even been formed.

Back in North London, the reserves were deputising for the first team in a Southern League fixture against Gravesend United (they won 5–0). Again, the Southern League had not allowed the game to be postponed. Needless to say, no-one was much interested in the result of that game, but the reaction of the crowd to the score from Bolton was a sight to behold. The team did not get back from Lancashire until 1 a.m. the following morning, but there was a massive reception on the High Road, with a band playing 'Hail the Conquering Heroes Come' and a firework display.

'Arbee', who had followed the Spurs faithfully in the Tottenham Weekly Herald for a decade and a half, quite lost control of himself in the following Friday's report. His piece, which ran to a full page, began: 'There are times in a man's life when he thinks a lot of things he can't give expression to, and that's just how I feel about last Saturday's magnificent accomplishment at Bolton. It really seems a hopeless task to adequately paint the picture in the way I would wish the Spurs supporters to read, mark, and learn. Our whole aim and ambition has been to bring that coveted trophy, the English Cup, to Tottenham, and yet their names are few who have ever thoroughly believed such would be the case. I know Bob Buckle was always very keen on seeing this happy state of affairs before he renounced active association with the team, and I can understand the feelings the same Bob, Jack Jull, Sam Casey, Jack Thompson, and Billy Mason must have had last Saturday evening. And again, one's mind turns to that little mound in Tottenham Cemetery, whereunder poor Frank Hatton (secretary of the club in the 1890s) sleeps, and deplores the fact that he wasn't spared to see the fruit blossom on the tree he did a deal to nourish and train. There are a whole flood of recollections come to one's mind in this hour of triumph. The early enthusiasm of our amateurs when men like Sykes, Briggs, Burrows, Jull, Cubberley, and Payne did their bit to push the club along, the subsequent advent of Jack Oliver with a wonderful wave of prosperity, and then the drastic change in our constitution by that big leap into professionalism. And after that! Well, dark days, but always a silver lining. We've had rare friends and staunch 'all weather' supporters like Mr Jull Senior, Mr Roberts, Harry Burton, T. Barlow, J. T. Thompson, and always the aforesaid Jack Oliver, and, to go further back, Johnny Ripsher – a name immortal to old Spurs. Yes, the management have been in tight corners financially. But that's a detail. Begone dull care! Let us live in the sunshine of the present and talk about what is more seasonable.'

The club held a celebration banquet a week later at the King's Hall in Holborn, where Bobby Buckle proposed the toast to the Cup winners and spoke of the club's history. No doubt he, like his listeners, found it astonishing that the boys' team he and ten others had founded a mere nineteen years before had just won the single biggest prize in the game. Charles Crump, a vice-president of the FA, responded by saying that he hoped the Cup would remain in the south. It didn't - indeed

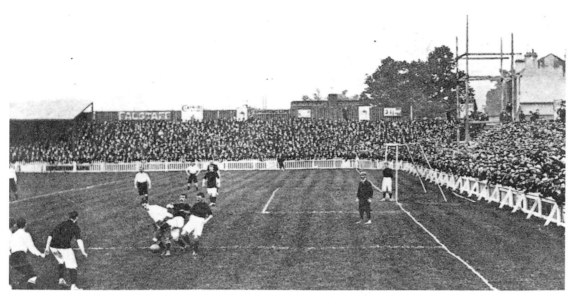

it was twenty years before it returned, and the team that was to bring it back was none other than Tottenham Hotspur.

THE JOINING OF THE LEAGUE

It seemed after the 1901 Cup success that Tottenham Hotspur must go from strength to strength and become one of the country's great sides. But, just as mysteriously as it had risen, so the Tottenham side declined. It was by no means a spectacular decline, rather a dull meandering without peaks or excitement. Cameron's failure to repeat his successes of 1900 and 1901 remains an enigma. Somehow it seems bound up with the departure of that remarkable talisman Sandy Brown. As has been mentioned before, the Southern League performances were acceptable, but in no way outstanding – second, fourth, second, fifth, fifth, sixth, seventh. The first team won the Western League (something of a misnomer as none of the premier division sides then came from further west than Bristol) in 1903–04 and the reserves had a particularly good season the year before, winning the top two divisions of the London League as well as the South Eastern League.

The Cup was unsatisfactory for the first eleven. In 1901–02 the holders, as many holders before and since, went out at the first attempt. It took three games for Southampton to dismiss them – the last one ending 2–1 in a snowstorm with the lines being continually re-marked as the game went on. Southampton were to go on to their second final, where they were beaten by Sheffield United. In the next six seasons Spurs reached the quarter-finals four times, but were to go no further until after the First World War.

Tottenham did figure in one interesting tie in that dull period, a second round match against Aston Villa at White Hart Lane. Spurs had won away at Goodison in the first round and, as a result, there was a feeling that this might again be Tottenham's year. The crowd for the Villa game was massive and the club put benches around the edge of the pitch to accommodate more people. Villa scored in the first half and, at half-time, a large part of the crowd invaded the pitch and refused to leave. It remains unclear quite what the purpose of the invasion was, but it seems likely that this was the first example of a crowd deliberately invading a pitch in the hope of getting a game abandoned because their team was losing. It has happened several times in recent years of course, notably at Newcastle. In this case the fans were remarkably successful. Referee Jack Howcroft could not get the pitch cleared and the game was abandoned. The FA ordered the match to be replayed at Villa Park the following Thursday (25 February) and fined Tottenham £350. To everyone's surprise Spurs won the replay 1–0, the goal being scored by Bristol Jones who was tragically to die of typhoid a few years later while still an active player. Having been transferred from Bristol Rovers, he was called Bristol to distinguish him from Jack Jones. Nowadays, no doubt, the FA would have awarded the game to Villa and fined Spurs much more severely.

At the time Spurs could afford the £350. They made a good profit every year between their first as a professional club (1898–99) and the First World War, when the finances of many clubs collapsed. The first six seasons in the League, 1908–14, were particularly profitable, the club making over £22,000 in all.

Money was, of course, a major reason for Tottenham's desire to join the footballing elite, but there was a stronger driving force. This

was sheer frustration with the attitudes of the Southern League. Conservative would probably be far too kind a term for its approach to twentieth-century football. Matters had come to a head between 1905 and 1907. Chelsea in 1905, and then Clapton Orient in 1906, had applied for membership, been refused, and had gone on to join the far more powerful Football League, which was happy to have members from the capital. In 1907 Fulham, champions of the Southern League the two previous seasons, joined them.

All of this was very worrying for the remaining major London clubs – Spurs, QPR, Millwall, Crystal Palace and West Ham. Leading Football League clubs were much big-

ger draws than their regular Southern League opposition (sides such as Leyton, Reading, Bristol Rovers etc) and Spurs were beginning to suspect a movement of their support to the Football League clubs in the metropolis. It might be added that the club's relatively poor playing record in recent years hardly helped crowds either. Spurs did try to overcome any financial problems a little by organising a baseball league at White Hart Lane in the summer. In the 1906–07 handbook they comment: 'Many supporters have got quite enthusiastic over the game...anyone who is desirous of playing should apply for a trial next spring.' To the regret of their baseball pitching chairman the scheme was a failure.

THIS PAGE: The programme from a London Challenge Cup tie against Chelsea on 10 October 1910, which Spurs won 3-0. This was the year in which the cockerel symbol became firmly established with the placing of bird and ball on the roof of the Main Stand, and this style of programme and newspaper illustration was common until after the Second World War. The caption 'I've got a terrible left!' presumably refers to the wing pair of Bert Middlemiss and Billy Minter which represented Spurs' major scoring threat at the time. Tottenham went on to win the London Challenge Cup (sometimes known as the London Charity Cup) this season, defeating Fulham 2-1 in the final at Stamford Bridge. It was, however, to be their last success in the competition until 1929.

OPPOSITE TOP & CENTRE: Two views of the players' social club, situated on the corner of the High Road and White Hart Lane, taken in 1904. Note the bar and the picture of the 1901 Cup winning team over the mantelpiece.

OPPOSITE BOTTOM: The home team changing room at around the same time; nearest the camera is Tom Morris, the most durable of the Cup winning team, who received two hefty benefits and was still playing for the first eleven at the start of the 1911-12 season.

Tottenham Hotspur Football and Athletic Company, Ltd.

Official Programme

And Record   of the Club.

Issued every Match Day.   PRICE ONE PENNY.

VOL. III. No. 9.   OCTOBER 10, 1910.

I'VE GOT A TERRIBLE LEFT!

REFEREE : Gentlemen : In this important Competition for the London Cup, I have pleasure in introducing the Competitors in the Second Round. On my left is "Old China" from Chelsea, and on my right is "Cocky," the Tottenham Bantam. Seconds out of the ring! Time!!

O. COVENTRY, Trade Union Printer, Lower Tottenham.

The Southern League refused to concern itself with the financial fears of its members and would not streamline its organisation or look to closer links with the Football League. It was a policy which was eventually to bring the Southern to a previously unimaginable low ebb in the 1920s. Spurs became so frustrated by all this that they decided to resign from the Southern in 1908. Queen's Park Rangers did the same. Unfortunately neither club had anywhere to go. QPR, then Southern League champions, changed their mind and asked to be readmitted, which they were but only on the financially crippling terms that they had to play all their home games in mid-week. Tottenham were rejected for Football League membership at the annual general meeting in summer 1908 (the voting was Grimsby 32, Chesterfield 23, Bradford Park Avenue 20, Lincoln 18, Spurs 14 and Burton United 1) but refused to go back cap in hand to the Southern. The result was that, as August approached, they had no fixtures except for friendlies and the FA Cup.

Fate smiled on them in a surprising way. Stoke (they did not become Stoke City until 1925) had been relegated to the Second Division in 1907 but found, after a season there, that crowds were not big enough to support the club. They decided on 17 June 1908 to resign from the League, a hasty move that the people of the Potteries were soon to regret. But, before doing so, the Stoke chairman got in touch with Charles Roberts to tell him of the decision. Some deal was struck between the clubs, possibly financial, and Stoke supported Spurs behind the scenes. By the time of the election, however, the Stoke board had changed its mind and decided to enter the new ballot. Nonetheless, a place had been created in the Second Division and Tottenham applied for it, as did Lincoln City. City's claim was good. They were founder members of the Division in 1892, had temporarily fallen on hard times being voted out in favour of Bradford PA in 1908, and were much closer geographically to most of the other clubs. Tottenham had only two advantages – they offered the potential of large crowds in London and they still had the mystique of that astonishing Cup win.

From a playing point of view Spurs had little or no claim – fifth, sixth and seventh in the last three Southern League seasons impressed no-one and they had lost in the first round of the Cup (1–0 at Goodison) the previous season. The voting could not have been closer: Tottenham and Lincoln tied twice (17 and 20 each) before the League Management Committee gave Tottenham their vote, 5–3. It was said later that it was the unspecified deal with Stoke which had swung the balance, but the reality is that nothing could ever compete with the lustre 1901 had added to Tottenham's name.

EARLY LEAGUE YEARS

Before the First World War, the football season began on the first day of September. On occasions the League treated that quite literally so, in 1908, Tottenham found themselves playing their first ever Football League game on a Tuesday afternoon, that day being 1 September. Their opponents could not have been more attractive, FA Cup holders

BELOW: Blackburn goal-keeper Arthur Robinson gathers the ball from Sandy Young during the FA Cup second round replay at White Hart Lane on Thursday 9 February 1911. Bob Steel, brother of cen-tre-half Dan, looks anx-iously. Blackburn won the game 2-0. Note the unusual method reserve forward Young is using to hold up his shorts.

Wolverhampton Wanderers, and a crowd of 20,000 turned out despite the pouring rain. The Midlanders, whose old strip Spurs had once worn, had just become only the second Division 2 side to win the FA Cup, and they had beaten hot favourites Newcastle United 3–1 to do so.

But Wolves were to find Spurs far trickier opposition, and the Londoners recorded their first League victory, 3–0, at the first attempt, Vivian Woodward scoring their first ever League goal after just six minutes. The side was interesting in that it contained only one member of the 1901 Cup-winning team; it was Hewitson, Coquet, Burton, Morris, Dan Steel, Darnell, Walton, Vivian Woodward, Macfarlane, Bob Steel and Middlemiss. Tom Morris was the sole survivor, though Sandy Tait, the club captain, had played on until the previous season aged 34. A fierce tackler, deadly serious on the field but apparently charming off it, Tait was an Edwardian Nobby Stiles and, by all accounts, the favourite of the crowd. Dan and Bob Steel were brothers, both from Glasgow, and Bobby Steel eventually took over his brother's key centre-half role. In those days this was not solely a defensive position, instead rather the link between attack and defence. The star of the 1908 side was, of course, Vivian Woodward.

Among Woodward's other accomplish-ments, and apart from scoring Spurs' very first League goal, he was, at the time, on the board of directors of the club – a remarkable combination. He was capped 23 times for the full England international side, 67 times for the England and United Kingdom amateur international teams, and captained the United Kingdom Olympic gold medal winning teams of 1908 and 1912. In his 23 full internationals he scored 29 goals, a record not bettered until Tom Finney scored his 30th in 1958. Tall and slim, he was a great dribbler, his style as well as his attitudes in some way belonging to the 1870s rather than the 1900s. It was said that he was never paid even the cost of a tram ride to the ground — an admirable amateur position, though one he could afford to adopt.

It was a great disappointment to the club when he decided to turn out for Chelsea in the 1909–10 season. Woodward remained on the Chelsea playing staff until the First World War, by which time he had scored 50 goals in 133 League games. There cannot have been many directors of League clubs who have played, even after their resignations, for another League club. Woodward, arguably the greatest centre-forward the club ever had, was to die on 31 January 1954, the same day as his friend and fellow director G. Wagstaffe Simmons, the club's first biographer and a

journalist on *The Sporting Life*. How strange that these two central figures in Tottenham's history should pass away on exactly the same day.

Wagstaffe Simmons' views about the game coincided closely with those one assumes Vivian Woodward held. In his 1946 *History of Tottenham Hotspur FC*, the first serious biography of the club since the *Tottenham Weekly Herald* had produced a series of articles in 1921, Simmons ranges far and wide over his own experiences as a referee and covers at great length the minutae of various contemporary political debates over entertainment tax and shareholder problems. It is interesting that in his section of 'Red Letter Events' he records such moments as '1924: First Annual Concert. Visit of T. R. H. Prince and Princess Arthur of Connaught' and '1926: Visit of H. R. H. Prince Feisal'.

With the deaths of Charles Roberts in July 1943, Arthur Turner in 1949 and Wagstaffe Simmons in 1954 it is clear that a whole era was put to rest. Between the First World War and the death of Charles Roberts in 1943 there was only one boardroom change, and that was caused by the death of one of the directors.

ABOVE: The Spurs side lines up at the Park Lane End before their first game of the 1912-13 season, versus Everton on 2 September. From left to right: Middlemiss, Darnell, Bliss, Tattersall, Rance, Collins, Lunn, Grimsdell, Lightfoot, Minter, Brittan. They lost the game 2-0 and did not win a League match until 23 November, after nine defeats and three draws. This remains Spurs' worst start to a League season, though they somehow ended it seven points clear of relegation.
LEFT: West Brom goalkeeper Pearson punches away a Spurs corner from the head of Billy Minter on 9 September 1911. Spurs won the game 1-0.

More than a whole generation of key Spurs figures was to be swept away soon after the Second World War.

Back in 1908–09, the first League season was a good one for Tottenham. They were unbeaten at home until 13 March, when West Bromwich won 3–1. With a week left Bolton, West Brom and Tottenham were neck and neck at the top of the division with just one game left each. By chance all three had to play Derby County! West Brom went first and lost; Spurs went second and drew 1–1 at the Baseball Ground; Bolton went third and won. So Spurs went up on goal average ahead of West Bromwich, who had led the table for most of the season, and Bolton were champions. But if Spurs had drawn 2–2 with Derby, rather than 1–1, they would not have been promoted, such was the closeness of the race and the idiosyncracies of the goal average system.

Promotion was a long awaited follow-up for the club, which was progressing in other ways. The old Main Stand, pulled down in 1980, took five years to build in all and was opened at the start of the 1909–10 season. It was on that stand that the cockerel and ball were first placed. These were transferred to the massive East Stand five decades later.

The origin of the cockerel symbol has never been satisfactorily explained. The Duke of Northumberland believes that Henry Percy became known as Hotspur because of the enthusiasm with which he led his troops into battle, digging his spurs deep into his horse's flanks to gain maximum speed. The spurs that were attached to the legs of fighting cocks (until the sport was outlawed) were very similar and the club's badge in the nineteenth century was actually a simple spur. It must be assumed that a link was made between the fighting cock and cockspur and the cockerel took over as the symbol. Certainly by the turn of the century newspaper cartoons were featuring Tottenham as a cock and this continued through to the early 1950s, when that kind of illustration began to die out.

SICK AS A PARROT

Winged symbols are not unique in football and Spurs might also lay claim to being the originators of the most ubiquitous of them all – the sickly parrot. This story begins at the same time as the cockerel and ball were put on the roof, and was told by G. Wagstaffe Simmons in his 1946 history. The club's first tour was to the Argentine in 1908. On the field things went successfully, the team losing only one game in seven, and that to fellow tourists Everton. Off the field things were less cosy. Several people were shot during a riot in a town where the team were attending a music hall, and during one game a troop of cavalry took to the pitch to beat back spectators with the flats of their swords. Apparently the gates had been broken down and the promoters wanted to drive the spectators out so that they would have to pay to get back in.

In those days, of course, journeys were by boat and it took weeks to reach South America. On the way home, one of the amusements the ship laid on for passengers was a fancy dress contest, which was eventually won by two of the Tottenham squad dressed as Robinson Crusoe and Man Friday. Suffering some

understandable confusion with the story of Long John Silver, they borrowed the ship's pet parrot to make their efforts more authentic and, in recognition of their success, the talisman bird was presented to the club by the ship's captain.

It apparently survived happily on the High Road for ten years, dying, according to Wagstaffe Simmons, on the day Arsenal were given Spurs' First Division place in 1919. Is it just possible that, in this incident, we find the roots of British soccer's most mysterious incantation: 'Sick as a parrot, Brian.'

Twelve months after promotion in 1909, Spurs were engaged in another tense battle, this time at the foot of the table. Again their fate was not resolved until the last match of the season, against neighbours Chelsea. Chelsea had 29 points, Spurs had 30 and, when the teams met at White Hart Lane one or other had to go down with bottom club Bolton. The unlucky ones were Chelsea, with Tottenham scraping home 2–1.

In some senses Tottenham's survival was of little significance. The club meandered along until the First World War, never rising above the halfway mark in the League, and it was honestly not a period which warrants much recalling. The Cup provides no more fertile ground for a historian, but there were a couple of games that deserve their place in the records. In the first round of the 1912-13 competition, Tottenham drew 1–1 with Blackpool at White Hart Lane. The Lancastrians, a Second Division club, were attracting poor crowds at the time, and agreed to sell their right to a home replay to Spurs. As a result the second game was played at Tottenham the following week and Blackpool, with two men off the field injured, lost 6–1.

The following year threw up a far more remarkable first round draw – away at Second Division Leicester Fosse's Filbert Street (they changed from Fosse to City after the First World War). That game resulted in Tottenham's highest scoring first–class draw, 5–5! Spurs won the replay 2–0 but went out to Manchester City at that club's old ground, Hyde Road in the second round.

Spurs played an annual charity game against the Edwardian equivalent of a showbiz eleven before the First World War. This particular picture was taken prior to the game on Thursday 5 March 1914, when Tottenham won 3-0. Few of the names would be familiar today, but seated in the centre is the great music hall star Marie Lloyd.

Despite the declaration of war in August 1914, the League and Cup were to continue for another season. This was, sadly, not to Tottenham's benefit. The club lost a disproportionate number of players who volunteered for the forces and this, added to the fact that the squad had never really got on top of First Division football anyway, meant that the club struggled from the start. The season's results make depressing reading: Sunderland won 6–0 at White Hart Lane and 5–0 at Roker, Liverpool won 7–2 at Anfield and Middlesbrough also scored 7. In the latter case Spurs did manage 5 by way of reply. The one bright spot was a Cup win over that same Sunderland side, a 2–1 victory being some con-

solation for all those League goals conceded. At the end of the season Tottenham finished bottom with 28 points, just one behind Chelsea and two behind Manchester United.

There was an interesting sequel to the season's final positions. Manchester United's last game of the season had been against Liverpool and it was later proved to have been fixed. When the League recommenced after the War this fact, plus Arsenal's intense ambition for First Division football, were to result in some very debatable manoeuvrings from which Spurs were clearly the losers. This story is told in full in the chapter on the North London rivalry, as is Arsenal's unwelcome arrival on Highbury Hill.

1921

Though it was not apparent at the time, Spurs' second great team was already largely built by the time British troops were fighting the first battle of the Great War, at Mons. Bert Bliss and Arthur Grimsdell had arrived in 1912, Jimmy Cantrell and Fanny Walden a year later, and John Banks, Bobby McDonald and Tommy Clay were signed before the outbreak of war. More important, Peter McWilliam, the Newcastle and Scotland half-back, became manager during the 1912–13 season. McWilliam had been left-half of that great Newcastle side which won three Championships and reached five Cup finals between 1905 and 1911. He was not a great tactical manager, but he was a good judge of men and of footballers. The story is told that, after the change in the offside law in 1925

(easily the most important alteration in the game this century), he held no team talks to work out new tactics. Rather he left Jimmy Seed, the team's key-man and scheming inside-forward, to drop back into midfield and work out the problem himself.

Interestingly, that first game under the offside law was against Arsenal at Highbury on 29 August 1925. Seed worked it out, and Spurs won 1-0. Given the direction the two North London clubs went in the next decade and a half (Arsenal won five Championships and two FA Cups, Spurs won nothing), plus Herbert Chapman's famed central role in developing the third-back tactic to counter the new offside rule, the result of the very first game under that revised system has a certain irony.

The Spurs team leaves Stamford Bridge with the Cup after the 1921 FA Cup final. The rain having finally stopped, the open topped charabanc drove through the West End and up the Seven Sisters Road to White Hart Lane.

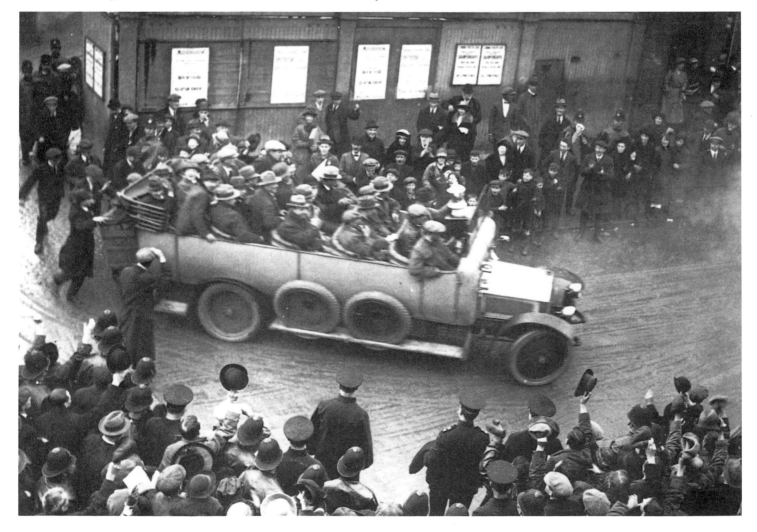

To today's ears McWilliam's lack of direction sounds vaguely unprofessional, but it was a structured era and one in which managers primarily picked men they thought could play and then let them get on with it. The manager was often also the secretary, though Tottenham had had a separate occupant of that position, Arthur Turner, since 1907. Turner had been one of the promoters of Rotherham Town FC and was a Yorkshire accountant. He remained at White Hart Lane for four decades, a critical influence behind the scenes.

The manager's skill was blending the right players into a particular pattern, as John Cameron did so successfully when he brought in Sandy Brown to complete his Southern League champions of 1900. Peter McWilliam was to do the same, only his key man was not a forward but a schemer, Jimmy Seed.

The parallels between Cameron's side and McWilliam's are uncanny. They both had a very brief flowering, spanning just three seasons. They both won a major League one season and the FA Cup the next. They both added a key member after winning the League but before embarking on their Cup run. But, on a less memorable note, neither really fulfilled their apparent promise and both sides faded, not spectacularly as some clubs do, but rather they gently subsided. Seed, always recognisable with his slicked-back, black hair

LEFT: A first team line-up from the record breaking Second Division season 1919–20. Standing (left to right); Archibald, Smith, Jacques, Grimsdell, Lowe, Brown, seated, McDonald, Banks, Seed, Cantrell, Bliss, Dimmock. Bert Bliss was the season's only ever present and scored 31 league goals. The team scored 102 goals and finished with a record 70 points.

ABOVE: Programmes from five of Tottenham's six Cup finals up to 1981, the 100th FA Cup final. Spurs have since appeared in the finals of 1982, 1987 and 1991. In fact all nine finals have been in years ending with 1, 2 or 7. They lost only one: in 1987.

was born in Durham but made his name with the Welsh club Mid-Rhondda. That unsung side was good enough to win the first ever Welsh League title after Seed had gone in February 1920, as well as one of the sections of the Southern League.

Jimmy Seed had been signed by his local club, Sunderland, at the start of the War but they released him after he had been gassed in France. Hence his arrival in Wales. After his playing career was over, he became manager of Clapton Orient, where he made headlines in his first managerial season. Arsenal were using Orient as something of a nursery club, guaranteeing debts and holding control over the player registrations. In 1931 the League ordered Herbert Chapman to stop this empire building and, as a result, Seed found himself managing a club without a single player on its books at the beginning of the next season.

Seed coped, and quickly moved on to humble Charlton Athletic. In 1935 Charlton were promoted as champions of Division 3 South. A year after that they were promoted straight through to Division 1, the first club ever to achieve this (only QPR have done it since). The following season Seed almost completed a spectacular treble when Charlton finished runners-up to Manchester City in Division 1. He took them to the FA Cup finals of 1946 and 1947 (when they beat Burnley 1–0) and, in all, he remained manager at The Valley for over 23 years, longer than any manager at any other English League club.

But to return to Spurs. After McWilliam had signed Seed he never again went scouting in South Wales without a wig and false beard, so violent had been the scenes when Seed's transfer was announced. After his last game for Mid-Rhondda, Seed had to address a crowd outside the dressing room, promising them that he was not being forced to leave. After this the crowd allowed the directors and players to leave the ground, though they missed Peter McWilliam, who was to be thrown into a nearby bog.

Jimmy Seed was at his best combining with Fanny Walden on the right wing. Walden, a tiny man who had first been signed by Herbert Chapman at Northampton, was capped in 1914 and 1922 but missed what should have been the most important game of his career through injury – the 1921 Cup final. He was also a county cricketer for Northamptonshire. Chapman, who unquestionably became the greatest manager in British football with Huddersfield in the 1920s and Arsenal in 1930s, had been on Spurs books (playing just 42 Southern League games) and his discovery joined Tottenham for £1,700 in 1913. Walden's place on the wing, after his injury in February against Arsenal, was taken by John Banks, a converted inside-forward, who took his chance well and ended with a Cup winners' medal to show for it. Apart from Seed, the team's other thinker was right-back Tommy Clay, who joined from Leicester Fosse in 1913.

On Saturday, February 5th —

Spurs v. Clapton Orient

LONDON COMBINATION.   KICK-OFF, 3.0.

On Monday, February 7th—

England v. South

INTERNATIONAL TRIAL.   KICK-OFF 3.0.

Second Round—ENGLISH CUP.   Kick-off 3.0.

TOTTENHAM HOTSPUR.

RIGHT WING.   LEFT WING.

GOAL
Jacques
1

BACKS

Clay   McDonald
2   3

HALF-BACKS
Smith   Walters   Grimsdell
4   5   6

FORWARDS
Walden   Seed   Cantrell   Bliss   Dimmock
7   8   9   10   11

Referee—Mr. H. RYLANCE.
Linesmen—Messrs. H. Miller and A. E. Betts.

12   13   14   15   16
Cook   Howson   Hibbert   Marsh   Poni

FORWARDS
17   18   19
McIlvenny   Storer   Duckett

HALF-BACKS
20   21
Boocock   Petts

BACKS
22
Ewart
GOAL

LEFT WING.   RIGHT WING.

BRADFORD CITY.

ANY ALTERATION WILL BE NOTED ON THE BOARD.

English League.—Division 1.

Made up to January 29th.

	P.	W.	D.	L.	For	Ag.	Pts.
Burnley	24	16	5	3	53	19	37
Newcastle United	24	13	5	6	47	26	31
Bolton Wanderers	25	11	9	5	46	29	31
Manchester City	24	13	4	7	49	30	30
Everton	26	10	10	6	41	36	30
Liverpool	24	11	7	6	41	23	29
Middlesbrough	24	11	7	8	37	21	29
Tottenham Hotspur	24	11	4	9	53	35	26
Arsenal	24	9	8	7	34	35	26
Manchester United	24	10	6	8	42	41	26
Aston Villa	25	10	5	10	41	43	25
Preston North End	24	9	5	10	37	35	23
West Bromwich Albion	23	7	9	7	31	36	23
Chelsea	24	8	7	9	26	36	23
Blackburn Rovers	21	7	8	9	25	36	22
Sunderland	24	7	8	9	29	34	22
Bradford City	23	7	7	9	32	34	21
Huddersfield Town	25	7	6	12	20	30	20
Sheffield United	27	4	10	13	24	48	18
Oldham Athletic	24	3	9	12	24	58	15
Derby County	24	2	10	12	18	34	14
Bradford	21	4	5	15	26	49	13

BEWARE!

The public is cautioned against buying "pirate" programmes. They are in no sense official. Our boys outside the Ground will in future wear caps labelled "Tottenham Hotspur Programme."

Seats may be reserved for any League Match on application to the Secretary, at 750, High Road, Lower Tottenham, enclosing P.O. for 5s. No seats can be booked by telephone.

London Combination.

Made up to January 26th.

	P.	W.	D.	L.	For	Ag.	Pts.
West Ham United	21	14	6	4	52	33	34
Tottenham Hotspur	24	12	5	7	61	32	29
Fulham	23	13	4	7	39	26	28
Queen's Park Rangers	19	10	6	3	47	25	26
Millwall	19	8	4	7	30	21	20
Crystal Palace	23	8	5	10	50	53	21
Chelsea	21	6	7	8	32	28	19
Arsenal	21	8	0	13	44	45	16
Clapton Orient	20	6	4	10	37	50	16
Brentford	22	2	4	16	24	72	8

THE BEST WAY HOME TO ALL PARTS OF LONDON

By Metropolitan Electric Trains from outside the ground to Finsbury Park Station and thence by

UNDERGROUND

LEFT: The programme from what became known as Jimmy Seed's game – the second round tie in 1921 between Spurs and Bradford City on 29 January 1921. Seed got a hat-trick in the second half, a 45-minute spell which he later called the best display of his life. John Banks, who had replaced Fanny Walden on the right wing, got a fourth and Spurs won 4–0. Apart from Alex Hunter replacing Jacques in goal when the latter was injured, the side was the same as the one which won the Cup. The numbers beside the players' names were of little practical help. Despite the efforts of Spurs and Arsenal, numbering was not introduced in League games until 1939.

FAR LEFT: Spurs supporters parade the short distance between Fulham Broadway underground station (then called Walham Green) and Stamford Bridge on the morning of the 1921 Cup final.

BELOW: Jimmy Cantrell breaks through the Southend defence during the 1921 third round tie at the Essex club's old Kursaal Gardens ground (the funfair can be seen in the background). Cantrell scored Spurs' equaliser to make it 1–1, but Southend then missed a penalty before Tottenham pulled away to win 4–1 in the second half.

45

BELOW: Arthur Grimsdell
holds the Cup outside
Stamford Bridge; after the
obligatory photo was taken
Grimsdell handed the Cup
to trainer Billy Minter and
caught a train home to
Watford, not taking part in
any of the celebrations
afterwards.
OPPOSITE TOP: Despite
the quagmire of a pitch,
both King George V and the
future George VI (then
Prince Albert, Duke of
York) came out to meet the
teams. Here King George is
shaking hands with Jimmy
Seed while full-backs
Tommy Clay and Bobby
McDonald wait their turn.
OPPOSITE CENTRE: An
hour and three quarters
later Arthur Grimsdell
receives the FA Cup from
the King.
OPPOSITE BOTTOM: A
very wet Stamford Bridge
during the final.

Not very quick, but extremely clever position-
ally, he was a great passer of the ball. Oddly,
the abiding White Hart Lane memory of Clay
was of a mistake. It was in the quarter-finals of
the 1919–20 FA Cup, against old enemies
Aston Villa. Spurs, running away with the
Second Division title, were well fancied to
achieve a rare double when Clay, faced with a
harmless ball and in no particular danger,
somehow sliced his clearance backwards into
his own net. It was the only goal of the game
and Spurs went out, 1–0. Nearly forty years
later, Tommy Clay remembered it as the single
most vivid moment of his career. The England
Selection Committee obviously didn't consider
it so important, for Clay was picked for his first
international two days later and he won four
caps in all.

No great side has eleven great players.
Apart from Clay and Seed, the Spurs of 1921
had perhaps two other stars, the left side partnership of Arthur Grimsdell and Jimmy
Dimmock. Grimsdell, club captain throughout
the 1920s, was born in Watford and was the
epitome of a scheming, attacking wing-half.
Spurs' single, most basic, movement was a
triangle formed by Grimsdell, Dimmock and
Bert Bliss. Grimsdell would play the ball
down the left wing to Dimmock, Dimmock
would beat the back, reach the goal-line and
pass it inside for inside-left Bert Bliss, or

centre-forward Jimmy Cantrell, to shoot home.
Julian Holland said of Arthur Grimsdell:
'When he was injured he was sorely missed.
He inspired his men, and he stamped his personality on them . . . he was a players' player.
Not only did he know what to do in any given
situation, he could also do it. He impressed
players and spectators alike with the *efficiency*
of his play . . . it was utilitarian football with
an emphasis on craftsmanship and it made
him the greatest half-back of the decade, if
not of all time.'

Seed, the counterbalance, was used not so
much as the creator but as the organiser. It
was Seed who had to drop back to cover the
space left by Grimsdell's constant foragings
down the left in support of Dimmock. And it
was Seed who had to drop back to play the
linkman after the offside law change. When
Spurs were not seeing enough of the game
(unlike Arsenal they have never been a side
content to absorb pressure and defend for
long spells; teams from White Hart Lane have
always sought out the ball, not just the result)
it was Seed who had to drop back to try and
win the ball more often.

Dimmock was the idol of the fans, a local
lad from Edmonton who was not yet 21 when
he won his first England cap and his Cup winners' medal. A classic flying left-winger, he was
the fourth of the side to be first capped in the

Cup winning year and there were seven caps in all – Clay, Grimsdell, Seed, Dimmock, Bliss, Walden and Bert Smith. It should be remembered that, at this time, the home countries played only three games a year, and to be capped was a far rarer achievement than it is today when international sides usually play four or five times as many fixtures.

Bert Bliss, at inside-left, was another great crowd-pleaser, the trigger man. He was small (5 ft 6 in) and balding, a West Midlander from Willenhall by birth. His 'glory' was really reflected glory. He succeeded because of the service he received from Dimmock and Grimsdell, a constant stream of passes which he converted to hammer-shots towards the goal or, more often, well wide or over it. One can see why he was such a crowd-pleaser. The other Bert, Smith, was actually signed on Bert Bliss's recommendation while the former was playing as a forward with Huddersfield. He was tried at right-half and succeeded well enough to play against Scotland in 1921 and against Wales a season later.

The four less well known members of the Cup winning side were goalkeeper Alex Hunter, signed from Queen's Park as an amateur, who took over from 26 February 1921 when regular keeper Jacques was injured against West Bromwich. Another Scot, Bobby

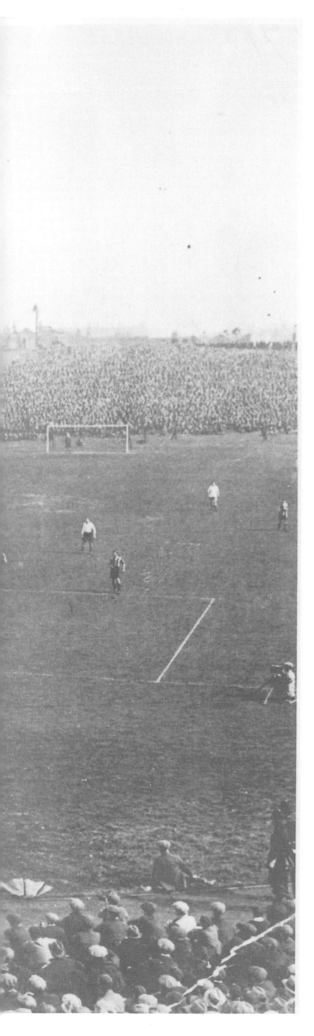

McDonald, was Clay's partner at left-back and, like Hunter, was an amateur when he signed from Inverness Caledonian. Centre-forward Jimmy Cantrell came from Notts County in 1913 and performed as something of a dual spearhead with Bert Bliss. Heaviest (12½ stone) and biggest (5 ft 11 in) was centre-half Charles Walters. Yet another amateur when he joined Spurs, Walters had made his name playing for Oxford City. With the exception of Seed (who replaced Banks in midfield) this was the team which walked away with the Second Division Championship in 1920.

THE 1921 FA CUP RUN

When Tottenham's lack of success in the pre-war First Division is considered, it is arguable that the Football League did the club something of a favour by refusing to elect it to that division in 1919. The injustice felt by club, players and fans was the perfect spur to show all concerned that a major mistake had been made. Tottenham ran away with the Second Division from the start. They won their first seven matches, scoring 28 goals and conceding just four. They dropped just two points at home (draws with Blackpool and Birmingham) all season and lost just four games away. All in all, they accumulated 70 points, easily the highest up to that time for any club in a season and not surpassed until Doncaster Rovers managed 72 in Division 3N in 1946–47. Tottenham's 70 points remained a record for the division until the end of the two points for a win system in 1981, and the club's 32 wins is still the highest number ever obtained in Division 2. Only one English club (Doncaster) has bettered it in a 42-match season. Of the club's 102 goals, 31 were scored by Bert Bliss, 19 by Cantrell, 14 by Grimsdell.

Hence Spurs had recorded their lowest ever League points total (28 in 1914–15) and their highest (70 in 1919–20) in consecutive League seasons.

The following season, 1920–21, the side settled down well in the First Division, eventually finishing sixth, but, as in 1900–01, it was the FA Cup that drew everyone's attention. This time Tottenham went right through the six rounds without a replay and the first two of these proved relatively easy. First round opponents on Saturday 8 January 1921 were Third Division Bristol Rovers (there was only one Third Division at the time). A crowd of 35,000 saw Spurs win easily 6–2, Rovers being further handicapped by having to play with ten men for virtually the whole game. Seed, Clay, Smith, Walden, Cantrell and Bliss got the goals.

Three weeks later First Division Bradford City should have proved tougher opposition at White Hart Lane in the second round, but a 39,000 crowd saw an equally one-sided match. This was Jimmy Seed's game for he scored a hat-trick (two within the space of 30 seconds) and ran the match. John Banks got the fourth from a Dimmock corner. Banks had come back into the side for Fanny Walden after the winger had been injured against Arsenal. All four goals came in the second half and Seed later said that it was probably the best 45 minutes he ever played. After the match Peter McWilliam ticked Seed off over his third goal – a 35-yard screamer – saying he should have dribbled it in and not shown off.

LEFT: The sole picture known to exist of the only goal of the 1921 FA Cup final. Jimmy Dimmock (white shirt, directly in line with photographers) ran down the left wing almost from his own half, somewhat fortuitously beat two Wolves defenders on the way, cut into the penalty area and hit a half-powered shot from around 15 yards out. The ball skidded in the mud just in front of keeper George and slipped underneath his diving arms. The ball can be seen entering the net just beside the left hand post. The two well placed Spurs players in the area are John Banks and, beside the penalty spot, Jimmy Seed. The picture on page 47, which shows Dimmock attacking down the left, was taken from the block of flats in the centre distance. The winning team was Hunter, Clay, McDonald, Smith, Walters, Grimsdell, Banks, Seed, Cantrell, Bliss and Dimmock. As can be seen from the two photographs, Stamford Bridge had virtually no cover from the elements at that time. The Chelsea ground, originally the home of the London Athletic Club, was opened for football in 1905 and was chosen for the first three post-war Cup finals because it had the largest capacity of all the London soccer grounds at that time. The crowd was 72,805 and the receipts (£13,414) were the highest then recorded for any football match.

The third round should have been easier than it proved. The draw took them down the Thames to Southend, then playing on their old Kursaal Gardens ground. It was a classic David versus Goliath Cup-tie – Southend running, harrying, tackling and putting Spurs off their game. The Londoners did not respond too well to the problems Southend set, and were a goal down within 15 minutes, scored for the Third Division side by winger Nicholls. This at least provoked a response and Cantrell quickly headed home an equaliser from a Banks corner. A quarter of an hour before the break Southend should have gone ahead. Smith fouled Nuttall on the goal-line and skipper Fairclough prepared to take the kick. The referee, however, had noticed that the ball was not on the spot and moved it himself. Fairclough walked up to reposition it (a nervous habit rather than anything else) but the referee would not allow him to touch it. After some arguing Fairclough took the kick and shot wide. That was the turning point and Spurs did not allow Southend to regain the initiative in the second half. Banks, Bliss

(with a 25-yard free-kick) and Seed settled matters at 4–1 and Tottenham were through to the quarter-finals. But what would have happened if Fairclough *had* scored from that penalty did not bear thinking about.

By an odd quirk of fate, Tottenham's quarter-final opponents were Aston Villa, who had put them out at the same stage the season before. And, as in 1919–20 and in that famous replayed game in 1903–04, there was only to be one goal in it. 52,000 fans paid £6,992 to see the game at White Hart Lane, both figures easily records for the club at the time and the receipts were actually the highest ever recorded for any club game (other than a Cup final) in England. Villa had won the Cup the year before and were favourites to become the first club since Blackburn in 1890 and 1891 to do so in consecutive years. The goal came from a Dimmock move on the left; he centred for Seed but the schemer dummied and allowed the ball to run through to his right for Banks to side-foot it home from a narrow angle. For a reserve winger Banks was remarkably effective. Seed said afterwards that he hadn't dummied at all, but had frozen and that Banks had had to kick both Seed and the ball to take advantage of the sudden confusion in the Villa defence. The shot had lacked power only because most of the force had been absorbed by Seed's back!

The semi-final was against Preston North End. The game was played at Hillsborough before a crowd of 44,668. It was actually a poor contest, Spurs being by far the superior team. In the first half they had two seemingly good goals disallowed (one when the referee, a Mr Forshaw of Birkenhead, brought play back to give Spurs a free-kick) and Dimmock hit the bar when he should have scored. Bert Bliss did better with two goals in the 51st and 56th minutes, both from moves set up by the magical Arthur Grimsdell. Preston replied once later in the game – an own goal off Tommy Clay's knee. Unlike his own goal against Villa the year before, this one fortunately didn't matter.

THE 1921 CUP FINAL
Crystal Palace, home of the Cup final between 1895 and 1914, had been requisitioned by the Army during the war as a munitions dump. No one had restored the ground after the war ended and the Football Association had to turn elsewhere for a venue. Indeed, Crystal Palace was never again used as a football ground; Selhurst Park, home of the current Crystal Palace club, has no connection with its far more famous predecessor. The FA chose Stamford Bridge, essentially because it had a bigger capacity than any other London ground. It nearly proved a big mistake, for Chelsea reached the semi-finals in 1920 and would have played the final at home had Villa not defeated them. In 1921 Spurs clearly enjoyed the advantage any London club holds in a Cup final – a shorter distance to travel and an inevitably friendly crowd. Their opponents were Wolves, the first club Tottenham had ever played in the Football League and semi-final victors over Cardiff City. They were a Second Division club, but so had they been when they won the Cup in 1908. The crowd for the final was 72,805, easily the biggest at the ground up to that time, and the

receipts were the biggest for any football match in history (though they were easily surpassed at the first Wembley final two years later). The crowds were so great that they were let into the ground at 10.30 a.m., hours before the kick-off at 2.55 p.m. It was not until 1924 that the Cup final became all ticket.

The match is perhaps best remembered for the weather. It had rained all day and, apart from a brief spell of sunshine just before the kick-off, it continued that way. Pictures of the two Kings (George V and the future George VI) shaking hands with the teams appear to show the Tottenham eleven lost somewhere in a paddy field. The weather also kept the photographers away. Only one picture survives of Jimmy Dimmock's goal, and that was taken from the terraces. In honesty, the conditions turned the game into something of a farce. Spurs were (and remained so throughout the next 40 or so years) a club which played the ball on the ground. A certain amount of rain was no disadvantage for them as favourites – it made defending harder – but a tropical downpour was a disaster. Strength would clearly tell over skill.

The game does not bear much recounting. The players slugged away, slipping and sliding in the mud, and, in general, Tottenham were the better side with Wolves creating hardly any chances. Tottenham took just one of the few good ones they created. Jimmy Dimmock was generally regarded by the following day's newspapers as having had a poor game, but in

the 54th minute, he took a pass near the halfway line from Bert Bliss. He ran the ball through the Wolves half, beat Gregory, but could not beat Woodward, who intercepted the ball. Unfortunately for the Wolves right-back, who had kept Dimmock quiet all afternoon, the ball bounced back off his legs before he could clear it and Dimmock was able to pick it up again. He cut into the penalty area and shot left-footed from about 15 yards. The ball skidded on the quagmire, kept artificially low, shot under the out-stretched arms of Wolves keeper George and just slipped inside the far post. Any goal that wins a Cup final is a good goal, but some are luckier than others and few can have been luckier than Dimmock's. It was also a selfish goal, for both Seed and Banks were well placed for a killing pass. On a good day Dimmock would probably not have beaten either Woodward or George, but then on a good day Spurs would probably have won in far more style and the fans would have been far better entertained into the bargain.

Wolves pressed but could achieve nothing, particularly with Charles Walters in inspired form at the centre of the Spurs defence. If it was anyone's match, it was his. In the very last minute, soon after Jimmy Dimmock had hit the crossbar, Wolves outside-left Brooks broke clear a few yards out. He should have equalised, but Walters got across fast enough to deflect the shot. Walters was never very creative, but he was very fast and that was his strength.

Keeper Herbert Blake and Bert Smith combine to clear a Cardiff attack during a third round FA Cup tie at White Hart Lane on 24 February 1923. Arthur Grimsdell (centre) looks unsure about Blake's punching abilities. Spurs won the game 3–2 but went out in the quarter-finals to Derby County.

So Spurs had yet again brought the Cup back to London, still the only professional southern side to win the game's greatest honour. It was a record they were to maintain until Arsenal won the 1930 final, though Cardiff City in 1927 might claim to be included. Celebrations were certainly different then. Captain Arthur Grimsdell, having collected the Cup from the King, handed it over to trainer Billy Minter and went back home to Watford. It was carried back to Tottenham, via Hyde Park, Camden Town and the Seven Sisters Road, in an open charabanc. Attached were the original ribbons from the rather more glorious moment of twenty years before. There was, as in 1901, a celebration dinner at the Holborn Restaurant. The whole of the 1901 team attended with the sole exception of goalkeeper George Clawley, who had died on 16 July 1920.

The Cup was paraded around the ground the following week, carried by groundsman John Over. Four decades earlier Over had laid out the pitch at Kennington Oval for the first England v Australia test match and had joined Spurs from Edmonton Cricket Club. No one was allowed to set foot on the White Hart Lane pitch while he remained in charge of it. Even stars like Seed and Grimsdell would be disciplined if they ignored this rule; it was even rumoured that Over had doubts about them trespassing on his pitch on Saturday afternoons. When he died, his son Will took over as head groundsman.

THE INTER-WAR DECLINE

When a club is only just over one hundred years old it may seem a little strange to concentrate only briefly on nearly a quarter of that whole period. But compared with what had gone before and, more significantly, what has happened since, the period from the 1921 FA Cup win through to Arthur Rowe taking over after the Second World War can only be called disappointing. The club reached the semi-finals of the Cup in 1921–22, and finished second in the League, but from here onwards it was down all the way. They did not finish above the halfway mark for the next six seasons and were relegated to the Second Division in remarkable circumstances in 1928. It took five years to get back again but, after a brief flowering in third place in 1933–34, Spurs went straight back down again. And there they stayed for another decade and a half until Arthur Rowe's push-and-run team took football by storm.

If the predominant reflection on Spurs' League performances in this period is one of mediocrity, then at least the Cup provided more than a little interest. A good run in the 1921–22 competition took Spurs to a repeat semi-final, against Preston at Hillsborough. It was a game that Spurs should have won. They were one up at half-time but Preston equalised after the break having (according to the Press) drunk champagne during the interval. Towards the end Bert Bliss scored with a blistering drive but, at the moment it entered the net, the referee blew for attention to be given to a Preston player near the halfway line. It was an odd decision, to say the least, and, according to Wagstaffe Simmons, the player was not even injured anyway. The incident threw Spurs and Preston got the winner near the end. Preston's

luck ran out in the final; they lost to Huddersfield after the referee gave a penalty against them for a tackle which was clearly outside the area.

Between 1922 and the Second World War, Spurs got no further than the quarter-finals, though they did that in three consecutive seasons (1935–36, 1936–37, 1937–38) while in the Second Division. There were certainly some interesting performances in that three-year spell. In the 1935–36 third round draw, Southend were drawn at White Hart Lane. Memories were revived of the same round in 1920–21, though this time Spurs' job was expected to be easier. It wasn't: Tottenham scored four goals just as they did in 1921 but, amazingly enough, Third Division Southend did the same. Spurs won the replay 2–1, this time at Southend Stadium, but lost 3–1 away at Bramall Lane to Sheffield United in the quarter-final.

The following season, 1936–37, saw one of the most exciting games the club has ever taken part in. In fact it is difficult to think of a more exciting match from the great days of the 1960s. It came in the fifth round. Spurs had been drawn away at Goodison. It was a poor game, which sprang to life in the last five minutes after Everton had been awarded a penalty for a foul on William 'Dixie' Dean. Dean took the kick himself, but his shot was saved by ex-Manchester United goalkeeper John Hall. Dean followed up on the loose ball, but Hall saved again and cleared downfield. Jimmy McCormick picked up the ball and Spurs, right against the run of play, were suddenly ahead. But that wasn't the end of it. Coulter equalised for Everton and the game was forced into a replay at White Hart Lane on Monday 22 February 1937.

This was the game that Joe Mercer later wrote about as the most memorable match he ever played in. Everton were leading 3–1 with just seven minutes left. It should have been 4–1 after a strange incident revolving around a throw-in by Mercer himself. The linesman flagged for a foul throw but the referee did not notice. Everton attacked down the left, winger Gillick was fouled in the area and Everton were awarded a penalty. At this point the referee spoke to the linesman – and decided to award Spurs a throw-in back where Mercer had taken his. While the referee's judgement on facts is always correct, of course, having let play go on so long the usual response would have been to continue as if the foul throw had never occurred. At the time it did not seem to matter but, with just six minutes left, centre-forward Jack Morrison made it 3–2. Two minutes later Joe Meek ran through to equalise with a solo goal. The relief on the terraces was enormous, but they had yet to witness the finale for, with the last kick of the game, Morrison got a fourth and Spurs had won a game (4–3) which was as unwinnable as any they had ever played.

Joe Mercer said afterwards: 'I stood there hardly able to realise that we had lost . . . Programmes were going up in the air, coming down and being thrown up again. Men and women and boys were dancing in circles, shaking hands and slapping one another on the back and throwing hats (which probably did not belong to them) in the air. I bet there were thousands of hats lost that day and I bet no-one cared. On the day it was played I hated

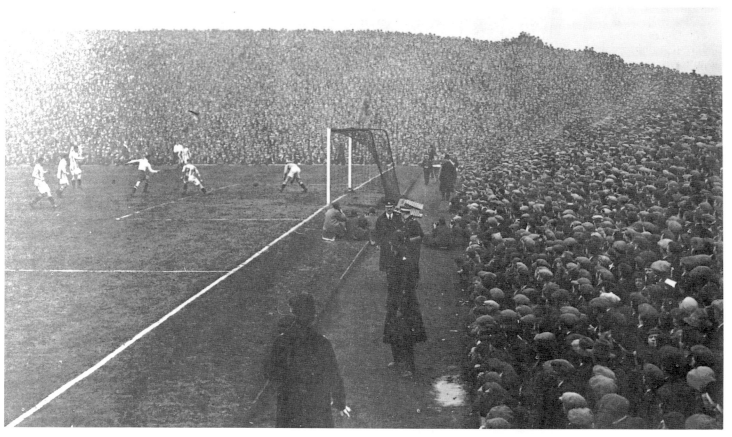

that game. Today it stands out as the greatest in which I ever took part, a belief in which I must be joined by everyone who was there.'

As Spurs had won a remarkable third round game away at Fratton Park (home of then highly rated Portsmouth) by a startling 5-0, hopes were understandably high for further progress. Sadly, there was no fairy story to follow, for Preston won 3-1 at White Hart Lane in the quarter-finals. It was the fourth time Spurs and Preston had met in the Cup since the First World War, and laurels had remained equal, a 2-1 and a 3-1 win each. 1938 saw another quarter-final, this time with considerably less drama. Spurs had struggled to get there, having been taken to replays by undistinguished New Brighton and Chesterfield. They were drawn against Sunderland at White Hart Lane in the sixth round, and the game drew the largest attendance in the club's history, 75,038. The technical capacity was even higher (78,000) but

this crowd will surely remain the largest ever to see a game on the High Road.

They were to be sorely disappointed, Sunderland winning 1-0. There was one odd incident in the game, however. Colin Lyman shot home for Spurs from an acute angle on the left and Alec Gibbons, sure that the ball was over the line, celebrated by punching it into the back of the net. The referee gave a goal, but a linesman flagged that the ball had not crossed the line when Gibbons handled it, though it was clearly on its way. It was a very strange incident indeed, and it probably cost Spurs a semi-final place.

Not all inter-war Cup matches were wine and roses. Lowly Crystal Palace beat Spurs 2-0 at Selhurst Park in 1923-24, while unlikely Reading did exactly the same in Berkshire five years later. Neither of these humiliations compared with the quarter-final tie at Huddersfield on Saturday 3 March 1928 however. The home side, League Champions in 1924, 1925 and 1926, and runners-up in 1927 and 1928, scored five goals in the first half and presumably let up only out of pity after the break. They eventually ran out winners 6-1 in a game best glossed over. The players were later to complain that they had been made to go out on long walks across the snow covered Derbyshire moors from their Buxton hotel and had all contracted colds.

Peter McWilliam had remained as manager of the club until February 1927, when Middlesbrough offered him £1,500 per annum to take over at Ayresome Park. Spurs were reputedly paying him only £850, but he would have stayed for £1,000. The Spurs board refused, for whatever reason, to give McWilliam that small rise and he left, only to be asked to return nearly a dozen years later.

THE SEED AFFAIR

Billy Minter, an inside-forward with the club in the pre-war years, had been trainer of the 1920-21 Cup winning side and took over as manager from McWilliam. It was soon afterwards that the club perpetrated perhaps its

A Tottenham Hotspur season ticket from their fiftieth season, 1931–32. The bearer simply showed the plastic disc and was allowed into the ground (by courtesy of Hugh Wrampling Esq).

biggest ever mistake on the transfer market. In recent years only the sale of Pat Jennings to Arsenal can remotely compare with Jimmy Seed's departure for Sheffield Wednesday.

Seed had been injured and a Welsh lad from the Northfleet nursery, Taffy (Eugene) O'Callaghan, had been promoted to the first team. O'Callaghan and Spurs colleague Willie Evans were later to be key members in Wales' Home Championship winning sides of 1932–33, 1933–34, and 1936–37. He was playing so well on the left side of the field, combining magnificently with the ex-Fulham forward Frank Osborne, that Seed could not get his place back from 'Boy Wonder' O'Callaghan. Of course a place should have been found for both of them, for no club finds players of their quality more than once or twice a decade. But Seed was given a transfer and went to apparently doomed Sheffield Wednesday.

Arthur Grimsdell had broken a leg in 1926 and missed nearly a whole season, after which he was never quite the same player as he had been in the early 1920s. The loss in such a short space of time of the two great orchestraters of the 1920–22 period (and remember that footballers' careers were much longer and took time to develop in those days), was too much for the club to bear. Seed, in his autobiography, said that he left Spurs basically because they reduced his wages from £8 per week to £7 while he played in the reserves.

It was unknown at the time, but Seed's departure was to have a far more immediate effect on Spurs' fortunes. He joined Wednesday during the 1927–28 season, when the Yorkshire side seemed certain of relegation from the First Division. With only ten matches left to play, they were five points behind the 21st club. But Seed's arrival rejuvenated them and, as Easter approached, they seemed to have a chance, if a faint one, of survival. Spurs, with just six games left to play, were in the top half of the table with 35 points. The League was so close that year that the players were thinking of perhaps just scraping into the 'talent money' places – the top four in the division where clubs were allowed to pay bonuses to their players over and above the maximum wage. It is doubtful that relegation had ever occurred to anyone at White Hart Lane, for in many ways the

season had been an encouraging one. Their best result was at Goodison where they had beaten League leaders Everton 5–2 and Taffy O'Callaghan had confirmed his continuing selection with four of the goals.

But Easter was to prove vital. Wednesday and Spurs had to play each other twice. On Good Friday, 6 April 1928, the Yorkshiremen won 3–1 at White Hart Lane. Seed scored. On Easter Tuesday, 10 April 1928, they also won, 4–2 at Hillsborough. Seed scored again. Wednesday could now save themselves. Spurs, still with no thought of relegation, finished their season earlier than most of the division (they were above the danger area) and went off to the Netherlands on a tour. They had drawn 2–2 at Burnley on 14 April, lost 4–1 at home to Bury on 21 April and lost again, 2–0 away at Anfield on 28 April. When they returned a few days later they were a Second Division club. The results had fallen in such a remarkable way that seven clubs had ended with 39 points. Tottenham had 38 and Middlesbrough 37, the highest points totals ever recorded by two relegated clubs from a 22-team division before the introduction of three points for a win.

The whole table was a complete statistical freak. Derby, who finished fourth, had just six more points than Spurs. A span of seven points covered all but three of the clubs in the division – and champions Everton managed only 53. Nothing like it had happened before nor has happened since. But it made little difference to Spurs – they were a Second Division club again. Wednesday and Seed had not only saved themselves, they finished a respectable 14th. The following two seasons, 1928–29 and 1929–30, Seed led Wednesday to the Championship. Taffy O'Callaghan and Spurs had done him a quite remarkable favour.

RISE AND FALL

Billy Minter's reign as manager did not last long. On the two previous occasions the club had been in the Second Division they were promoted at their first attempt But Spurs could finish only 10th in 1928-29 and 12th in 1929-30 (still the worst performance in the club's League history) and Minter, who remained as an assistant secretary until his death, was replaced by Bury manager Percy Smith. Smith rapidly remodelled the side – its most

notable members being centre-half Alf Messer from Reading, Taffy O'Callaghan at inside-forward, and Eddie Harper at centre-forward. Harper had been the First Division's leading scorer with Blackburn in 1925–26, and was capped against Scotland the same year. He had been bought from Sheffield Wednesday in 1929, and, though past his best, scored 36 goals in 1930–31. No Spurs player beat this in a single season until Jimmy Greaves got one more in 1962–63. Yet within 12 months Harper had been replaced by the 'Chesterfield Tough', George Hunt.

The last survivor from the great side of the early 1920s left the same season. That was Jimmy Dimmock, who now weighed 13½ stone and who had been having problems for some time. And while the older fans mourned his passing, they could not fail to be delighted by the very promising team that Percy Smith was building. George Greenfield, a local boy from Hackney, was really the greatest talent and the man who paved the way for promotion in 1933. But before that season was even halfway through he broke a leg at Fulham and his career never flourished again. Smith replaced him immediately with the remarkable Willie Hall, who was to find lasting fame with his five goals in 28 minutes for England against Northern Ireland at Old Trafford on 16 November 1938. Three of those goals came within 210 seconds and no other player has ever scored more than five for England in a single international.

He was playing inside-right for his country that day, and was obviously helped in no small way by Stanley Matthews' performance on the wing. Hall scored seven goals for England that season, only two less than he managed for his club! Hall, who came from Nottingham and had previously played for Notts County, was also remarkable for his build. The inside-right was only 5 ft 7 in tall but weighed 11½ stone. This rather rotund, muscular shape was easily distinguishable to crowds not yet assisted by numbers on the back of shirts. For that improvement, incidentally, they have Spurs to thank, for the club pushed the change through a previously reluctant League before the beginning of the ill-fated 1939-40 season. Hall, whose name has happily lived in the record books, had a less happy sequel to his distinguished career. He was afflicted by disease and eventually lost both his legs. The club gave him a testimonial in 1946 which raised a hefty sum for the times. After their unhappy five-year sojourn in the Second Division, Percy Smith's Spurs eventually fought their way back up on 29 April 1933. Their elevation was not very impressive and, though the highlight of a 25-year period, was rather in keeping with the mood of that quarter century. Spurs lost 1–0 at Upton Park on that day while their only challengers, Fulham, went down by the same score at home to Grimsby. Stoke were champions, just one point ahead of Spurs, who at least had the distinction of being the only team in the top two divisions not to lose at home. Tottenham had started the season appallingly and were in the relegation zone in October. But they lost only three of their last 35 games, didn't once lose at home, and slowly pulled themselves up through the table. To celebrate both promotion and the club's

OPPOSITE PAGE:
Managerial comings and goings at White Hart Lane during the late 1920s and early 1930s. Billy Minter resigned in November 1929, going onto the club's administrative side, and on 1 January 1930 greeted Percy Smith from Bury (right, top picture) to the club in his place. After Tottenham's relegation in 1935, Smith was replaced by Jack Tresadern (middle, centre picture). He was welcomed to White Hart Lane on Monday 1 July 1935 by trainer George Hardy (left) and chief scout Ben Ives (right). Three years later, at the start of the 1938–39 season, Billy Minter welcomed back Peter McWilliam to the club. McWilliam had been manager of the Cup winning side in 1921 and had left to manage Middlesbrough in February 1927.

ABOVE: One of the most dramatic matches Spurs ever contested was a fifth round FA Cup replay against Everton on 22 February 1937. Spurs scored three goals in the last six minutes to win 4–3. In the picture Everton goal-keeper Ted Sagar clears a corner from the threat of Spurs forwards Jack Morrison and Joe Meek.

ABOVE LEFT: Spurs supporters leaving Euston on Saturday 20 February 1937 for the first tie at Goodison.

50th anniversary, the 1933-34 handbook tells us that '. . . a Grand Concert was held at the Municipal Hall.'

The club's successful spell continued into the following season. George Hunt, not at all cowed by the First Division, scored another 32 League goals to add to his 32 of the previous campaign, Willie Hall and half-back Arthur Rowe received their first caps, and the side finished an excellent third. They were ten points behind Arsenal and it must be admitted that they never really looked like actually winning the Championship after losing first place on 25 November. Nonetheless, portents were good for the future.

Portents may have been good, performance was anything but. The side fell apart almost from the start of the following season, 1934–35. In 1933–34 the goal record had been 79–56. In 1934–35 it was virtually the reverse, 54–93. The problem was in defence, where Cecil Poynton had gone (to Ramsgate), club captain Frank Felton had been released, and Arthur Rowe was injured so badly that his career never recovered. Suddenly the Spurs defence found itself without enough experience and took on the properties of a sieve. In all, 36 players were tried in the team during the season, but the problems were never really solved. Arsenal beat them 5–1 at Highbury and 6–0 at White Hart Lane, one of the most humiliating results in the club's history.

Taffy Day (left) and the 'Chesterfield Tough', George Hunt, on their way from Kings Cross to Bradford for a fifth round FA Cup tie against Park Avenue on 15 February 1936. Spurs drew the game 0–0 and won the Monday afternoon replay 2–1. They then travelled back to Bradford the following Saturday and won 5–2 in the League – a rare trio of games in one week for the same clubs. In the background is Fred Bearman, who was chairman of the club during the Double season.

Between 26 December 1934 (when they beat Grimsby 2–1) and 19 April 1935 (when they beat Blackburn 1–0) Spurs did not win a League game. This run of 16 matches remains an unequalled spell of failure in the history of the club, though, oddly, they won two Cup games in January. The board and the manager had been squabbling all season, and Percy Smith's departure at the end of it was singularly ungracious, considering that he had taken them to third place in the League but 12 months before. But then these things often are.

It was hardly a good time to open the new East Stand, then easily the most impressive structure on any English League ground. The cost was a staggering £60,000, largely financed through the support of Barclays Bank. As an illustration of just what an investment that was, £60,000 was almost exactly the same amount as the club's total aggregate profits (meaning annual profits minus losses) since the First World War. The most they had ever made in a single season was £17,417 in 1921–22 and in 1934–35 the club made only £8,777. Of the previous ten seasons, Tottenham had lost money in four.

Jack Tresadern, manager of Crystal Palace, took over for three seasons. He is best remembered for captaining West Ham United at the 1923 'White Horse' Cup final. He complained after that game that, when David Jack had scored Bolton's first goal, he was trapped in a section of the crowd which had prevented him getting back on the pitch after he had taken a throw-in. Sadly, his three years at White Hart Lane produced little to compare with that famed occasion. Tresadern's most memorable decisions were the sales of George Hunt to Arsenal, where he found a place in that all-conquering club's First Division line-up, and Taffy

O'Callaghan to Leicester. O'Callaghan proved a critical factor in Leicester's subsequent promotion to the First Division a season later in 1937 but he, like Willie Hall, did not survive to celebrate a comfortable middle-age for he was prematurely dead within a decade. The shades of Seed and Jennings did not go unnoticed by the fans, who never forgave Tresadern for seeming to blame these two great performers for Tottenham's troubles. Their later successes hardly assisted the manager's cause either, and his departure was inevitable.

Peter McWilliam came back to his old job for the last season before the Second World War, but time was obviously too short to work the miracles of 1920 and 1921. There were parallels with that period, however. Just as the post-Great War team had been emerging before it, so it was with Arthur Rowe's push-and-run side. McWilliam had sensibly decided that the team he inherited would not do the job, and he began to promote youngsters from the Northfleet nursery through the combination side. Les Bennett, Ted Ditchburn, Bill Nicholson and Ron Burgess all had their first taste of senior football before the War. Arthur Rowe had gone (to take a coaching job in Hungary) but he would be back.

THE WARTIME YEARS

The War was a bleak period for most clubs. Spurs had already been in relatively poor financial straits – by 1940 they had lost money in as many years as they had made it since their loss of permanent First Division status in 1928. Indeed, in 1929–30 they lost over £10,000 for the first time ever. Secretary Arthur Turner organised the side during the War and the club had some fleeting success in reaching the semi-finals of the London Cup in 1941 (they lost to Brentford). Later on in the War the club was clearly finding its feet, winning the Football League South in both 1943–44 and 1944–45. In the latter season, Spurs lost only one of their 30 games. All in all, these wartime results should not be taken too seriously. They obviously reflected the availability of players and the particular skills and positions of key individuals – some clubs had more players in the forces than others for instance. It is no coincidence that Aldershot, with so many army bases nearby, were the best side of the period. We have, nonetheless, included all first-team results from this period in the appendix for they do make interesting reading. One other intriguing event in the war years was the expulsion of Spurs, among a dozen London clubs, from the Football League in 1941. These clubs had refused to travel long distances for some games arranged by the League (on the grounds that they could not get their players released from war duties for long journeys) and organised their own League instead. The breach was healed quickly enough, though it generated a remarkable amount of heat for a time.

1951

Arthur Rowe • Push-and-run • Semi-final blues • Eddie Baily • Second Division champions • Make-it-simple, make-it-quick • Champions at last • Danny Blanchflower

In the annals of Tottenham Hotspur the immediate post-war era will always be associated with Arthur Rowe and 'push-and-run'. The phrase originated in Spurs style: push because it was a short, accurate passing game where the ball was pushed for exactness, run because the three-man triangle and 'wall pass' (often described as a 'one-two' or, in America, as 'give-and-go') were an integral part of the style and required the man passing the ball to run immediately into a new position to receive it back. As it happens, Rowe never liked the phrase 'push-and-run', thinking it descriptively inadequate.

The memory is often deceptive in football. It was, in fact, almost exactly four years after VE-Day that Arthur Rowe returned to Tottenham. Nor did he build that great team of the era; it was already there. He basically gave it confidence, moulded its talents, and directed its style of play. And within twelve months Spurs were back in the First Division.

The Second World War had brought changes to Tottenham. When first-class football emerged from the gloom in 1946, the club had a new chairman and a new manager. Chairmen can be remarkably important, equally they can be irrelevant. At White Hart Lane, Charles Roberts had been the dominant force for over four decades. He had taken over the club in the previous century, at a time when the balance sheet showed a deficit of £501 and there was great concern for its financial future. One wonders what he would make of the expenditure of £4,000,000 on a new stand.

His right-hand man for virtually the whole period had been secretary Arthur Turner, who was to die six years after Roberts in 1949. And while their era had begun so well, with the 1901 Cup win, the entry to the League and the excellent side of the post-Great War years, the subsequent quarter-century must have proved a great disappointment to them both.

The team that is always associated with push-and-run and the 1951 Championship; standing left to right: trainer Cecil Poynton, Bill Nicholson, Alf Ramsey, Harry Clarke, Ted Ditchburn, Arthur Willis, Ron Burgess and Arthur Rowe; seated left to right: Sonny Walters, Les Bennett, Len Duquemin, Eddie Baily and Les Medley. Missing from the picture is Peter Murphy, who made 25 appearances that season. No other players made more than seven.

Doubly so, one assumes, because of the astonishing success of neighbours Arsenal. The Gunners in the 1930s were the most successful team in soccer history and only Liverpool in the 1970s and 1980s can be said to have surpassed them domestically since.

And it was to Arsenal's memory that Spurs went for their first post-war manager — specifically to Joe Hulme. He had appeared in five Wembley Cup finals, for Arsenal and Huddersfield, a record only Pat Rice has equalled since. For Hulme, the club and football generally, the immediate post-war years were an unreal period. Though, unlike the Great War, few British players had actually died in the fighting, the disruptions to home life had been much greater, and the experienced, talented players of 1939 had lost their late twenties and early thirties to the war. The younger players had had no concentrated experience of first-class football, and in this context the younger players were now aged between 24 and 30.

Hulme never blended the old and the new quite well enough. Spurs were often in with a chance, but always flattered to deceive, finishing sixth, eighth and fifth in their first three post-war Division 2 seasons. The 1948 FA Cup semi-final was the bitterest moment. Spurs had fought their way past Bolton, West Bromwich, Leicester and Southampton to reach Villa Park for their first semi-final in nearly three decades. Blackpool were the opposition after a simpler trot past Leeds, Chester, Colchester and Fulham.

It was a semi-final Spurs seemed to have won in the 63rd minute when centre-forward Len Duquemin scored after a goalmouth melee. But with four minutes left that marvellous imp Stan Mortensen went past four defenders and goalkeeper Ted Ditchburn and squeezed the ball home from an impossible angle on the goal-line. In extra-time Mortensen scored twice more and Spurs' season collapsed. Mortensen scored in every round that year, though Blackpool lost the final to Manchester United, and then became the only man to score a Wembley FA Cup final hat-trick in 1953; Spurs were just one of the clubs whose dreams were shattered by the England centre-forward. In Julian Holland's beautiful metaphor: 'Their paws buttered, they slipped helplessly down the rungs of the League ladder. . .' They did not score in their next four games, and well founded hopes of promotion disappeared with the April winds.

That single moment was really the end of Joe Hulme's managership, though Arthur Rowe did not take over until the end of the following season, on 4 May 1949. To Hulme's credit, it must be pointed out that the great side of the early fifties was already playing for him. Eddie Baily, energetic, enthusiastic, perhaps the key man, and Les Bennett were at inside-forward, Les Medley and Sonny Walters were on the wings, Harry Clarke, at 6ft 3in, had joined as the solid stopper centre-half from Lovell's Athletic in the March (Spurs, despite their cultured traditions elsewhere, have no history of stylish centre-halves), Ted Ditchburn was in goal, Bill Nicholson and Ronnie Burgess firmly established at half-back, and Channel Islander Len Duquemin

was a brave, tough and willing, if not skilful, centre-forward.

At the end of Hulme's last season, after the transfer deadline, assistant manager Jimmy Anderson went down to Southampton and brought back the final link. He was the latest in a long line of thinking Spurs full-backs, following in the pattern of Sandy Tait and Tommy Clay and he was later to make something of a name for himself as a manager – Alf Ramsey. At age 29 Ramsey might reasonably have assumed that his brief first-class career was not far from an end, but he was to have five marvellous years with Spurs and England and it must have been a spell that taught him much that he was later to put into practice at Ipswich and at Wembley.

We are now entering a period when it is possible at last to let the actors speak for themselves. Before this date today's historian has only written memories, newspaper reports, second hand conversations; the principals of this post-war era were still, happily, with us as this book was written and wherever possible, it is best to let them tell their own stories.

ARTHUR ROWE — ONE MAN'S SOCCER VISION

It was a handful of sugar cubes spread round a table in the dining car of a London-bound express that originally brought the speaker's point home. That scene was recalled by neat soft-spoken Arthur Rowe, folding back almost half a century as he tells you what happened: 'We were returning home from a match at Bradford Park Avenue and were all dead

pleased at our £2 win bonus, talking over the game and the last-minute goal which had done the trick for us. I spread the sugar around, trying to map out the moves leading up to our goal. It was one to savour because there were about seven passes starting out from our own penalty area. I argued that if we could plan moves like that instead of just hoping for it to happen we would score more often.'

So spoke a man with a vision, a man born just 10 minutes away from White Hart Lane. Even in the thirties push-and-run soccer was taking shape in the mind of the Tottenham centre-half, the club captain who was honoured once by his country, against France, and in time was destined to retrace his steps and manage his old club, his only club as a player. When he arrived at White Hart Lane the prodigal was firmly on trial as the manager of his first League club. Rowe had done things and won things as the secretary-manager of Chelmsford City, had been a big success. But that was the Southern League. It had brought him recognition and awards, but had it geared him sufficiently for a much greater challenge?

He spent the close season of 1949 planning the spreading of the soccer gospel according to Arthur Rowe. Modestly he now says: 'Our style was basically the method of Spurs football taught down the years . . . with variations. Tottenham had always tried to play football to entertain. When you can get both, entertainment with effectiveness, you are on the right road. Push-and-run, that was the label they came to pin on our style although, quite

OPPOSITE PAGE: Bill Nicholson won just one cap for England – on 19 May 1951 against Portugal at Goodison – but he certainly made the best of it, scoring with his first touch of the ball after 19 seconds. It was the fastest debut goal ever scored by an England player. 'I was picked again more than once' says Nicholson now, 'but I always seemed to be injured. It was very disappointing not to play again, but Billy Wright was a very good right-half in those days.' Number 6 in the picture is Henry Cockburn of Manchester United.
BELOW: 'Reliable' Len Duquemin heads Spurs second goal past keeper Jim Sanders of West Brom at White Hart Lane on Saturday 17 March 1951. Spurs won 5–0 and centre-forward Duquemin scored hs only hat-trick of the season. 'We called him Reliable because if everyone else was off form, you could usually rely on Len to come up with a goal, ' said Baily.

61

honestly, I was never very fond of it. You
often saw something like our style happening
in a match, any kind of match; a side
suddenly stringing together short, quick passes
and players moving intelligently to give and
take them. It's as if the game suddenly got an
electric shock. The thing about the Tottenham
side I had was that we tried to make it happen all the time.'

He makes a surprising admission: 'I never
told anybody how to play, I just made sugges-
tions on playing patterns, put up ideas. I'd ask
players if they had ever tried a certain move,
talk it over with them, get them to discuss
between themselves...then we'd try it out.'

'Make it simple, make it quick' was the
maxim Rowe endlessly pumped into his men.
That was the content of a famous telegram
Rowe sent to ex-Spur Vic Buckingham on the
eve of an Amateur Cup semi-final.
Buckingham was managing Pegasus, the intel-
lectual Corinthians of the mid-twentieth
century. Pegasus beat Hendon in the semi-final
and then went on to win the final against
Bishop Auckland. As Rowe says: 'I took our
style back to the streets, the way we played it as
kids – off the kerb, off the wall, taking the ball
at different angles, enlisting the kerb as a team-
mate who let you have the ball back immediately after you had played it quickly . . . the
quicker the better. And all the time you were
tailoring your ideas, your hopes to the limits or
the limitations of your players, not asking them
to do the things they could not do.'

Arthur Rowe had stored admiring memories of an old rival, Clem Stephenson, the star
of a Huddersfield Town which had won a
hat-trick of League Championships in the
1920s. Said Rowe of Stephenson, whom the
England selectors of the time also only remembered to honour once: 'He was great. I was
enthralled when I played against him, he best
illustrated the style I wanted my teams to
play. He played everything off quickly, you
didn't catch him in possession. He was like
Alex James but did things faster. I saw how
much trouble he caused and thought "What if
you get them *all* playing it like that?"'

'So many players wanted to show their
individual skills in those days, but it's a team
game, everybody had to come into it. I tried
to build a side who would play for each other
because that's what the push-and-run style
demanded if they were to get the most out of
it. Some players had greater skills than others
but you had to try and make all of them feel
that they had a big part to play. For instance,
I asked Sonny Walters if he was prepared to
work harder by coming back more into our
half . . . not something wingers reckoned to
do in those days. I told him that he would
have to defend more but he would also get
more of the ball. I put it to Alf Ramsey that
while I knew he was brought up on using
long, measured passes, these tended to leave
him out of the action once he had played
them. But had he ever thought how much
more accuracy was guaranteed, how much
more progress could be made, if he pumped
15 or 20-yard passes to a withdrawn Walters?

'The opposing left-back would hesitate to
follow Walters back into the Spurs half, which
was definitely no-man's-land to the full-back
then, thus giving Walters the vital gift of
space. And Sonny could also now make an

inside pass if Alf followed up and made himself available. We had one more option; with
Ramsey's precision, once advanced he could
drive the ball down the right for Les Bennett,
coming to the near post, to turn the ball
inside with his head. And Bennett created
numerous chances doing just that. Ramsey's
advances would throw a heavier load in
defence on Bill Nicholson but he was the
ideal cover at half-back – sound, solid and a
rattling tackler.'

Ramsey at the back and Bill Nicholson in
front of him patrolled the right-hand side of
the field and remain the best known of that
great side. But they were arguably not the
stars. Captain was Ronnie Burgess, the successor to the great Arthur Grimsdell, and also
left-half and captain for his country, Wales.
While Nicholson kept back, protecting the
flank and allowing Ramsey more freedom,
Burgess played the roving half-back. He was
always happier in attack, utilising a remarkable burst of speed for a nominal defender,
and it took years of coaching, first from Peter
McWilliam and then Arthur Rowe, to persuade him to curb this tendency when it was
in the team's best interests.

INTERNATIONAL HONOURS

Eddie Baily, at inside-left, was the crowd's
favourite. A local from Clapton he was the
effervescent enthusiast – always running,
always willing, always involved. A great dribbler, a great passer of the ball, possessor of an
excellent shot, perhaps his one fault was confidence – he could so easily lose it, become
unsure of himself. But it was around him that
Rowe really built his team, for 'push-and-
run', or whatever nomenclature one may wish
to use, was virtually Baily's natural game. He
was to win nine England caps, scoring five
times. Nicholson, oddly, won only one, though
he scored against Portugal in the opening seconds of that game. Ramsey won 31 caps while
with Spurs, and scored three times from the
penalty spot for England. They were not the
only members of that side to be capped; Ted
Ditchburn eventually appeared six times for
England, Les Medley the same number, and
full-back Arthur Willis, not an absolute regular in the side, picked up a cap against France
in 1951. Ron Burgess appeared for Wales on
32 occasions, as well as for Great Britain
against the Rest of Europe in 1947. Billy
Rees, another reserve, won a Welsh cap in
March 1950 — making eight internationals in
all, a remarkably high number for a club gathered together in the middle of the Second
Division and with virtually no
outside purchases.

The team also had its unsung members —
particularly inside-forward Peter Murphy,
signed from Coventry, who played 25 times
in the Championship season and yet whose
name is rarely remembered. Arthur Rowe
knew the way he wanted to play the game
and he longed to try out his ideas with good
players. That chance came, but he never
believed it would be his old club which gave
it to him or that any club could provide such
talent: 'Not just good players, I took over
some *marvellous* players. Eddie Baily, a
natural one-touch player. I never saw a man
who could play a moving ball either way and
with either foot as quickly or as accurately.

Where would you find an inside-forward like him now? Then there was the skipper, Ronnie Burgess, brilliant, a great player. And I don't use that word easily. I wanted the ball moved at speed from the midfield and that is what this priceless pair did for me. Then there was Alf Ramsey who gave us our momentum . . . from the back.

There was no finer competitor than Ted Ditchburn in goal, nor did I think there was a better keeper to be found. Ditchburn, Baily, Ramsey and Burgess . . . they played as you wanted them all to play. They were the ones who most used their abilities to the full.'

Eddie Baily tells of the lead-up and the outcome of that first season under the new Spurs boss: 'There were a lot more instinctive players about then than now. That team just came together and you really didn't know why. When Arthur took us over he had players with a lot of natural ability. He was a kindly, amiable man who soon saw that they could play the way he wanted the game to be played, the way it ought to be played. So he gave us every encouragement.

'He would encourage the simple principles, on and off the ball and the urge to play this more exacting but much more exciting game took us along with the obvious enthusiasm of the man. There was no coaching to it, we improved and improvised as we went along. We just did things instinctively and being good players – and we were – we chose to do the

right things more often than not. Basically, we played our game in a series of triangles, moves involving three players at a time with each learning and getting to know each others' parts. The whole thing became very fluid, there were no attackers and defenders, in a given situation we all became defenders or attackers.'

This was most obvious with Ted Ditchburn. Today the tactic of retaining pocession by having the goalkeeper throw the ball to a full-back is commonplace. When Ditchburn and Alf Ramsey did it consistently in the 1950s it was a remarkable departure in approach. Ditchburn would rather deflate the budding tactician Ramsey when he was asked how the ploy developed: 'Simply because I was such an awful kicker,' he would explain.

'We changed things,' says Baily today. 'We gave the ball to the man who was marked. But other players slipped into support positions to give the man with the ball more options. That in turn depended on how the ball had been given and we had to guarantee that our man received it. It was the kerb or the wall game with players in support to allow the man in possession a choice of angles. It drew defenders, it got our rivals chasing as well. Fine players like Joe Harvey of Newcastle and Pompey's Jimmy Scoular, always tough competitors, would have a few choice words to say as they tried to close you down. Joe used to call across to me at the start of a game: "We'll get you today, you little —" It wasn't meant as a threat

SECOND DIVISION CHAMPS

Rowe's push-and-run stylists swept Spurs to the top. Nobody could have bargained for such a dramatic impact in the new manager's first season. There was a home stutter in a 2–3 defeat by Blackburn Rovers in their third match, after delighting supporters with 4–1 victories over both Brentford and Plymouth Argyle. Then Burgess and his boys powered away on an unstoppable run from the 2–0 return win at Plymouth on August 31 until Leeds United halted them with their 3–0 success at Elland Road on 14 January 1950, an unbeaten sequence of 22 League matches at the end of which was a Cup win over Stoke City to make it 23 games in a row.

It meant that from the beginning of September until the season closed for them on May 6, they stood astride the Second Division, a nine-month reign at the close of which their rivals only got within a distant nine points as the rampant Spurs eased down on the home straight. For over the regulation promotion course of 42 League matches from August to May, Spurs had jinked their way clear of all opposition to burst into the 1950s with a lead of ten points, and then went on to stretch it to a runaway thirteen as April brought its usual clutter of games before the close down. And

the crowds crammed into White Hart Lane as Rowe's side stormed on. Loyal fans were rewarded for their patience as Tottenham served out the end of the fifteen-year exile in the Second Division.

Lukewarm followers saw a light rekindled, others came in from the fringes of North London and beyond for the first time as Spurs and their winning ways became the capital's leading attraction. North London indeed had become the mecca of football with the Tottenham home gates for that glorious season returning an average of 54,405, an incredible figure as you look at it now, and the next highest in the League having been established across at Highbury where Arsenal had totalled 51,381. White Hart Lane attendances topped 50,000 on no fewer than 15 occasions; the Southampton visit on February 25 brought the season's biggest gate . . . 70,305; 66,880 came to the April match with Hull City and the meetings with Queen's Park Rangers, Chesterfield and Leicester City all passed the 60,000 mark. More than a million and a half customers passed through the Tottenham turnstiles that season, still a record for the club. The return to the First Division could not have been gained in more conclusive fashion. Spurs scored more goals (81) and conceded fewer (35) than any of their rivals in the Second Division. The fans' cheers were particularly sweet music for Arthur Rowe. Though injured for several

Confusion at the back as Ditchburn fails to gather the ball from West Brom right-winger Griffin and Nicholson and Ramsey prepare to clear the danger area. Spurs' 3–1 win in this 9 October 1954 fixture was more than welcome; it was their first for ten matches and only their second at home since the season began. Ted Ditchburn and Ron Reynolds shared the goalkeeper's jersey, rather unsatisfactorily, for the next four seasons.

THE GOAL!

TOTTENHAM HOTSPUR FOOTBALL CLUB

LEAGUE CHAMPIONSHIP

F.A. CUP

...WHILE THE SPURS GO MARCHING ON

ABOVE: The rather premature cartoon which appeared in the club programme on Tuesday 26 December 1950, showing Arthur Rowe dreaming of Ron Burgess leading the side to the Double. The dreams and hopes were to be shattered just a week and a half later at Huddersfield, on 6 January 1951, when Spurs went out of the Cup 2–0 at the first hurdle. But perhaps it was really a premonition of ten years later . . .

OPPOSITE PAGE: Ted Ditchburn at his best, diving to save a Burnley shot on 27 October 1956. He kept a clean sheet that day, Spurs winning 2–0 against a side which was to figure prominently in the dramas of the next few seasons. Ditchburn was the last survivor of the push-and-run side.

months, he had played 18 games fifteen years before in that last season in Division 1.

Now they were back – and with a bang. In the Cup they had taken on First Division opposition in beating Stoke in the third round. For Sunderland in the fourth round there was an enormous crowd of 66,246, and Spurs turned the tap full on.

Sunderland, good enough to end the season third in the League, were simply swamped in a breath-taking home display, especially in the second half. Coming up after the interval with a 2–1 lead Tottenham then bewitched, bothered and bewildered a Sunderland defence which was laboriously slow and had the fact rubbed home by the speedy switchings up front and the rapid change of the points of attack by quicksilver Spurs forwards. Sunderland were run ragged as Tottenham piled up a 5–1 win, Sonny Walters and Les Bennett having helped themselves to two goals apiece and Les Medley getting the other. But Goodison Park in round five saw Everton in no mood to share a fate as bad or worse than Sunderland's. The Liverpudlians retained their Cup interest by the only goal scored, and a disputed penalty at that. Big Harry Clarke was ruled to have handled in the early minutes. Spurs protested at the penalty award but it made no difference. And they bade their Cup farewell when Wainwright rapped in the spot kick.

The return to the First Division lifted the spirits of everybody and everything connected with the club. Now there was an expectancy, a feeling of things about to happen. The lengthening queues for advance ticket sales heightened interest and hopes. Baily harks back to the players' mood at that time: 'You felt that you couldn't get started quickly enough. Remember, none of us had sampled the First Division before. We didn't fear it, we knew we were a very good side now. But we were impatient to find out just how good.' All the time Arthur Rowe fed his players virtual 'Sunday school' tracts; 'Make it simple, make it quick'; 'A rolling ball gathers no moss'; 'He who stops is lost'. 'I said them so often the boys must have got sick of hearing them,' he admits. He even had them printed

and scattered around wherever the players might appear. Said Eddie Baily: 'It got so that we were making them up ourselves.'

But what could have sounded very much like children at school repeating parrot-wise after teacher was apparently very real to the Tottenham players. Baily readily admits to chanting them aloud as reminders in the hottest of practice matches. There were cartoons, too. Rowe had one printed which showed a burglar with customary swag-bag at the ready, hurling a brick through a jeweller's window. The inevitable policeman approaches and over the shattered window we read, 'If we make space'; down to the second cartoon and a judge proclaiming 'three years' over the burglar with caption, 'We get time', and the last strip shows our hero, arrowed suit and all, breaking stones in a vast wilderness which could only be Dartmoor and the final lesson: 'And time means space.'

Spurs had never been able to boast a League title when they set out in the 1950–51 season. Their best effort had been as runners-up to Liverpool in 1922, six points adrift. Rowe himself was in the 1932–33 team which won promotion to the First Division, a point behind Stoke City, and then the following season did well enough to take third place in the title race behind Arsenal and Huddersfield Town, the dominant teams of the era. Some thought that there might have been some cracks showing in the side after their finish to the 1949–50 campaign, given the fact that they lost four of their last five matches and drew the other. Were they too casual or too arrogant in believing they had already done their job, it was asked?

Arthur Rowe shrugged it off: 'We had won the Second Division with six or seven games to go and if we had finished the job in the manner in which we had been playing up till then we must have ended up with a record points total. I don't think the players knew, or felt, that they were easing up. And I don't think that I was aware of it either. It happened, and that was it. It wasn't that we just didn't care once the title had been won. But there was a lesson there for us.'

The summer which intervened between Tottenham's Second and First Division Championships had seen what still has to be regarded as England's greatest humiliation – the 1–0 defeat by the United States in Belo Horizonte, Brazil. Ramsey, Baily, Ditchburn and Nicholson were all part of that discredited squad and they returned home to a still soccer-obsessed nation which was asking just where English football went next. The answer was to White Hart Lane.

THE LEAGUE CHAMPIONSHIP
Spurs had marked the opening of the season with a 1–4 home deflation by Blackpool. It furrowed the brows of the faithful. Then things began to fall into a more fruitful pattern four days later with a similar score, this time in their favour at Burnden Park with Bolton as the victims. A 2–2 away draw with Arsenal, four more goals against the unfortunate Bolton side, another away point at Charlton and it left no doubts. Tottenham were well able to take care of themselves in this more rarefied football atmosphere and their slick, slippery soccer, their punchy pace, sent out danger signals to

every team in the First Division.

Their hurricane broke with a run of eight straight victories between the very last kick of September and mid-November. It was devastating and deadly, nothing could stem its force. Everything came together at once in a sustained, co-ordinated spell unparalleled by even the best this now great side had shown up to then. At the end of it all, 28 goals had humiliated such teams as Aston Villa, Burnley, Chelsea and Stoke City, West Bromwich Albion, Portsmouth, Everton and Newcastle United. The eight opponents among them mustered a feeble six scoring efforts in reply. And felt as if they had been through a threshing machine.

Said Eddie Baily: 'I have been lucky to have been in the right place at the right time to give me a lifetime of football satisfaction, but this was something else again.' The centrepiece of it all was three consecutive home performances, virtuoso stuff which stunned Stoke City with six goals, then rattled home a further five past proud Portsmouth, League Champions in the two previous seasons, and finally flattened luckless Newcastle United, who were to win the FA Cup that season but

failed to raise a whisper of defiance when seven successful scoring attempts filled the net behind them.

Baily himself and left-wing partner Les Medley each helped themselves to hat-tricks from this harvest, and Eddie tried to keep the pride from his voice in remembering: 'Our style commanded a lot of respect from others because of its freshness, because of the way it was played and the men who played it. You felt that you were helping to lift the tone of the game and so you got that respect from crowds as well. Other players would quiz you on it, and discuss how they might combat a team which moved all the time and always seemed to have more men than they did . . . the true yardstick of a great team.'

Arthur Rowe, the quiet genius behind it all, swallowed hard at the recollection: 'I never had more pleasure from the game than that team gave me,' he stated. 'When it was flowing like that and all going right I would sit transfixed at some of the football they put on. I was jealous for them, anxious that they should do justice to themselves. That was the only pressure, the rest was sheer pleasure.'

*OPPOSITE PAGE: Ron
Burgess and Ted Ditchburn
combine to repel a
Blackpool attack during the
FA Cup semi-final at Villa
Park on 21 March 1953. On
the left is Stan Mortensen,
who was to go on to score
the only hat-trick ever
recorded at Wembley in an
FA Cup final as Blackpool
beat Bolton 4–3. For Spurs,
the semi-final was sup-
posed to be revenge for
their extra-time defeat at
the same venue by the
same side in 1948, when
Mortensen had also scored
a hat-trick. In the 1953
game, Bill Perry had put
Blackpool in front, Len
Duquemin had equalized
and the game was almost
in extra time when Ramsey
played a back-pass too
short, Jackie Mudie picked
it up and Blackpool won
the game 2–1. It was the
last throw of the dice for
the great side of 1949–51.
Bill Nicholson said of
Welshman Ron Burgess,
captain of that team: 'Of all
the men I played with and
managed at White Hart
Lane, I think he was the
best. Once Arthur Rowe
had persuaded Ron about
push-and-run, then we had
no more trouble in getting
it to work.' Managers,
though, had terrible trouble
persuading Burgess to curb
his attacking instincts.
After one pre-war game he
complained to Peter
McWilliam about how
badly his shins had been
bruised in tackles. 'That'll
teach you to get rid of the
ball then, won't it?' was the
unsympathetic reply.*

Tottenham's programme for Boxing Day, 1950, and the home match with Derby County contained a cartoon of manager Rowe, sur-rounded by the seasonal festive drinks and eats and snoozing by the fire with his feet up. He's dreaming a dream which has Burgess and his men marching towards a twin goal of the League Championship and the FA Challenge Cup. Perhaps it was not a dream at all, but a premonition of ten years hence. Within a fortnight Huddersfield Town had brought a rude awakening to at least the Cup part of the dream. They tumbled Tottenham out with a 2–0 third round eclipse on their own Leeds Road pitch, seemingly always a bad ground for Tottenham.

The Town, in fact, paid scant respect to Tottenham's soaring reputation that season for they beat them in three straight sets, 3–2 in their first League meeting, 2–0 in the Cup (both at Leeds Road) then 2–0 at White Hart Lane to end another Spurs run of unbeaten games late in the season and so dilute and delay the Tottenham title hopes. Not that the Yorkshiremen were any great shakes them-selves; they had all their work cut out to avoid relegation at season's end, finishing 19th in the table.

A look on the Tottenham line-ups of the time proves how successful was the youth policy of the club, begun in the old Northfleet nursery era and, it must be said, in the days when clubs appeared to be able to find the time to wait for youngsters to come through. The worth of such a policy together with a tight talent net spread locally by the club scouts meant that an astonishingly high pro-portion of seven first team players came from London, or within a few miles of the capital, and most of the others came up through the Spurs farm teams: keeper Ted Ditchburn came from Gillingham, Bill Nicholson was born in Yorkshire but at Northfleet from school, Charlie Withers (Edmonton), Alf Ramsey, bought from Southampton but hail-ing from Dagenham, Harry Clarke from Lovell's Athletic but first from Woodford, Ronnie Burgess, belonged to Cwm, Monmouth, but another nursery graduate, Les Bennett came from Wood Green, Sonny Walters from Edmonton, Eddie Baily was a native of Clapton and his wing twin Les Medley was another of the Edmonton crop.

And checking down the playing staff we find Vic Buckingham (Greenwich), striker Jack Gibbons (Charlton), dapper little Tommy Harmer (Hackney), George Ludford (Barnet), Tony Marchi – Edmonton once more, Sid McClelland, a Rowe buy from Poplar, reserve keeper Ron Reynolds, from Aldershot, and Sid Tickridge from Stepney in the East End. By any standards that was a tremendous haul of local and home-grown talent, both in quality and quantity, and said much for the alert coverage of the Tottenham scouts under the shrewd chief spotter, Ben Ives.

Baily talked of the great bond between the players fostered by Rowe which came to mean equally as much as any other part of the team's preparation. 'It meant so much to us all,' he said. 'We were always playing for each other, it was genuine team spirit. We gave and accepted criticism of our game, of our-selves that was honest and well-intended. You played with a pride in yourself and the team.

And all that for a win bonus of two pounds.' He smiled wryly and added: 'You know I never had a car until I was 34 years old; the only players I can recall owning one then were Ronnie Burgess and Ted Ditchburn. I believe it was Ted who had a big old thing that came straight out of the American bootlegging days . . . we called it "Dillinger" because Ted looked for all the world like the gang leader Jack Dillinger when he set off in it . . .

'I lived in Clapton and on match days I used to walk up the road and queue with the fans waiting to catch a bus to our ground. On the journey you would have to settle playing queries, chat about football generally and then give an optimistic forecast of the afternoon's game, and often having to stand all the way. Then, because the crowds were so great, you would have to drop off some way down the High Road and try and thread your way along the jammed pavements. But, at the end of the day, you might be two pounds better off.'

ROWE THE PLAYER

Arthur Rowe himself came up through the ranks like most of his team. He went to, and through, the Northfleet nursery after joining Spurs as a teenager when Peter McWilliam was still manager. But with a young eye on security he kept up his apprenticeship as an upholsterer until he had passed out. At 20 he felt that his football career was not taking off fast enough and he asked the then manager, Billy Minter, about it. To which he was asked quickly: 'What do you mean, has somebody been getting at you?' Then thinking on, Minter added: 'Come and see me next week.' And that's how young Rowe forced through his ambition to become a Spur, which he did after signing on at White Hart Lane for £4 a week.

He got his League chance, and took it, in the 1931–32 season and Spurs won promotion in 1933, ascending to the First Division with their young, attacking centre-half now firmly established in a very good side. Rowe gained his one England cap on his native White Hart Lane pitch on 6 December 1933 against France, a match which the pow-erful English side won 4–1 with two goals coming from George Camsell, of Middlesbrough, one from dynamic Eric Brook, the Manchester City winger, and the other from Birmingham's strolling Tom Grosvenor at inside-right. Club-mate Willie Hall was in that same English side and the names of the rest of his colleagues that day sound like a roll of drums in soccer history . . . goalkeeper Harry Hibbs, uncommonly short of stature for a keeper, this Birmingham star, but rated by many as the greatest we have ever had; full-backs Roy Goodall, of Huddersfield, and Newcastle's Dave Fairhurst (Goodall, it transpired, was getting the last of his 25 caps that day while for Fairhurst, like Rowe, this was to be a once-in-a-lifetime appear-ance); Alf Strange, of Sheffield Wednesday, and the fearsome Wilf Copping played either side of new boy Rowe at right and left-half respectively.

Rowe played adventurously at centre-half in accordance with Spurs wont to take the fight to opponents; he was never shackled by plans or areas of the playing pitch, the whole arena was his domain. So when England began to over-run the struggling French, Rowe was

in close support to a raid down the right-wing, much to the amazement of Strange, then gaining what was to be the last of his 20 caps. 'What are you doing, coming over to my side of the field?' he demanded of England's newcomer. 'I came over to see if you wanted any help,' was the cheeky answer Strange apparently received. The following season Rowe and Hall both suffered cartilage operations and Spurs went back to Division 2 and stayed there until Rowe regained the reins.

Rowe's playing career ended in 1938–39 when he lost his battle against injuries. He had played more than 200 League matches for Tottenham and took up a coaching appointment in Hungary, thus following in the footsteps of pioneer Jimmy Hogan some years earlier. He thoroughly enjoyed his stay at a Budapest college and was in the process of negotiating a three-year contract to become Hungary's national coach when the war clouds blew up even more menacingly. He said: 'I felt I was lucky to have got away before someone blew the whistle on me. I would liked to have stayed under different circumstances but it was obvious by then that something was going to happen.'

So instead of helping to loose a stream of future Hidegkutis, Puskases and Bosziks on unprepared Englishmen, Arthur Rowe went off instead to the Army to become one of the many sportsmen organising training, recreation and entertainment for the troops and travelling extensively. With the war over and football literally trying to find its feet again, he landed his job with Chelmsford City, to the great advancement of himself and the non-League club. The City, under Rowe, began in stirring fashion, winning both the Southern League title and the Southern League Cup in their first season together. And so it was that he was recalled to White Hart Lane and a team that was already waiting for him. 'Watching them was nothing short of uplifting,' said Rowe. 'I used to wish that all teams could have played like it for the benefit of the game. The fans at White Hart Lane loved us and that was a crowd that was well educated because they had seen good football through the years. Fathers watched it and brought up their sons on it; that was the Tottenham tradition. And it's so good to have seen it happening again in more modern times. There was no thuggery in our game, it had no part. You played football and you won the ball by positional sense. You played them out of the game. We did it in style, no jealousies, all pals together. It would have been great to have had all those wonderful games on tape so that you could take them down when you wanted and enjoy them all over again.'

CHAMPIONS AT LAST

Among those on the shelf above the video machine would surely have been the highlights from that last third of the season, while Spurs were still in the championship foothills. They had gone to the top of the First Division on 30 December 1950, the first time for 17 years. Tottenham held on to a one-point lead over Middlesbrough going into February of 1951 and Manchester United were lurking on the premises. But Spurs had given off the glint of champions and were to save themselves for a finishing burst in true Lester Piggott fashion. With the Easter matches

included, they had to play seven matches in March, which meant them rounding off the month with four games in nine days, a stiff programme. Altogether they then had twelve matches left to play.

Taking a leaf from Lewis Carroll, they became football's March Hares as they scudded ahead of their rivals with a powerful surge which saw them whip through the month's seven barriers with hardly a falter. Playing as confidently and as consistently as prospective champions should they gathered in twelve of the fourteen points the month had offered, a fitting tribute to their skill and dedication. First Chelsea were set aside 2–1 at White Hart Lane, next Stoke City held 0–0 in the Potteries. West Bromwich Albion were crushed in the capital, Len Duquemin notching a hat-trick in a 5–0 romp, and Fulham were 1–0 victims on Good Friday at Craven Cottage. On the Saturday, Portsmouth were held to a 1–1 draw at Fratton Park, Fulham seen off again, this time 2–1 in the Easter Monday return fixture, before the curtain came down on a prolific month's work with a 3–0 home beating of Everton.

Against that Tottenham run of success, the strength of Manchester United's challenge is clearly shown by the fact of their getting within three points of the leaders with just two games left to play. And this even though Tottenham had taken nineteen points from their last dozen matches – eight wins, three

draws and one defeat against, of course, their bogey team, Huddersfield Town. That three-point gap left Tottenham in the fortunate position of having to play both their last two matches at home, against Sheffield Wednesday and Liverpool, the very last on 5 May.

But on Saturday 28 April 1951, it mattered little to visiting Wednesday that Spurs were at home with a crowd that had turned out solely to cheer them on to their first title success. Wednesday had their own worries how to win so that they could stay in the First Division (they failed on goal difference). But they meant to sell the pass dearly. Duquemin ('Reliable Len we used to call him because when all the other forwards were off the mark it was usually old Len who saved our faces,' said Eddie Baily) looked to have set Tottenham on the right road when he gave them the lead in the first half. As the game went on, however, a one-goal lead seemed a none too safe anchorage as desperate Wednesday fought to save First Division football for Hillsborough.

Then, with a quarter of an hour to go, the Tottenham roar began to well up, slowly gaining in power and rising to a pitch as the crowd sent out an urgent 'Hold out' demand to their favourites. The roar was at its height when a massed case of heart failure was avoided with the final whistle. Seven decades after playing on the Marshes, the British game's ultimate prize had at long last found its way to White Hart Lane.

That defeat of Wednesday meant Tottenham still had three points more than Manchester United so there was nothing left to play for in the final game except the credit of a job well done. Ironically enough, as Spurs were making hard work of removing lowly Wednesday from their path, the United were ramming six goals past Huddersfield Town. Alas for Matt Busby's side, they were to finish as runners-up for the fourth time in five years, having previously had a hat-trick of near misses as they finished below Liverpool in 1947, Arsenal in 1948 and Portsmouth in 1949.

A week later, after Spurs had beaten Liverpool 3–1 to close the season, Arthur Drewry, President of the Football League, made the presentation to skipper Ronnie Burgess, as a year earlier he had done with the Second Division Championship Shield. And the most rewarding part of his short speech was again, as the year before, the President's reference to the manner of the title achievement. Said Mr Drewry: 'I not only congratulate them on having won it, but also on the manner in which they did so.'

SECOND AGAIN

Spurs were unable to maintain their momentum in the following season. They swapped places with Manchester United and finished second. There were those who were ready to make excuses and blame the very heavy pitches of the season's winter months for Spurs not

OPPOSITE PAGE: At
£30,000 Danny
Blanchflower was the most
expensive wing-half in
Britain, a distinction he
held until Dave Mackay
joined Spurs four years
later. Blanchflower's first
game for Tottenham after
his move from Villa was on
a muddy day at Maine
Road, 11 December 1954,
which ended in a goalless
draw. While the new sign-
ing guards keeper Ron
Reynolds, left-back Mel
Hopkins heads clear and
Harry Clarke keeps an eye
on proceedings.
Blanchflower was pur-
chased by Arthur Rowe as
the central cog of what the
manager hoped would
become a team to rival the
push-and-run side. But it
was to be five often controversial years, and two
changes of manager, before
Blanchflower was to really
fulfil that role for
Tottenham Hotspur.
Nonetheless, Arthur Rowe
described this game against
Manchester City as: 'The
first I had been able to
enjoy for weeks.'

being able to produce one more League title.
There was substance in it but in truth football
clubs, like people, get the weather they get and
have to make the best of it.

That being said, it could be argued that, of
all the major teams, Spurs, geared to a moving
style and a ball coming through quickly, would
most likely suffer when the ground was stodgy,
as it most surely was in the last quarter of
1951. And those who so believed were able to
chide: 'What did I tell you?' when they
received the news that the White Hart Lane
pitch, because of the difficulty of proper
drainage through a hard topsoil, was to be
ripped up. It duly happened at the 1951-52
season's end and 3,500 tons of what had, in
many eyes, prevented a second title was borne
off and dumped on Hackney Marshes to make
way for 2,000 tons of special new topsoil and
nearly 25,000 turves.

Nor were there the happiest of auguries for
the season when the stolid, dependable Harry
Clarke was missing for the start after being
injured in a practice match. Clarke had not
missed a game in the two previous seasons; this
time he was out of action for nine matches.
'Harry was a miss because he was such a great
fellow to have around', said Eddie Baily. 'He
was one of the blokes who did so much to
make up the real spirit of the side. Funnily
enough he never believed he should have been
in the team. He didn't think he was good
enough. On the pitch he was a hard, determined player, off it he was an old
sentimentalist. He was a much better player
than he realised.' Arthur Rowe agrees with that
assessment of the towering pivot, who was
bought by Jimmy Anderson just before Rowe
took over. 'He was a determined old-time stopper and we all believed in him. He was very
strong on his left side and this helped him a lot
because most centre-forwards tend to swivel to
the right and in doing so they ran into Harry's
stronger side . . . and knew all about it.'

During that shaky start Newcastle United
put seven September goals past Spurs at St
James' Park . . . sweet revenge for the seven
slammed past them a year earlier at White Hart
Lane. Rowe's famed team talks probably had
some positive effect, but from the end of
November, in worsening weather, until the first
League games of February the results were
appalling . . . of twelve matches played they
won four, drew one and lost seven. They
rallied but by now it was too late and they fell
four short of Manchester United's winning
total and pipped Arsenal into second place by
decimals.

The season's end saw one remarkable game
which is worth recalling. This was Tottenham's
1-0 defeat of Huddersfield Town on 2 April,
which helped send the Yorkshire club down to
the Second Division. That solitary goal caused
all the trouble. Tottenham had struggled
against a Town side desperate to win points
and keep themselves in the First Division. It
had been a tough tussle, without a goal from
either side to show for it, when Tottenham
won a corner almost in the last minute. Eddie
Baily took the kick.

The referee, who had just ticked Baily off,
was along the bye-line, between the kicker and
Huddersfield's near post. Baily, curling the ball
in, struck the back of the referee and the ball
rebounded into the path of the Spurs' forward.

So Baily moved to the ball, centred into the
Town goalmouth and there was the alert
Duquemin to head the ball home. That's when
the storm broke . . .

Huddersfield players rightly claimed that the
goal should not stand because the same Spurs
player had touched the ball twice without
another player intervening. The referee consulted the linesman nearest to the happening
and maintained his ruling of a goal to
Tottenham. The Huddersfield chairman, a
gentleman of considerable proportions, hurried
angrily down from the directors' box to the
referee's dressing room and brushed all the
waiting reporters aside as they lined up to get
the referee's account of the incident. 'You can
all wait, I'm seeing him first,' he stormed.

The air around was blue and the Town
chairman announced that he would appeal to
the League to have the match replayed. Which
he did and everybody interested – and that
meant every soccer fan in the country – took
their different sides. Eventually the Football
League Management Committee turned down
Huddersfield's request for a replay and the
Town then went to a Board of Appeal set up
by the Football Association for an inquiry into
all the evidence regarding that goal. But this
was turned down too . . . and Huddersfield in
due course went down as well. The conclu-
sions were relatively simple. The referee said
that he thought another player had touched the
ball before Baily centred, though, as he was
presumably face down on the pitch, no-one
explained how he could have seen this. The
fact that he was incorrect was irrelevant. If he
said he thought another player had intervened,
then his judgement was final.

By 1952–53 the great Spurs side was beginning to show the same signs of decline as had
the League winning sides of 1900 and 1920.
Despite a very successful close-season tour of
North America, during which Spurs beat
Manchester United 5-0 and 7-1 on successive
evenings, they could finish only tenth in the
First Division. Meanwhile the Cup was to
revive memories of that melancholy semi-final
in 1948. Tottenham began with two games
against Tranmere Rovers, about halfway up the
Third Division North at the time, then two
very tough ties with Preston North End, due to
lose the League title only by decimals; next
came a softer touch in turfing out Halifax
Town, also of the Third North, at their Shay
Ground and then three encounters of the
closest possible kind in the sixth round against
Birmingham City, finally concluded by a late
Sonny Walters goal at Molineux.

RAMSEY'S SLIP

Blackpool in the semi-final was supposed to be
a revenge performance for the tragedy of 1948.
Eddie Baily, a central figure in the terrible conclusion for Tottenham, years later still found it
difficult to talk about his greatest disappointment as a player – not getting to a Wembley
final. 'I've been there seven or eight times with
Spurs and West Ham since, but always to
watch. Yet that was the time we should have
made it, and we really thought we were going
to . . .'

The story of this meeting, of course, was of
the slip by the usually so immaculate Alf
Ramsey, when his pass back to Ted Ditchburn
was too short. Jackie Mudie nipped in, fastened

onto the chance and put Blackpool into the final for the third time in five years. Baily takes it up: 'We knew there wasn't long to go and we began to think about extra-time. I don't think any of us were worried about that because we felt that we had been the better team and would still pull it off. Alf took all the stick for us not making it — on TV and the radio, in the papers all over the weekend and for years afterwards. Everybody blamed him, every headline reminded him — him, an England full-back, a man of his experience, and so on. The fans laid the defeat unquestionably at his door.

'But he took it all marvellously, and he needn't have done really. There was no better student of the game than Ramsey. He could go over a match and tell you everything that had happened in it. He often did so in our dressing-room. And he did just that at Villa Park, where we must have been the most miserable bunch of players in football history. Without any recrimination or attempt to shift the blame he told me where I had gone wrong on that goal. He went over every sickening moment . . . how I, having conceded a free-kick and stood there disputing it, argued with the referee that I had not handled the ball. Then how Blackpool rushed the kick to Bill Perry on their left wing who in turn was challenged by Ramsey . . . then that back pass.

'Alf made his point, telling me that if I had not stopped to dispute the referee's decision I would have been back deeper in our half and helping provide cover against the free-kick. As it was, I left a gap. And, as he always was, he was right this time. That might not have prevented Mudie's goal but we asked for trouble by not maintaining field discipline. I accepted Ramsey's findings, just as the rest did. Just as we always did when we criticised each other. None of it was made because of the sheer frustration of losing. It was a hard and bitter lesson and it was the first time I'd seen that team with their heads down. They were down because of the manner of our defeat and because we realised that it could well be the last real Cup throw for many of the side.'

Baily was right about the last throw of the dice for the great side of the 1950s. The second semi-final was to be their last flirtation with greatness. The records simply say that Perry's first half goal put Blackpool in front, that Les Bennett made the leveller for Duquemin in the second and that Spurs then lost Bennett as an effective unit for the last half-hour after he had had to go off following a violent knock in the face. But the real story of that game was of Ramsey's back pass, and it will always be recalled as one of those matches that one side loses rather than the other wins. The team then broke up fast. Les Medley left to live in Canada, the appearances of the great names became fewer and fewer, the side struggled in a First Division dominated by the youthful Manchester United – 16th, 16th and 18th between 1953 and 1956.

Rowe took the gradual break-up of his ageing side to heart and suffered more than anybody realised for the men who had been through so much with and for him. The fifth round Cup defeat by Third Division York City in 1955 at Bootham Crescent was the final blow — he was a sick man and had to rest. It was his second breakdown. He never went back to White Hart Lane.

But just before Rowe handed over to long-serving Jimmy Anderson, with Bill Nicholson becoming club coach, Arthur Rowe completed the transfer of Robert Dennis Blanchflower from Aston Villa, his most inspiring, most successful transfer and a testimony to the historical continuity that has always been evident at White Hart Lane.

FROM ROWE TO ANDERSON

Blanchflower serves as the bridge between the fade out of the fifties squad and the re-found glories that the sixties were to bring. For now the push-and-run conquerors were moving out and moving on . . . after Medley's departure came that of the magnificent Burgess and that neat little left-back Arthur Willis, the pair joining Swansea; Bill Nicholson's role now was clearly to show others the way; Les Bennett went to West Ham. The two North London First Division clubs were the chief rivals for the signature of the slightly built Blanchflower and the late Tom Whittaker was favourite to bring him to Highbury and make amends for an earlier missed opportunity to sign the now 29-year-old Northern Ireland captain. This happened when a much younger Blanchflower was playing for his Irish club, Glentoran, but Highbury moved too slowly and he went to Barnsley instead.

Managers Rowe and Whittaker, firm friends for all the intense rivalry of their clubs' followers, also had a great professional respect for each other. Aston Villa were reportedly asking £40,000 for Blanchflower and the fee frightened off most clubs. But neither Rowe nor Whittaker had any intention of going so high and, because they wanted no part of an auction, the two came to a gentlemens' agreement that they would not go beyond £30,000 on any account. And if both clubs made the same offer then it would be left to the player to make his choice of a move. The managers agreed to keep in touch and to keep the fee at around £28,000. They had the field to themselves.

Rowe badly wanted to enrol the classic wing-half skills of the cultured Blanchflower. Equally he needed the leadership he was sure he would get if the lively, loquacious Irish star would take over the captaincy of a Spurs team struggling to regain an identity. Rowe had already realised that Blanchflower was a one-off, a midfield thinker probably without a parallel in the twentieth century. With this argument he won his case for increasing his club's bid by £2,000 to reach the £30,000 ceiling he and Whittaker had agreed. Then Rowe, incredibly by any standards today, rang the Arsenal manager and told him the position; that if Arsenal wanted to match Tottenham's bid of £30,000 then it would be up to the player himself. But Arsenal stuck on £28,000 and Blanchflower had to take what had originally appeared second best. He was the most expensive half-back in soccer history and he began his Spurs career on 11 December 1954, playing at Maine Road against Manchester City and helping his new club to gain a much needed point from the 0–0 draw.

'The first match I'd been able to enjoy for some weeks,' recalled Rowe. And the lift in Tottenham's form went on so that they lost only one of the first ten League matches in which the new man played. 'I got Danny because the team was running down. I knew that we had to change the pattern; other teams had been latching onto our game and getting to know it too well. Nor had we the players left to carry on as we were even if we had wanted to keep the pattern going. The team I had in mind was Blanchflower at right-half with little Tommy Harmer at inside-left as the axis of another, somewhat different, side. Those two had the combined skills to carry us forward. I was ready to throw the responsibility on them to pull us round.'

Rowe had been criticised over Tottenham's slump in form. He was found guilty of being too loyal for too long, that he did not make changes, or at least not quickly enough. He was accused of not playing Harmer early or often enough. Nothing or nobody split the fans as much as the abilities of the little genius who looked on field for all the world like some white-shirted scarecrow that had been left there by mistake. He was an impish football conjuror, a frail, pale wisp of a man who scaled 9st. when wet through and could see over a five-barred gate if he stood on tip-toes. 'Harmer the Charmer' he was dubbed and he could be sheer soccer magic to his supporters. Quiet, shy and nervous off the field, he could bestride a match like some colossus with touches to illuminate the bleakest winter afternoon. But his detractors thought otherwise, that he was too small, lacked the stamina for heavy grounds and the strength to resist cynical and calculated tough tackling.

Rowe thought the world of him but looking back was as firm in his conviction as he had been then: 'With Blanchflower in the same side another pattern of play might have been created . . . that was my hope. But I couldn't see Tommy in the other (push-and-run) side. That was unfortunate for him. It also caused more argument than enough with those who wanted him in and could not see why he wasn't playing regularly. I told him, "You can rest assured that if any clubs come in for you and you wish to go, you can – with my blessing. And if you go somewhere and don't like it there, I'll gladly have you back." He was a most gifted player and it was quite sad because

he was such a lovely little fellow. In different circumstances he would have been your first choice. But, as it was, I never really got the Blanchflower-Harmer tie-up working before my health broke and I had to give up the Spurs altogether.'

Harmer had joined Tottenham as an amateur in 1945, turned professional in 1948 and made his League debut early in the 1951–52 season when he played 13 games; but over his first five seasons he averaged only ten League matches. Amid other disappointments his biggest was surely being dropped during the 1955–56 season and before the club's third post-war FA Cup semi-final, against Manchester City, a match which had fierce repercussions.

Manager Jimmy Anderson, a cheerful, popular man but perhaps now too old and too inexperienced tactically, was installed for his second and more prolonged term of office following Arthur Rowe's departure; Bill Nicholson was appointed his right-hand man. Alf Ramsey, who had been left out towards the end of the previous season made his move to fame, glory and Ipswich Town in the close season; Eddie Baily also went, to Port Vale, and Anderson bought Maurice Norman from Norwich City and Bobby Smith from Chelsea as 1955 drew to its end. Only Duquemin and Clarke survived in the first team from the push-and-run days.

Anderson had done virtually everything at Spurs except play. He had come to White Hart Lane before the club had even joined the League and, just before he left, a party was held to celebrate his 50 years service. The situation with Ramsey was an odd one. Within the club it was known that he was keen to go into management, but Bill Nicholson, who had considerable coaching experience during his army days and had kept it up by looking after the Cambridge University side, was firmly established as coach. There could never be room at that level for both of them but, even forty years later, it is easy to see what a difficult choice it would have been. There were Spurs with the two greatest English managers of the next decade, both hoping to be asked to make Spurs a great club again. Not only were they contemporaries and team-mates, they had played together for so long, the one in front of the other. It was a situation that was to add poignancy to the tactical Spurs v Ipswich clashes of the early sixties, when Nicholson and Ramsey were fighting each other for the Championship.

The League performances were moderate

enough for most of season 1955–56, but the Cup still stirred. Non-League Boston United were 4–0 home victims in the third round; Middlesbrough fell 3–1 at White Hart Lane in the fourth; Doncaster Rovers were beaten 2–0 on their Belle Vue ground and the short hop to Upton Park saw West Ham removed in the sixth after a 3–3 draw at White Hart Lane had seen Spurs pull two goals back in the dying minutes. So for Manchester City on 17 March, St Patrick's Day, and the semi-final at ill-omened Villa Park. After the West Ham triumph Spurs travelled with high hopes that they could reach their first final in nearly 40 years.

Micky Dulin was on the Spurs right wing for the Boston success, Dave Dunmore took over there when beating the Boro. Then Harmer was tried as a deep lying outside-right against Doncaster, proved a success, was there for a solid 4–0 League win over Chelsea and stayed for the victory over the Hammers. The tactic was to play Harmer in a withdrawn position, tempting the full-back forward. To have played him way up on the wing would have invited his disappearance from the game as well as some physical treatment from the era's backs. Blanchflower recalls how Anderson, following the League game before

the semi-final, had seen Harmer take enough tough tackling from Portsmouth to raise the manager's doubts about playing him against the likes of the Manchester City hard man, Roy Paul. He told his captain he was thinking of playing Alfie Stokes for his speed. But after a midweek reserve match in which both Dunmore and Stokes played, it was Dave Dunmore who got the vote, the dropping of Harmer clearly disrupting the team's rhythm. That semi-final provided a third defeat in eight years at Villa Park for the luckless Spurs, a Bobby Johnstone header deciding the game in City's favour. But there was no doubt in Tottenham ranks that they would have earned a draw if German goalkeeper Bert Trautmann had been penalised for holding the legs of George Robb as the left-winger was about to knock the ball into an empty City net. Blanchflower has told his own story of that dejected Villa Park dressing-room . . . of the gamble which failed in the last twenty minutes when he pushed big Maurice Norman up in attack, dropping Johnny Brooks back . . . then, still hoping to drive Spurs level in the last minutes, he sent Brooks forward again . . . of how he had tried and failed. It seemed that Spurs could never hope to break the Cup hoodoo

A worm's eye view of the end of the Anderson era as Spurs entertain Burnley in the 1957–58 season. Spurs players in the picture include Peter Baker, Cliff Jones, Ron Reynolds, John Ryden, Terry Dyson and Maurice Norman. On top of the East Stand sit the cockerel and ball, which had been transferred from the Main Stand at the time the first floodlights were erected. Manager Jimmy Anderson had served the club for over 50 years in virtually every capacity except that of player. During this season a special presentation was made to him in recognition of his service, which began before Spurs had even entered the Football League.

that appeared to have settled on the Tottenham High Road.

In the League, Tottenham now needed a point from Cardiff and their final home match against Sheffield United, who in due course were relegated with Huddersfield, to be safe. But Blanchflower did not take part in the 0–0 draw with Cardiff, the result which meant safety. Manager Anderson gave out that he was injured, Blanchflower, when asked, said that he was fit. Manager and player discussed the captaincy before that last game with the Yorkshire club. Blanchflower said he could not be captain if he wasn't trusted with authority on the field. So the captaincy was taken off him for the game with Sheffield United. Harry Clarke started as captain the following season. Then Marchi, Bobby Smith and John Ryden took turns. But Blanchflower was still in the wings, waiting for his time to come.

Jimmy Anderson did almost every job there was to do at Tottenham in his fifty splendid years with the club. Twice he stepped into the breach when Arthur Rowe was ill, the second time for some three and a half years when he had to see off the rear end of the miserable 1954–55 season, with Spurs taking a moderate 16th place in the table. Despite the captaincy problems, Anderson was actually fitting the pieces well; Harmer and Blanchflower could work together and the pair of them turned in virtually a full complement of League matches

in 1956–57. This in itself was a great tribute to their staying powers, their skills having long been accepted and admired. But here they were, successful too as Spurs recovered and ended the season as runners-up again to Manchester United. Essentially Spurs were still an attacking side, and their century of goals was the first by any club in the First Division for two decades.

And that welcome improvement by the team was maintained sufficiently for Spurs to finish in third place a year later behind Wolves and Preston North End. It was a good return for Anderson in his second term of office (he had been in charge at the end of the War) but it took its toll. As with Rowe, the strain of big-time managership, and the need for the 24 hours-a-day application it brings, laid him low only weeks into 1958–59 when a familiar early season slump had settled in and the Tottenham defence was having one of its most harrassing times anybody could remember. Second and third in the League was hardly a disgrace, but it is also necessary to remember Anderson's good stewardship down the years, the manner in which he fashioned a side to trouble the best in those two previous seasons; besides which there were his shrewd signings... Maurice Norman . . . Bobby Smith . . . Cliff Jones . . . Terry Dyson . . . Terry Medwin . . . Jim Iley . . . John Ryden. Already the best side Spurs, and perhaps the Football League, has ever had was in the making.

1961

Nicholson's ten-goal debut • White, Mackay and Allen • Dreams of the Double • A Molineux close shave • Team of the Century • Benfica • Glory, Glory, Hallelujah • Dyson's match • Sadness and sorrow

Remarkable though Bill Nicholson's managerial career at White Hart Lane was, nothing ever really matched his very first game in charge. At lunch-time on Saturday 11 October 1958, Nicholson was called to the Tottenham boardroom and appointed manager of the club in succession to Jimmy Anderson. In itself, this was no great surprise. He had been coaching the first team for three years and Spurs have ultimately always preferred to promote those they know (Minter, Rowe, Anderson, Burkinshaw to name other obvious examples).

The fixture that afternoon was not an attractive one. Spurs, with only nine points from eleven games, were sixteenth, a point clear of the bottom three. Everton were actually one of that bottom trio. What happened is history, for the game was to produce the biggest aggregate score of any ever played in the First Division – its 14 goals equalling a record set up when Aston Villa beat Accrington 12–2 a mere 66 years before. Spurs got ten of those goals and, as one paper reported: 'Tommy Harmer scored one and made nine.'

It was perhaps the peak of Tommy Harmer's amazing career, yet he had approached it with trepidation: 'All I can remember is feeling miserable that morning. I had been dropped for the previous four games and it was in the balance whether I'd get my place back.' Harmer's goal, Spurs' eighth, was as uncharacteristic as the day: 'The ball just bounced towards me and I hit it first time, on the half-volley, from 20 yards and it flew into the top corner of the net. I hardly ever scored from that range. It was just one of those days when everything goes in.'

A winning Spurs' side in the bath early in 1960. Clockwise from the top: Danny Blanchflower, Cliff Jones, Dave Mackay, Terry Medwin, Bobby Smith, Bill Brown and Mel Hopkins.

RIGHT: Bobby Smith heads home a centre from Alfie Stokes for the third of his four goals against Everton on 11 October 1958. It was Bill Nicholson's first game in charge and Spurs won 10–4, easily a record managerial debut. It also equalled the record aggregate score for any First Division game. Spurs' other goals were scored by Alfie Stokes (2), George Robb, Terry Medwin, John Ryden and Tommy Harmer. As the teams left the pitch Harmer commented to his new manager: 'We don't score 10 every week you know.' Alfie Stokes was a fine goalscoring inside-forward, finding the net 40 times in only 65 League games.

BELOW RIGHT: More mudlarking at White Hart Lane for Bobby Smith, who has just beaten Preston keeper Fred Else to make an easy goal for right-winger Terry Medwin. The game, on 18 January 1958, ended 3–3. Smith finished 1957-58 with 36 goals, equalling the club record in a season of League games. He eventually broke the club aggregate record as well, ending with 176 goals from 271 League appearances. This season was also to be Preston's last as a truly great club – they finished second, eight points ahead of Spurs, but within four years were playing Second Division football and the nostalgic clashes between two sides which had shared the same strip and contested so many dramatic Cup ties were to be no more.

Harmer's last comment probably sums the game up. For Spurs Bobby Smith got four, Alfie Stokes two, George Robb, Terry Medwin, the injured John Ryden and Harmer one each. For Everton Jimmy Harris joined the select band (possibly the only member) of those who have scored a hat-trick and still seen their team lose by six clear goals, and Bobby Collins got the fourth. Everton reserve keeper Albert Dunlop had let in four against a South African touring team in a friendly three days before; in one week he had thus picked the ball out of the net fourteen times. 'We must protect this man from lumbago,' wrote one witty Merseyside journalist on the Monday.

Harmer was nothing if not sanguine: 'We don't score ten every week you know,' he said to Nicholson as the sides left the field. Nicholson, as befitted his slightly pessimistic character, was equally cautious: 'I've been in this game long enough to know you can be in the clouds one minute and down to earth the next.' In this ease, he was quite right. The next Saturday, Spurs did almost as well, winning 4-3 at Leicester, but Nicholson was more interested in his defence's porousness than his attack's magnificence. In his first four games, including these two, they let in 15 goals and, after the Leicester match, won only one of their next 11 League fixtures. The phrase 'false dawn' could almost have been invented for Nicholson's managerial career.

FOOTBALL CORNUCOPIA

Though matters improved, the 1958–59 season was to all intents and purposes a write-off. It was an odd interlude in a period of dramatic success – their League positions went 2nd, 3rd, 18th, 3rd, 1st, 3rd, 2nd between 1956 and 1963, when the great days were to come to an end. Blanchflower and Harmer were dropped in turn, and with both of them out of touch Spurs were a pallid shadow of the side which had, for instance, taken two points away from pre-Munich Manchester United in a 4–3 thriller at Old Trafford, the first time a London club had won there for 19 years. Blanchflower had been a delight that previous season. As well as leading Northern Ireland to a highly improbable quarter-final place in the World Cup finals in Sweden, he had become the first Spurs player to be elected Footballer of the Year (he was to win the award again in 1961 and thus become, with Stanley Matthews, Tom Finney and Gary Lineker a near immortal). It is possible that Blanchflower was playing even better than in the Double year at this time. Julian Holland said of his displays in the 1957–58 season that: 'The football poured out of him in a ceaseless irresistable profusion, as though his genie had been taking lessons from the sorceror's apprentice. He was a footballing cornucopia . . . at this stage in his career he was the unfaltering dynamo tirelessly feeding the striving attack.'

But Blanchflower and Harmer were not the only ones suffering a few months later. Cliff Jones, the wonderful, direct winger from Swansea was finding it difficult to carry the game's most expensive player (£35,000) tag. Like his uncle Bryn, who had moved to Arsenal twenty years before for £14,000, Jones was thoroughly uncomfortable with the expectations this distinction carried. The Spurs crowd was not noted for its generosity to new signings

('I wouldn't say they were impatient' said Terry Venables a decade later, 'they wait till the third game before they give you the bird.') It was almost Jones' good fortune that he collided with Peter Baker in an early season practice match and broke a leg. He returned half-way through the season, when the crowd had forgotten his earlier fumblings, and he was allowed to develop, with Dave Mackay behind him, to become almost the definitive flying, goalscoring winger. Certainly it is hard to think of a better one since the Second World War. And while, strangely, Jones is somehow remembered as a left-winger, he wore the number seven shirt far more often than the eleven and rarely played for long on either wing anyway. Rather he was the most mobile of the prompting second line – starting anywhere and finishing anywhere.

To add to Nicholson's early season problems in 1958–59 Ted Ditchburn's career had been finished with a bad injury and reserve keeper John Hollowbread was in goal. Things were so difficult that Nicholson decided to put Blanchflower in the reserves where, at 33, the Irishman was trying, and failing, to raise any enthusiasm as a late developing inside-right. It was Nicholson's idea that he should try this out while the club tried to find a more defensive right-half for the League team in order to put a few more mines in the ever open pathway to the Tottenham goal area. The transfer request which followed, and Nicholson's solemn declaration that he would have the board turn it down, was in fact the end and the beginning of the matter. Blanchflower decided that he could work with, and for, the new Tottenham manager. There is no record of any real differences between the pair from that day forward. Their respect for each other and their close friendship remained till Blanchflower's death.

It was on 2 March 1959, before a drawn game at Wolverhampton, that Nicholson publicly acknowledged he needed Blanchflower. Spurs had not won one of their last four home matches. With the Irishman restored as captain they crushed Leicester 6–0 at home five days later. It was the turning point. From here onwards the only way was up.

Mel Hopkins was then injured on duty for Wales and this provided a long sought chance for the tidy Ron Henry at left-back. Hopkins had given fine service to Tottenham but soon the Baker–Henry full-back partnership took off and became one of the solid essentials in the Nicholson build-up.

Having squirmed through season 1958–59 the way ahead began to take on a more hopeful hue. Just before Easter Nicholson had set off on the sort of journey which was to become more frequent over the years, the kind of trip about which no-one knew anything but the closing of the door as Nicholson disappeared. This, one of his earliest, was supposed to have ended with him returning with Mel Charles. Instead of Charles, brother of the great John, the Nicholson capture came from over the other border, Dave Mackay from Hearts. At £32,000 he took over Blanchflower's mantle as Britain's most expensive half-back. It was the first of many transfers to be completed by Nicholson while others waited and wondered'. Mackay and Blanchflower took to each other from the off. Spurs headed for the sixties with higher hopes than the previous season could

RIGHT: Exchanges in the *RIGHT: Exchanges in the dressing-room during the 1959–60 season, when Spurs would have taken the Championship had they won either of their two home games over Easter. Here Medwin, Mackay, Smith, Jones and Baker listen to Bill Nicholson's plans for getting outside the opposing full-back. Walter Winterbottom, England team manager at the time, said of the side Nicholson was building: 'His system had individual expression, but it was based on team-work. The great personalities had been harnessed to be unselfish and, above all else, the team effort made the lesser players look so good.'*

substantiate. Eighteenth in the table was far from being the surest way of keeping the customers happy. Even less promising was a defence like a sieve which had 95 goals sunk past it, the worst defensive League offering anybody at White Hart Lane could remember. But Nicholson had begun to ring the changes. After Mackay he bought another Scot, another keeper to make a third along with Ron Reynolds and John Hollowbread, Scottish international Bill Brown of Dundee for £16,000. Tottenham had also bought back the commanding Tony Marchi from Italian football, where for two years he had effectively been on loan to Lanerossi Vicenza and Torino.

Outgoings there had to be to keep a balance and there was a warm, sentimental farewell to the last remaining players of the fabulous push-and-run team . . . Ted Ditchburn, twenty years with Spurs and with a club record of 418 League appearances, who went to Romford . . . gangling Harry Clarke, who left to enter management, and the 'quiet man', Len Duquemin, who left behind him a mark of 135 goals in League and Cup as he joined Bedford Town. These three left indelible memories and hard to follow standards. Other less significant actors were also to leave, Jim Iley to Nottingham Forest, Alfie Stokes to Fulham.

Blanchflower had been among the first to spot the new signs of hope in that past season, but few would have believed that the glory to be won would have much to thank for its lift-off to the playing fields of the USSR. Bill Nicholson himself was ever-grateful for the bond he was able to build in Russia between his players. Of that twelve-day close season tour he said: 'I was glad of the opportunity of getting the players together. I had said that we would go to see what it was like there. "It's a lot different," I had told the boys. There wasn't much chance for entertainment, so we had every day for training. We trained hard and we played three matches. I cannot overstate the value of that trip in terms of getting things together. And we still had a very enjoyable time, very enjoyable.'

Medwin scored the only goal against Moscow Torpedo, Johnny Brooks got two against Kiev (Spurs winning 2–1) and then he also got the only reply as the third game was lost 3–1 against a national squad in Leningrad. The full benefits of that Russian tour and of the understanding built up in advance of the new season came to fruition at the gateway to the sixties as Tottenham were caught up in a League title race with Burnley and the Wolves.

On 3 October 1959, Danny Blanchflower was in the Northern Ireland team which took a 4–0 home beating at Windsor Park, Belfast, from the Scots. In the Scottish side were his Spurs colleagues, Bill Brown and Dave Mackay. There was also a slim, pale youngster from Falkirk named John White, who scored one of those four Scottish goals. Blanchflower remembers his return from that debacle for the Irish and the greeting from Nicholson: 'What did you think about young John White?' Among the hints, the guesses and the crystal-bowl guidelines of the soccer gossip columns he had seen a vague reference connecting the youngster, unknown south of the border, and the Spurs.

When Nicholson filled in the gaps by telling his skipper that he could get White for a bar-

gain £20,000, Blanchflower told him to grab the next plane bound for Scotland. Mackay and Brown backed up the Irishman's high regard for their young countryman so that manager Nicholson was up and away and within the next 24 hours the signing was all but complete. All but, because ex-Scotland keeper Tommy Younger, the old Hibs and Liverpool favourite who was then managing Falkirk, having brought his player down to White Hart Lane to finalise the deal, saw that Nicholson was not happy with progress. He discovered the reason when he took White aside to ask him what was holding up the deal. He got the surprising answer: 'I'm not good enough for here, I'll never fit in with these players.' Younger said that he had never known a worse case of an inferiority complex: 'He had become a luxury for us because he was thinking two

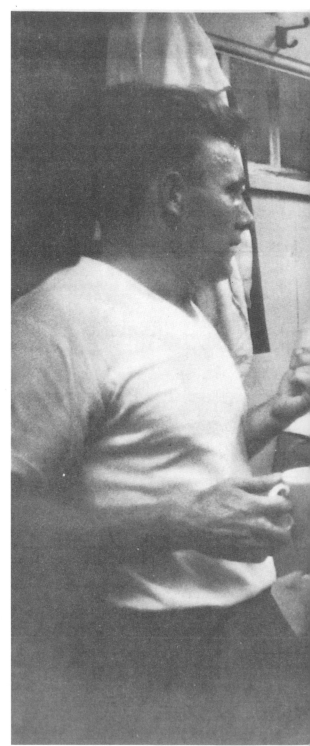

and three moves ahead and his passes were not being picked up,' understood the Falkirk manager.

And exactly as if to prey on those early fears of John White came Tottenham's first defeat of that 1959–60 season. It was Tottenham's 13th League match and was also White's debut, at Hillsborough against a powerful Sheffield Wednesday side . . . and Spurs were missing three regulars in Hopkins, Jones and Medwin, all playing for Wales that afternoon. White did manage to score the solitary Tottenham goal in their 2–1 defeat, but did little more. Two months later Nicholson swooped again to add striker Les Allen to his squad as Johnny Brooks crossed to Chelsea in an exchange deal. Allen and Bobby Smith were essentially similar – they were both goalscorers. Both could look clumsy out of the

penalty area, but they were part of a necessary mixture. A team cannot be composed entirely of John Whites. Swiftly, shrewdly, Bill Nicholson had, did we but know it, put together a collection powerful enough to tackle the world. It had taken him just a year and the mixture was now formed. For three months of 1959–60 – from December to March – Spurs led the way at the top of the First Division, their elevation coinciding with Allen's two-goal debut in the 4–2 Boxing Day success at Elland Road. In the return two days later Leeds United hammered Spurs 4–1 at White Hart Lane; it didn't help the Yorkshiremen to avoid relegation, but it showed that Spurs did not yet have the consistency of a great side.

That was one shock result for Tottenham. Two more at Easter, just as big, ended any

title hopes. Spurs had three Easter fixtures, then two more to complete their programme. But just as their own 3–1 win at Molineux was to rob Wolves of an historic League and Cup Double in the last but one match of the season, so did two unaccountable home beatings in 48 hours – 0–1 to Manchester City on Easter Saturday, and another 0–1 to Chelsea on Easter Monday – end any Tottenham title chance.

Tottenham lost the Championship by just two points, and they should have had them both against Manchester City. Cliff Jones' penalty, at the end of the first half, was well saved by goalkeeper Bert Trautmann but the Welshman, following up, tapped home the rebound. Unfortunately for Spurs, the referee had added time on for the penalty to be taken and the goal did not stand. Had it done so, they might have approached the second half differently and not conceded City's vital single goal. That being said, no team which loses its last two home matches deserves to win anything very much.

WOLVES AND THE DOUBLE

The Championship is always a matter of ifs and buts, never more so than in 1960 when Burnley's success was unquestionably unique. The Lancastrians never led the League until after their, and the Division's, final game, which they won at Maine Road. Burnley had actually lost 6–1 at Molineux only weeks before and, with just three weeks left, were little more than hopeful outsiders behind Spurs and Wolves. Wolves themselves had thrown away a

Championship which seemed to be theirs for the taking when Spurs came to Molineux on Saturday 23 April 1960. This was one of the truly critical games of Spurs' great years ranking alongside the Cup ties against Aston Villa and Sunderland, the European Cup semi-final with Benfica and the last gasp of the era, the European Cup Winners Cup final against Atletico.

Wolves were not only running strongly for the Double (and odds-on with the bookmakers to become the first team this century to achieve it) but were also on the verge of equalling Huddersfield's and Arsenal's record of a hat-trick of Championships. But even on the edge of such an achievement, it was clear to some that Molineux's great days were at an end – Wright, Swinbourne, Hancocks, Mullen and Wilshaw had all gone. Stan Cullis's long ball game remained, but the replacements were not as good as their predecessors. That being said, Wolves were now four points clear of Burnley and three clear of Spurs. If they beat Tottenham they had only Chelsea to overcome and the Championship was theirs. If Burnley did not get maximum points, then just beating Spurs would be enough. It did not seem too great a task for a team that was to walk over Blackburn Rovers in the Cup final two weeks later – particularly as opponents Spurs had lost their last two games, both at home.

But this was to be one of those moments when an observer can actually sense history turning. Spurs were relaxed, their chances of winning the League virtually gone. Blanchflower held his team talk in the middle

of the pitch rather than in the dressing-room and, within two minutes, had created the first goal. Feinting to put Cliff Jones away on the right, he changed direction and centred for Bobby Smith. The centre-forward did the rest while the Wolves defence still covered the threat from Jones. Broadbent equalised but Mackay, with a rare header, put Spurs back in front. Their third, and final, goal was a classic: Terry Dyson flying down the left wing, a perfect cross and there was Jones with a full-length header.

Wolves did beat Chelsea at Stamford Bridge, 5–1, but Burnley pipped them anyway and the hat-trick and the Double had both gone. Wolves had been as baffled by Barcelona in the European Cup as they had by Spurs (who had also beaten them 5–1 at White Hart Lane). It was a decisive end to Wolves' great era. They have not won the League or Cup since.

Though everyone had hoped for better, third place behind champions Burnley and Wolves was still a boost for Bill Nicholson and Spurs. The rise from eighteenth in the table to third place a season later was improvement indeed. So was the performance of the defence, which had 45 fewer goals rattled past it this time. There was also proof that Tottenham were giving the fans what they wanted – they were the best supported home side in the country with an average of 47,948, a total only seriously challenged by Manchester United. It was also the season which brought the club's record victory . . . the 13–2 swamping of little Crewe Alexandra in an FA Cup fourth round replay in February 1960. Mighty Spurs had stuttered

and spluttered at Gresty Road. Blanchflower said that the Crewe supporters worked themselves up to a belief that they could provide a Cup shock and Spurs played so cautiously as to fumble over scraping a 2–2 draw in the first meeting. Only a shot which bounced back off a post saved Spurs from their fourth humiliation in six years – Third Division York, Bournemouth and Norwich already being in the record books.

The outcome of the Tottenham visit was a record 20,000 home gate for Fourth Division Alexandra, the reward for making Spurs play it again at White Hart Lane on the following Wednesday a massive 64,365 gate to share. But that and a rare look round the capital were all poor Crewe were allowed as Spurs turned cold killers under the arc lights to pile up the agony of a 10–1 half-time lead. Only a second-half easing down spared further torture for Crewe and unfortunate keeper David Evans, who had picked the ball out of his net 15 times (his only concession from fortune being two scores which were ruled out). Les Allen got five, Bobby Smith four, Cliff Jones three and Tommy Harmer the other goal. The story, perhaps apocryphal, is still told of how Crewe arrived on platform 2 at Euston and went home from platform 13. Poor Evans; he afterwards admitted to fearing seven or eight home efforts going past him, but 13! 'I don't know WHERE those other five goals came from,' he said, 'and I didn't feel too good about it.' But that was the end for Tottenham too, and on an off day in the next round Blackburn Rovers took away a 3–1 victory at the Lane.

ABOVE: A flying Bill Brown fails to connect with a Blackburn centre at Ewood Park on 27 August 1960. While Maurice Norman, now restored to his rightful centre-half spot, heads away, captain Danny Blanchflower appears to look on amused. Spurs won the game easily 4–1.

OPPOSITE: An unusually
relaxed team shot taken
towards the end of the
1960-61 season. From left
to right the eleven players
who formed the Double-
winning side are: John
White, Les Allen, Ron
Henry, Peter Baker, Terry
Dyson, Dave Mackay, Bill
Brown, Cliff Jones, Danny
Blanchflower, Bobby Smith
and Maurice Norman.
Terry Medwin was the only
other player to appear
more than half-a-dozen
times during the season.
Deryk Brown wrote of this
side afterwards: 'One
always wondered why
Tottenham did not
regularly reach double
figures against some set of
unfortunates. Surely one
day the team would troop
off the pitch at half-time
and the loudspeaker would
announce that
Blanchflower had declared
or that the opposition had
sent a white flag to Bill
Nicholson.'

DREAMS OF A DOUBLE

Blanchflower, looking back, remembered how the team's new-found power began to give him ideas, how the all-round strength of the squad had increased, the force of 5–1 victories gained against Newcastle United at St James' Park, at Old Trafford when meeting Manchester United and of similar home wins over Preston and Wolves . . . days when everyone and everything moved in harmony. He could see only the Double, the Double which both Manchester United and Wolves had missed so narrowly in the past four seasons.

The 'impossible' Double was a far more common topic of football conversation then than it had been, say, thirty years before or was twenty years later. That was largely because both Manchester United and Wolves had come so close to achieving it within the space of three years. Both had failed by a single match – United in a Cup final they couldn't possibly lose, Wolves by conceding a home game to a side which had just lost two consecutive home matches. These amazingly close-run attempts had apparently proved one of two things to soccer journalists – that the Double certainly was possible or, alternatively, that it obviously wasn't. The latter school of thought quoted the psychology of the four-minute mile; that the mental barriers became so great in the home stretch that few athletes could break through them. But, up in North London, sat football's own squad of Roger Bannisters.

Joe Mercer recalled coming back from Sweden after the World Cup in 1958. On the plane, said Joe, Blanchflower could talk of little else to himself and Stan Cullis. It went on in the taxi from Heathrow. 'He told us over and over again that it was going to be done. "And we'll be the ones to do it," he had promised.' The Spurs captain repeated the vow when the elderly club chairman, Mr Fred Bearman, asked him what 1960–61 might bring for Tottenham. 'We'll get the Double for you this time . . . the League and the Cup,' came the confident answer. In fact Blanchflower had originally been confident about the Double before 1959–60. Looking back he said: 'We could have done it then, but we hadn't been there before, hadn't had the experience. The following season we were able to pace ourselves better.'

'That third in the League table was a boost,' said Bill Nicholson. 'We were getting it together, getting the team working and playing for one another and getting to know each other. Ron Henry for Mel Hopkins at left-back was an important change. Then Terry Dyson came in for Terry Medwin. I felt that we would have a good shout in the League, but in the Cup . . . well, who knows about the Cup? One afternoon on a strange pitch, an awkward ground, one or two little things going the opposite way and bingo! You're gone. It's different again, the Cup.'

Then, very firmly, he added: 'Anyway, I never did make predictions, it wasn't my job to. And it's not a thing I'd lend myself to, the game is so fickle. If Danny liked to say it . . . well, that was Danny. He should have known by then that teams often win games they don't deserve to win.'

Nicholson took a deep breath after this, as if trying to summon memories, those magical moments from perhaps the greatest single season in any English club's history, to feel for an echo of a sustained season of soccer classics and maintained at a pitch of performance no year had ever previously seen. Smooth, soft skills . . . perfect patterns . . . tenacity of purpose laced with hard discipline . . . still with a stylish swing to refresh their every game. And all the threads painstakingly pulled together by the stolid Nicholson, dependable as man and player, who had always performed within his own honest limitations, few as they were, forever pursuing excellence in his teams.

'I tried to keep our football as simple as possible,' he recalled. 'We had good players but I didn't want them to indulge themselves too much as individuals. "We've got to be effective, not exhibition players" I used to tell them. "You've got to involve other players like the 1950 side." You are always preaching involvement but the situations come on the field and the player has to do it himself. The good player will always know what it is best to do.

'In the 1950 side we played the short game. If you kick the ball any length there's a good chance the other side will intercept, and naturally you cannot be so accurate. It was so different from the long game favoured by the Wolves who lashed the ball from side to side and reckoned that long stuff to forwards, if not getting on the mark, did enough to unsettle defenders. Then they always had players coming through quickly, either to close down rivals or ready to snap up any half chances their assaults might have given them to feed on.

'In the 1960 side we had the skill to play balls first time, like the Rowe side did, but also the skill to play the longer game.' It is a theme he no doubt developed on many occasions, with him loyally insisting on including a salute for his old comrades in arms. 'Harry Evans, once the Aldershot manager, joined me as my assistant. He took a lot of work off to leave me free for the real job of preparing a team.' Unhappily, the popular Harry was to die in harness after a brief stay with the club, sorely missed by Nicholson.

GLORY, GLORY, HALLELUJAH

'I felt in 1960 that I had a side well prepared to do something. You cannot put it into words, it's a feeling you get. And I had this strong feeling around that time.' The result was that: Spurs became the first club to take the League and Cup Double this century; their 66 points total equalled the First Division record set up by Arsenal in 1930–31; their 33 away points also equalled Arsenal's of the same season; eleven consecutive victories from the start of the season bettered the record of Hull City, with their nine opening successes in 1948–49; the total of 31 winning matches was a First Division record, as was the 16 victorious away matches; Spurs achieved 11 doubles over their League rivals, which equalled the First Division performances of Manchester United (1956-57) and Wolves (1958-59); they attained 50 points in 29 games, faster than any club previously; and their 115 goals was a club scoring record for a season.

Statistics are a mundane wrap-around for a glorious season played out to the challenging background of 'Glory, Glory, Hallelujah', but they help us take in the picture more readily. Like the 31 points from the first 32 when only Manchester City's 1–1 draw at the Lane in October had temporarily stubbed a toe before sturdy Sheffield Wednesday ended that unbeaten run at Hillsborough on 12 November.

Spurs had opened up a seven-point lead over Wednesday, their nearest challengers, but the eight previous clubs that had journeyed to Hillsborough had not taken a single point away. Fittingly it was a giant of a match, tough, mean, abrasive with the 56,363 crowd stoking up a furnace-like atmosphere. Wednesday were nothing if not a defensive side. The strapping Peter Swan blocked the goal-path to Bobby Smith, who earlier in the season had hat-tricked his way against Blackpool into being Tottenham's best-ever goalscorer with 141 goals in his five years since joining from Chelsea. Alongside Swan, and soon to suffer with him in a bribery scandal, was red-headed firebrand Tony Kay. With burly Don Megson behind it was mainly these three who turned the tide against Spurs and their unbeaten record.

Billy Griffin's goal near half-time stilled the Tottenham roars. Maurice Norman set them off again when he equalised from a quickly taken Dave Mackay free-kick. But, with some 20 minutes to go, Megson attacked and crossed down the left for John Fantham to get the home winner. So Spurs had fallen at the 17th hurdle, after taking a record 31 points from the first 32. If anything, they were pleased. The tension of waiting for the inevitable defeat had been massive. It was a surprisingly cheerful team coach which left Hillsborough that evening, some of the players singing on the way to Sheffield Midland station. Long before this defeat they had earned a glowing tribute from that stern taskmaster Stan Cullis, manager of Wolves, after Spurs had buried them again, this time 4–0 on their own Molineux turf. 'They are the finest club side I've ever seen in the Football League – even better than the great Spurs of ten years ago.'

Three weeks later came the unforgettable meeting with Burnley, the reigning champions, an epic 4–4 clash which first established Tottenham as true heirs-apparent to the League throne and then fully proved that the crown

had been worn well, and not uneasily, by the Lancastrians.

Tottenham halted any early Burnley aggression on a miserable, rainy December afternoon, then struck three times in three minutes, first through Norman then with two breakaway efforts by Jones. And when Mackay came up with a fourth goal inside 40 minutes it was as certain as anything could be that Burnley were to be added to the list of Tottenham scalps. Even Bill Nicholson himself admits that he could not imagine soccer turning so fickle. But, before the interval, winger John Connelly strode through the home defence to pull one back and battle recommenced with Burnley drawing on pride and pedigree to push Blanchflower and company completely out of their stride. Next, Jimmy Robson, then the blond Ray Pointer, nipped in for Burnley goals and the noise was truly deafening when, with only a dozen minutes left, the elusive Connelly was again haring up the middle to present the crowd with an incredible draw. Few could quite remember the like of this remarkable match, or such a turnabout result. It was more a lesson for the prospective champions than the resilient title-holders but Bill Nicholson proved typically phlegmatic with his defence: 'We scored eight goals and still only drew,' he commented in the dressing-room.

Half way to the title finish there was no longer a bookmaker who would accept money on Tottenham. It was a one-horse race. The point and poise of the side was the Blanchflower-White axis, the wry, pale Scot having taken over Harmer's role ('Scottish waif for Cockney wisp' wrote one journalist) to add a more urgent, broader sweep to a side now better able to vary pace and power. Mackay, who seemed to play with a skirl of bagpipes in his game, was the ideal blend of flinty, foraging pirateer opposite his skipper, and the so brave Jones with his jet speed was a scimitar aimed at the heart of any defence. And now Smith and Allen were proving Nicholson's point, that with all the style in the world it was still goals which won matches in the end.

Little Dyson, small enough to be the son of his father, a leading northern jockey, had wrested the other wing place from Medwin with a bit more dash and unorthodoxy, while the defence had now bedded solidly down from keeper Brown and outwards to Baker and Henry, with Norman commanding in the air if occasionally reluctant to tackle on the ground. For the first three seasons after he had moved from Norwich, Maurice Norman had played at full-back, somewhat uneasily for much of the time. He was now in his prefered position in a defence which was, unlike the middle and front lines, built on extremely conventional principles.

In the 1960–61 season's first half they scored 21 more goals and gained 10 more points than they did in the second half. And they won five more games. The point is made for interest, not contention. By kinder weather alone the going should be more favourable, played mostly as it is in the autumn. But in any case, those who had been trying to pick the flaws in Tottenham's runaway leadership had seen ample evidence presented to them that the heavier going would not – and did not – really clog up the Tottenham works. But the fact was that they lost two of their first three League

games in the New Year, 0–2 at Old Trafford against Manchester United, then a 2–3 beating by Leicester City at White Hart Lane. They also finished their greatest ever season with another wobble, beaten 2–4 at Burnley and then by West Bromwich back at the Lane in two of their last three League matches. The West Brom game, played before 51,880 people on 29 April, was a particular disappointment. One more point would have broken Arsenal's First Division record. Instead, Spurs lost 2–1. But they were still masters enough of the First Division to bridge a ten-year gap in the club's history and reclaim the Football League Championship trophy for the Tottenham sideboard as they finished eight points ahead of Sheffield Wednesday and nine in front of Wolves. Appropriately the trophy was won by beating Wednesday.

It was against the Wednesday on 17 April that Spurs avenged their first defeat of the season with the same 2–1 scoreline, this time in their favour. But, as last time, it was no match for the faint-hearted and skill came second to all-out, full-blooded effort which had the smile freezing on the face of 'Smiler' Tommy Dawes, the Norwich referee. He booked both Mackay and Wednesday's Peter Johnson and Spurs fans were to suffer a slight case of shock when Megson, villain of the piece at Hillsborough, smashed home a first half free-kick to give his side the lead. The evening was one of roaring sound as 62,000 bayed for blood and goals; they had come to see Spurs win the Championship, not to appreciate a great football match. The home crowd, silenced momentarily, then set up even greater roars for Spurs to hit back. They did so almost immediately . . . twice. First Bobby Smith flipped the ball over England's Swan and slammed it home on the half-volley. And they were still acclaiming that goal when Blanchflower's free-kick was headed sideways by the lurking Norman and Allen thumped in a terrific, shoulder high volley. The match got even hotter in the second half; Smith charged Wednesday keeper Ron Springett into a post and the keeper was carried off, only to insist on returning within minutes. Some nail-biting moments for Tottenham's hopes ended with the crowd pouring onto the pitch at the final whistle and sheer pandemonium until skipper Blanchflower led out his players to take the crowd's thanks and appreciation.

'DANNY, DANNY'

The crowd had little doubt where the credit lay, calling specifically for 'Danny, Danny' to come out and take the victory salute. 'Footballer of the Year' for the second time in four years, the judgement of the fans was surely correct, though it is difficult to pin down exactly how Blanchflower made it all work. He was part of the team, but, probably uniquely, not of it; essentially he was the deputy manager. And while many managers would not (and did not) tolerate Blanchflower's insistence on having his own way, Bill Nicholson had the sense and the confidence to harness it rather than fight it. It was probably the best intuition Nicholson ever had. Blanchflower assessed his own contribution in relatively few words: 'I could change the rhythm, change the pace, slow it down if necessary, speed it up when we needed to. I also had the ball much more often than anyone else – so I should have done something with it shouldn't I? And I was a lot older than the rest – 34. I had learned how to play by then, and, at Villa, how not to play.

'Most of all I could read the team as players and as men. I think I knew how to bring out the best. I would never, for instance, direct Maurice Norman openly on the field – I'd ask Peter Baker or Ron Henry to talk to him. But with Dave Mackay you never had to worry about confidence or ego. I remember Terry Medwin getting injured once, being unhappy about staying on. Dave and I suggested Terry go out to the right-wing, where we used to put people who'd been in the wars, for a few minutes till he recovered. Five minutes later he came haring back: "Did you say go on the right-wing? I was on the right-wing!" I think I knew the team.'

Blanchflower had long since ceased to be a mere footballing figure and was a publicly feted 'personality'. His television advertisements for a breakfast cereal led to an Irish accented 'Hullo there' becoming a public catch phrase alongside such gems as Bruce Forsyth's 'I'm in charge'. His refusal to appear on *This is Your Life* (the programme's first such embarrassment) was front page news. 'I did it for personal reasons,' he said afterwards. 'If I told you what they were they wouldn't be personal any more would they?' Blanchflower, like many footballers, has remained unimpressed by television, questioning the apparent assumption that man's

BELOW: *Perhaps the single most worrying moment during the Double season, McPheat's shot flashes into the net for Sunderland to make it 1–1 in the FA Cup quarter-final.*
Playing at Roker on 25 February 1961, Spurs had taken an early lead through Cliff Jones but Sunderland eventually scored after four corner kicks in a row. The crowd invaded the pitch (BOTTOM) and this helped the players calm down. Blanchflower, seen about to pick the ball out of the net with Maurice Norman, told the referee: 'Let the fans work it off, we don't mind.' Spurs won the replay 5–0. Nicholson's greatest fear was just this sort of Cup upset: 'Who knows with the Cup? One afternoon on a strange pitch, an awkward ground, one or two things go the opposite way and bingo. You're out.'

primary goal in life should be to appear on the small screen. His later career with such programmes as *Sportsview* was short-lived and not marked by outstanding displays of harmony with producers and directors who would not allow him the same creative freedom he enjoyed on the Tottenham pitch.

Bill Nicholson, the other half of this on-field/off-field relationship was blunter: 'In a poor side Danny was a luxury. That's why I dropped him. But in a good side his creativity, his unorthodox approach, was priceless – a wonderful asset.' Together they thought about the game and moulded that great side, the one that won the Double.

Nor did the Tottenham triumphs, or Tottenham-connected triumphs, end at that in 1961. With the FA Cup final still to come there was ex-Spur Alf Ramsey guiding his Ipswich Town side into the First Division for the first time in the club's history, plus Nicholson and Ramsey's mentor Arthur Rowe, thankfully back at work again, managing Crystal Palace from the Fourth to Third Division. And, not to be left out of the celebrations, the Spurs reserves were runners-up to Chelsea in the Football Combination and the third team romped away with the Eastern Counties League.

In achieving their League triumph, Tottenham spread their fire-power right across their attack; all five forwards were into double figures even before the halfway stage, proof that the canny Nicholson had the front blend about right. It pleased him that he was carrying on a Tottenham tradition in doing so.

'Supple and imaginative, that's how the game has always been played at Spurs. Or how they have always tried to play it over my years here. It's the man without the ball who is the most important. I can remember an old schoolmaster who tried to show me the way. His words stuck and they always apply: "When not in possession get into position." I never forgot that phrase. You should never be just watching. I used to say when any of my players erred in this way, "If I catch you doing that again I'll charge you admission. If you want to watch, then you should pay".'

THE OTHER HALF

There was motivation enough for the Cup, the other leg of the impossible. They had eased the load by piling up the League points until that title was virtually assured well before the season was completed. From the New Year on the Cup trail opened up, with Second Division Charlton pressing Spurs, on an off day, far too close for comfort before going down 3–2 in the third round at White Hart Lane. Crewe Alexandra travelled down again in sheer terror for a fourth round set-to, and, although escaping the 13–2 annihilation of their previous visit, were not exactly flattered at 5–1.

A trip to their Cup bogey ground of Villa Park was the reward in February's fifth round draw. But the fixture list provided first a full dress rehearsal for that match in the shape of a League meeting between the clubs the previous Saturday. Spurs were happy enough with their League returns from Villa Park games (where they had not lost since Blanchflower moved down), distinctly not so when it came to the Cup, where they had, of course, been beaten in the semi-finals of 1948, 1953 and 1956.

The League match suffered from a lot of sparring and weighing-up by both teams trying to learn something for the more glamorous Cup tie ahead, and although there was effort enough there was not much more. Even so, Spurs made history by a 2–1 victory which took them to the fastest 50 points yet achieved. It was the barrel-chested Mackay who took the chief honours a week later in the Cup as Aston Villa went down again, this time 2–0, before an enormous 69,000 crowd. The goals, both from Cliff Jones and one in each half, were first a somewhat fortunate deflection off full-back John Neal, later Middlesbrough and Chelsea manager, the other an unstoppable drive to round off a smooth five-men Tottenham move. Julian Holland said of the astonishingly fast, direct Jones: 'More than any other player, it was he who made Blanchflower's old age comfortable.' No longer burdened by the most expensive footballer tag, Jones was now doing just what he had been bought for.

It was another Jones goal which held Sunderland to a 1–1 draw at Roker Park in the sixth round. Sunderland jolted Spurs out of their elegant stride in a rugged second half fight-back but later, with a packed 64,797 looking on at the White Hart Lane replay, the

Wearsiders were right up against it as five home goals poured past them without reply. And for conclusive proof that the Villa Park pitch held no more Cup terrors for them, Tottenham stilled a gusty, swirling wind sufficiently long enough to tame Jimmy McIlroy and the rest of the renowned Burnley team into a 3–0 submission in the semi-final. McIlroy and Blanchflower were close friends and shared the scheming role for Northern Ireland. The Burnley star was not, however, always entirely overwhelmed by his colleague's charms: 'People ask me why I often don't play as well for Ireland as I do for Burnley. It's simple – Danny always keeps me up all night talking.' Bobby Smith's two goals and a late one from Jones were the passport to a Wembley meeting with Leicester City in the final. The semi would have made a better final, and for Burnley the match was poorly timed, being just three days after their 4–1 European Cup defeat by Hamburg.

Unfortunately the final itself, on 6 May, was spoiled as a spectacle, or the spectacle it should be, by the injury to City's right-back Len Chalmers. He was hurt in a tackle by Les Allen in the 19th minute, a hard tackle but nothing more than a clumsy one, as Chalmers himself was quick to point out later. There are those who believe that in those early minutes, and with Chalmers still in action, Leicester looked the better bet as Cup winners; that Spurs did little justice to themselves as the heralded Team of the Century until the last twenty minutes of the match, and that was when tiredness had taken toll of a City side which battled helplessly against the odds of having Chalmers,

when he returned to the fray, limping bravely but ineffectively along the left wing.

Leicester could only hope to keep some self respect from the result. They did this by holding out until Smith, with a dummy, feint and cracking 67th minute shot which rocketed past young keeper Gordon Banks, and ten minutes later little Dyson, with a deliberately placed header from a precise Smith cross, enabled skipper Blanchflower to lead the way up to the Royal Box to redeem the pledge which he had made to his chairman at the start of the season – the League and the Cup. Forty-eight hours before he had received his second 'Footballer of the Year' award. It was a time for silverware.

Though it had to be whispered at the time, many found the final something of a disappointment. Everyone, except a few unfortunates from the Midlands, had wanted to see Spurs win, and win in style. At White Hart Lane, however, they remembered what had happened to Manchester United just four years before, when they were even hotter favourites for the Double. Certainly Leicester's chances in 1961 looked better than had Villa's in 1957, even if City had taken three appallingly poor games (0–0, 0–0, 2–0) to get past Sheffield United in the semi-finals.

For Spurs it had been a season of Cup finals; every side was desperate to beat them and the opposition raised its game time after time. This is why Blanchflower's ability to change the pace was so important – to slow everything down, absorb pressure, consolidate any gains they had made. In the 1970s, particularly with European teams away from home, such tactics became commonplace; in 1960

Before the great days began. From left to right: Peter Baker, Bill Brown, Dave Dunmore, Danny Blanchflower and a preoccupied Tommy Harmer, apparently concerned about his toes. Full-backs Peter Baker and Ron Henry were actually the only locally born members of the Double-winning team. At the beginning of the 1960–61 season Blanchflower had told chairman Fred Bearman that he thought the side could do the Double. 'In our last League match of the previous season at Wolverhampton we had been clearly better than the best of the competition, and this was the basis of my confidence,' Blanchflower was to say years later.

they were never really understood. Spurs approached the Cup final in 1961 in a more conservative frame of mind than for any other game they had played all season. It was, for instance, the only match during which Maurice Norman did not go up for corner-kicks. Certainly it is possible that Chalmers' injury was critical, Spurs only taking control in the last half hour when Leicester had been worn down by the combined burdens of knowing that, unlike most underdogs, they would not be popular winners, the understandable apprehension about their opponents, and, much the most relevant, playing with a man short.

Blanchflower felt the anticlimax as much as anyone in the stadium and made a more general point: 'I did not feel the same emotion before or after as I had with previous rounds. There were too many people there who did not care about the result and, at the end, I didn't have much heart for running around the stadium. I looked upon it as a duty rather than an enjoyment. For the player the reality of a Cup final can never live up to the dream, the promised land, anyway. The dreams are for the fan, not the player, for the lover of the game who will never know what it is like out there. Cup final day is the fans' day.'

Nicholson also mentioned disappointment before glories. 'Looking back now the Double

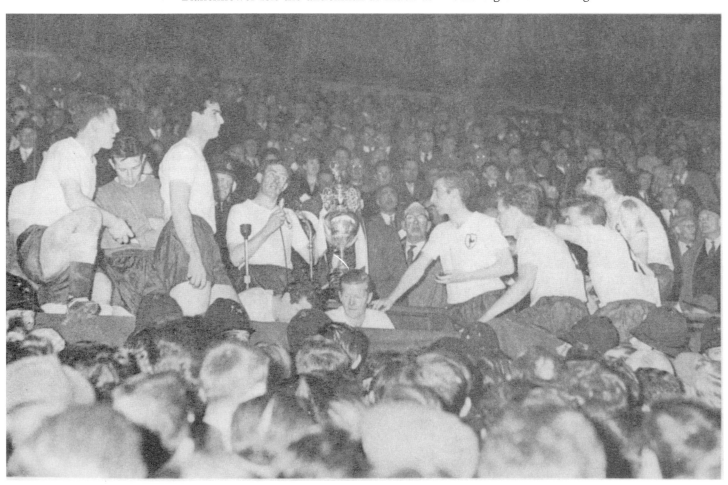

was fabulous,' he said reflectively, 'but there was also disappointment for me when we did not put our Double feat right out of anybody's reach – remember that Arsenal caught up with us ten years later – by doing it for a second year in succession. Which we should have done.' The key to this regret was his old colleague Alf Ramsey and one game in 1962.

IPSWICH AND RAMSEY

Nicholson explained: 'We were due to play Ipswich and in our team chat before the match I was keen that we should change marking tactics and have our wing-halves mark their wingers instead of the full-backs doing the job. This was because they had wily Jimmy Leadbetter pulling the strings back from deep and I believed that if our half-backs could do a smother-job it would enable us to raid forward while, we hoped, Blanchflower and Mackay throttled them before they could set up anything.

'But there was a disagreement about playing it that way and I conceded the point because I did not want them trying to play a tactical plan they were unhappy about. They beat us home and away, 3–1 on our own pitch. If we had beaten them 3–1 at White Hart Lane we would have done the Double again; it is just as simple as that. It was all a question of tactics.

'But the sequel is interesting . . . as Ipswich won the League title and we again won the Cup, we had to meet for the Charity Shield at the start of the new season, 1962–63. Alf Ramsey won the toss for the game to be played at Portman Road. There was no nonsense this time. I put my foot down and told them very firmly that we would play this one my way. Which we did and we beat them by 5–1.'

The tactics of these two clashes are worth a diversion, for they highlight the astuteness of Nicholson, the reasons why Alf Ramsey was able to win a World Cup and, more pertinently, the relative tactical illiteracy of most English managers at the time. Ipswich, newly promoted, had a mediocre squad at best. It is not too much of an exaggeration to say that Alf Ramsey won the Championship with just two strengths; one was the fact that hardly anyone in the division had met the Ipswich team before, the other was the use of slightly built Jimmy Leadbetter as a

withdrawn left-winger. Instead of pushing Leadbetter to the goal-line, Ramsey had him use the ball in a variety of ways, often slotting it diagonally into the penalty area from up to 50 yards out from goal. The opposing full-back, conventionally believing that the number 11 was nowhere near the danger-area, generally held off. But Leadbetter was a remarkably accurate kicker of the ball and his target was almost invariably the battering ram of a dual spearhead – Ray Crawford and Ted Phillips. Neither was at all subtle, but attacking the centre-half together (this was before the days of twin centre-backs and, remember, the full-backs had stayed wide) they were remarkably effective. Phillips scored 28 goals in his only First Division season of note (the next two years his tally dropped to 9 and then 4), Crawford 33. And no one really found them out until Nicholson revealed the simplicity of the tactic in that Charity Shield match. He brought the Spurs full-backs infield to outnumber Crawford and Phillips, and had the half-backs mark Leadbetter out of the game. Spurs won 5–1.

FIRST DIVISION 1960–61

	P	W	D	L	F	A	W	D	L	F	A	PTS
Tottenham	42	15	3	3	65	28	16	1	4	50	27	66
Sheff Wed	42	15	4	2	45	17	8	8	5	33	30	58
Wolves	42	17	2	2	61	32	8	5	8	42	43	57
Burnley	42	11	4	6	58	40	11	3	7	44	37	51
Everton	42	13	4	4	47	23	9	2	10	40	46	50
Leicester	42	12	4	5	54	31	6	5	10	33	39	45
Man Utd	42	14	5	2	58	20	4	4	13	30	56	45
Blackburn	42	12	3	6	48	34	3	10	8	29	42	43
Aston Villa	42	13	3	5	48	28	4	6	11	30	49	43
WBA	42	10	3	8	43	32	8	2	11	24	39	41
Arsenal	42	12	3	6	44	35	3	8	10	33	50	41
Chelsea	42	10	5	6	61	48	5	2	14	37	52	37
Man City	42	10	5	6	41	30	3	6	12	38	60	37
Nottm F.	42	8	7	6	34	33	6	2	13	28	45	37
Cardiff C.	42	11	5	5	34	26	2	6	13	26	59	37
West Ham	42	12	4	5	53	31	1	6	14	24	57	36
Fulham	42	8	8	5	39	39	6	0	15	33	56	36
Bolton	42	9	5	7	38	29	3	6	12	20	44	35
Birmingham	42	10	4	7	35	31	4	2	15	27	53	34
Blackpool	42	9	3	9	44	34	3	6	12	24	39	33
Newcastle	42	7	7	7	51	49	4	3	14	35	60	32
Preston	42	7	6	8	28	25	3	4	14	15	46	30

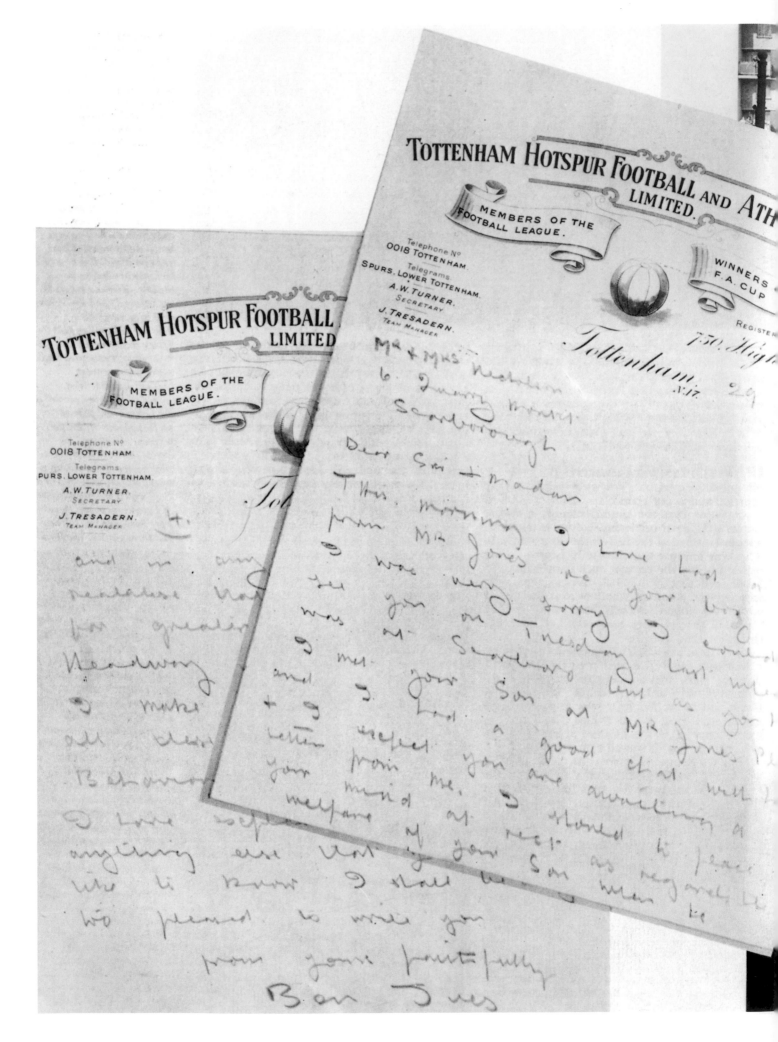

OPPOSITE PAGE: The letter that changed, and made, Tottenham's history. Written by chief scout Ben Ives on 29 February 1936 it invited Bill Nicholson's parents to send their son down to White Hart Lane for a month's trial. While Ives mentions having had a chat with Nicholson, the future manager has no recollection of the meeting. The Mr Jones mentioned was the organiser of Nicholson's local team. The letter came as a complete surprise to the Nicholsons. 'My parents had never seen me play; they knew I was keen but had no idea whether I was any good or not. We weren't even exactly sure where Tottenham was, ' says Nicholson. The letter goes on to reassure the 16-year-old's parents that. 'You need not fear about him as at present we have about 20 boys his age and we get them good lodgings with personal friends of mine . . . Mr Jones will put him on the night train at York and I shall meet him at Kings X, or should Mr Nicholson like to bring him down himself he would be welcome. The boy seems to be very bright and I am sure he will get on (here) and in any case I trust you realise that he must have a far greater chance of making headway in London than elsewhere.' Nicholson came and, 25 years later, so did the trophies. In the space of three years there were to be four of them.
LEFT TOP: Ron Henry and Peter Baker hold the Championship trophy and FA Cup respectively as the Double winners parade up the High Road.
LEFT BOTTOM: A year later the FA Cup, in the capable hands of Maurice Norman and Danny Blanchflower, takes the same route after Spurs had become only the fourth club in history to retain the trophy. They missed another Double by one game – when Ipswich beat them at home.
BOTTOM CENTRE: There'll be another bus along next year . . . this time carrying the Cup Winners Cup. Though the crowds couldn't know it, an era was at an end.

It was a vindication of manager Nicholson's tactical know-how and one could understand the disappointment of a man who had always aimed to be a winner. But it might also have been true to say that Tottenham took their eye off the ball over the last few laps of the League race. Five crucial home points were dropped in the last six matches to be played at White Hart Lane and that was definitely not championship form. Amazingly West Brom yet again beat them in the season's last home match – and again the score was 2–1. It was all too late when, faced with the most difficult ending possible to their programme, they rattled-off three away victories at Blackburn, Birmingham and Leicester. That only underlined what might have been. Ipswich and Burnley slugged it out in the final matches, both dropping points all over the place, but Ramsey clinched the title at the end with a convincing 6–2 win over the Lancastrians.

Almost as an afterthought, Spurs did win the Cup again – only the fourth club (after Wanderers, Blackburn Rovers and Newcastle United) ever to do so in consecutive years. The draw was not an easy one for them but they handled it in style. In the third round they drew 3–3 at St Andrew's and won the replay 4–2. The fourth round saw a 5–1 walkover at Plymouth, the fifth 4–2 at The Hawthorns. Spurs' only home draw was in the quarter-finals, when they beat Villa 2–0. Hillsborough, a favourite semi-final ground for the club (they were to win there in 1967 and 1981), was the venue for the penultimate round, and a relatively easy 3–1 defeat of Manchester United. It was a quiet campaign. Fans and Press were diverted by the drama of the European Cup and the intrigue of pursuing incomprehensible Ipswich in the League.

The final was a much better game than the previous year's, and brought together the best two teams of the period. Burnley, without an FA Cup win since 1914, were probably slightly favoured. Like Burnley when the clubs met in the previous season's semi-final, Spurs had just been knocked out of the European Cup (but by the odd goal only), and the general assessment was that Spurs were past their peak and coming downhill. The pundits were wrong. Jimmy Greaves, a member of the team for six months now, scored an early goal. Robson pulled one back but Smith scored an excellent second and Blanchflower made it safe at 3–1 with a late penalty, only the fourth ever given, and converted, in a Wembley final.

But, as in 1961, there was just a slight sense of anticlimax. Not because of the game, which was a good one this time, but because this wasn't really the Cup players and fans had

wanted to win. The 1962 FA Cup often appears as little more than a footnote to the Double because the real prize, the one that was never won, was the European Cup.

AND SO TO EUROPE

No British club has ever entered the European Cup with more confidence than did Spurs on 13 September 1961 against Gornik Zabrze of Poland. At no time were the supporters of Liverpool, Manchester United or Nottingham Forest ever as sure that this was their year as were the Spurs fans of 1961. This was not only because of the unquestioned excellence of their team, but also because the competition was, at last, wide open. Read Madrid had been beaten, by Barcelona, for the very first time the previous season. Benfica were the new champions – a good side to be sure, but surely not one to live with Spurs?

It was Tottenham's first trip to Europe, and their inexperience showed. Bill Nicholson told of his advance trip to Poland to have a look at the training facilities and hotels: 'They took me to this terrible place, and told me this is where we would be staying. I told them they would stay at the best hotel in England when they came to us, so I wanted Spurs to stay at the best hotel in Katowice (Gornik's home). They said this was the best hotel in Katowice. So we tried nearby Chorzow, but there were no decent hotels at all there, and Warsaw was hours away.' Spurs were one of the first British clubs to experience the total disorientation that trips behind the Iron Curtain can bring. Blanchflower told more of the story: 'There were prisoners in the streets digging up cobblestones, guarded by men with machine-guns. Going through the park leading to the Slaski Stadium we could see women, on their hands and knees, cutting the grass with what seemed to be large pairs of scissors. The stadium, massive, lit and tall like a distant castle, was the only welcoming thing about the whole place.'

Apparently no-one had told Gornik that this was Spurs' year for the European Cup. Within an hour the Poles were 4–0 up and Tottenham were as good as dead. 'I was bloody upset,' said Nicholson. 'We showed no determination or discipline.' But Jones and Dyson got two late goals back when the Poles let up and Spurs were in with a chance back home.

Perhaps the fondest memory of the great Spurs years of the early sixties is of the magical European nights. Twenty years later men from all over London still speak with damp eyes of those tremendous occasions — the first London had ever experienced and in an era, of course, when European Cup ties were not televised as a matter of course. It was not until these wonderful Wednesday nights that *Glory, Glory, Hallelujah*, the four-sided Tottenham wall of sound, really became established as the most individual and evocative of all English club tunes. As it happens, the club played *McNamara's Band* as the 'official' song at the time. 'The sound came from everywhere,' says Blanchflower, 'It was marvellous. When they sang, they all sang together fathers and sons, old and young. A local vicar used to complain that the whole thing was like a substitute for religion, and I suppose it was in a way. A century before those

OPPOSITE PAGE: The Double team. Standing left to right: Bill Brown, Peter Baker, Ron Henry, Danny Blanchflower, Maurice Norman, Dave Mackay; seated left to right: Cliff Jones, John White, Bobby Smith, Les Allen, Terry Dyson. This is the team that won the Cup in 1961. The following season's final saw Medwin and Greaves replace Dyson and Allen. At the end of the 1960–61 season Blanchflower paraphrased Nicholson's low-key approach saying: 'We've had what our manager might call a rather good year . . . '

fathers and sons would have sung in church together – but it wasn't in any way irreligious.' It was rather a sad reflection on all this that two decades later the Tottenham crowd at Wembley for the 1981 Charity Shield were singing 'Can you hear us on the box?' with barely a Glory, Glory to be heard.

To hear tell of it now, one could be excused for thinking that the great European nights went on for years. In actual fact there were really just two seasons and seven games (four in the European Cup and three in the Cup Winners Cup) and the legends that surround them really grew up from one particular game – the return leg against Gornik on 20 September 1961.

This was the night when the Poles found themselves outnumbered 60,000 to 11, when, as they admitted later, the noise from the crowd (who were much closer to the pitch than they were used to) battered them into submission. And yet they scored first through the appropriately named Pohl, and Tottenham, 5-2 down, were yet again up against the wall. The ferocity of their support drove them on – frightening the Spurs players almost as much as their opponents. Blanchflower got a penalty, and then the flood gates opened; three for Jones, two for Smith, one apiece for Dyson and White. At the end the crowd slumped back limp just from watching. Sitting or standing it had been an extraordinary experience and anyone who was there will talk about it with the same intensity today.

Nicholson's reactions to the first leg problems were characteristic. Never again would Spurs be caught out that way. Preparations for away legs became intense, every detail was covered, never again would Spurs players find themselves covered in flea bites from bug-ridden beds, or bemused by the social conditions of the countries they had to visit. As Blanchflower repeated: 'You had to go there once, to experience it. It's difficult to win anything first time round.'

The next two legs were much easier. In nearby Rotterdam Feyenoord went down 3–1 (Dyson and young Frank Saul, with two, getting the goals) though Spurs disappointed their fans by playing safe for a 1–1 draw at home. Dyson again got the goal. In the quarter-finals Tottenham lost 1–0 in Prague to Dukla, playing much more cautiously than in Poland, and won 4–1 at home; Smith and Mackay both scored twice.

THE DREAMS DIE
In the semi-finals Spurs drew Cup holders Benfica. The other tie was between Real Madrid and Standard Liege. The prize, then, was as great as could be imagined – almost certainly a final against Real in the Olympic Stadium in Amsterdam.

This is the fourth of those critical five games with which one can write the Spurs story of the early sixties. It is also the only one they lost and, in so doing, robbed the story of its expected denouement. When all is said and done Spurs did not, like Liverpool, Manchester United and Forest after them, reach the ultimate goal. They came as close as the woodwork on three occasions, and suffered almost certainly incorrect offside decisions twice, but that often tends to be the margin by which great stories are never told and by which great

prizes are never won.

Nicholson prepared himself well for the tie. He watched Benfica in Nuremberg and took the trouble to see Real beat Juventus in Madrid. 'Real were not the side they had been. I came back thinking that we would beat Real in the final if we could get past Benfica,' he remembers. Bela Guttmann, the Hungarian exile who was coaching that side of Portuguese and Mozambiquans and who had just acquired a young black player called Eusebio, agreed with Nicholson's assessment. He was proved correct – despite a Puskas hat-trick Benfica were to win one of the great finals, 5–3.

Nicholson's tactical planning was also more sophisticated now. For away games he would generally play Tony Marchi as an extra defender. The player left out from the Double side was Les Allen, meaning Spurs had one less attacker. Medwin, who could cover back better than Dyson, generally got the vote to play alongside Smith and Jones up front. Dyson, who had scored in each of the first four European Cup games, was never to play in that competition again. For the semi-final, however, Greaves was eligible, and he took the remaining place in Lisbon in a formation which was effectively a pioneering 4-3-3.

Tottenham always preferred to bring their opponents back to White Hart Lane for the second leg, knowing then what they needed to do. This allowed them to use the first match to get to know their opponents, the initial 45 minutes being played extremely cautiously. The whole scheme fell apart in Lisbon. Within 20 minutes Aguas and Augusto had put Benfica two ahead. Smith got one back, but Augusto headed his second to make it 3–1. The talk was not of the goals that were scored, but of the two that were disallowed – one by Greaves and one by Smith. Greaves, not a bad loser, says now: 'I reckon to this day the Swiss ref, Muellet, refereed us out of the final. I beat the full-back before I scored and was still given offside. Nine minutes from the end I crossed for Smithy to score and Muellet pointed to the centre-circle for 3–2. Then he saw the linesman flagging and disallowed the goal without even talking to him. But I was *ahead* of Smithy when I crossed.' Nicholson was brutal about the defeat: 'We gave away two vital goals because three players in a row made stupid mistakes.'

Spurs had already pulled back a two-goal deficit against Gornik and the crowd expected them to do so again. The ground was packed for the return leg on 5 April 1962, the noise terrifying. The average attendance for these four European Cup matches worked out at 60,430. Twenty years later David Miller of the *Daily Express* called the Benfica game '. . . the most electrifying ninety minutes of European football I have seen on an English ground,' and few who were there would ever question these sentiments. Bela Guttmann brought his extraordinary tactical and human know-how to succeed in one of his greatest tasks.

Guttmann himself deserves a diversion. He was a member of the Hungarian Olympic team in 1924, and went on to coach in America and the Netherlands before being imprisoned in a Second World War concentration camp. Having survived that, he took Ujpest to the Hungarian championship, coached Kispest

(who, renamed Honved, created something of a stir) and moved on to Italy. Here his AC Milan won the championship and were leading the Italian League when he was sacked for his pains, and he then took over the touring Hungarian side which had escaped the 1956 revolution. Having thus arrived in South America, he coached Sao Paulo to the 1958 Brazilian Championship, and almost certainly created the 4-2-4 system which Vicente Feola adopted for the Brazilian national squad in the World Cup in Sweden that year. Having thus learned to speak Portuguese, he ended up in Lisbon with Benfica.

Guttmann was a worthy opponent for Nicholson and Blanchflower. His gamesmanship was subtle but not extreme. He complained loudly about the physical excesses of Smith and Mackay, and the resulting Press comment seemed to intimidate Danish referee Aage Poulsen (certainly Guttmann thought it worked; he said afterwards: 'Yes, we got more than our share of free-kicks'). He knew the crowd would overawe his players, so he refused to let them warm up. They went straight out to the kick-off so that the atmosphere was not allowed to get to them before the game began.

Within 15 minutes a thoroughly underawed Aguas played a one-two with Simoes and slid the ball home across the rain-sodden six-yard box. Spurs were 4–1 down on aggregate. Then came a replay of one of the disallowed goals in Lisbon. White to Smith to Greaves, who, running between two defenders, scored from close in. The referee gave it, then consulted a linesman who had briefly raised his flag and the goal was disallowed. It was the third marginal decision that had gone against Spurs and it raised justifiable doubts afterwards.

After 38 minutes White finally made a goal for Smith, and then Blanchflower calmly converted another penalty four minutes after the break. Costa Pereira went the wrong way, Spurs were only one goal behind and there were 40 minutes left. History says they did not succeed, that their frantic attacks left them with no reward other than muddy woodwork – three shots that would have gone in another day came back off the posts and bar (though, to be fair, Aguas also hit the bar in the first half). Nicholson and Blanchflower both said afterwards that they thought Spurs were probably a goal better, over the two legs, but they wouldn't have changed their tactics if they had to do it again. 'I lost count of the near misses,' says Nicholson, 'but the one I'll always remember is when Dave (Mackay) hit the crossbar right at the end.' Blanchflower conceded Benfica's abilities: 'You have to remember that Pereira was magnificent against Bobby Smith and that Coluna was marvellous in midfield. I think Guttmann was sharper than we thought. All those years in Europe and South America, all that experience. He told me that Benfica would do it after the game in Lisbon.' Guttmann resigned the Benfica job after the final, eschewing a possible hat-trick, and moved to Penarol in Uruguay. He eventually went to live in Vienna where, so legend has it, he became a pool hustler. The destroyer of Spurs' most cherished dreams was to die there in August 1981.

Spurs themselves did not despair and the following season was to see them become the first British club to win a European trophy, the Cup Winners Cup. This was a new trophy, only three years old, and had yet to acquire its later status but Spurs were, nonetheless, impressive winners.

Nor was their League performance much behind when they finished runners-up to Everton for the Championship. They were six points in arrears of the Merseyside club with Burnley, always their close rivals, a further point behind. But the Lancashire side sampled some revenge for this and that Cup final defeat of the previous year by inflicting Tottenham's first FA Cup defeat for three years when they went to White Hart Lane for their third round meeting and came away clear 3–0 winners. No hat-trick here for Nicholson.

It was a season in which Spurs, with 111 goals, were the liveliest attackers in the Football League, Jimmy Greaves leading the way with a club record 37 goals which beat the jointly-held previous best of 36 by Ted Harper and Bobby Smith. This brighter if not quite as consistent Spurs side scored in each of their first 19 League games and it took new champions Everton to check them in the twentieth, when they earned a 0–0 draw from their visit.

THE CUP WINNERS CUP

In one glorious autumn seven game spree they averaged five goals a go, including nine rammed home against Nottingham Forest (Forest winger Trevor Hockey said afterwards: 'We scored first and last and they got nine lucky ones in between'), six against Manchester United, five against Leyton Orient away and the sharing of a 4-4 draw with Arsenal. They later hit West Ham for six, Liverpool for seven and Ipswich Town for five and Jimmy Greaves scored four goals against both Forest and Liverpool. The two Liverpool games were particularly entertaining. Having lost 5-2 at Anfield on Good Friday, Spurs won 7-2 at home on Easter Monday. But their failure to stay the course strongly, the 62 goals conceded, and the reallocation of matches following the worst hold-up which League football has ever experienced after the appalling 1962–63 winter, put paid to another title chance. From their last ten matches they took only eight points, winning three, drawing two and losing five of the games. It was the second consecutive season in which a terrible finish probably cost them the title.

The season was, in retrospect, one of hanging on for the final prize. The Cup Winners Cup final against Atletico Madrid in Rotterdam was the fifth and last of the era's critical games, partially because it was literally the last gasp of the Double side and the glory that had gone with their achievements.

The route to Rotterdam had not been a long or exhausting one, consisting of only three preliminary rounds for Spurs. Glasgow Rangers were poor opposition, going down 3-2 at home and 5-2 in London. Two of their defenders did, however, make their mark. A violent sandwich on Blanchflower damaged his knee and the cartilage came out. At his age (37) it took time to repair and he was to miss 22 games in all. John White's growing importance to the team is indicated by how well they played in Blanchflower's absence. The next round saw more Iron Curtain travels

OPPOSITE TOP: On 30 November 1961 Bill Nicholson made perhaps his best ever signing, bringing Jimmy Greaves back from Milan for £99,999. The fee was set at that figure so that Greaves would not have to carry the tag of being the first player to have cost an English club £100,000. Here the new boy listens with team-mates Blanchflower, Henry, Hopkins, Dyson, Hollowbread and Eddie Clayton to Nicholson's instructions at the Cheshunt training ground. Greaves' first senior game for the club was on 16 December 1961, against Blackpool. He got a hat-trick and maintained a record of scoring in every debut game of his career.
OPPOSITE BOTTOM: Greaves and ball in a familiar position - the back of the net. The date is Saturday 24 November 1962 and Greaves has just put Spurs 1-0 ahead at Burnley, despite the efforts of defenders Brian Miller, Alex Elder and John Angus (number 2). The day was not to end happily for Spurs, however, Connelly and Pointer scoring in the second half to give Burnley victory. Seven weeks later the Lancastrians were to inflict Spurs' first FA Cup defeat for three years – 3-0 at the Lane.

with a match against Slovan Bratislava. By now Spurs were almost seasoned travellers in Eastern Europe, but Slovan were to pull them apart. Bill Brown, his nose all plastered up after one particularly brave dive at a forward's feet, kept them in the game. Spurs were lucky to keep the score down to 2–0. Blanchflower, from the previous year's experience with Gornik and Dukla, knew that Western Europe disorientated Iron Curtain sides even more than the reverse trip upset Spurs. 'We were never happy over there,' he says, 'but they couldn't believe their eyes when they came to London. We rarely had any trouble at home.' Blanchflower was right, Spurs scoring six without reply in the second leg.

The semi-final against OFK Belgrade was most notable for Jimmy Greaves being sent off – the first man in a Tottenham shirt to be dismissed since 27 October 1928. Greaves played at outside-right, John Smith moved to inside-forward and Maurice Norman turned out with an injured foot. Missing were Cliff Jones and Blanchflower when Tottenham arrived for the first leg in the Red Army Stadium, Belgrade. Greaves was sent off in the 55th minute for retaliation, and one man who could clearly remember the last time it happened, 35 years before, was Spurs trainer Cecil Poynton, for he was the unfortunate it had happened to. Greaves admitted later that he had taken a swing at Krivokuca, the home defender who had been trying to kick lumps out of him. Earlier there had been a free-for-all with the Hungarian referee roughly manhandled when trying to sort things out. The cause of it all was the senseless figure of wing-half Maric lying flat out in the home penalty area after a free-kick had been awarded against him for a horrific tackle on Smith. No-one in London had much doubt as to who had laid him out. Sixty thousand fans still gave ten-man Spurs a stirring

farewell as they left 2–1 winners through White and Dyson and thanks to heroic defence inspired by play-everywhere Mackay. Blanchflower returned for the second leg to make the first goal for Mackay . . . Belgrade pulled that back; then Jones and a Smith header meant the first one-legged European final for any English club on a 5–2 aggregate.

It was harsh on Nicholson that Dave Mackay, of all people, should miss the final against the holders, Atletico Madrid, in the Feyenoord Stadium in Rotterdam, a stomach injury keeping him on the touchlines. It was certainly not his week . . . he also came second to Stanley Matthews as 'Footballer of the Year'. Marchi made an admirable deputy for the Scot.

It was the prospect of Mackay's absence which troubled Spurs most as they waited for the final on 15 May 1963. 'With Dave in the team we feel we can beat anyone,' said Cliff Jones before the match. 'He makes things happen. He makes us go. Without him, the odds change.' The odds had changed and Mackay did not play, added to which Spurs lost their last domestic game 0–1 to already relegated Manchester City. Blanchflower was still not fit but, officially now assistant to the manager (not assistant manager), he preferred Bill Nicholson to make the critical decision. 'It's a simple choice', he said, 'either me on one leg or John Smith (a skilful reserve bought from West Ham) on two.' Nicholson ordered pain-killing injections for Blanchflower's knee and had him play. He was 37 and this, to all intents and purposes, was his last major match.

The Atletico match has gone down in folklore as the game Blanchflower won without kicking a ball. Nicholson, says David Miller, gave an almost funereal team-talk. 'Nick's confidence seemed to have gone,' said Jimmy Greaves afterwards, 'because we'd lost Dave Mackay and he was our best player. He just went through the Spaniards, player by player, pointing out their strengths. But he just made us worry whether they *were* as good as he had painted them.' Blanchflower took over from Nicholson and told them to listen to what *he* had to say. Greaves recalls the captain's own brand of team-talk: 'He said that if their centre-half was big and ugly then ours, Maurice Norman, was even bigger and uglier. That if they had a fast winger called Jones

ABOVE: The moment of truth for the great Spurs' side of the early 1960s came on Thursday 5 April 1962, when Benfica came to White Hart Lane to defend a 3-1 lead gained in the first leg of the European Cup semi-final. Twenty years later David Miller of the Daily Express was to call the game '. . . the most electrifying ninety minutes of European football I have seen on an English ground.' Benfica went 4–1 up on aggregate early in the game, Smith scored after 38 minutes and then Blanchflower made it 4–3 with this penalty, sending Costa Pereira the wrong way.

ABOVE LEFT: Maurice Norman cannot prevent Aguas getting in a flying right-footed shot in the second leg, but the ball hit the bar. Aguas scored in both games and got another in the final against Real Madrid.

FAR LEFT: Tottenham attacked throughout the second half, hitting the woodwork three times. 'I lost count of the near misses,' said Nicholson afterwards, 'but the one I'll always remember is when Dave hit the crossbar right near the end.' A few moments later the referee blew for time and, while keeper Pereira crosses himself, a sporting Dave Mackay turns back to congratulate the Benfica defenders. Near the edge of the area Bobby Smith congratulates the Benfica captain Coluna who, Blanchflower said afterwards, '. . . was marvellous.'

OPPOSITE TOP: The goal that made the Double safe. In the 77th minute of the 1961 FA Cup final Bobby Smith (furthest left in picture) crossed for Terry Dyson to head past a despairing Gordon Banks.

OPPOSITE CENTRE: Ten minutes earlier Bobby Smith (just rising from ground) had feinted one way, turned the other and put Spurs 1–0 ahead against a Leicester City side reduced to ten men after an injury to Len Chalmers. Danny Blanchflower said that the final was probably Spurs' worst performance of the whole season.

CENTRE: The two scorers after the Cup win of 1961; Terry Dyson (left) and Bobby Smith, plus the photographer catching himself in the mirror and, also reflected in the mirror, John White bending over the table.

OPPOSITE BOTTOM: A year later and Bobby Smith scores a similar goal against Burnley after a John White run down the left. Smith's goal made the score 2–1.

THIS PAGE TOP: Jimmy Greaves (far left) scores the first goal of the 1962 final after just three minutes. This was the first medal Greaves had won – two more coming in the Cup Winners Cup and the FA Cup final of 1967.

THIS PAGE CENTRE: Jimmy Robertson (right) raises his arm in triumph as the ball hits the back of Peter Bonetti's net and opens the scoring in the 1967 final against Chelsea. In the 40th minute Alan Mullery's shot had rebounded off Chelsea defender Allan Harris and left Robertson with a clear opening from the edge of the penalty area.

THIS PAGE BOTTOM: After 67 minutes of the 1967 final Frank Saul put the result beyond reasonable doubt with a hooked shot inside Bonetti's near post. Saul, who was standing with his back to goal, is not in the picture, but looking on are John Boyle, Jimmy Robertson, Allan Harris, Jimmy Greaves and Marvin Hinton as Spurs' last Cup final goal of the decade buries itself in the net.

OPPOSITE TOP: Bill Brown in pensive mood. Signed from Dundee in June 1959, Brown was already a Scottish international and went on to win 28 caps in all, his last against Italy in November 1965.

OPPOSITE BOTTOM: The fluke goal which restored Tottenham's composure midway through the second half of the European Cup Winners Cup final against Atletico Madrid in Rotterdam on 15 May 1963. Though they were leading 2–1, Spurs were struggling against the Spaniards when Terry Dyson slung over a high cross from the left. It seemed to swerve late and the Atletico keeper, Madinabeytia, lost its flight and could do nothing but flap at the ball as it dropped over his head into the net. Afterwards Dyson claimed he had seen the keeper move out a fraction and decided to shoot; that might even have been true judging by his later goal, a 30-yard run and 25-yard shot which made the score 5–1 and completed a game forever remembered as Terry Dyson's night. 'Terry would do anything for the team and, in particular, for Dave Mackay,' said Nicholson. 'That's why we had such a good left side for three years – they were wonderful together.'

(which Atletico did – a strange coincidence), then ours was so fast he could catch pigeons.'

That pigeon-catching Cliff Jones played on the right-wing, Terry Dyson on the left, and it was to be Dyson's night. Spurs' first goal came in the 16th minute, a cross from Jones to the impeccable Greaves and into the net. Sixteen minutes later Dyson made it 2–0, but Ron Henry had to give away a penalty at the start of the second half and Collar made it 2–1. Spurs were on the ropes for perhaps twenty minutes, but were saved by a bolt from a highly unlikely source. Dyson, who had been having a good, teasing match against full-back Rivilla beat his man again and slung over a high, teasing cross. It went too close to the keeper, Madinabeytia, but somehow the goalie lost it in flight and it squeezed over his head at the near-post. Dyson claimed this fluke among flukes was the result of his quick thinking when he saw the keeper move out two yards, but it certainly inspired the winger to believe anything was possible. Ten minutes from the end he sent over the cross from which Greaves made it four and then, in the 87th minute, Dyson made the night his by running 30 yards with the ball, dummying right and left and finishing with a 25-yard screamer. He had the immense satisfaction of playing the game of his career at the perfect time, a privilege few footballers ever enjoy. As the 5–1 victors walked back to the dressing-room Bobby Smith said to Terry Dyson: 'You'd better retire now, you'll never play better.'

THE OLD GUARD GOES

Dyson may not have decided to retire, but the next three years was not much more than the gradual dissolution of Nicholson's first great side.

Little Harmer had departed the Tottenham scene just before Spurs hit their jackpot years. At 32 he had to abdicate in favour of the younger White after some 15 years at White Hart Lane, the longest-serving active member of a squad which had seen many changes under the demanding Nicholson. Many clubs were still ready to make room for him in their first teams when Spurs put a £6,000 transfer fee on his head, including his old team-mate Alf Ramsey at Ipswich. Harmer chose Watford, where he had worked in a print shop, but the move was not a success for the Third Division was not equipped to follow the advanced promptings of the wee fellow. His still bright talents were not being fully utilised until manager Tommy Docherty stepped in. He saw Harmer as the mastermind to lead his young Chelsea fledglings upwards and into the First Division. It proved to be a master stroke. Besides coaching and spreading his soccer lore around the Stamford Bridge dressing-rooms and training areas, he played in just five of that season's League matches, but was on the winning side every time to make a joke of the £3,000 fee he had cost Chelsea. And the one goal he scored came in the closing game of the season . . . to beat Sunderland, his club's nearest rivals for promotion, at Roker Park. He converted a centre into a goal with what might euphemistically be called his private parts. With that goal Chelsea went into the First Division, while Sunderland had to wait one more season.

There was satisfaction for Tiny Tom the fol-

lowing season when he went back to the Lane with Chelsea and had a leading part in both the Chelsea goals which brought a 2–1 away success over his old club. It's an echo of a favourite story of Eddie Baily about Harmer, his old colleague of the Arthur Rowe days and much later. According to Eddie: 'I thought I had been put out to grass when I was transferred from Tottenham to Port Vale. We played Nottingham Forest, then around the top of the Second Division, and we beat them 3–1. I must have impressed Forest's manager Billy Walker. I was told he wanted me to join him.

'Freddie Steele, the Port Vale manager, had me in his office and asked if I was willing to go. He received more than the £6,000 he paid for me . . . and a fair bit besides. We won promotion at Forest, I got a Second Division medal and so in no time I was back at the Spurs, in the First Division. We went to White Hart Lane leading the division in October 1957 and Tommy Harmer was in the Spurs team. I was then 36 and was captain for the day against many old pals I had left behind . . . I remember when the score was at 2–2 Tommy coming near to me and calling out, "I don't think much of your team, Eddie." But as we went off at the end I caught him up to tell him, "I think even less of yours, Tom" – we had won 4–3 and stayed top!'

In April 1964 the club lost a much-loved figure, its president, Fred Bearman, at the great age of 91. He had begun as a Spurs director 54 long years before, in 1910, was made chairman in 1943 and president in 1961 after retiring from the board. He had been a real tower of strength during his long association, a caring chairman. Three months later, just as the players were due to report back for pre-season training in July, came the tragic news of John White's death while sheltering from a storm during a round of golf at Crews Hill, Middlesex. It was a sickening blow to all who knew him. The pleasant, friendly, freckle-faced young Scotsman left a wife and young family and a great host of friends and admirers. In his near five years since joining from Falkirk he lit many of the fuses which set off the power drive of this great club side.

In a season in which he was to be tested by taking almost every bad knock that could be handed out, Bill Nicholson broke down and wept over the death of the slight 26-year-old young man of so many talents. He had been asked by the police to identify the body and had kept his feelings under his usual iron control until talking to his players after they had reported back.

He had already lost his right-hand man, Danny Blanchflower, who, at 37 and still feeling the recurring effects of that injury against Glasgow Rangers en route to lifting the Cup Winners Cup, had called it a day to switch sideways to reporting and talking football both in print and on television.

But the sad, bad news did not end there. Terry Medwin, on the summer tour of South Africa in 1963, had been injured in the very first match. That more or less ended the tour for him. But, worse for Nicholson's plans, he lost the services of the adaptable Welshman for the whole of 1963–64 season. Came December 1963 and their defence of the Cup Winners Cup. It did not last long, not even beyond the first challenge, despite the two-goal lead gained on the first leg of a domestic dust-up with Manchester United. A week later at Old Trafford the Nicholson furrowed brow took on another line of worry as United wiped out their two-goal deficit and finished 4–1 victors (4–3 on aggregate) to end any further Spurs interest in Europe. But they suffered a far deeper cut after only twenty minutes play when they lost Dave Mackay with a broken leg and inevitably, even though it was ironman Mackay, for the rest of the season. Within a year Nicholson had lost his whole midfield of White, Blanchflower and Mackay, that magical trio which had surely been the key to the Double. A month after Mackay's injury, Chelsea held a patched up Spurs 1–1 at White Hart Lane in the FA Cup, then put them out 2–0 in the Stamford Bridge replay.

Determined to get back in the senior line-up, Mackay put everything into his efforts to win the thumbs up for a return. He had been out of action for nine months when he turned out against Shrewsbury Town reserves . . . and that same left leg was broken again. And who else but the indestructible Mackay, with painful sweat pouring down his face, could beg his bearers, 'Don't let Bill Nicholson know, not yet,' thinking of the boss's preoccupation with first team troubles.

Nicholson had a special regard for Mackay, his first signing and the man he called the 'heart' of his teams. The loss of both Blanchflower and Mackay at the same time was like taking the works out of a watch; two players, two men who, in their own individual way, had meant so much and given so much to Tottenham and Bill Nick. He was interesting when he spoke about players like these: 'The character of a player meant as much to me as his skill,' he said. 'After all, he was going to represent my club and me. Most of my fellows were truly genuine. They were good to have around and ready to serve you fully. When the going became tough or rough you could still bank on them. That's when they proved you, and themselves, right or wrong. I pulled out of several deals for top players because I saw that I could not have them around this club. I like to think that I was consistent as a player, and I like consistency in players. You would have a job to go through my lot and say, "He was an inconsistent player."

'Danny Blanchflower was a fine captain. He was respected and could carry out any orders to the team. He was a class player and we always worked together very well. I admired him and still do, as a player and as a man. Dave Mackay was the complete professional, the heart-beat of a team with his fierce will to win in every game of every kind.'

BAILY RETURNS

Towards the mid-sixties Eddie Baily got the call from his old club. 'Bill Nick asked me to join him as coach and assistant manager. I got back just when the great Double side was beginning to break up. I've been so lucky to have been with clubs whose teams had been brought up in the best footballing traditions . . . Spurs, Nottingham Forest and West Ham. And I happened to be coach when manager Johnny Carey took Leyton Orient to their only season in the First Division back in 1962–63.

We went up with Liverpool and came down with Manchester City!'

He had a long ten-year partnership with Nicholson, his old playing colleague of the push-and-run days, before their break-up in September 1974. Baily was on the outside of the game looking in for two years during which time he worked as a games instructor, at a school in Enfield, teaching both football and cricket. He had been scouting for Chelsea along with the schools job, longing to get back, when Ron Greenwood rang to ask him if he would become West Ham's chief representative as that doyen of soccer scouts, Wally St Pier, was about to retire. When Greenwood took over the job of England manager, Baily was one of his first appointments as an observer, weighing up England's rivals in advance.

Later he would tell you: 'The game hasn't changed much, only people have. It's the same ball, same markings, the game's the same. One-touch football is what they are teaching and coaching now, we called it push-and-run so maybe we were a bit ahead of our time. We had forwards, now there are strikers, hit-men, target players; there are numbered formations, it's all done by numbers.' He was being more reflective than critical when he said it. 'Great players are players who haven't got the ball, the hardest thing in the game. But when they've got it, it is simply doing the right thing, picking the right thing to do, not the hard thing. Lesser players shun doing the simple thing.'

The Spurs break-up continued. Peter Baker went off to play in South Africa, Tony Marchi became player-manager of Cambridge City, unlucky Terry Medwin had to call it a day after that injury in South Africa, Terry Dyson joined Fulham, Les Allen went to QPR, where son Clive was to make a name for himself fifteen years later. 1965–66 was really the end of the old days. Bill Brown handed over to Pat Jennings, Ron Henry played just once, his place filled by the 'nice one, Cyril' Knowles, and the old-timer helped coach the reserves and the youngsters. A badly broken leg finished Maurice Norman's career, Cliff Jones found he could no longer catch pigeons and in 1968 contented himself with whatever feathered varieties they have at Fulham. Only Jones and Dave Mackay were left when the decade's final trophy was carried round Wembley, the FA Cup of 1967.

Mackay broke the final link in 1968, a good time to go: 'I could do nothing more for them, nor they for me. If I had stayed I would have got a share of the blame. It meant a new challenge.' He joined the star of the new generation, Brian Clough, at Derby. Far from being finished, he helped Clough bring Derby back to the First Division, and shared a long-deserved 'Footballer of the Year' award with Tony Book in 1969. On 20 September 1969, the Baseball Ground saw its largest ever crowd (41,826) and they saw Derby annihilate Tottenham 5–0. It was a magnificent moment for Mackay, who stayed around the East Midlands during that area's great decade, first to manage Nottingham Forest and then supersede Clough at Derby, where his side won the 1975 Championship, before Mackay drifted away from the limelight.

But all was not gloom and depression in the mid-1960s. Spurs did not cease to exist as a footballing force, and they maintained a respectable League position throughout these years of turbulent change – second in 1962–63, fourth in 1963–64, sixth in 1964–65 and eighth in 1965–66. The addition of Jimmy Greaves was, of course, the first, the most exciting and most significant change to the Double-winning side.

The addition of the goal-power of Jimmy Greaves towards the end of 1961 was simply a case of the alert Nicholson taking his chances as swiftly as the little striker himself took them on the pitch. 'He came in November, but his registration was held up for a time by the Football League,' said Nicholson. 'What a great player he proved for us and he seemed so happy here after the misery of his stay with AC Milan and his fall-outs with trainer-coach Rocco.

'I went for Jimmy because of something I had stored away in my mind, something he had said when I met him going to a dinner at the Cafe Royal. We got talking and it came up about his proposed transfer from Chelsea to a continental club. He told me that night that he would have loved to have played in our Double team. I stored that away. It wasn't too long after he went to Italy that we began to hear stories of how difficult he was finding trying to settle in Italy. How his game had suffered and that he was homesick. Then I heard he might be available for transfer and that's when I began to get things moving. He had such talent, such wonderful anticipation that he was on the right spot at the right time – the real art of the great striker. His timing was perfect and he was deadly. Once he lined up a goal in his sights the biggest certainty was that he would get it, he was such a deadly finisher.'

Greaves proved all this with his goal-a-game beginning with Tottenham and 20,000 turned out to see him score for the reserves at Plymouth. He hit a hat-trick in his first League match, a 5–2 home win over Blackpool, then went on to score 30 goals in the 31 games, League and Cup, he played in the second half of the 1961–62 season. His third goal against Blackpool was recently recalled by one national newspaper as being one of the greatest ever scored in post-war football, an overhead bicycle kick which made the £99,999 Nicholson had paid appear absurdly cheap. Greaves' goalscoring for Spurs in the next eight seasons was astonishing. His League tallies alone were 21 (in 22 games), 37, 35, 29, 15 (in 29 games), 23, 23 and 27. He led the First Division scorers an unprecedented six times between 1958 and 1969 and is the only man to have headed that list in three consecutive years.

There has not been another goalscorer like him in the post-war game, despite the effort and money the major clubs have put into trying to find a successor. Despite the goals, his relationship with Bill Nicholson was not always perfect. There is the famous story of a game during one of Tottenham's leaner spells. The manager was trying to get Greaves to come back and help the midfield more often, or to run into space more effectively. On one particularly lazy day Greaves' finishing was at its sharpest. He would score a goal, only to disappear for twenty minutes, and then pop up with another. After the game Nicholson

OPPOSITE TOP: Part of a famous photographic sequence showing Leeds' Billy Bremner fouling his Scottish team-mate Dave Mackay and the Tottenham skipper's less than friendly reaction. Referee Norman Burtenshaw moves in to separate the two as soon as possible while Terry Venables, recently signed from Chelsea, looks on.
OPPOSITE BOTTOM: Mackay had the last laugh; he and Mike England congratulate Alan Mullery after Spurs' first goal. Gilzean and Greaves went on to add others and the game, played on 20 August 1966, ended 3–1. It was to be a good season for Spurs; they finished third in the League, a place above Leeds, and Mackay lifted the FA Cup after the club's third Wembley success of the decade. Nicholson always regarded Mackay as the heart of the Double side. 'He was such a strong, skilled left-sided midfield player and one who could score goals. That is probably the rarest kind of player in the game today, because of the natural left-sidedness. We had one particular training routine where players volleyed against a wall from about 30 to 40 feet and had to keep the ball in the air all the time. If you could do it six times on the trot without it hitting the ground you were good; I remember Dave doing it 36 times.'

was heard to comment: 'All he did this afternoon was score those four goals . . . ' Spurs now had three ex-Chelsea forwards – Allen, Smith and Greaves – and it was Allen who had to make way in the established first choice team.

During the mid-sixties there were other major additions. In 1966 Terry Venables also came from Chelsea, where Tommy Docherty had seemingly dismissed his key playmaker in a fit of disappointment after Chelsea had lost their second consecutive FA Cup semi-final. Venables, the only footballer ever to be capped at every international level for England (Schoolboy, Youth, Amateur, Under-23, Full), was essential to fill the creative hole in midfield, but he found the going difficult. At Chelsea he was in charge of a team of younger players who had been brought up on a faster, longer-ball game. The shorter, subtler Spurs style was not suited to Venables spraying long passes from the centre-circle and, though he won an FA Cup winners' medal against his old club, he never really fitted in as Nicholson had hoped. He and Mullery, signed from Fulham in 1964 for £72,500, suffered most at the hands of the Tottenham crowd and both had some cynical things to say about their experiences. It was their misfortune, of course, to have to try and step into the shoes of Blanchflower, White and, in Mullery's case later, those of the great Mackay. It is no disrespect to them both to suggest that this was simply not possible, that Spurs have never had, nor will probably ever have again, a centre-line quite like that one. No players in the world could have filled that gaping hole and it was unfortunate that the crowd needed the enchantment of distance, via a few years, to appreciate the fact. 'It was bloody awful at the time,' says Mullery now. 'It took me at least two years to win the crowd over and get accepted and I'd have gone anywhere else for a time. I won them over in the end, but it was hard going.' Mullery recalls that he had gone to Tottenham because of Nicholson, and that the manager had predicted well ahead that Spurs would win the Cup again by 1967, which is one reason he had moved from Fulham.

The other major signings were Mike England, £95,000 from Blackburn Rovers to fill Maurice Norman's place, and the man with the three-penny bit shaped head, Alan Gilzean. Gilzean had starred in Dundee's surprise run to the semi-finals of the European Cup in 1963 when they beat FC Koln 8–1, Sporting Lisbon 4–1, and Anderlecht 4–1 away but went out to AC Milan at the penultimate stage. Gilzean had scored hat-tricks against Koln and Sporting, two against Anderlecht and the only goal of the home leg against Milan. His ability to head the ball in any direction was priceless, though Spurs did not reap maximum dividends from it until he was playing slightly behind Chivers in the early 1970s, a time when Gilzean's back header from a long throw into the penalty area might almost have been copyrighted. Like Blanchflower, Gilzean became an old war-horse, continuing until he was 36 in 1974.

There was a negative side to the transfer

market, both financially and domestically. Nicholson never found another really successful winger – going through the likes of Robertson, Saul, Morgan, Coates, Possee, Weller and Pearce. By the late 1960s, after Ramsey's 'penguin side' ('the wingless wonders' as parts of the Press had called them) of 1966 had sown its tactical seed, no major club was regularly playing more than one winger, and the one that remained was often having to double as a marking-back wide midfield man as well. Roger Morgan, one of celebrated identical twins from QPR, was the North London crowd's biggest disappointment. At £110,000 the fans thought they should have got Rodney Marsh (the joke on the terraces was that Rangers had wrapped Morgan in a paper bag and told Spurs they were getting Marsh, only they couldn't open the bag until they got home).

Domestically the problem was that youngsters were put off by Spurs image as the big-money club. Like Liverpool in the 1970s, it seemed that Spurs would always buy to fill the gaps – so what chance did youngsters have of coming through from the ranks? Nicholson denies it, but the fact is that only two of the 1967 Cup winning team (Jennings, Kinnear, Knowles, Mullery, England, Mackay, Robertson, Greaves, Gilzean, Venables and Saul) had come up through the juniors. Those two 'outsiders' were Kinnear and Saul, and the other nine had cost over half a million pounds. In present day terms that does not sound a lot but at the time no other club in the country could come near it. One of Spurs' problems

was their sheer success – buying a player a year used up the profits and brought the corporation tax bill down. Under the somewhat absurd Inland Revenue regulations, buying players was tax deductible whereas ground improvements were not, so while profits were good there was actually a need to buy expensive players.

1967 – ANOTHER FA CUP

The 1967 Cup win was a surprise, and all the more welcome for that. It is unusual for a club which has had such spectacular success to rebuild a team and come back for a major prize so quickly. Wolves did it in the 1950s, but the Spurs fans of 1967 appreciated the difficulty of the feat and the crowds that greeted the team and the trophy were even bigger than they had been in 1961 and 1962.

The third round draw was away at Millwall – actually a much harder prospect than it sounds. At the time the numbers came out of the hat Millwall had gone 59 League games at The Den without defeat, a record run that had lasted thirty-two months as they rose from the Fourth to the Second Division. As chance would have it, Millwall lost that record to Plymouth Argyle the Saturday before the third round, but Spurs had to weather a hard, goalless draw nonetheless. The replay was almost as tight, Gilzean getting the only goal.

The fourth, fifth and sixth rounds also threw up Second Division opponents. Gilzean got two and Greaves one to remove Portsmouth 3-1 and Bristol City then went down 2-0, both

OPPOSITE PAGE:
Saturday 29 April 1967 and Spurs are back in the FA Cup final. A 2–1 defeat of Nottingham Forest at Tottenham's favourite semi-final ground Hillsborough (where they won in 1921 and 1981) was inspired by a Jimmy Greaves snap shot in the first half and cemented by another from Frank Saul with 15 minutes left. Here Saul challenges full-back Peter Hindley while keeper Grummitt gathers the ball. Looking on are Alan Gilzean and Bobby McKinlay. It was the critical game on the road to Wembley for Spurs, Forest being favourites and finishing one place above them in the League.
BELOW: Jimmy Greaves after the game, talking with Terry Venables (left). Greaves was a constant nightmare to Forest, scoring 29 first-class goals against them in his career including four on no fewer than three separate occasions.

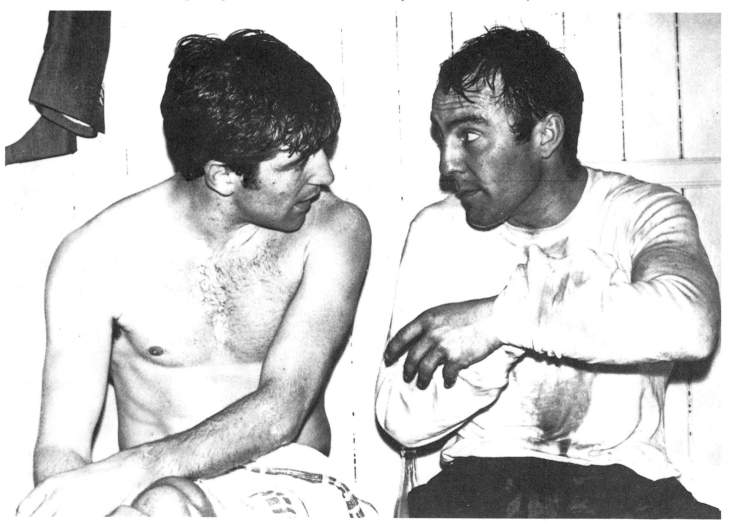

111

Jimmy Greaves somehow contrives to scoop a shot over the bar at Craven Cottage during a First Division game on Saturday 4 September 1965. Spurs won the game 2-0 with goals from Eddie Clayton and Dave Mackay. Nicholson, speaking about Greaves, said: 'Occasionally players would ask me to give Jimmy a kick in the pants to get him working a bit harder. Fair enough, but I would always tell them to start complaining when he stopped scoring goals. Because that's the hardest thing in the game. I used to ask them whether, if Jimmy stopped scoring and we dropped him, would they like to go up front and get 25 goals a season for us? I didn't get many takers . . .'

games being at White Hart Lane. Birmingham at St Andrew's in the quarter-finals was much tougher and Spurs were lucky to escape with a goalless draw. Despite Jimmy Robertson's speed on the right Greaves and Gilzean could do little that matched the winger's penetration, and all the good chances fell to Birmingham. The closest was when Jennings dropped a Fenton centre on the line and everyone joined in with their opinion as to whether it was over or not.

To their evident relief Spurs escaped with the draw and then crushed the Midlanders 6–0 on a White Hart Lane paddy field the following week. Venables scored straight from the off, unusually adding his name to the sheet, but soon added a second and Gilzean finally made use of one of Robertson's constant stream of crosses for a third before half-time. Birmingham got no better after the break and virtually gave up trying to control Greaves, who got two, with Frank Saul adding the sixth.

The semi-final at Hillsborough was the season's critical game. Nottingham Forest, second in the League and chasing Manchester United hard, were favourites, but they had lost

Joe Baker in their classic quarter-final defeat of Everton and this was to disrupt their whole pattern of play. Despite having three other current or future England internationals up front (Hinton, Wignall and Storey-Moore), they depended on Baker's speed on the turn to win games no less than Spurs needed Greaves.

This game was, indeed, to produce one of Greaves' most memorable goals, a killing psychological blow as much as a single score because of his strange affinity for Forest. During his career Greaves scored far more goals (29) against Forest than any other club – including four on three occasions. Clearly he terrified the Nottingham club and his thirtieth-minute goal demoralised them so much that they lost a game they really should have won. As a goal it was probably not as classic a moment as three others that will always live in the memory – his bicycle kick against Blackpool in his first game for the club, his turn and dribble past four Manchester United defenders at White Hart Lane on 16 October 1965, and his run and shot past three Forest defenders when he never touched the ball but beat them simply by letting it run, dipping his shoulders and dummying left and right. But the semi-final goal was a great goal because of its context, because it got Spurs to a Cup final, because it was one of those goals that only Greaves seemed to be able to score, and because it was proof, if it was needed, that a single player can occasionally win for a team trophies that they would not otherwise have won. In recent years only Jimmy Greaves and George Best fall unquestionably into this category.

Greaves' goal came out of the blue at a time when Forest were clearly on top. A long clearance from Mike England was headed side-ways by Gilzean. As the ball bounced at Greaves' feet, he suddenly twisted and hit it left-footed on the half-volley from about 25 yards. The ball shot along the ground, snicked Grummitt's right-hand post and settled in the far corner of the net. The Forest defence never moved. With a quarter of an hour left Frank Saul robbed Terry Hennessey in the defender's half, set off for goal and whacked a magnificent shot into the net. Forest attacked frantically but could only reply once, from Hennessey himself, and Spurs were through. It was probably the best of all their semi-finals.

They found themselves facing Chelsea in the final; the Pensioners had, at the third consecutive attempt, managed to win a semi-final at last by beating Leeds 1–0. It was the first all-London professional final, which was excellent for the two competing sides but which somehow robbed the game of its national stage – the rest of the country was clearly indifferent to the whole thing. Deryk Brown wrote of the game: 'It was supposed to have been drab, which it wasn't, and supposed to have lacked atmosphere, which it did. This was Tottenham's fault only in that they were too good.'

Spurs did not break their routine at all. They trained as usual and spent just one night away. For the club it was not an overwhelming moment, being their fourth cup final in six years. For Chelsea's youngsters, however, it was rather too much; the Spurs players watched their opponents on television on the morning of the match and were delighted to observe nerve ends showing.

That Tottenham judgement on the Chelsea side was proved accurate; the younger team never settled, nor once looked like winning the game. Only Ron Harris, who kept Greaves out of things, enhanced his reputation. After 40 minutes Jimmy Robertson scored a well deserved goal. Mullery ran at the defence, his shot hit Allan Harris and Robertson buried the rebound from the edge of the area. After 67 minutes Frank Saul, with his back to goal, somehow hooked a shot into the corner of Peter Bonetti's net after a Dave Mackay throw. It was all over, Bobby Tambling's 85th minute header (Jennings effectively punched the ball at his head) barely even being a consolation for Chelsea. It was now Dave Mackay's turn to collect the silverware and Cliff Jones became the first substitute ever to collect a Cup final winners medal. It was more easily earned than his other mementos – he never left the bench.

The most significant benefit was, of course, that Spurs were back in the Cup Winners Cup. This time things did not end so happily. Their first rivals were the Yugoslav side Hajduk Split and they returned from the first leg with a 2–0 lead. It all seemed so easy. Then in the return the Spurs fans rejoiced as their team sailed on with a three-goal lead, then got another in the dying minutes. But not before the tough Yugoslavs had bounced back to grab three goals for themselves in a late rally which caused many palpitations.

Alan Mullery was sent off in a riotous second round away clash with the French club Olympique Lyonnais which saw Spurs defeated 1–0. The home side also lost their international centre-forward, Andre Guy, sent off in the scuffle with Mullery. A series of battles broke out round the terraces and spectators piled onto the pitch. The second leg resulted in a 4–3 success for Spurs but they went out on the away goals counting double rule. After 1962 and 1963 it was a terrible anticlimax.

The crowd, by now having got used to the fact that they were not going to be watching Blanchflower and White every week, were disappointed rather than depressed. Bill Nicholson remained the biggest critic having reached the summit it was hard for him to remain camped on the slopes.

A TOTTENHAM LEGEND

A hard man but a fair man was Alan Mullery's summary of Nicholson the manager at this time. There was little artistry but a lot of honesty in his game. But he always wanted to see his teams doing it in style. Ask him, looking at it as a player and a manager, did he enjoy football and he says: 'Enjoy . . . that is not a word I would think of using. You cannot do that, playing or watching with a direct interest, until after a match. As a player there is the preparation, the feeling of being keyed up, the bending of all your thoughts to the game. You carry these through any game. Same with a manager, there is too much else on when things are happening to say you enjoy it. Only if your side is playing exceptionally well and have gone well in front – very well in front – then maybe you might enjoy it as it happens. But enjoy . . .' and he leaves the thought in mid-air.

The stories of Tottenham Hotspur and Bill Nicholson are now so intertwined that it is virtually impossible to separate them. For the record, the future manager was born in Scarborough, one of a family of nine. His father was a groom and horse cab driver and Nicholson was a little special even then, passing scholarship examinations to go to Scarborough High School.

Leaving at 16 he went to work in a laundry and played soccer at weekends for a local team, the Young Liberals. He had no thoughts of becoming a professional footballer at this stage but, out of the blue, Spurs asked him to come for a trial in 1936.

'When the letter came no-one knew what to do. We weren't even sure exactly where Tottenham was. My mother and father had never once seen me play football. They knew I was keen, but they had no idea whether I was any good or not. I honestly had no idea what the world of professional football was about. Our heroes were the local Midland League side – none of my friends had even been to see Hull or York.'

Nicholson's opinion was that the local Spurs scout, based in York, had heard about him and Ben Ives, the chief scout, then took a trip to see for himself. Nicholson was probably introduced to Ives but retained no recollections of the meeting and certainly had no idea of what it might lead to. No other club had ever shown any interest, and from this point on his life in football was to be committed to the cause of Tottenham Hotspur.

He had a month's trial at White Hart Lane, and was taken on as a ground staff boy. 'We were cheap labour really,' he said later, 'I think I painted every single girder under those stands out there, eight to five we worked, every weekday. We trained two afternoons a week, including a lot of running round the pitch. There was no tactical discussion, just what we were able to organise ourselves. But it wasn't all bad, of course. I remember that Willie Hall, who was club captain at the time, was very kind and always took a great interest.'

Nicholson played for the nursery side, Northfleet, and signed as a full professional at 18, on the same day as Ronnie Burgess. The Welshman retained a warm spot in Nicholson's memory: 'If I had to pick out one player in all my time here, a player who had it all, I think I'd pick Ron Burgess. He could do anything. Once Arthur Rowe had sold Ron on his methods then he had no trouble with push-and-run. Convincing Burgess was the most difficult thing Arthur ever had to do, but once it was done, well . . . yes, if pushed I'd even put him above Blanchflower.'

Burgess and Nicholson had started to play odd games for the first team before 1939, but on the outbreak of war Nicholson joined the Durham Light Infantry. Because he was known to be a professional footballer, he was sent on a PE course and soon became a sergeant-instructor. He continued training new intakes throughout the War, eventually ending up in Italy where he took over a rest camp in Bari from Stan Cullis and then going on to Geoff Dyson's physical education headquarters at Udine.

He probably lost half his playing career to the War but doesn't regret it because he is convinced that it was those wartime experiences which made what came afterwards possible. 'It was invaluable. What I did for six years in the army taught me how to handle

OVERLEAF: Like virtually all other successful teams of the post-war era, Spurs great spell lasted just three years, during whch they won four trophies. The last was the Cup Winners Cup, photographed here with the squad at the beginning of the 1963-64 season. Standing left to right: Cliff Jones, Ron Henry, Mel Hopkins, Maurice Norman, John Hollowbread, Bill Brown, Bobby Smith, John White, Jimmy Greaves and John Smith. Sitting left to right: Frank Saul, Peter Baker, Dave Mackay, Danny Blanchflower, Tony March, Les Allen, Terry Dyson and Eddie Clayton. The only player from the great days not in this line up was Terry Medwin, who had been injured on a close season tour of South Africa and was never to play for the first team again. Within a year far worse was to have happened: John White was killed by lightning on a golf course, Dave Mackay was out having broken his left leg twice, Blanchflower had to retire after being given a terrible run-around by Denis Law at Old Trafford and Brown, Baker, Smith and Allen were no longer first choices.

people and how to talk to people. It obviously taught me how to get players fit, and I began to think about coaching routines – not in a very organised way, but how it could be done. After the War Freddie Cox asked some of the lads to go on a coaching course, and, with all those years in the army, I didn't find it too difficult. Gradually I got to think more about it.'

In 1946 he went straight into the Tottenham first team at centre-half for two seasons. He moved to right-half and stayed there until Danny Blanchflower took over the position in 1954. Nicholson had suffered a knee injury and had already said to Arthur Rowe that he felt the time had probably come to find a replacement.

They were good years for Nicholson, though not without their regrets. He was a member of the disastrous World Cup party in 1950 and won only one cap overall, basically because

Billy Wright held the right-half spot throughout Nicholson's career. That debut was as spectacular as his managerial one however; he scored against Portugal after just 19 seconds with his very first kick in international football.

Nicholson became the Spurs first-team coach in 1955. He had already helped Walter Winterbottom on England tours and courses ('He was a wonderful coach, taught me an enormous amount,' said Nicholson) and had trained the Cambridge University side for a time. He went with the England side to Sweden for the 1958 World Cup and, when Jimmy Anderson resigned a couple of month's later, the Tottenham board apparently asked the FA to help in making recommendations for the succession. It is possible that the board were just asking for confirmation of what they already knew. The reply soon came back, probably from Stanley Rous thought Nicholson,

that the club had already got the very man at White Hart Lane, that they did not need to search any further and that Nicholson had already proved his abilities to the FA, never mind the club.

Bill Nicholson was regularly described as dour and pessimistic during his period as manager, adjectives which were impossible to apply and barely possible to believe talking to him later. The only hint of pessimism came when discussing the game's present state and prospects for the future: 'I go and watch Second and Third Division games nowadays and I think to myself: "How can even the managers of these teams bear to watch them 46 times a year?" It can be terrible. There's no point anyone pretending that the game has not lost a lot of what made it worth watching.'

Otherwise he was nothing if not positive, particularly about the 1980s side at the time of the interview. His pride also shone through when he spoke of the academic successes of his daughters and of his then five-year old grandson's enthusiasm for football, but, above all else, when he described how the Double side came together.

'People talk about the team's skills, rightly, but they don't seem to recall that the team succeeded because it was very fit and very well organised. That was almost disguised *behind* the skill. People used to come to Cheshunt from all over Europe to watch our training routines – stood there with stop watches and notebooks in their hands, writing it all down.'

When Nicholson became coach the players still often trained at the ground. When it rained they had to train under the stand where there were girders all over the place. 'Because of those years in the army, I could

work out indoor routines where the girders didn't get in the way. But I pushed for the indoor training pitch (opened in the early 1960s) and that made a big difference.' Nicholson clearly loved the coaching; devising new routines, analysing how best to coach two-on-one situations, or how to tackle, making defenders play as forwards or vice versa, so that they could appreciate better their own roles. He would look at every facet of the game. Most things could be improved, could be broken down so that they could be coached; he would not accept that players either had or did not have certain skills and could not get better with the right routines.

'I was never a desk manager, like many were at that time. I would tell the directors that they could get me in the office before a quarter to ten. After that I would be out with the team, coaching'.

The side Nicholson took charge of already contained most of the Double side, but there were two or three vital additions to be made later. 'I'd been chasing Dave Mackay for some time but there seemed to be no chance; the club had enough money for a big signing, the directors wanted one and the transfer deadline was coming up. I went down to Wales to see Mel Charles. He wasn't sure and said he'd ring me at the weekend. Then, out of the blue, my sources in Scotland told me that Mackay might just be available. Only I couldn't do anything because of Charles – I couldn't buy them both

and I'd given my word and had to hope he'd say no. So I waited until Saturday night, when Mel Charles thankfully rang to say he wasn't going to sign. I got the sleeper to Edinburgh, signed Mackay from Tommy Walker at Hearts the following morning (which was the deadline) and brought him back. I remember the station-master at Edinburgh nearly went through the roof when he saw us together and realised what had happened. Nobody else got a whisper.

'With John White the problem was stamina. He seemed so frail I wasn't sure he was tough enough. Then someone – Danny, I think – mentioned that he was a cross-country runner. So I rang up White's army unit (he was on national service at the time) and talked to his commandant. "Yes, he's a bloody good footballer," said this officer, "but he'll not be playing football on Saturday. He'll be running for us in a race." We talked about John White and I soon discovered that he was an excellent cross-country runner. That convinced me.'

Les Allen's arrival was also a little different from the way it was reported at the time. 'Actually,' says Nicholson, 'Ted Drake [the Chelsea manager] rang me and said he needed Johnny Brooks. Ted was in trouble fighting relegation at the time, and I didn't really feel Brooks was the right man for his team then. But Ted persisted so I looked at their squad. Les Allen was in the reserves and it struck me as a good swap. Chelsea wanted money as well but I told them what they could do about that. What I liked about Les was that he could ghost into scoring positions, like Martin Peters.' Allen had already been on Spurs' books once, as an amateur, but had preferred to sign professional forms with Chelsea.

'So there was the Double side. There was no single secret to it, just as there's no school for managers where you can go and be told how to win things. The players in that side didn't get the rewards they should have though that wasn't clear at the time. I'm sorry about that, and that I was always too busy to appreciate the small things about people and about our success, which is a great pity.'

He still lived in the small house close to the ground which had been home to his wife Darkie (so called because she was the darker of twins) and himself for years and remained a positive presence at the club, without in any way casting shadows over the manager as Matt Busby did over his successors. Indeed, it was Keith Burkinshaw who insisted that Nicholson rejoin the staff in 1976. 'It's been my life, Tottenham Hotspur, and I love the club,' he readily agreed and he made the parallel between the Tottenham sides he served as a player and as a manager. Of the 1950 champions he said: 'Other clubs got to know our style . . . it was only for a short time. But the chief factor was that a lot of us went over the hill together. It was impossible to replace them. In a good side you can paper over the cracks with one or even two good players and the loss is not allowed to show too much. You can still play well and get by. But when it involves a lot of players going, then it's a real problem. It happened to me with the 1960 team . . . a lot of them finished at around the same time. That was the saddest thing, but I wouldn't have missed a moment.'

1971

**The Glory Game • The numbers game •
Four seasons, four finals • League Cups • Chivers
and troubled times • Rotterdam again • Nicholson
resigns • Terry Neill • Relegation and renewal**

On Wednesday 29 May 1974, against a background of rioting by their supporters, Spurs lost the second leg of the UEFA Cup final 2–0 against Feyenoord in Rotterdam. With a 2–2 draw at White Hart Lane eight days earlier paving the way for a Dutch victory, Spurs had, for the first time in their history, lost a major cup final. Suddenly it was the end of Europe and conspicuously the end of an era, the Golden Age of Bill Nicholson. In fifteen glorious years, he had led them to the Double, two more FA Cup wins, two League Cup wins, the Cup Winners Cup and the UEFA Cup. The heights had been intoxicating, so falling from them was all the harder.

Spurs fans had not only come to expect success, but to demand it. And in 1974, after a decade and a half dominating the breeze, the

bubble finally burst. Almost exactly three months after the UEFA final defeat, on 28 August, Nicholson resigned after the club's worst start to a League season in 62 years. 'Success in soccer,' as he rightly said, 'comes in cycles. It can't go on forever. You must have experienced players to win things, but the problem is that they all grow old together.' By the start of the 1974–75 season, the players who had helped Spurs win three major titles in the early seventies and reach the final of a fourth were, by soccer standards, growing old. Mike England was 31, Martin Peters and Cyril Knowles were 30, Phil Beal and Martin Chivers 29. Only a few weeks earlier Alan Gilzean had played his last game for the club, retiring just before his 36th birthday.

Nicholson realised that to prolong the cycle, or preferably break it, he needed to introduce

Alan Gilzean goes up with Denis Smith (right) and Alan Bloor of Stoke City during a League game in February 1972. Gilzean was signed from Dundee in 1964 and played for Tottenham for ten successful years, retiring at the age of 36. 'Football's not a job or a career – you're meant to enjoy it,' he said in 1972, 'I get paid to enjoy myself!'

new blood. But times in soccer were changing and for a collection of reasons, some external, some stemming from the character of the man himself, Nicholson was unable to sustain a youth policy as he wanted it, or to buy in the players who could realise his constant vision of new and successful Spurs sides rising out of the ashes of the old. Abolition of the maximum wage had made players wealthy. And the younger ones were impatient for their share of the riches. They were no longer content to sit around waiting for their first team chance. Few were willing to weigh the glorious traditions of White Hart Lane against the lure of hard cash.

'We couldn't keep our young reserves,' says Nicholson, recalling the name of one outstanding Scottish Youth international midfield player who signed as an apprentice in 1969 but left four years later, still hungering for his first team chance. His name? Graeme Souness. There were others like him, too. Derek Possee and Keith Weller, who went on to win England honours, were on Spurs books in the late sixties. 'We didn't want to lose any of them,' says Nicholson, 'but they just wouldn't wait.' To an extent the problem was of Nicholson's own making. The pressures on him for success were enormous. But in his pursuit of excellence, he was caught in a trap: to gain the necessary experience, you need to be playing; to be part of a regular side, you need to play well and the team needs to win; to be winning, you need the experience. In consequence, his younger players were depressed by expensive new signings and held back to the point where the more talented and ambitious simply drifted away.

Nicholson was also frustrated in his attempts to recreate the magic of his Double winners. As a perfectionist who measured all performances by the standards set by Blanchflower's side, he often rejected signings better than the players he had because they were not as good as those he wanted. Those he did sign were not so much replacements for the Double heroes as copies, and as such they suffered in comparison. Chivers on his day was more skilful than Smith but surely lacked his dogged determination and courage; Coates never approached the heights of a Jones; Mullery was never quite in the Blanchflower or Mackay class and would complain of incessant reminders of what Mackay might have done in a given situation. Nicholson summed it all up when he said, 'I can't sit and watch them in comfort, not the way I've done with other teams I've had.'

As they entered the seventies, Spurs also suffered at the hands of changing playing styles, or the 'numbers game' as Nicholson called it. The days of 3-2-2-3 were long gone, even 4-2-4 was well past its peak. This was the era of defensive football, the day of the spoiler, a time epitomised by Arsenal and Peter Storey, Leeds and Norman Hunter. The one-touch game employed by Spurs over nearly two decades was an easy target, open to exploitation and destruction by less ambitious, more ruthless teams. It was also a style which did not lend itself to players whose skills could probably not match those of an earlier generation. It merely added to Nicholson's frustrations to have to change to a safer percentage game, where long passes were driven upfield for target men. As the

new decade opened in August 1970, with Spurs suffering their worst start since 1958–59, it was being asked whether they had players with the heart for this type of game.

After a 1–0 fourth round FA Cup replay defeat at Crystal Palace on 28 January 1970, Nicholson made sweeping changes. The Palace defeat was a watershed for Jimmy Greaves whose great goalscoring skills had rapidly gone into decline. It was his last game for Spurs, dropped along with Gilzean, Knowles and Kinnear. But Nicholson's revamped side fared no better in the next League match against Southampton, losing 1–0. In March Nicholson moved into the transfer market in a deal which brought England World Cup star Martin Peters from West Ham for £200,000. It was ironic that, in breaking the British transfer record for the second time in a decade, Nicholson should part with the player for whom he broke it the first time nine years before. For the deal included Greaves in part-exchange. Greaves' departure cut a further tie with past glories. He'd joined Spurs in November 1961 and, as Spurs' new chairman, Sidney Wale, wrote in the 1970–71 handbook: 'We shall always remember the joy and pleasure Jimmy gave us.' In just over eight years, Greaves scored 267 goals in senior matches, leaving behind him two club records which are still unbroken: his 37 First Division goals in a season (1962–63) and his aggregate League goals, 220 between 1961 and 1970. In his place, Nicholson went for experience rather than promise. Peters, still only 26, with his subtle ball skills and brilliantly timed blindside runs, was a goal-taker and goal-maker who had match-winning experience at the ultimate level. There were, after all, only two players in England who had scored a goal in a World Cup final.

Spurs finished the 1969–70 season eleventh in the First Division, their lowest for eleven years. The stigma of failure was felt most by Wale, who was in his first year as chairman following the death of his father, Frederick. 'This,' he wrote afterwards, 'is obviously not good enough for Tottenham Hotspur.' Spurs responded in the tradition set by their uncanny knack of winning major titles at the start of a new decade. And their victory in the 1971 League Cup final over Aston Villa heralded a revival in their fortunes. They won the new UEFA Cup the following season and the League Cup again in 1973. But none but the most blindly fanatical supporters could pretend that the quality of these latter-day triumphs could match the flair and brilliance shown by Nicholson's earlier sides. A look at Tottenham's for and against columns in the early sixties and seventies is most revealing. In the seasons between 1960 and 1965 they scored 115, 88, 111, 97 and 87 League goals. A decade later the tally was 54, 63, 58, 45 and 52, an average reduction of nearly half. And Spurs were by no means a negative or unsuccessful side by the standards of the early 1970s. In defence the figures were 55, 69, 62, 81 and 71 against 33, 42, 48, 50 and 63, an average fall of over 30%. So while Tottenham's notoriously porous defence (only three other clubs conceded more than fourth-placed Spurs in 1963–64) had certainly tightened up in keeping with the times, the attack had ceased to be the rock on

which success could be guaranteed. It was no criticism of Tottenham, still one of the more popular and entertaining sides, to suggest that football's authorities needed to look no further than the goals scored column to discover why the game was losing its popularity. Not only that, but rather than ask why fans were voting with their feet, it might have been more interesting to find out why so many still bothered to watch at all.

FOUR SEASONS: FOUR FINALS

Nonetheless, trophies came at a time when the emphasis in soccer had shifted even further from entertainment towards success. Winning was clearly the name of the new game; it wasn't just the main thing, for a time it became the only thing. And though it hurt Nicholson to suffer mediocrity while he was searching for perfection, major trophy wins in 1971, 1972 and 1973 were more than any other club could offer its fans. It was a sign of the times when he was forced to admit: 'A bloke is measured by what he wins.' In 1970–71 they were propelled towards Wembley by a mixture of good luck and a change of playing style which saw them perform more as a team than as a team of individuals. If the sum of the individual parts of the Double side had been greater than the whole, the reverse was surely true of Spurs in the early seventies. The last ties with individual flair had been cut with the departure of Greaves. Their style with him up front had been geared to providing chances for the game's greatest goal poacher to polish off. But Greaves' partnership alongside Gilzean had never blossomed, mainly because the Scottish forward wasn't suited to the role of target man and provider. Finding the right position for the gifted Gilzean had also been a problem for Scotland, but at club level it was solved with the switch of Chivers to centre-forward and Gilzean to his preferred position just behind the two front men. With Peters in close support, and Perryman and Mullery adding thrust from midfield, Spurs found a style which at last began to pay dividends in the First Division's new, relentless long-ball, target-man game.

Spurs reached Wembley via four consecutive home ties and a semi-final against a Bristol City side struggling in the Second Division. It was a time when the word 'lucky' switched from its more familiar Highbury home to White Hart Lane. Spurs' final opponents, too, weren't the most awesome in the world – Third Division Aston Villa. But a team that had defeated Manchester United to reach Wembley was not to be treated lightly and there was the added ill-omen for Spurs in recent successes by the Third Division over the First in League Cup finals, namely Queen's Park Rangers against West Bromwich and Swindon against Arsenal.

Like their Third Division predecessors, Villa proved no pushovers but, despite hitting the woodwork and forcing a goal-line clearance from Perryman, they couldn't make history repeat itself. With 12 minutes remaining and Villa holding a grip in midfield, Spurs broke the deadlock with two goals from Chivers to win 2–0. It was a drab final but, spectacle or not, victory meant everything to Tottenham: another major trophy, their first League Cup win, success in their lucky year, and to Nicholson, most of all, it meant Europe once more. For him, matches against continental opposition were the only occasions when Spurs rose above the mundane and appeared to relish the battle. They were occasions when, for Nicholson, expectation and achievement more nearly matched one another. As he was so fond of saying: 'Spurs are not Spurs anymore without Europe.'

With Chivers shaking off the effects of a bad knee injury, sustained three seasons earlier, to produce his best form – 29 goals from 54 games – Spurs enjoyed a resurgence in the League and FA Cup too. Only an inspired performance by Ray Clemence in a quarter-final replay at White Hart Lane prevented them from reaching the FA Cup semi-final at the expense of Liverpool, while in the League a much improved defensive record (33 goals conceded against 55 the previous season) lifted them to third, their best position since 1967. How ironic that their last home game should have been against Arsenal, who were seeking a goalless draw or victory to clinch the Championship and first leg of their own Double exactly ten years on from Spurs' more historic achievement. From the glories of one-touch, the game had deteriorated to a monotonous succession of high balls to a couple of big front-runners and, in John Radford and Ray Kennedy, Arsenal had two worthy masters in heading and shooting. Spurs were reduced to trying to beat Arsenal at their own game and came off second best when George Armstrong eventually found the head of Kennedy to give Arsenal the winning goal they needed to bring the title to Highbury. The contrast in playing styles between 1961 and 1971 was completed five days later when Peter Storey ruthlessly marked Liverpool's Steve Heighway in the Cup final to help Arsenal to a 2–1 extra-time victory which clinched the Double. In ten years, soccer had arguably gone from its most sublime to its most cynical phase.

Wingers had rather gone out of fashion at international level with Ramsey in 1966. Spurs fans used to joke that, as a full-back himself, he had never liked wingers anyway, but they remained a tradition at Tottenham throughout the sixties and into the seventies. From Cliff Jones through Jimmy Robertson to the 1970s crop of Roger Morgan, Jimmy Neighbour and Jimmy Pearce, Spurs had won all their trophies playing with wingers. But as they approached the 1971–72 season it was a position where Nicholson had neither experience nor outstanding talent. Morgan, who had been bought from Queen's Park Rangers for £110,000 in 1969, promised much but delivered little, partially because of injury, while home-grown youngsters Neighbour and Pearce always gave the appearance of being in the first team only as stop-gaps. When Burnley's England winger, Ralph Coates, came up for sale at the end of the 1970–71 season following his club's relegation to the Second Division, Nicholson moved swiftly. In a characteristically cloak-and-dagger deal Coates' move was finalised on a May night at the Staffordshire Post House, just off the M6. One of the reasons for all the secrecy was because both clubs wanted to avoid a public auction for the player, Spurs because they feared his price could go considerably beyond the £190,000 they'd agreed, and Burnley because they wanted to honour their long-standing promise to give Spurs first option.

Coates' arrival brought Tottenham's England international contingent to five (Peters, Mullery, Knowles and Chivers were the others) and with Gilzean (Scotland), England (Wales), Jennings (Northern Ireland) and Kinnear (Republic of Ireland) completing their international line-up, Spurs had a wealth of experience with which to march again into Europe. The new season saw Chivers continue his prolific goalscoring form – 44 goals in 64 matches – and Spurs create another British club record. On 17 May 1972, they won the new UEFA Cup, the successor to the defunct Inter-Cities Fairs Cup, thus becoming the first British club to win two of the European trophies. Only Liverpool and Manchester United have ever matched this feat. But during a season in which they also finished sixth in the League, reached the quarter-finals of the FA Cup and the semi-finals of the League Cup, the first cracks were beginning to appear in the Nicholson renaissance.

It is a measure of how high standards had been set at White Hart Lane when, in a season as apparently successful as 1971–72, finishing sixth in the League should have been considered only adequate. But as Sidney Wale would never cease reminding everyone, the League was the club's bread and butter. It was vital to do well. When the end came for Nicholson two years later, it wasn't Spurs' failure in Europe, the FA Cup or League Cup which was at the root of the problem, but their inability to win a League match. The paradox of the club's contrasting fortunes at European and domestic level was never more clearly illustrated than by the ten games it took Spurs to reach the UEFA final and, for example, their first ten League games of 1972. In the former they scored 27 goals and conceded just four while in the latter they scored 12 and conceded seven. The anomaly was frequently remarked on but never

satisfactorily explained. Nicholson was aware of it but could only say: 'For such an experienced team, a lot of them are not consistent,' while chairman Wale had a reason but no cure: 'It was as if the players had got such a taste for Europe that it was the only competition in which they could raise their game.'

In his controversial book *The Glory Game* journalist Hunter Davies made the same point: 'There seemed something lacking in the team's character all season which made them fade in ordinary League matches . . . but almost every big occasion had been a joy to watch. During the season Spurs produced consistently high form in every cup match. Was their failure in ordinary matches a group weakness or a weakness in certain individuals in the group?' The question was left unanswered. With the benefit of greater hindsight, it is clear that three factors emerged during that season which were to begin undermining the club's achievements. They were Nicholson's growing disenchantment with the game as a whole, a real disaffection between Nicholson and at least one of his players, and the ageing process which was catching up on his current team. All this could be set aside in European matches, however, as it was in the Battle of Bucharest.

On a cold December afternoon in the Rumanian capital, Spurs once again rose out of their League doldrums to inflict another impressive defeat on European opposition. But it was almost a pyrrhic victory. Against a Rapid Bucharest side determined to kick and punch their way back into the match (they were 3–0 down from the first leg) Spurs had seven players injured and Jimmy Pearce sent off along with Rapid's right-back. Spurs won 2–0 to finish 5–0 aggregate winners, but it was only due to the discipline and self-restraint drummed into the team by Nicholson that their casualties weren't higher. Afterwards

Cyril Knowles chases Liverpool left-winger Steve Heighway during the goalless draw at Anfield on 17 April 1971. A Yorkshireman who had worked in the mines before becoming a professional footballer, Knowles won four England caps. He is, nonetheless, probably best remembered as the inspiration for the record 'Nice One, Cyril' which reached number 14 in the hit parade just before the 1973 League Cup final.

Gilzean and Jennings combine to clear an Ipswich corner on 10 April 1971. The Ipswich defender is Derek Jefferson. Spurs won the game 2–0 (with an own goal and one from Chivers) and finished a creditable third in the League behind Arsenal and Leeds.

Nicholson, normally a restrained man in front of the Press, was moved to say: 'Rapid were the dirtiest side I've come across in 30 years of football. If this is European football, I'd rather have a Combination match.'

Even victory in the UEFA Cup final itself couldn't raise Nicholson's enthusiasm. After Spurs' heady European campaigns, it was a bit of an anticlimax to be facing less than exotic Wolverhampton Wanderers. In a match the Press rightly dubbed 'The Forgotten Final', Spurs survived a tremendous Wolves onslaught in the second leg at White Hart Lane to emerge 3-2 aggregate winners. There was plenty of tension but little good football to excite a purist like Nicholson. Hunter Davies, in *The Glory Game*, remarked that Nicholson was relieved but far from ecstatic. 'As a European final,' said Nicholson, 'it was nothing like our 1963 win. That really was a wonderful occasion. Winning 5–1 against Atletico Madrid was winning in style.' Once again Nicholson's fate had been to suffer mediocrity in success while seeking perfection.

"THE GLORY GAME"

The publishing of *The Glory Game* deserves a diversion in itself. A minor sensation when it appeared, it remains the most controversial inside view of how any Football League club works. At the time journalist Michael Hart commented: 'The exposure is total and absolute. No one is spared. As one player put it to me: "He has dug his holes too deeply. I am surprised the club passed the transcript." Understandably the hierarchy at Tottenham were not happy with Mr Davies. The players, too, had a few choice phrases for him . . . (but) as one observed: "There's nothing we can do. It's all true".' But Mike Langley in *The People* said on 29 October 1972: 'The book has been scourged over the past few days by reviews of staggering naivety . . . it's been suggested that Chivers, Mullery and even Mrs Nick might make . . . a point of smashing Mr Davies's front teeth down his throat. But no one mentioned that he'd an arrangement with the club. That each player, and fan Morris Keston, read and approved his individual chapter. That the entire book was scrutinised . . . by club chairman Sidney Wale.' Langley went on to say that the management and players were taking part of the profit from the book (implying that it was to their benefit to make it more spicy than usual) and concludes, interestingly, that: '. . . far from doing Spurs down I'd say he's glossed over a few sensitive details.' The club's only deep sensitivity was for Eddie Baily, a Tottenham stalwart for so long, whose contribution and warmth seemed to have been ignored in favour of rather isolated quotations and observations which, while no doubt being strictly accurate, were perhaps prejudicial by being selective.

Nonetheless, reading it more than two decades later, it is difficult to see what the fuss was all about. Apart from revealing that some of the players and staff had the average man's human prejudices, and that the team did not like garlic on its food, there is little that comes as a surprise. In fact it is almost totally silent on what had already become the most sensitive issue at Tottenham and throughout senior football – the financial demands of the players. And on the positive side it is a book with very real heroes – primarily Bill Nicholson, whose dedication to the club and unstinting effort on its behalf shines through on every page, Pat Jennings and Steve Perryman, who emerges as a thoughtful, generous and devoted player, the kind of hero every father would want for his son. Twenty-odd years on, it actually reflects extremely well on the club that the author was allowed the freedom of a whole season with the side to write the book, and that the publishers were allowed to sell it without any of the devaluing censorship that so often accompanies anything written about football.

Spurs achieved their European successes by Nicholson's shrewd tactical planning, playing 4-3-3 in the home legs while smothering the opposition's 4-2-4 line-ups in the away leg by packing midfield with a 4-4-2 formation. For these games Chivers and Gilzean were the front men, feeding off crosses from Coates and the overlapping full-backs Knowles and Kinnear. Coates had a disappointing debut season. He was tried in midfield and on the wing but, like many players coming to a new club, he was slow to settle in. It is fair to say, with hindsight, that Coates never fulfilled the promise he had shown at Burnley. With Spurs he was always adequate, and often valuable, but just missed out on being a really great club player.

Up front Chivers had his best season to date in terms of goals, but he tended to have too many anonymous matches and was frequently the focal point of Nicholson's criticisms. Constant carping was the manager's way of trying to rouse and motivate the infuriatingly inconsistent striker. On his day, Chivers was a match-winner, as his two excellent goals in the first leg of the UEFA final proved. But too often he faded out of matches altogether, as England were to find to their cost in that astonishing World Cup qualifier against Poland at Wembley. Nicholson's attacks ('He never stopped moaning' Chivers complains in *The Glory Game*) did not reduce the mounting antagonism which was eventually to prove a factor in Nicholson's resignation. For the manager's part, he felt he had just cause in requesting more effort from Chivers. He did not ask for goals every week from the centre-forward, who was hardly a players' player anyway, but he felt entitled to ask for the energy and co-operation which regularly appeared to be lacking.

However, the Spurs manager was faced with a player problem of a different nature as the 1971–72 season drew to a close. In an unprecedented revolt over pay, no less than nine first team players, including Chivers, were in dispute over their contracts. To the consternation of the board there were revelations in the Press about how poorly players were paid in comparison with the rest of the First Division (if not with the country at large) and, worst of all, that players at (admittedly highly successful) Arsenal were paid nearly twice as much. Led by Welsh international centre-half Mike England, the Spurs players optimistically demanded parity with Highbury.

The UEFA final was a personal triumph for club skipper Alan Mullery. Already 30, Mullery's England and Spurs career looked to be coming to a close when he lost his international and club place midway through the season and was shipped back to Fulham on loan. But, in typically tenacious style, Mullery battled his way back. He returned to score a vital long range equaliser in the away leg of the UEFA Cup semi-final against AC Milan (Spurs drew 1–1 to win 3–2 on aggregate) and scored again, fairy tale like, in the 1–1 home draw against Wolves which clinched the Cup. It turned out to be a glorious swan-song for

'Mullers'. In the summer he made a permanent move back to Fulham – the first of the new victims of Nicholson's old enemy, time.

It had been more than a year since Nicholson's last big purchase and with the fans coming to expect the arrival of a big expensive new star at the start of every season, and the club eager to oblige if only to keep the money from the tax man, the one manager in Britain to have spent a million pounds on new players was ready to take another massive plunge into the transfer market. Nicholson had already broken the British transfer record twice with Greaves and Peters and, armed with more than a quarter of a million pounds as the rich pickings of Spurs' European crusades, he had more than enough to do it again. On this occasion, however Nicholson became the victim of his own big spending. In pushing transfer fees well into six figures, he had been one of the principal causes of inflation in the game. Quality players were scarce and clubs were asking astronomic fees. Even Spurs did not have a bottomless well of money, although they were undoubtedly one of the richest clubs in the country. Frustrated at not being able to buy the players he wanted, Nicholson kept faith with his experienced players, despite their growing age and inconsistency, at the expense of his own frustrated reserves.

WEMBLEY AGAIN

The following season repeated the pattern of 1971–72 – good cup performances contrasting with poor league form. The difference this time was that the levels of achievement on all fronts were that much lower. They finished eighth in the League, two places lower than the previous season, were knocked out by Derby in the fourth round of the FA Cup (losing 5–3 in a home replay after leading 3–1 with five minutes to go), lost to Liverpool in the semi-finals of the UEFA Cup on the away goals rule (despite winning 2–1 at White Hart Lane), yet still managed to pull a rabbit out of the hat by lifting the League Cup for the second time in three years when they beat Norwich 1–0. The final was an individual success for Ralph Coates, who came on as substitute for John Pratt to score the winning goal, but was one of the most tedious Wembley finals in history (if not the most tedious) and the club was widely criticised as yet again achieving success at the expense of entertainment. As Sidney Wale remarked, with considerable understatement, in the handbook for the following season: '. . . the final . . . was not the classic we should have liked to witness. 'Spurs were stifled by Norwich's defensive approach, but they still managed to breathe enough air to keep themselves alive in Europe for just one more season.

Events in football were now being influenced by the country's worsening economic climate. Big pay packets and spiralling overheads were eating into the profits of those clubs lucky enough to be still making money at all, while others plunged inexorably into the red or were forced to sell their star players to stay solvent. Even a club as rich and successful as Tottenham, with a healthy balance in the bank, was about to feel the pinch. And since a job at Spurs was generally a job for life, there was never any question of Nicholson selling any of his star names. Falling attendances throughout the game, as much a sign of the diminishing entertainment value of soccer as of the general effects of inflation and tight money, added to clubs' financial worries. And, for all their success, Spurs were as badly hit as anyone. In two seasons average home attendances declined from 38,000 in the 1971-72 UEFA Cup winning season to 26,000 in 1973-74, and that after winning the League Cup again and proceeding to the final of the UEFA Cup. Spurs fans demanded success, but not so many were willing to pay for it any more.

The result was that from a profit of £300,000 in their League Cup season of 1972-73, proceeds from the following season tumbled to a mere £35,000. Worse still, forecasts for the following season, 1974-75, when Spurs would be out of Europe for the first time in four years, were for a loss of £250,000. And the club was already committed to spending £200,000 on ground improvements.

August 1973, and for the second season in succession Spurs kicked off without a new signing. Unable to get the players he wanted, Nicholson decided to concentrate instead on his home-grown youngsters. Ray Evans established himself in the right-back position occupied for eight seasons by Joe Kinnear, Cyril Knowles was to make way for Terry Naylor and, in midfield, Nicholson gave an extended run to Chris McGrath, a promising young Belfast boy who had turned professional only 18 months earlier. This belated attempt to rejuvenate his ageing team had mixed results for, despite the weight of experience which again carried them to another European final, Spurs' League form continued its alarming downward trend.

RIOTS IN ROTTERDAM
The disparity was at its greatest in March 1974, when they won even greater admiration in Europe with a memorable fourth round UEFA Cup victory over West Germany's FC Cologne (2-1 away and 3-0 at home) while at home their image was being further tarnished by the threat of relegation. They recovered to finish eleventh in the League but Nicholson admitted: 'It was the most disappointing season since my first as manager,' and he talked of a lack of determination and slipping standards. The side scored only 45 League goals, the same as in 1912-13 and their worst total ever. His three-times cup winners were for the most part approaching the autumn of their soccer careers and, while it may be a harsh judgement on the younger players Nicholson was now drafting in, they could not show the skill and application of their predecessors, because, in the final analysis, they were not the creme de la creme Spurs were accustomed to. In failing to buy new quality players, and neglecting the best of his youngsters, the Sounesses, Wellers and Possees, Nicholson had fallen between two stools. For the first time in 15 years, there was serious talk of resignation. Sidney Wale hinted that not even the great man's job was safe when he said: 'There will have to be changes one day. It's a question of time and timing.'

For his part, Nicholson considered the board might take the pressure off by making him general manager and appointing a younger man to look after team affairs. One of the criticisms levelled at Nicholson in the Press was that he hadn't already pressed for a younger man to be brought in to bridge the growing generation gap between himself and his younger players, the role that he himself had filled for Jimmy Anderson in the 1950s. Nicholson was 55 and finding it increasingly difficult to maintain a rapport with his team. His assistant, Eddie Baily, was no better placed, being of the same generation as Nicholson and, like him, Spurs man and boy. 'It's more difficult to get loyalty, respect and honesty from players,' said Nicholson at the time. His long-running feud with Chivers was smouldering on, ready to erupt in a final showdown during the summer of 1974; he was still having no success in the transfer market, and, most critical of all at this stage in his career, he lacked a strategy. He could see no long-term solution to the club's problems, as he said in retrospect: 'What could I do? Just carry on. There was no turning point, so you just change gradually to suit your own problems.' Had Spurs beaten Feyenoord in the UEFA Cup final in May 1974, Nicholson says he had intended to resign there and then. 'You're only as good as your last result,' he philosophically reiterated.

But he was denied that coup de grace when, in a grisly sequel to the Battle of Bucharest, Spurs were traumatically beaten in the Riot of Rotterdam, their first defeat in ten major cup finals spanning 73 years. Feyenoord were formidable opposition. They had just won the Dutch championship and in de Jong, Rijsbergen, van Hanegem and Jansen they had four internationals who, two months later, were to help take Holland to the World Cup final against West Germany. By comparison, Spurs went into the first leg at White Hart Lane on 21 May with a mixture of youthful inexperience in players like Evans, Naylor and McGrath, none of whom had ever played in a cup final before, and seasoned campaigners whose international careers (with the exception of Jennings) were drawing to a close; England was out of the Welsh team; Chivers had made his last England appearance in the fateful World Cup qualifier against Poland seven months earlier, and his intermittent career was well past its peak; Coates hadn't played for England since 1971 and Peters' 67th appearance for England, in the Home International against Scotland only three nights earlier, was to be his last. Spurs also preferred young Chris McGrath, who, by contrast, had just won his first three caps for Northern Ireland in the same Home Internationals, to the ageing Gilzean.

Spurs needed a decisive victory to stand any chance of maintaining their record of cup invincibility. But a downpour just before the kick-off made the surface slippery and immediately upset their passing. They were frequently caught by Feyenoord's offside trap, and, though scoring twice, through England and an own goal by van Daele, were finally outmatched by the physical strength and resilience of the Dutch. With four minutes left and Spurs leading 2–1, de Jong stole a late equaliser. The writing was on the wall and everyone at White Hart Lane knew it. The 2–0 defeat at Rotterdam eight days later against a team of Feyenoord's quality was, on Sidney Wale's admission, no disgrace – that belonged to the so-called fans who brought mayhem to the match and to the streets of Europe's biggest port in a night of mindless violence and vandalism.

Thousands of pounds worth of damage were caused to shops and cars during a rampage which resulted in 70 arrests and 200 injuries. Nicholson personally appealed to fans at the match to stop fighting, but to no avail. The hooliganism merely became one of a list of similar outbreaks of violence perpetrated by British fans abroad in the face of defeat and was strangely out of character for a group of supporters which had never been associated with the Shedites of Chelsea or the Stretford Enders of Manchester United. That Spurs followers might have joined the ranks of those who had done so much to destroy the traditional pleasures of English football was perhaps the most depressing lesson of a thoroughly depressing episode. Now, it had to be assumed, no club was safe from the mindless minority. Because Nicholson went out to talk to the crowd he was unable to give his usual half-time team talk. That did not help the side's composure and everyone was disturbed by what was going on outside. When Nicholson came back Steve Perryman thought he detected tears in the manager's eyes. It must have been one of the final straws for a man who had always acted in the most decent and straightforward way, a terrible climax to an increasingly difficult season.

UEFA's punishment, ordering Spurs to play their next two European home ties at least 250 kilometres from White Hart Lane, was largely academic. There was no more Europe for Spurs in the 1970s, and in 1980 came UEFA's 25th anniversary amnesty. For some reason Spurs were left out of the general lifting of such punishments, and director Geoff Richardson had to appeal on behalf of the club before they were included. 'I think they just forgot about us,' he said.

NICHOLSON'S LAST STAND

Nicholson, his resignation plans temporarily shelved, returned to try and pick up the pieces. He faced problems on nearly all fronts, most of all with Chivers, who had finally made it clear that White Hart Lane was no longer big enough for both of them. It had been Chivers' goals which had kept Spurs afloat over the past few seasons but now his feud with Nicholson erupted into another bitter pay row. Chivers publicly called Spurs' offer 'rubbish' and demanded a transfer. He was joined by one of Nicholson's young proteges, defender Mike Dillon, who had made a handful of senior appearances and was now demanding suitable reward. Nicholson gave the same reply to both: 'No one leaves until I've found replacements.' That was the rub. Replacements were proving almost impossible to find. Nicholson tried to sign Duncan McKenzie from Nottingham Forest, David Hay from Celtic and Chelsea's Bill Garner. But they all said no, McKenzie preferring Leeds, Hay Chelsea and Garner staying where he was.

Nicholson's one transfer success in the summer of 1974 was persuading Alfie Conn, a young left-sided midfield player with hippie-length hair, to sign from Glasgow Rangers for £150,000. Nicholson had £500,000 to spend on

John Toshack tries to evade Alan Mullery in another Anfield clash of the early 1970s. Spurs did not win a match there for 73 years. Mullery joined the club from Fulham in 1964 and returned there eight years later, but not until after a fairy tale return to the side which saw him score a vital semi-final goal against AC Milan and another against Wolves in the final to help lift the UEFA Cup. Mullery suffered during his early days at the club by being compared with the great half-back line of the Double year: 'People always told me what Dave Mackay had done. Like telling me the wonders he performed after his injury. You wanted to say it's me, it's my injury, this is how I feel and I'm not putting it on.' Mullery, as Spurs' captain, lifted the club's second European trophy at White Hart Lane on 17 May 1972. It was also, as it happened, his last ever game for the club.

RIGHT: Mike England gets above AC Milan defender Karl-Heinz Schnellinger during the UEFA Cup semi-final first leg in London on 5 April 1972. The Italians went into a 1–0 lead but Steve Perryman scored twice, once from 20 yards and again from nearly 35 yards, to give Spurs hope for the second leg. Despite England heading against his own crossbar at the San Siro, Tottenham came away from Milan with a 1–1 draw and were through to the final, where they met Wolves.

RIGHT BELOW: The clock at Molineux shows 8.40pm as Martin Chivers rises to meet a Mike England free-kick (one of Spurs' rehearsed moves), outjump Frank Munro and put the Londoners 1-0 ahead in the UEFA Cup final first leg. Woves equalised from a McCalliog free-kick, but Chivers made it 2-1 with perhaps the best goal he ever scored for the club. Picking the ball up near the half-way line, he went past two defenders and shot on the run from all of thirty yards. The return leg was a perfect finale to the season for Spurs, the last game and the biggest crowd – 54, 303. Mullery's headed goal made it 1-1 and the trophy was Spurs' – their eighth victory in their eighth cup final.

new players but, as the new season opened with a series of calamitous defeats, revelations were made in the Press about one of main reasons pinning Spurs to the foot of the table. Nicholson claimed that several top-class players (not those mentioned here), and especially those from London, were demanding five-figure sums 'under the counter' to move. It was Spurs' persistent refusal to pay these sums, as Sidney Wale confirmed, that lay behind Nicholson's failure to bring star names to White Hart Lane in recent years.

Here one reaches one of the game's most delicate areas, one that most fans were unaware of during the 1970s and which was not revealed publicly in all its details until Terry Yorath's attempts to negotiate his own departure from White Hart Lane in 1980. It is a subject which everyone in the game is extremely sensitive about (under-the-counter payments are dubious because they are out-side the tax system though, as Nicholson points out, a player can ask for a tax-free sum quite legitimately – as long as the club is prepared to pay the massive resulting Inland Revenue bill itself) but which has come to dominate the movement of players. Several seemingly incomprehensible moves, and numerous disputes, would be made only too comprehensible if the full financial details were revealed. Spurs have maintained an excellent reputation through this period, being among the foremost of those clubs which have unsuccessfully tried to outlaw illegitimate, unnecessary and excessive payments. In the late 1970s this attitude also began to extend to transfer fees.

When Spurs, clearly in need of a goalscorer, were linked with Andy Gray and, as the traditional Bank of England club, were expected to pay £1.5 million for him, Sidney Wale became exasperated by newspaper pressure on the club to bid. 'We are expected to pay out more than one and a half million pounds for a single player, plus wages. That is more than we took at the gate in the whole of last season. Is it sane economics to spend more than your entire gate money on one man?' It was a policy Spurs pursued with some success and it was not until 1988 that they paid £1 million for a player (Paul Gascoigne). The attitude to advertising was also conservative. They were the last of the major clubs to hold out against making their ground a TV-inspired billboard, not allowing hoardings around the pitch until as late as 1972.

Back in 1974 the strain of the Chivers dispute, coupled with the club's deepening League crisis, reached breaking point for Nicholson in a week when Burnley's Martin Dobson became the fourth player to reject a move to White Hart Lane and Spurs, without a point, plunged to their fourth successive League defeat. Dobson, a cultured England player whose pedigree would have brought some much-needed class to the weak midfield, preferred to stay in Lancashire with a £300,000 move to Everton, where he failed to fulfil his massive earlier promise. At White Hart Lane, Spurs, who had lost 1–0 in midweek to newly promoted Carlisle, faced their fourth match of the season at home to Manchester City. It was 28 August, and Nicholson's last stand. He recalled Martin Chivers, who had been dropped for the first three matches, replaced Pratt with McGrath, and, with the exception of Neighbour, fielded the side which had lost in Rotterdam. A crowd of 20,079 watched in dismay as Spurs lost 2–1. It equalled their worst ever League start 62 years before. For Nicholson defeat was the final straw. On the Saturday evening, after 38 years with Tottenham, the last 15 of them as the most successful manager in their history and as one of perhaps the three most successful with any British club ever, he resigned.

'You're only as good as your last result' . . . no-one except a perfectionist such as Nicholson himself would say that his reign had been anything other than outstanding. Yet now there was the danger that, if he stayed any longer, the club and the man would destroy each other. 'The pressures had been building up over several months,' said Sidney Wale. 'Few people knew it at the time but Bill was under a lot of strain. He'd had a bad time over contracts and some players really got him down. The opening results of the season finished him. He felt he just couldn't take any more.'

Although Wale wouldn't say so publicly, there is no doubt that the contract dispute which upset Nicholson most was with Martin Chivers. A passage from *The Glory Game* gives an idea of the two men's relationship. After a poor Spurs performance in a 0–0 draw against Nantes in the 1971–72 UEFA Cup, Chivers called Nantes a poor team: "You mean *we* had some poor players" said Bill. He was looking straight at Chivers. He hadn't named any names, but there was no doubt which poor player he was referring to. "What do you mean?" said Chivers, becoming suddenly violent and animated.'

Chivers' love-hate relationship with the club through this period was its most intriguing feature. Probably against his own wishes, Chivers became the dominant factor in its success. When he was playing well, and scoring goals, Spurs could win trophies. When he wasn't, they didn't. It is inconceivable that Spurs could have reached those four finals without Chivers up front, and his two goals at Wolverhampton in the UEFA Cup final could probably not have been scored by any other player of the period. Yet this placed too much responsibility on him. If he had a bad game the team tended to have a bad game, because they had lost their goalscoring threat (the need for defences to mark him closely was the primary means Spurs used to create space for *other* players to score goals, particularly at set-pieces). So his bad games were much more noticeable than those of other players, and he would receive much more criticism, both inside and outside the club, because of that. In Chivers' case there can be little doubt that matters were out of balance – the team was simply too dependent on him – and similar recriminations were to be heard after his performance for England against Poland in 1973.

The other strange, almost unreal, factor about Nicholson's (and his team's) perceived problems at this point was that they had reached a cup final in each of the previous four seasons, and won three of them. This, while not unprecedented, is very rare in the modern game. Reactions to the side at the time were a statement about Nicholson's past successes, and the levels of expectation which he had engendered in the club and its supporters, rather than any detached view of the club's actual situation or the team's abilities. As Nicholson said at one point in this period: 'Here I am contemplating problems and so called failure while someone like Matt Gillies (then manager at Nottingham Forest) would give anything to be in my shoes.' In addition to the four cup finals, Nicholson's side had reached the semi-finals of the League Cup in 1968–69 (beaten 2–1 by Arsenal) and in 1971–72 (beaten 5–4 by Chelsea) as well as the UEFA Cup semi-finals in 1972–73. Seven semi-finals in six seasons was surely enough to keep the most fickle fan interested.

Despite the board's request that he reconsider, Nicholson's decision was final. He would never be thought of as anything but a success, but now he was tired and not a little disillusioned and he was surely right in thinking that the time for a change had come. Geoff Richardson, then a director of the club, stressed that the board never asked Nicholson to resign, nor did it ever wish him to leave.

The option of general manager was never seriously considered by Nicholson, no matter how hard the Press may have pushed it. He had resigned and expected to leave the club. He had no desire for an administrative post and Tottenham, with the example of Matt Busby at Manchester United in the immediate past, would not necessarily have thought it the best solution. If a new man was to come in, faced with the near impossible task of following the legendary Bill Nicholson, then there would have to be changes made.

Nicholson's first choice as successor was his assistant, Eddie Baily. 'The age difference was the same as Shankly and Paisley,' says Nicholson, 'and it worked well enough there.' After Baily he supported Blanchflower and Johnny Giles, either individually or as a team.

Kevin Keegan and Alan Mullery take off during a League game on 4 September 1971. Spurs won 2–0 with goals from Chivers and Peters. Nicholson said of Mullery: 'He was honest and dedicated and, of course, he was there at just the right time in 1972. It couldn't have worked out better for him.'

It would be foolish to pretend that such a successful era ended, or could have ended, without some regrets and not a little hurt. A new manager, if any outsider took the job, would inevitably be walking on eggs, trying to take account of the sensitivities of staff who had, in some cases, been with the club for decades.

But even the greatest of institutions do have to undergo change from time to time though it is certainly true that the change-over might have been handled more smoothly if one or other of the alternative candidates had been given the job. As it was, the Press, at least, seemed convinced that Danny Blanchflower's time had come.

BLANCHFLOWER REJECTED

The next seven seasons took Spurs through troughs of depression to achievements that didn't seem possible in their darkest hours. There was another change of manager, relegation to the Second Division for the first time since 1935, instant promotion, the arrival of the Argentinian World Cup stars, Ardiles and

Villa, and finally, in 1981, the magical first year of the new decade, victory in the FA Cup. Spurs were back in Europe. But success took years of painstaking work and as Spurs crashed from one disaster to another in that traumatic 1974–75 season, Brian James, in his *Daily Mail* column, asked how different things might have been had Nicholson been allowed to name his own successor. He raised the point as Spurs, still struggling near the foot of the First Division under the new managership of Terry Neill, faced a Liverpool side challenging Derby for the League title. Ten months earlier, Spurs and Liverpool had met more nearly as equals, watched and presided over by the two men who had created them, Nicholson and Shankly. A few months later both would be gone. One difference was that Shankly sat in on the board meeting which selected Bob Paisley as his successor, while Nicholson had no say at White Hart Lane. James argued, fairly, that if Spurs had only groomed a successor in the way the well-oiled Liverpool machine had groomed Paisley, the White Hart Lane change-over could have been made without the traumas which followed.

Spurs didn't ask Nicholson's advice because, in the words of Sidney Wale, 'It was the manager's job to manage' and, in keeping with their conservative image, they attempted to make the appointment as straightforward as possible by advertising the post and choosing a successor from the applicants. But they had to contend first with a massive Press campaign in favour of the man said to be the number one choice of the fans, and arguably the one everyone was expecting to take over, Double hero Danny Blanchflower. Victor Railton confidently predicted in the *London Evening News* that Blanchflower would be appointed, while other names being touted for the job included Gordon Jago of Queen's Park Rangers, Dave Mackay of Derby and Johnny Giles, player-manager of the Irish Republic and soon to retire at Leeds. Of all the likely candidates, Blanchflower was the most obvious, though he himself would have preferred Johnny Giles alongside him as coach. Immediately identified with the glory years, Blanchflower was a man who shared Nicholson's idealism but was still young enough, at 47, not to share his despair. He had retired from the game in 1964 vowing never to go into management and spending the years instead trying to put an errant soccer world to rights from the platform of sports journalism in the *Sunday Express*.

Nicholson possibly believed he could play king-maker by spending several hours persuading Blanchflower to become a candidate. Plans were hatched, prospective transfers tentatively negotiated. In one deal, Don Givens and Gerry Francis were to come from QPR in exchange for the still uncontracted Chivers. A whole new side was being planned. But at the end of the day, Blanchflower didn't get the job because he didn't apply for it. That, however, was arguably a convenient escape route for the board, who had not been pro-Blanchflower from the outset. 'I know Bill wanted Danny to have the job,' said Wale, 'and I know they discussed it together. I told Bill that if he wanted Danny to be considered, Danny would have to apply like the others. He never did. It's as simple as that.' Wale did not try to hide his own reasons for not being a Blanchflower enthusiast, although he claims: 'I could have been persuaded either way.' Wale said he believed that Blanchflower had been out of the game too long to make a return at the highest level of management without any experience. 'I felt he was out of touch,' said Wale later. 'Also, over the years I'd come to look on him, through his columns in the *Sunday Express*, as more of a football critic than a prospective manager. I believe, too, that his subsequent records in charge of Chelsea and Northern Ireland proved me right.'

Privately, the board had other reasons for opposing Blanchflower. They feared that he would challenge their authority as he had done constantly as a player (they remembered how he gave up the club captaincy in that row about how far he could extend his responsibilities), and that he would ruffle the hitherto calm waters of White Hart Lane. Under Nicholson, Spurs had had a low profile manager. ('I'm not a man who's desperate to see his name in the papers' Nicholson once said.) The only news, until the recent troubles, had been good news and directors could sleep soundly at night knowing they wouldn't find the club's name plastered all over the back pages. With his own Press connections, and a long standing dislike of Football Association regulations which in theory prevented any manager or player going into print without his club's approval (when he was a player Blanchflower discussed his newspaper pieces with the club only after insisting that he would not change anything anyway), he could have proved a very independent force. No greater change from the Nicholson era could probably be imagined.

'I know it sounds hopelessly optimistic,' said Wale, 'but the type of manager we were looking for was someone like Bill, a man who could take over and get on with the job. I don't know if the idea of following in Bill's footsteps put anyone off, but we were very disappointed with the response to our advert.' In light of their requirements, and in what was perceived as a snub for Blanchflower, the board's subsequent appointment was a paradox. Not only that, it upset Nicholson, angered Spurs fans and stunned the soccer business.

In naming Hull City's Terry Neill the board had chosen someone with a good deal more in common with Blanchflower than with Nicholson; moreover, as a former and recent long-serving Arsenal player, Neill was among the very last people the fans wanted. Nicholson's pride was obviously hurt by the board's decision. 'I thought they'd appoint Danny,' he said. 'I don't even know Terry Neill.'

Capped a then record 59 times for Northern Ireland (thus beating the record held by Blanchflower and Billy Bingham), Neill had spent 12 years as centre-half at Arsenal before serving his 'apprenticeship' player-managing Second Division Hull and the Northern Ireland team. Like Blanchflower, Neill came from Belfast, shared the same energetic enthusiasm for the game, though not Blanchflower's brilliance, and had also captained club and country. And, while not as articulate as Blanchflower, he still had plenty to say for

himself; indeed arguably rather too much, as the Spurs board would find to their regret.

Neill's four years at Hull were, by his own admission, an undistinguished start to his new career. The best Hull finished was fifth, and that was in his first season. After his period in charge they slowly descended to the Fourth Division. He was 32 when he applied for the Spurs job, offering a happy-go-lucky football philosophy that was in stark contrast to the austere regime of Nicholson. It was Bill Shankly who once said: 'Football's not a matter of life and death – it's more important than that'; Neill said of the Spurs' job: 'If I fail, I've got a wonderful wife and two beautiful daughters to go back to.' And, good for him, he meant it.

His Arsenal connections didn't bother the board for the simple reason that, unlike the fans, they've generally got on well with their Highbury counterparts. So why in the end did Spurs appoint him? Said Sidney Wale later, perhaps with a touch of sadness: 'He was clearly the best candidate.' But Neill's selection was a unanimous decision (he was hardly responsible for the quality of the opposition) and he took over as the First Division's youngest manager with a simple but daunting brief: to keep Spurs up. It was 13 September; Spurs were still bottom with just two points from their first six League games and had just been knocked out of the League Cup 4-0 at home by Middlesborough.

Neill's relaxed approach ('I want you all to go out and enjoy yourselves' he started by telling his struggling team) brought mixed results. They began Neill's term with a 2–1 win over West Ham and a 3–2 away success at Wolves, going on to collect 15 points from their next 13 League matches. Helped by some points-earning goals from his new striker John Duncan, bought from Dundee on 19 October for £125,000, they slowly began to edge away from the bottom. But a New Year relapse once again brought back the spectre of relegation and questions began to be raised in the Press about Neill's apparently unconcerned attitude in the face of crisis.

Neill was under constant fire from the fans, too. 'They made it clear they didn't want me from the outset,' he says. 'My every word and action was scrutinised for its level of devotion towards Tottenham Hotspur. It was a test of loyalty. In other words, what was I doing with THEIR club. During his early months in charge, Neill correctly identified and tried to rectify one of the malaises which had developed under Nicholson, the problem of over-staffing. 'Competition for first team places was healthy,' said Neill, 'but in Spurs' case, places in the reserves which should have been for up-and-coming players, the Glenn Hoddles, Steve Walfords and Neil McNabs, were being taken by players who had no future at the club. The paths to the top were being blocked.' McNab was a case in point, says Neill. Signed by Nicholson from Morton in February 1974, the teenage Scottish youth international midfielder had been playing games in the South East Counties League for the youth side when he should have been on the fringe of the first team.

For season 1974–75, the staff numbered 32 professionals and 13 apprentices, but by the end of the season those totals would be

OPPOSITE TOP: Ralph Coates is hugged by an admirer at the end of the second leg of the UEFA Cup Final in 1972. Coates' arrival from Burnley was a matter of some secrecy and he actually signed for the club in the back of a car outside a Staffordshire hotel. At the time there was talk of Burnley wanting to keep Arsenal out of the bidding, but Nicholson insists that Burnley manager Jimmy Adamson was simply determined to honour his promise that Spurs could have first option on Coates.

OPPOSITE BOTTOM: Alan Gilzean and a very young Steve Perryman celebrate the 1972 UEFA Cup victory over Wolves.

considerably fewer as Neill cleared the decks for his younger players to emerge and time caught up with the remaining stars from Nicholson's final days.

First to go of the old guard were Martin Peters and Mike England. Following a 3-0 home defeat by Leicester in February, which left Spurs even more firmly embedded in the relegation struggle, Neill sold Peters to Norwich for £40,000 – where he was to enjoy a renaissance under John Bond – while England walked out after a row, to retire from the English game at the age of 32. The normally placid Peters had refused to watch a game against Stoke after rowing about tactics and being substituted. Back in the League, Spurs' dismal run of only three points from their first ten New Year games was halted by three successive wins over Easter. But they continued to live dangerously until the very last game of the season. The drama did wonders for the gates. Only six months earlier, for the home game against newly promoted Carlisle on 16 October, Spurs had been watched by a mere 12,823 fans, their lowest League gate since the Second World War (though it should be said that it was a mid-week game, it had rained all day and Carlisle did not exactly pack the grounds they played). For their penultimate home game against Chelsea, 50,998 watched Spurs win 2–0. A week later 43,762 were at Highbury for a 1–0 defeat by Arsenal which left Spurs needing victory in their last match, at home to Leeds two days later on Monday 28 April, to stay in the First Division. Anything less and they, not Luton, might be relegated. Neill's preparation included calling in a hypnotherapist to convince the team they were going to win. The idea worked, or rather it didn't fail, because in front of a 49,886 crowd Spurs stormed to a 4–2 win with two goals from a back-in-favour Cyril Knowles and one each from Conn and Chivers. It was the sort of Spurs performance of which Nicholson would have been proud. But for Neill victory was a bitter sweet sensation. 'It was as if we'd won the Cup,' he says, 'but I'd worked 24 hours a day, seven days a week to keep Spurs in the First Division and I'd taken a lot of stick from the fans for my trouble. Yet here they all were chanting my name and calling for me to go out on to the pitch and acknowledge their cheers. Did I go? I went straight home. I'd paid my dues.'

BURKINSHAW'S ARRIVAL

Spurs fans don't thank Neill for very much these days but one of his appointments which must warrant their gratitude is Keith Burkinshaw, brought in as coach during the summer of 1975 (Neill's Hull coach, Wilf Dixon, who'd replaced Eddie Baily as assistant manager in the change-over, was moved to youth recruitment). Burkinshaw had been sacked by Newcastle following defeat by Liverpool in the 1974 FA Cup final and, though he didn't know him personally, Neill had heard enough about his qualities to want him at White Hart Lane.

Perhaps it was because the fans couldn't find it in their hearts to say a good word about Neill, that Burkinshaw got much of the praise for helping the club finish a respectable ninth in the First Division the following season and reach the semi-finals of the League

Cup. Certainly Neill didn't do his Tottenham cause any good by disappearing to Highbury so soon after joining, but the facts are that with him Spurs returned from the brink of relegation to within 90 minutes of another cup final, while without him they sank like a stone. The fairest assessment is that, together, Neill and Burkinshaw would have struck up a very successful partnership. In his seven years at Newcastle, the last four of them as first team coach, Burkinshaw's side enjoyed a spell as a First Division force, reaching the FA Cup final in 1974, and, even after his departure, maintaining enough momentum to reach the 1976 League Cup final (ironically, at Spurs' expense in the semi-final). Two seasons later they were relegated. When Burkinshaw arrived at Spurs, Neill had already had five years' managerial experience at Second and First Division level to Burkinshaw's none. The partnership equation of good coach plus experienced manager equals successful team starts to make sense when it's remembered that, after Neill teamed up with Don Howe at Arsenal, the Gunners had their greatest run of success since their own Double year. Burkinshaw would have his day but, like Neill before him, it would take five years.

A combination of economic factors and Neill's desire to streamline his squad saw the turnaround in their fortunes on a playing staff reduced from 32 professionals the previous season to 26 for 1975–76. Their number was strengthened by the arrival in September 1975 of a tall, powerful if inelegant central defender, Willie Young, who cost £80,000 from Aberdeen, and, two months later, striker Gerry Armstrong from Irish club Bangor. As essentially a players' manager, Neill had a cordial but distant relationship with the board. 'During the first 18 months they let me get on with the job without interference,' he said later. But three events during the spring and summer of 1976 brought Neill's brief Tottenham reign to a swift and sour finale.

OVER TO HIGHBURY

First, in autumn 1975, the board heard from the Press (and vetoed) plans to try and bring Dutch star Johan Cruyff to Tottenham (they needn't have bothered, since if subsequent attempts to bring Cruyff to a British club were anything to go by, Neill was on a wild goose chase). The incident which followed in the spring of 1976 was a far more serious challenge to Neill's authority, not so much in its nature as in the manner in which it was done. It happened on the morning of Sunday 25 April, as the players prepared to set off on their close-season tour of Australia and the Pacific. Neill had promised a seat on the coach to Heathrow Airport for the only fan travelling with the party, 78-year-old retired bookmaker Mr Fred Rhye, a devoted follower who had missed only three of their matches in 40 years and was popular throughout the club. Rhye's standing at White Hart Lane can be gauged by the fact that he was the only fan to have a place in the official car park. Yet Sidney Wale, for reasons which he went to some lengths to explain, chose the occasion to embarrass Neill by publicly countermanding his orders. Rhye was told he would have to find alternative transport to the airport (he was paying his own way to follow Spurs) and Neill was left to hurriedly organise a taxi.

London clubs often have difficulty with enthusiastic fans, and the arranging of rival celebration parties after Cup wins has caused both Arsenal and Spurs considerable heartaches in recent years. Rhye was never in this category, though the incident does bring to mind the fact that, when the Supporters Club was founded in 1948, it had to be called the Spurs Supporters Club because permission to use the official club name was withheld.

Wale defended his action by saying: 'It was always a firm club rule that fans were not allowed to travel on the team coach, for insurance reasons among others. If we made an allowance for one fan, we'd get everyone climbing aboard. I knew Fred Rhye well, and, among other things, felt that we were being rash in encouraging him to undertake such an arduous trip when he was ill.' (Rhye subsequently decided to return from Canada.) The incident brought to the surface the personality clash which had been underlying Neill's presence at Spurs almost from the day he arrived. Neill's expansive, aggressive approach was always bound to be at odds with the more cautious Wale and his colleagues and it needed only a contretemps like this to bring it into the open. Neill recalled: 'I'd been aware for some time of a growing aloofness by the board towards myself and it made it very difficult for me to go into the job with all my heart and soul. The coach affair was the beginning of the end. When a manager can't decide who can and can't travel on the team coach, what next?' The very same point might have been made, of course, by the directors.

With relations soured before the tour had even got under way, and a long and tiring itinerary ahead taking in Canada, New Zealand, Fiji and Australia, the outlook was stormy. Neill won't admit to deliberately provoking the showdown which led to the final breach, but his actions at the end of the tour had that effect. As a reward for winning all nine matches, Neill wanted to give some of his players and backroom staff a bonus out of the proceeds of the tour. He maintains that perfectly straightforward means could have been found to make such payments, but the directors, and Wale in particular, were not prepared to sanction them. Wale insists that Neill was rash in promising the players something he could not guarantee they were going to get – hence the untenable situation in which Neill then found himself. The party arrived back in England on 24 May and Neill handed in his resignation a fortnight later. It was another three weeks, on 30 June, before the board unanimously accepted it after a four-hour meeting. They were not hoping Neill would change his mind, rather the delay was because Sidney Wale was not prepared to cut short his holiday to resolve the matter sooner. The parting of the ways was thus mutual. 'I didn't feel it was up to me to ask Terry to change his mind,' said Wale. 'He was still under contract and he'd walked out on us.' Neill said 'They didn't take me seriously. I was treated like a naughty schoolboy who didn't know how lucky he was.'

As soon as news of Neill's resignation reached Highbury, Arsenal chairman Denis Hill-Wood telephoned Wale to see if the

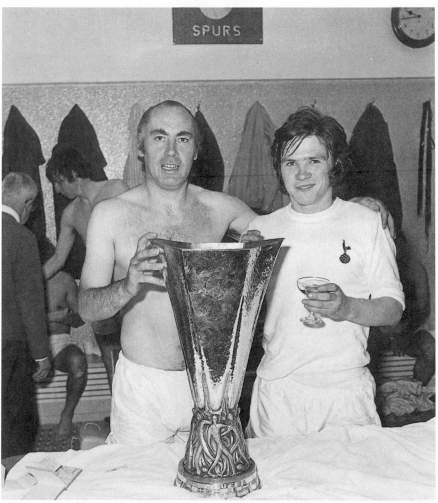

way was clear to offer Neill a job, and, within a fortnight of quitting Spurs, he was installed as Arsenal manager in succession to Bertie Mee. If it seems strange how, with two clubs as close and as big as Arsenal and Spurs, one should be almost relieved to see the back of their manager while the other strives to take him on, Wale summed up the reasons when he said: 'Terry wasn't the sort of manager we were used to. But as an Arsenal player and club captain, he was highly thought of by Denis Hill-Wood, and rightly so.' Neill was predictably branded a traitor by Spurs fans, but he still insists: 'I know a lot of people thought I was an opportunist and was using Tottenham for my own ends, but I can say in all honesty that I had already made up my mind to resign from Spurs before I knew of the Arsenal vacancy. Spurs still mean something very special to me and I was proud to be asked to manage them.'

Wale was understandably bitter about the Neill affair, writing in the 1977–78 handbook: 'It can be seen that the decline of our club was not halted by the appointment made following the resignation of Bill Nicholson in August 1974.' He might have been more favourably disposed if Neill's brief reign had not merely postponed the inevitable. After 15 years with one manager, the club could not absorb the shock of having three in under two years. The season after Neill's departure they were relegated to the Second Division for the first time since 1935.

Keith Burkinshaw, whose only other claim to fame prior to joining Spurs was that he had been in the same form as Michael Parkinson at Barnsley Grammar School, had stayed well in the background throughout the Neill dispute. He had played mainly for Workington, where he had scored one of the goals in that unsung club's 9–1 defeat of Barrow in the Football League Cup in 1964, a record victory in the competition which lasted nearly 20 years. He had gone on to enjoy brief managerial experience at Workington and Scunthorpe and he clearly had aspirations of his own. When Neill took him on as coach, Burkinshaw was shrewd enough to get an assurance that Neill would not stand in his way if a manager's job came up. He could scarcely have believed it would be the Tottenham job itself that he would be applying for inside a year, or given much for his chances of getting it. His only experience in the transfer jungle, for instance, was spending three months trying to raise the £300 Workington needed to pay for a Scottish junior. With Neill's exit leaving the rest of the Spurs backroom staff exposed to a new manager's purge, Burkinshaw acted quickly to leave the directors in no doubt where his loyalties lay. By applying for Neill's job he effectively killed two birds with one stone.

As one of the game's quiet men, Burkinshaw already had a lot going for him so far as Spurs were concerned. A workmanlike wing-half of moderate ability as a player, he had been rejected by Wolves before joining Liverpool. He made a handful of first-team appearances and spent most of his time in the reserves. He had just concluded a seven-year spell as a coach at Newcastle, the last four of them, between 1971 and 1975, in charge of the first team. In his final full season at St James' Park, Newcastle reached the FA Cup final – their first since 1955. His reward was the sack.

Burkinshaw believed that the good working relationship he had established with the Spurs players helped his claim to the managership. But what clinched the job for him in the summer of 1976 was the impression he made on Sidney Wale during the fateful close season tour. While relations between Wale and Neill were at their lowest ebb, Burkinshaw was quietly getting on with the job in the background. 'Doing the work while Terry appeared on television,' was how Wale put it.

'On the tour I got the chance to get to know Keith,' said Wale. 'I found him hard-working, honest and I knew he was well-liked by the players. It was those qualities which convinced the board when we considered his application.' Burkinshaw's ideas about attacking football were also very much in the Spurs tradition, although it was to take five long years to bring them to fruition.

'I grew up in the era of Read Madrid, di Stefano, Puskas – they were my heroes and they influenced me more than anyone else influenced my approach to the game. My philosophy has always been that you've got to entertain, but you can only play like that nowadays if you've got players willing to get back when it matters.'

Burkinshaw's ideal had to be put into cold storage in his first season in command. Spurs were playing with their backs to the wall from the moment they lost 3–1 at Ipswich in the first match of the season. Burkinshaw analysed the problem simply when he said: 'We just weren't good enough.' More specifically they were weak at the back and were beset by problems in attack. John Duncan, who had been top scorer for the previous two seasons, missed the first eleven games with a back injury which limited his first team appearances that season to just nine games, and in which he scored only four times. Defensively, the team started badly and then got worse. In consecutive away games in October and November they conceded 13 goals, including the club's then heaviest defeat when they went down 8–2 at Derby. The one defender who emerged with his reputation unscathed from the winter blitzkrieg was goalkeeper Pat Jennings. 'He didn't stand a chance,' said Burkinshaw.

Burkinshaw's early forays into the transfer market came before the full extent of the team's shortcomings were apparent. His first buy was £75,000 forward Ian Moores from Stoke in August. Peter Taylor, a winger of capricious skills who had played for England while still in the Third Division, and whom Neill had already tried to sign, came from Crystal Palace for £125,000 in September. When his defence crumbled, Burkinshaw imported John Gorman from Carlisle in November, but still the defeats piled up. On the cup front, the team suffered the ignominy of losing at home to Third Division Wrexham in the third round of the League Cup, and equally embarrassing was their exit at the first hurdle from the FA Cup when they lost 1–0 at Second Division Cardiff.

For the League game against Birmingham on 19 March Burkinshaw played his final card. Steve Perryman, club captain and mid-field ever present, was switched to the back four where Burkinshaw felt his leadership qualities, quick reading of the game and overall purposefulness could marshal a department which had lost all coordination and confidence. The move

helped bring about 12 points from the last 13 League games of the season, but it came too late to save Spurs. The killer result was a 5–0 defeat at Manchester City in the penultimate match. Spurs were relegated for the first time in four decades.

If anyone's knives were out for Burkinshaw, Wale did a remarkably good job of keeping them out of his manager's back. 'I didn't expect the sack,' said Burkinshaw, 'but in view of our performance that season, they would have been justified in getting rid of me. I didn't think I was a failure. I knew where we were going and that what I was doing was right. I could only hope that the board thought the same way.'

Spurs means different things to different people but it is generally a club where players and staff, once settled, stay for a long time. Throughout Burkinshaw's season as manager, he had always received the backing of Wale, even when relegation looked a certainty. 'I remember travelling by car to Manchester City with Keith on the day we were relegated,' recalled Wale. 'It was one of the saddest days of my life. But as soon as we got home, the first thing I did was to phone Keith's wife Joyce and reassure her that his job was safe.'

At the next board meeting, Wale told his four fellow directors: 'I don't know if any of you have any idea about trying to get rid of Keith Burkinshaw, but one thing I must remind you of is that it was we five who appointed him.' Not another word was spoken on the subject.

Despite the setbacks of that season, Wale had continued to be impressed by Burkinshaw's dedication and hard work. 'He showed many of the qualities of Bill Nicholson. Like Bill, he was never a publicity-seeker. He was honest, hard-working and, in short, more the sort of manager we'd been used to and we liked.'

THE JENNINGS THUNDERBOLT

Two decisions in his first year in charge, which were to prove of long-lasting significance, reflected Burkinshaw's awareness as a tactician, but his lack of experience as a manager. The single most contentious issue of the decade was, of course, Pat Jennings' sale to Arsenal and it still seems surprising that the club should have allowed the deal to go through. It wasn't so much the sale itself, which on the face of it seemed reasonable at the time, but the buyers which should have caused alarm. Given Burkinshaw's relative inexperience in the transfer market, someone should have at least given him the benefit of one timeworn business dictum: 'Don't sell on your own doorstep.' The repercussions of the Jennings sale rebounded on Burkinshaw with three-fold force. He had already sold Willie Young to Highbury in March 1976, and Jennings's departure was coupled with the sale, also to Arsenal,

Gerry Armstrong and Leicester's Steve Sims fight for the ball on 14 May 1977, Spurs' last day in the First Division for over a year. They won the game 2–0 with goals from Jimmy Holmes and John Pratt but it did them little good. They were already condemned to Second Division football for the first time in nearly three decades and eventually finished the season in bottom position. Armstrong had joined Spurs late in 1975 from Irish club Bangor but, with the arrival of Archibald and Crooks, was to move to Watford.

133

of defender Steve Walford. All three proved bargain buys for Terry Neill, none more so than Jennings, as Spurs fans were never to let Burkinshaw forget. Neill said of the deals: 'They were good for me, but I was conscious that Keith was inexperienced.'

Young was sold right at the climax of the relegation battle because, despite his aerial strength, he possessed few of the ground skills a purist like Burkinshaw required in his players. At 6ft 3in and 14 stone, Young made up in energy and enthusiasm what he lacked in finesse. Fans love a trier, and Young was immediately adopted by Highbury's North Bank in the way he had been by the Park Lane End. But Burkinshaw remained unimpressed. As a former player who perhaps shared Young's relative lack of natural ability, it was all the more important to Burkinshaw to create a team without such shortcomings. With Spurs' defence taking most of the rap for their dismal performances that season, Young was sacrificed when Perryman was switched into the back four. Terry Neill had bought Young in the first place and was still an admirer of the big man's capabilities, so a move to Highbury suited all concerned.

The sale of Jennings was under very different circumstances. He was 31 at the time and the previous season had set a new club appearance record of 449 League matches, passing Ted Ditchburn's total of 418. He'd been voted Football Writers' Footballer of the Year in 1973, the Professional Footballers' Player of the Year in 1975–76 and had been made an MBE in the Queen's Birthday Honours List the same year. He was also Northern Ireland's most capped player, having passed Terry Neill's record of 59 caps in the 1975–76 season.

Standing 6ft tall with hands as big as frying pans, he was the complete goalkeeper, probably the best in Britain and perhaps the world throughout the 1970s. Bought from Watford by Bill Nicholson in June 1964, for a bargain £30,000, Jennings had spent twelve illustrious years at White Hart Lane, collecting an FA Cup winners' medal in 1967, League Cup winners' medals in 1971 and 1973 and a UEFA Cup winners' medal in 1972. 'Pat,' says Sidney Wale, 'had seen it all and done it all.' Although Jennings never asked for a transfer, it was almost an embarrassment for Spurs to have to ask a goalkeeper of his calibre to play in the Second Division. Understandably, he didn't want to leave the top division.

There were other factors to be considered, too. Cuts would have to be made to help the club pay their way on projected lower gates, and Jennings would be an expensive item on the wage bill. Spurs also believed they had a capable deputy in Barry Daines, and adequate cover in Welsh Under-21 international Mark Kendall. A former Spurs apprentice, Daines was seven years younger than Jennings and had stood in competently for him 19 times during the 1976–77 season when the senior player was injured. More to the point, Daines had told Spurs that he could see no future for himself at the club if Jennings stayed. The club saw it as something of a rerun of the Banks/Shilton debate at Leicester.

Wale later agreed that Spurs were wrong in believing Jennings was approaching the end of his career and Burkinshaw is the first to admit that, in the light of experience, he wouldn't do the same thing again. It is interesting that it was Jennings' high quality performances for Arsenal through into the 1980s that finally convinced most league managers that keepers could go on, and arguably get better, into their mid- and even late-thirties. That changing attitude received an ironic twist, of course, when Spurs bought 33-year-old Ray Clemence from Liverpool in August 1981 to replace the more than competent Milija Aleksic. Burkinshaw pointed out, with some justification, that the consequences of the Jennings' sale would not have rebounded so hard on him if Daines' progress as goalkeeper hadn't been hampered by injury. Said Burkinshaw ruefully: 'Barry never came near to fulfilling his potential, while Pat went from strength to strength. I don't regret my decision, because I thought it was right at the time, but knowing what I now know, I wouldn't do it again.'

Burkinshaw's new tactical plan was drawn up simply to get Spurs out of the Second Division at the first attempt: in a sense, it didn't much matter how. Nonetheless, Burkinshaw's scheme was founded on his faith in attacking football, a brave philosophy in the Second Division, where it is often said that the only successful method is to kick your way out. By contrast Burkinshaw was determined that Spurs would 'play our way out.' To that end he retained the industrious Perryman in the back four, turned Terry Naylor and Jimmy Holmes into a couple of overlapping full-backs ready to attack down

LEFT: Pat Jennings saves his second penalty of the match against Liverpool on 31 March 1973. This one was taken by Tommy Smith, the first by Kevin Keegan. Other players in the picture are, left to right; Chris Lawler, Brian Hall, Larry Lloyd, Keegan, Smith, Steve Perryman, Alec Lindsay, Alan Gilzean, Martin Peters, Joe Kinnear, Phil Beal and Emlyn Hughes. It is interesting that Beal ('The best close marker I ever had,' said Nicholson) is the only defender to have rushed in with the intention of clearing any rebound. The game ended 1–1, Keegan scoring for Liverpool and Gilzean for Tottenham. Liverpool won the Championship that year, while this display virtually assured Jennings of the 'Footballer of the Year' award a few weeks later.
OPPOSITE BELOW: Martin Peters, who moved to Spurs from West Ham in an exchange deal with Jimmy Greaves in 1970, ghosts behind the Derby defence to get in a header. The game, played on 29 September 1973, was won 1-0 by Spurs with a Ralph Coates (left background) goal. Peters remained an England regular until the end of this season, eventually winning 34 caps during his time with the club. Only Mullery (with 35), Waddle (36), Lineker (38) Greaves (42) and Hoddle (44) have been picked for England more often while on Tottenham's books.

John Duncan (far left) slots home his second goal of the game against Stoke at the Victoria Ground on 2 November 1974. Defending are Mike Pejic, Denis Smith, John Marsh and Alan Dodd. The game ended 2–2. Joining Spurs from Dundee on 19 October for £125,000, Duncan went on to score 12 much needed League goals in 28 appearances. Chivers' (second from right) tally was dropping rapidly at this stage; he managed just 11 in all first class games this season. Chivers was eventually to finish with 118 goals from 278 League appearances for Spurs, while Duncan got 53 in 108 games.

the flanks, and took the team on a close-season tour to Scandinavia to see how the experiment worked. Results proved encouraging enough for Burkinshaw to pursue the plan in the club's pre-season triangular tournament at Umea in Sweden against Leicester, who finished eleventh in the First Division the previous season, and Royale Union of Belgium. Spurs won the tournament, defeating Royale 2–0 and Leicester 2–1, and Burkinshaw was ready to put the scheme to the real test in the Second Division. He later recalled the reaction of Leicester after seeing the new-style Spurs in action: 'You'll never get away with playing in the Second Division like that.' But Burkinshaw was convinced he'd got it right, and so were the team. 'Everyone was right behind it,' he said.

He didn't have to wait long to be vindicated. In their first match of the new season, Spurs beat Sheffield United 4–2 with goals from John Duncan, Chris Jones and two penalties from Keith Osgood. And that really was the story of their season. Spurs amassed 83 goals for their highest total since 1965, but their attacking style took its toll in defence where 49 goals were conceded. The result was that, despite being the Second Division's top scorers, Spurs were involved in a nail-biting race for the promotion line with Brighton, Southampton and Bolton. The issue was not resolved until the last Saturday of the season, with Spurs playing at Southampton and needing a draw to be certain of going up at Brighton's expense. With news reaching The Dell that Brighton were beating Blackpool, the wait for chairman Sidney Wale became sheer agony. 'I remember looking at my watch with about a quarter of an hour to go, and again at what I thought was at least five minutes later and the minute hand hadn't moved a millimetre!' His match was still scoreless.

If both scores stood at the final whistle, Spurs would be promoted on goal difference over Brighton. Victories like the 9–0 demolition of Bristol Rovers, the club's biggest win since their record 13–2 victory over Crewe, had given them a comfortable goal advantage over Brighton but the one thing they couldn't afford to do was lose. By a happy coincidence, Southampton also needed only a point to be sure of their promotion place so, with both teams content to defend, the match ended in the goalless draw. It was a result which drew more than a little cynical comment, particularly from along the South Coast at the Goldstone Ground, and an impartial observer who was not aware of all the circumstances would certainly have found it difficult to believe that Spurs and the Saints were desperately battling for a First Division place. If Wale offered a silent prayer of thanks afterwards, he would almost certainly have mentioned Southampton winger Tony Funnell: 'How he missed a couple of chances for them, I just don't know,' he recalled.

So Spurs were back in the First Division at their first attempt. And their return was a triumph not only for Burkinshaw's tactics but for Spurs' attacking style of play. For far from playing to smaller houses in the Second Division, they maintained the upward trend in their gates that Burkinshaw had managed to accelerate even in their relegation season. From a home average of 27,836 in Terry Neill's last season, attendances rose to 30,173 in the season Spurs went down and were swollen by an extra 68,119 fans in the Second Division for an average of 33,417. It was a figure bettered by only six other clubs in the Football League and came at a time when attendances generally were falling fast. 'I suppose people must have liked something we were doing,' said Burkinshaw afterwards.

1981

Two Cup wins in succession • Steve Perryman • Glenn Hoddle • The new stand • Chris Waddle • The return of Venables • The beginnings of financial problems

'*Wherever Spurs play, whether it's Manchester, Malta or Mauritius, we're famous. Soccer is about big clubs and star names, but most of all it's about people. You can be playing for the biggest club in the world with the biggest stars in the game, but if you don't enjoy it, if you don't get on with the people around you, you're wasting your time. I enjoy Spurs because at this club everyone, from the humblest backroom boy to the highest-paid player, is treated with equal respect. They're all equally important to our success. That's what makes Tottenham Hotspur a great football club.*'

Steve Perryman, club captain in the centenary season.

The transfer market is as much part of the mystique of the soccer world as magical goals and memorable cup wins. It figures every bit as much in the fan's imagination as, say, scoring the winning goal at Wembley. It is every schoolboy's dream for his favourite club to sign a star player. For fans in the fifties and sixties, the transfers to Italy and back of Jimmy Greaves, John Charles and Denis Law were just as exciting as almost anything that happened on the pitch. In the seventies the outstanding memory is unquestionably the coup which Keith Burkinshaw pulled off in the summer of 1978. Just as Bill Nicholson had changed the face of soccer 17 years earlier with his Double-winners, so Burkinshaw changed it that July. It was a time when virtually no foreigners played it the Football League, though no one who saw Argentina win the World Cup a month before could have failed to be impressed by the

Osvaldo Ardiles, Ricky Villa, Terry Yorath and Glenn Hoddle, four of the eight internationals on the club's books that season, line up against Crystal Palace on 6 October 1979. Villa scored the only goal in a 1–1 draw.

bewitching skills of their diminutive midfield player, Osvaldo Ardiles.

Every World Cup throws up a star or two who, through the worldwide media of television, radio and newspapers, suddenly become household names. The mesmerising one-twos Ardiles played with Mario Kempes instantly raised the hitherto unknown Argentinian schemer into the superstar bracket. But unlike many World Cups, where the victors merely pack up their kits and silently slip away, heroes today, gone tomorrow, the impact of Ardiles

was to reverberate around the clubs, shops, offices, pubs and homes of England like no other soccer event since the 1966 World Cup win. The first inkling that a sensational transfer deal was in the offing came in the few lines Fleet Street newspapers gave to a news agency report from Buenos Aires on Wednesday 28 June that Ardiles was to sign for Manchester United. Indeed the papers that did mention the item turned it into an emphatic denial from Sir Matt Busby that United knew anything about such a deal.

The next report to hit the teleprinters in Fleet Street came on the evening of Tuesday 4 July, nine days after the World Cup final. Again, Spurs were not mentioned. Ardiles' club, Huracan, was reported from Buenos Aires as saying that he had been transferred to Sheffield United for £530,000. The same report quoted Ardiles' World Cup teammate, Ricardo Villa, as saying he had been transferred from Racing Club, Buenos Aires, to Manchester City for £315,000. Several papers ignored this dispatch altogether. Ardiles coming to play in England? At Sheffield United? It must be a joke. Only *The Times* carried the report in full. It was not until three days later, on Friday 7 July, that the real news came out and this time it was on every front page. Ardiles and Villa were joining Spurs in what Jeff Powell in the *Daily Mail* called (with little if any exaggeration – only the transfer of Tommy Lawton to Third Division Notts County is comparable) the most sensational deal in British soccer history. David Lacey summed up a common reaction when he wrote in *The Guardian*: 'When Keith Burkinshaw went shopping and brought back Ardiles, it was as if the janitor had gone out to buy a tin of paint and had returned with a Velasquez. Astonishment that the Argentinians were coming at all is equalled by the incredulity that they were going to play for Spurs, who seemed to have lost faith in major transfers following the muted success of such purchases as Coates, Conn and Taylor.'

How did it all come about? Perhaps it was Bill Nicholson, the man responsible for so many sensational soccer transfers himself, who played the talisman at Tottenham on the morning of Thursday 29 June, a few days after Argentina's 3–1 win over Holland. Nicholson was sitting in his office just across the corridor from where Burkinshaw was having a meeting when the phone rang. It was the Sheffield United manager Harry Haslam on the line, asking to speak to Keith. Burkinshaw, who only minutes earlier had returned from giving his manager's report to the monthly board meeting, takes up the story. 'Bill came in, told me Harry was on the line and I had to go into his office to take the call. Harry told me that both Ardiles and Villa were available for transfer and wanted to play in England. The tie-up was through Antonio Rattin the old Argentinian captain, who was acting as agent but who is obviously still best known here for being sent off at Wembley in 1966. He was a big mate of Harry's and Harry was phoning a few clubs to see if they were interested. Like everyone else I'd watched Argentina in the World Cup. You dream about having players like that in your side but you never think it could come off.'

Burkinshaw lost no time. He went straight

back to the board meeting, which was still in progress, got the directors' blessing to fly out to Buenos Aires to pursue the deal and began to make the necessary preparations. The League ban on overseas players had been lifted a couple of seasons earlier, but Burkinshaw still needed to be certain that the necessary work permit could be obtained and one of his first calls was to the Department of Employment, who told him there should be no problem with a player of that ability. At that stage he was going with the intention of signing just Ardiles. He was due to fly out to Buenos Aires on the Friday evening, a plan which very nearly ran into trouble when he heard that Arsenal's Terry Neill might be intending to do the same.

'I obviously wanted this one all to myself,' said Burkinshaw, who was relieved to find later that the Arsenal manager had decided against the trip. Whether the Arsenal board vetoed the idea has never been revealed, but in conceding this particular victory to his North London rival, Neill subsequently maintained that, already having Brady and Rix, he didn't need Villa and Ardiles.

Burkinshaw caught the Friday night flight, arrived in Buenos Aires on Saturday morning and checked into the Hotel Libertador. Within a matter of hours he had his first meeting with Ardiles. 'It was one of those occasions when you immediately know something is right,' said Burkinshaw, 'there was an instant rapport. Within twenty minutes of meeting him, he'd agreed to sign.' Ardiles' next words took Burkinshaw by surprise. 'He told me he had a friend, Ricardo Villa, who also wanted to play in England. Could be come too?' At that time Villa was assuming he would be going to Arsenal, and that the two could effectively come to London together.

One of the reasons why Burkinshaw was able to win his board's immediate approval for the trip was because Haslam had told him that Ardiles could be bought for around £350,000 – a bargain price by English standards, even in 1978. With the bankrupt state of Argentinian soccer and the virtually permanent devaluation of the Argentinian peso, clubs were prepared to let their players go for under their international market value just to reduce debts. Perversely, it also meant that they wouldn't then go to any domestic rival. For their part, the players were so poorly paid that, even under the British taxation system, they'd be ten times better off than staying at home. Burkinshaw didn't know much about Villa except that he was the big, bearded player Cesar Menotti had twice sent on as substitute (once for Ardiles) to add some steel to the midfield in two crucial group matches. What he did know was that for around £700,000 he could have two leading members of the squad that had just won the World Cup. To put the figure in perspective, it was £250,000 more than Manchester United had just paid Leeds for Gordon McQueen, whom Burkinshaw had failed to sign earlier in the summer.

Back in England, on the Sunday morning, Sidney Wale was about to have a drink with his wife before lunch when the phone rang. 'It was Keith calling from Buenos Aires,' recalled Wale, 'He told me he had a bit of a problem. There was another player who wanted to come too. Well, we'd agreed as a board on one but since Keith wanted an answer straight away, I told him to hang on, and did some quick mental arithmetic. I worked out how much the bank would allow us on overdraft, how much extra we could expect to raise from season ticket sales with all the interest that was bound to be aroused, and I thought, we'll take a chance, so I gave Keith the go-ahead. We were both putting our heads on the chopping block. It was a big gamble to take, but looking back on it now, it was the best decision I ever made.'

Burkinshaw reached agreement with Villa even more swiftly than with Ardiles. 'Within a minute of meeting him, he'd agreed to sign,' says Burkinshaw. The stories about the Argentinian team being keen to get away were obviously no more than the truth. Not only were Spurs able to pay cash on the nail, but in the best traditions of Nicholson's cloak-and-dagger transfers, not a word came out about the true nature of the historic deal until Burkinshaw was ready to announce it.

The arrival of Ardiles and Villa was initially opposed by a PFA fearful of an invasion of foreign stars depriving their British members of a job. One can think of many other unionised trades and professions where such protests would have succeeded, but it is to the credit of football that the voices of welcome far outweighed those of dissent. At the same time, Spurs took no chances. With Keith Burkinshaw having already done his homework on the work permits, chairman Sidney Wale smoothed the path at Home Office level by marshalling some powerful voices to ensure there were no hiccups along the way.

By the time the new League season came around on 19 August, the soccer-going public's attention focused with excitement and eager anticipation on the debuts of Ardiles and Villa. And the two Argentinians couldn't have asked for a sunnier South American day on which to make their entry into British football. A crowd of 41,223 turned out on a magnificent summer's afternoon at the City Ground, Nottingham, to watch the new champions Forest do battle with the most talked-about team in the League, Tottenham Hotspur. Without TV cameras present, those fans alone had the privilege of witnessing a sensational start to the Argentinians' League careers.

With 26 minutes gone, Spurs were trailing 1–0 to a goal by Martin O'Neill when Peter Shilton was drawn out to a low cross from Ian Moores. But with a deft skill which belies his massive stature, Villa teased the ball away from Shilton's grasp and flicked it past the outstretched leg of Archie Gemmill into the corner of the net.

Villa would have to wait almost three years to score another goal with such public acclaim. But this was more than enough to be going on with. Spurs collected a well-deserved point in their opening match back in the First Division, the Sunday papers proclaimed the result with predictable headlines like 'Viva Villa', and already Spurs were rather prematurely being tipped to win the Championship.

But the honeymoon was soon over. Only four days later, Spurs were brought down to earth with a bump. Playing their first home match before a crowd of 47,892, who laid on a South American-style confetti welcome for their new heroes, Spurs were roundly beaten 4–1 by Aston Villa. A 2–2 home draw against Chelsea followed and then a result which in

OPPOSITE TOP: Ricky
Villa beats Middlesbrough's
Tony McAndrew in
August 1981.
OPPOSITE BOTTOM: Don
McAllister and Paul Miller
appeal to the referee while
West Brom's Ali Robertson
and Gerry Armstrong size
each other up.
BELOW: Osvaldo Ardiles,
the most sensational
arrival in British football of
the decade. 'If Spurs had
bought Batman and Robin
they could scarcely have
created greater curiosity,'
said Brian James in the
Daily Mail. Surprisingly
Spurs paid slightly less for
Ardiles than for Villa and
the two cost around
£600,000 in total, arguably
the best deal of the decade.
Ardiles soon became
known as one of the club's
humorists. When asked
whether Keith Burkinshaw
gave him more or different
tactical instructions than
Cesar Menotti he quickly
replied. 'It is the same in
both countries. The only
difference is that in
Argentina I understood
them.'

two words and two figures rudely shattered Burkinshaw's brave new world; Liverpool 7 Tottenham 0. It is the only time in their history that Spurs have been defeated by a margin of seven goals in a Football League match. But their fans did at least see the next League champions that September day – Liverpool. For Keith Burkinshaw, the problem of grafting South American skill on to the muck and nettles of English league soccer was only just beginning.

Looking back on that new era in Spurs' history, Burkinshaw explained the dilemma in which he found himself. 'Over there,' he said, metaphorically pointing to a distant corner of the globe, 'all the attackers attack, and the defenders defend. That means all your midfield players attack as well. Ossie and Ricky didn't know the meaning of the word defend when they first came here. It's a coach's nightmare when you've got five against three – and the three are your's because the midfield's in attack. That's what happened to us at Liverpool and they're the sort of team who punish you for it.'

Ex-Spurs and England winger Peter Taylor asked an obvious question at the time when he said: 'Argentina won the World Cup not picking anyone up, so who's wrong?' Burkinshaw draws this distinction between the way the game is played in South American countries and the English concept of midfield players who combine defence with attack: 'The South Americans have defenders who all have as much skill as Glenn Hoddle. They don't need the support our defenders need because they're so much better equipped. We don't have these players, so we've got to get extra men back.'

Spurs continued to win friends, if not as many matches as they would have liked, throughout the season. The curiosity factor of Ardiles and Villa swelled gates wherever they played, making Spurs the top away attraction in the League. While Villa struggled to secure a regular first team place, Ardiles delighted fans with his darting runs, perceptive passing and use of space. Pictures frequently show him with the ball glued to his right instep, while his eyes are glancing about to see who's in space.

'It's his terrific skill combined with the ability to play with his head up which makes him a world-class footballer,' said Burkinshaw when Ardiles had settled in. 'He's 5ft 6in and weighs under ten stone. People said he would be knocked all over the place when the pitches got heavy here in winter. But he's proved them all wrong. He's hardly had an injury since he arrived. There's a very tough character inside that little frame.'

Indeed, it was Ardiles' ability to ride heavy tackles and still maintain his superb balance which won him almost as much admiration as his marvellous ball skills. But despite his individual success, Spurs finished a moderate 11th in their first season back in Division One. They reached the quarter-finals of the FA Cup before going out 2–0 to Manchester United in an Old Trafford replay, but overall their achievement fell short of the high expectations held for them after such a sensational summer. And Burkinshaw still hadn't solved the problem of how to make the best use of his new acquisitions.

They were tried in defensive midfield, attacking midfield, left midfield, right midfield and central midfield. But Spurs were forgetting

one vital point as they searched for the magic formula. In Argentina's World Cup-winning side, Ardiles was working with two highly mobile, skilful ground players in Leopoldo Luque and Mario Kempes, two players with the acceleration and speed on the turn to make the most of Ardiles' through balls and lightning-quick one-twos on the edge of the box.

Spurs skipper Steve Perryman summed up the problem: 'We'd come up from the Second Division using a winger and overlapping full-backs to provide crosses for tall front men who were good with their heads. But with Ardiles and Villa, we naturally channelled everything through midfield. We were playing shorter, quicker balls, changing our game to a style which our strikers just weren't used to. It was unfair to expect them to play that way.'

Spurs added the combative talents of Welsh international captain Terry Yorath to midfield for the 1979–80 season as they continued to juggle with the permutations. But even Yorath's ball-winning ability – a quality rather lacking in Spurs' armoury until then – failed to make much impression on their overall performance. Unlike the previous season, when their home form let them down, this time it was Spurs' away form which was dis-

appointing, and the club slipped to 14th, scoring a meagre 52 goals while conceding 62.

The season was, however, memorable for one match: Spurs' third round FA Cup victory over Manchester United in yet another titanic struggle between the two clubs. United had beaten Spurs in the previous season's quarter-final replay, knocked them out of the current season's League Cup after two hectic second round legs, and here they were again, poised for their sixth cup meeting in two seasons after United had forced another 1–1 draw and another Old Trafford replay.

Ardiles had often been quoted about his dream of appearing in a Wembley final, but it seemed the chance had once again eluded him. And the prospect of a Spurs victory looked even more improbable when, midway through the Old Trafford match, goalkeeper Milija Aleksic, who had made a brilliant reflex save from Sammy McIlroy earlier in the game, was stretchered off with serious chest and head injuries after a collision with Joe Jordan. But after 'the save of the season', as Aleksic's effort was later voted by the BBC, came 'the goal of my life' by Osvaldo Ardiles.

With Glenn Hoddle in goal for the injured Aleksic, and the game heading for a second replay after 119 minutes without a goal from either side, Villa received the ball on the edge of the United penalty area. What happened next was a piece of South American magic, pure and simple. As Ardiles said: 'Most English players would have gone to the bye-line and crossed. But I knew Ricky's play. I knew he wanted to lay the ball back and I darted back to find space just inside the box. Just as I anticipated, Ricky saw me, rolled the ball back, and I looked up and with all my strength aimed for the top corner.'

The ball curled beyond the despairing Bailey and into the exact spot Ardiles had picked. Seconds later the whistle went and jubilant Spurs had won a match they were expected to lose. Victories followed over Swindon and Birmingham, but again the quarter-finals proved the bogey round. In a tense home game against Liverpool, they lost by the only goal, a typical opportunist effort from the edge of the box by Terry McDermott which won the BBC's 'Goal of the Season' award. Ardiles' dream would have to wait another season . . . but just another season.

Burkinshaw recognised that if his bold experiment was not to fizzle out in anticlimax, if his cherished vision of a truly great Spurs side was to be accomplished with his current squad, time was running out. Ardiles and Villa each had just one more season of their contracts remaining, while Spurs' other prize possession, the richly gifted Glenn Hoddle, was also approaching the end of his contracted period.

Hoddle, so often an enigma with his breathtaking skills alternating with long periods of anonymity, had just enjoyed his most successful season. He increased his work-rate, conquered his frequently criticised habit of fading from matches well before the final whistle, and scored an impressive 22 goals in all. What was remarkable about Hoddle's feat was that not only did he score them playing from midfield, but that so many came from outside the penalty area. The point was never more clearly illustrated than when he scored on his England debut on 22 November 1979, with a superb 20-yard volley in the 2–0 win over Bulgaria at Wembley.

It was a dream start to an international career, but somehow Hoddle was unable to establish his England place, a fact that puzzled Burkinshaw as much as Hoddle's many admirers. 'He's so good that by now he should be among the world's best,' said Burkinshaw. 'Just talk to Ossie Ardiles. He says that Glenn is one of the best players he had come across in world football, and that's some accolade.' Burkinshaw believed Hoddle should have been given an extended run in the international team to give him the chance to realise his potential: 'Glenn needs to come into the England side on a regular basis for a chance to produce two or three top-class performances and get himself established.'

In May 1980, with the backing of Spurs' new chairman, Arthur Richardson, Burkinshaw made the first of two new purchases that took Spurs' spending that summer to £1.5 million. Sidney Wale, who had surprised everyone at the club with his decision to resign from the board at the end of the 1979–80 season, admitted that the advent of the million-pound transfer was one of the reasons that caused him to retire from a soccer world he saw becoming increasingly inflationary. An accountant by profession and a sensibly cautious man with money, Wale liked to try to balance the books and he said: 'It alarmed and saddened me to see so many clubs going deeper and deeper into the red.' Ironically one of Wale's last decisions before his retirement and subsequent appointment as the club's life president was to sanction the building of Spurs' £41 million stand, an act he acknowledged, looking at the problems that clubs such as Chelsea, Sheffield United and Wolves had, could make or break Spurs.

But he said: 'We had little choice with the building of a new stand, although we could have settled for something a little less ambitious and grandiose. The original stand had wooden floors and was a potential fire hazard. The time had come when we had to do something.'

Whatever Wale's reservations about spending huge sums of money on new players, Arthur Richardson had no such inhibitions. Although then 76, he was unusual among chairmen in having been a competent player himself, good enough to have a trial for London Schoolboys at one point – though he never appeared for the side as their fixture against Glasgow Schoolboys was called off because of a railway strike. With their new chairman, if there is any truth in the saying that fortune favours the brave, then Spurs reaped an instant dividend. Steve Archibald, bought in May from Aberdeen for £800,000, and Garth Crooks, a £650,000 August arrival from Stoke, struck up an explosive partnership which yielded 46 goals and helped the club to its first major title for eight years. Having correctly diagnosed Spurs' problems in attack, Burkinshaw had gone for two quicksilver strikers, essentially ground players with the ability to play with their backs to goal, fit into the new midfield pattern, turn their marker, and, above all, score goals. In other words players who could profit from the split-second timing of Ardiles' short-ball game.

Archibald's name had been linked with Spurs for some time but the deal wasn't concluded until Aberdeen's shrewd manager, Alec Ferguson, had made certain of only Pittodrie's second Scottish League championship, and thus a hefty transfer fee for his twenty-goal star. England Under-21 striker Crooks had been a consistent scorer for Stoke over the previous three seasons with nearly fifty goals but, with the Potteries club anxious to pay off some of their debts and Spurs looking for a hunting partner for Archibald, a deal was swiftly concluded which meant that, in the best Spurs tradition, the club was once again starting a new season with a couple of exciting and expensive new stars.

Even skipper Steve Perryman, who saw so many big names come and go while making a record number of appearances for the club, admits Spurs wouldn't be Spurs without their star signings. 'Our fans have come to expect it, I've come to expect it, I think most of the players have come to expect it,' he said. 'It brings an air of excitement to be club, fans talk about it, it brings them in each season and it means they know we're always trying to get things right.'

Crooks and Archibald got things right from the opening day of the season. Crooks marked his debut with a goal in the 2–0 win over Forest, and propelled by his August hat-trick in the 4–3 win over Crystal Palace, Spurs led the First Division for the first time in nine years. But it was in the FA Cup that they enjoyed their finest hour. Said Perryman: 'We'd felt for a couple of seasons that our best chance of

success was in the Cup. We knew our League form wasn't consistent enough to win the First Division but we thought we had the individual talent in the one-off games to go all the way.'

Playing now with short one-twos around the penalty area to the nimble Archibald and Crooks, Spurs had the agility and mobility to go through defences rather than have to battle it out in the air. Defensively, however, they remained suspect, a price they would have to pay for a team so committed to attack. But while Crooks and Archibald were scoring goals, it was a price they could afford.

Tottenham began their Wembley odyssey without Ardiles, who had been given leave of absence to play for Argentina in the Gold Cup in Uruguay in January 1981. In a defensive match at Loftus Road, Spurs were held to a 0–0 draw by a Queen's Park Rangers side hoping to sneak into the fourth round on the break. Rangers went into the return with the same approach, confident that having stretched Spurs' shaky defence on the first occasion they could breach it on the second. But Tottenham opened up their game at White Hart Lane and, though they were clearly not playing with much confidence, scored a decisive 3-1 victory. The game was a personal triumph for winger Tony Galvin, who scored on his return after eight months recovering from a pelvis operation.

Spurs were next drawn at home to Hull, who, despite their Third Division ranking, held out for 84 minutes before succumbing. The match marked the return of Ardiles, though not without a ripple of controversy.

In his absence Spurs had gone six games without defeat, including their first victory over
Arsenal in four seasons. Ardiles didn't help his
case by returning several days late from South
America and promptly found himself dropped
for the Arsenal match. The matter was quietly
forgotten but Ardiles also sounded a warning
about his personal future at the club: 'Spurs
want me to stay and I want to play for them for
another two years. But we can't agree on a new
contract. We're not even close on the financial
aspects.'

If Galvin was the success of the third round,
it was 20-year-old Garry Brooke who was the
star of the fourth. Demoted because of Ardiles'
return, there was still room on the substitute's
bench because of a knee injury sustained by
Villa in the tie with Rangers. Brooke, a home-
grown youngster with a deceptively powerful
shot from a very short back-swing, broke Hull's
resistance after coming on in place of Ardiles.
Brooke was to figure in a rather more important substitution later in the Cup, but on this
occasion he gave due warning of his ability by
shooting Spurs ahead in the 84th minute and
laying on their second for Archibald four minutes later. Even Ardiles was impressed: 'He
made the difference. I love the way he plays.
He's a brilliant prospect.'

Spurs were drawn at home a second time
with a fifth round tie against Coventry, a team

much vaunted for having the youngest average
age in the First Division. But a week when they
had just been denied their first-ever Wembley
appearance by West Ham's League Cup semi-
final victory was probably not the best of occasions to pitch a team of shell-shocked teenagers
against an increasingly confident Spurs. The
result was never in doubt with Ardiles,
Archibald and Hughton contributing to the
3–1 victory. Spurs were now in the quarter-
finals, the round they'd stumbled at in the previous two seasons.

'We'd had Liverpool and Manchester
United those times so we were due a bit of
luck,' said Perryman. Spurs duly got it when
the draw was made: a home tie with Third
Division Exeter. 'We knew then that we could
win the Cup,' said the captain. Conquerors of
Newcastle and Leicester in the previous
rounds, Exeter were no push-overs. Indeed it
took a second half injury to midfield player Ian
Pearson to throw Exeter's defence into sufficient confusion to allow Spurs to score.
Perhaps it was only delaying the inevitable
since, while they held Spurs at bay for an hour,
Exeter seldom looked likely to score themselves. However Spurs could scarcely have rel-
ished the prospect of a trip to Exeter's tiny
ground – scene of the Leicester and Newcastle
defeats – so it brought some considerable relief
when Graham Roberts headed them in front.
Paul Miller completed what was then a formality
and Spurs marched 2–0 victors into the semi-
finals .

THE YEAR OF THE COCKEREL

For those who believe in omens, Tottenham
Hotspur's progress towards the winning of the
hundredth FA Cup was little less than
inevitable. It was, after all, the 'Year of the
Cockerel', thoughbeit in the Chinese calendar. Then there were the vagaries of the draw,
so unfavourable in the disastrous campaigns
between 1974 and 1978, but now producing
only one game out of nine away from London.
The superstitious pointed to the catalogue
of major trophies gathered to White Hart
Lane in the first season of each new decade,
and any casual observer could point out
that Spurs, of all the major clubs, were

the only one never to have lost a game at Wembley (a record which lasted to the following season's League Cup final). Above all else, perhaps, there was Tottenham's amazing propensity for winning major cup finals. This would be their eleventh, and they had previously lost just one out of ten (against Feyenoord in the 1974 UEFA Cup). Spurs had never lost a single-leg cup final, nor any final match played in England. No other club came near to matching this amazing record.

Within the dressing-room, however, an overwhelming sense of realism prevailed, primarily because of Keith Burkinshaw's painful experiences seven years earlier. As coach to Newcastle United he had been on the wrong end of the FA Cup's most one-sided post-war final. Liverpool, inspired by Kevin Keegan, had overrun players who had been drained not just by the occasion but also by an over-lengthy and too open-housed preparation.

Determined that his Tottenham of 1981 should not fall into this trap, Burkinshaw established some ground rules in the week leading up to the semi-final against Wolverhampton Wanderers at Hillsborough. One day, but one day only, was set aside for the requirements of television, radio and newspaper reporters, an exercise to protect the squad which was successfully repeated before the final.

At Cheshunt on that final press day, Ricky Villa, an absentee from the Cup since an injury in the third round, confirmed his fitness to return; Steve Perryman chatted happily of his memories of significant Spurs victories over Wolves in the 1972 UEFA Cup final and 1973 League Cup semi-final, while Milija Aleksic pondered on the prospect of his first FA Cup tie since his shuddering, jaw-breaking collision with Joe Jordan at Old Trafford more than a year before.

Semi-finals often live in the memory more for the result than for the quality of the contest. This one, however, transcended the limits normally imposed by the importance and tension of the match. Tony Galvin established the tone with the first incisive break after just four minutes. From his cross Steve Archibald had only to stretch forward to turn the ball over the line for his 25th goal of the season. But, only minutes later, Wolves were level. Andy Gray, patched up on the morning of the match, guided down the type of header that was to trouble Spurs all afternoon and Ken Hibbitt's low shot arrowed inside Aleksic's left-hand post. Yet by half-time Tottenham were back in the lead with a goal that generated some considerable heat. As Osvaldo Ardiles surged purposefully towards the extremities of the penalty area, George Berry's tackle sent him flying into the area. The Spurs appeals were for a penalty, the Wolves defenders believed the challenge to be fair. Referee Clive Thomas judged that a foul had been committed, but just outside the box.

Glenn Hoddle could have been excused some relief at the decision. On the morning of the match he had recalled that the last penalty he had missed had been saved by Paul Bradshaw. But now, from seven yards further out, he totally deceived the goalkeeper. Bradshaw's awareness of the danger from a direct shot over the wall sucked him in right behind his

Club captain Steve Perryman and Villa's Tony Morley contest the Spurs' right flank during a First Division game on Saturday 5 September 1981. Villa won 3–1, Ricky Villa scoring the only home goal against hs namesakes. Keith Burkinshaw said of Perryman at the time: 'He's just as important as Ardiles or Archibald. The big clubs . . . Leeds, Liverpool . . . they've all enquired about him at some time. They'd take him tomorrow. He knows the game inside-out and can apply that knowledge on the field. The other players know this and listen when he talks.'

line of defenders. Hoddle deftly guided the ball into a vacant corner.

In the second half the tempo understandably dropped, only to reach a new crescendo in the final minute of normal time. Television's much-used replay of the central incident clearly showed that in a tackle on Hibbitt, by unlikely Hoddle of all ironies, the ball had been played well before the man if, indeed, the man had ever been touched at all. The tackle was entirely fair. Referee Thomas, without the aid of technological assistance and from a different angle, signalled dramatically for a penalty. Mayhem followed. Archibald and Ardiles argued their claims of injustice to such lengths that they might have been sent off, instead of merely becoming two of the game's eight cautioned players. Burkinshaw intervened to pacify his team before the start of extra time. Meanwhile Willie Carr had produced an unerring touch from the spot, remarkable circumstances for his first goal of the season. The newspapers the following day were full of admissions – from Hibbitt that it was natural to fall in the area when tackled, from Wolves manager John Barnwell that the game was 'professional' and teams had to do what they had to do, particularly in the closing minutes of a semi-final when they were a goal down. No-one questioned that Clive Thomas had been deceived.

Neither side could muster their flagging resources to settle the tie in the additional thirty minutes, but Tottenham's desperate disappointment was partially mollified by the venue for the replay. At Highbury, it was

virtually a home match. Shortly before the replay's kick-off came significant news on the Wolves team sheet; this time the battle-scarred Gray had not made it, and his influence would inevitably be missed. Soon after the start, Garth Crooks picked up a ball that Wolves should have cleared and Tottenham established a lead that was rarely threatened. On the stroke of half-time the same striker settled the outcome in glorious fashion. Hoddle released a through pass of stunning accuracy and Crooks provided a sprinter's pace and a perfect finish. The final goal belonged to Villa, from a lazy swing of his left foot some thirty yards out that emphasised the latent power of the Argentinian, a power that was too often hidden. So uncertain was his future at the time, it could have provided an epitaph for his days in English football. As it turned out it was just a rehearsal for an even greater spectacular.

WEMBLEY AGAIN

Villa and Ardiles thus became the first two Argentinians to play in an FA Cup final, with Manchester City the opposition after surprising favourites Ipswich Town 1–0 in the other semi-final at Villa Park. Keith Burkinshaw kept faith with his semi-final selection, which meant a Wembley disappointment for important squad members like Don McAllister, Gordon Smith, the injured John Lacy and, particularly, Barry Daines in his testimonial year. So often playing the bridesmaid to victorious goalkeepers, in all those years he had still won nothing of note. The green jersey went to Milija Aleksic, just

past his thirtieth birthday, a self-confessed 'nervy player' who could draw confidence, though, from a Wembley appearance nine years earlier for Stafford Rangers in the FA Trophy final when he kept a clean sheet and Rangers beat Barnet 3–0. Steve Perryman, unselfishly accepting any role if it suited the team, had now been switched to right-back and had just broken the club appearance record previously held by Pat Jennings. Chris Hughton, naturally right-sided, was happier at left-back, though he worried that his only attack of cramp had come at Wembley when playing for the Republic of Ireland fifteen months earlier.

The centre of the defence had come under continual scrutiny in a season in which Tottenham's attractive philosophies had often been at the expense of a vulnerability at the back. The frailty had arguably owed more to their style of play than to individual weaknesses, but persistent pre-match comments on defensive problems exerted extra pressure on the two young centre-backs. At twenty-two Paul Miller had risen from the ranks of the apprentices, and had won back his place just at the right time, before the third round. Alongside him Graham Roberts, a year younger, had proved a versatile acquisition from Weymouth in his first full League season, and was desperate to show Southampton, Bournemouth and Portsmouth how wrong they had been to discard him. Roberts' selection added a romantic note to the hundredth final. Thirteen months earlier he had been working as a fitter in a shipyard with only the memory of a 1973 appearance at Wembley to cherish . . . as a ballboy !

In midfield Osvaldo Ardiles was living out a dream held since he had watched the 1979 final between Arsenal and Manchester United, a sentiment that provoked a highly successful record which swelled the funds of the players' pool of commercial earnings from their achievements. References to Ossie going all trembly and Tott . . . ing . . . ham can probably bear omission from the story, though the demands of the players' pool did bring forth some unflattering comments; *The Observer* suggested that Ossie's knees had probably gone trembly at the thought of the demands (into four figures) for player interviews. Unlike Ardiles, Ricky Villa had not been selected for the 1978 World Cup final and, surprised that he had bounded back so quickly from three months absence with injury, he described the prospect of the final as the greatest day of his career.

To the right in midfield of the two South Americans Glenn Hoddle could point to two unusual statistics. He had scored in both his Wembley internationals for England, and had contributed a goal in each of his last four games against Manchester City. Hoddle's personal situation within the club led to an even greater desire for victory from Tottenham followers; many believed that a place in Europe the following season would persuade him to decline a number of rich European clubs to whom he would be available at the end of his contract. In the event, all was to be well on that front.

Tony Galvin attracted much less publicity than Hoddle as the final approached, yet his role in the pattern of play had become barely less important. His commitment and energy on the left showed no signs of a major groin operation at the start of the season, although it still gave him considerable pain. The younger brother of a professional, Leeds' and Hull's Chris Galvin, Tony had arrived in the big-time via a Russian degree at Hull University and Goole Town of the Northern Premier League – which was no doubt a unique combination.

For Steve Archibald and Garth Crooks, the Cup campaign provided a splendid climax to a season in which their talents had blended superbly. The investment of almost a million and a half pounds for their services, from Aberdeen and Stoke respectively, had produced its dividends in goals from the quiet Scotsman and the articulate, ebullient Crooks, who never seemed happier than when leading the singing on the team coach. The substitute's shirt went to Garry Brooke, who had marked his first full league game in December with two goals against Southampton. Now twenty, his development had been aided by a spell on loan in Sweden, and coming off the bench he had already contributed a number of impressive performances.

In the knowledge that Tottenham had never lost a game at Wembley, Keith Burkinshaw took his side away to the seclusion of the Ponsbourne Hotel in Hertfordshire, where the club's own security force protected their privacy. So settled was the base that the manager could happily slip back to his own nearby home on the night before the big game. As usual the television cameras provided the players with a diversion from the pressures, the highlight being a Friday evening link-up between Villa and Ardiles and their families in Argentina.

Saturday morning was a time to keep to routines. Assistant manager Peter Shreeves drove off to Cheshunt to supervise a light training session preferred by Perryman, Miller and Aleksic. The rest of the squad with Mike Varney, the physiotherapist, at the helm set off for a gentle stroll around the extensive grounds of the hotel. At 1pm they left for the forty-minute drive which transferred them from the hotel's tranquillity to the electricity of the greatest occasion in the domestic game. The occasion was more significant than usual, for it was the 100th final and it was fortunate that the draw had brought together two of the game's greatest names and provided a London v Lancashire clash for such a historic match.

Manchester City, meanwhile, were crossing London on their journey north from their headquarters at the Selsdon Park Hotel in Surrey. David Bennett, the young striker who had vowed never to go to the Empire Stadium until he played there, had survived a rigorous examination on a thigh strain, and took his place in the team which had come alive since the November arrival of John Bond in the manager's chair. His side was also that which had won the semi-final: Joe Corrigan, Ray Ranson, Nicky Reid, Tommy Caton and Bobby McDonald, Tommy Hutchison, Steve Mackenzie, Gerry Gow and Paul Power, Dave Bennett and Kevin Reeves, with Tony Henry as substitute.

History will record that the one hundredth FA Cup final lived up to its billing, but not before it threatened to fall horribly flat. The events of Saturday 9 May lasted wearily for two hours with the most memorable experience being that of Tommy Hutchison, who became only the second man ever to score for both sides in a Cup final. City began with the midfield industry that had stifled Ipswich in the semi-final, not to mention the enthusiastic tackling of Gerry Gow. On a pitch dampened by morning rain their cohesive effort created an atmosphere in which the skills of Hoddle and Ardiles were not allowed to flourish. Archibald and Crooks were left isolated, their supply cut off. Without being able to use their possession to dominate, City could still stifle Spurs and deserved the lead they edged into on the half-hour. Hutchison's superb near-post header produced a goal in the same unlikely vein as that of Trevor Brooking's which had won the Cup for West Ham United a year earlier. Most neutrals saw the comparisons being exact, that City would sneak it 1–0 despite Spurs having been everyone's favourites.

Keith Burkinshaw recalled the half-time discussion: 'We felt that they couldn't keep running like that. We had to make sure we played through the middle of the park. We didn't do it enough, though give credit to Manchester City – they didn't give us any space.' As Tottenham initiated some improvements in the second half, they clearly owed nothing to Villa, an anonymous figure to both his own dismay and to that of the millions watching the match live in Argentina. Brooke's arrival in his place offered a perkier alternative, and the replaced Argentinian sought to hide

LEFT: Graham Roberts seems almost to be protecting the body of a fallen colleague at White Hart Lane late in 1981. Rejected by his three local south coast clubs (Southampton, Bournemouth and Portsmouth), he eventually joined Spurs from Weymouth for £35,000, then a record fee for a non-League player.

LEFT BELOW: Ricky Villa powers past Sammy McIlroy, perfectly illustrating the combination of speed and strength which enabled him to score the winner in the 1981 FA Cup final. He joined Spurs from Racing Club of Buenos Aires and, until the transfer of Diego Maradona, was the most costly player in Argentinian football history. Oscar Arce, an Argentinian coaching at Sheffield United, provided the first link in the chain that was to bring Villa and Ardiles to White Hart Lane.

TOP RIGHT: The aggressive side of Glenn Hoddle; Ardiles' arrival was a great plus for the England midfield player. 'Glenn has shown greater maturity since they arrived,' said Burkinshaw a few months later, 'He's really begun to turn it on. Ardiles thinks he's a must for England.' Hoddle was to win 53 caps, all but nine while a Spurs player.

OPPOSITE RIGHT: Hoddle brings the ball away from England colleague Bryan Robson, then with West Bromwich Albion.

OPPOSITE BOTTOM: Ricky Villa takes on Villa's Gordon Cowans.

THIS PAGE CENTRE: Garry Brooke gets in a fierce left foot shot at Middlesbrough. Another local, born in Bethnal Green, he scored a vital goal against Hull in the fourth round of the triumphant 1980–81 Cup run, but was granted a free transfer at the end of the 1984–85 season.

THIS PAGE BOTTOM: Tony Galvin contests possession with Geoff Palmer of Wolves.

THIS PAGE TOP: Trainer Johnny Wallis, manager Keith Burkinshaw and physio Mike Varney in the dug-out before kick-off. Burkinshaw had a relatively undistinguished career as a professional, as he recalls: 'As a 15-year-old I went to Wolves. When you were 17 they decided whether or not they would take you on they decided against me. So I went to a Midland League club called Denaby United for about 13 weeks when Liverpool took me as a full-time pro. I was also working down the pits at the time.' I was at Liverpool for four years but still in the reserves so I asked for a transfer and went to Workington for eight years. Ken Furphy was manager and we got promotion. After he left I took over as manager for 3 or 4 months, but left after a disagreement with the club and went to Scunthorpe with Freddie Goodwin. After three years I ended up as acting manager but at 33 cartilage trouble made me quit as a player and I went to Newcastle as a coach for Joe Harvey.'

his disappointment in the dressing-room rather than watch the remaining minutes of what he was sure would be Tottenham's first FA Cup final defeat. His lonely and very public walk, which ended tearfully in the dressing-room, had reached the mouth of the tunnel when he checked to watch a free-kick ten minutes from time.

With one hand on the Cup, Manchester City lost that grip in a freak moment. Just as, in the semi-final, the threat of Hoddle at free-kicks produced an irrational response from the Wolves defence, this time it was Hutchison who opted to move from his allotted defensive task to run behind the wall and cover the swerve round the outside of the line of defenders. His reading of Hoddle's intentions was exactly right, but with Corrigan covering any danger from the free-kick, the goalkeeper was left stranded as the ball spun off Hutchison's shoulder and into the other corner. Ten minutes from being crowned the hero, Hutchison's unnecessary intervention had made him at least part villain.

The most relieved player in the ground was the one who had just left the pitch. Gradually Ricky Villa swallowed his pride and, by extra time, had marched back to the bench. On the field the additional period produced little to remember, and John Bond lamented at the end of the affair: 'We could have had penalties, or even played until somebody scored, though it might have ended up two-aside the way every-one was dropping in extra-time. Everybody was wandering around not knowing what to do. I think that if a game of this importance, with a crowd of this size, ends in a draw, it is an anti-climax.' It was only the second Wembley FA Cup final ever to need a replay.

On the coach back to the post-match ban-quet at London's Hilton Hotel, Garth Crooks quickly broke the atmosphere by encouraging raucous renditions of *Ossie's Dream*. Graham Roberts, who had lost two front teeth in a collision with Chris Hughton, suffered further pain when an emergency stop by the bus induced a bout of cramp. At the front Keith Burkinshaw was already affirming, despite the poor form of Villa, that his side would be unchanged when the battle continued.

The first ever Wembley replay of an FA Cup final took place on Thursday 14 May, with a controversial edict from the Football Association that penalties would decide things if the match was again drawn after extra-time. With England at home to Brazil on the Tuesday night, and the European Cup Winners Cup final between Dinamo Tbilisi and Carl Zeiss Jena televised from Dusseldorf on the Wednesday, there was enough alterna-tive football to take the limelight from the players for a welcome few days. Recharged, Tottenham Hotspur and Manchester City pro-duced an enthralling contest, arguably one of the great finals.

This time both sides scored inside the open-ing ten minutes, the first from Villa, whose show of temperament at his substitution five days earlier had looked like a thoroughly unwise snub to his manager. But Burkinshaw's wise reaction to the affair could not have pro-duced a better ending. Villa's goal had its roots in the work of Ardiles, whose attempted shot struck Archibald. The Spurs leading scorer, who was to have no personal good fortune in

either match, swung quickly to shoot. The ball ricocheted off the body of Corrigan straight to Villa and, from just outside the six-yard box, he drove it straight into the unprotected net.

Steve Mackenzie's equaliser now lies buried among a welter of memories of this marvellous match. In the context of most other games it would have lived as the abiding memory. Mackenzie, hauled into prominence two years earlier as a seventeen-year-old when Malcolm Allison paid £250,000 before he had played a league game, must have made his mentor smile in satisfaction at a goal of the highest calibre. From just outside the Spurs' penalty area, Hutchison nodded the ball down and Mackenzie's right-footed volley sped past Aleksic. It was to be City's strange fate in this final to score two of the best goals ever seen in an FA Cup final – by Hutchison and Mackenzie – and still finish with the losers' medals.

Though Corrigan continued to be the busier goalkeeper, it was City who made the next inroad early in the second half. Bennett's speed uncovered a soft centre in the defence and Miller and Hughton converged for a combined challenge that demolished the progress of the City striker. Referee Keith Hackett from Sheffield awarded only the fifth penalty in the history of Wembley FA Cup finals. Kevin Reeves joined the names of Mutch, Shimwell, Allen and Blanchflower and kept up the unfail-ing record by placing his shot to the goalkeeper's left with sufficient power, though Aleksic guessed the right way.

So lethargic in adversity in the first match, Tottenham now produced a response far more in keeping with the quality of their players. Hoddle had already enjoyed a much more productive game when he lit the flame under a grand finale. A controlled lofted pass caught City coming out and found Archibald onside. The Scot was not able to fully digest the offering but the defenders could not recover, and the crumbs were devoured by Crooks for his 22nd goal of the season. Twenty minutes left and at two goals each the ebbs and flows of this captivating match had pushed the miserable memories of Saturday far from the mind.

What followed has now passed into the folk-lore of the competition; a denouement in the tradition of the Matthews final of 1953 and Everton's comeback in 1966. The very nature of the winning goal would have deserved all its accolades, but the Cup so often reaches beyond the pure world and drama of football to create an extra dimension. Now the same brooding, bearded Latin America figure who had sulked away to the Wembley dressing-room the previous Saturday was to place his name on that roll-call of legendary figures whose deeds will be remembered long after they have gone.

In the 76th minute Ricky Villa collected the ball on the Spurs left outside the penalty area, a long way from, and no direct threat to, Joe Corrigan's goal. Caton and Ranson were the defenders caught momentarily off their guard by the audacity of an Argentinian who was in no mood to settle for a safe square pass. The two young City players were entangled as Villa worked a magical web, with sure-footed changes of direction this way and that and which were coupled with the physical power

Tottenham's somewhat fortuitous equalising goal in the 81st minute of the first game at Wembley in 1981. Just as Spurs' fans were beginning to believe that they were about to witness Tottenham's first ever FA Cup final defeat, their side was awarded a free-kick on the edge of the penalty area. As Hoddle stood over the ball, City winger Tommy Hutchison took up his appointed position on the left-hand edge (TOP) of the Manchester City wall. But as Hoddle took the kick (CENTRE) Hutchison ran behind the wall, presumably to cover any shot which might curl into the top right corner. In fact, at this stage, there was no danger; keeper Joe Corrigan had that side of the goal well protected and the free-kick was going wide. A few moments later (BOTTOM) the ball struck Hutchison on the angle of shoulder and head and was neatly deflected into the other corner of the net. Joe Corrigan had already made a safety dive and could do nothing. Hutchison thus became only the second man (Bert Turner of Charlton in 1946 was the other) to score for both sides in an FA Cup final, and at a time when he must have begun to think that his excellent first-half diving header had won the trophy for City.

156

that had always made him such a difficult player to knock off the ball. Corrigan advanced to try to halt the trail of devastation, but Villa retained his balance and took advantage of the goalkeeper committing himself: 3–2. Wembley roared its appreciation of a superb solo goal, and Villa raced away totally unstoppable in his triumph. It was not that it was just an outstanding goal – more, it was a courageous goal. To have the courage to hold onto that ball with 15 minutes of an FA Cup final replay left – that was the ultimate significance of the moment.

'It's great after last Saturday,' enthused Villa, whose command of English was now vastly improved from the silent days of his arrival in 1978 alongside the more talkative Ardiles. 'The ball seemed stuck to my feet. I don't know how many players I beat but the thrill was terrific when the ball went into the net. I just wanted to run anywhere. I say thank you to the manager. He took big chance on me for the semi-final. Before tonight I have not much luck in England, I think.'

Steve Perryman, who had begun to worry as to whether the side would ever win a major trophy under his leadership, collected the FA Cup from Princess Michael of Kent, a reward for his twelve years of unquestioned loyalty to Tottenham Hotspur. Keith Burkinshaw, controlled in the fashion of his native Yorkshire, had seen his team selection vindicated: 'How can you leave out a player of his quality? Ricky showed all his skill tonight. He was pleased that I had so much faith in him. But above all I am thrilled for our fans who have waited a long time for success and now they have their pride back. They did not desert us when we slipped into the Second Division. I hope we

have repaid them for their loyalty.'

John Bond retained his dignity, and humour, in defeat: 'This was a magnificent match in terms of what English football is all about. Whatever I feel personally it's been a tremendous night for the game. But you know I said right at the start of the season that it might be Tottenham's year for the Cup. For once I wish I hadn't been right.'

THE CENTENARY SEASON

The centenary season, 1981-82, started in tremendous style. Though attendances were dropping elsewhere in the country, Spurs had become the League's biggest drawing card. Their football was often a delight to watch. Patrick Barclay said in *The Guardian* after one of the season's first games, a Cup final repeat at Maine Road, that: 'If every team played like Tottenham Hotspur, football's only problem would be in pacifying the hordes of supporters unable to get into packed grounds. They bring beauty to the game, and people like that. If all the public wanted was to see one side win and another lose, they would go to the nearest park and save money.'

John Bond was no less complimentary: 'However long you look at football and think of all the great teams, you won't find any who could knock it about better than Tottenham did today. They are not necessarily a great team, they might not win the Championship because they are a bit vulnerable when they haven't got the ball, but they are great for the game.'

Spurs' two major signings before the season began had been the England goalkeeper Ray Clemence, for £300,000, and the Welsh international defender Paul Price from Luton.

With Corrigan already committed, Garth Crooks slides home the rebound from a Steve Archibald shot and Spurs draw level again at 2–2 in the 1981 Cup final replay on Thursday 14 May. This was the first time that an FA Cup final replay had ever been played at Wembley. Indeed, it was only the second replay that had been necessary since the stadium was built nearly 60 years before. The players, left to right, are: Ranson, Perryman, Caton, Hutchison, Corrigan, Miller, Crooks and Archibald.

The Cup final replay of 1981 was to be Ricky Villa's day. A quarter of an hour from time, with the score 2-2, Villa dribbled the ball in from the left touch-line, weaved his way past (TOP AND CENTRE) Ranson, Caton and Reid, and (BOTTOM) drew Joe Corrigan out far enough to slip the ball into the net. It was one of Wembley's truly great goals and one certainly fit to win the 100th FA Cup final.

Unfortunately Price was injured early on and Clemence took time to settle into a new defensive pattern, having left such a familiar one behind on Merseyside.

This was never clearer than at Wembley for the 1981 Charity Shield, when his uncharacteristically poor handling helped Aston Villa achieve a 2-2 draw they probably did not deserve. The clubs shared the trophy and Spurs continued their amazing Wembley record – this was the eighth game they had played there and they had yet to be defeated. Clemence also set up a personal record that day – it was his sixth appearance in the season's annual opener. Spurs had now contested the annual Shield (both the Charity and its forerunner the Sheriff of London's) on eight occasions, winning five and drawing two.

The Charity Shield was also notable for the display of a Spurs reserve, Mark Falco, who scored his side's two goals. Deputising for Garth Crooks, who had undergone a cartilage operation, Falco went on to score nine goals in the season's first twelve games, before suffering a ligament injury himself.

Falco's most notable performance was in Amsterdam, where he scored twice in the highly creditable 3-1 Cup Winners Cup win over once mighty Ajax. The club was concerned that its first European trip since the disaster at Rotterdam should be back to the Netherlands – it would have been preferable to play rather further away where fewer of the troublesome element could afford to travel. There was happily little trouble, though it is a comment on the current interpretation of the term that Jeff Powell could write in the *Daily Mail*: 'Thirteen arrests, mostly for window-breaking and car-scratching, one unconfirmed minor stabbing and the separation of two small groups of squabblers on the terraces were no more than a routine night's work for the Dutch police.'

A £4 MILLION INVESTMENT

The return at White Hart Lane was no less easy – Spurs winning 3-0. Little Dundalk, runners-up in the League of Ireland, proved far tougher opposition in the second round of the Cup Winners Cup, holding Tottenham 1-1 in Ireland and going down to a single goal from Garth Crooks in the return. It was enough, however, to put Spurs through to the quarter-finals in March 1982.

Although Tottenham's signing of Ray Clemence received the summer's headlines, far more significant to the club was the fact that Hoddle, Villa and Ardiles had all renewed their contracts. Vice-chairman Geoff Richardson rightly pointed out that: 'In the current climate, with some players looking to European salaries and with others exercising their new freedom to move where they like at the end of a contract, this was as important as signing three new stars.'

CUPS AND MORE CUPS

As the centenary season settled down, it seemed to North London that Spurs were contesting one non-stop cup tie.

From the beginning of October through to the middle of February, when the League Cup finalists and FA Cup quarter-finalists were decided, Spurs played 25 games of which 12 were cup ties. They were already in process of establishing a record for modern times

when, on February 13, they beat Aston Villa in an FA Cup fifth round tie to establish a run of 23 consecutive cup matches without defeat. This covered three competitions – the FA Cup, the League Cup and the Cup Winners Cup. At this stage their last cup setback had been a League Cup tie at Upton Park on 2 December 1980. Far more remarkable, the last occasion on which Tottenham had been drawn away in a cup tie was in the third round at Queen's Park Rangers on 3 January 1981. They had obviously had to play two-legged matches and semi-finals away from White Hart Lane, but had not otherwise had to travel. Fortune indeed seemed to be favouring them. It must have bought tears to the eyes of the push-and-run side who, between 1953 and 1955, played away in 10 consecutive FA Cup rounds, then a twentieth-century record.

The Centenary Year, 1982, could not have got off to a more dramatic start. After nearly one hundred years of almost totally ignoring each other in the FA Cup, Arsenal and Spurs were drawn together at White Hart Lane in the third round on 2 January. It was to be a one-sided game, Garth Crooks winning it with the only goal, as well as hitting a post and bar. It will always be remembered, however, for the manner of the goal. An Ardiles pass gave Crooks the chance of a weakly hit left-footed shot. Jennings, returning to his old stamping ground, had the ball well covered, but it somehow slipped under his arm and dribbled over the line. To make the day thoroughly forgettable for Jennings, he later suffered a groin strain in a wild chase and tackle outside the penalty area with Crooks, had to leave the field and was to be out of the game for months. He said afterwards, with no overstatement: 'It's the worst goal I've let in during the whole of my career.'

The one-sided, rather dull (if extremely satisfying for the home supporters) fixture allowed many to reminisce about the only other occasion the two clubs had met before in the Cup – at the same stage 33 years and two Doubles before. The following day one or two reporters seemed to devote more space to the earlier game than the one they had just witnessed. Said Brian Glanville in the *Sunday Times*: 'On that remote afternoon, Tottenham inexplicably dropped their star inside-forward Eddie Baily, replacing him with an obscure reserve called Harry Gilberg, who did nothing. Ronnie Burgess, their attacking wing-half, ran wild, giving the freedom of the park to Arsenal's Jimmy Logie, who then ran them ragged. Roper and Lishman, if I remember correctly, ran in to drive ground shots home in the first half and Ian McPherson was on the far post to head the ball past the celebrated Ted Ditchbum in the second.'

That paragraph was an excellent cameo of the strengths and weaknesses of Spurs' creative department in the 1950s, as well as revealing a tremendous affection for the Tottenham, and the football, of the time.

In 1982 Spurs won just as easily as had Arsenal in 1949, and just as they would do again in the next two rounds, against Leeds (Crooks again scoring the only goal) and against League Champions Villa. The latter game was yet another 1-0 home win, the goal coming from a Falco diving header after an

excellent Paul Price run and a Crooks' centre.

For the moment though, attention returned to the League Cup, where the whole country was gearing up for perhaps the most attractive final ever in this previously poor relation of a cup competition. It was to be a clash of the country's best and most popular sides of the moment – Liverpool and Spurs. The Merseysiders had convincingly ejected Ipswich in the League Cup semi-final and, until losing to Chelsea in the FA Cup, had gone undefeated through 1982.

Spurs, for their part, had undergone a difficult path to Wembley. The home and away second round tie was against Manchester United – the fourth time the two sides had been drawn together in Cup competitions in the space of four seasons.

It was inevitably a tight tie. In the first leg Steve Archibald scored the only goal; in the away return, before 56,000 people, Mike Hazard volleyed one in early on and it was all over bar the glum Old Trafford obituaries. The next two rounds were easier – Second Division Wrexham succumbed 2-0 to Hughton and Hoddle goals, while Third Division Fulham conceded just one, again to Mike Hazard, but it was one too many for them. The fifth round, again at home, against Nottingham Forest was the toughest tie. Forest had the best record of any club in the League Cup, having reached three of the previous four finals. This time it was Spurs against Peter Shilton, the only goal eventually being a mis-hit shot by Ardiles. The game's talking point was, however, a thrice

taken penalty by Glenn Hoddle. Shilton saved Hoddle's first effort, diving to his right, but the kick was ordered to be retaken because Forest defenders had been encroaching; Hoddle succeeded with the next, to Shilton's left, but again had to retake it because Mark Falco had entered the area; Hoddle changed direction again, put it just inside Shilton's right-hand post – and this time saw the England keeper save it again. Hoddle's face was saved by Ardiles in the second half and it proved a happy day for the 6,000 fans who occupied the new West Stand for the very first time.

The League Cup semi-final was against West Bromwich, again another tight and hard fought tie and against a side Spurs had not defeated for three seasons. The first leg, in the Midlands, ended goalless after seven names had been taken and Galvin and West Brom's Jol were sent off in the closing minutes. Galvin was singularly unlucky to be dismissed for nothing much more than an arm wave of exasperation after he had been impeded. The second leg, a week later, was far more dignified. After 56 minutes Falco back-headed a ball from Hoddle and Mike Hazard added to his tally of valuable goals. Yet again a single goal won it and, with the same result removing Villa from the FA Cup three days later, Spurs had played their tenth domestic Cup game of the 1981–82 season without defeat. Far more remarkable was the fact that they had yet to concede a goal in either the FA Cup or League Cup. So far, ten games had seen ten goals for and none against; eight had ended 1-0, one

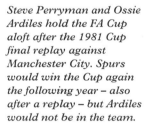

Steve Perryman and Ossie Ardiles hold the FA Cup aloft after the 1981 Cup final replay against Manchester City. Spurs would win the Cup again the following year – also after a replay – but Ardiles would not be in the team.

2-0 and the other was goalless. The decision to buy Ray Clemence was looking better by the Saturday.

The remarkable sequence of nine consecutive home ties was finally broken for the FA Cup quarter-finals. Even so Spurs still remained in London. They had played 29 cup matches since they had last been drawn to play outside the capital in a normal domestic single legged tie. That was way back on 26 January 1980 when they had drawn 0-0 at Swindon in the fourth round of the FA Cup. Of those 29 matches all had been played on London grounds except the first semi-final in 1981 against Wolves (at Hillsborough) and the away halves of the two legged League Cup ties against Manchester United and West Bromwich.

The FA Cup quarter-final against Chelsea was perhaps the most exhilarating of all their cup ties in a cup-packed season. Spurs went in for half-time having conceded their first cup goal of the season – a quite magnificent 25-yard free-kick from Mike Fillery. But the Pensioners' hopes were to be short-lived for, within a quarter of an hour of the restart, Spurs were 3–1 ahead and cruising. The goals came in quick succession from Archibald (after Francis failed to hold a Hoddle shot), Hoddle himself after a delightful cross-passing sequence from Archibald to Hazard to Hoddle, and then a third from Mike Hazard. Alan Mayes made it 3–2 but Spurs had made Chelsea's earlier hopes of a repeat of their win against Liverpool look rather foolish. A few

days later Tottenham patiently awaited their chances in the first leg of the Cup Winners Cup quarter-final against Eintracht Frankfurt. Miller and Hazard took their openings late in the second half and Spurs had a two-goal lead to take to Germany for the second leg. Talk had now, a little late but the more insistently for that, turned to the apparent possibility of Spurs winning four prizes. Everyone at the club dismissed this as pure fantasy – it was only a few days before that view was to be confirmed.

THE RECORDS TUMBLE

On Saturday 13 March 1982 Spurs lost their first ever domestic Cup final, at the ninth time of asking; they lost for the first time at Wembley, also their ninth appearance; their run of 25 consecutive cup games without defeat came to an end, though it went into the record books as the longest ever, beating Blackburn's run of 24 set up only four years after Spurs were founded; and, of course, they lost any chance they might have had of winning four trophies in a season.

It was a game with the usual ironies. The two captains, Steve Perryman and Graeme Souness, had played together in Spurs' youth team in 1970 when it had won the FA Youth Challenge Cup (the success was repeated in 1974). Less well known was that Keith Burkinshaw had played just one League game for Liverpool, at the end of 1954, and this was his sole first-team appearance in the upper reaches of the English game. Joining Liverpool in November 1953, he had stayed until December 1957 when, with that one memory, he had gone off to Workington. Bob Paisley, by contrast, had given up playing in 1954 and gone on to the coaching staff at Anfield at the same time.

And it was Liverpool who were to get the cream at the end of the newly-named Milk Cup final, but not before Spurs had appeared to be on their way to a famous and un023charac-teristic success until just three minutes from the end of normal time. The details of the game are easily told. Steve Archibald scored after just 11 minutes when he somehow managed to latch on to a lofted pass from Glenn Hoddle, persevere rather than dribble his way past the Liverpool defenders Thompson and Lawrenson, and then beat keeper Grobbelaar, who had already committed himself. For the next 76 minutes Spurs defended, getting behind the ball, bringing forwards back into midfield, closing down the Liverpool power-house. It was not a particularly attractive display but it appeared to be effective, bringing back memories of the titanic struggles between Liverpool and Forest in the late 1970s when Forest kept winning with just those tactics.

Had the game ended three minutes early, the following day's reports would have been full of just this kind of praise for Spurs; that Liverpool were never easy to beat, but that there were ways and means of doing so and Spurs had found the right one. Not a great game, but well done Tottenham.

But in that 87th minute concentration lapsed just long enough. Substitute David Johnson, on for McDermott, crossed from the right. Somehow or other the Spurs defence let it through, and there was young Ronnie Whelan, Liverpool's discovery of the season, to place it to Clemence's right.

From that moment on the result never seemed in doubt. At the end of 90 minutes the Liverpool players seemed exuberant, raring to go; by contrast the Spurs seemed exhausted. Hoddle had had a poor 90 minutes, apparently suffering from a bruised rib, while Tony Galvin had not proved his superiority over Phil Neal as predicted, perhaps because of an early injury after a tackle by Graeme Souness.

Twenty minutes into extra time, Ossie Ardiles, clearly the best of the Spurs players on display, gave the ball away to Ian Rush near the penalty area. The ball passed quickly from Rush to Dalglish to Whelan and into the back of the net. Rush added a third in the dying seconds but by then it was all academic. The writing had been on the milk bottle from the moment Whelan scored his first goal. Spurs were brave in the unaccustomed role of vanquished; in a history lasting 99 years and 6 months there had never been the need to hand down lessons on how to be good final losers.

For most clubs, such a traumatic Wembley defeat would have been both the highlight and the end of their season. For Spurs, though naturally disappointed by the result, it was very much business as usual. There were still three prizes to be pursued and such a log-jam of fixtures that many wondered whether they could possibly end the season with even eleven fit professionals; in April and the first three weeks of May alone Tottenham had an absurd 18 fixtures.

It was the familiar failing of British football, simply too much pressure for the better teams, and all the worse for the fact that it was World Cup year as well. Clemence, Hoddle, Archibald and company would be playing first-class English football only two weeks before the start of the World Cup. Argentina, by comparison, had refused to allow their squad to play any club football since mid-February, the only exceptions being the exiles Ardiles and Bertoni.

The Championship remained the most alluring prize, if certainly the toughest. Because of their run of Cup matches, plus exceptional problems during the winter's cold spell, Tottenham had spent most of the season four or five games in arrears of the other challengers. Theoretically they were almost always in a position to eventually head the League, but they would have had to win most of their games in hand to do so – a near impossible feat in modern times.

The attempt was to be a brave, if doomed, one. Excellent results such as a 3-2 defeat of Southampton, at a time when the Saints headed the League, a 1-0 Easter win over Ipswich, then second in the division, and a sweet 3-1 success at Highbury two days later, clearly left Spurs in with a chance. But inevitably they were occasionally erratic; a 1-0 defeat at The Hawthorns on 27 March was their first League setback away from home in six months, but a 2-2 home draw with Sunderland just after Easter was rather more crucial. The 1981–82 season was the first which awarded three points for a win, and to take only one point from the then bottom club in the division (particularly after being 2-0 up at half-time) was careless in the extreme. Even so, Spurs might still have won (or, more crucially at the time, might have believed they could have won) the

Championship if Liverpool had not run into such devastating form from the turn of the year after having fallen to 12th.

By the time Spurs arrived at Anfield on 15 May, the last Saturday of the season, their chance had gone and, ironically, Liverpool needed to win to secure a record 13th Championship. Spurs had not won at Anfield for 70 years and this was no moment to break the sequence. A glorious Hoddle goal, from nearly 40 yards out and swerving left to right over Grobbelaar's head, provided a delightful memory but Liverpool won 3-1 and confirmed Keith Burkinshaw's prediction made ten games earlier. After a crucial 2-0 defeat for Spurs at Old Trafford he had said: 'Liverpool are such a good team for getting these 1-0 wins, aren't they? I can't honestly say we stand a great chance of catching them now.' And so it was to prove.

It is not really surprising that Spurs could not sustain enough of a challenge to win the League. Bill Nicholson said of his teams in 1961 and 1962 that, as soon as they had won their FA Cup semi-finals, it was almost impossible to keep their minds on League matches. Indeed, in both years Spurs had a very poor spell leading up to Wembley.

Burkinshaw's team appeared slightly less vulnerable to this fluctuating form because of the extremely strong defensive base which had been laid down. The midfield and forward line had developed the confidence not to panic in search of a first goal in even the most vital games – largely because they had developed a reliance on the defence keeping its domain intact during the mid-season run of ten cup games without conceding a goal.

As 1982 progressed, injuries to his front runners meant that Burkinshaw had to be able to permutate Crooks, Archibald, Falco and Chris Jones almost game to game. In midfield things were even more fluid – a choice being made among Ardiles (before his return to Argentina), Villa, Hazard, Brooke, Hoddle, Perryman and Graham Roberts depending on who was fit. Roberts' play was a revelation. He proved that he was not only a strong, forceful centre-back, but also a rather subtle, hard-working midfield tyro when given the chance. Against Southampton he even contrived to score a hat-trick, all three goals coming from open play. This may well be the only occasion in first-class soccer history that a centre-back, playing in midfield, has scored a hat-trick – and against the League leaders.

Tony Galvin's role on the left was also perceived as more critical. With neither Archibald nor Crooks being a natural target man, Galvin's speed down the wing was the essential variety in a mix which would otherwise have depended too heavily on a skilful midfield pushing ground-balls through the middle to utilise the speed of the front-runners. The full-backs also proved themselves valuable overlappers. Chris Hughton had long performed that role, and scored the occasional goal into the bargain, but Steve Perryman's ability to read Glenn Hoddle's intentions became almost telepathic. Perhaps Spurs most delightful move of the season was Hoddle's dropping of a long ball, or quick reverse pass against the direction of play, into the last few yards of the right hand side of the field for Steve Perryman to run on to and centre.

CUP WINNERS AND CUPS

If the Championship was to slip slowly from Spurs grasp, perhaps the single most likely prize – the European Cup Winners Cup – shot dramatically from that of Ray Clemence in one dreadful moment.

Tottenham had survived the quarter-final second leg away at Eintracht Frankfurt somewhat fortuitously. Two-nil up from the first leg, they conceded two goals very quickly to Eintracht's Borchers and the Korean Bum Kun Cha and seemed on the way out. However a slow, cautious recovery in the final 45 minutes was rewarded when, ten minutes from time, Hoddle delicately placed a 20-yard shot into the corner of the net to put the Londoners into the semi-final.

Initially they seemed fortunate to draw Barcelona in the last four, partially because it meant avoiding favourites Dinamo Tbilisi, but, more relevantly, because Barcelona were to host the final in their own Nou Camp Stadium and it seemed preferable to face them over two games than in a single one on their own patch. As it turned out, that reasoning was defective. Standard Liege won both legs against Dinamo and Barcelona came to London obsessed by the need not to lose.

Playing the final at home would mean a full house for the Spaniards at Nou Camp extended to hold 120,000 spectators for the World Cup opening match being held there only a couple of weeks later – and almost one million pounds for the club. They therefore arrived in London with a succeed-at-all-costs attitude.

The result was 'the most cynical game I've seen for 10 years,' according to Frank McLintock. Barcelona manager Udo Lattek ('the match was sometimes too violent') had sent out a hit-squad very reminiscent of the bunch of Atletico Madrid thugs which disgraced Celtic Park in the 1974 European Cup semi-final. In both cases, the Spaniards did their job. Barcelona went home with a 1-1 result and only one man – Estella – sent off. He was later

suspended for two matches (meaning he missed the final) while both clubs were fined, Barcelona much the more heavily.

Despite all this, Spurs might have survived had it not been for a terrible error by Ray Clemence, his first critical mistake since the Charity Shield eight months before. A speculative 35-yard shot from Barcelona full-back and captain Olmo was aimed straight at the keeper and looked totally harmless. As Clemence stood and gathered the ball it somehow squirmed from his grasp and over the line. It should be said, in mitigation, that it was Clemence's excellent performance in Germany in the previous round that had kept Spurs in the competition at all. Graham Roberts popped up for a late equaliser but it was not to be enough. 'We didn't expect them to play like that,' said Keith Burkinshaw, 'we had heard so much about them being a good side technically, but it never showed through.' A fortnight later in Barcelona Spurs, who had thus far lost only four games away from home all season and hence had cause for some hope, went down 1-0.

The goal was a bad one for Spurs; Quini headed on a free-kick, Ray Clemence apparently yelled 'Away!' but defenders Hughton and Roberts thought he said 'Leave it' in the noise and confusion. As a result no-one went for the ball and Allan Simonsen nipped in to push it home.

It was a sad moment, with inevitable memories of another semi-final in the Iberian peninsula exactly twenty years before, when Benfica denied the seemingly unstoppable claims of Glory, Glory, Hallelujah to a first European prize.

But the Spurs of 1962 were to bounce back from their European Cup semi-final defeat, were to finish third in the League and were to go on to retain the FA Cup they had won the year before. The parallels and omens seemed remarkably close.

After Spurs FA Cup quarter-final defeat of

Chelsea the semi-final draw threw up two rather poignant games, while leaving open the possibility of the first all-Second Division final or the attractive and intriguing re-run of the League Cup semi-final between Spurs and West Brom.

Queen's Park Rangers, playing in their first FA Cup semi-final, and West Brom were to meet at Highbury. They had met in only one other crucial game in their history – the first Wembley League Cup final in 1967, when Third Division QPR beat their First Division opponents 3-2. Playing for QPR that day was one Les Allen, of Double fame. Fifteen years later the Londoners upset the bookies again when one of their forwards stuck out a leg to deflect a defenders' clearance into the West Brom net and win the game 1-0. The forward's name was, of course, Clive Allen and he was the son born to Les Allen and his wife exactly two weeks after Spurs beat Leicester to win the Double. It was Clive's seventh goal in the Cup run, including four against Blackpool in the fourth round.

The other semi-final brought back even stronger memories of that same Double, for Spurs were to play against the very side they had defeated in the 1961 Cup final – Leicester City. The similarities did not end there either. The game was at Villa Park, traditionally Spurs' unlucky semi-final ground after the 1948, 1953 and 1956 defeats, though they had won their semi-final there in the Double year. More significantly, Leicester were to go down by the same score as in the 1961 final – 2-0. Like that game at Wembley twenty-one years before, it could hardly be called a classic. Spurs were trying to reach Wembley for the fifth time in a year; Leicester were hopefully trying to make it fifth time lucky, for they had lost their previous four FA Cup finals. The first half was tight, the most newsworthy item being the Leicester crowd's continual booing of Ardiles.

Argentina had invaded the Falkland Islands

24 hours before the game and there was considerable speculation about what would happen to that country's most popular exports to Britain – Ardiles and Villa. Ardiles was due to return to Buenos Aires the following day anyway but Cesar Menotti, the Argentine manager, had indicated that he might be prepared to let his key midfielder return to England for the Cup final. Menotti was quoted as saying: 'Keith Burkinshaw and all the people at Tottenham are my friends. Always Tottenham have said Yes, Yes and Yes again to Menotti. Now it is impossible for Menotti to say No if they need Ardiles for the Cup final. Ardiles will decide.' The crisis obviously put Ardiles' eventual return in doubt, as did an interview given at Buenos Aires airport on his arrival there.

But if the Villa Park semi-final was eventually to be remembered as Ardiles' last game for Spurs, he certainly made his mark on it. In the 56th minute he moved towards Hoddle as the latter took a corner on the right. In a clearly set-piece move, Hoddle pushed the ball short to Ardiles, who, having lost his marker, was able to turn and put across a low centre for Crooks' to volley home from the six-yard line. Leicester's troubles mounted. In yet another incident reminiscent of 1961 (when they had lost right-back Len Chalmers for most of the final) an innocuous collision between Galvin and Leicester's current right-back Tommy Williams left the defender with a hairline fracture of the shin and his side with ten men.

Even more was to come. In the 76th minute, a Galvin cross went begging and was collected about 20 yards from his own goal by Ian Wilson. The Leicester man was under no pressure and had any number of options. He chose a back pass to Mark Wallington, but got too much of his foot under the ball and clipped it perfectly over the goalkeeper's head into the net. It was, if nothing else, one of the most memorable goals scored in a semi-final in

ABOVE RIGHT: The 1982 FA Cup semi-final at Villa Park on 3 April brought back memories of the Double for Spurs' opponents were Leicester and City lost by the same score as in the 1961 final, 2-0 Garth Crooks (out of picture ABOVE) scored the first goal but it was made by Ossie Ardiles (celebrating background right) after a Glenn Hoddle corner. This was to be Ardiles' last game for Spurs before his return to Buenos Aires. Argentina had invaded the Falklands the previous day and Ardiles left to join his country's World Cup squad the following morning. ABOVE LEFT: An unusually sombre conversation between two goalscorers in a semi-final Garth Crooks consoles Leicester's Ian Wilson after the latter had finished his club's chances of reaching their fifth FA Cup final with a spectacular lobbed own-goal in the 76th minute.

years and it guaranteed Tottenham's tenth game at Wembley, their thirteenth cup final and a chance to equal the performances of 1961 and 1962 in retaining the FA Cup.

So the final was an unexpected and unpredictable one against Queen's Park Rangers, and it clearly had more than its fair share of interest. It was the fifth time in ten seasons that a Second Division side had reached the final and no-one at White Hart Lane needed reminding that three of the previous four (Sunderland, Southampton and West Ham) had come away with the Cup. It was also the fourth all-London professional final in fifteen years (Spurs had figured in the first, against Chelsea in 1967), a factor which increased the interest in the capital but rather tended to diminish the event for the country as a whole.

On the personal level, and in addition to the Allen connection, Rangers' manager Terry Venables had, of course, played for Spurs in that 1967 success, while, by coincidence, Rangers were also celebrating their centenary.

Tottenham had no illusions about the task ahead. As recently as the third round in 1981, they had found it no easy task to squeeze past Rangers – drawing 0-0 at Loftus Road and winning the replay 3-1 at home. Rangers run to the final – past Middlesbrough (winning 3-2 away after drawing 1-1 at home), Blackpool, Grimsby, Crystal Palace and West Bromwich – was impressive enough. And it was rather odd, travelling to Wembley, to consider that QPR had almost withdrawn from the 1981-82 FA Cup over their synthetic pitch. The FA would not give them an absolute guarantee that it could be used for Cup matches for more than one season and chairman Jim Gregory had to be dissuaded from withdrawing in protest.

Playing a Second Division club at Wembley was certainly going to be no walkover. Spurs knew they would face a tight midfield and a very committed defence. They had also experienced a very lop-sided approach to Wembley. The first three rounds were against relatively strong First Division sides, the next three all against Second Division clubs. Since the formation of the Football League in 1888, only one other club has completely avoided First Division opposition from the last eight onwards.

That club was Newcastle United, who had faced Grimsby, Fulham and Wolves in 1908, and actually lost the final 3-1 to the latter. Strangely, Newcastle enjoyed the same good fortune two years later, in 1910, when they played Leicester Fosse, Swindon and Barnsley. Again they failed to win the final (drawing 1-1 at Crystal Palace) but eventually won the replay 2-0 at Goodison. Spurs share another statistical oddity with Newcastle. They are the only clubs to have retained the FA Cup in the twentieth century. Newcastle did so in 1951 and 1952, Spurs in 1961 and 1962. In the first two years of another decade Spurs were set to maintain the sequence.

But as the club approached the 1982 FA Cup final there was a very real fear that Burkinshaw's side had peaked too early, that it had seen its period of excellence around the middle of what had been an over-long and over-strenuous season. Ardiles had gone back to Buenos Aires, Hoddle seemed prone to nagging injuries and, perhaps, concern about his England place. In attack neither of the strikers had been as consistent as in the previous year and Archibald had had no better than a mediocre 1982, scoring just six league goals in an injury-upset season.

At the back the best combination had yet to emerge – the mixture of Roberts, Miller and Price suffered a string of injuries and even gave way, as late as the beginning of May, to a further centre-back pairing in the shape of John Lacy and Pat Corbett.

Any instability in the centre of the defence put even more pressure on the side's cornerstone and captain, Steve Perryman. Often referred to at the time as the best uncapped player in the country, Perryman at last won the recognition he deserved, when coming on as a substitute for England against Iceland in Reykjavik in June 1982.

Perryman played his last game for England Schoolboys just days before joining Spurs as an apprentice in 1967. He progressed easily into the Under-23 team, winning 17 caps, and was undoubtedly being groomed for the senior team when a pair of unconnected events robbed him of his inheritance.

First Ramsey was sacked from the England job after the failure to reach the 1974 World Cup finals. Then Perryman had to switch positions as Spurs went through their relegation traumas in the mid-1970s. 'I won the Under-23 caps playing in midfield, then I changed to the back four. I realised then that if England wanted two big men at the back, capable of winning everything in the air, I'd never get a look-in,' Perryman reasoned.

Brian Glanville, then of the *Sunday Times*, believed the Ramsey era had a lot to answer for in failing to help a player of Perryman's ability make the international grade. 'We paid a heavy price for World Cup success in the awful sterile years of work rate, neglect of wingers and the primacy of effort over style and skill,' said Glanville. 'At the time Perryman was encouraged to toil and graft rather than to express his natural skill.'

Throughout his career, Perryman remained, in Glanville's words, the eternal cherub. In 18 years at the club, he passed Pat Jenning's record of 472 League appearances and established the current record of 655, before joining Brentford as player-manager. When he signed as a professional in 1969, he joined names like Gilzean, Greaves and Mullery. 'Spurs were the team to play for then. I was in four finals in my first five years,' he recalls. Perhaps Perryman's greatest qualities were his versatility and durability. Keith Burkinshaw said he was one of the best speed-readers of a ball in the game, but his ability to play a variety of roles to great effect was probably a reflection of his tremendous staying power as much as anything else.

There were to be other tangible rewards as well. Two weeks before the FA Cup final he was voted Sportswriters Footballer of the Year, the third Spurs' player to win the award after Blanchflower and Jennings. Glenn Hoddle was a close second, reflecting the impression the Spurs side had made on the country through an excellent season. Perryman also joined Hoddle in Ron Greenwood's final forty for the World Cup finals.

In a sense, the real story of the 1982 Cup final had been told before a ball had even

been kicked. Just as Spurs had played their semi-final the day after Argentina invaded the Falklands, so Keith Burkinshaw was faced with a decision whether or not to play Ricky Villa the day after the British task force had landed there. At 11.30am on the morning of the match Burkinshaw was forced to concede that both he and the player felt the situation had become too tense for Villa to play. In itself that was a terrible decision to have to make. What made it so ironic were the memories of a year before, of a Cup final replay in which Villa scored twice and won the match with perhaps the most memorable individual goal scored at Wembley since the War.

Villa himself stayed at home with his family to watch the game on TV – not to avoid the fans or his team-mates, but to try and keep away from insistent media pursuers. At the ground the fans chanted his name with affection and sadness, hoping that they had not seen the last of the two symbols who had so dramatically placed Spurs back on centre-stage four years before.

Sitting on the coach on the way to Wembley Burkinshaw must have been pondering on a fraught end to a strange season. Three months before Spurs might have won four trophies. Now here he was, having agreed a new three-year contract with the club the night before, forced to resign himself to the probable loss of the two talismen who had first brought him to managerial prominence, and also having to cope with three troublesome injuries to the players he did have left. Ray Clemence had a calf injury, Tony Galvin an uncertain knee after a month out of the game, and captain Steve Perryman, who had not missed a match all season, a pulled thigh muscle.

In the event all three took the field, the team having Clemence back in goal; Perryman, Price, Miller and Hughton at the back; Graham Roberts pushed into midfield to join Hazard and Hoddle, and the front runners were the season's first choices – Galvin, Crooks and Archibald.

The clubs may have only played each other once before in the FA Cup (in 1981) but the team members knew each other well enough. Like Graeme Souness, Mike Flanagan had also played with Steve Perryman in the Spurs team which won the 1970 FA Youth Cup. Les Allen, Clive's father, was manager at QPR when

Terry Venables followed him from White Hart Lane to Shepherd's Bush in 1969. Not surprisingly, young Clive had trained for a time at Spurs and had even scored a hat-trick in Tottenham colours when playing for London Schools against Coventry at the Lane.

Before the game David Miller said in the *Daily Express* that: 'Together Ardiles and Burkinshaw have made a statement of principle (about the game) which has possibly been the most important in English football since the era of Moore-Hurst-Peters at West Ham. At an admittedly lean time in the game, Burkinshaw has more than deserved his success and it is what he has done for the game as much as it is for Tottenham that we should be celebrating today.'

But as Danny Blanchflower said after the 1961 final, the talking was rather better than the playing. Few finals can possibly live up to their previews, but this one was perhaps more guilty than most. It was one-sided but unconvincing. Spurs were playing their 65th first-class game of the season and, particularly in the second-half, looked it. For 115 minutes Ray Clemence (who was equalling Pat Jennings' record of four goalkeeping appearances in FA Cup finals) had just two real shots to stop – and both of those looked marginally off target. QPR were hampered by an early injury to Clive Allen, but Spurs were equally affected by Steve Archibald's poor finishing. Twice he was put through clear, twice he failed to score. Ironically, on the one, similar, occasion he did find the net he was very debatably ruled offside. It was 0-0 after 90 minutes but Spurs eventually broke the deadlock with ten minutes of extra time left. Glenn Hoddle played a one-two with Graham Roberts, hit a low shot from 20 yards and saw it go through Tony Currie's legs, take a slight deflection, and beat Rangers' excellent keeper Peter Hucker.

It seemed all over but, with just five minutes left, Spurs were suckered by a QPR set piece. A Stainrod long throw was back-headed by Bob Hazell and nodded in by an unmarked Terry Fenwick. It was the first goal ever scored from open play by a full-back in a Cup final. To nostalgic eyes looking back ten years the whole move could have been a Chivers throw, a Gilzean back-header and a ghosting Peters, but that was hardly an excuse for Spurs being caught out.

Glenn Hoddle's 110th minute shot passes through Tony Currie's legs, takes a slight deflection and beats man-of-the-match Peter Hucker to put Spurs 1-0 up in the first game of the 1982 FA Cup final. It was the second consecutive year that a Hoddle shot had been deflected into the net by an opponent in the Cup final. Spurs, playing in yellow because of the colour clash, held that lead for just five minutes before Terry Fenwick equalised for QPR and, for the second consecutive year though only the third time since the final moved to Wembley in 1923, the match went to a replay.

Seven finals and seven victories as Glenn Hoddle slots home his second goal of the 1982 FA Cup final, a penalty in the sixth minute of the replay. It was his third scoring shot in the four games that had made up Spurs' two consecutive FA Cup successes, but this one did not need a deflection on the way. It was to be the only goal of the game and Tony Currie was again involved, conceding the penalty when he brought down Graham Roberts just inside the area.
Fortunately, as it was to decide the game, there was no doubt about the decision, though Queen's Park Rangers had cause to feel that their aggressive, dominating performance perhaps deserved some reward other than the losers' medals. It was, in fact, only the third FA Cup final to be decided by a single penalty goal – the other two being the famous games between Huddersfield and Preston in both 1922 and 1938. In 1982 the FA had already decided that, should scores be level after extra time, then the final would be the first major match in Britain to be concluded by penalties anyway. How right they were . . .

So for the second year running, and for only the third time since the final moved to Wembley, there was to be a replay. And this time the problems were to be QPR's. Clive Allen's ankle injury ruled him out while Glenn Roeder was suspended after an earlier sending off at Luton and so Tony Currie captained the side. Gary Micklewhite and Warren Neill came into the QPR team while Spurs remained unchanged.

And, at 9.15pm on Thursday 27 May, only one thing really mattered; that was that Spurs had retained the FA Cup and won the trophy for the seventh time in seven appearances equalling the record then held by Aston Villa. But it is fair to add that not even the most blinkered Tottenham fan could have argued that it was one of his side's greatest performances, certainly not one to compare with a year before, or that QPR did not deserve something more from their replay performance.

There was to be just one goal, scored after a mere six minutes before either side had settled. Graham Roberts set off on a surging run into the right side of the penalty area; three yards inside his legs were swept away by Tony Currie; it was a clear penalty, as QPR manager Terry Venables agreed at half-time. Glenn Hoddle took the kick without any preamble, placing it in the corner to Hucker's right. This time he didn't need a deflection. As an attacking force, Spurs' final virtually ended there. As on the previous Saturday, they looked like a team that had been playing flat out for months, as indeed they had. Not until the very last minute, when Steve Archibald was put through yet again and this time hit the post, did they look like scoring a second.

But the essence of football is that the better team is the one which scores more goals. The simple fact was that QPR, after attacking for the greater part of the match, did not manage to do so once. Nonetheless they seemed to have succeeded in the 43rd minute when a Gary Micklewhite shot was disallowed because Terry Fenwick was judged to have been offside for an instant. The decision was a let-off – the Spurs players had not protested and it was the sort of goal which would have been allowed on a different day. After 65 minutes QPR went even closer when John Gregory hit the crossbar with a beautifully volleyed chip and for most of the second half it was really a matter of Spurs holding out, not so much for the FA Cup but

for some tangible reward at the end of an impossibly exhausting season. Paul Miller and Graham Roberts were the heroes, though, even with Garry Brooke on again as substitute, it was clear that Ardiles was going to be sadly missed.

But if both games left something to be desired there could be no denying that Spurs deserved their prize after a string of six convincing wins on the way to Wembley, achieved without a single replay. The fact that the season and the tiredness had finally caught up with them could not take away the memories and the quality that had achieved all those magnificent results against Ajax, Manchester United, Chelsea and many others.

It was, in fact, the sixteenth time that Spurs had taken the field (including replays) for a cup final match played in England. Astonishingly they had lost just once, the Milk Cup final against Liverpool.

Nonetheless, a strangely quiet Thursday night with the exhausted Cup holders hanging on to a one goal lead is not the archetypal image of the English season's dramatic conclusion. The air of unreality was highlighted by the empty spaces on the terracing. For the only time in the 60 years since the very first Wembley game in 1923, it had been possible to buy tickets at the gate for an FA Cup final. Even then, the stadium was not full. The official attendance was given as 90,000, but it was clearly considerably less. Perhaps this was not so surprising. It was Spurs' sixth appearance at Wembley in two seasons (four FA Cup finals, the Milk Cup final and the Charity Shield), an all-London tie generates little provincial interest and QPR could not expect to carry more than 25,000 supporters at the most.

But, at the end, there could hardly be a more fitting conclusion to the centenary season than the winning of a record seventh FA Cup. It is the FA Cup that has been Spurs' symbol, almost as much as the cockerel. It was their astonishing win in 1901 that gained them not only a place in the history books but a place in the Football League. It was the glory of 1921 which proved the answer to Arsenal's stealing of their First Division place. It was the moment in 1961 which placed the crown on the best club side the country had ever seen; it was 1962 and 1967 which saw Jimmy Greaves in his rightful place; and it was to be 1981 which left the game with the enduring memory of one

glorious goal and two Argentinians. The uncanny sequence was extended with victory over Nottingham Forest in 1991.

So the 1982 Cup celebrations surely seemed a fitting finale to the centenary story and yet, at that very moment, events were in train to prove that no story ever ends. As the actual centenary date was reached, in September 1982, negotiations which were to have a far wider effect on the club than any FA Cup win were being quietly concluded.

The symbol and the spur had been the new stand. The intention to build it, declared in mid-1980, had already caused the resignation of one chairman, Sidney Wale. Wale had, however, remained the biggest shareholder. And while the building had gone reasonably to schedule, there was no disguising the fact that the father and son team of chairman and vice-chairman Arthur and Geoff Richardson were, despite their confident earlier assertions, increasingly worried about matching costs with revenues. A basic part of the plan had been to sell the 72 boxes for £30,000 each, covering a three-year lease. That would, in theory, have covered nearly half the cost of the whole enterprise. The problem was that, with the recession deepening and companies becoming very sensitive about visible directors' perks (this was the period when numerous chairmen's Rolls-Royces were quietly sold), the boxes were just not moving. Having set the price at £30,000, it also became very difficult to reduce this figure to create more interest. Those that had committed would, not unreasonably, expect a similar deduction. And, as the bills rolled in, it also became clear that the original estimate of £4 million had been somewhat unrealistic. When

the final reckoning came to be made the overall costs were nearly £1 million higher, and the club was faced with interest and repayments on the loan of around £800,000 per annum. To make matters worse, despite reaching two Cup finals and taking £3 million in receipts (easily their highest ever), the club's profit on the 1981-82 season was only £200,000.

All of this was probably manageable, but it was seen to be combined with a standard of public relations and organisation off the field which bore no relation to that achieved by Keith Burkinshaw and the team on it. At a meeting to discuss the new stand, a prospective purchaser of a private box asked for confirmation that it would be available for European matches, a point which should have been rhetorical. Arthur Richardson seemed unsure, giving an answer that gave an impression of poor planning and even poorer salesmanship, and this was compounded by an unconvincing and uninspiring appearance on a televised brains trust on the future of football. The move into the new stand had thrown the ticket office and administration into ill-disguised chaos. Season ticket holders had first been moved out of the old main stand and then back again, but the new systems were poorly installed and numerous seats were double, and even treble, booked. Given the fact that this coincided with a run of big attendances and major Cup games, the organisation was clearly beset with problems.

Despite all this, the board still felt secure. There had never been a takeover attempt at the club, partially because of its traditions but largely because of the article of association which required that any share transfer had to

Alan Brazil celebrates his recent signing by Spurs with a header which hit the Watford bar on 19 March 1983. The rebound was knocked in by Mark Falco and Spurs won the game 1-0. After a brief career Brazil went (at a profit to Spurs) on to Manchester United where he was unable to find a place in the first team.

be authorised by the board. The consequence was that this article of association (effectively a rule of the club) could only be overturned by a vote of the shareholders. But, and here was the catch-22, the board knew all the shareholders, controlled a large percentage of the shares itself and, by its veto, could theoretically prevent any outsider from buying any shares anyway.

The board's confidence was eventually shown to be misplaced in the face of a clever assault by two rich young fans, 31-year-old Paul Bobroff and 35-year-old multimillionaire property developer Irving Scholar. Scholar had approached the Richardsons back in 1980, genuinely worried about matters prior to the stand being built, and offering his services as a property consultant free of charge. His motivations were concern for the club as a fan, but his interest was not reciprocated. Bobroff later also offered his company's computer facilities to sort out the problems in the ticket office, but this was not to be taken up either.

By February 1982, while Spurs ploughed on to two Cup finals on the field, matters were equally intense off it. Scholar and Bobroff had devised a plan to get round the problem of the articles of association. They could buy shares – the problem was that the board did not have to recognise the purchase. So, in addition to the shares, they also acquired the proxy voting powers of the previous owner. In other words, they could use the votes whether the board recognised the purchase or not. With half the shares, they could overturn the old rules at the next meeting. At the rapidly escalating share

price (which reached £300 per share) it would cost around £500,000 to buy up enough, always assuming the owners would sell.

The critical moment was when ex-chairman Sidney Wale decided to sell. His son-in-law, Douglas Alexiou, was already on the board and was to become chairman when the coup was carried through. Wale had always disagreed with the building of the stand and, while too gentlemanly to bear a grudge, bore the current board little personal goodwill after his replacement as chairman. By November 1982 Richardson realised that Bobroff and Scholar had enough promises and proxy votes to call an extraordinary general meeting and unseat him. He had no choice but to resign and allow Bobroff to join the board. Scholar, the effective owner of the club with Bobroff, remained in Monte Carlo for the time being.

For the next year and a half Spurs made more news off the field than on it. Ossie Ardiles had, of course, gone back to join the Argentinian national squad before the 1982 World Cup, had supposedly commented at Buenos Aires airport that the Malvinas were Argentinian (a perfectly understandable sentiment for anyone of his nationality, especially so public a figure) and that he would never play in England again. As the Falklands War continued through the summer of 1982 it did indeed seem unlikely that he could ever return. Keith Burkinshaw arranged a year's loan to Paris St Germain, supposedly for £100,000, and it was assumed that that was the last of Ardiles.

Keith Burkinshaw's relationship with the

TOP: A foggy day in Munich; Chris Hughton scores Spurs' only goal in a 4-1 Cup Winners' Cup defeat at the hands of Bayern on 3 November 1982. Spurs lost the tie 5-2 on aggregate.
BOTTOM: Chris Hughton in European action again, this time with happier results. Tottenham had drawn Feyenoord, the team which beat them in the 1974 final, in the second round of the 1983-84 UEFA Cup. Having won the first leg 4-2 at home, Hughton (with this goal) and Galvin gave Spurs a 2-0 victory in Rotterdam.

Argentinians had always contained a large element of chance, and so it was to prove again. Spurs had invited the Luxembourg national team, who had just played England at Wembley, to come to the Christmas 1982 party at White Hart Lane. The Luxembourgeois interpreter also acted in the same capacity for Paris St Germain, and had been involved in the Ardiles transfer. He told Burkinshaw that Ardiles, who had not settled well, was prepared to return and that the French club would probably agree. Burkinshaw flew off again on his second Argentinian-chasing odyssey, concluded the deal, gave St Germain their money back, and Ardiles was at home in Hoddesden by the New Year, 1983.

The Ardiles story did not continue quite so happily. In only his second game back in England he broke a leg. In a friendly six months later, shades of Dave Mackay, he sus-

tained another fracture. A year later there was an operation for cartilage trouble. He was now 32, a difficult age to make a comeback after three such disturbing blows. But Ardiles himself was philosophical, as he told Brough Scott of the *Sunday Times*: 'Alas, people are entitled to think I can't come back. Maybe sometimes I think it myself. But I don't have economic problems and more than anything I love to play football. All my life, from six or seven, I can play very, very good, but they always say I am too small. Now they say I am too old. We'll see.' Indeed, Ardiles had few problems compared with most footballers contemplating the end of their careers. He owned a 1,500-acre farm and other property in Argentina, and was close to his final qualifications as a lawyer. It was nonetheless not until the end of the 1983-84 season that he was again seen in the first team, making a particularly important contribution to the second leg of the UEFA

On 11 January 1983 Ossie Ardiles made his return to English football. The Falklands crisis had led to the midfielder being transferred to Paris St. Germain but Keith Burkinshaw eventually brought him back from abroad for a second time. He made a cautious return – playing for the reserves against Luton at Cheshunt in front of a few dozen spectators.

Cup final when he came on as a substitute. But, because of cartilage trouble, little was to be seen of him the following season either until well into 1985, and just months before his £80,000 per year contract was due to expire.

Off the field, the club were making an equally controversial, and noticeable, impact. One of the early decisions of the new board was that the club should advertise its 'product' like any other commercial organisation. A relatively sophisticated television and radio campaign, based on the theme of individual fans taking the field against next Saturday's opposition, was mounted on Thames and London Weekend Television, and via the local commercial radio stations, Capital and LBC. As an idea it received a considerable amount of attention and comment; arguably, in a peculiar twist of public relations logic, the discussions about the campaign had more overall impact than the campaign itself. It has to be said that the expenditure on advertising cannot really be counted a success. One of the problems was that it was impossible to guess how many people would have gone to the game if there had not been any advertising anyway (always an acid test of the effectiveness of any form of advert) and, in addition, attendances were being compared with the very successful spell the club had enjoyed through 1980, 1981 and 1982. By the beginning of 1984 crowds were significantly down and the idea had been quietly put to one side.

Questions were beginning to be asked about the team and the direction the club was going in 1984, as the cold wind of the recession seemed to be affecting Spurs more than other major sides. While they tried to match the expenditure and the ambitions of Liverpool, Manchester United and Arsenal, the other members of the current unofficial elite, it did

seem that Tottenham's base support fell below that of their rivals. Between mid-January and May 1984, with the club well out of the Championship race, there were only two gates above 25,000 and several below 20,000, well under the effective break-even point. It had become a simple truism that the club needed at least one good Cup run each season to hope to balance its books.

Happily, the overhang of financial worries had been largely solved by a brave and unique step taken by the new board. The decision was made to become the first club to take a full stock-market listing, which meant, simply enough, that absolutely anyone could buy shares in the club through their local bank manager. The new board had already put £1,150,000 into the club early in 1983, and they then raised another £3,800,000 by selling shares to the public. The two injections of cash largely eliminated the bank borrowings, causing many people elsewhere in the game to ask why such a simple and relatively obvious idea had not been tried by other clubs in difficulty. Perhaps the answer was the massive depth of support for the club, particularly in relatively financially sophisticated North London. The shares were put on sale at 100 pence each (3 million in all) and, though they were sold easily enough, the price soon dropped to the 75p-80p level where it has largely remained since.

Despite this fall, the shares and financial state of the club remained something of a favourite with the *Financial Times*. 'Spurs set for promotion' and 'Spurs score in strong second half' became popular if predictable headlines in the normally conservative pink pages, and the results were always treated kindly. 'To the average fan, who completely dominates the share register, the news that Glenn Hoddle has

Ardiles' return was not trouble free. Two fractures and knee problems meant that he rarely appeared for the first team in 1983 or 1984. A rare foray was against Leicester on 11 February 1984, where he is seen battling with Steve Lynex.

signed a new contract probably means more than the disclosure that the club has beaten its flotation target by 6 per cent,' said the FT about the first year's results. But, more positively, they concluded: 'The annual results show that, with the elimination of the previously crippling burden of debt, playing costs have been strictly controlled in line with operating revenues and to cover the dividend with something to spare. That, if nothing else, is a measure of the new team's [meaning the board's] strike rate this far.' The second year, with a profit of nearly £1 million, was equally encouraging financially and equally well received. 'I've never known a fan or a shareholder complain about the dividend', said Paul Bobroff. 'I don't think that's why they bought the shares.'

Well before the end of the 1983-84 season it had become clear that Keith Burkinshaw would leave at its end. The reasons were complex. He had been in effective control for

some time, had been conspicuously successful and was rightly noted as a man who spoke his mind and stuck by his own beliefs. The fall in attendances in 1984 was financially worrying, and the board's frank and publicly stated view was that the football team, while the necessary core of the whole business, was only part of the business and that other sectors, such as the development of the property on the High Road, were financially significant as well. Expenditures on the team had to be viewed in that light.

Burkinshaw also suffered a season-long running argument with his main striker, the unpredictable Scot Steve Archibald, who continued to play for the team having vowed at one point never to speak to the manager again. At season's end the club conducted a number of financially astute deals, especially in obtaining a remarkable £1¾ million by selling Alan Brazil (who

173

begun to succeed since his arrival from Ipswich) to Manchester United and Steve Archibald to Terry Venables in Barcelona where, it must be said, the Scotsman surprised everyone by leading the Spanish scoring list as Barcelona and Venables ran away with that country's League Championship. Peter Shreeves, the new manager, spent some of the cash in bringing Clive Allen to his father's, club from QPR. Allen had thus perambulated from Loftus Road, to Highbury, to Crystal Palace, back to QPR and on to White Hart Lane in a very brief career which had, for a striker who had cost in aggregate some £3,500,000, supplied relatively limited highlights. While Allen's early linking with the other new purchase, Notts County winger John Chiedozie, seemed encouraging, injuries and loss of form soon led to the striker being replaced up front by the old team of Falco and Crooks.

But this is to run ahead of the highlight of 1984, yet another trophy for the departing Burkinshaw. While domestic events had provided little cheer (Spurs going out to Norwich in a fourth round FA Cup replay and to Arsenal in the third round of the Milk Cup), there was always the UEFA Cup. Their run through the competition was not noticeably easy, though it started in style.

In the first round they amassed 14 goals without reply as the Irish part-timers of Drogheda were despatched 6-0 on their own ground and 8-0 at White Hart Lane. A superb performance by Glenn Hoddle, upstaging a much publicised return to the European arena by Johan Cruyff, paved the way to victory in the second round over Dutch side Feyenoord. Spurs couldn't stop Cruyff scoring, however,

and their 4-2 home win was more precarious than it looked until Hughton and Galvin put the result beyond doubt in Rotterdam. Once again there were the same scenes of violence which had marred Spurs' previous visit to the Dutch port in the final of the same competition back in 1974. Tottenham fans left a trail of destruction and 30 injuries. In the event the club was probably fortunate to escape with an £8,000 fine by UEFA.

Spurs scored their most impressive victory in the third round. A goal by Michael Rummenigge, brother of West Germany's World Cup star and European Footballer of the Year Karl-Heinz, gave Bayern a 1-0 home win. Steve Archibald levelled the scores in the home leg and Mark Falco, who was to score another vital goal in the semi-finals, hit their winner.

Security problems dominated the quarter-final tie against Austria Vienna, whose unprotected ground looked a sitting target for trouble-makers. Spurs gave themselves a comfortable 2-0 home lead and the away leg passed without incident except on the pitch, where the Austrians fought to a 2-2 draw after Brazil and Ardiles had inflicted further damage.

Spurs were frankly lucky to win their semi-final, against the perennial Yugoslav challengers Hajduk Split. Losing 2-1 on the Adriatic, Falco getting the priceless away goal, Tottenham crept through 1-0 at home when Mike Hazard hit a low, hard drive into the right-hand corner from 20 yards after just six minutes. Roberts, Miller and Garry Stevens all performed sterling roles in the middle of the field and at the back to close Split down for the remaining 84 minutes.

Steve Archibald in action against Feyenoord in the second round of the UEFA Cup in 1983.

Tottenham's opponents in the final, the club's fourth in Europe, were to be the holders of the trophy, Anderlecht of Brussels. The Belgians, like Spurs, were a little fortunate to be there. Having lost 2-0 at Nottingham Forest in the first leg of their own semi-final, they had won the home half 3-0 after a peculiar long shot from their Italian prodigy Scifo beat Forest's Van Breukelen early on, and the referee had then awarded them a travesty of a non-existent but game-winning penalty in the last minute. No doubt Spurs were relieved; it would have been a peculiar coincidence if they had had to play another European final, like that against Wolves in 1972, against a second Midlands club.

The first leg of the UEFA Cup final was in Brussels. It was a hard game, with Spurs pleased to come away with a 1-1 draw. They were leading through a 58th-minute Paul Miller header – another vital away goal which was to prove Spurs' passport right the way through the competition – and held on until 6 minutes from the end when Anderlecht forced an equaliser. Once more crowd trouble dominated the tie and a Spurs fan was shot dead in a Brussels bar after a disturbance.

The return, and Keith Burkinshaw's last game as manager of the club, was memorable essentially for its conclusion, yet another penalty shoot-out. Almost unknown prior to 1982, these events had become increasingly and irritatingly familiar after the France v West Germany World Cup semi-final that year. In 1984, two of the three European competitions (Liverpool defeated Roma in the Champions Cup the same way) went to the same unsatisfactory conclusion. The actual result after 120 minutes was again 1-1, but this concealed the fact that most independent observers thought Anderlecht the better team. 'Roberts, who scored the first penalty kick, as much as Parks and the rest of them hung on to beat a better team for Burkinshaw's sake,' said Jeff Powell in the *Daily Mail*. 'It may seem a little churlish to focus attention on the ugly character of Spurs' defensive play in their hour of triumph,' wrote Robert Armstrong in *The Guardian*, 'but there is no doubt that the London side would not have reacted with the same stoical fortitude shown by the Belgians, who declined to retaliate under extreme provocation. The fact that Spurs could muster only a single goal in two hours – and that from Roberts – indicates how fortunate they were to topple Anderlecht.' Indeed, it is odd that a European trophy should be won with just two goals from the two centre-backs, but then Liverpool's full-backs had a similar habit of winning European Cups for their side.

The Belgians had actually gone ahead after an hour when Morten Olsen's beautiful through ball put Alex Czerniatinski away and the Polish miner's son flicked the ball past keeper Tony Parks, who had been standing in for the off-form Ray Clemence towards the season's end. The Belgian side, incidentally, was composed of Danes, Dutch, Italians, Icelanders and various other combinations of European blood. Tottenham continued to battle. Roberts, captaining the side in Perryman's absence, was in the thick of everything, his enthusiasm carrying him beyond the bounds of most players' normal physical endurance and often beyond the bounds of most referee's notebooks. He was probably lucky the West German Mr Roth seemed to view his antics benignly. With just a few minutes left, and the game increasingly looking all over for

Mark Falco shoots past Bayern Munich's Soren Lerby during the UEFA Cup tie on 23 November 1983 but fails to score. Spurs had lost the first leg 1-0 but won the tie 2-1 on aggregate with goals from Archibald and Falco. It was adequate revenge for the previous year's defeat in the Cup Winners' Cup.

175

Steve Archibald powers a shot towards the FK Austria Memphis goal during the first leg of the UEFA Cup quarter-final at White Hart Lane on 7 March 1984. Spurs won the game 2-0 and the tie 4-2 on aggregate. Archibald left for Barcelona at the end of the season, netting Spurs £1,160,000 – the most they received for a player until they sold Richard Gough to Rangers in October 1987.

the home side, Burkinshaw made his very last decision as Tottenham manager – he sent on his talisman. Off came Miller and Mabbutt, on went Ally Dick and the man whose own career had been so closely linked to Burkinshaw's, Ossie Ardiles. As if by pre-arrangement with the gods, it worked.

Ardiles, with one of his earliest touches, hit the crossbar, the ball came back into a crowded penalty area and Roberts somehow forced it home. There were just six minutes of normal time left. 1-1 and the teams were level on aggregate, 2-2.

The half-hour of extra time produced numbing tiredness but no goals, leaving 21-year-old Tony Parks to face the remarkably daunting task of penalties to decide the destination of the trophy. Roberts took the first and scored. Then the Anderlecht and Danish captain Morten Olsen struck his shot well to Parks left, but the young keeper surprised the whole ground by saving it. 'I could see in the Anderlecht player's eyes where he was going to go,' said Parks afterwards, 'so I just dived to the left.' Falco, Stevens and Archibald scored for Spurs, de Groote, Scifo and Vercauteren did the same for Anderlecht. That meant that if Danny Thomas, signed from Coventry the year before, scored from the fifth kick, the trophy was Spurs'. In the kind of moment which can live with a player for the rest of his career, full-back Thomas ran up, shot unconvincingly, and Munaron saved. It was now 4-3 on penalties and there was only one of the original 10 penalties left. If Anderlecht scored it would be 4-4 and go

to sudden death. Parks said later: 'I'd dived left for all four penalties so far, so I thought it was best to change my mind.' Icelander Arnor Gudjohnsen took the kick, Parks threw himself to his right and palmed it away. Up jumped the young reserve and hared off down the pitch. 'You read about this sort of thing in comics,' he said later. 'It's a lovely feeling. I started playing at nine on Hackney Marshes – now all this. I'm only 21 and not so long ago I thought I'd have to move to another club to get a chance.' It was very much Parks' night, and Burkinshaw's.

The manager was going out on a high note, winning a European trophy and having reached four finals in four years. The parallels with Bill Nicholson a decade before were uncanny. He too resigned after reaching four Cup finals in four seasons. He too won three of them, including the UEFA Cup. He too had spent a season in dispute with his principal striker.

Debate about a successor ranged far and wide. Terry Venables, David Pleat and Graham Taylor were favoured. In the end the club maintained its tradition of promoting within. An intelligent new broom has the sense to preserve those ideals which have worked in the past. The man who got the job was Burkinshaw's assistant, Peter Shreeves. Like Burkinshaw, Shreeves had not had a particularly distinguished playing career – appearing or coaching at Reading, Chelmsford, Charlton and Wimbledon. At the tender age of 18 he was just three days away from a Welsh under-23 cap when he broke a leg playing for Reading. The chance never came again. He is

Welsh because his parents were evacuated from Islington to Neath and he was born there during the Battle of Britain. Perhaps the most quoted fact about him is that he has been a taxi-driver, which he was while coaching Chelmsford in the late 1960s. He had to retire from playing at the age of 28 with cartilage trouble and had coached ever since, though John Pratt was by now (acting as) trainer of the Spurs first team. Terry Neill brought Shreeves to Spurs in 1975, as youth team coach, and one of the advantages he had was that many of his early charges had grown with him into the first team.

That was certainly something of benefit as the Spurs team went through a fair number of permutations in the first half of the 1984–85 season. Up front Allen, Falco, Crooks, Galvin and Chiedozie fluctuated without any set of three settling down. In midfield none of Hoddle, Stevens, Ardiles, Mabbutt or Hazard was exactly a permanent fixture. But this did not serve to greatly upset the way the team played. Though they were unexpectedly knocked out of the Milk Cup at home by Sunderland, and almost inevitably lost 1-0 at Anfield in the FA Cup, the League remained open and Spurs well placed in the top three. The fact that the League was, for perhaps the first time since 1981, of interest outside Merseyside was actually due to Liverpool starting the season very badly. Missing Graeme Souness, with Sampdoria, it took some time for the Red machine to move into gear. The championship had gone to Liverpool in the three previous seasons, and in 1984-85 it certainly looked likely that the trophy would

return to the said city, if not club. FA Cup holders Everton led the League from early on, with Spurs a steady second in a well-paced chase. The critical day could well have been Saturday 2 March. While Spurs won 1-0 at Stoke, Garth Crooks capitalising on a dreadful goalkeeping error by his old club, Everton let go a golden opportunity to keep the gap dangerously wide and effectively eliminate the third club, Manchester United, from the chase at the same time. With the score 1-1 at Old Trafford, and less than ten minutes left, Everton were awarded a penalty. Bailey saved from Sheedy and Everton got one point out of United rather than three. Suddenly the race was wide open and, almost as suddenly, Spurs were favourites. Ten of their remaining 15 games were at home.

Two weeks later the omens seemed to have gone into reverse. Having lost 2-1 at home to Manchester United in the interval, Spurs had to travel to a resurgent Liverpool. It was exactly 73 years to the day – 16 March 1912 that they had last won at Anfield. If Liverpool won, and took the three points, then their claim to a fourth successive championship would begin to look very substantial indeed. If they lost, they would be around ten points adrift, surely too big a gap to make up in a dozen or so games. No one, understandably, thought the latter scenario a possibility. To place Spurs' sequence at Anfield in context (it was the longest of its kind in British football), the last time Spurs won there was the year the *Titanic* sank and, even more remarkably, Barnsley won the FA Cup, having applied for re-election the year before. To the amusement of some

Spurs' new signing Gary Stevens causes Pat Jennings a little discomfort during the Boxing Day game between Tottenham and Arsenal at White Hart Lane in 1983. Arsenal won 4–2.

Archibald slides the ball across the face of goal during Spurs victory over Hajduk Split.

Liverpool had just beaten the very same Barnsley 4-0 in the FA Cup, though as it happened their memories would be closer to the iceberg that was Clemence.

Early in the second half, with the score at 0-0, Hoddle nodded a subtle header to the edge of the penalty area, Mike Hazard hit a scorching volley to Grobbelaar's right, the keeper palmed the ball out but there, as he had been at Stoke, was Garth Crooks and Spurs were 1-0 up. Thanks to excellent Clemence goalkeeping (he emphatically denied having been the Liverpool keeper when Spurs last won at Anfield) that's the way the score stayed. Spurs were level top, had thirteen games to play and nine were at home. Everton, ahead on goal difference, had injury problems, and were still in the FA Cup and Cup Winners Cup.

One of Spurs' advantages seemed that they had nothing else to concentrate on. The attempt to retain the UEFA Cup had collapsed at the quarter-final stage. Opponents Real Madrid were thought to be little more than a shadow of their former glorious selves; domestically they were far behind the Barcelona of Venables and Archibald. But the current Spurs could not exercise the domination of their old days. The tie was unsatisfactory in almost every sense, there being just a single goal in the whole 180 minutes. It was an owngoal at that, Steve Perryman deflecting a shot past Ray Clemence in the first leg at White Hart Lane. Spurs were the better team in the Bernabeu Stadium two weeks later and suffered from a disgraceful refereeing decision when an excellent Falco header was disallowed by a referee who was presumably momentarily hallucinating. But even had the goal been

allowed, it would only have brought the scores level. With three minutes left the frustrations boiled over and Steve Perryman ended a tie he will hope to forget by being sent off for a frankly dreadful tackle on Valdano. This time no one could argue with the referee's decision.

Before the game, it had been the general view among the British press that Spurs would probably win. This highlighted one peculiarity of their season so far – they had played better away from home than at White Hart Lane. It was a difficult phenomenon to explain, except in terms of their now being a strong defensive unit, capable of absorbing pressure, and a good side on the break. Traditionally these were qualities associated more with near neighbours Arsenal than with the more cultured Spurs. If it was the case, then it does not seem to have been part of any tactical change by Peter Shreeves. Nonetheless, with so many home games left there were real concerns about form at the Lane.

Sadly, these fears were to prove only too justified. In the space of five days what had seemed to be so firmly in Spurs' grasp melted away like an early summer mist. In the space of five days on the cusp of March and April two disastrous home defeats left them clutching at straws rather than rungs on the ladder. First came Aston Villa, an admittedly poor side lacking both their regular goalkeeper and central defender Allan Evans. Two breakaway goals, a frustrated Spurs attack and a 2-0 home defeat looked ominous. Five days later came the crunch – the visit of leaders Everton to White Hart Lane. Everton scored twice, from Andy Gray and Trevor Steven, and though both goals were aided by defensive errors they were

very well taken and a late Roberts goal could not conceal the fact that Everton were by far the better side. In retrospect, it was probably the leg injury to Gary Stevens a month before which had been the turning point. Now virtually an England regular, his ability to play either as central defender or in midfield was invaluable to the team.

Spurs' loss of form was a huge disappointment to the club and its fans. Between 1 January and 4 May 1985 they played eight home games, lost six, drew one and won just once. There were four consecutive home League defeats – against Villa, Everton, Arsenal and Ipswich. But there are seasons and seasons. Even if they had won most of those games it wouldn't actually have won them the trophy. Everton had gone into one of those sequences which make a club unstoppable. Heading for an undefeated run of 30 matches, chasing three trophies and already well past the previous highest ever points total, they were uncatchable and clearly the best side in the country. Another year Spurs' efforts would have won them the Championship; this year Everton brooked no real contenders.

Chairman Irving Scholar was philosophical about the season's end: 'Ever since I first watched Spurs from the terraces in 1954 I've believed that if the club wins a trophy it is essential that it deserves to win it and is seen to deserve it. This is Everton's year – but it's also our best League performance for around 15 years. Don't forget that.'

Since his arrival at the club at the end of 1982, Scholar's main priority had been putting the financial side in order. He had already had informal discussions in the City about a public flotation prior to the takeover. As soon as there was a change of control he was quick to introduce an efficient computer-controlled ticket system (long Spurs' Achilles' heel) and arrange a testimonial for Bill Nicholson, who celebrated 50 years with the club in February 1986.

The biggest problem was paying for the stand, something Scholar's business career well suited him for: 'It is interesting that every club which has gone in for a major new stand since the early seventies has had major problems as a result. Chelsea and Wolves both nearly went out of business, Forest were fortunate to have the revenue from that amazing spell of theirs. Spurs were in a similar position. The reason is quite simple; a new stand is a capital asset and has to be paid for out of capital. A player isn't – you can pay for him out of profits and deduct the transfer fee before paying tax. Basically, if a stand costs, let's say, £5 million, then you need to make profits of around £10 million to pay for it. And who can make that sort of money in football nowadays? The reason we went public was very straightforward; money raised in a share flotation is capital. Hence it could all be used to pay for the capital cost of the building. It made perfect sense. '

Scholar was surprised no other clubs had followed Spurs' route: 'Every kind of business is represented on the Stock Exchange – why not football clubs? It's a conservative game, but the advantages are enormous; not least that you give the fans a chance to have a share, and, as a result, a say in *their* club.'

In May 1985 the club received permission to develop its valuable Cheshunt training ground, a plan which should be worth at least £3 million to Spurs. 'We may develop it ourselves,' said Scholar. 'Why not? It's very sensible for the club to have interests outside football because they provide other sources of income. Of course, football will always be the basis but if we can make money elsewhere then it is bound to benefit the club. The key is to do things gradually, steadily, not to rush major decisions. We are going to continue developing the ground, but a step at a time like Manchester United at Old Trafford. I would like to do something about the corners first, then perhaps move on to a new stand on the East side. But we'll take it slowly – and, until we reach the

ABOVE LEFT: Keith Burkinshaw says his farewells to the Tottenham crowd before the UEFA Cup final on 23 May 1984. It was a fitting end, Spurs winning the trophy on penalties. Irving Scholar said of Burkinshaw that he constantly needed new challenges: 'It must be very difficult for a manager to come up with new ideas all the time to keep players interested . . . Keith was always looking for something new, and he's done well'
ABOVE: Burkinshaw's assistant and successor, Peter Shreeves.

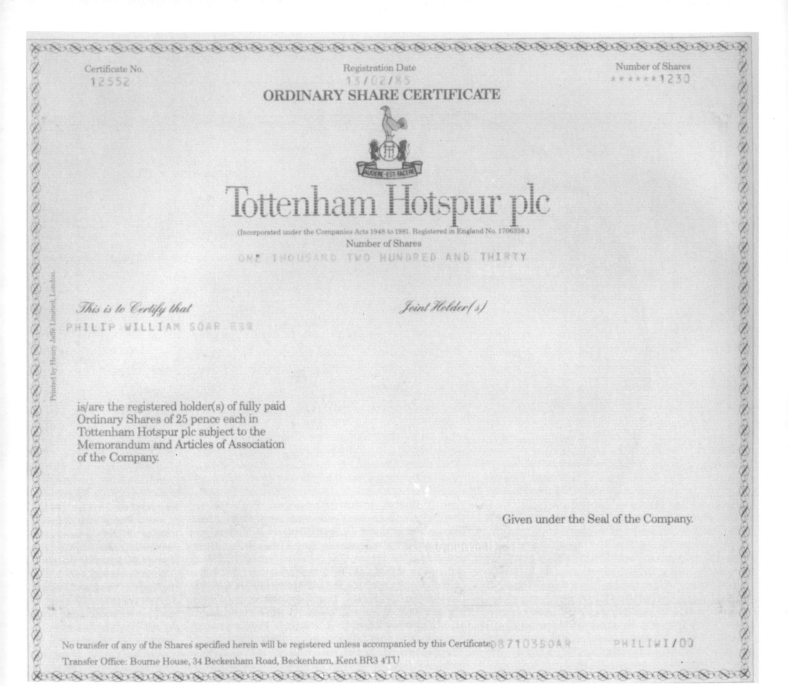

ORDINARY SHARE CERTIFICATE

Certificate No.
12552

Registration Date
13/02/85

Number of Shares
******1230

Tottenham Hotspur plc

(Incorporated under the Companies Acts 1948 to 1981. Registered in England No. 1706358.)

Number of Shares

ONE THOUSAND TWO HUNDRED AND THIRTY

This is to Certify that
PHILIP WILLIAM SOAR ESQ

Joint Holder(s)

is/are the registered holder(s) of fully paid
Ordinary Shares of 25 pence each in
Tottenham Hotspur plc subject to the
Memorandum and Articles of Association
of the Company.

Given under the Seal of the Company.

No transfer of any of the Shares specified herein will be registered unless accompanied by this Certificate 08710350AR   PHILIWI/00

Transfer Office: Bourne House, 34 Beckenham Road, Beckenham, Kent BR3 4TU

Printed by Henry Jaffe Limited, London.

One thing that can make a Tottenham follower's lot a happy one compared to that of the supporters of many teams . . . a part ownership of the club. This modest share certificate is the author's.

point when everyone wants to sit down, there will always be standing accommodation at White Hart Lane.

'The traditions of the club are vital to me. I've always believed in the way the club plays the attacking game, the style, the fact that we have always been known as a *positive* club. That will never change while I'm chairman. You have to take the responsibility personally and very seriously. You can never think, or let anyone else think, that the club is not bigger than any individual. The club must always come first and we only want players at White Hart Lane who want to play for Spurs. I remember a discussion with one player recently. It wasn't a serious problem but he wanted a meeting. I said to him straight away: "Do you want to play for this club?" "Yes, absolutely," he replied, and after that no problem is too difficult to solve. But if he had said no then I wouldn't have wanted him ever to play for Spurs again. That's why we spend as much time, more in fact, investigating a player *off* the field than on it when we make a new signing.'

In 1985 the problems of football were indeed rather more off the field than on it. While Spurs had certainly experienced a reasonably satisfactory season, the game itself was in turmoil. 1984-85 would not be remembered for Everton's Championship or Norman Whiteside's astonishing FA Cup final winner, rather it would go down in the history books as the year of Luton and Chelsea, of Bradford and Birmingham and, of course, the ghastly culmination of so many ills at the European Cup final in Brussels. And while Spurs had been relatively blameless in recent seasons, they soon became one of the clubs most affected by the dramatic and entirely understandable public reaction to this final tragedy.

The first thing to go was Spurs' hard-won place in Europe, not just for one season but perhaps for a footballing generation. As with the other major clubs, revenues from television, sponsors and, for that matter, week-by-week gates were suddenly also brought into question. Few major clubs could afford the consequences that loomed before them – Spurs alone would almost certainly be several

ABOVE: With just six minutes of the UEFA Cup final against Anderlecht left on 23 May 1984, Graham Roberts forces the ball over the line and gives Spurs the chance of extra time.

BELOW: As Tony Parks makes his historic save from Arnor Gudjohnsen's penalty, the Spurs players (from left to right) Ardiles, Stevens, Roberts and Hughton rush to congratulate their young keeper. Spurs beat Anderlecht 4-3 in the penalty shoot-out.

A sight for sore Spurs eyes: Chris Waddle bearing the Tottenham logo with the ball at his feet. At White Hart Lane he matured from an unpredictable talent, prone to wrong decisions, to an incisive world-class performer capable of destroying the best of defences with mazy dribble or visionary pass. Indeed in the later stages of the 1988–89 season he gave perhaps the best midfield displays by a Tottenham player since John White. What might have happened had he stayed – alongside fellow Geordie Paul Gascoigne and with Gary Lineker to feed – is painful conjecture; Spurs needed the money and he journeyed south to the Riviera, winning a French League championship medal with Olympique Marseille. On his return to England, still only 31, he went to Hillsborough.

OPPOSITE TOP: Spurs' recent history is littered with ifs and buts, none more so than in the case of David Pleat. His effect on Tottenham was not only fast but very nearly fruitful – in normal circumstances a place in Europe would have been his least reward – and no one can tell what he might have achieved had he remained in office beyond October 1987. With the climate of sleaze that engulfed football over the next few seasons his indiscretions now seem paltry; perhaps he could have ridden out the press storm, but it was typical of the man that he felt the right course of action was to resign. Pleat was widely linked with a return to White Hart Lane in October 1994, but, like Waddle, Sheffield Wednesday were to be his first Premiership employers.

hundred thousand pounds worse off than they had projected by losing European competition in one season alone. It induced a sense of real sadness in more than one way.

Only a year before Spurs had effectively won a European trophy in that very Belgian capital. Their return leg against Anderlecht had, unusually for an English club game, been televised live throughout Europe. While it lacked the quality of European matches two decades before, it certainly compared for excitement. 'It was a wonderful advertisement for the club and for the English game,' said Irving Scholar. 'It was fast, thrilling and tense. In many respects it was probably the best game seen at White Hart Lane since the legendary Benfica match.' It was sad that it would be many years before we could expect to see its like again.

After the horror of Heysel, Peter Shreeves began his second season robbed of the UEFA Cup place his third place had earned in May 1985. Following four successive years of European competition that involved 32 games and saw the likes of Barcelona and Real Madrid, Bayern Munich and Eintracht Frankfurt, Ajax and Feyenoord at White Hart Lane, Spurs fans would have to be content with the fare offered by the domestic scene – a situation which put even more emphasis than usual on the two cup competitions.

It was especially galling for the talented Chris Waddle, 24 and already an England regular with eight caps when he signed from Newcastle for a tribunal-fixed fee of £590,000 in July. One of the most enigmatic players ever to wear the Spurs colours, Waddle was a unique amalgam of vision and waywardness, a combination that could send supporters, colleagues and managers into paroxysms of pleasure or the depths of despair.

Aptly named, Waddle cut an unlikely figure for a football hero, round shoulders hunched over ungainly gangling gait as he ambled, aimlessly it seemed at times, across the White Hart Lane turf. Even when he received the ball he hardly looked a 'natural': yet there were times, plenty of them, when there was no-one in England to touch him.

He had deceptive skill, a wicked change of both pace and direction, the ability to pass and cross with both feet – and, above all, vision. On his day he could leave bemused opponents helplessly in his wake or slit a defence open with a raking pass; on others, however, he would be a proverbial 'waste of time', exasperating fans by disappearing up blind alleys of his own making. Shy, taciturn and sometimes difficult, he struggled with lack of confidence, but gradually he won over the fans (his Spurs displays were invariably better than his patchy performances for England), and with his fellow Geordie Paul Gascoigne alongside him he would perhaps reach the peak of his contribution in 1988–89.

Waddle began his Spurs career in style, heading two goals on his League debut in a 4-0 drubbing of Watford at the Lane on the opening day of 1985–86 – the first having come from fellow debutant Paul Allen. But then came the first poor spell of what was (as so often with Tottenham) a season of baffling spells: four straight League wins in September, only one point from six games after Boxing Day, just one defeat in the last 12 matches, with 14 goals in the last three.

Though the late run took Tottenham to 10th place in the League, their chase for honours had finished back on 4 March when Everton – the only class opposition encountered in the cup competitions that season – beat them at White Hart Lane in the fifth round of the FA Cup in what proved to be captain Steve Perryman's last match for the club. It was the fourth year in a row that Spurs had failed to get past the last 16, and coming on top of a miserable League run – itself prefaced by a fourth round League Cup exit at the third attempt at the hands of Second Division Portsmouth – it undermined Peter Shreeves' tenuous position.

Shreeves had bought well, securing not just Waddle (second top scorer on 14 behind Mark Falco's 21), but also the hard-working, ball-carrying services of Paul Allen, snatched from West Ham under the noses of Arsenal and Liverpool for £400,000, again set by a tribunal. Paul was the third member of his family to sign for Spurs, following uncle Les and cousin Clive; Bradley, Clive's younger brother, was a junior prospect at the club as a 13-year-old but chose to join QPR.

Clive's continued absence until late November with a groin injury didn't help Shreeves' cause, and put added pressure on the willing Falco to produce the goals; nor did the persistent injuries to Ossie Ardiles (only 20 League games) and John Chiedozie (13). He also made sensible deals in the transfer market, Micky Hazard moving to Chelsea for £310,000 in September 1985 after growing frustrated with failure to command a regular first-team place; he would return, after visits to Portsmouth and Swindon, in 1994.

A former player with Reading and, after injury, with Southern League sides Chelmsford and Wimbledon, Shreeves had moved up through the coaching ranks under Keith Burkinshaw and he stayed faithful to his predecessor's attempts to play flowing, attacking football. Indeed, his teams scored four goals or more seven times in 1984–85 and no fewer than 11 times the next season; with 14 of those 18 occasions at home, no fan could claim his sides didn't entertain.

But the board – and perhaps many supporters – were in no mood for explanations: they wanted success. Although the players generally held him in high regard, at least as a coach, liking his emphasis on skill and invention in training, he was sacked.

If Peter Shreeves had been more of an entertainer himself he might have survived a good deal longer. Plenty of more vocal managers have had worse records and lived to tell the tale (as would Terry Venables), but Shreeves was no Allison or Docherty, no Atkinson or Clough, and he went across London to become assistant manager to Jim Smith at QPR. However, like Perryman, Ardiles and Hazard, he would be back.

PLEAT'S NEW APPROACH

Shreeves' replacement at White Hart Lane was somewhat different – a confident talker at home with players, coaches, directors and the media. David Pleat was chairman Irving Scholar's first choice, a tried and tested operator who for eight years had kept lowly Luton in the First Division by playing attractive, entertaining football, despite meagre resources and a continual leak of good players to bigger clubs. Friendly and amusing (he became a regular TV and radio pundit during his several subsequent spells out of management), Pleat took up where Shreeves left off – and added his own special ingredient.

The season began with a 4-4-2 system, with average results. Always willing to experiment, Pleat introduced a new approach at Oxford on 22 November, inspired by the French team in the 1984 European Championships and both France and Belgium in the 1986 World Cup, with a mobile five-man midfield supporting a lone striker of pace, Clive Allen. Allen scored twice and Waddle, played by Pleat in a roving role on the right rather than on the left or down the middle, notched the others in a 4-2 win. The display received rave reviews and though the day was marred by a hamstring injury to the recent £600,000 signing from Standard Liège, Nico Claesen, the system would bring Spurs a chain of good results – only four defeats in the next 19 League matches – with Paul Allen, Glenn Hoddle, Ossie Ardiles, Tony Galvin and recent England cap Steve Hodge (like Claesen 24 years old but costing £50,000 more from Aston Villa) the usual candidates for the five places.

Players also departed, Mark Falco going to Watford for £300,000 on Claesen's arrival and Graham Roberts moving to Glasgow Rangers in December for £450,000. Both were large, well-built men who had given their all for six years, but while local product Falco (despite ceaseless endeavour and a respectable tally of 68 goals in 174 League games) had never won over the White Hart Lane crowd, Southampton-born Roberts had become a Tottenham folk hero.

While he will always enjoy a place in the

hearts of fans as the man whose dogged performance against Anderlecht was capped with a match-saving goal, Roberts will be generally recalled as a ruthless ball-winner, the toughest tackler at Tottenham since the incomparable Dave Mackay. Roberts could dish it out, too: the challenge that put Arsenal glamour boy Charlie Nicholas into the Highbury stand on New Year's Day 1986 is set firmly in club legend.

Pleat's first major signing would eventually follow Roberts to Ibrox. Richard Gough of Dundee United was Scotland's regular right-back when he preferred Spurs to Chelsea for £750,000 in the close season, but he could

THIS PAGE: Clive Allen slots home a penalty against Southampton at the Lane on 12 September 1987 – a 2-1 win that was part of a start to a season which brought 20 points from 10 games and where the tenth game (a 2-0 victory over Sheffield Wednesday on 3 October) set a club record of 14 consecutive home League wins. But the bubble soon burst: within weeks David Pleat had gone and despite the arrival of Terry Venables the season was disappointing, with just seven League wins after September and defeat at Port Vale in the 4th round of the FA Cup.
OPPOSITE TOP: As manager of Luton, David Pleat had been more used to the role of underdog than that of favourite, but at Wembley on 16 May 1987 his side were firmly fancied to beat a club out of form and appearing in their first FA Cup final. On the day, however, Coventry would nick the match 3-2, and a season which had promised so much ended merely with a great record on paper – third in Division 1, FA Cup finalists, League Cup semi-finalists – and a rich promise for the future.
OPPOSITE CENTRE: Coventry celebrate and Spurs heads drop as Lloyd McGrath's cross is deflected past a hapless Ray Clemence. For even the oldest of Tottenham fans it was a bitter pill to swallow: all previous seven FA Cup finals, including five at Wembley, had ended in victory.
OPPOSITE BOTTOM: The 1987 FA Cup final defeat was particularly poignant for Glenn Hoddle, playing his last game before moving to Monaco for £1 million in the summer. Not yet 30, his wonderful talent flourished in France, and he returned to England in 1991 to player-manage Swindon to promotion from Division 1. In 1994, managing Chelsea, he would play his fourth FA Cup final, putting himself on as substitute in the 4-0 defeat by Manchester United. A marvellous craftsman, his skills were displayed in 490 matches for Tottenham.

play anywhere – and though he was not the manager's first choice for centre-back (that was Ipswich Town's Terry Butcher, who ironically went instead to Rangers), this was the position he filled to such effect. He formed a fine understanding with Gary Mabbutt – like many supporters, Pleat thought that centre-back was Mabbutt's natural position – and when Gough was appointed captain on New Year's Day Spurs fans imagined the 24-year-old had taken the job for several seasons to come.

With Ray Clemence in continuing good form and injuries blissfully absent – the trio missed only nine League games between them – the goals-against column was reduced to 43 in 42 First Division games. They were helped by solid performances from the three full-backs – Gary Stevens, Danny Thomas and Mitchell Thomas – and the cover of a five-man midfield.

Pleat's plan would work, of course, only if there was a striker of class to finish the job. And, unlike the luckless Peter Shreeves, he was blessed with a fit and on-song Clive Allen. The man had a phenomenal season, scoring 33 goals in the League (in 39 games), 12 in the Milk Cup (nine) and four in the FA Cup (six). Even without his seven penalties, the total would still have bettered Jimmy Greaves' record tally, though he couldn't touch the 37 League goals notched up by Greaves in 1962-63.

The 5-0 thrashing of West Ham in the fifth round League Cup replay at White Hart Lane on 2 February was perhaps the best of many fine team performances during the season. A semi-final with Arsenal was the prize and Spurs grabbed it with both hands; and even if the Hammers were hit by injuries, few teams could have lived with Tottenham that night.

They scored after just six minutes, Claesen taking Ardiles' chipped pass on his chest before flicking it past Parkes; a rare occurrence, this, since 13 times that season Clive Allen opened the scoring for the hosts at the Lane. For more than an hour Spurs then played the most delightful cultured football, Waddle baffling defenders, Ardiles and Claesen displaying foreign skills, Hoddle probing with telling passes, Paul Allen harrying and carrying everywhere.

In the 70th minute Hoddle placed a sweet shot past a helpless Parkes for the second, surprising the crowd as much as the retreating defenders. As West Ham pushed forward, Clive Allen took full advantage: first he converted a low cross from Claesen, then scored from the spot after Alvin Martin had brought down cousin Paul, and finally put away Paul's far-post cross to complete a great night in front of 41,995 spectators.

The match came during a purple patch for Spurs that included a run of five unbeaten games in the League, during which they scored 12 goals and conceded none – all of this at home because of several weather postponements away – as they vied with Everton, Liverpool and Arsenal for leadership of the First Division.

And Clive Allen just went on scoring, including all nine games of the League Cup run. With solid progress in the FA Cup, the treble wasn't out of the question. But while Allen would win both the FWA and PFA Footballer of the Year awards, he would end up with no winner's medal. Spurs failed, if that's a fair word, on all three fronts.

In the League Cup, having scored five goals in three earlier games, and despite Clive Allen netting in each of the three semi-final games against Arsenal, the Gunners nicked the 4 March replay at the Lane with a wicked deflection off Danny Thomas' heel that set up David Rocastle for the last-ditch winner. Over five hours of football, Arsenal had been ahead for just one minute – unfortunately it was to be the last minute.

Three days later the home crowd saw a tackle from Gavin McGuire of Queen's Park Rangers put an end to the footballing career of Danny Thomas, who had proved a great favourite since his move from Coventry for £250,000 in June 1983. A disappointing month ended on a sour note, the result of the 3-1 defeat at Luton being overshadowed by demonstrations aimed at both David Pleat and his club.

In the League, where Pleat raised the club's average home attendance by 5,022, Spurs were to prove the victims of a fixture backlog that saw them play 14 League and Cup games in five weeks, falling behind Everton and Liverpool during a run-in which gleaned only five wins in 13 matches. Indeed Spurs were later to be fined £10,000 for fielding what was effectively a reserve side against the new champions at Goodison five days before the FA Cup final.

CUP FINAL OWN-GOAL DEFEAT

It wasn't a year ending with a '1', but it was 20 years since Dave Mackay lifted the trophy when Spurs beat Chelsea. Their run had been comfortable (Scunthorpe, Crystal Palace, Newcastle, Wimbledon), but their semi-final opponents were Watford, then a respectable First Division side. At Villa Park, however, Tottenham hit top form, Steve Hodge grabbing two goals and the Allen boys one apiece to crush Graham Taylor's men (including Mark Falco and John Barnes) by 4-1. The Watford scorer was also an Allen – Malcolm.

Spurs were in their seventh final and their phenomenal unbeaten record looked unlikely to be broken. Their opponents, the journeymen from Coventry, had scraped through the last four with a 3-2 extra-time win over Leeds and, though they finished 10th in the table, they had won only three League games away from home all season. Yet while manager John Sillett looked to be enjoying every moment of the day at Wembley on 16 May, David Pleat (more used to being an underdog in big games with Luton) appeared strangely nervous.

He must have felt a lot better after just two minutes, when Clive Allen headed his 49th goal of the season, and a lot worse when Dave Bennett levelled nine minutes later. But when Spurs regained the lead at the perfect moment – skipper Gary Mabbutt claiming what's usually recorded in the football bibles as an own goal by Brian Kilcline – they were again firm favourites. But it wasn't to be: Keith Houchen brought Coventry back with a marvellous diving header, taking the final to extra time for the fifth time in seven years.

Substitutions of Claesen in place of Hughton and Stevens in place of Ardiles made little impact, and as so often at Wembley it was a bizarre goal that settled it, Lloyd McGrath's cross being firmly deflected over the despairing Clemence by Mabbutt's attempted interception. Poor Clemence: he had been beaten 16 years before by a deflected winner (albeit slightly) when Charlie George's fierce shot nicked Larry Lloyd's foot.

The immediate aftermath was at best muted, at worst acrimonious. Richard Gough, who had played well below par and had become the first Spurs captain to lead his team to defeat in an FA Cup final, stormed out of the dinner after a row with David Pleat. There were inevitably plenty of recriminations, not all of them so public. A massively promising season had finished in cruel anti-climax.

PLEAT HOUNDED OUT

It would not be players who gave David Pleat grief the following season, however: it would be the tabloid press. *The Sun* began its lurid allegations about his private life in July, but

ABOVE: Clive Allen pursues his 50th goal of the season early in the 1987 final. Allen scored with a glancing header after just two minutes to take his season's tally to 49, but the afternoon was to prove a fruitless chase for honours. Notice the fact that Allen's shirt bears the Holsten logo while Hoddle's does not. In one of the most unlikely errors of this commercialized era, half of the Spurs' team took the field in plain shirts. It was a mistake that gained Holsten enormous publicity.

RIGHT: A Scholar and a gentleman? The strangest of handshakes presages what was to become an increasingly uneasy relationship between the Spurs chairman and Terry Venables following this photo-shoot to celebrate Terry's arrival at the club on 23 November 1987.

after his wife and family stood by him the paper's attention appeared to drift elsewhere. With several big changes at White Hart Lane – Glenn Hoddle moving to Monaco for £750,000, Chris Fairclough coming from Nottingham Forest for £500,000, along with former Real Madrid star Johnny Metgod for £250,000 – there was indeed much to talk about.

And it did look as though 1987–88 was going to be a classic season for Spurs fans. Their side won six and lost two of their first 10 games, Nico Claesen matching Clive Allen goal for goal, and the 2-0 defeat of Sheffield Wednesday on 2 October set up a club record of 14 successive home League wins. A new era was looming.

But so was *The Sun* and the most scandal-seeking of the tabloids returned, visiting Pleat more than once at unreasonable hours and making fresh allegations. In his view, his position became untenable, and in the great tradition of British public figures he was obliged to step down, tendering his resignation at an emergency board meeting on the evening of 23 October.

The fans had seen Pleat as a permanent fixture, building on the near-misses of the previous season to lead London's assault on Merseyside (10 Championships in 12 seasons) and take Tottenham back into Europe. Despite the flagrant summer stories chairman Irving Scholar wasn't alone in still being stunned by events: 'I'd believed he was going to be the Spurs manager for many years to come. I went home [from the board meeting] and felt completely numb.'

Pleat's replacement was chosen for Scholar, not only by the clamour of the press and supporters but also by the League club bosses' recent 'agreement' not to approach contracted managers during the season. Thus there was no leading, proven coach available in England.

Terry Venables was on holiday in Florida when Pleat resigned, and Scholar flew out to sign him. It was good timing: despite huge success in Spain – he was hailed as a saint after taking Barcelona to their first League title for 11 years in his initial season and to the European Cup final the following year – the rapport with the Nou Camp crowd was long gone and the club was happy to release him by mutual consent, making room for Johan Cruyff. Thus on 27 October, in the American autumn sunshine, the man who had played for Spurs in their record triumph at Wembley in 1967, by now acknowledged as one of Europe's finest football thinkers and twice the unsuccessful target of approaches from Arsenal, agreed to become the manager of Tottenham Hotspur, to take over in December. It would be the start of the most traumatic, topsy-turvy and at times tiresome period in the club's history.

By contemporary English standards Venables' terms were extremely generous: a three-year contract with a salary of £150,000 and a signing-on fee of £50,000. But he would have to earn it. After Pleat's departure assistant manager Trevor Hartley and coach Doug Livermore had taken over, with team selection somewhat confused and at times even passing to a coterie of senior players. The team's form was by now quite appalling: having narrowly lost their last two League games under Pleat – the first of which saw the groin injury to Ray Clemence at Norwich which would end his career – they went down 3-0 at Forest the day after his resignation and then, five days later at Villa Park, the day after Venables had signed, they went out of the League Cup 2-1 to Graham Taylor's Aston Villa. Defeats by Wimbledon (3-0 away) and Luton, and draws with Portsmouth and QPR followed. Richard Gough, who had followed Graham Roberts to Rangers for £1.5 million in September for family reasons, and Chris Waddle, out with heel and hernia problems for much of the season, were being sorely missed.

TEL TAKES CHARGE
Though hardly a hero as a Tottenham player, 'Tel' was now seen as a managerial saviour and when he took over earlier than expected, White Hart Lane's best crowd since the visit of Everton in April 1985 (47,362) turned out on 28 November to witness his first match in charge, and the expected instant miracle – against a Liverpool side unbeaten in the League all season.

The game was a gross disappointment, Steve Hodge being sent off before half-time in a 2-0 defeat, and worse was to follow a fortnight later with a 1-0 home defeat by lowly Charlton. With Allan Harris alongside Venables, the slide was halted just in time for Spurs to finish in a deceptively comfortable 13th place. Hopes of Wembley had crashed at the end of January, when Third Division Port Vale beat a lacklustre team 2-1 in the Potteries, Spurs' goal coming from a raw 19-year-old called Neil Ruddock.

Goals were indeed hard to come by: Spurs scored only 26 in 25 matches that season under Venables, and the League total of 38 was the lowest since the club had joined the League in 1908. Clive Allen lacked support, touch and luck, Waddle was nagged by injury, Claesen slid in and out of form and favour, and Metgod's potential influence was restricted by injury to a dozen appearances, mostly as substitute.

While able to wield the chequebook, however, Venables opted for a cautious approach, encouraging youth (Vinny Samways, Brian Statham) as well as buying: goalkeeper Bobby Mimms from Everton (£375,000), Paul Walsh from Liverpool (£500,000) and, first and most controversial in December 1987, his old skipper Terry Fenwick from QPR (£550,000). Fenwick was not only a dodgy purchase in the eyes of most fans; he also persuaded Venables to agree to terms that radically pushed up the salary structure at White Hart Lane, with the utility player actually earning more than Chris Waddle. Meanwhile, in the spring of 1988, Venables loaned the 35-year-old Ossie Ardiles to Blackburn. Not for the first time, fans at a Venables club sometimes found the manager's strategy difficult to understand.

Though on the high side by the standards of the time, these transfers were merely a prelude to a summer of 'super signings' – 21-year-old Paul Gascoigne from Newcastle for a British record of £2 million and 23-year-old Paul Stewart from Manchester City for £1.5 million – though Mark Hateley had been first choice here. Neither had yet been capped at full level by Bobby Robson, but for Gascoigne an England debut was imminent, and in a rather stale era his remarkable skills on the ball were a breath of fresh air for a flair-starved football public.

Some of this vast outlay was recouped with the sale of four players. Out of contract Clive Allen went to Bordeaux for £900,000 after a relatively poor tally of 13 goals in 37 games, and three players went 'home' – Nico Claesen to Antwerp for £550,000, Steve Hodge to his

Clive Allen celebrates yet another accolade. Following his 49 goal haul in 1986–87, the former QPR striker received both the PFA and FWA Player of the Year awards. He is seen here with the Spurs Supporters' Club Award.

native Nottingham with Forest paying £550,000, and Dutchman Johnny Metgod to Feyenoord for only £175,000.

Fleet Street dubbed Venables 'Mr Moneybags'. On 28 July the *Daily Mail* said that 'no one in football has spent so extravagantly as Venables this summer,' and Spurs were regarded as big if not profligate spenders – in sharp contrast to neighbours Arsenal's highly geared youth system.

For Spurs fans, however, the prospect of the new season was mouth-watering, and the opener at home to Coventry couldn't come quickly enough. Unfortunately, they would have to wait until 23 November (a 1-1 draw) because the East Stand was not ready in time. After all the vast expenditure on players, over £5 million, and all the hype through the summer, this was a humiliating experience for those in the dock. You could almost hear the laughter from Highbury.

The East Stand story went back some way. Everyone at the club was aware that the old steel-framed structure, with its appalling toilets and smell of horses from the under-stand police stables, with its wooden seats at the upper end and its wooden floorboards, had to go. But with tax relief and 'easy terms' available on players and not on facilities, it was always tempting to splash out monies on staff rather than the supporters. The Bradford fire of 1985, in which 56 people died, changed all that: Haringey Council began to enforce strict controls and in January 1988 the London

Evening Standard revealed that Spurs were preparing to develop the East Stand.

Some fans were hostile; they were treated simply as 'turnstile fodder', claiming that the ordinary fan was being railroaded or ignored in the new age of corporate hospitality. The biggest bone of contention was the proposal to end the life of The Shelf, the upper standing level of the East Stand and part of Tottenham folklore. Chairman Scholar and his board failed badly to communicate with the supporters generally, but especially over this issue, and they found themselves facing an organisation called LOTS (Left On The Shelf), mainly young supporters objecting that the hallowed shrine was to be replaced by 'boxes and executive seating'. After several hostile meetings a compromise emerged, with standing room for 3,000 season ticket holders allocated below the boxes.

While this and other hiccups delayed the start of work, contractors George Wimpey were convinced that the new stand would be ready for the first match of 1988–89, and the debuts of Gascoigne and Stewart, on 27 August. Indeed, Wimpey experts were there with local safety officers at 4pm the day before, but despite the assurances given and ceaseless overnight work the new structure was not granted a certificate the next morning and there was no alternative but to postpone the game.

Later, at a meeting in the Warwick Hilton on 17 October, the three-man management committee of the Football League decided that Tottenham were guilty of breaching Regulation 24, and were 'unprepared for the eventuality'; furthermore, the club had notified neither Coventry nor the League. Two points were to be deducted from their season's total. On appeal to the FA (on the grounds that the two-point penalty was not mandatory) these were reinstated – and Spurs ordered to pay a £15,000 fine.

Under the aegis of a friend of director Paul Bobroff the work was renewed in February 1989, the later estimate being £400,000 to finish the job on top of the existing estimate of £2.3 million for the first phase. However, when that bill finally came in the total had risen to an astonishing £5.6 million – and that without legal fees. Revised estimates now saw the costs of the whole project, executed during the ludicrous property and building boom of the late 1980s, reaching into the stratosphere with a final figure of some £6.9 million. If the much-criticised large columns supporting the roof had been removed and replaced by a cantilevered roof the cost would have shot up to some £9.4 million. The stand was eventually reopened for the visit of Arsenal on 18 October, 1989, witnessing a 2-1 victory.

The refund of the two points was welcome news for a club that had made a dreadful start to the season, bottom of the table with just one win in 10 League matches – the worst performance for 13 years. A potentially prolific attack missed a genuine proven striker, while a defence that looked good on paper just leaked goals (22 in those 10 games, for example). Then in the 11th game, a 3-2 defeat of Wimbledon, Gary Stevens sustained a knee injury in a challenge from Vinny Jones which put him out for the rest of the season.

Gascoigne started well – both he and his pal

Waddle scored on his home debut, a 3-2 defeat by Arsenal – but he would not really warm up until later in the season. A Spurs recovery in November was devalued by a poor performance in the League Cup, where after needing extra time in a replay to get past Blackburn they lost 2-1 to Southampton at The Dell. But worse, far worse, was to follow.

Gascoigne was unavailable for the awkward third round FA Cup tie at Second Division Bradford City on 7 January , a game that could either set Spurs on the way to Wembley or effectively finish their season. It would do the latter. On a day no Tottenham fan wants to recall Bradford won 1-0, a result that (coming a year after the ignominious defeat at the hands of Port Vale) had even the most committed Venables admirer questioning whether he should have stayed in Spain.

Another man who must have had his doubts was the man who signed him. According to Irving Scholar 'The season had by now been even more dismal than the previous one – if that was possible. We had touched bottom in

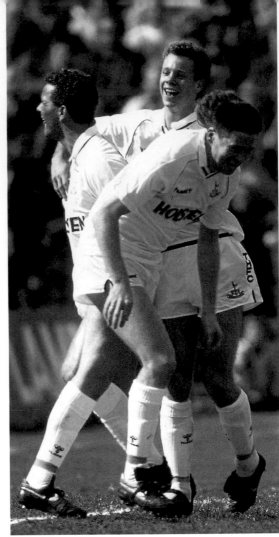

ABOVE: Gazza strikes a pose after scoring on his home debut: 10 September 1988 against Arsenal no less. The looks on the fans' faces say it all – a footballing god has arrived at White Hart Lane – and Mitchell Thomas appears unsure whether he should actually touch him. However, the Waddle-Gascoigne-Stewart partnership hardly clicked straight away, and this 3-2 defeat was the second in a 10-match start that brought a paltry seven points.

RIGHT: Mellow yellows: Stewart, Howells and Waddle celebrate Stewart's winner against Wimbledon on 15 April 1989, towards the end of a marvellous run that began in February and registered nine victories in 13 League matches to take Tottenham from the edge of relegation to a respectable sixth place in Division 1. Waddle's form was devastating. For Venables, however, his main problem was a reliable scorer: Waddle himself topped the season's totals with 14 goals.

the League, and although we had climbed up from there we were still drifting.'

With no Cup run and the East Stand fiasco, money was short and clearly going to get shorter. At the board meeting a month after the Bradford debacle Venables was understandably told he would have to sell before he could buy, whereupon the manager produced a list of candidates. Top of the pile to pay for his intended purchases – Coventry's midfielder Steve Sedgley, Sheffield Wednesday left-back Nigel Worthington and Wolves striker Andy Mutch – were Chris Fairclough (valued by Venables at £500,000) and Gary Mabbutt (£600,000), the latter's inclusion being baffling to the directors, most notably Scholar. Venables' obvious down on the captain's playing style had always puzzled observers (he considered Mabbutt sluggish and prone to positional lapses), and was yet another irritant in the deteriorating relationship between chairman and manager.

Scholar may have won the day (Mabbutt did not make the mooted move to Steve Coppell's Crystal Palace for £750,000), though Enfield-born Sedgley would finally move to Tottenham for that price in July. Fairclough went to Leeds, first on loan in March and later permanently for £500,000, and at Elland Road he reproduced the style he had shown as a youngster at Forest and which inexplicably deserted him at White Hart Lane and he became a key member of Leeds' Championship winning team. Bobby Mimms didn't move on until December 1990 (Blackburn Rovers for £250,000), making only four further first-team appearances. The reason was the the arrival of Erik 'the Viking' Thorstvedt, an extrovert

Norwegian international who, after a disastrous televised debut against Forest on 15 January, conceded only 16 goals in 17 games to become a firm favourite of Lane loyalists. Another factor in Spurs' spring revival was the arrival of 'Nayim' (real name Mohamed Ali Amar, born in the Spanish enclave of Ceuta, on the Moroccan mainland) who added a continental dimension to midfield while on loan from Barcelona – a move made permanent in June.

These two, with Fenwick moving into the back four alongside Mabbutt, helped (yet again) to transform a miserable season into an encouraging one. From the fringe of relegation and a double cup exit the club clawed its way up the table, first to safety and then to what would have been, in normal circumstances, the fringe of Europe in sixth place. Between the 1-0 defeats at Old Trafford on 5 February and Loftus Road on 13 May, Tottenham won nine and drew four of their 14 matches, the only defeat in a sparkling sequence that registered a goal tally of 27-10 being at the hands of title-chasing Liverpool.

It was the sensational form of Chris Waddle that was the most salient feature of this run. In one three-game spell, especially, he was simply breathtaking, scoring four goals that Spurs fans will always savour: the dribble and angled drive against Norwich, the chip in the mud at Southampton, and the magnificent pair that sank Aston Villa at White Hart Lane. It was the kind of consistent brilliance that drew the European scouts like bees round a honey pot.

Helped too by Gascoigne bubbling and Stewart starting to score, the climb up the table removed any danger of serious criticism of

only go to £900,000 and Gary had made his way to Goodison.

The 1989 deal was nevertheless a comprehensive coup for Venables – Spanish under-21 cap Nayim was a further £400,000 in the package – but despite the modest fee it would trigger a series of unforeseen events in the boardroom. At the ratifying meeting Paul Bobroff, chairman of the public holding company, emphasised to his colleagues, including Venables, that the money had to be recouped as soon as possible: the first payment of £600,000 was due on 1 August, the balance a year later. But after the manager left the room, Bobroff announced there was no money at all for the deal, and Scholar had guaranteed the deal from his own resources. The truth, hidden from many at the club for a long time, was that Spurs were not just short of immediate funds, but in serious debt.

All this meant little to the ecstatic fans; to them the prospect of England stars Gascoigne, Waddle and now Lineker in the Tottenham team would represent no less than a holy trinity of talent in residence at the cathedral of cultured football. For Irving Scholar, however, the possibility lasted only days. Just minutes before the press conference for Lineker's arrival there came a phone call from a Paris middle man representing Bernard Tapie's Olympique Marseille, offering first £2½ million and then £3 million for Chris Waddle. While the chairman continued to play hard to get, the manager, somewhat characteristically, suggested a cheeky 'pay now, move later' deal.

But Tapie wanted Waddle right then. And when Scholar later asked for £5 million (only Ruud Gullit had moved for more at that time), the Marseille boss didn't wince; he would certainly pay that for Waddle and Walsh, and £4 million for the one player. It was an offer Scholar simply couldn't refuse.

Waddle might object, of course, and most observers were surprised when the player, happy at Tottenham and with six years of a seven-year contract to run, jumped at the chance to hone his skills in the south of France. Spurs supporters were even more dumbfounded. Venables used the potential

Venables. Not that he had ever been under great pressure, even when the star-studded team sank to the foot of the First Division. Terry enjoyed not just the knack of talking his way out of trouble – Scholar called him 'the man with the silver tongue' – but he also managed to inculcate the idea that despite blips, however large, he was the man with the master plan, the right notions regarding the necessary players and tactics to bring lasting success. Pressmen, supporters and, particularly, directors were made to feel inadequate; he had played for England at every level, he had won the FA Cup, he had already won honours at places as different as Selhurst Park and Barcelona.

Still, it didn't need that much appreciation of the game to see that what he lacked was a genuine goalscorer. Waddle topped the list in 1988–89 with 14, one ahead of Stewart, but third was Fenwick, seven of his nine coming from penalties. Paul Walsh, while a tireless user of space, managed only six goals in 37 games.

LINEKER COMES, WADDLE GOES

Venables found his striker all right: the best this country has managed since Jimmy Greaves and, arguably, the most lethal finisher in Europe since Gerd Müller. In June he signed Gary Lineker; after three years at Barcelona, England's favourite son was coming home. And at £1.2 million the 28-year-old must have been one of the bargains of the century. In 1984, when Spurs sold Steve Archibald to Barcelona, they could have got Lineker from Leicester for £1 million, but Scholar would

LEFT: Nurtured by Terry Venables at Barcelona, Nayim came first to Tottenham on loan before joining permanently in the Summer of 1989. Nayim spent much of his time at White Hart Lane as a substitute and being substituted. But though prone to anonymous passages of play, he could play some spectacular stuff, whether in Southend or Paris. The former was a stunning piece of improvisation in the League Cup in October 1989, when with his back to goal he flicked the ball over his head, turned and slotted home an extra-time winner; the latter was the amazing long-range top-spin lobbed volley in the dying moments of the 1995 European Cup Winners' Cup final that gave Real Zaragoza a deserved victory over Arsenal.
BELOW: First the good news. The signing of Gary Lineker for £1.2 million from Barcelona in the summer of 1989 was the transfer coup of the decade – a proven, virtually injury-proof scorer, with a reputation as England's most fair and honest player to boot, for the price of a decent midfielder. The bad news was that finances were so parlous that Waddle had to go to pay for him.

Pat Van den Hauwe shows his versatility by covering at right back in a game against Sheffield United. Though he usually operated on the left side, he filled the No 2 spot several times in the 1991–92 season and later in his career at Millwall he was used to good effect at the heart of the Lions' defence. A tough, uncompromising Welsh international, of Belgian birth (he was dubbed 'Psycho-Pat' at Everton), Van den Hauwe was the second major signing after Waddle's departure, for £575,000. The first was Steve Sedgley, an Enfield boy and former junior player at Tottenham, who cost £750,000 from Coventry.

profits cautiously, signing only Sedgley and, just after the season's start, 28-year-old Welsh international left-back Pat van den Hauwe from Everton for £575,000. What later hurt the fans was that having bought Lineker at a bargain price, sold Waddle for a fortune and not spent in the interim, the club was still in deep financial trouble.

Back in July, however, the supporters were suffering from a shattered dream. They had seen the dawn of a new era, with Gascoigne, Waddle and Lineker playing the roles of Best, Law and Charlton to take Spurs to the apex of Europe. Now it had been blacked out, apparently by mismanagement, and seemingly by greed. The fans could not know how the cost of the new stand had restricted the club's ability to manoeuvre. And the feeling of anti-climax was deepened by a miserable start to the 1989–90 season, with only one win (against Luton in the opening game) in the first six League matches.

While Lineker hit a hot streak, with eight goals in seven League and League Cup games, to ease Tottenham out of their embarrassingly lowly position in the autumn, success in the cup competitions would elude Venables for yet another season. The patience of supporters starved of European action was tested further. Nor did it help Venables' public relations that this year both exits were at home – a 3-1 humbling by new bogey team Southampton in the third round of the FA Cup on 6 January and then, at the end of a dire month in which they took only two points from three League games, a 3-2 defeat by a fast and skilful Forest side who made Spurs look pedestrian.

Indeed Spurs were somewhat fortunate to

make it that far, because apart from a marvellous 3-0 win over Manchester United at Old Trafford in the third round they had really struggled, beating plucky Fourth Division Southend only on the away goals rule in the second round and needing an own goal to gain a replay against Tranmere in the fourth round of the competition.

After another frustrating period on the slide it was left to Lineker to lift the spirits – and the club up the table. His seven goals led to a final flourish of eight wins in 10 games to take Tottenham to third in the table behind Liverpool and Aston Villa. In better times, and had UEFA relented, it would have meant the passport to Europe.

The role of Gary Lineker in saving Spurs' season, involved as he was with England's crucial build-up to the World Cup in Italy, cannot be overrated. With constant changes in personnel behind him (only some of which were enforced by injury), and often feeding only on scraps, he scored 24 out of Spurs' 59 League goals – Stewart was second with only eight, Gascoigne next with six – and he stayed remarkably free of injury trouble; indeed, he was the only player to complete the League programme.

With Chris Waddle enjoying a free role and helping Marseille to their second consecutive French Championship, Spurs fans were left wondering just what their talented trio may have produced at White Hart Lane. To see them play together they would have to wait a few weeks – until the nail-biting passage of England to the verge of the World Cup final. No marketing man would quarrel with having the name Tottenham beamed round the globe.

1991

An eighth FA Cup • Extinction looms with bankruptcy • Sugar takes over • Gascoigne and Lineker follow Waddle abroad • Legal and financial strife • Sugar ousts Venables • Banned from the Cup • Ardiles and Francis • The year of Klinsmann

England's unexpected World Cup exploits guaranteed renewed interest for the 1990-91 season, as well as a crop of offers from abroad for Lineker and Gascoigne. Venables toyed with the idea of selling Lineker to Torino to pay for Dean Saunders and Mark Wright from Robert Maxwell's Derby County but the deal fell through, not least because of hearty boardroom opposition, notably from Scholar. But the fuse that had been lit on the club's finances in 1989 was burning ever faster, and apart from small moves all deals appeared to be off.

Thus Tottenham kicked-off the 1990–91 season with essentially the same side; yet the campaign was to be the complete antithesis of 1989–90. Instead of starting badly, leaking goals, then pulling themselves up, they began with an unbeaten run of 10 games, during which a notoriously porous defence permitted just four goals; it was the best defensive run since the spring of 1967, when one Terry Venables was in the team. But then came an almighty slide: in the 24 League games over the six months from December to May Spurs won just three (Luton, Derby, Southampton), with only their 10 draws keeping them in mid-table. Lineker, troubled by a rare injury in the spring, managed a relatively modest total of 15 League goals (three of them penalties).

The League Cup, too, had started in great style, with five goals against Hartlepool at the Lane, and progress was steady until they met Chelsea in January, with a goalless draw in the fifth round at Stamford Bridge in front of 34,178. Tottenham's humiliating 3-0 defeat in the replay was the seventh cup exit at home in the nine seasons since Spurs had last won silverware at Wembley. If ever a football manager needed a good run in the FA Cup, Venables needed it now.

ANOTHER YEAR ENDING IN '1'

And he got it – after all, it was a year ending in '1'. Venables, at his fourth attempt, steered Spurs into the fifth round, by way of Paul Stewart scoring the goal that beat his old club Blackpool in Tottenham's voodoo scenario – away to a lowly club in the third round – and Oxford duly being despatched at home 4-2 in the fourth, a result significant for the rebirth of Gascoigne. 'Gazza' had been prominent in the League Cup run (his six goals including a haul of four at home to Hartlepool), but in the relentless League programme his form had been patchy and lacking the expected lustre. Against Oxford he really turned it on, creating two goals and scoring two himself

(one a beauty) and throughout displayed his extravagant skills.

In the fifth round Gazza again dazzled by scoring both goals to beat Portsmouth; in the quarter-final against Notts County he conceded the lead by failing to clear his lines, then won the match with a superb late hit. All this time he was carrying the burden of constant European club and press attention (partly a result of his famous World Cup tears in Turin) and, to cap it all, he was suffering from an

In an era of big-name signings David Howells has been a welcome echo of a creature from football's past – the home-grown, loyal, one-club man, in his case one who could play up front, in the middle or at the back despite being dogged by a succession of injuries.

injury that would need an operation before the semi-final with Arsenal.

The Cup run was played against the backdrop of mounting debt and boardroom wrangles, and with European competition back on the agenda it took on more than its usual significance. In addition, speculation had been rife since before the turn of the year about Gazza's imminent departure, his name being linked with almost every wealthy continental club. One approach that was serious came from Lazio, who offered £5 million; Scholar, with no intention to sell (at least yet), had asked for twice that sum, and thought it was the end of the matter. As it was, the Gascoigne deal with Lazio would be a key part of the complicated in-fighting at Tottenham that would end with Alan Sugar becoming chairman at the end of the season.

The semi-final was a monumental clash of the great North London rivals, their first meeting in the FA Cup since Garth Crooks' goal won the third round in 1982. They had met twice since in the League Cup, the Gunners going through in both 1983–84 and 1986–87. Top of the table with just two League defeats all season and five points clear of Liverpool (even after two points had been deducted for a brawl at Old Trafford), Arsenal were chasing their second Double and were clear favourites against a Spurs side who had won only twice in the League that year.

In addition David Howells had been absent for 11 weeks, returning to the first team just four days before, in the match against Norwich, and Gascoigne had played only an hour of that game following his operation. Both were risked from the start by Venables. The FA had both the common and commercial sense to stage the match at Wembley, the first ever semi-final there, and the 77,893 crowd was one of the highest ever to attend a semi-final. The Hillsborough tragedy was still fresh in everyone's memory and it wasn't until 1995 that the FA felt confident enough to return FA Cup semi-finals automatically to the provinces.

Though both League encounters between the clubs had finished scoreless that season, the first goal came after just five minutes, when Paul Stewart was needlessly brought down 30 yards from goal by Anders Limpar. Gascoigne's free-kick was unstoppable; nobody, least of all David Seaman, who had confidently lined up a two-man wall, anticipated that he would strike the ball with such venom. Powerful, deadly accurate and with a slight bend, the ball flew into the top corner of Arsenal's net for one of Wembley's best strikes. It remains one of the most memorable goals of the 1990s.

It was a sensational start, and just four minutes later it was 2-0. A neat exchange of passes between Gascoigne and Allen ended with Allen's cross eluding Howells but finding the chest of striker Alan Smith, who had tracked Gary Mabbutt back to the six-yard box; his poor control near the line let in Lineker, who poked the ball home from close range. Arsenal had conceded only 16 goals in 31 games before the final; now they leaked two in 10 minutes.

For 20 minutes and more Arsenal could find no answer to Spurs' neat, fluid, short-passing game as time after time the five-man midfield supported Lineker and drove holes into the Gunners' defence. Tireless work by Howells and Allen on the flanks pushed Winterburn and Dixon back into their third of the pitch, blunting one of George Graham's strongest attacking options. Above all (and a surprise to many), there were the neat touches, lay-offs and passes of man-of-the-match Vinny Samways. He gave perhaps his most dazzling performance for the club – suggesting that rather than being sold (he had recently been linked with Villa and Forest), he could take over the creative mantle of Gascoigne when inevitably he flew south to warmer climes.

Just before half-time, and very much against the run of play, Arsenal scored, Smith atoning by beating Mabbutt to a Dixon cross – though

Thorstvedt had come and then, fatally, retreated. With Gascoigne and perhaps Howells bound to tire, Tottenham would be in for a tough 45 minutes. But in the second half their defence proved as classy as their attack had been in the first.

While Pat van den Hauwe had seen it all several times before, and nullified the threat posed by Limpar (he was replaced by substitute Groves), Justin Edinburgh had only 23 first-team starts behind him and a year previously was toiling in the Fourth Division with Southend, but he played with assurance. Experience and youth blended in the middle of the back, too, with Mabbutt and Sedgley seeing off the menace of Smith and Kevin

ABOVE: Paul Gascoigne's free-kick is already there before David Seaman has had a chance to put out his right hand, and Spurs are ahead in the 1991 FA Cup semi-final after just five minutes. This early strike forced Arsenal to push forward, giving the Spurs five-man midfield the space and time to kill the game off. LEFT: Context is crucial. Gazza, returning after an operation, produced his magic after just five minutes, against Arsenal and in front of almost 78,000 spectators at Wembley. Small wonder that he jumped for joy.

Campbell. And, after his moment of indecision, Thorstvedt was commanding.

Gascoigne lasted 15 minutes longer than his manager had intended, and as he went off on the hour to a tumultuous reception from the Spurs fans the energetic Nayim came on. It was the cue for Tottenham to score again, Mabbutt winning the ball in the middle of the park to set Lineker off on a run against a retreating defence. Samways drew Steve Bould and Lineker had too much pace for Tony Adams; though he didn't finish in characteristically clinical fashion, his shot was enough to enter the net via Seaman's hands.

A final Arsenal assault, including a brief scare when Campbell hit the bar and Paul Merson failed to net the rebound, was followed by elation: Spurs would be returning to Wembley on 18 May, and they had spiked their rival's Double.

There was no question of Gascoigne going anywhere, not before that crucial day. Spurs played five meaningless League games in the interim, including a 1-1 draw at the Lane against Nottingham Forest, who had beaten West Ham in the other semi-final.

The strange hiatus that is the period between the semi-final and the final was taken up with more power struggles and disputes over finances, this time directly concerning Venables' future as manager. While to many supporters his departure would be unthinkable, especially at this juncture, Venables himself had always maintained that no one at a football club was indispensable, and there was no shortage of top-class replacements. Indeed just one name was enough: Kenny Dalglish had resigned as Liverpool boss at the end of February.

Meanwhile, the financial crisis deepened inexorably, and offers to take over Tottenham's holding company were now on the table. *The Sunday Times* had originally broken the story by revealing that Irving Scholar was having exploratory talks with Robert Maxwell. The funds for the Lineker transfer had been provided by Maxwell via a loan to

Scholar and, since then, the possibility that Maxwell – already the owner of both Derby County and Oxford United – might bid for Spurs had been discussed.

As the Wembley final approached, Spurs supporters little realised that their treasured institution faced liquidation. Then, just days before the game, new bankers Midland (Bobroff had switched from the traditional Barclays) extended their facilities until the end of August. By then, it was argued, pre-season ticket sales would be in – and there would be the prospect of large sums from a good run in Europe.

The restitution of European football – following UEFA's decision that a five-season ban on English clubs in all three competitions was sufficient punishment for Liverpool's involvement in the Heysel disaster – gave the 1991 FA Cup final added spice. Not that it was short of drama: it already had the stormy background at Tottenham, the personalities of Cockney Venables and dour northerner Brian Clough, the flair of two 'footballing' sides, the attraction of England regulars Lineker, Gascoigne and Pearce, and the tension of Clough's first FA Cup final. Under him Forest had won the League Cup four times in five finals, but never the big one. It would be his last chance.

The night before the Cup final has its own mythology. On one celebrated occasion Arsenal's Alex James disappeared completely from the Regent Palace Hotel, but there could have been few eves to compare with 17 May, the night before the 1991 final. The players had been booked into the Royal Lancaster Hotel, a football favourite because of its close proximity to FA Headquarters at Lancaster Gate. But the day was to be taken up by negotiations on two fronts – firstly the efforts by Terry Venables to acquire the club, and secondly by the continuing saga of where Gascoigne would play in the future. With the players resting upstairs, it seemed almost certain that the Saturday would see Gascoigne play his last game for Spurs, and certainly possible that it could be the last game Spurs ever played as a first-class club.

Between 4.30 pm and 10 pm on Friday Irving Scholar and Terry Venables sat in the hotel trying to reach an agreement on the sale of Scholar's shares from chairman to manager. Gascoigne complicated the issue – Scholar had offered to sell at a lower price if Gascoigne could be kept at the club. Scholar's control had really disappeared by the last day of 1990, when he stood at the back of the room as Spurs held their Annual General Meeting. He was no longer on the board of the holding company, and, though still chairman of the football club, his influence now essentially extended to where and to whom he chose to sell his shares.

By 10 pm it was clear that there were no deals to be struck. And though both Venables and Scholar sought any means possible to keep Gascoigne at White Hart Lane, the prime asset had already gone. Gascoigne was the difference between a future and bankruptcy and, by the eve of the Cup final, he had already committed himself to Lazio.

So, with just 17 hours to go to kick-off, the talks were called off and the fate of Tottenham Hotspur remained in the balance. Venables returned to his players and, in particular, Gascoigne.

In an interesting paragraph in his own book *Venables: The Autobiography*, the former manager notes that: ' . . . for once the team doctor was not required to fire his usual "tranquilliser dart" into Gazza to put him to sleep.' Venables goes on to say that Gazza never needed anyone to hype him up, and all of the efforts before the Cup final, in particular, were designed to calm him down, not wind him up. But, as Venables also says about Gascoigne that day:' . . . it looked like his mind was somewhere else . . . the transfer might have been on his mind . . . in any event he was not as hyped up as normal and certainly nothing like he had been before the semi-final.'

Wembley that day was to be a breeding ground for memories that few finals provide.

Most FA Cup finals are anti-climaxes; few provide talking points that will outlive their participants. Since the Second World War there have been only a handful that truly met everyone's hopes – 1948, 1953, perhaps the first game in 1970, 1973, Ricky Villa's game in 1981. But 1991 was to be as dramatic as any. It may well have contained the worst foul ever seen in a Cup final, it saw only the second ever penalty save, it saw an indisputably good goal disallowed, it had the emotion of Brian Clough's failure, and, of course, it had Gascoigne's self-destruction.

Forest were favourites. It was the third time in four years they had reached the semi-final stage and this time they finally made Wembley by disposing of West Ham 4-0 at Villa Park. Historically Forest have a record almost as good as that of Spurs in Cup finals –

ABOVE: Gascoigne makes the most of the adulation after starring in Spurs' handsome victory against the odds. It was the crowning glory of his days at Tottenham. He lasted an hour (15 minutes longer than planned by Venables) and left the field to a hero's reception – a very different exit to the one he would make a few weeks later from the same arena.
LEFT: Gazza takes on Forest's Brian Laws in the League match that preceded the Cup Final. The fixture computer had drawn the two clubs together in a dress rehearsal just days before the showpiece in which the real drama was to unfold.

THIS PAGE: Hand in hand, arguably the two most charismatic managers in the English game lead out their sides for the 1991 FA Cup final at Wembley. OPPOSITE PAGE: Gazza, still apparently hyped up beyond belief crunches his right leg high into the path of Forest right-back Gary Charles, who was making an innocuous run across the edge of the box. Down he goes (TOP RIGHT), having tried to battle on for several minutes. The club physio rushes to the aid of the stricken star (CENTRE). But his work is in vain and Gascoigne is forced out of the match – courtesy of a severed cruciate ligament. For Spurs the damage was immediate – they were losing 1-0 as a result of the free-kick conceded by Gascoigne – and permanent, since that one moment of madness cost the club £3 million in lost revenue from the Lazio transfer.

this was their tenth major final and they had previously lost just one (the League Cup to Wolves in 1980).

Forest were also the emotional favourites – Brian Clough never having won the FA Cup and still being enormously popular. But Clough, unlike Venables, had crucial selection decisions to make and history was to suggest he probably made the wrong ones. Unlike many Cup finalists, Forest had finished their League season in fine style with five wins out of six games. This sequence included a 7-0 defeat of Chelsea, 5-0 against Norwich, 2-1 against Liverpool and 4-3 against Leeds. Perhaps unsurprisingly Clough chose to stick with his winning team – including youngsters Ian Woan and Lee Glover. Current England midfielder Steve Hodge and Nigel Jemson, who had scored a fifth round hat-trick against Southampton and had won the League Cup with his goal against Oldham two seasons earlier, were left out. Viewed from a Forest perspective, the consequent lack of experience in the team showed.

The game was to engender rare emotions and the experience and calm of Hodge, in particular, would arguably have been invaluable. The fact that Hodge had, of course, been a Spurs player should also have counted in his favour – the law of the football returnee.

As the teams took to the field the Forest manager grabbed Venables' hand and held onto it. As Venables said later: 'He wouldn't

let go, so I made him laugh, which at least made it look as if we were joking and not a couple of lovers.' Just as they reached the edge of the playing area, Venables brought his hand up as if to wave at someone and Clough was forced to let go.

It remains very difficult to think of any other important English football match which had become, in advance, the story of one player. There may be international comparisons – Maradona and the 1986 World Cup final, Puskas and the 1954 final perhaps – but no FA Cup final had been previewed this way; even 1953 became the Matthews final after the event.

But Gascoigne had become a football celebrity the like of which had not been seen since the peak of George Best's career 20 years before. Since the famous tears in Turin and Lineker's frantic finger pointing gestures to Bobby Robson, Gazza had become public property. The run to the Cup final had reached an almost dreamlike quality, capped by that astonishing free-kick in the semi-final. 'Many players can bend a ball from 30 yards – take Ronald Koeman. Many players can hit a ball hard from 30 yards – look at Stuart Pearce. But to hit the ball that hard with that curl, from that distance is very rare indeed . . . ,' said one writer afterwards.

So the game had become Gascoigne's final even before it kicked off. The fact that it was almost certainly his last game in England, at least for a while, and no-one knew when anyone might play in a Tottenham shirt again, added piquancy to an already over-tense build up. The Prince of Wales meets the Prince of Wails, as John Motson's well rehearsed (and impossible not to repeat here) line went as Gascoigne cheerfully shook hands with the Prince and Princess of Wales and the Duke and Duchess of Kent.

UNPUNISHED FOUL

The game was just 90 seconds old when Gascoigne confirmed with his studs what everyone in the ground suspected - that he was hyped up to a level that was beyond anyone's control. Out on Spurs' right Gascoigne tackled the Forest midfielder Garry Parker. In truth, to call it a tackle is to flatter Gascoigne's behaviour. As Parker moved towards him Gascoigne lifted his leg to the horizontal and simply kicked Parker at chest height. It was an astonishing act – totally out of keeping with the setting, the mood and the excellent reputation of the two clubs. Parker went down in a heap. The reaction of everyone watching was identical: 'He'll be very lucky to stay on the field'. Terry Venables said afterwards that the tackle was vicious and his first thought was: 'Christ, that's him booked.' As Venables said: 'Gazza was still looking wild. I don't know whether he was anxious or what the reason was, but he did himself no favours'.

In the short database of memorable Cup final fouls it is impossible to find anything comparable. The only man sent off in an FA Cup final was Kevin Moran for a tackle on Peter Reid in 1986, but that was genuinely mild, by comparison, and certainly not intended to damage flesh. Many will remember Willie Young's trip on Paul Allen after 87 minutes of the 1980 final, for which Young received a yellow card. That was a 'professional' foul par

excellence, but it was committed without any personal malice and with little danger of injury, even if today Young would be immediately sent off. Peter McParland's tackle on Manchester United goalkeeper Ray Wood in the 1957 final, which broke Wood's cheekbone, left United with 10 operating players and helped McParland score two goals later in the game, looked nasty, though McParland was not booked. Looking at replays today one believes the referee was correct – that McParland was

Forest keeper Mark Crossley emulates Dave Beasant and saves a penalty in an FA Cup final, guessing correctly to go left for Gary Lineker's kick. The England striker had earlier scored a perfectly good 'goal' – referee Milford took the linesman's decision for offside – and at this point, 30 minutes into the game, it looked as though it just wasn't to be Tottenham's day.

challenging hard rather than unfairly, that Wood stood his ground, and that both expected to bounce off the other.

It was the post-match consensus, and one which has grown with time, that not only was Gascoigne's tackle on Parker the worst ever seen in a Cup final, but also that Roger Milford's decision not even to book him has few competitors as the worst refereeing decision ever seen in the showpiece of the English game. The closest comparison is probably Dutch referee Charles Corver's decision not to send off German keeper Schumacher after he had knocked out Battiston in the 1982 World Cup semi-final. What remained astonishing back at Wembley was that Milford never even showed Gascoigne the yellow card. Perhaps the referee had also been carried away on the wave of sentiment about Gascoigne's last game.

Gascoigne's madness was to strike again after just 12 minutes of the match. Forest's young right-back Gary Charles ran right to left across the edge of the penalty area and was tackled by Gascoigne, who simply kicked him viciously on the right knee after the ball had gone. Charles got up without a murmur, Roger Milford chuckled and Gascoigne was treated for an apparent injury to his own knee.

Stuart Pearce took his trademark free-kick, left-footed into the top left-hand corner.

Thorstvedt was even standing at that side of the goal knowing exactly where the ball would go, but could barely move as Pearce's shot rocketed past. It was Pearce's 16th goal of the season, all from left-back, and none of them a penalty. That was an English record for a defender. As Forest celebrated, Gascoigne collapsed in the middle of the field clearly unable to play on. The players gathered around him, Venables came onto the pitch. Suddenly everything was in the balance – Gascoigne's future, Spurs' future, the fee for Gascoigne, Venables' future at White Hart Lane – even whether there was a future at White Hart Lane at all.

Nayim came on as substitute, but the reality was that Spurs should have been down to ten men. Roger Milford said later that he didn't feel it was necessary to take any action with Gascoigne because the Spurs player was clearly not able to continue. But that was hardly fair to Forest.

Venables did not appear particularly panicked. There were still 75 minutes to go and, as he commented afterwards, until Gascoigne went off the balance of the side was not quite right. As Venables said: 'Forest normally played wingers so wide it drew the full-backs out with them and left large spaces through the middle for Nigel Clough to exploit. So I took

David Howells from the left to play in front of the two centre-halves'. Venables had a problem about whom to leave out of the centre, having too many midfield players who were playing well. Samways had been in good form and Venables eventually preferred him on the left side to Nayim. But, as Venables said: 'My difficulty was that Samways did not really like playing on the left and he soon began to follow the ball and vacate his position. It could have cost us the game, because Gary Crosby got through where Samways had gone into midfield a few minutes later and Crosby was one-on-one with the keeper. If Crosby had scored [as he should have done] I don't think we would have been able to come back and, apart from the goal it was the only real chance they had'. Thorstvedt competently made the save that was required from him.

When Gascoigne came off, Nayim took over on the left and Samways occupied Gascoigne's more central role. With Stewart moving to the right side of midfield, this gave Spurs a considerably better balance and helped to reduce the threat from Crosby and Charles on the Forest right. The game settled down to a more even contest and, after 25 minutes, Paul Allen put Gary Lineker through to score a classic sharp Lineker goal. Lineker was clearly onside, but the linesman made the most public mistake of his career, and it was disallowed. Five minutes later Lineker was through again, this time from Paul Stewart.

Mark Crossley, in the Forest goal, brought Lineker down and was arguably lucky not to be sent off himself. The penalty was indisputable and Lineker took it well, putting it in the corner to Crossley's left. Unfortunately for Lineker, Crossley guessed correctly and turned

the ball away. It was only the second time in the 120-year history of FA Cup finals that a goalkeeper had saved a penalty – the other being Dave Beasant for Wimbledon from John Aldridge of Liverpool in 1988. It was also only the third time in an FA Cup final that a penalty had been missed – Charlie Wallace of Villa had shot just past the post in 1913 and cost his side the game.

So at half-time Forest were 1-0 ahead and the 80,000 crowd had surely seen one of the most dramatic 45 minutes of football in the history of the competition. It would not have been possible for the next 45 to be so exciting, but they were to be no less interesting as Spurs gradually clawed their way back into a match which seemed to have stored up a season's misfortunes in a single afternoon.

Venables spoke to Gascoigne, by now in a hospital bed, at half-time. The medical team already knew that Gascoigne had torn his cruciate ligaments. He certainly wouldn't play for at least six months, Lazio would presumably not now pay for him, and it was quite possible he would never wear a football shirt again. It was the very same injury that had ended Brian Clough's magnificent playing career.

But it took Spurs just seven minutes of the second half to equalise. Nayim put Stewart through and the midfielder capped what was surely his best ever performance for Spurs with a beautiful cross-shot goal. Forest, with Spurs keeping Nigel Clough well under control, did not have a clear-cut chance in the second half and, by the end of 90 minutes, the pendulum had firmly swung towards Tottenham.

Venables talked to his players before extra-time. 'We're back in the game and it's got "WIN" written all over it. The only thing that

Lineker watches Paul Stewart's angled shot head for the corner of the net to pull the scores level after seven minutes of the second half.

RIGHT: Paul Allen (11) and Lineker congratulate the scorer. If Vinny Samways had enjoyed his best game for the club in the semi-final, Stewart reserved his for the big one. He would continue his good form through 1991-92, gaining full England recognition.

BELOW: The expressions of Stuart Pearce, substitute Steve Hodge and Nigel Clough need no explanation as Des Walker's attempted clearance goes into the Forest net. It was a remarkably sweet irony for his challenger Gary Mabbutt (arm aloft), whose own o.g. had given Coventry victory during extra time four years before.

can stop us is if we stop ourselves. They're on their heels, they don't know if they have got anything left in them.' Venables' assessment was correct, and Brian Clough sat on the bench chatting to a policeman while Archie Gemmill and Alan Hill tried to inspire a flagging Forest in the five-minute break.

There was just the one goal in extra time. Nayim put in a corner from the right, Paul Stewart flicked it on and Mabbutt came charging in on the far post. In attempting to head the ball out for another corner, Des Walker managed to put it just inside the post, for an own goal. Mabbutt, the loser via his own o.g. in 1987, went up to collect the trophy. Spurs thus became the first club to win the FA Cup eight times and no one had missed the fact that the year ended in a one. It was the first domestic trophy that Venables had ever won as a manager.

Venables says: 'It was the most action-packed, incident-filled final that I can remember. It seemed as if it needed something to go wrong – Gazza's injury – to bring it to the boil'.

The pre-match had all been about Gazza and the game lives in the memory as his match, despite his positive contribution being zero. The memory, of course, can become blurred. Because the semi-final was also held at Wembley, the images of Gascoigne's free-kick, the fouls on Garry Parker and Gary Charles, Gascoigne being carried off and Pearce's answer, Lineker's penalty, his good goal disallowed and his winning shot past Arsenal's David Seaman all become jumbled - as if it were a single game. The team and their wives got on to the club coach and took the Cup to hospital for Gascoigne to see. Gascoigne, whom Venables says was crying, received his medal in his hospital bed. That was the end of his Tottenham career.

It was a poignant moment. In many ways Gascoigne had carried the club's hopes through the whole season. His performances had got them to the final, and it was the prospect of the transfer fee he might command which had underpinned the club's financial survival. Yet here he was, after what should have been the game of his career, lying in hospital with the distinct possibility that his golden career might be at an end. Indeed, four years later, it was easy to argue that Gascoigne has never come near reclaiming the heights of those 12 months between the Turin of 1990 and the 1991 FA Cup final. The real tragedy was that the damage was self-inflicted.

FINANCIAL PROBLEMS MULTIPLY

The euphoria of the Cup final was soon to be replaced by the realisation that all the problems had not gone away. Indeed, they had suddenly got significantly worse. Lazio had been prepared to buy Paul Gascoigne for £8 million, now it was not certain that he would ever play football again. The new stand – having cost £9 million – still had largely to be paid for and there was no acquirer on the horizon who came close to being acceptable to the banks and the current shareholders. Amazingly, when viewed from the perspective of just a few years later, the disgraced Robert Maxwell still seemed the most likely purchaser of Irving Scholar's shares.

Scholar and Maxwell had served together on the aggressive FA committee handling negotiations with the television companies in the mid-1980s, and Scholar appeared to have developed a high opinion of Maxwell's skills at that time. The situation for Spurs had become even more critical because, after their failure to negotiate a deal in the days before the Cup final, it was clear that Venables and Scholar could no longer work together.

With Lazio reducing the amount they were now prepared to pay for Gascoigne to £4.85 million (though the actual sum was the subject of intense dispute later) and with no other bidders for the player even remotely likely, the Midland Bank became more crucial in the tempestuous mix. The pressure to conclude matters – one way or the other – was intense. But the Cup success had simply complicated matters even further. A successful bidder would not only have to satisfy the Midland Bank, and get the support and shares of Scholar and Bobroff, but would also risk losing the manager who had just won the FA Cup.

It was at this point that Alan Sugar stepped up on stage. He was 46 years old and his company, Amstrad, had been one of the success stories of the Thatcher years. His speciality was today's technology at tomorrow's prices – in other words, bringing the very latest electronic products to a mass market at affordable prices. He was not a soccer obsessive in the sense that Irving Scholar was, but his sons Simon and Daniel and his brother Derek were all fans. The first Amstrad offices had been in Tottenham, near the ground. Sugar and Venables had met some time before when Venables had taken part in an Amstrad advertising campaign. It is interesting that Venables said in his book *Venables: The Autobiography* (page 302) that : 'I had known Sugar slightly for several years, but had taken an instinctive dislike to him...'

Alan Sugar contacted Terry Venables 48 hours after Spurs had won the trophy. Venables returned the call and within days the two were negotiating with Scholar and Bobroff. Venables declared himself prepared to invest £3 million in the club, which impressed Sugar, but Sugar was clearly going to be the financially senior partner and made it clear that he saw the arrangement as a business transaction. Alan Sugar said to Irving Scholar during their negotiations that Terry Venables saw himself as an entrepreneur, a view Sugar was not in agreement with. Nonetheless, Sugar was sensibly quite prepared to leave Venables to handle all the football aspects of their joint venture.

With Alan Sugar now a credible and wealthy bidder the Midland Bank were considerably more relaxed and, on 12 June, gave the club a year's extension on their £11 million overdraft. Sugar and Venables were negotiating to buy the stakes of both Scholar (who owned 26 per cent) and Bobroff (11 per cent). Together, while not 50 per cent, these two stakes would give them effective control of the company and the club. Right up to the very last minute Scholar was still talking to Robert Maxwell, who also still seemed to want to buy the club.

Unfortunately for Maxwell, and very fortunately for Spurs, Maxwell's ownership of Derby County meant he could not control Spurs as well. The League had put their collective foot down over Maxwell's activities when he appeared to be trying simultaneously to acquire stakes in Watford, Reading, Manchester United, Oxford and Derby County. He ended up with the last two – but that was enough for the League.

Maxwell had even contacted Sugar to suggest that: 'Spurs could have two Sugar daddies'. Sugar told Maxwell in no uncertain terms that it was laughable to believe that Maxwell would be a passive investor in Tottenham (or indeed in any company), but that, as the company was public, he could always buy shares through the stock market. Eventually Sugar was able to persuade Paul Bobroff to sell his stake and Irving Scholar, who was in Monte Carlo, chose to sell to Sugar as well when it finally became clear that Maxwell could not deliver.

Because Venables could not come up with his promised £3 million immediately, Sugar financed the whole deal for the first 10 days. And while Sugar had funded his share from his own bank account, Venables had to borrow most of his £3 million. The two parties held 17.8 per cent of the shares each. On 6 December 1991, however, Tottenham decided to issue more shares to raise money as it still did not have the necessary funds to repay the overdraft. The consequence of this was that Alan Sugar's percentage of the company rose to 48 per cent while Terry Venables' increased to just 23 per cent. This was because Sugar could afford to buy any available extra shares while Venables could only buy a relatively small extra number. So, to all intents and purposes, it was now Alan Sugar's company.

SUGGESTIONS OF SLEAZE

In the next three years, an almost interminable series of television programmes and newspaper articles were to attempt to delve into the sources of Terry Venables' funds, the details of Paul Gascoigne's sale to Lazio and the decline and collapse of the relationship between Sugar and Venables. Even four years later, towards the end of 1995, these programmes and articles are the subject of a number of lawsuits and libel actions and a level of animosity rarely seen either in sporting or in financial circles.

The details, in themselves, are ultimately not important to the story of Tottenham Hotspur. It is clear that the trust between Alan Sugar and Terry Venables broke down over a number of issues and, given that fact, there was always only going to be one winner. It was, and in 1995 still is, Alan Sugar's company and if he chooses to dismiss his chief executive, then that is his prerogative.

Matters came to a head at a board meeting on 6 May 1993. Though the club had been doing much better financially because of the sales of Gascoigne and Lineker and the arrival of the new Sky Television contract, on the field results had not been exceptional and attendances were down on 1991. At the conclusion of the board meeting Sugar handed Venables a letter which suggested for the first time that Venables sell back his shares, at their original purchase price, and resign as chief executive. Another board meeting was arranged for Friday 14 May at which the formal termination of Terry Venables' contract was discussed. The board voted two to one in favour of Venables leaving, with one director (Tony Berry) abstaining. Because of his personal interest in the issue, Venables was not allowed to vote.

Venables went straight to the courts to seek an injunction stopping the board's vote coming into effect. Venables was successful in doing so in the short term, but the situation was clearly an impossible one for the club.

The various hearings in the High Court were nothing if not a circus, and an unpleasant one at that. Venables was clearly portrayed in the popular press as the hero, with groups of spectators appearing noisily outside the court to back up their opinions. Sugar, by comparison, found himself continually intimidated by hate mail, death threats, demonstrations outside his home, obscene phone calls and abusive verbal attacks outside the court. Ultimately this was not to Venables' benefit – though there is no suggestion he was ever involved in orchestrating it – and Sugar, on legal advice, generally kept his own counsel and did not talk about the reasons for Venables' dismissal.

And, in the end, Venables' decision to go to the courts was to prove to be a misjudgement.

Sugar never wanted a court battle and Tottenham were probably unlucky that Venables got his vital injunction: 'We got a freak decision at eight in the evening from what we could see was a lady judge under great pressure,' Sugar is quoted as saying. 'We cannot blame her for her making the decision she did . . . (but) there erupted months and months of work.' And as Sugar quite rightly says: 'There was never any court case. There were just court cases to decide whether there should be a court case.' That point is quite correct – the matter of Venables' dismissal has, at the time of writing, never reached a judgement in court.

An injunction is, essentially, an attempt to prevent something happening. Venables was trying to get the courts to agree that Spurs could not dismiss him until he had gone to court to challenge the legality of his dismissal. He wanted matters to remain as they were until the courts had decided whether his dismissal was proper and legal. None of the court hearings ever addressed whether or not Venables was fairly or unfairly dismissed, or what the alternatives might be. The courts were simply debating whether Venables could remain as chief executive until a future court hearing. The point may seem a fine one – but Alan Sugar is correct. All the courts ever discussed was whether there was going to be a court case.

After three days the judge observed that 'There was nothing to suggest that the board of directors did not have the normal right to hire and to fire the company's chief executive or that if Mr Sugar and Mr Venables should fall out, they were nevertheless bound to continue to support each other indefinitely.' He went on to later add that: 'Whether Mr Venables' dismissal was in the best interests of Tottenham is

The saga of the East Stand somehow seems to symbolise the mismanagement of the later Scholar era at White Hart Lane: soaring costs, uncompetitive contracts, poor planning, internal disputes, lack of consultation with the fans and, ultimately, public embarrassment. The stand was not ready for the heralded home debuts of Gascoigne and Stewart in August 1988, the game was cancelled at the last minute and Spurs were fined by the football authorities.

RIGHT: New chairman Alan Sugar and director Tony Berry flank Terry Venables following the Amstrad boss's acquisition of control of the board in 1991. Sugar had contacted the manager within 48 hours of the Cup final, but it was only after several months of tortuous wrangling that he got his way. To the very last, beleaguered chairman Irving Scholar was still negotiating with Robert Maxwell to buy Tottenham – a course ultimately not possible because of the Mirror Group's chairman's associations with several other Football League clubs.
RIGHT, BELOW: The media circus gathers at White Hart Lane for the 'takeover press conference'. Left to right: Ian Gray, Tony Berry, Terry Venables, Alan Sugar, Nat Solomon, Douglas Alexiou, Frank Sinclair.

not a matter for the court to decide. That is a matter for the Tottenham board, to whom this matter is entrusted under the company's constitution, although it is a matter on which the shareholders can express their views to the board.'

That was both a fair summation of the truth and the end of Terry Venables' association with Tottenham Hotspur. The club's lawyers presented him with a bill for an astonishing £400,000 to cover their legal costs, while Venables' own costs were probably not less than another £200,000. Soon afterwards, he sold his stake in Spurs for £3 million.

By April 1994, he had been appointed coach of England, an accolade which clearly seemed to suggest that if Venables was to be accused of anything it was not much more than bad judgement. His personal financial affairs would continue to be a matter of speculation and will no doubt be so for a very long time. To some extent, by the first half of 1995 they had become subsumed in a wider debate about

football and morality, highlighted by the dismissal of George Graham by Arsenal in February 1995. There was something of an irony in both North London rivals dismissing their managers, close friends of course, in such a short space of time.

Sugar was reluctant to press his attack personally or even in court. Any revelations which appeared critical of Venables would, almost by definition, be damaging to Spurs in both the short and long term and it was hard to see how Sugar or the club could gain from that. After the deal was originally done, Irving Scholar had rung Sugar from Monte Carlo to wish him well: 'Alan, I wish you the best of luck and hope you get as much enjoyment out of it as I did, but without the aggravation.' 'Don't worry about me', Sugar is said to have replied, 'I won't get any aggravation.' But by 1993 Sugar had become irritated by where the credit for saving the club, and returning it to the black, was going: 'Terry Venables did not save this club. Twelve million saved this club. And I put up most of it.' Of the 1993 profit, some £3 million came from the sale of Gascoigne and about £1.4 million as Spurs' share of the Sky Television deal.

The legal and press battle seemed to have the stamina of Paul Allen in his prime – it just ran and ran. Venables' autobiography, published in September 1994, was another opportunity for old wounds to be opened, scraped and to have salt rubbed into them. Happily, a certain amount of humour was now creeping in. *The Sunday Times* asked Alan Sugar to review the book (his fee going to Great Ormond Street Hospital for Sick Children) and his two-page piece was a rare opportunity to enjoy the conflict and their jokes. He worries about whether prospective buyers will be able to find the book at all because they weren't to know whether to look in the fiction or non-fiction sections. His concluding line was also a delight: 'The book is certainly guaranteed an immediate sale of at least 10,000 copies because, with so many allegations lodged against so many people, I should imagine every law firm in the country will buy.'

A RETURN TO FOOTBALL AND SHREEVES

While all of this was going on, Tottenham had been playing football. Only days after his takeover, at the press conference of 22 June 1991, Alan Sugar stated: 'I will look after the £11 million at the bank, while Terry Venables will look after the 11 players on the pitch'. A neat line, and an assurance also given to Irving Scholar, but within weeks Peter Shreeves had returned as first-team coach and then manager, with Venables abdicating direct team responsibility on his appointment as chief executive of Tottenham Hotspur plc.

Shreeves, who since leaving White Hart Lane in 1986 had been assistant and then caretaker manager at QPR (then passed over for Trevor Francis) and later No. 2 to Steve Perryman at Watford, returned to take control of what was essentially Venables' 1990–91 squad but with two notable differences: Gascoigne had gone, laid up for more than 12 months before he could play for Lazio or England, and Gordon Durie had arrived, signed from Chelsea for £2.2 million (a million more than Lineker in 1989).

This Anglo-Scottish strike force began well, registering five wins in seven games and Lineker in a real purple patch with 11 goals, Durie chipping in with two. Then, inexplicably, a 2-1 defeat by Manchester United signalled a

BOTTOM LEFT: Peter Shreeves, back for a second spell as team manager, welcomes Gordon Durie to White Hart Lane in August 1991 – the club record fee of £2.2 million standing until the purchase of Ilie Dumitrescu three years later and Chris Armstrong for £4.5 million in June 1995. Neither man would have a particularly happy time in what was a fairly lacklustre period on the field and a distinctly uneasy one off it. The retiring Shreeves was in an awkward position: if the team did badly, he took the brunt of the brickbats, but if it did well then Terry Venables was more likely to be awarded the accolades.

TOP RIGHT: Gordon Durie pops in Spurs' second goal against Sheffield United at White Hart Lane on 2 September 1992 – the club's first win in six League games under the new management team of Doug Livermore and Ray Clemence. Durie combined well with Teddy Sheringham after the latter's arrival from Nottingham Forest in 1992, but his season fell apart after he was charged by the FA with feigning injury (subsequently cleared) and then hampered by fitness problems. Ossie Ardiles, 'dissatisfied with his commitment', finally sold the Scottish international to Rangers for £1.2 million in November 1993.

BOTTOM RIGHT: In a season riddled with home defeats (11 in the League) the most difficult to take was the 1-0 win by Villa in the FA Cup third round replay on 14 January 1992. Here Dwight Yorke challenges Mabbutt. Gary Lineker's 33 goals in 40 matches kept them alive, but even he failed in both games against Villa. It was Tottenham's third first hurdle exit in four seasons.

ABOVE: Gary Lineker scores his second against Porto in the Cup Winners' Cup match on 23 October 1991. It was a goal that represented Spurs at their best – a one touch move involving practically every Spurs' player. After six blank years Tottenham were back in Europe and they rose to the occasion: after three successive League defeats, two of them at home, they put themselves on course for the third round with a 3-1 win. RIGHT: Gordon Durie had scored three vital goals in six Cup Winners' Cup matches in 1991–92, but neither he nor any Tottenham player managed it in Rotterdam on 4 March against a defence superbly marshalled by sweeper and former Spur Johnny Metgod. It was revenge for the club Tottenham had beaten 6-2 on the way to taking the UEFA Cup in 1983–84.

ghastly sequence of only five wins in 25 League games to leave Spurs in danger of relegation. To make matters almost intolerably worse was yet another home defeat in the third round of the FA Cup, the club relinquishing control of the trophy with a spineless 1-0 home defeat in a replay with Aston Villa. It was the home form that was crippling: 11 defeats in the League, plus that loss in the FA Cup and, on 1 March, another in the second leg of the League Cup semi-final against Forest, avenging their Wembley defeat of the previous year. Small wonder that Lane regulars were worried.

Without Lineker the Second Division would have been almost a certainty. But while Durie experienced a six-month goal drought in the League, and Stewart, Walsh and the rest registered no more than a handful each, the England striker struggled on magnificently, scoring 28 goals in 35 League games and five from as many matches in the League Cup. It was a phenomenal performance in a struggling team lacking the flair of Hoddle, Waddle or

Gascoigne, and that this was an even better achievement than the 24 goals that took Spurs to third place in 1990 was recognised by the Football Writers Association, who voted him their footballer of the year.

There was always the excitement of Europe to fall back on. Spurs had missed out in both 1987 and 1990, but with the UEFA ban now over they found themselves with successive trips to Austria in the European Cup Winners Cup. First there was a faltering, early-season performance against Sparkasse Stockerau of Vienna in the preliminary round, goals coming in each leg from Durie and Mabbutt. Then there came more formidable opposition in the form of Hajduk Split, the Croatian side having to play in Linz because of the war with Serbia – and winning 1-0 in front of only 7,000 people. In the second leg, goals from Durie and defender David Tuttle, a fine drive, saw Tottenham through at White Hart Lane.

Three weeks later Spurs shrugged off their appalling League form to beat Porto 3-1 at

White Hart Lane, with Durie and Lineker (2) reviving their earlier form, and a solid defensive display in Portugal for a goalless draw gave Spurs supporters some comfort during the long winter months. When they played Feyenoord on 4 March they had last tasted victory on 8 January – a 2-1 win over Norwich in the fifth round of the League Cup.

Like Hajduk, Feyenoord had been victims of Spurs on their way to UEFA Cup success in 1984, but this time the Dutch side would be no 6-2 pushover. Largely responsible for Tottenham struggling were two fine displays by ex-Spur Johnny Metgod, now 34, first in front of 48,000 in Rotterdam (1-0) and then when Feyenoord successfully defended their lead with a goalless draw at White Hart Lane.

Spurs were left to aim for respectability in the League. After yet another defeat (2-1 by Liverpool), they won five out of their next seven games (nine goals for Lineker) and finished 15th. The fans remained loyal, at least to Lineker: his farewell home appearance before moving to Grampus 8 (a 3-3 draw against his old club Everton) pulled in a crowd of 34,630.

It was hard not to feel sympathy for Shreeves. If the team did well, it was Venables' side; if they performed badly, it was down to the coach. But although he was hampered by lack of money and forced to operate against a background of boardroom battles he was nevertheless guilty of being overcautious at times and some of his team selections baffled the most trusting of fans, while an increasing dependence on the long ball did nothing to earn respect in the cradle of cultured football. A pleasant enough man, he did not have his tenuous one-year contract renewed in the summer of 1992 and, for the second time in six years, drifted away from White Hart Lane to other venues.

A TOUCH OF THE CONTINENT – AND SHERINGHAM

With Venables' target of 'turning the club's finances around' almost achieved – Alan Sugar's rights issue in December 1991 raised £7 million – the chief executive took a more active role in team affairs for 1992–93, creating a continental-style structure by appointing Doug Livermore (chief coach) and Ray Clemence (his assistant) as his right-hand men; he would remain in overall control of team affairs while they would be responsible for day-to-day matters – and team selection.

The season, according to Venables, would be a 'transitional' one. Yet again. Certainly there was a flat feeling around White Hart Lane after a quartet of genuine footballing folk heroes (Hoddle, Waddle, Gascoigne, Lineker) had been lured away to foreign parts in just five seasons. Even the internationals that remained were, or could be, on the move.

First Stewart, having come good in 1991 with a fine season capped by his FA Cup final goal, and consolidating his contribution with three England caps in 1991–92, was forced to move back north for family reasons and joined Liverpool for £2 million.

Icelander Gudni Bergsson came under increasing pressure, as Dean Austin, a classy attacking full-back, followed in Justin Edinburgh's footsteps from Southend for a fee of £375,000 in June, and decided to leave. Also arriving were centre-backs Jason Cundy (signed from Chelsea for £800,000 after a promising period on loan at the tail-end of 1991-92), and Neil 'Razor' Ruddock, back for a second spell for a tribunal-fixed £750,000 in May having shown growing maturity at Southampton.

All three moves were set up by Shreeves, as was the loan of Andy Gray from Crystal Palace, Steve Coppell getting a useful price of £900,000 in the summer of 1992. Even in goal there were changes, Ian Walker continuing to chase Shreeves' estimation back in 1985 that he was 'the next Peter Shilton' by allowing the

Gunners won their second semi-final with Spurs at Wembley, a crowd of 76,263 seeing a goal from Tony Adams putting his side through. Forest had earlier rubbed in their success by knocking Spurs out of the League Cup for the second year running – this time with a 2-0 win in the fifth round in December.

That Spurs had a reasonable season was due (as so often before) to the goalscoring exploits of one man. Bought just after the start of the season to do the impossible – follow in the formidable footsteps of Gary Lineker – Teddy Sheringham was a very different kind of striker, but at 26 he had learned to play both the long-ball game (at Millwall) and the short-passing game (at Forest).

At Tottenham, after his £2.1 million move in August, he combined them well, savouring the role of saviour following Spurs' sloppy start of two draws, two defeats and only two goals. Sheringham scored 21 goals in the 38 remaining League matches to lead the Premier League list, with four more in five FA Cup appearances and three in four League Cup ties (he didn't miss a game). And he didn't just stop at chasing Lineker's club achievements: despite fierce competition (Shearer, Wright, Smith, Ferdinand) he won a place in the England side.

Sheringham played 17 games alongside Gordon Durie but the partnership failed to flourish, first because the Scot's form faltered following allegations that he had feigned injury and, in the spring, through genuine injury. In November 1993 he would return to Scotland and to Rangers, still only 27 and a Scotland squad regular.

Help for Sheringham up front came from a very different source – the 18-year-old Nick Barmby, a product of the FA's School of Excellence. Very unlike Sheringham in size, shape and style, Barmby complemented the No 10 nicely in a limited number of outings and his surprisingly mature play – his precocious talents were shown to good effect in the televised 2-0 win over Norwich in the fourth

ABOVE: Nick Barmby, Teddy Sheringham, Darren Anderton and Neil Ruddock: a cameo of the mix of youth and experience that began to work so well for Livermore and Clemence in the spring of 1993. If consistency was not exactly their watchword (five times Spurs scored four goals or more, twice they conceded six), the football their side played in that period was in the best traditions of White Hart Lane.
RIGHT: Return to Wembley: Spurs walk out for the FA Cup semi-final with Arsenal on 4 April 1993, two years after the club's classic victory in the same fixture. Six players (Thorstvedt, Edinburgh, Mabbutt, Howells, Nayim, and Allen) survived from that day, but this time there was no magic Gascoigne free-kick or Lineker double. Unable to score, Spurs surrendered the chance of a 10th final to a goal from Tony Adams.

experienced Thorstvedt between the posts only when he was injured.

Certainly there were upheavals in this 'transitional' season. But was it transition or indecision? Livermore used 34 players for 42 League and five FA Cup games, plus Jeff Minton for the first League Cup tie against Brentford – the highest total since the special demands of wartime (39 different players were used in the 36 matches of 1941–42).

Considering the constant changes, not all of them enforced by injury, Spurs did well to finish eighth in the new Premier League and have a good run in the FA Cup. This time it was Arsenal's turn to get even for their 1991 FA Cup defeat, but unlike Forest's revenge at White Hart Lane this one was an eye for an eye: robbed of their double chance in 1991, the

round of the FA Cup – had many critics hailing him as a future England star. In fact he would make his full debut under Terry Venables against Uruguay in March 1995 – as Peter Beardsley came off.

Both players benefited from the arrival of Darren Anderton, a rangy 20-year-old winger whose performances in Portsmouth's 1992 FA Cup run had persuaded Venables to part with £1.7 million – another signing that must have made Peter Shreeves seethe with envy. If Sheringham had to follow Lineker then Anderton, equally unfairly, was often compared with Waddle. While he struggled with a nagging injury in the early weeks, his later form

was confident, then at times sparkling after his return following a hernia operation around Christmas. He, too, would get an England call-up under Venables.

From the end of January these three and the rest of the side gelled as Spurs, playing the kind of exhilarating football for which the club is renowned, enjoyed six successive victories, five in the League and one in the FA Cup. Sheringham scored 10 of the 19 goals in that sequence, and it was his tally of 16 in the last 17 League matches that gave Spurs a respectable eighth place – comfortable if well outside Europe.

Given the relative success of an exciting side, with youngsters like Barmby, Anderton and Austin grafted on to the experience of Mabbutt, Allen and Samways (now a midfield regular), the future on the field appeared rosy. The positions of Livermore and Clemence seemed safe, too; but if the management structure at Tottenham was 'continental', the next stage of English soccer's longest-running lager saga was straight out of a Jeffrey Archer novel.

ALL CHANGE AGAIN

In the record of his time at Tottenham, former chairman Irving Scholar, writing a year after his removal from the boardroom in the autumn of 1992, bemoaned the betrayal of the legendary love of flair, the end of the aristocratic Spurs, the lack of creative class players – citing, for example, the failure of any move to re-sign Chris Waddle from Marseille.

'Many of its best sons are in exile,' he wrote. 'Ossie Ardiles is receiving rave reviews as manager of West Bromwich Albion; Glenn Hoddle proving a wonder player – and a very good manager – at Swindon; and Steve Perryman in command at Watford. These three, and in time Waddle, form a Spurs management in exile. Surely their talents, their expertise, their skills, would be better employed at White Hart Lane? I have nothing against Doug Livermore and Ray Clemence, now the coaching duo managing Spurs, but why should Spurs, whose old boys show such continuing gifts, have to go to Liverpool Old Boys to get their football management input? I just can't understand that . . . Of course, all these questions would

LEFT: 'Razor' Ruddock tangles with Arsenal striker Kevin Campbell in the 1993 FA Cup semi-final at Wembley. After just two League games at Millwall the centre-back moved to Southampton, maturing in both play and attitude before being brought back to White Hart Lane for £750,000. But after only one season at Spurs, he chose to seek his fortune on Merseyside and was transferred to Liverpool for £2 million.

BOTTOM LEFT: Nayim comforts Justin Edinburgh after the 1993 FA Cup semi-final. The game triggered a strange end to the 1992-93 season: Spurs recovered to trounce Norwich 5-1 five days later and finished by beating Arsenal 3-1 at Highbury, but in between they lost four of their six matches, including a 6-2 defeat at Liverpool.

BOTTOM RIGHT: Doug Livermore and Ray Clemence had no chance to pursue their promising policies. Terry Venables' legal battle with Alan Sugar over his role at the club was resolved on 14 June 1993 and their positions as his protegees were untenable. Five days later Sugar appointed West Bromwich Albion boss Ossie Ardiles as manager and the Argentinian installed two former Spurs players on his staff: Steve Perryman (assistant manager) and, pictured here with Ardiles, Pat Jennings (goalkeeping coach).

Paul Allen may not have scored as many goals (23 in 292 League games for Tottenham) as his uncle Les and his cousin Clive, but he certainly enjoyed them when they came. But while not a striking mid-fielder he made an enormous contribution to the club for eight seasons, ball winning, ball carrying, ball providing, before Ossie Ardiles sold him to Southampton in September 1993.

be irrelevant if Terry Venables had stayed in charge of the team.'

In fact, they became relevant when the esteemed Terry Venables ceased to be in charge of anything. Better late than never, perhaps, the chairman in exile would see his wish fulfilled of a Spurs-style 'locker-room' – during what would prove to be the first of two bizarre but intriguing seasons in N17.

Following a falling out on the eve of the FA Cup final, Venables was sacked by Alan Sugar as chief executive and overall manager in May 1993, a move that may well have had its roots in the very move which rescued Spurs' season. Venables became the subject of press allegations about a 'bung' (illegal payment) arrangement with Forest boss Brian Clough over the transfer of Teddy Sheringham – a similar allegation would, ironically, lead to the eventual sacking of Arsenal manager George Graham in February 1995.

Venables finally lost his legal battle with Sugar on 14 June – and only five days later Ossie Ardiles was installed as team manager at the Lane. The situation was full of ironies: not only did West Bromwich Albion threaten to sue Spurs for poaching the Argentinian, but they appointed his assistant as manager at The Hawthorns. His name was Keith Burkinshaw.

By now Alan Sugar, also mindful of the need for experienced business management, had already strengthened the 'team behind the team' with the appointment of Claude Littner as Chief Executive. Littner, with his back-ground in crisis management, had previously demonstrated a tough results-orientated approach as Managing Director of a number of Amstrad's European subsidiaries. His success in organising the management team and getting the financial side back on an even keel and into an extremely healthy position in such a relatively short time, was to provide the foundation for future multi-million pound deals and the continued development of the stadium, facilities and the business in general.

On 6 July Ardiles sacked Clemence and made Steve Perryman his assistant, with Pat Jennings coming in as goalkeeping coach. Livermore was retained as 'first team coach and chief scout'.

The first signals for Spurs supporters, who were split on the events, were very mixed, with the hosts beating Paul Gascoigne's Lazio 3-2 in the opener of the pre-season Makita tourna-

ment but then crashing 4-0 to Chelsea at home in the final. Ardiles, strangely, began in classic Venables signing style, taking Jason Dozzell from Ipswich for £1 million (later increased by tribunal to £1.75 million) and Colin Calderwood from Swindon for a tribunal-fixed £1.25 million (three times the amount Ardiles had offered his old club).

Despite losing Nick Barmby for the first couple of months of the season with shin-splint trouble and Anderton only appearing as a substitute in August, Tottenham started in promising form, winning five and drawing three of the first 10 League matches. The prolific Sheringham averaged a goal a game; he kept that up in the League Cup, too, scoring twice against Second Division Burnley. It was a remarkable sequence, beginning with an excellent win at Kevin Keegan's newly-promoted Newcastle and including a 2-1 success at Liverpool, where Spurs had won only twice in 81 years. Irving Scholar was perhaps entitled to feel a little smug about his prescription.

In statistical terms the most remarkable result was the 5-0 trouncing of Joe Royle's Oldham at White Hart Lane on 18 September, when Tottenham totted up what must surely be one of the fastest three-goal bursts in the League's history: Sedgley (5min 2sec), Sheringham (6min 48sec) and Sedgley again (7min 36sec) scored to record the team hat-trick time of 2 minutes and 35 seconds, grabbed during a frantic opening spell where two of the goals were gifted by misplaced clear-ances from poor Latics keeper Paul Gerrard. The down side of this thrilling match – Durie (his last goal for the club) and Dozzell (his first) scored the others – was the loss of the promising Dean Austin with a broken leg.

The run ended with a 2-1 defeat at champi-ons Manchester United, a game that saw Teddy Sheringham carried off with a knee injury which, with complications, would keep him out for a crucial five months. Without his goals, and his underrated general forward play, Spurs struggled, securing three points only twice in the next 18 League games and finding the going tough in both knockout competitions.

In the League Cup, 1-0 wins over Derby and title-chasing Blackburn (Barmby and Campbell the scorers) were followed by a home defeat by Aston Villa, the eventual winners.

In the FA Cup Spurs needed not only a replay but a 5-4 penalty decider to get past a plucky Peterborough side who would finish the season at the foot of Division 1 (the old Second Division). This was the first shoot-out at White Hart Lane since the UEFA Cup final of 1984, and like that one it was won by a Spurs save, on this occasion when Ian Walker shut out 16-year-old sub Andy Furnell. Spurs then crashed 3-0 at Portman Road to a pedestrian Ipswich team fighting relegation from the Premier League.

Thus Ardiles' first quest for honours finished on 29 January, and the complexion of Spurs' season had now radically changed. It wasn't until 2 March that Ronny Rosenthal, signed from Liverpool for £250,000 in January, secured the first point of the year in a 1-1 draw with Villa, following seven successive League defeats. Draws against fellow strugglers Sheffield United and Ipswich weren't enough to allay fears of the worst, despite Sheringham's return, and the situation eased only after surprising away wins at Everton and Norwich. But consecutive defeats by West Ham (4-1 at home), Coventry and Leeds put Tottenham firmly back in trouble, and the relegation battle on 23 April against Southampton (including Paul Allen, who had moved for £550,000 in September) became a genuine 'six-pointer'.

Nearly 26,000 saw goals from Sedgley, Samways and Anderton haul Spurs up from 18th to 16th place, but then a defeat at Wimbledon left them still with the unholy possibility of Endsleigh League Division 1 football in 1994–95. It took a gritty 2-0 win against a battling Oldham on 5 May (goals from Samways and Howells condemning the hosts to Division 1) to preserve Spurs' precious Premier League status – and, if in the record books 15th slot in the table now looks comfortable, the management, players and above all the fans knew just how tight the dog fight had been. Their great club was only three points and a healthy goal difference away from the dreaded Endsleigh League.

The season had been beset by problems, and supporters could only speculate on what might have been were it not for the injury to Sheringham and, later, the loss for long periods of Austin, Howells, Mabbutt, Thorstvedt and Calderwood, though Micky Hazard's return from Swindon helped compensate for the absence of Howells and the signing of Kevin Scott from Newcastle for £850,000 helped plug the hole at the back for the last vital stages.

The attitude of Gordon Durie didn't help, either. After the Coca-Cola Cup game with Burnley at White Hart Lane – when Caskey was sent off at 1-1 – Ardiles confirmed that he would fine the Scot the maximum amount for his abusive reaction on being replaced by substitute Howells (who scored), and later put him up for sale 'dissatisfied with his commitment'. Rangers paid £1.2 million in November to take him back to Glasgow.

While Durie was hardly missed for his goals (he managed only one in his last 12 games), with Sheringham injured Spurs were now relying on a permutation of Barmby, Anderton, Sedgley, Samways, Dozzell and new boy Caskey to play at strikers, a problem illustrated with a tally of 19 goals in 19 games between October and February. Indeed it was stand-in

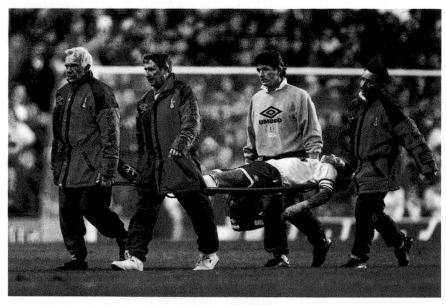

forward Sol Campbell who scored the goal that knocked Blackburn out of the Coca-Cola Cup in December.

The last thing Spurs needed around this time was a major problem at the back, but on 24 November their faltering season turned positively ugly when captain Gary Mabbutt sustained a fractured cheekbone from John Fashanu's elbow during a more than usual fractious clash with Joe Kinnear's Wimbledon. Later the same week (following a PFA decision to launch a campaign to outlaw the so-called 'lethal elbow'), Spurs officially reported the incident to the FA, accompanying their case by video evidence of a 'dangerous challenge'. Meanwhile, Wimbledon reiterated their observation that referee Keith Hackett awarded no foul and saw no reason to reappraise that decision having seen the replay.

Mabbutt, one of the few totally fair-minded defenders left in the game, was diagnosed as carrying no fewer than four fractures of the cheekbone and three fractures of his eye socket. It was not a pretty sight – and, to many football

Serious faces. The White Hart Lane backroom staff stretcher off Gary Mabbutt following the Spurs' captain's clash with John Fashanu's errant elbow in the game with Wimbledon on 24 November 1993. The injury was as serious as it was senseless, Mabbutt sustaining four fractures of the cheekbone and three of the eye socket. The ugly incident led to a hearing before the FA and a serious crackdown by referees, but for Spurs the absence of their skipper was crucial as they lost eight of their 13 League matches while he was out of action. Mabbutt made a typically brave return with the reserves only three months after the Fashanu clash, having been awarded the MBE in the New Year's Honours list. Just over two weeks later he was back in the first team for the 4-3 defeat by Chelsea, and was then everpresent as Spurs hauled themselves to safety in a tense and tight relegation fight.

Danny Blanchflower, who retained a very special place in the affections of all Spurs fans, died on 9 December 1993, aged 67. Coming as it did only weeks after the demise of Arthur Rowe, manager of the great 'push and run' side of the 1950s, it seemed to symbolise a change of era. Now the game is dominated by sponsorship deals, multi-million pound transfers and live television, and seems a far cry from the days of brown balls and black and white photographs.

fans outside north-east London, nor was the prevarication of the FA. Their commission decided, after 4½ hours of videos and interviews, that they needed more time to consider whether to charge Fashanu with misconduct.

The next day – Christmas Eve, as Mabbutt prepared to undergo further surgery – the commission decided not to charge Fashanu because they could not be sure there was 'sufficient intent' – this despite the fact that referee Hackett now conceded there was 'a measure of intent'. It was hardly a seasonal gift for the Spurs skipper, but he did receive some comforting news the following week when he was awarded an MBE in the New Year's honours list. Mabbutt's absence was crucial, though Steve Sedgley filled in admirably before returning to midfield and scoring vital goals against Everton and Southampton. Wearing a 'phantom' mask to protect his appalling injuries, Mabbutt made a typically brave return in the reserves on 10 February and resumed his place in the first team 17 days later against Chelsea to help in the fight against relegation.

While one fine Tottenham captain was honoured, another – indeed perhaps the club's greatest – had died. Danny Blanchflower, one of the tiny handful flatly to refuse the unexpected invitation to parade his past on *This Is*

Your Life, had passed away on 9 December. When approached by Eamonn Andrews with the words: 'Danny Blanchflower, this is your life,' Blanchflower simply replied: 'Oh no it isn't,' and walked away. Coming only a month after the death of 'push and run' manager Arthur Rowe, aged 85, it seemed somehow to signal yet another aspect of a club in a state of change. New ownership, an Argentinian manager – and, the following season, a veritable invasion of European stars.

Tottenham's bad luck – and poor form – continued into 1994, with Erik Thorstvedt ruled out for several weeks after damaging knee ligaments during a depressing defeat by bottom club Swindon on 22 January, the fourth match in a miserable sequence of seven consecutive League defeats. Not surprisingly, attendances at White Hart Lane began to fall, only 17,452 turning out for the visit of Villa on 2 March.

The season was bedevilled by events off the field, too, with the legal battles over management of the club becoming something of a football soap opera that first enthralled and then bored the average non-Spurs fan. On 2 September Venables resigned from the Tottenham board, having sold his 23.3 per cent shareholding for £3 million; a fortnight later a much-publicised *Panorama* programme was broadcast, containing allegations about his business dealings, the nub of which was the source of the money used to buy his stake in Spurs.

In January the police apparently cleared him of any illegal dealings in his business affairs – the move took him a vital step nearer the England job vacated by Graham Taylor, a choice supported publicly by Alan Sugar – but two days later Tottenham presented a petition to the High Court to wind up Venables' company Edennote in order to recoup the estimated costs of £350,000 caused by his previous legal action. Despite the allegations still hanging over his reputation, Venables took over as the national coach on 28 January. Exactly a month later he would include Darren Anderton as one of three uncapped players in his squad for the visit of European champions Denmark, and the winger made an emphatic debut in a 1-0 win at Wembley.

The petition was far from the first litigation of the season, involving Spurs. The FA charged Spurs with misconduct over the appointment of Ossie Ardiles – the day before the club announced profits for 1992–93 of some £3.3 million. In November Spurs were found guilty, fined £25,000 plus costs, severely censured and warned over 'future conduct in such matters'.

Even during the gruelling, nail-biting end to the season Tottenham's torrid affairs in court were far from over. While the hearing for the claim against Edennote was deferred, Tottenham were fighting a claim for £500,000 from the Inland Revenue over signing-on fees and pursuing a claim against Bill Jenkins, architect of the £6million East Stand reconstruction, for £700,000 repair bills the previous year.

And hanging over the club was the big one: the array of tawdry allegations during the Scholar era first rumoured back in February. On 12 May, only five days after their last game (a rather prophetic 2-1 home defeat by Gerry Francis' QPR), and ironically the very same

TOP LEFT: The transfer dealings of Ossie Ardiles caused constant consternation for many Spurs fans. His first two purchases were seen as dubious and both were inflated by the FA tribunal – Jason Dozzell (Ipswich) from £1 million to £1.75 million and Colin Calderwood (Ardiles' old club Swindon) from £450,000 to £1.25 million. While Dozzell (pictured) started promisingly and ended the season as second top scorer he faded into the background the following season under Gerry Francis; Calderwood, by contrast, suffered from lack of form and injury early on but in 1994–95 matured into a Scottish international.
BOTTOM LEFT: Crystal Palace midfielder Andy Gray had won an England cap when Peter Shreeves negotiated his loan in February 1992, a move made permanent for £900,000 in the summer. A combination of injury and stiff competition for midfield places kept his first-team appearances to just 33 before he drifted off to Swindon on loan.

day that Edennote was finally wound up in the High Court by Sugar and Spurs, the FA formally charged the club with misconduct concerning alleged irregular payments to an array of players after studying documents handed over voluntarily by Sugar.

The charges didn't relate to 1993, nor even the 1990s: these 'interest-free' loans were said to have been made between 1985 and 1989. As far as the average football fan was concerned, the dates may as well have been 1885 and 1889. Certainly Sugar was seen as in no way connected – surely the old regime responsible for the payments in question should carry the can.

On 25 May the FA announced that if Spurs were found guilty and punished by demotion, relegated Sheffield United, who finished 20th, would take their place in the Premiership. It seemed that the FA were determined to make Alan Sugar pay for remarking, during his court battle with Venables, that football is 'riddled with corruption'. The date of the inquiry was set for 14 June. The allegations concerned 40 charges of malpractice involving 15 players and a total of £545,000 between 1983 and 1989, the 6 most serious relating to alleged transfer rule breaches between 1985 and 1989 during the purchases of Paul Allen, Chris Fairclough and Mitchell Thomas. Despite Gascoigne being listed among the recipients, the biggest single sum involved was an interest-free loan of £75,000 to Paul Stewart.

Even in the build-up to the World Cup finals, this case was big news. On the whole the press was sympathetic, though on 12 June the *Daily Mirror* called Spurs 'the club that is dying of shame'. Later that day Tottenham were cleared of the claims made by the Inland Revenue. Swindon chairman Ray Hardman contended that if the club were found guilty they should indeed be demoted, just as Swindon were after winning promotion (under Ossie Ardiles) in 1990, and threatened to sue the FA for £4million if Spurs were not.

There had been widespread sympathy for the Wiltshire club then, and the prevailing mood now was that the allegations had little or nothing to do with the present regime or players, and that punishing the club with relegation or points deduction was not an apt response; and if the public were understandably sick of the relentless series of sleaze stories emanating

from White Hart Lane, they still felt that in this case the wrong people – present chairman and, inevitably, long-suffering fans – were in the dock. There were exceptions: *Today* recommended a ludicrous demotion by two divisions, pointing out that: 'Arsenal have long had a reputation as strict disciplinarians in this area.' Not so their manager, apparently, as later events were to suggest.

In the *Sun* on the day of the hearing Jimmy Greaves made a passionate plea for his old club to retain Premier League status, and for the real culprits to be brought to book. He was granted his first wish, but there was a massive price to pay: the FA not only deducted 12 points from the club's total for the coming season but also banned them from the FA Cup. The £600,000 fine, though a record (the previous largest was the £105,000 levied on Chelsea for similar offences in 1991) was almost an irrelevance considering the economic implications of the first two stipulations. Oh yes, and Spurs had to pay considerable legal costs.

The reaction was one of shock, almost disbelief: 'Sentence of Doom', 'Gutted', 'Sugar Caned for £7m', 'Cheating Spurs in Disgrace' ran the tabloid headlines, with the club dubbed Tottenham Dropspur and Tottering Hotspurs. Few people had genuinely expected demotion to the Endsleigh League, and the consensus was for a hefty fine, but the 12-point penalty was viewed as excessive (it would mean needing to finish in the top half in 1994–95 to avoid relegation) and the FA Cup ban was a crippling blow to a club who had won the trophy eight times.

Former player Garth Crooks described the sentence as 'Draconian' and likely to 'blow the game apart. The FA have opened up a can of worms.' Gordon Taylor of the PFA claimed 'the FA have done everything but relegate them.' With four clubs facing the drop in 1995, it was seen as especially harsh. The players' reaction was predictably one of disbelief and dismay, with David Howells' observation that it was 'slow torture . . . worse than relegation' widely quoted. The club's share price plummeted on the Stock Market and the bookies lengthened the odds on Spurs winning the Championship from 50-1 to 250-1.

It was also ironic that the hearing should be held at the Wembley Conference Centre, just 200 yards from the scene of Spurs' greatest Cup triumphs; seven of the 1987 Finalists were recipients of unauthorised payments, and now Tottenham suffered the indignity of being banned from the oldest football competition in the world.

Nor was it lost on the public that the chairman had cooperated fully in the FA investigation. 'When Alan Sugar brought the word "bung" into public parlance in his High Court battle against Terry Venables in June 1993, he can have no idea what he had started,' wrote John Duncan in *The Guardian*. 'Four television documentaries, countless newspaper revelations and an FA Commission of Inquiry later, his club start the 1994-95 season with minus 12 points . . . the story started in court, and it will probably end there.'

Sugar was understandably angry, stating: 'I'm not going to be intimidated by these archaic and barbaric methods.' The FA's stance represented a 'deliberate vendetta

against our club and against me personally'. Some cynics suggested that he had opened up the issue in order to get Venables discredited, and it was widely assumed that at least 15 of the Premier League's 22 clubs were involved in 'improper payments'.

Despite the risks of a possible harsher sentence, Sugar received broad backing for his appeal to a three-man FA tribunal. For the hearing, at St Albans on 2 July, Sugar ditched his heavyweight team, conducted his own case – and came away with a substantial prize. In effect he clawed back six points at £150,000 apiece, the tribunal reducing the penalty from 12 points to six but increasing the fine from £600,000 to £1.5 million. However, the FA Cup ban was still in place.

It was a critical change, not least in trying to attract new players. In *Today*, two days after the initial hearing, Alan Hansen's article was headlined 'What player in his right mind would join Spurs now?', the former Liverpool player arguing that 'Tottenham should forget about next season and what seems inevitable relegation, and start planning for a future two years ahead.' He was, eventually, wrong on both counts, but it was certainly the case that Ardiles had problems trying to persuade class players to join Spurs.

It was a problem he could have done without. The feeling was that the manager had bought badly and that his signings, expensive or otherwise – Dozzell, Calderwood, Kerslake, Hazard, Rosenthal, Scott – amounted to £5million of almost wasted money, and indeed they made less than a handful of appearances between them in the last crucial League games. Speculation about new players had been rife ever since Sugar publicly promised the manager money to spend in early May (Richard Gough was then a candidate), but the 12-point penalty and then the World Cup finals had held things up. Now, with Sugar saying he would spend £13 million of his own money 'to make the club great again' the race was on for a star name; prime among the targets was Romania's midfield genius Gheorghe Hagi valued by Barcelona at around $4million (US).

Players were on the move, too. Two days after the swingeing penalties on Spurs, Steve Sedgley's transfer to Ipswich recouped a million and on 7 July Vinny Samways put in a transfer request. However, such domestic changes were overshadowed on 27 July when Ardiles' patient search was rewarded with the arrival of Ilie Dumitrescu, one of the leading lights of Romania's run to the World Cup semi-finals, for $4.3million (US).

The quiet, intelligent forward signed for Spurs on 29 July, but his transfer was that day eclipsed by another – one of the most astonishing deals in the history of English football. A day before his 30th birthday, Jürgen Klinsmann became a Spurs player. For the second time in six weeks an event involving the club had rocked the football public. 'Alan Sugar pulled off English football's transfer coup of the decade yesterday by signing charismatic German World Cup star Jürgen Klinsmann for Tottenham,' led off Brian Scovell in the *Daily Mail*. The Spurs chairman went to Monte Carlo to put the finishing touches to the $3.3million (US). capture of the former German Footballer of the Year.

'Most of the negotiations were conducted from the communications room of Sugar's yacht *Louisiana*,' continued Scovell. 'The White Hart Lane chief planned his holiday in the Mediterranean to ensure he would be in the right place at the right time to negotiate directly with the German, who steers clear of agents.'

The signing of Klinsmann and Dumistrescu – plus another possible World Cup star Ardiles was reluctant to name – gave the close season at Spurs, and indeed across the country, a fresh angle. Not since Keith Burkinshaw brought over Ardiles and Ricky Villa in 1978 had foreign investment attracted so much attention. A

Spurs go international as the Argentinian boss signs Romanian midfield star Ilie Dumitrescu for a club record $4.3 million (US) on 29 July 1994. Though exciting, the signing was overshadowed the same day by the leaking of another deal which was the story of the year in English football. For just $3.3 (US) million Sugar had secured the services of Jürgen Klinsmann, one of Europe's top strikers.

player of genuine international class, with 25 goals in 65 matches for his country (five of them in the recent World Cup), Klinsmann had been a huge success at both Inter Milan and Monaco after leaving VfB Stuttgart, but his reputation in England was shallow: here he was seen as a talented creator and masterful taker of goals who tarnished his performances with clever con-tricks to elicit free-kicks from less astute referees. And while mature fans might speculate on everything from the strengths of the potential Sheringham Klinsmann strike partnership to the arrival of a blond German at a club with such strong Jewish associations, the newspapers just couldn't resist having a go; indeed several of them featured step-by-step diagrams on how to follow the Klinsmann 'dive'. Jürgen himself, full of charm and diplomacy, first parried questions on the subject and then joked about it in near-perfect English, disarming both press and public.

This man was no 'over the moon' player. Fluent in four languages, a supporter of Greenpeace, driver of an ageing VW 'Beetle', impeccably behaved at all times, here was a refreshing antidote to the yobbish, spoilt-brat antics of many British soccer stars – both past and present. This was to be a new kind of football hero.

The level of interest was staggering. 'Since news of the signings was announced our phones have been jammed,' explained the ticket office 'At the time of the punishments we were all down in the dumps. But this has given the place a spark. The news has tipped the balance and suddenly there is a wave of optimism.'

A few observers sounded a more cautious note, pointing out that Premiership survival and a good run in the League Cup was about the best that could be hoped for, even if both chairman and manager did hold out secret hopes of an FA Cup reprieve. 'To fail last season, with the number of injuries, was almost understandable,' pointed out John Ley in *The Sunday Telegraph*. 'To fail with Klinsmann, Dumitrescu, Sheringham, Barmby and Anderton leading the line would be unforgivable. Early shortcomings in the campaign could determine Ardiles' fate before Christmas.' Prophetic words.

Meanwhile, and on the back of his brave fight against the FA's harsh punishments, the position of Sugar had changed dramatically with the signings. From being a hard-nosed businessman with no real passion for the game – let alone a love of the club so professed by his predecessor – he had for the supporters become a saviour, prepared to bend his holiday round the pursuit of his prey and pump his personal millions into the purchase of top players. He made no bones about his vengeful feelings towards the FA – but to the fans what counted was commitment.

The admiration for Sugar's deal was emphasised only days later with the sale of Vinny Samways to Everton for £2.2million, some £200,000 more than the fee for Klinsmann. Personal terms and one-year opt-out clauses notwithstanding, followers of the game were left wondering why Premiership clubs were paying so much for British players (£5million for Chris Sutton, for example) when experienced foreign stars like the Spurs signings, Stefan

Schwarz at Highbury and several others were available for far less. Samways was a talented, hard-working 25-year-old with reasonable, perhaps even international prospects, but there was no way he would ever be a World Cup star like those for whom he made way at White Hart Lane.

More column inches were devoted to Klinsmann than any other pre-season topic, including Manchester United. Everything from his impact on share prices (Spurs' rose 21% in the week after the double signing) to his ability to handle Vinnie Jones was considered, though for most football writers there was one key area. Mick Dennis caught the mood well in the London *Evening Standard* as early as 4 August: '. . . although Spurs supporters are salivating at the prospect of a glut of goals, the rest of the country wants to boo him.'

All eyes were on Hillsborough and its sell-out crowd on 20 August for the opener against Sheffield Wednesday. Ardiles did indeed play his five-man attack, answering critics' predictions of defensive frailty by deploying Calderwood in front of a back four that featured Stuart Nethercott alongside Sol Campbell in the middle. The line-up was completed by Ian Walker in goal, with David Kerslake and Justin Edinburgh filling the full-back positions; Micky Hazard and former captain Gary Mabbutt formed a venerable pair on the bench.

The Hollywood script – blighted only by the absence of Chris Waddle in the home team – continued to be written for Spurs as they beat Wednesday 4-3 in one of the finest games of the season. Four of Ardiles' 'famous five' scored, Klinsmann losing Des Walker to head in Anderton's cross and make it 4-2 before wheeling round and lurching into a studied dive along the turf – to be followed by Sheringham and the rest of the team, including Ian Walker. Remarkably, the vanquished home fans appreciated the parody, and when the striker hurt his face in an ugly clash of heads with Des Walker shortly afterwards, and was stretchered off with blood pouring from his mouth, the Yorkshiremen gave him a standing ovation. No mean feat: in less than 90 minutes he had become the most popular German in the north of England since Bert Trautmann.

What's more, his overall performance (full of commitment and free of con-tricks), his goal, his antics and his heroics – he was back after the match and 11 stitches in his lip giving interviews to the media – did much to endear him to the rest of the nation. Klinsmann's arrival was already giving the season a much-needed lift.

Was the result a flash in the pan or, as David Lacey's headline had it in *The Guardian*, was it 'New era dawns for Spurs'? Wednesday boss Trevor Francis reckoned it was 'the most adventurous team I've seen in my time as a manager,' but most pundits harped on the problems of defence, Alan Hansen claiming that Ardiles was 'brave but misguided'. The acid test, he said, would come against champions Manchester United in the third match. Spurs fans weren't looking that far ahead; indeed it was a shame that only 25,553 could squeeze into White Hart Lane for the midweek visit of Everton. The unchanged team again delivered in dangerously exciting style,

Klinsmann getting both goals (a volley and a header) in a 2-1 win, achieved despite a missed Sheringham penalty.

If Spurs supporters were ecstatic, the chairman was pretty pleased too. The next day the share price shot up 14p, adding £1.6million to the club's Stock Market value to take it past £20million. In the 27 days since the signings of Klinsmann and Dumitrecsu the valuation of Spurs had gone up by £5million, and by some £8million since the initial FA decision to dock 12 points. But this, of course, is the real world: Tottenham had two wins in two games and were still at the foot of the table.

Hansen was right. On the following Saturday a dull United still beat Spurs 1-0 to bring fans down to earth a little, that feeling helped by another missed Sheringham penalty. For many, however, this was merely a blip, the roller-coaster returning to the rails for a 3-1 win at Ipswich on the Tuesday for Spurs' first 'real' points, with Klinsmann notching two goals to take his tally to five in four games.

The 'third man' mentioned by Ardiles after the signings in July turned out to be Romanian World Cup star Gica Popescu from PSV Eindhoven, who pushed the Spurs club record up to £2.9 million. Understandably, Popescu took a little time to settle, but under Gerry Francis he would emerge as a vital part of the Spurs game plan. First, however, he would suffer the agony of a humiliating defeat at Notts County in the League Cup.

Spurs then lost twice in six days to lowly opposition: first Matt Le Tissier outgunned a below-par Klinsmann at the Lane to give Southampton their first win of the campaign and then, more worryingly, they went down 3-1 at Leicester. Klinsmann scored again, but the defence was looking increasingly leaky. Leicester would win only six League games all season.

Any sane fan realised now that dreams of the League title were sheer fantasy, and that the League Cup was indeed a crucial lifeline. So when Spurs went behind to Watford after just 26 seconds at Vicarage Road in the first leg of the second round there was more than a little concern on the terraces. New boy Giga Popescu, signed from PSV Eindhoven for £2.9million and replacing Calderwood to play behind his countryman Dumitrescu, must have wondered what was happening. The other starters (Mabbutt for Nethercott, Hazard for Barmby) must have been nearly as perplexed. But it was all right on the night: Spurs ran out 6-3 winners, with Klinsmann grabbing a hat-trick.

If Popescu was the last piece in Ardiles' jigsaw – Sugar revealed that he had spent £8 million of his own money over three years – there was little evidence of the finished article working well against Nottingham Forest at White Hart Lane on the Saturday. Indeed it was Dutchman Brian Roy, not Spurs' imported stars, who stole the limelight, and the 4-1 drubbing highlighted what the press had been saying since the season's start: a team needs to

be solid at the back and winning the ball in midfield before it can exploit its rich diversity of talent in attack. With three successive League defeats and 12 goals conceded in four games, Ardiles' future was again put firmly on the line.

The heat might have eased for Ardiles with a gutsy 2-1 win over an understrength Wimbledon at Selhurst Park on 4 October, Popescu getting the winner, as Ardiles finally abandoned his five-man attack, but in a week of hiccups Barmby and Edinburgh both demanded clarification of their future, the team lost 3-2 at home to Watford in the League Cup return (a restored Barmby scoring the first), assistant manager Steve Perryman split with his wife after 22 years, blaming the pressures of work for the breakdown, and the Sugar-Venables tiff continued, this time with the England boss infuriating Spurs' chairman by saying Spurs players could suffer from his exclusion from White Hart Lane.

All this helped undermine Ardiles, and many were named as likely successor, among them Souness, Hoddle and even Beckenbauer and Cruyff. Under mounting pressure Ardiles maintained his calm – 'I'm surprised by all the speculation surrounding my position' – as he looked to the match with Gerry Francis' QPR for his first home victory in five attempts.

It was hardly surprising that the team peformed poorly in a scruffy 1-1 draw (Kevin Scott and Les Ferdinand were sent off), with Jason Dozzell and Danny Hill in a line-up featuring neither Romanian, ironically as a result of injuries picked up on international duty against England. The next game, Leeds away, elicited a more creditable 1-1 draw, with Dumitrescu judged man of the match in spite of his almost total lack of comprehension at team talks. Ardiles, having been backed both by the PLC's AGM and the local paper that week, could breathe a little easier.

Manchester City at Maine Road should have been a chance to consolidate, but it wasn't taken: Spurs lost 5-2 to a side for whom old boy Paul Walsh did much of the damage, scoring two of the first three goals and making a couple more. The only consolation for Spurs was that they finally found a penalty taker, Dumitrescu succeeeding after Sheringham had missed his third in a row.

Scott, incidentally, was playing after an FA Commission had reduced his three-match suspension to a four-point booking after video evidence clearly showed he should not have been sent-off for his scuffle with Les Ferdinand during a League match.

Maybe the team would have in any case been better off relying on the experience and temperament of Mabbutt, but the longest-serving Spur could not even find a place in the team for the tricky Coca-Cola Cup third round tie against Notts County the following Wednesday, and this despite the fact that Ardiles made three defensive changes (Walker, Kerslake and Scott making way for Thorsvedt, Austin and Calderwood).

Despite the obvious pressure on this game – the League Cup was Tottenham's only realistic chance of a trophy and of entry to Europe – the manager remained in an upbeat mood. But if the matches against Forest and Manchester City had been embarrassing, the result against a County side propping up the Endsleigh

LEFT: Notts County striker Tony Agana hits a firm shot past Erik Thorsvedt in the third round Coca-Cola Cup tie on 26 October 1994. BELOW: Ilie Dumitrescu is sent off by referee Ken Burge after his second bookable offence at Meadow Lane. However, the writing was already on the wall: two goals down against a team who hadn't won a League game at home for six months and was propping up the First Division. BOTTOM: For Ossie Ardiles and assistant Steve Perryman it was a living nightmare. Plenty of Spurs managers had been the victim of giant killing acts, but with no entry in the FA Cup and six points to be deducted in the League the Coca-Cola Cup had been the only path to glory that season. Or so it appeared at the time as both men saw their careers at Tottenham in tatters.

League Division 1 was positively numbing. Not only did Spurs lose, but they lost calamitously, 3-0.

For County it was not so much giant-killing as taking candy from a big baby. For Spurs, playing a side who had not won at home in the League for six months, it was perhaps the most humiliating night in the club's history. Their lowly opponents (despite Howard Kendall's brief managerial rescue bid County would still drop a division in April) appeared more committed and better prepared, and Spurs were already 2-0 down before Dumitrescu was sent off for his second bookable foul well before half-time. The 10 men of Tottenham, even more confused, had no answer.

Nor did Ardiles afterwards. The press had universally seen it as his last-chance game, and they were right. Henry Winter pointed out in *The Daily Telegraph* that the reasons for Ardiles to resign multiplied by the match: 'Wednesday night's Coca-Cola Cup ignominy at Notts County confirmed that Ardiles is ill-equipped to coach a club of Spurs' tradition and ambition. Likeable man, limited manager is the gathering consensus...'

While tabloid headlines bayed for blood, neither Ardiles nor his chairman panicked. But it was clear to many observers that even a win against West Ham at home would not save the manager. Ardiles sensibly put his faith in experience, starting Hazard and Mabbutt for the first time in the season. A 3-1 win looked good (the first in six games), but victory was no more than a temporary stay of execution. Though Ardiles remained calm and refused to contemplate resignation – '. . . reports of my funeral have been greatly exaggerated' – his departure was widely expected to be announced at the next board meeting the following Thursday.

It didn't take that long. Having been called to Sugar's Essex home on the Monday night,

ABOVE: Ossie Ardiles leaves White Hart Lane. The Notts County result sealed his fate, and, despite a 3-1 win over West Ham three days later, the die was cast, and on the Tuesday he confirmed his departure. OPPOSITE PAGE: Teddy Sheringham greets the incoming Gerry Francis to the training ground. Francis' task wasn't easy: stopping the leaks at the back, winning more possession in midfield and keeping the goal tally going up front, all with the same squad. No one's play improved more under Gerry Francis than that of Colin Calderwood, whose displays at the back during the middle of the season earned him a Scotland call-up.

Ossie's contract was 'terminated with immediate effect' and he left the club the next day. If he blamed the grinding Venables-Sugar row for some of his troubles ('I was the pawn in the middle of their battles'), Ardiles left White Hart Lane as he had played and managed there, with dignity, honesty and a touch of humour. It was ironic that the same day, November 1, after yet more allegations about his predecessor's dubious business dealings, Venables was given unequivocal backing by the FA.

Ardiles had remained true to his beliefs right to the bitter end. 'I'll never change my principles. Brazil in 1970 were the best team I have seen, the paragon. They had no great defenders and only one defensive midfielder. They showed what attacking teams can do. I don't want to apologise for a very exciting Spurs team. This is the way forward.' Brazil won, of course: Tottenham's record under Ardiles was hardly in the same vein, with just 20 wins in 65 matches.

While David Pleat and former England captain Gerry Francis emerged from the pack of possibles as favourites for his job, assistant manager Steve Perryman took over for the thankless task of taking a dispirited side to title-chasing Blackburn. To lose 2-0 wasn't too bad – in the circumstances – even if Alan Shearer and Chris Sutton did run Mabbutt and Popescu ragged. But according to Ian Ridley in *The Observer* the new manager's mission was to 'turn a group of disparate, disjointed talents into a football team. The current collection has a tendency to self-destruct in eight minutes.' Eight minutes was the time of the first Blackburn goal.

The same day, Pleat's allsorts of a Luton team were winning at Wolves, whose managerial vacancy had previously been spurned by Francis. Pleat's vast experience, not least in a highly successful sojourn at White Hart Lane, made him the logical choice for Alan Sugar, but there appeared to be technical hitches.

Events elsewhere – including the sacking of Mick Walker at Everton and Ron Atkinson at Aston Villa, and the breaking of the Bruce Grobbelaar bribes scandal – diverted football's attention for several days. When it returned to Spurs, Francis was a clear favourite. Having resigned from his job (apparently on the rumour of Rodney Marsh being installed as general manager) to put himself firmly in the frame, he eventually took on the mountainous task of reviving Tottenham's flagging fortunes. Interestingly, while Alan Sugar mused on winning the League within three seasons, Francis signed up only on a one-year 'rolling' contract. One result of his arrival and the choice of his back-up team was to be the departure of assistant manager and former captain Steve Perryman, whose association with the club had begun in 1967.

Francis' first match was a salutory lesson on Spurs' problems, a 4-3 home defeat by an Aston Villa side lacking a manager. Francis had reversed Ardiles' philosophy, playing five central defenders across the back and a sweeper (Popescu) in midfield. 'Quite how Francis can teach these hapless defenders to master the art of keeping the ball out of the net remains to be seen,' quipped Christopher Davies in the *Daily Telegraph*; yet within days he did just that.

On 23 November Tottenham drew 0-0 at home to Chelsea to record their first clean sheet of the season – no fewer than 18 matches. The price was a lack of flair and entertainment, but for Francis and Sugar, whose prime concern was Premiership survival, it was a reasonable price to pay. A bonus was how Gica Popescu was becoming an increasingly creative and influential figure in midfield.

Things now began to look up for Spurs off the field. On 25 November, just ten days after Francis' appointment, the FA announced following an arbitration hearing that a new commission would shortly review the club's summer punishments – widely interpreted as code for a likely reprieve on the FA Cup ban. Ossie Ardiles was entitled to feel a tad aggrieved.

It was Francis who had whatever luck was going. At Anfield the next day an own goal from old boy Neil Ruddock gave them an unwarranted 1-1 draw against Liverpool, and the new manager was relieved that the only goal his side gave away was a penalty.

Francis was hardly having easy opposition to

start with. After Liverpool came Newcastle, and though weakened by injuries the visitors still posed a real test, notably through the probing of the irrepressible Peter Beardsley. The crucial 4-2 victory – another turning point in Tottenham's topsy-turvy season – owed much to a hat-trick from Sheringham, but there was the selfless work of Klinsmann, the guile of Anderton and a handsome performance in the defensive wedge by David Howells, who had found his niche for the rest of the season. With six points deducted, Spurs now moved a couple of places above the relegation zone.

The forthright Francis had been working mostly on defensive duties in training but, vitally, he had simply made the players fitter for football, too. 'I don't think it's something they've done here, that kind of running, for three or four years, if at all,' he said, referring to area-to-area sprints. "It's bloody hard work. There aren't too many players, if any, who want a ball afterwards. Mostly they want a basin.'

They would need champagne glasses for the next twist of fate; on 3 December they were drawn at home to Altrincham in the FA Cup, a clear signal that entry in the competition would follow. Six days later it did, with the arbitration tribunal going all the way, also reinstating the six deducted points in the League. The £1.5 million fine imposed at the July appeal remained – an average international's transfer fee being viewed as more than fair for a wealthy club guilty of illegal payments, even if the wrong directors were being penalised.

While most supporters had been unaware of the situation, this decision was almost inevitable once Alan Sugar put his lawyers to work and the matter had gone to arbitration. Indeed the tribunal's verdict on the FA's disciplinary committee was damning: the charges against Spurs were 'misconceived, bad in law and should not have been proceeded with . . . and it was irrational to impose any penalty other than a fine.'

Irrational is the word; and as a result the papers portrayed the decision as a crushing victory for the Amstrad and Tottenham chairman over the serried ranks of the stuffy football establishment. 'Some of us were always anxious that the nature of Tottenham's punishment smacked of a desire to put Alan Sugar in his place,' recalled Patrick Barclay in *The Observer*. 'My complaint about the FA, however, is not so much that they were too tough in this case as they have been too weak in previous ones.'

Few complaints were coming from White Hart Lane. There was a new determination at the club not only to take full advantage of the break and build on the foundations laid by Francis, but also in some way to repay the dedication and not inconsiderable skill displayed by Sugar behind the scenes. He had considered taking the FA to the High Court but instead agreed to go to arbitration in keeping with FIFA guidelines; now nothing would give him more satisfaction than to hold the FA Cup aloft at Wembley on May 20.

It was poor Sheffield Wednesday who, for the second time in four months, caught Spurs in upbeat tempo. For a second time, too, Jürgen Klinsmann was the key to success, eclipsing Chris Waddle's warm return to White

Hart Lane by helping to make goals for Barmby and the fast-improving Calderwood and in between rifling a fierce right-foot shot past Pressman to score his first goal in four matches.

Tottenham continued their improvement throughout December, moving up the table with two wins and two draws; amazingly, not a goal was conceded, and they finished the year with a 4-0 win at Coventry (their biggest away win for nearly two years) to move into sixth place in the Premiership. There was talk of Europe. A miracle was in the making.

The only casualty of the resurgence had been Ilie Dumitrescu. An adventurous free spirit, he found it difficult to tie down a place in the first team and suffered most from the departure of Ardiles, finding the going tough in the high workrate policy of Francis, who preferred the reliable down-to-earth performances of Howells and, latterly, the committed power of Ronny Rosenthal.

Under Ardiles the Romanian scored five times in 13 games; under Francis he played only an hour in the unbeaten run of five matches. Just before Christmas he asked for a transfer and on 30 December he was sent on loan to Seville in the Spanish League until the end of the season.

For the rest of the squad the New Year kicked off with the traditional fixture against Arsenal, still reeling from the revelations about Paul Merson's drug taking and, far more importantly, the allegations about manager George Graham's taking of large 'bungs'. Spurs began 1995 where they had left off in 1994 – winning and not conceding goals – with Popescu popping up to convert Anderton's cross.

Next came perhaps the sweetest moment of the season: the FA Cup third round tie against Altrincham. Though the visitors were among the leaders of the Vauxhall Conference and had something of a giant-killing tradition, the game was virtually a bye for Spurs, but there

was an edge to the hosts' play early on; imagine the reaction if, after all the fuss, Spurs were to be knocked out at the first hurdle by non-League opposition. However, goals from Sheringham, Nethercott and Rosenthal steered them safely through.

The following week they completed the double over West Ham with goals from Sheringham and Klinsmann, the German's first in seven games. A minor blemish (how times change) was a conceded goal – again the first in seven games. Gerry Francis' record was now nothing short of astonishing: P12, W7, D4, L1, F23, A9. It was Championship form.

The marvellous run came to a halt in front of more than 40,000 at Villa Park, where the home team (now under Brian Little) recorded only their third home League win of the season with a slender 1-0 victory. (The setback to Tottenham's fortunes was overshadowed that night by events at Selhurst Park, which resulted in both Eric Cantona and Paul Ince facing assault charges – the former with grave consequences for Manchester United.)

Spurs' own confidence was soon restored with a fine performance in a difficult fourth round tie at Sunderland, struggling in the Division 1 of the Endsleigh League. The spectre of Meadow Lane hung over the travelling fans at Roker Park, but professionalism won the day 4-1 with Klinsmann getting his first two FA Cup goals, one a penalty.

If proof were needed of Spurs' resurgence – they had not played a club from the top five since early December – it came with the visit of League leaders Blackburn to White Hart Lane on 4 February. The eventual champions looked vulnerable to Spurs' snappy, accurate and imaginative first-time passing, and goals from Klinsmann, Anderton and Barmby completed a convincing 3-1 win that threw the title race wide open.

Here was the fusion of talent, toil and tactics that Francis was seeking, and the covering of Anderton and Barmby in defensive positions

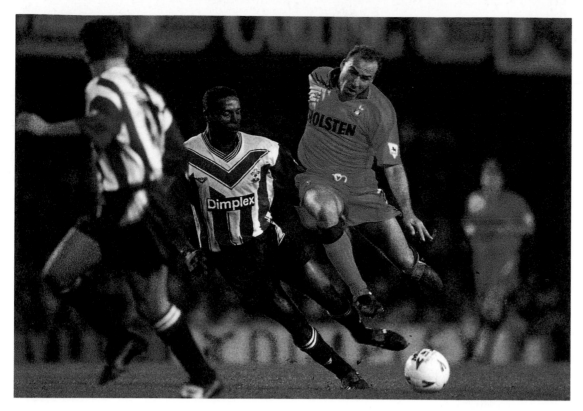

illustrated the approach to good effect. Barmby's reward was to be called into Terry Venables' England squad (along with Sol Campbell, and joining regulars Anderton and Sheringham) for the ill-fated game with the Republic of Ireland in Dublin, which was abandoned due to hooliganism. The experience of Colin Calderwood was much happier – he was in the Scotland team which earned a draw with Russia in Moscow in March, thus graduating from a man with an unsure future under Ardiles to an assured international in three months.

The victory over Blackburn, perhaps Spurs' most complete League performance of the season, was followed by a patch of three disappointing results. First came a repeat 1-1 draw with a Chelsea side on the slide at Stamford

RIGHT: With just two minutes left Sheringham returned the favour, setting up Klinsmann with a neat flick and the German captain scored with power and panache. It was a sensational victory against a side in form and at a ground where a draw is a great result. After the comeback at Southampton people were starting to say that Spurs' 'name was on the Cup'; now, with lowly Everton their semi-final opponents, their name was almost being inscribed on the trophy in the public imagination.

Bridge, then a worrying stutter against Southampton with the same score in the Cup at White Hart Lane, and a 2-1 home defeat by Wimbledon a result that let Leeds steal sixth place in the table. Such placings had become even more important since the decision by UEFA, taken a fortnight before, to increase the English allocation in the UEFA Cup from three to four clubs for 1995–96.

But if doubts were creeping into the squad's thinking they were banished during March, a spectacular month that kicked off with a most remarkable Cup replay at The Dell. In a pulsating match it was an unsung journeyman, Ronny Rosenthal, who kept Spurs' Cup dreams alive, scoring a stunning hat-trick that took them into the lead from being 2-0 down at half-time. Missing Campbell and Popescu through injury, Tottenham totally lost their new-found shape and organisation in the first half as Southampton's pace and panache proved too much. Two down, Francis was man enough to abandon the ploy even before half-time and sent on the former Liverpool player.

It was the substitution of the season. In the 56th minute he swept in Barmby's awkward cross over the amazed Grobbelaar; two minutes later the keeper was non-plussed again as Rosenthal unleashed an angled shot from well out on the right; then, in the 11th minute of extra time, while moving down the inside-left channel, he let a shot go from over 25 yards that flew into the top corner of the Saints' net. Spurs added three more against a demoralised opposition, but it was the Israeli's night: he just couldn't put a foot wrong, and if he had taken a corner (probably even a goal-kick) he probably would have scored that evening.

There was a growing feeling now, after the nature of this incredible comeback, that Tottenham's 'name was on the Cup', that somehow the club would win it by predestination; but any such theories were tempered by the quarter-final pairing with Liverpool – at Anfield. Spurs warmed up well, securing a 2-2 draw at better-placed Forest to regain sixth spot and then ambling past table-propping Ipswich 3-0 at home only four days after poor Town had conceded no fewer than nine to Andy Cole and Manchester United.

Francis kept faith with the team that did so well against Southampton. Liverpool, beaten only once at home in the League, went ahead late in the 38th minute through Robbie Fowler, but Klinsmann cleverly set up Sheringham to level on the stroke of half-time with a beautifully flighted shot into the corner. Spurs won on points in the second half, and with two minutes left – and Liverpool hanging on for the replay – Sheringham returned the favour with a deft flick and Klinsmann coolly finished the move in style. The strikers took the accolades – rightly so, when Anfield had been such a graveyard for Tottenham in recent years – but the whole team played magnificently and no one better than Howells, who gradually wrested control of the game from Liverpool's powerful midfield. Klinsmann was tearful after the final whistle as he celebrated with thousands of ecstatic travelling fans at the Anfield Road end. And he was not alone in being moved by the generous ovation given his team by the Kop.

'Nothing short of a royal decree, it seems, can prevent Tottenham reaching Wembley in search of a record ninth FA Cup triumph,' Joe Melling wrote in the *Daily Mail*. It certainly appeared that way, and it was a fantastic moment for Gerry Francis, whose only pledge to Alan Sugar had been to keep Spurs in the Premier Division.

Francis had benefited hugely from the lifting of the FA Cup ban and the restoration of the six points in the League, but it must be said that his team were improving well before that. 'When I came here we were four points off the

LEFT: Unlucky 13: full-back Matt Jackson's shot beats Ian Walker to put Everton ahead in the FA Cup semi-final at Elland Road on 9 April 1995. Spurs fans looked to their side for the reasons for the surprise defeat – a struggling Anderton, discomfort at the choice of the venue by the FA, perhaps even over-confidence – but Everton had done their homework and executed their strategy well on the day.

BELOW: Jürgen Klinsmann's penalty past Neville Southall was the only goal Everton conceded in the competition. Klinsmann rushed to collect the ball from the net so that Spurs could get on with their quest for an equaliser. But Everton quickly restored their two goal lead and for the German and his team the Wembley dream was gone.

bottom, and we were out of the Cup. Morale was low and there was no money to spend. But the players have worked hard and applied themselves. It's down to them, not me . . . You need to have passion in your game. It's about winning the ball and then playing your football – and then working hard again to get the ball back if you lose it.' It was a simple philosophy, modest in both senses, and one espoused by many a manager; the difference was that Francis seemed to make it work.

David Lacey in *The Guardian* was not alone in applauding his astonishing effect on the club since his arrival: 'It's possible to argue that, had Gerry Francis been organising the team from the start of the season, Spurs might now be heading towards a second Double. For consistent quality of performance they are now up there with Manchester United, Newcastle, Blackburn and, as this match showed, ahead of Liverpool.'

Yet that game was to prove the zenith of Tottenham's season. Over the next 11 days

they would play goalless draws with both
United (away) and Liverpool (at home), the
matches sandwiching a laboured 1-0 win over
bottom of the table Leicester. But with the
teams above them making few mistakes these
five points were worth little. Leeds slipped
back into sixth place and the UEFA Cup
became a receding target. All eyes were now
on Elland Road – an unpopular choice of
venue for both Spurs fans and for Francis,
who quite rightly wanted the bigger stage of
Wembley – and the FA Cup semi-final against
Everton on 9 April.

Meanwhile they had one more League
game, away at Southampton and, though few
expected a repeat of the eight-goal thriller at
The Dell a month before, the crowd were
treated to seven. Unfortunately four of them
went to the Saints, Le Tissier taking his tally
against Spurs in the season to six goals in four
games. It was the first time since mid-
November, in Francis' first game, that the
defence had conceded more than two goals,
and it was strangely portentous of what was to
come a week later.

For reasons that would frustrate Spurs fans
for years – should Francis have really brought
back Nethercott and Popescu after six weeks,
for example? – Everton not only won but won
fairly comfortably. Could it be that Spurs, firm
favourites against a side battling against
relegation every week, and with their name
now virtually inscribed on the Cup in the
public imagination, had been lulled into laxity
by the dominant mood? Millions in Britain had
moved from wanting, to almost expecting
Jürgen Klinsmann to walk up the Wembley
steps to shake a royal hand. After all, Spurs
had lost only three times in 25 games.

But this is the Cup. In any case, such
theories ignore the performance of Everton,

who had yet to concede a goal in the competition. They showed all the determination, industry and discipline brought to their play by Joe Royle since his arrival in November (and which they would demonstrate again in the final with Manchester United), and they didn't allow Spurs to play their flowing game. In addition, the defence gave away sloppy goals. Two late scores from substitute Daniel Amokachi sealed the victory – Royle admitted he was on the pitch in error – but Klinsmann's penalty had been little more than a token comeback. If any club's name was on the trophy in 1995, it was that of Everton.

The dream had ended not with a thunderous climax but with a dark cloud. Seven points adrift of Leeds (even with two games in hand) and almost certainly out of European contention, it would have been easy for Spurs to become maudlin. They are a club unused to FA Cup semi-final defeats (only their sixth of 15 semi-finals in their great history), and the chance of glory had gone. The next day, £5million was slashed from the club's Stock Market value in the wake of the failure to reach Wembley, shares falling 23 pence to 141p.

But this was a new Tottenham, with backbone. Two days later they repaired some of their lost pride with a 2-1 win over Manchester City in front of the White Hart Lane fans, with two heroes of their recent 'success', Howells and Klinsmann, getting the goals. Yet the season, inevitably, had lost much of its sparkle, and the last of their several memorable games – a 3-3 draw at Newcastle, when a missed Klinsmann penalty would have made it 4-2– presaged anti-climactic defeats by QPR (now managed by Ray Wilkins) and Coventry (Ron Atkinson).

Only a week after the semi-final exit, allegations broke that Dumitrescu had pocketed some £550,000 from Steaua Bucharest on his move to Tottenham, and White Hart Lane grew increasingly impatient with the rumoured transfer of Jürgen Klinsmann.

While he was initially expected to stay for two seasons the German captain had stated on 27 March that he had turned down Inter Milan and Bayern Munich – but the latter 'only for the present'. In the first week of May it surfaced again and finally, after days of speculation, he announced on 11 May that he was indeed returning home to play for Bayern in the 1995–96 season. Good news for Spurs came the same day when Gerry Francis agreed to be team manager for another year. This followed the good news for Spurs fans which had come two days earlier, when their former favourite Nayim scored a last-minute-of-extra-time goal from long range for Real Zaragoza to wrest the European Cup Winners Cup from the holders Arsenal in a dramatic final.

Two days later Klinsmann bade farewell to 33,040 sad fans in his last game, failing to score in a 1-1 draw with Leeds; indeed he had been stuck on 29 goals for more than a month, and the penalty at St James's Park would have made it 30. But it wasn't that important. Sure, it would have been good to score, but Klinsmann had been making as well as taking goals all season, including a critical part in many of Sheringham's tally of 23. Now the formidable partnership was to be parted and with it, thought many Spurs fans, the best chance of success in 1996.

Klinsmann's decision to leave may have been puzzling, but no less so than his decision to join, given Spurs' position at the time. He had been the leading character in the most fascinating, twisting season in the club's long history – the Double notwithstanding – in a few months metamorphosing from a loathed cheat to a univerally liked sportsman voted Footballer of the Year by the Football Writers Association.

The irony was not lost on the majority of caring football fans in England. During a season that saw their beloved sport riddled with almost endemic sleaze and corruption – endless stories of bungs, bribes, drugs, riots, assaults, dissent, poor administration and even the death of a fan – it took a distrusted foreigner to show us how to play and how to enjoy our national sport. Few footballers have made such an impact in so short a space of time as Jürgen Klinsmann did in England in 1994–95. Alan Sugar's sensational gamble paid massive dividends both for his club and the game in general, and it very nearly brought off a miracle.

The sport must move on. And so must the club. On 22 May, Gica Popescu signed for Barcelona as a $4.3million (US) replacement for Feyenoord-bound Ronald Koeman, he of the sinister foul and the sensational free-kick. All three foreign visitors to White Hart Lane, it seems – Dumitrescu, Klinsmann, Popescu – had been one-season wonders. But what a season.

Tottenham Hotspur is now an institution well into its second century. No one survives who can tell us about those days spent playing on the Tottenham Marshes, or even about the way the club eventually arrived at White Hart Lane. Few of us will be there to celebrate the Bicentennial in 2082. But there is one thing that we can be sure of: that as long as football continues to be played, then the Spurs will go marching on . . .

OPPOSITE PAGE , TOP: Klinsmann was made captain for his final game, a 1-1 draw with Leeds. He had frustrated Alan Sugar by not confirming that he would stay for the second year of his contract. Three days before the Leeds game Jürgen Klinsmann announced that he would indeed be leaving for Bayern Munich. Spurs fans were, to say the least, disappointed at his departure.
OPPOSITE PAGE , BOTTOM: Bouquets, not brickbats. While it was a crying shame that the phenomenal, phoenix-like story of Spurs in 1994-95 was rewarded with neither Wembley nor Europe, it is difficult to exaggerate the impact Jürgen Klinsmann made on Tottenham and on English football in less than nine months. In a season riddled with stories of sleaze and corruption, he brought a refreshing breath of fresh air to the ailing sport. For Spurs fans, however, the news on 12 May was not all bad; Gerry Francis, himself on a one-year rolling contract, agreed to a further season as manager.
LEFT: Farewell to Holsten, main sponsors of the club since their name first appeared on Tottenham shirts for the game at Old Trafford on 16 December 1983. On 10 March 1995 Alan Sugar announced a new four-year deal with computer giant Hewlett Packard. Chairman of Amstrad, Sugar admitted that the arrangement involved 'some conflict of interest', but added that 'the two companies are not really in head-to-head competition'. Tottenham also announced a new four-year deal with strip manufacturers Pony.

TOTTENHAM HOTSPUR —
the complete first class record

The Hotspurs did not have a recognised fixture list until their third season; the first official 'list' was published in the *Weekly Herald* on 24 October 1884. Between their formation in 1882 and season 1892–93, all games can be classified as friendlies except for a small number of appearances in local cup competitions, when the specific competition is mentioned. Between 1884 and 1892 only games which were included on the fixture list at the beginning of the season and were reported by the *Herald* have been included. For the other seasons prior to 1896–97, when the club joined the Southern League, only games covered by the *Herald* as first team matches have been included. The club obviously arranged other games on free Saturdays, but there are no means of distinguishing, at this distance, whether those games were first, second or third team fixtures. In seasons where the *Herald* gives the team's final record as including more games than were actually reported, then this fact has been noted. Again, it is probable that the paper included some second team matches in its summary. The *Herald*, incidentally, is referred to in various sources as the *Weekly Herald*, *Tottenham Herald* and *Tottenham Weekly Herald* but these are all the same newspaper. In 1882–83 only one game, against Latymer, was reported by the *Herald* and it is therefore more than likely that the team's other fixtures were against local scratch sides. The Latymer fixture was only covered because the Edmonton club was quite prominent at the time — otherwise the Hotspurs' first season would have been ignored completely.

In a number of cases in the first decade, games were definitely played but no record of the result remains. This is usually because the *Herald* did not cover the game, but occasionally it was because the result was disputed and the paper did not wish to offend either team by stating one result. At other times, games had to be called off because of bad light and, on at least two occasions, because the ball burst and there was no replacement.

Between 1896 and 1908, Spurs played in at least two first class leagues and sometimes in three. In theory all of these games were first class, for the reserve teams contested other leagues such as the South East Counties and the London Combination (reserve leagues and games are not covered here). It does not seem possible, however, that all of the Thames and Medway League, United League, Southern District Combination or even Western League games can have been contested by the first team. They were, nonetheless, published as first team fixtures and have been included here. The same problem applies to friendlies, which are always difficult to classify. In general, friendlies where it is known that most of the first team turned out have been included, but the reader must assess for himself or herself how seriously these games would have been taken by the club.

Several discrepancies in the various league tables, particularly prior to 1900, have been identified but not always altered. These generally occur when the for and against columns do not add up (or do not correspond to those results which are known), or where some results are missing or are contradictory in different sources. While every effort has been made to ensure that the Spurs figures are correct, at this distance it is impossible to find the missing information, or to resolve contradictory scores and results for other clubs. Given the choice between leaving these tables out or reproducing them as published at the time, with their errors,

we have chosen to do the latter. The same problems apply to early Southern League appearances and to goalscorers (who were occasionally not recorded as late as 1939). Even in the 1970s, there are goalscoring discrepancies between newspaper reports, club programmes and annual aggregates. These often arise through interpretation of what constitutes an own goal. We have tried to be as accurate as is now possible in all these cases but there are occasions where, for instance, early appearances do not add up to the required totals and there is no way of correcting the figures. In recent seasons substitutes have added a further complication, and our rule has been to include a substitute as having made an appearance if he actually came on the field. The appearances and goals columns apply only to Southern League and Football League matches throughout.

Key to Competitions

AC	Amateur Cup
CS	Charity Shield
CUP	Minor wartime cup competitions
EC	European Cup
ECWC	European Cup Winners Cup
EEC	East End Cup
f	Final (of a Cup competition)
F	Friendly
FC	FA Cup
FLC	Football League Cup
LCC	London Challenge Cup (sometimes referred to as London Charity Cup)
LCup	London Wartime Cup
LGC	Wartime League Cup
Lge	Football League (or, in wartime years, whichever League was operating [Football League South, London Combination, Regional League South, London League] as shown by the League table that season).
LLge	London League
LnC	London Cup (known also as the London Association Cup and the London Senior Cup)
LPCF	London Professional Charity Fund
LSupp	London Supplementary Wartime Competition
LuCC	Luton Charity Cup
MC	Middlesex Cup
r	Replay (of a Cup tie)
SAll	Southern Alliance
SCC	Southern Charity Cup
SDC	Southern District Combination
SDCC	Southern District Charity Cup
sf	Semi-final (of a Cup competition)
SLge	Southern League
SLS	Sheriff of London's Charity Shield (occasionally referred to as Dewar Shield)
TEX	Texaco Cup
TLge	Thames and Medway League
UEFA	UEFA Cup
ULge	United League
VC	Victory Cup
WDC	Wolverton and District Charity Cup
WLge	Western League
WRF	War Relief Fund

Blank spaces in early years represent local friendlies — the only sort of game at that time apart from occasional cup matches.

The columns in each league table are, in order, played, won, drawn, lost, for, against and points.

SEASON 1882/83

Date		Venue	Opponent	Result	Score
30 Sep		*	Radicals	L	*
6 Jan		A	Latymer	L	1-8

* Venue and score unknown, but lost by two goals

SEASON 1883/84

Date		Venue	Opponent	Result	Score		Date		Venue	Opponent	Result	Score
6 Oct		H	Brownlow Rvs	W	9-0		29 Dec		H	Star	W	3-0
13 Oct		H	Evelyn	W	5-1*		12 Jan		A	Woodgrange	L	0-1
20 Oct		A	Grange Pk	L	1-3		19 Jan		A	Grafton	W	1-0
27 Oct		H	Leyton Rvs	W	1-0		26 Jan		H	Albion	L	0-1
10 Nov		A	Brownlow Rvs	W	1-0		2 Feb		A	Clarence	W	1-0
24 Nov		H	Sekforde Rvs	W	2-0		9 Feb		H	Albion	W	3-0
1 Dec		A	Sekforde Rvs	W	1-0		16 Feb		H	Hanover Utd	L	1-2
8 Dec		A	Leyton Rvs	L	1-3		23 Feb		H	Grange Pk	W	1-0‡
15 Dec		H	Claremont	W	2-0†		8 Mar		A	Hanover U 2nds	W	2-0
26 Dec		H	Oak	W	6-0		15 Mar		A	Latymer	W	2-0
27 Dec		H	Latymer	W	2-0		22 Mar		H	Remington	W	2-0

* Hotspurs score recorded as 'five goals and one disputed goal'
† Game lasted only 60 minutes
‡ Grange Park played with only 10 men

SEASON 1884/85

Date		Venue	Opponent	Result	Score		Date		Venue	Opponent	Result	Score
27 Sep		*	J. Jull XI		5-4		3 Jan		A	Hadley		‡
4 Oct		H	Remington	W	4-0*		10 Jan		A	Abbey	D	1-1
11 Oct		H	Abbey	W	1-0		17 Jan		A	Grange Pk	L	0-1
18 Oct		H	Woodgrange	L	4-5		24 Jan		H	Victoria	W	5-0
25 Oct		H	Grange Pk	W	4-0		31 Jan		H	St Martins		‡
1 Nov		A	Sekforde Rvs	W	4-0		7 Feb		H	Fillebrook	W	3-0
8 Nov		H	Marlbro Rvs	W	1-0		14 Feb		H	Latymer	D	0-0
15 Nov		A	Latymer	W	2-1		21 Feb		H	St Peters		‡
22 Nov		H	St Peters	W	3-2		28 Feb		A	Bedford Rvs	D	1-1
29 Nov		H	Hadley		‡		7 Mar		A	Marlbro Rvs		‡
6 Dec		H	Tottenham	W	4-0†		14 Mar		A	Victoria Wand		‡
13 Dec		A	Woodgrange	D	0-0		21 Mar		A	Remington		‡
20 Dec		H	Sekforde	W	5-0		28 Mar		A	St Martins		‡
26 Dec		H	Grove		‡		4 Apr		H	Mars		‡
27 Dec		H	Enfield	W	3-0		11 Apr		A	Grove		‡

* Jack Jull's XI versus Billy Harston's XI
† Tottenham were a different side from Hotspurs
‡ Scores either unknown or disputed by the two clubs

SEASON 1885/86

Date		Venue	Opponent	Result	Score		Date		Venue	Opponent	Result	Score
3 Oct		A	Silesia Coll	W	4-3		6 Feb		H	Edmonton Ind	W	4-1
10 Oct		A	Grange Pk	L	0-3		13 Feb		H	Grange Pk 2nds	L	0-3
17 Oct	LnC	H	St Albans	W	5-2		20 Feb		H	Sth Hackney	W	8-0
24 Oct		H	Westmstr Rvs	W	*		27 Feb		H	Silesia Coll	D	1-1
7 Nov	LnC	A	Casuals	L	0-8		6 Mar		H	Ilford	W	6-1
14 Nov		A	Fairfield	L	0-1		13 Mar		H	Rutland	W	5-0
28 Nov		H	Dalston Rvs	W	3-0		20 Mar			Upton Excelsior		*
26 Dec		H	Bowes Pk	W	2-0		27 Mar		H	Enfield Lock	W	6-1
2 Jan		H	St Martins	W	3-0		3 Apr		H	Park	W	8-0
9 Jan		H	Woodgrnge Pk	*	*		10 Apr		H	Park	W	8-0
16 Jan		A		L	0-2		17 Apr		H	Hermitage	W	3-0

* Score not available
According to the Tottenham Weekly Herald a total of 37 games were played at all levels this season, of which 24 were won and only 11 lost. Total goals for were 111 with 51 against. Nonetheless, the Herald only records the results of the 22 matches above.

SEASON 1886/87

Date		Venue	Opponent	Result	Score		Date		Venue	Opponent	Result	Score
2 Oct		H	Sth Hackney	W	13-1		15 Jan	EEC	H	Park	W	2-0
9 Oct		H	Woodford Bdg	W	2-0		22 Jan		H	Foxes	W	2-1
16 Oct	LnC	A	Upton Pk	L	0-6		5 Feb		A	Park	W	4-1
30 Oct		H	Old St Pauls	D	1-1		12 Feb		A	Fillebrook	W	3-0
13 Nov		A	Silesia Coll	L	2-3		19 Feb	EEC	A	St Lukes	W	2-1
27 Nov		A	Fillebrook	L	1-4		5 Mar		H	Edmonton Ass	W	2-1
4 Dec		A	Iona	W	5-0		16 Apr	EEC	A	Caledonians	L	0-1
18 Dec	EEC	H	Phoenix	W	6-0		23 Apr	EECsf	H	Enfield Lock	W	6-0*
27 Dec		H	Dreadnought	W	6-0							

* Herald gives score as 'six goals and one disputed goal to nil'. The Herald gives the club's record for the season as played 20, won 14, lost 5, against 22. Results of two games against City Ramblers and another possibly against Silesia College were not recorded by the Herald.

SEASON 1887/88

Date		Venue	Opponent	Result	Score		Date		Venue	Opponent	Result	Score
1 Oct		H	Buckhurst Hill	W	6-1		31 Dec		H	St Martins	W	3-0
8 Oct	LnC	A	Hendon	L	0-6		7 Jan		H	St Brides	W	3-2
29 Oct		H	St Augustines	W	5-1		14 Jan		A	Bowes Park	D	2-2
12 Nov		H	Nondescripts	W	6-1		21 Jan		A	Old St Pauls	W	2-1
19 Nov		H	Royal Arsenal	W	2-1*		4 Feb		A	Royal Arsenal	L	2-6
3 Dec		A	Luton Town	W	2-1		18 Feb		A	Olympic	W	5-1
10 Dec		A	Priory	W	3-0		17 Mar		A	St Brides	W	3-0
24 Dec		H	Balmoral	D	1-1		2 Apr		A	Clapton	L	1-6

* Abandoned after 75 minutes because of bad light

SEASON 1888/89

Date		Venue	Opponent	Result	Score		Date		Venue	Opponent	Result	Score
22 Sep		A	Royal Arsenal	W	1-0		26 Dec		H	Orion Gym		*
13 Oct	LnC	H	Old Etonians	L	2-8		10 Jan	MC	H	Civil Engineers	D	0-0
20 Oct		H	Clapton	L	2-5		16 Jan		A	Windsor Phnx	L	1-2
17 Nov		H	Millwall Rvs	D	1-1		19 Jan	MC	A	Civil Engineers	L	1-4
24 Nov		H	Plaistow (Knt)	W	4-0		1 Mar		A	Windsor Phnx	L	1-2
1 Dec		H	Old St Marks	W	5-1		9 Mar		H	Royal Arsenal	L	0-1
8 Dec		H	Upton Excelsior	D	3-3		16 Mar		H	Edmonton	D	1-1
15 Dec		A	Plaistow	W	2-1		13 Apr		H	Orion Gym	W	6-1
22 Dec		A	Bowes Pk	W	4-0							

* Result not available

SEASON 1889/90

Date		Venue	Opponent	Result	Score		Date		Venue	Opponent	Result	Score
21 Sep		A	Royal Arsenal	L	1-10		11 Jan		A	Romford	D	0-0
28 Sep		H	Westminster	W	13-0		18 Jan	MC	A	Old St Stphns	W	4-2
5 Oct		H	Vulcan	W	5-1		1 Feb		H	Robin Hood	W	1-0
12 Oct		H	Iona	W	10-0		8 Feb		H	Vulcan	W	2-1
19 Oct		A	Edmonton	L	2-3		15 Feb	MC	H	Clapton	L	†
2 Nov	LnC	A	Old St Stphns	l	0-4		1 Mar		A	Swindon	L	1-2*
9 Nov		H	Clapton	W	5-3		8 Mar		H	Unity	W	3-1
16 Nov		A	Finchley	D	1-1		15 Mar		H	Edmonton	L	1-4
23 Nov		H	Hampstead	W	1-0		4 Apr		H	Dreadnought	L	0-1
30 Nov		H	Sutherland	W	1-0		5 Apr		A	Uxbridge	D	2-2
4 Jan		H	Foxes	D	1-1		7 Apr		A	Maidenhead	W	3-2

† Score not available
* According to the Herald Swindon won by 'one goal and one disputed goal to one'. The Herald says that the club played 45 games in all this season, winning 22 and drawing 10, but they record only the results of the 22 above.

SEASON 1890/91

Date	Comp	H/A	Opponent	Result		Date	Comp	H/A	Opponent	Result	
27 Sep		H	Hampstead	W	6-3	22 Nov	LnC	H	Barking	W	3-0
4 Oct		H	Grove House		*	6 Dec		A	Unity	D	1-1
11 Oct		A	Edmonton	L	4-6	24 Jan	LnC	A	Barnes	W	1-0
18 Oct		A	Luton Town	L	1-4	31 Jan	LnC	A	Millwall Ath	L	1-5
25 Oct		H	Northumbrlnd	W	1-0	7 Feb		H	Orion	W	7-1
	LnC		Fusiliers			14 Feb	MC	H	Clapton		*
1 Nov	LnCr	A	QPR	D	1-1	21 Feb		H	Vulcan	W	6-0
8 Nov		A	QPR	W	2-1	28 Feb		H	Old St Stphns	W	3-0
15 Nov		H	City Ramblers	W	1-0						

* Result not available

SEASON 1891/92

Date	Comp	H/A	Opponent	Result		Date	Comp	H/A	Opponent	Result	
26 Sep		H	Hampstead	W	6-2	26 Dec		A	Kings Lynn	L	*
3 Oct		H	Grange Pk	W	4-2	2 Jan		H	Uxbridge	W	3-0
10 Oct	LnC	H	Caledonian Ath	W	4-3	9 Jan		H	QPR	L	1-2
24 Oct		H	Clapton	L	1-2	23 Jan		H	Westminster	D	2-2
31 Oct	LnC	A	Hampstead	W	3-2	30 Jan		H	Old St Lukes	W	3-1
7 Nov	LuCC	H	Coldstream	D	3-3	6 Feb		A	St Albans	L	1-2
14 Nov	LuCC	H	Coldstream	W	7-2	13 Feb		A	Clapton	D	1-1
21 Nov	LnC	A	City Ramblers	L	1-4	20 Feb		H	City Ramblers		*
28 Nov		H	Old St Stphns	D	0-0	27 Feb		H	Grenadier Gds	W	9-0
5 Dec	MC	A	Minerva	L	0-2	12 Mar		H	Casuals	W	3-1
12 Dec		H	Forest Swifts	D	1-1	26 Mar		A	Luton	L	1-3
19 Dec		A	1st Scots Gds	L	0-4						

* Result not available

SEASON 1892/93

Date	Comp	H/A	Opponent	Result		Date	Comp	H/A	Opponent	Result	
17 Sep		H	Paddington	W	10-0	26 Dec		H	Edmonton		*
24 Sep	SAll	A	Polytechnic	W	2-1	14 Jan	SAll	A	Erith	L	1-2
1 Oct		H	Royal Arsenal	W	3-0	21 Jan	SAll	A	Slough	D	3-3
8 Oct		H	Coldstrm Gds	W	6-0	28 Jan	LnC	H	Casuals	L	0-1
15 Oct	SAll	A	Old St Stphns	W	3-0	4 Feb	SAll	H	Slough	W	5-2
22 Oct		H	Coldstrm Gds	W	3-2	11 Feb	SAll	H	Polytechnic	D	2-2
29 Oct		H	2nd Scts Gds	L	2-4	18 Feb		H	London Welsh	D	2-2
5 Nov	SAll	A	Windsor	W	2-1	25 Feb	SAll	H	Upton Pk	W	1-0
12 Nov		H	Clapton	L	1-2	4 Mar	SAll	H	Windsor	W	5-2
19 Nov	SAll	H	Erith	W	3-2	11 Mar		H	QPR	W	1-0
26 Nov		H	Caledonian Ath	W	5-0	25 Mar	SAll	A	Old St Stphns	L	1-2
3 Dec	LnC	A	Polytechnic	D	2-2	1 Apr		H	City Ramblers	W	1-0
10 Dec		H	Hampstead	D	1-1	8 Apr	SAll	A	Upton Pk	L	1-4
17 Dec	LnCr	H	Polytechnic	W	3-0	15 Apr	WDC	†	Smethwick	L	0-2
24 Dec		H	Coldstrm Gds		*	22 Apr		H	London Welsh	W	4-1

† Played at Wolverton
The Herald gives Spurs full first team record for the season as played 31, won 17, drawn 6, for 79 and against 46. They fail to record the results of five of these matches, however.
* Result not available

Southern Alliance 1892–93

1	Old St Stphns	12	10	1	1	44:15	21
2	Erith	11	8	1	2	29:14	17
3	**TOTTENHAM**	**12**	**7**	**2**	**3**	**29:21**	**16**
4	Polytechnic	8	4	0	4	18:12	8
5	Slough	11	2	2	7	21:33	6
6	Windsor/Eton	10	2	1	7	14:37	5
7	Upton Pk	10	1	0	9	7:36	2

Only two other fixtures were known to have been played–Slough v Upton Park on 29 April and Windsor v Polytechnic on 23 April. The results of these games are not recorded and, as far as known, the league was left incomplete. The Southern Alliance was disbanded at the end of this season

SEASON 1893/94

Date	Comp	H/A	Opponent	Result		Date	Comp	H/A	Opponent	Result	
16 Sep		A	Enfield	L	1-5	20 Jan	MCr	H	3rd Gren Gds	L	0-2
23 Sep		A	Romford	D	2-2	27 Jan	WDC	H	Chesham	D	2-2
30 Sep		H	Casuals	L	0-1	3 Feb		H	City Ramblers	D	0-0
7 Oct		H	City Ramblers	W	2-0	8 Feb		H	London Hospital	D	1-1
14 Oct		H	London Welsh	W	1-0	10 Feb		H	Polytechnic	W	5-0
21 Oct	LnC	H	Old St Marks	D	0-0	17 Feb		H	Highland Iftry	D	2-2
28 Oct	LnCr	H	Old St Marks	L	1-6	24 Feb	WDC	A	Chesham	W	3-1
4 Nov		H	1st Scts Gds	L	1-2	2 Mar		H	Uxbridge	D	1-1
11 Nov	AC	H	Vampires	W	3-1	10 Mar	WDC	*	Smethwick	L	0-1
18 Nov		H	London Welsh	W	2-1	23 Mar		H	Scots Gds	W	3-1
9 Dec	LCC	H	Crusaders	L	2-5	24 Mar		H	Slough	W	3-0
16 Dec		H	Erith	L	0-1	26 Mar		A	N/Brompton	D	3-3
19 Dec		H	Friars	W	2-1	31 Mar		H	Polytechnic	D	0-0
23 Dec		H	Wolverton	D	2-2	7 Apr		H	Old St Stphns	D	1-1
26 Dec		A	Southampton	L	0-1	14 Apr		H	Ilford	L	0-1
30 Dec		A	Uxbridge	L	0-1	21 Apr		H	Crouch End	D	2-2
13 Jan		H	3rd Gren Gds	D	1-1						

* Played at Wolverton

SEASON 1894/95

Date	Comp	H/A	Opponent	Result		Date	Comp	H/A	Opponent	Result	
15 Sep		A	Uxbridge	L	0-2	29 Dec		H	Vampires	W	4-1
22 Sep		H	Casuals	W	3-1	5 Jan	ACr	H	Lon Welsh	D	3-3
29 Sep		A	Lon Calednian	L	1-3	19 Jan	ACr	*	Lon Welsh	W	4-2
6 Oct		H	3rd Gren Gds	D	1-1	26 Jan	LnC	H	Lon Welsh	W	5-0
13 Oct	FC	H	West Herts	W	3-2	23 Feb	AC	H	Beeston	2	2-0
20 Oct	AC	H	O/Harrovians	W	7-0	2 Mar	LnC	A	Old Westmster	D	3-3
27 Oct		A	Crouch End	D	2-2	9 Mar	LnCr	H	Old Westmster	L	4-5
3 Nov	FC	H	Wolverton	W	5-3	16 Mar	AC	H	O/Carthusians	L	0-5
10 Nov	AC	H	City Ramblers	W	6-1	19 Mar	LCC	H	O/Carthusians	L	0-3
17 Nov		H	Hglnd Lt Ifnt	D	1-1	23 Mar		H	Lon Calednian	W	5-1
24 Nov	FC	A	Clapton	W	4-0	30 Mar		H	City Ramblers	W	2-0
1 Dec	AC	A	Romford	W	8-0	6 Apr		H	Casuals	L	1-2
8 Dec	LCC	H	Crusaders	W	4-2	12 Apr		H	Lpool Casuals	W	6-0
15 Dec	FC	H	Luton Town	D	2-2	13 Apr		H	2nd Scts Gds	D	1-1
22 Dec	AC	H	Lon Welsh	D	1-1	16 Apr		A	Bristl Sth End	W	7-0
25 Dec		H	Sheff & Dist	W	7-1	25 Apr		A	Lon Calednian	W	2-0
26 Dec		H	Wst Liverpool	W	3-0	27 Apr		A	Brimsdown	W	2-0

* Second replay at Spotted Dog Ground

SEASON 1895/96

Date	Comp	H/A	Opponent	Result		Date	Comp	H/A	Opponent	Result	
7 Sep			Royal Engs	L	0-3	8 Feb		H	Royal Scots	W	2-1
14 Sep	AH		Royal Scots	W	3-2	10 Feb		A	Luton Town	L	0-9
21 Sep		H	Casuals	W	3-2	15 Feb		A	Ryl Ordnance	L	1-2
28 Sep		H	Ryl Ordnance	W	2-0	22 Feb		H	Clapton	W	4-0
5 Oct		A	Claptn Orient	L	4-5	29 Feb		H	Burslm Prt Vle	W	3-1
12 Oct	FC	A	Luton Town	W	2-1	4 Mar		A	Gravesend	D	1-1
19 Oct		H	Ilford	W	2-0	7 Mar		H	1st Scts Gds	W	8-0
26 Oct		H	Ryl Artillery	L	1-2	9 Mar		A	Ryl Ordnance	L	1-3
2 Nov	FC	A	Vampires	L	2-4*	14 Mar		H	Uxbridge	W	4-0
6 Nov		H	Luton Town	L	0-2	16 Mar		A	Woolwich Asnl	W	3-1
9 Nov		H	Old Westmstrs	W	2-1	19 Mar		H	Ryl Ordnance	D	2-2
16 Nov	FC	H	Vampires	W	2-1	21 Mar		H	Manctr Reg	W	8-0
23 Nov	FC	A	Ilford	W	5-1	26 Mar		A	Woolwich Asnl	L	1-3
30 Nov		A	Lon Welsh	W	3-2	28 Mar		A	Lon Calednian	W	5-0
7 Dec		H	Caledonian	L	0-3	3 Apr		A	Reading	W	3-2
14 Dec	FC	H	Old St Stphns	W	2-1	4 Apr		H	Ostwsle Rvs	W	4-0
21 Dec		H	Casuals	W	3-1	6 Apr		H	Middlesbrough	W	5-0
25 Dec		A	Millwall Ath	L	3-5	7 Apr		H	Swindon	L	2-3
26 Dec		H	Accrington	W	3-0	11 Apr		H	Aston Villa	L	1-3
28 Dec		H	Freemantle	D	2-2	15 Apr		A	Swindon	W	2-0
4 Jan		H	Reading	L	1-4	18 Apr		A	Southampton	L	1-4
11 Jan		H	Millwall	D	1-1	22 Apr		A	Gravesend	D	1-1
18 Jan		H	Ilford	W	2-1	25 Apr		H	Wellingboro	W	3-0
25 Jan		H	Notts County	L	1-5	30 Apr		H	Woolwich Asnl	W	3-2
1 Feb	FC	A	Stoke	L	0-5						

* Replayed because Vampires pitch was 'improperly marked'

SEASON 1896/97

Date	Comp		Opponent		Score
3 Sep	F	H	Rossendale	W	7-0
5 Sep	SLge	A	Sheppey Utd	D	3-3
10 Sep	F	H	London Caled	D	3-3
12 Sep	SLge	A	Wolverton	W	1-0
17 Sep	F	H	Casuals	W	4-0
19 Sep	ULge	A	Millwall	L	5-6
24 Sep	F	H	Luton Town	D	0-0†
26 Sep	F	A	Casuals	W	4-1
1 Oct	F	H	2nd Cold Gds	W	4-1
3 Oct	SLge	A	Gravesend	W	3-1
8 Oct	F	H	Royal Scots G	W	5-0
10 Oct	SLge	H	Chatham	L	2-3
17 Oct	SLge	H	Gravesend	W	4-0
24 Oct	SLge	A	Ryl Ordnance	W	2-1‡
29 Oct	F	H	Southampton	W	3-1
31 Oct	SLge	H	Chatham	W	2-1
2 Nov	ULge	A	Rushden	L	0-2
7 Nov	SLge	H	Sheppey Utd	W	3-2
9 Nov	ULge	A	Woolwich Asnl	L	1-2
14 Nov	SLge	H	Swindon	W	3-1
16 Nov	F	A	Luton Town	L	0-3
19 Nov	WDC	H	Gravesend	W	3-2
21 Nov	F	H	Blackpool	L	0-2
28 Nov	SLge	H	Millwall	L	1-3
5 Dec	SLge	A	Reading	L	1-2
12 Dec	FC	H	Old St Stphns	W	4-0
16 Dec	WDC	A	Wolverton	W	2-0
19 Dec	F	A	Clapton	W	2-1
25 Dec	SLge	A	Millwall	L	0-4
26 Dec	F	H	Vampires	W	4-0
26 Dec	F	H	3rd Gren Gds	L	2-3
29 Dec	F	H	Northfleet	W	4-0
6 Jan	FC	H	Maidenhead	W	6-0
9 Jan	SLge	A	Swindon	L	0-1
11 Jan	F	A	Chatham	L	1-2
16 Jan	FC	A	Luton	L	0-3
23 Jan	F	H	Aston Villa	D	2-2
28 Jan	F	H	Chatham	D	2-2
30 Jan	ULge	A	Wellingbro'	D	2-2
6 Feb	F	H	3rd Gren Gds	W	9-3
10 Feb	F	A	Gravesend	W	3-1
13 Feb	SLge	H	Northfleet	W	5-0
15 Feb	F	A	Southampton	L	0-2
20 Feb	SLge	A	N/Brompton	L	1-2
25 Feb	ULge	H	Woolwich Asnl	D	2-2
27 Feb	ULge	A	Loughbrough	L	1-2
4 Mar	ULge	H	Rushden	W	5-1
6 Mar	SLge	A	Northfleet	L	0-2
9 Mar	F	A	Eastbourne	W	1-0
13 Mar	ULge	H	Luton	L	1-2
15 Mar	ULge	A	Kettering	D	1-1
20 Mar	SLge	H	Reading	D	4-4
25 Mar	F	H	Gravesend	W	3-2
29 Mar	ULge	A	Southampton	D	1-1
1 Apr	SLge	H	Wolverton	W	2-0
3 Apr	ULge	H	Millwall	L	1-3
5 Apr	WDCsf	*	Rushden	W	2-1
8 Apr	SLge	H	Southampton	D	2-2
10 Apr	ULge	A	Luton	L	1-2
16 Apr	F	H	Nottm Forest	D	1-1
17 Apr	F	H	Kettering	D	1-1
19 Apr	ULge	H	Wellingbro'	D	1-1
20 Apr	F	H	Blackburn	L	1-2
22 Apr	F	H	Everton	W	2-1
24 Apr	ULge	A	Loughbrough	L	2-3
26 Apr	F	A	London Caled	D	1-1
29 Apr	WDCf	A	Wellingbro'	L	0-2

* at Wellingborough
† abandoned
‡ void after Royal Ordnance resigned from Southern League

Player	Lg App	Goals	Player	Lg App	Goals
Allen	9		Lanham	1	
Almond	16	1	McElhaney	19	8
Ambler	19		Main	1	
Briggs	7	1	Markham	3	
Burrows	16		Milliken	19	7
Clements	20	10	Montgomery	20	
Collins	2		Newbigging	9	2
Crump	18	2	Payne	18	5
Devlin	20	1	Robertson	1	3
Fleming	2	2	Wilson	5	1
Hatfield	1				

United League 1896–97

1	Millwall Ath	14	11	1	2	43:22	23
2	Luton	14	10	1	3	51:16	21
3	Woolwich A	14	6	3	5	28:34	15
4	Loughborough	14	6	1	7	29:31	13
5	Rushden	14	6	1	7	25:42	13
6	Kettering	14	4	4	6	23:24	12
7	Wellingborough	14	3	3	8	17:39	9
8	**TOTTENHAM**	14	1	4	9	25:34	6

Southern League 1896–97

1	Soton St Marys	20	15	5	0	63:18	35
2	Millwall Ath	20	13	5	2	63:24	31
3	Chatham	20	13	1	6	54:29	27
4	**TOTTENHAM**	20	9	4	7	44:32	22
5	Gravesend Utd	20	9	4	7	35:34	22
6	Swindon	20	8	3	9	33:37	19
7	Reading	20	8	3	9	31:49	19
8	N/Brompton	20	7	2	11	32:42	16
9	Northfleet	20	5	4	11	24:46	14
10	Sheppey Utd	20	5	1	14	34:47	11
11	Wolverton	20	2	0	18	17:74	4

SEASON 1897/98

Date	Comp		Opponent		Score
2 Sep	F	H	Glossop	W	3-2
4 Sep	SLge	A	Sheppey Utd	D	1-1
9 Sep	F	H	Ryl S. Fuslrs	W	12-0
11 Sep	F	H	Chorley	W	3-1
16 Sep	ULge	H	Kettering	D	1-1
18 Sep	SLge	H	Southampton	W	2-0
23 Sep	F	H	2nd Scts Gds	W	4-1
25 Sep	SLge	H	Millwall	W	7-0
29 Sep	ULge	A	Loughbro'	W	2-1
2 Oct	SLge	A	N/Brompton	L	0-1
7 Oct	F	H	3rd Gren Gds	W	4-0
9 Oct	SLge	H	Gravesend	W	2-0
11 Oct	ULge	A	Luton	L	0-5
16 Oct	ULge	A	Millwall	D	0-0
20 Oct	F	H	Reading	W	2-1
23 Oct	SLge	A	Southampton	L	1-4
30 Oct	FC	A	Southampton	L	1-4
2 Nov	F	A	Eastbourne	W	2-0
6 Nov	SLge	A	Reading	D	3-3
9 Nov	F	H	N/Brompton	W	3-0
13 Nov	SLge	H	Bristol City	D	2-2
20 Nov	FC	H	Luton	L	3-4
27 Nov	SLge	A	Bristol City	L	1-3
1 Dec	F	A	Gravesend	W	2-1
4 Dec	ULge	H	Wellingbro'	W	5-0
11 Dec	F	A	Kettering	D	1-1
18 Dec	SLge	A	Wolverton	W	2-1
25 Dec	ULge	H	Woolwich Asnl	W	3-2
27 Dec	F	H	Ilkeston	W	4-2
28 Dec	F	H	Stockton	W	3-0
1 Jan	ULge	A	Fushden	L	2-5
8 Jan	ULge	H	Rushden	W	3-1
10 Jan	ULge	A	Kettering	L	2-4
15 Jan	SLge	H	Northfleet	W	4-0
19 Jan	ULge	A	Southampton	D	2-2
22 Jan	SLge	H	Wilverton	W	7-1
27 Jan	F	H	Gravesend	L	1-2
29 Jan	SLge	A	Chatham	L	2-4
3 Feb	ULge	H	Luton	D	2-2
5 Feb	SLge	A	Swindon	L	0-3
9 Feb	F	H	Sussex	W	2-1
12 Feb	F	H	Sheff Utd	D	1-1
15 Feb	F	H	St Bernards	W	4-0
19 Feb	SLge	A	Northfleet	W	3-1
26 Feb	SLge	H*	Reading	D	1-1
28 Feb	F	A	Chesham	W	4-2
5 Mar	SLge	A	Gravesend	W	2-1
9 Mar	F	A	Tunbridge W	W	5-0
12 Mar	ULge	H	Millwall	W	3-2
17 Mar	ULge	A	Loughbro'	W	5-0
19 Mar	SLge	H	Sheppey Utd	W	4-0
24 Mar	ULge	A	Southampton	W	7-0
26 Mar	F	H	Sunderland	L	0-2
2 Apr	SLge	A	N/Brompton	W	3-1
8 Apr	ULge	A	Woolwich Asnl	W	1-0
9 Apr	F	H	Chatham	W	2-1
11 Apr	SLge	H	Swindon	W	2-0
12 Apr	F	H	Lincoln	W	2-0
16 Apr	SLge	A	Millwall	L	1-3
29 Apr	F	A	Reading	D	3-3
23 Apr	ULge	A	Wellingbro'	D	2-2
25 Apr	F	H	Aston Villa	L	2-3
28 Apr	F	A	Woolwich Asnl	L	0-3
30 Apr	F	H	Bolton	D	2-2

* Game versus Reading played at Millwall as Northumberland Park suspended after attacks on Luton players

Player	Lg App	Goals	Player	Lg App	Goals
Ambler	1		Jones J.L.	20	1
Black D.	20	8	Joyce W.	19	16
Briggs S.	1		Knowles J.	19	
Burrows L.	9		Madden J.	2	
Cullen J.	21		Meade T.	10	5
Crump	11		Montgomery J.	16	
Davidson J.	17	8	Stormont R.	22	3
Downie	7		Tannahill R.	11	3
Hall A.	21		Own Goal		1
Hartley A.	15	7			

United League 1897–98

1	Luton	16	13	2	1	49:11	28
2	**TOTTENHAM**	16	8	5	3	40:27	21
3	Arsenal	16	8	5	3	35:24	21
4	Kettering	16	8	1	6	28:25	19
5	Rushden	16	9	1	8	24:26	15
6	Southampton	16	7	3	7	23:28	13*
7	Millwall	16	6	4	8	27:27	12
8	Wellingborough	16	4	3	10	17:41	9
9	Loughborough	16	1	2	13	8:42	4

* two points deducted

Southern League 1897–98

1	Southampton	22	18	1	3	53:18	37
2	Bristol City	22	13	7	2	67:33	33
3	**TOTTENHAM**	22	12	4	6	52:31	28
4	Chatham	22	12	4	6	50:34	28
5	Reading	22	8	7	7	39:31	23
6	N/Brompton	22	9	4	9	37:37	22
7	Sheppey Utd	22	10	1	11	40:49	21
8	Gravesend	22	7	6	9	28:39	20
9	Millwall Ath	22	8	2	12	48:45	18
10	Swindon	22	7	2	13	36:48	16
11	Northfleet	22	4	3	15	29:60	11
12	Wolverton	22	3	1	18	28:82	7

Thames & Medway League 1898–98

1	N/Brompton	16	13	1	2	47:15	27
2	Gravesend	16	12	1	3	53:21	25
3	Chatham	16	10	3	3	41:11	23
4	**TOTTENHAM**	16	11	0	5	34:28	22
5	Thames Irnwks	16	7	2	7	23:24	16
6	Sheppey Utd	16	7	1	8	31:31	15
7	RETB	16	2	2	12	24:49	6
8	Grays Utd	16	2	2	12	11:42	6
9	Dartford	16	2	0	14	21:64	4

SEASON 1898/99

Date	Comp	H/A	Opponent	Result
1 Sep	F	H	Gainsbro'	W 6-2
3 Sep	TLge	H	Thames Iron	W 3-0
5 Sep	ULge	H	Luton	W 1-0
10 Sep	SLge	H	Bedminster	D 1-1
12 Sep	F	H	Surrey Wandrs	W 5-0
17 Sep	SLge	H	Sheppey Utd	W 3-2
19 Sep	ULge	A	Luton	W 4-3
24 Sep	SLge	H	Warmley	W 7-1*
26 Sep	TLge	A	Sheppey Utd	W 3-2
1 Oct	F	H	Burton Wand	W 5-2
3 Oct	TLge	H	Gravesend	W 3-1
5 Oct	ULge	A	Brighton Utd	W 2-1
8 Oct	SLge	H	Chatham	W 2-0
10 Oct	ULge	H	Southampton	W 4-0
15 Oct	ULge	A	Bristol	W 1-0
17 Oct	TLge	H	N/Brompton	W 2-1
22 Oct	SLge	A	Millwall	L 2-4
26 Oct	TLge	A	Dartford	W 3-2
29 Oct	FC	H	Wolverton	W 4-0
2 Nov	TLge	A	RETB	W 6-2
5 Nov	SLge	H	Reading	W 3-0
9 Nov	ULge	A	Reading	L 0-1
12 Nov	ULge	H	Bristol City	W 2-1
19 Nov	FC	A	Clapton	D 1-1
23 Nov	FCr	H	Clapton	W 2-1
26 Nov	SLge	A	Ryl Artillery	W 3-2
3 Dec	SLge	A	Bristol City	L 1-2
5 Dec	ULge	H	Kettering	W 3-0
10 Dec	FC	H	Luton	D 1-1
14 Dec	FCr	A	Luton	D 1-1
17 Dec	SLge	A	Sheppey Utd	L 2-3
19 Dec	FCr	A	Luton	W 2-0
21 Dec	F	A	Surrey Wandrs	D 1-1
24 Dec	SLge	A	Warmley	W 5-1*
26 Dec	SLge	A	Southampton	D 1-1
27 Dec	F	H	Ilkeston	W 1-0
31 Dec	SLge	A	Swindon	L 3-4
2 Jan	TLge	A	Chatham	W 5-0
7 Jan	SLge	H	Ryl Artillery	W 1-0
9 Jan	TLge	H	Chatham	L 0-4
14 Jan	SLge	A	Gravesend	L 2-4
16 Jan	TLge	H	Sheppey Utd	W 3-0
21 Jan	SLge	A	Brighton Utd	W 1-0
23 Jan	ULge	H	Reading	D 1-1
28 Jan	FC	H	Newton Heath	D 1-1
1 Feb	FCr	A	Newton Heath	W 5-3
4 Feb	SLge	A	Reading	L 0-2
6 Feb	TLge	H	Grays Utd	W 2-1
11 Feb	FC	H	Sunderland	W 2-1
15 Feb	ULge	A	Southampton	L 1-2
18 Feb	SLge	H	Bristol City	W 3-2
20 Feb	ULge	H	Rushden	L 1-2
25 Feb	FC	A	Stoke	L 1-4
27 Feb	ULge	A	Kettering	W 1-0
4 Mar	ULge	H	Millwall	L 1-2
8 Mar	TLge	A	Gravesend	W 3-0
11 Mar	ULge	A	Woolwich Asnl	L 1-2
13 Mar	SLge	A	N/Brompton	D 1-1
16 Mar	TLge	A	Thames Iron	L 1-2
18 Mar	SLge	H	N/Brompton	W 3-0
20 Mar	TLge	H	RETB	L 1-2
22 Mar	TLge	A	Grays	L 0-1
25 Mar	SLge	A	Brighton Utd	L 1-3
27 Mar	ULge	A	Rushden	D 0-0
31 Mar	SLge	H	Southampton	L 0-1
1 Apr	SLge	H	Gravesend	W 3-0
3 Apr	SLge	H	Swindon	D 1-1
4 Apr	ULge	H	Brighton Utd	W 3-0
8 Apr	SLge	A	Chatham	L 0-1
10 Apr	TLge	A	N/Brompton	L 4-5
13 Apr	TLge	H	Dartford	W 9-0
15 Apr	SLge	A	Bedminster	L 0-1
17 Apr	ULge	A	Wellingbro'	L 1-3
22 Apr	SLge	H	Millwall	W 3-1
24 Apr	ULge	H	Wellingbro'	W 5-2
26 Apr	ULge	A	Millwall	L 1-3
29 Apr	ULge	H	Woolwich Asnl	W 3-2

*Warmley resigned from Southern League on 21 January 1899 so their results void

Player	SL App	Goals		Player	SL App	Goals
Ambler	2			Leach	4	2
Atherton	2			McKay C.	17	4
Bradshaw	22	3		McNaught J.	19	
Cain R.	22			Meade T.	5	
Cameron J.	23	11		Melia J.	13	
Cullen J.	19			Rule A.G.	3	2
Downie E.	4			Smith T.	24	5
Erentz H.	22			Stormont R.	21	
Hall A.	2			Payne E.	1	
Hartley A.	3	1		Waller W.H.	3	
Jones J.L.	14			Own Goals		2
Joyce W.	19	10				

United League 1898–99

1	Millwall Ath	20	14	3	3	42:19	31
2	Southampton	20	12	1	7	53:32	25
3	Woolwich Asnl	20	10	4	6	30:30	24
4	**TOTTENHAM**	**20**	**11**	**2**	**7**	**36:25**	**24**
5	Bristol C	20	11	0	9	43:31	22
6	Reading	20	8	5	7	36:25	21
7	Brighton Utd	20	10	1	9	41:42	21
8	Wellingborough	20	7	1	12	32:40	15
9	Kettering	20	8	1	11	25:38	15*
10	Rushden	20	6	1	13	26:45	13
11	Luton Town	20	2	3	15	24:71	7

* two points deducted

Southern League 1898–99

1	Southampton	24	15	5	4	54:24	35
2	Bristol C	24	15	3	6	55:33	33
3	Millwall Ath	24	12	6	6	59:35	30
4	Chatham	24	10	8	6	32:23	28
5	Reading	24	9	8	7	31:24	26
6	N/Brompton	24	10	5	9	38:30	25
7	**TOTTENHAM**	**24**	**10**	**4**	**10**	**40:36**	**24**
8	Bedminster	24	10	4	10	35:39	24
9	Swindon	24	9	5	10	43:49	23
10	Brighton Utd	24	9	2	13	37:48	20
11	Gravesend Utd	24	7	5	12	42:52	19
12	Sheppey Utd	24	5	3	16	23:53	13
13	Ryl Artillery	24	4	4	16	17:60	12

SEASON 1899/1900

Date	Comp	H/A	Opponent	Result
2 Sep	SLge	A	Millwall	W 3-1
4 Sep	F	H	Notts Co	W 4-1
9 Sep	SLge	H	QPR	W 1-0
13 Sep	F	A	Richmond	W 3-1
16 Sep	SLge	A	Chatham	W 3-2
18 Sep	SDC	H	Portsmouth	W 2-0
23 Sep	SLge	A	Reading	W 2-1
26 Sep	F	A	Clapton	W 4-1
30 Sep	F	A	Southampton	L 1-2
2 Oct	SLge	H	Gravesend	W 4-0
7 Oct	SLge	H	Brighton Utd	W 6-1†
11 Oct	SDC	A	Reading	L 1-2
14 Oct	SLge	A	Bedminster	L 1-2
16 Oct	SDC	H	Millwall	L 1-2
21 Oct	SLge	H	Bristol Rvs	W 1-0*
23 Oct	SDC	A	QPR	W 3-1
28 Oct	F	H	Southampton	W 4-3
30 Oct	SDC	H	Reading	W 3-0
4 Nov	SLge	H	Thames Iron	W 7-0
6 Nov	SDC	H	Chatham	W 8-0
11 Nov	F	H	Ilkeston	W 7-0
15 Nov	SDC	A	Bristol City	D 3-3
18 Nov	F	A	Bolton	W 4-0
20 Nov	SDC	H	QPR	W 3-1
25 Nov	F	H	Corinthians	W 5-1
27 Nov	F	H	Kaffirs	W 6-4
2 Dec	SLge	A	Swindon	W 2-0
4 Dec	SDC	A	Chatham	W 1-0
9 Dec	SLge	H	Bristol City	D 2-2
11 Dec	F	H	Players/South	W 3-2
16 Dec	F	A	Cowes	W 6-1†
18 Dec	F	H	HRBourkesXI	W 12-2
25 Dec	SLge	H	Portsmouth	W 3-0
26 Dec	SLge	A	Southampton	L 1-3
30 Dec	SLge	H	Millwall	W 2-1
1 Jan	F	A	Middlesbro'	D 2-2
2 Jan	F	A	Sunderland	D 3-1
6 Jan	SLge	A	QPR	D 0-0
8 Jan	SDC	H	Southampton	W 3-2
13 Jan	SDC	H	Chatham	W 2-1
17 Jan	SDC	A	Portsmouth	D 2-2
20 Jan	SLge	A	Reading	W 1-0
27 Jan	FC	A	Preston	L 0-1
3 Feb	SLge	A	Sheppey Utd	W 4-1
5 Feb	F	H	Oxford Univ	W 7-2
10 Feb	SLge	A	Brighton Utd	W 3-0†
17 Feb	SLge	H	Bedminster	W 5-2
24 Feb	SLge	A	Bristol Rvs	D 2-2
3 Mar	SLge	A	Portsmouth	L 0-1
5 Mar	F	H	Stoke	W 6-0
10 Mar	SLge	A	Thames Iron	D 0-0
12 Mar	SDC	H	Bristol City	W 2-0
17 Mar	F	A	Corinthians	W 3-1
19 Mar	SLge	H	Bristol Rvs	W 5-1
24 Mar	SLge	A	N/Brompton	W 1-0
31 Mar	SLge	A	Gravesend	W 6-2
2 Apr	F	H	Thames Iron	W 3-0
7 Apr	SLge	H	Swindon	W 3-0
13 Apr	SLge	H	Southampton	W 2-0
14 Apr	SLge	A	Bristol City	L 0-3
16 Apr	SLge	H	Sheppey Utd	W 3-0
17 Apr	SDC	H	Woolwich Asnl	W 4-2
21 Apr	F	A	Aston Villa	L 3-4
24 Apr	SDC	A	Woolwich Asnl	L 1-2‡
26 Apr	SDC	A	Millwall	D 0-0
28 Apr	SLge	A	N/Brompton	W 2-1
30 Apr	SDC	A	Southampton	W 4-1

* Abandoned after 55 minutes

† Games void: Brighton United resigned from Southern League on 10 March, Cowes resigned from Southern League on 18 December

‡ Game not completed because of crowd trouble

Players	SL App	Goals		Players	SL App	Goals
Cameron J.	25	11		Melia J.	12	
Clawley G.	7			Morris T.	20	4
Copeland D.	24	12		Munro	1	
Chapman	1	1		Pratt T.	26	19
Erentz H.	16			Riley	2	
Haddow D.	20			Rule A.G.	4	
Hughes E.	1			Smith T.	24	6
Hyde L.	6	2		Stormont R.	22	1
Jones J.L.	18			Tait A.	28	
Kirwan J.	26	10		Waller W.H.	1	
McNaught J.	24			Own Goal		1

Southern League 1899–1900

1	**TOTTENHAM**	**28**	**20**	**4**	**4**	**67:26**	**44**
2	Portsmouth	28	20	1	7	59:29	41
3	Southampton	28	17	1	10	70:33	35
4	Reading	28	15	2	11	41:28	32
5	Swindon Town	28	15	2	11	50:42	32
6	Bedminster	28	13	2	13	44:45	28
7	Millwall	28	12	3	13	36:37	27
8	QPR	28	12	2	14	49:57	26
9	Bristol City	28	9	7	12	43:48	25
10	Bristol Rvs	28	11	3	14	46:55	25
11	N/Brompton	28	9	6	13	39:49	24
12	Gravesend Utd	28	10	4	14	38:58	24
13	Chatham	28	10	3	15	38:58	23
14	Thames Irnwks	28	8	5	15	30:45	21
15	Sheppey Utd	28	3	7	18	24:66	13

Southern District Combination 1899–1900

1	Millwall	16	12	2	2	30:10	26
2	**TOTTENHAM***	**15**	**10**	**3**	**2**	**40:16**	**23**
3	Portsmouth	16	9	2	5	30:16	20
4	Woolwich Asnl*	15	7	1	7	25:21	15
5	Bristol C	16	5	3	8	25:32	13
6	Southampton	16	5	2	9	23:30	12
7	Reading	16	4	4	8	16:28	12
8	Chatham	16	5	2	9	12:35	12
9	QPR	16	4	1	11	19:28	9

* Match between Woolwich Arsenal and Spurs at Plumstead abandoned after 55 minutes because of crowd trouble (score stood at 2-1). Never replayed.

SEASON 1900/01

Date	Comp	H/A	Opponent	Result	Score
1 Sep	SLge	H	Millwall	L	0-3
3 Sep	F	A	Bristol Rvs	L	0-1
8 Sep	F	A	Southampton	W	3-1
10 Sep	F	H	Reading	D	3-3
15 Sep	F	H	Chatham	W	5-0†
17 Sep	F	A	Millwall	W	2-1
22 Sep	SLge	A	Bristol City	D	1-1
24 Sep	F	H	Richmond Ass	W	8-0
27 Sep	F	A	Notts Co	L	1-4
29 Sep	SLge	H	Swindon	W	2-0
3 Oct	F	A	Reading	D	1-1
6 Oct	SLge	A	Watford	L	1-2
8 Oct	F	H	Notts Co	D	1-1
13 Oct	F	H	Corinthians	D	2-2
15 Oct	F	H	Millwall	W	2-1
20 Oct	SLge	A	QPR	L	1-2
22 Oct	F	H	Luton	L	1-3
27 Oct	SLge	H	West Ham	D	0-0
31 Oct	F	H	QPR	W	7-0
3 Nov	F	A	Portsmouth	W	3-1
5 Nov	F	A	Camb Univ	W	3-1
10 Nov	SLge	A	N/Brompton	W	2-1
12 Nov	F	A	Luton	L	0-1
17 Nov	WLge	H	Portsmouth	W	8-1
24 Nov	SLge	A	Reading	L	1-3
26 Nov	WLge	H	Bristol City	W	4-1
1 Dec	SLge	H	Kettering	W	1-0
5 Dec	WLge	A	Swindon	W	1-0
8 Dec	WLge	H	Millwall	D	1-1
10 Dec	WLge	H	Bristol Rvs	W	6-0
15 Dec	SLge	A	Millwall	W	2-1
17 Dec	F	H	Preston	D	1-1
22 Dec	WLge	H	Southampton	W	2-0
25 Dec	SLge	H	Portsmouth	W	4-1
26 Dec	SLge	A	Southampton	L	1-3
29 Dec	F	H	Newark	W	3-0
5 Jan	F	H	Clapton	W	3-0
8 Jan	F	H	German XI	W	9-6
12 Jan	SLge	A	Swindon	D	1-1
14 Jan	F	H	CWBrowns XI	W	4-2
19 Jan	SLge	H	Watford	W	7-0
26 Jan	SLge	H	Bristol Rvs	W	4-0
4 Feb	F	H	Oxford Univ	W	5-2
9 Feb	FC	H	Preston	D	1-1
13 Feb	FCr	A	Preston	W	4-2
16 Feb	SLge	A	West Ham	W	4-1
18 Feb	WLge	H	Reading	W	3-2
23 Feb	FC	H	Bury	W	2-1
27 Feb	WLge	H	Swindon	W	5-0
2 Mar	SLge	H	N/Brompton	W	2-1
6 Mar	WLge	A	Reading	D	1-1
9 Mar	SLge	A	Bristol Rvs	L	0-1
11 Mar	WLge	A	Southampton	D	1-1
16 Mar	SLge	H	Reading	W	1-0
18 Mar	WLge	A	QPR	D	1-1
23 Mar	FC	A	Reading	D	1-1
27 Mar	WLge	A	Bristol City	L	1-4*
28 Mar	FCr	H	Reading	W	3-0
30 Mar	FCr	H	QPR	W	4-1
3 Apr	SLge	A	Gravesend	L	1-2
5 Apr	SLge	H	Southampton	W	1-0
6 Apr	SLge	H	Bristol City	W	1-0
8 Apr	FCsf	‡	WBA	W	4-0
13 Apr	WLge	A	Millwall	W	1-0
15 Apr	WLge	H	QPR	D	2-2
17 Apr	WLge	A	Portsmouth	L	0-1
20 Apr	FCf	‡	Sheff Utd	D	2-2
22 Apr	WLge	A	Bristol Rvs	L	0-4
24 Apr	SLge	A	Portsmouth	L	0-4
25 Apr	SLge	H	Luton	W	3-2
27 Apr	FCfr	‡	Sheff Utd	W	3-1
27 Apr	SLge	H	Gravesend	W	5-0*
29 Apr	SLge	A	Luton	W	4-2
30 Apr	SLge	A	Kettering	D	1-1

* Reserves played these fixtures as first team playing Cup tie
† Match void as Chatham resigned from Southern League on 20 December 1900
‡ Semi-final played at Villa Park, Cup final at Crystal Palace and Cup final replay at Bolton

Players	SL App	Goals	Players	SL App	Goals
Anson	2		Jones J.L.	17	3
Brown A.	20	10	Kirwan J.	20	5
Burton	3	1	McNaught J.	18	
Buckingham	5		Melia J.	10	1
Cameron J.	21	6	Moffat	5	3
Clawley G.	25		Moles J.	3	
Erentz H.	21		Morris T.	19	3
Forthum	2	1	Pangbourn T.	2	
Haddow D.	3		Smith T.	17	2
Hawley	3	2	Stevenson	3	
Hudson	1		Stormont R.	22	5
Hughes E.	19	2	Tait A.	22	
Hyde L.	8	4	Woodward V.J.	2	2
Jones A.E.	6	1	Own Goal		1

Southern League 1900–01

1	Southampton	28	18	5	5	58:26	41
2	Bristol C	28	17	6	6	54:27	39
3	Portsmouth	28	17	4	7	56:32	38
4	Millwall	28	17	2	9	55:32	36
5	**TOTTENHAM**	**28**	**16**	**4**	**8**	**55:33**	**36**
6	West Ham	28	14	5	9	40:28	33
7	Bristol Rvs	28	14	4	10	46:35	32
8	QPR	28	11	4	13	43:48	26
9	Luton Town	28	11	2	15	43:49	24
10	Reading	28	8	8	12	24:25	24
11	Kettering	28	7	9	12	33:46	23
12	N/Brompton	28	7	5	16	34:51	19
13	Gravesend Utd	28	6	7	15	32:85	19
14	Watford	28	6	4	18	24:52	16
15	Swindon	28	3	8	17	19:47	14

Western League 1900–01

1	Portsmouth	16	11	2	3	36:23	24
2	Millwall	16	9	5	2	33:14	23
3	**TOTTENHAM**	**16**	**8**	**5**	**3**	**37:19**	**21**
4	QPR	16	7	4	5	39:24	18
5	Bristol C	16	6	4	6	27:24	16
6	Reading	16	5	5	6	23:31	15
7	Southampton	16	5	2	9	19:29	12
8	Bristol Rvs	16	4	1	11	18:42	9
9	Swindon	16	2	2	12	9:35	6

SEASON 1901/02

Date	Comp	H/A	Opponent	Result	Score
2 Sep	F	H	Hearts	D	0-0
7 Sep	SLge	H	Millwall	W	2-0
9 Sep	WLge	H	Reading	W	4-0
14 Sep	SLge	H	QPR	W	2-0
16 Sep	LLge	A	Woolwich Asnl	W	2-0
21 Sep	SLge	A	Reading	D	1-1
23 Sep	F	A	Sheff Utd	L	1-3
28 Sep	WLge	H	Southampton	W	5-0
30 Sep	WLge	A	QPR	W	3-1
5 Oct	SLge	A	Bristol Rvs	W	2-1
7 Oct	WLge	H	Millwall	W	3-1
12 Oct	SLge	A	N/Brompton	W	3-1
14 Oct	WLge	A	West Ham	W	2-1
16 Oct	F	H	Rest Sth Lge	W	2-0
19 Oct	SLge	A	Northampton	L	1-3
21 Oct	WLge	A	Bristol Rvs	W	4-1
26 Oct	SLge	A	Watford	W	8-1
2 Nov	SLge	A	West Ham	W	1-0
4 Nov	LLge	A	Woolwich Asnl	W	5-0
9 Nov	SLge	A	Wellingborough	W	1-0
11 Nov	WLge	A	Swindon	W	6-0
13 Nov	F	A	West Norwood	W	3-1
16 Nov	WLge	A	Portsmouth	L	1-3
18 Nov	WLge	A	Bristol Rvs	W	4-0
23 Nov	SLge	A	Swindon	W	3-1
2 Dec	F	H	Army Assoc	W	2-1
7 Dec	SLge	A	Kettering	W	2-0
9 Dec	WLge	H	QPR	W	3-2
14 Dec	F	A	Corinthians	L	0-3
16 Dec	LLge	A	West Ham	L	1-3
21 Dec	SLge	A	Millwall	D	1-1
25 Dec	SLge	H	Portsmouth	L	1-2
26 Dec	SLge	A	Southampton	L	0-1
28 Dec	SLge	A	QPR	W	3-0
1 Jan	F	A	Everton	L	1-3
2 Jan	F	A	Hearts	L	1-3
4 Jan	SLge	H	Reading	W	4-2
6 Jan	LLge	A	Millwall	D	1-1
11 Jan	WLge	A	Southampton	L	1-5
13 Jan	WLge	A	Reading	D	1-1
18 Jan	SLge	H	Bristol Rvs	W	1-0
25 Jan	FC	H	Southampton	D	1-1
29 Jan	FCr	A	Southampton	D	2-2
1 Feb	SLge	H	Northampton	W	1-0
3 Feb	FCr	*	Southampton	L	1-2
8 Feb	SLge	A	Watford	W	3-0
10 Feb	LLge	H	QPR	L	1-5
15 Feb	SLge	H	West Ham	L	1-2
17 Feb	WLge	A	Millwall	W	3-1
22 Feb	SLge	A	Wellingborough	W	3-0
1 Mar	SLS	H	Corinthians	W	5-2
8 Mar	SLge	H	Swindon	W	7-1
10 Mar	WLge	A	West Ham	D	1-1
15 Mar	SLge	A	Brentford	L	1-2
17 Mar	WLge	H	Portsmouth	D	0-0
22 Mar	SLge	H	Kettering	W	4-0
24 Mar	LLge	A	Millwall	D	1-1
28 Mar	SLge	H	Southampton	D	2-2
29 Mar	SLge	A	Luton	D	0-0
31 Mar	SLge	A	Portsmouth	L	0-1
1 Apr	F	H	Sheff Utd	W	3-2
5 Apr	SLge	A	N/Brompton	D	0-0
9 Apr	WLge	A	Swindon	W	1-0
12 Apr	SLge	H	Luton	D	0-0
14 Apr	LLge	A	QPR	W	2-1
21 Apr	LLge	H	West Ham	D	2-2
23 Apr	SDCC	A	Woolwich Asnl	D	0-0
26 Apr	SLge	H	Brentford	W	3-0
28 Apr	F	H	Preston	L	1-2
29 Apr	SDCCr	H	Woolwich Asnl	W	2-1
30 Apr	F	A	Portsmouth	W	2-0

* FA Cup 2nd replay (at Reading FC)

Player	SL App	Goals	Player	SL App	Goals
Barlow J.	3	1	Hyde L.	2	
Brown A.	26	18	Jones J.L.	26	1
Burton J.H.	2		Kirwan J.	28	10
Cameron J.	24	13	McNaught J.	17	
Clawley G.	20		Moles J.	1	
Copeland D.	29	9	Morris T.	26	3
Erentz H.	30		Soulsby T.	1	
Fitchie T.T.	1		Smith T.	23	4
Gilhooly P.	9	1	Stevenson	1	
Griffiths F.J.	9		Tait A.	26	
Haig-Brown A.R.	2		Woodward V.J.	2	
Hughes E.	22	1			

Southern League 1901–02

1	Portsmouth	30	20	7	3	67:24	47
2	**TOTTENHAM**	**30**	**18**	**6**	**6**	**61:22**	**42**
3	Southampton	30	18	6	6	71:28	42
4	West Ham	30	17	6	7	45:28	40
5	Reading	30	16	7	7	57:24	39
6	Luton Town	30	11	10	9	31:36	32
7	Millwall	30	13	6	11	48:31	32
8	Kettering	30	12	5	13	44:39	29
9	Bristol Rvs	30	12	5	13	43:39	29
10	N/Brompton	30	10	7	13	39:38	27
11	Northampton	30	11	5	14	53:64	27
12	QPR	30	8	7	15	34:56	23
13	Watford	30	9	4	17	36:60	22
14	Wellingborough	30	9	4	17	34:72	22
15	Brentford	30	7	6	17	34:61	20
16	Swindon	30	2	3	25	17:92	7

Western League 1901–02

1	Portsmouth	16	13	1	2	53:16	27
2	**TOTTENHAM**	**16**	**11**	**3**	**2**	**42:17**	**25**
3	Reading	16	7	3	6	29:22	17
4	Millwall	16	8	1	7	25:29	17
5	Bristol Rvs	16	8	0	8	25:31	16
6	Southampton	16	7	1	8	30:28	15
7	West Ham	16	6	2	8	30:20	14
8	QPR	16	5	1	10	17:43	11
9	Swindon	16	0	2	14	8:53	2

London League 1901–02

1	West Ham	8	5	1	2	18: 9	11
2	**TOTTENHAM**	**8**	**3**	**3**	**2**	**15:13**	**9**
3	Millwall	8	2	4	2	9:13	8
4	QPR	8	2	2	4	11:14	6
5	Woolwich A	8	2	2	4	9:13	6

SEASON 1902/03

Date	Comp	H/A	Opponent	Result	Score
6 Sep	SLge	H	QPR	D	0-0
8 Sep	SCC	A	West Ham	W	2-1
13 Sep	WLge	A	Southampton	D	1-1
15 Sep	WLge	H	Millwall	W	4-3
20 Sep	SLge	H	Wellingborough	W	6-1
22 Sep	WLge	A	QPR	W	2-0
27 Sep	SLge	A	Bristol Rvs	L	2-3
29 Sep	WLge	H	Reading	W	2-1
4 Oct	SLge	H	Northampton	W	2-0
6 Oct	LLge	A	Brentford	W	5-1
11 Oct	SLge	A	Watford	W	2-1
13 Oct	WLge	H	Bristol Rvs	L	0-1
18 Oct	SLge	H	Brentford	W	3-1
20 Oct	LLge	A	West Ham	D	0-0
25 Oct	SLge	A	Millwall	L	0-2
29 Oct	WLge	A	Reading	L	0-3
1 Nov	SLge	H	West Ham	D	1-1
3 Nov	WLge	H	QPR	W	3-0
8 Nov	WLge	H	Portsmouth	D	0-0
10 Nov	F	H	Camb Univ	W	2-1
15 Nov	F	A	Corinthians	W	3-1
17 Nov	LLge	A	Woolwich A	L	1-2
22 Nov	SLge	H	Swindon	W	2-0
24 Nov	SCC	H	Reading	D	1-1
29 Nov	SLge	A	Portsmouth	D	2-2
1 Dec	LLge	A	Woolwich A	W	1-0
6 Dec	SLge	H	Luton	D	1-1
8 Dec	F	H	London FA	D	2-2
10 Dec	F	A	West Norwood	W	9-0
13 Dec	F	H	Corinthians	D	2-2
15 Dec	LLge	H	West Ham	W	4-0
20 Dec	SLge	A	QPR	W	4-0
25 Dec	SLge	H	Portsmouth	D	2-2
26 Dec	SLge	A	Southampton	W	1-0
27 Dec	WLge	H	Southampton	D	0-0
3 Jan	SLge	A	Wellingborough	W	2-0
5 Jan	SLge	H	N/Brompton	W	3-1
10 Jan	SLge	H	Bristol Rvs	W	3-0
12 Jan	LLge	H	Brentford	W	1-0
14 Jan	SCC	A	Reading	L	2-3
17 Jan	SLge	A	Northampton	L	1-3
22 Jan	F	A	Camb Univ	W	1-0
24 Jan	SLge	H	Watford	D	1-1
28 Jan	WLge	A	Millwall	D	1-1
31 Jan	SLge	A	Brentford	D	1-1
7 Feb	FC	H	WBA	D	0-0
11 Feb	FCr	A	WBA	W	2-0
14 Feb	WLge	A	West Ham	L	0-1
16 Feb	WLge	H	West Ham	W	1-0
21 Feb	FC	H	Bristol City	W	1-0
23 Feb	WLge	A	Bristol Rvs	L	0-2
2 Mar	LLge	A	Millwall	W	3-0
7 Mar	FC	H	Aston Villa	L	2-3
19 Mar	WLge	A	Brentford	D	0-0
14 Mar	SLge	H	Kettering	W	4-0
16 Mar	LLge	A	QPR	L	0-1
19 Mar	WLge	A	West Ham	D	0-0
21 Mar	SLge	A	Luton	L	0-3
23 Mar	LLge	H	Millwall	W	1-0
26 Mar	WLge	H	Brentford	W	4-0
28 Mar	WLge	H	Reading	W	2-0
30 Mar	LLge	H	QPR	W	3-0
4 Apr	SLge	A	Reading	D	0-0
6 Apr	F	H	QPR	W	1-0
10 Apr	SLge	H	Southampton	W	2-1
11 Apr	SLge	A	N/Brompton	L	0-3
13 Apr	SLge	A	Portsmouth	L	0-2
14 Apr	SLge	H	Millwall	W	2-0
22 Apr	SLge	A	Swindon	L	0-2
25 Apr	SLge	A	Kettering	L	0-1
30 Apr	F	H	Nottm Forest	W	2-1

Player	SL App	Goals	Player	SL App	Goals
Barlow J.	4	1	Houston R.	9	4
Brown C.	12		Hughes E.	20	3
Burton J.H.	11	1	Jones J.	8	3
Cameron J.	14	2	Jones J.L.	17	
Chalmers J.	4		Kirwan J.	26	7
Clawley G.	30		Morris T.	27	1
Copeland D.	28	8	Tait A.	25	1
Dryburgh T.	17	2	Warner A.	20	8
Erentz H.	25		Watson J.	13	
Fredericks	1		Woodward V.J.	12	2
Gilhooly P.	6	3	Own Goal		1
Haig-Brown A.R.	1				

Southern League 1902–03

1	Southampton	30	20	8	2	83:20	48
2	Reading	30	19	7	4	72:30	45
3	Portsmouth	30	17	7	6	69:32	41
4	TOTTENHAM	30	14	7	9	47:31	35
5	Bristol Rvs	30	13	8	9	46:34	34
6	N/Brompton	30	11	11	8	37:35	33
7	Millwall	30	14	3	13	52:37	31
8	Northampton	30	12	6	12	39:48	30
9	QPR	30	11	6	13	34:42	28
10	West Ham	30	9	10	11	35:49	28
11	Luton Town	30	10	7	13	43:44	27
12	Swindon	30	10	7	13	38:46	27
13	Kettering	30	8	11	11	33:40	27
14	Wellingborough	20	11	3	16	36:56	25
15	Watford	30	6	4	20	35:87	16
16	Brentford	30	2	1	27	16:84	5

Western League 1902–03

1	Portsmouth	16	10	4	2	34:14	24
2	Bristol Rvs	16	9	2	5	36:22	20
3	Southampton	16	7	6	3	32:20	20
4	TOTTENHAM	16	6	7	3	20:14	19
5	Millwall	16	6	3	7	23:29	15
6	Reading	16	7	0	9	20:21	14
7	QPR	16	6	2	8	18:31	14
8	Brentford	16	3	4	9	16:34	10
9	West Ham	16	2	4	10	15:29	8

London League Premier Division 1902-03

1	TOTTENHAM	10	7	1	2	19: 4	15
2	West Ham	10	5	3	2	15:13	13
3	Woolwich A	10	6	0	4	14:10	12
4	Millwall	10	3	4	3	18:14	10
5	QPR	10	2	3	5	9:15	7
6	Brentford	10	1	1	8	9:28	3

This was the last season in which the first team contested the London League. From 1903-04 onwards it was a reserve team league.

SEASON 1903/04

Date	Comp	H/A	Opponent	Result	Score
5 Sep	SLge	A	Fulham	D	0-0
7 Sep	WLge	H	Reading	W	3-1
12 Sep	SLge	H	Millwall	L	0-1
14 Sep	SLge	A	Brentford	D	0-0
19 Sep	SLge	A	QPR	L	0-2
23 Sep	F	A	N/Brompton	L	0-3
26 Sep	SLge	H	Plymouth	L	0-2
28 Sep	SCC	A	Millwall	L	1-3
3 Oct	SLge	A	Reading	D	2-2
5 Oct	WLge	H	QPR	W	3-0
10 Oct	SLge	H	Wellingbor'	W	1-0
14 Oct	WLge	A	Reading	W	2-0
17 Oct	SLge	A	Bristol Rvs	L	0-1
19 Oct	F	H	N/Brompton	W	4-2
24 Oct	WLge	H	Brighton	D	2-2
31 Oct	WLge	A	Portsmouth	W	3-0
2 Nov	WLge	H	Brentford	D	1-1
7 Nov	SLge	H	Northampton	W	2-1
9 Nov	WLge	A	QPR	L	0-2
21 Nov	SLge	H	West Ham	W	2-1
28 Nov	F	H	Brighton	W	7-0
30 Nov	WLge	H	Bristol Rvs	W	2-1
5 Dec	SLge	A	Luton	L	2-3
7 Dec	F	A	Burnley	W	4-0
12 Dec	F	A	Corinthians	W	5-1
14 Dec	WLge	H	West Ham	W	4-1
19 Dec	SLge	H	Kettering	D	3-3
25 Dec	SLge	H	Portsmouth	D	1-1
26 Dec	SLge	A	Southampton	L	0-1
28 Dec	WLge	H	Southampton	W	1-0
2 Jan	SLge	H	Fulham	W	1-0
9 Jan	SLge	A	Millwall	W	1-0
16 Jan	SLge	H	QPR	D	2-2
23 Jan	SLge	A	Plymouth	W	3-1
30 Jan	SLge	H	Reading	W	7-4
6 Feb	FC	A	Everton	W	2-1
13 Feb	FC	H	Bristol Rvs	W	5-1
20 Feb	FC	H	Aston Villa		0-1*
22 Feb	SLge	H	Swindon	W	1-0
25 Feb	FCr	A	Aston Villa	W	1-0
27 Feb	WLge	H	Portsmouth	D	1-1
29 Feb	WLge	H	Plymouth	W	5-1
5 Mar	FC	H	The Wednsdy	D	1-1
10 Mar	FCr	A	The Wednsdy	L	0-2
12 Mar	SLge	H	Brentford	D	1-1
19 Mar	SLge	A	West Ham	W	2-0
26 Mar	SLge	A	Swindon	D	0-0
28 Mar	WLge	A	Brentford	W	2-1
1 Apr	SLge	H	Southampton	W	2-1
2 Apr	SLge	H	Luton	D	1-1
4 Apr	SLge	A	Portsmouth	L	0-1
5 Apr	SLge	H	N/Brompton	W	1-0
9 Apr	SLge	A	N/Brompton	W	1-0
13 Apr	SLge	A	Brighton	W	2-1
16 Apr	SLge	H	Kettering	W	5-1
18 Apr	WLge	A	West Ham	W	1-0
20 Apr	WLge	A	Plymouth	D	0-0
23 Apr	WLge	A	Southampton	L	0-1
25 Apr	SLge	A	Northampton	W	1-0
27 Apr	WLge	A	Bristol Rvs	W	4-2
30 Apr	SLge	A	Wellingbor'	D	3-3

* Abandoned after crowd invasion. FA ordered replay to be played at Villa Park and fined Spurs £350

Player	SL App	Goals	Player	SL App	Goals
Berry	3		McConachie A.	6	
Brearley H.	16	3	McNaught J.	13	
Brown C.	2		Mapley	5	
Burton J.H.	5		Mearns F.	5	
Burton O.	15		Milton	1	
Cameron J.	3		Morris T.	22	2
Chalmers J.	6	1	Quinn	1	
Copeland D.	32	5	Tait A.	25	
Erentz H.	16		Walton J.	12	4
Gilhooly P.	1		Warner A.	17	3
Hughes E.	24		Watson J.	17	
Jones J.	25	15	Williams C.	29	
Jones J.L.	20	1	Woodward V.J.	17	10
Kirwan J.	28	4	Turner A.D.	5	5
Leach-Lewis A.	1		Own Goal		1

Southern League 1903–04

1	Southampton	34	22	6	6	75:30	50
2	TOTTENHAM	34	16	11	7	54:37	43
3	Bristol Rvs	34	17	8	9	66:42	42
4	Portsmouth	34	17	8	9	41:38	42
5	QPR	34	15	11	8	53:37	41
6	Reading	34	14	13	7	48:35	41
7	Millwall Ath	34	16	8	10	64:42	40
8	Luton Town	34	14	12	8	38:33	40
9	Plymouth	34	13	10	11	44:34	36
10	Swindon	34	10	11	13	30:42	31
11	Fulham	34	9	12	13	34:35	30
12	West Ham	34	10	7	17	39:44	27
13	Brentford	34	9	9	16	34:48	27
14	Wellingborough	34	11	5	18	44:63	27
15	Northampton	34	10	7	17	36:60	27
16	N/Brompton	34	6	13	15	26:43	25
17	Brighton	34	6	12	16	45:69	24
18	Kettering	34	6	7	21	39:78	19

Western League 1903–04

1	TOTTENHAM	16	11	3	2	32:12	25
2	Southampton	16	9	3	4	30:18	21
3	Plymouth	16	8	4	4	22:18	20
4	Portsmouth	16	7	2	7	24:23	16
5	Brentford	16	6	4	6	19:22	16
6	QPR	16	5	6	5	15:21	15
7	Reading	16	4	4	8	16:26	12
8	Bristol Rvs	16	4	3	9	29:29	11
9	West Ham	16	2	4	10	13:31	8

SEASON 1904/05

Date	Comp	H/A	Opponent	Res	Score
3 Sep	SLge	H	Fulham	L	0-1
7 Sep	WLge	A	Reading	W	1-0
10 Sep	SLge	A	Watford	W	1-0
12 Sep	F	H	Brighton	W	3-1
17 Sep	SLge	H	Plymouth	W	2-0
19 Sep	WLge	A	QPR	W	4-1
24 Sep	SLge	A	West Ham	D	0-0
26 Sep	WLge	H	Bristol Rvs	W	1-0
1 Oct	SLge	H	Reading	L	1-3
3 Oct	WLge	A	Millwall	L	2-3
8 Oct	SLge	A	Bristol Rvs	L	1-3
10 Oct	SCC	A	Woolwich Asnl	W	3-1
15 Oct	SLge	H	Northampton	L	0-1
19 Oct	WLge	A	Plymouth	L	0-5
22 Oct	WLge	A	Portsmouth	L	0-1
24 Oct	WLge	H	West Ham	L	0-1
29 Oct	SLge	H	Brentford	D	1-1
31 Oct	F	H	London FA	W	4-1
2 Nov	F	A	Littlehampton	W	7-0
5 Nov	SLge	A	QPR	W	2-1
7 Nov	WLge	A	Reading	D	2-2
12 Nov	SLge	H	Millwall	W	1-0
12 Nov	WLge	A	Fulham	D	0-0*
19 Nov	SLge	A	Brighton	D	1-1
21 Nov	WLge	H	Plymouth	W	2-0
26 Nov	SLge	A	Luton	L	0-1
28 Nov	F	H	Camb Univ	D	2-2
3 Nov	SLge	H	Swindon	W	6-3
5 Dec	F	H	G. Robey's XI	W	2-1
10 Dec	SLge	A	N/Brompton	D	1-1
17 Dec	SLge	H	Wellingboro'	W	8-1
26 Dec	SLge	A	Southampton	D	1-1
27 Dec	SLge	H	Portsmouth	D	1-1
31 Dec	SLge	A	Fulham	L	0-1
2 Jan	WLge	H	Fulham	L	0-5
7 Jan	SLge	H	Watford	W	2-0
9 Jan	SCCsf	H	West Ham	W	10-0
19 Jan	F	H	Corinthians	L	0-2
21 Jan	SLge	H	West Ham	W	1-0
24 Jan	F	A	Camb Univ	D	4-4
28 Jan	SLge	A	Reading	L	2-3
4 Feb	FC	A	Middlesbrough	D	1-1
9 Feb	FCr	H	Middlesbrough	W	1-0
11 Feb	SLge	A	Northampton	W	3-0
18 Feb	FC	H	Newcastle	D	1-1
22 Feb	FCr	A	Newcastle	L	0-4
25 Feb	SLge	A	Brentford	D	0-0
27 Feb	WLge	H	Millwall	W	4-1
4 Mar	SLge	H	QPR	W	5-1
6 Mar	WLge	A	Bristol Rvs	L	1-2
11 Mar	SLge	A	Millwall	W	2-0
18 Mar	SLge	H	Brighton	D	1-1
20 Mar	WLge	A	QPR	D	1-1
25 Mar	SLge	H	Luton	W	1-0
27 Mar	WLge	A	West Ham	D	1-1
29 Mar	WLge	A	Southampton	D	1-1
1 Apr	SLge	A	Swindon	L	1-2
3 Apr	WLge	A	Brentford	L	0-2
5 Apr	SLge	A	Plymouth	L	1-2
8 Apr	SLge	A	N/Brompton	W	2-0
11 Apr	WLge	H	Brentford	D	0-0
15 Apr	SLge	A	Wellingboro'	W	1-0
17 Apr	WLge	H	Portsmouth	L	0-1
21 Apr	SLge	H	Southampton	L	1-2
22 Apr	WLge	A	Southampton	L	0-1
24 Apr	SLge	N	Portsmouth		2-3
25 Apr	F	H	Sheff Utd	D	0-0
27 Apr	SCCf	N	Reading	D	0-0
29 Apr	SLge	H	Bristol Rvs	W	1-0
4 May	F	A	Hohen Warte	W	6-0†
7 May	F	A	Everton	L	0-2†
10 May	F	A	Vienna Ath	W	4-1†
12 May	F	A	Torna	W	7-1‡
14 May	F	A	Testgyakor	W	12-1‡
16 May	F	A	Everton	L	0-1‡
21 May	F	A	Slavia	W	8-1‡

* Reserve team appeared at Fulham † In Vienna ‡ In Budapest N at Fulham

Player	Lg App	Goals
Berry	8	
Brearley H.	19	3
Bull W.	26	2
Burton J.	9	
Chapman H.	3	1
Copeland D.	18	2
Eggett	27	
Freeborough	1	
George	3	1
Glen	19	11
Hughes E.	15	2
Kirwan J.	26	3
McCurdy	12	

Player	SL App	Goals
McNaught J.	8	
Morris T.	29	3
Murray	8	
O'Hagen	14	5
Stansfield H.	23	5
Swann	2	
Tait A.	24	1
Walton J.	19	6
Warner A.	10	6
Watson J.	25	
Williams C.	7	
Woodward V.	20	7
Own Goal		1

Southern League 1904–05

1	Bristol Rvs	34	20	8	6	74:36	48
2	Reading	34	18	7	9	57:38	43
3	Southampton	34	18	7	9	54:39	43
4	Plymouth	34	18	5	11	57:39	41
5	TOTTENHAM	34	15	8	11	53:34	38
6	Fulham	34	14	10	10	46:34	38
7	QPR	34	14	8	12	51:46	36
8	Portsmouth	34	16	4	14	61:56	36
9	N/Brompton	34	11	11	12	40:40	33
10	Watford	34	15	3	16	43:45	33
11	West Ham	34	12	8	14	48:42	32
12	Brighton	34	13	6	15	44:45	32
13	Northampton	34	12	8	14	43:54	32
14	Brentford	34	10	9	15	33:38	29
15	Millwall Ath	34	11	7	16	38:47	29
16	Swindon	34	12	5	17	41:59	29
17	Luton	34	12	3	19	45:54	27
18	Wellingborough	34	5	3	26	25:107	13

Western League 1904–05

1	Plymouth	20	13	4	3	52:18	30
2	Brentford	20	11	6	3	30:23	28
3	Southampton	20	11	2	7	45:22	24
4	Portsmouth	20	10	3	7	29:30	23
5	West Ham	20	8	4	8	37:43	20
6	Fulham	20	7	3	10	29:32	17
7	Millwall Ath	20	7	3	10	32:39	17
8	TOTTENHAM	20	5	6	9	20:28	16
9	Reading	20	6	3	11	28:37	15
10	QPR	20	6	3	11	27:45	15
11	Bristol Rvs	20	7	1	12	32:44	15

SEASON 1905/06

Date	Comp	H/A	Opponent	Res	Score
2 Sep	SLge	A	Reading	D	1-1
4 Sep	WLge	H	Reading	W	5-1
9 Sep	SLge	H	Watford	W	1-0
11 Sep	WLge	A	QPR	D	1-1
16 Sep	SLge	A	Brighton	L	0-2
23 Sep	SLge	H	West Ham	W	2-0
25 Sep	WLge	H	Bristol Rvs	L	0-1
30 Sep	SLge	A	Fulham	D	0-0
2 Oct	WLge	H	Plymouth	L	0-2
7 Oct	SLge	H	QPR	W	2-1
11 Oct	WLge	A	Reading	D	0-0
14 Oct	SLge	A	Bristol Rvs	W	2-0
16 Oct	WLge	H	Fulham	W	1-0
21 Oct	SLge	H	N/Brompton	W	6-0
23 Oct	WLge	H	Millwall	W	5-0
28 Oct	WLge	A	Portsmouth	D	0-0
4 Nov	SLge	H	Swindon	W	2-1
6 Nov	WLge	A	West Ham	L	1-4
8 Nov	SCC	H	QPR	W	2-0
11 Nov	SLge	A	Millwall	L	1-2
13 Nov	WLge	H	Brentford	L	2-3
18 Nov	SLge	H	Luton	W	1-0
20 Nov	WLge	A	Fulham	W	3-0
25 Nov	SLge	H	Northampton	W	2-0
27 Nov	F	H	Camb Univ	W	2-1
2 Dec	SLge	A	Brentford	W	3-0
9 Dec	F	H	Corinthians	W	3-1
16 Dec	SLge	A	Plymouth	L	1-2
23 Dec	WLge	H	Southampton	W	5-0
25 Dec	SLge	H	Portsmouth	W	3-1
26 Dec	SLge	A	Southampton	L	0-1
30 Dec	SLge	H	Reading	W	1-0
6 Jan	SLge	A	Watford	D	0-0
13 Jan	FC	H	Burnley	W	2-0
20 Jan	SLge	H	Brighton	W	3-1
24 Jan	F	A	Camb Univ	L	1-4
27 Jan	SLge	A	West Ham	W	1-0
29 Jan	WLge	H	QPR	L	1-2
3 Feb	FC	A	Reading	W	3-2
10 Feb	SLge	A	QPR	D	0-0
12 Feb	SLge	H	Fulham	L	0-1
17 Feb	SLge	H	Bristol Rvs	D	2-2
19 Feb	WLge	A	Millwall	D	1-1
24 Feb	FC	H	Birmingham	D	1-1
26 Feb	WLge	H	Brentford	W	1-0
28 Feb	FCr	A	Birmingham	L	0-2
3 Mar	WLge	A	Portsmouth	D	1-1
5 Mar	SLge	H	N/Brompton	L	0-1
10 Mar	SLge	A	Swindon	L	0-2
17 Mar	SLge	A	Millwall	W	3-1
19 Mar	WLge	A	Bristol Rvs	D	0-0
21 Mar	WLge	A	Plymouth	D	0-0
24 Mar	SLge	A	Luton	L	0-2
26 Mar	WLge	A	West Ham	W	1-0
31 Mar	SLge	A	Northampton	D	0-0
7 Apr	SLge	A	Brentford	W	4-1
13 Apr	SLge	A	Southampton	D	1-1
14 Apr	SLge	H	Norwich	L	1-4
16 Apr	SLge	A	Portsmouth	L	0-1
17 Apr	SLge	A	Norwich	W	3-0
21 Apr	SLge	H	Plymouth	L	0-1
23 Apr	SCCsf	H	Woolwich Asnl	D	0-0
25 Apr	WLge	H	Southampton	L	0-1
28 Apr	SCCsfr	A	Woolwich Asnl	L	0-5

Player	SL App	Goals
Berry	4	1
Brearley H.	16	1
Bull W.	30	2
Burton O.	6	
Carrick C.	15	4
Chaplin	2	
Chapman H.	28	11
Darnell J.	10	
Derry	1	
Eggett	34	
Freeborough	1	
George	1	
Glen A.	14	2
Hughes E.	22	

Player	SL App	Goals
Kyle	25	8
Leach-Lewis A.	2	2
Morris T.	32	2
Murray	13	
O'Hagan	7	
Page G.	1	
Shackleton	3	1
Stansfield H.	7	1
Tait A.	27	1
Walton J.	21	5
Watson J.	33	
Whyman A.	7	
Woodward V.J.	12	5

Southern League 1905–06

1	Fulham	34	19	12	3	44:15	50
2	Southampton	34	19	7	8	58:39	45
3	Portsmouth	34	17	9	8	61:35	43
4	Luton	34	17	7	10	64:40	41
5	TOTTENHAM	34	16	7	11	46:29	39
6	Plymouth	34	16	7	11	52:33	39
7	Norwich	34	13	10	11	46:38	36
8	Bristol Rvs	34	15	5	14	56:56	35
9	Brentford	34	14	7	13	43:52	35
10	Reading	34	12	9	13	53:46	33
11	West Ham	34	14	5	15	42:39	33
12	Millwall	34	11	11	12	38:41	33
13	QPR	34	12	7	15	58:44	31
14	Watford	34	8	10	16	38:57	26
15	Swindon	34	8	9	17	31:52	25
16	Brighton	34	9	7	18	30:55	25
17	N/Brompton	34	7	8	19	20:62	22
18	Northampton	34	8	5	21	32:79	21

Western League 1905–06

1	QPR	20	11	4	5	33:27	26
2	Southampton	20	10	5	5	41:35	25
3	Plymouth	20	8	8	4	34:23	24
4	TOTTENHAM	20	7	7	6	28:17	21
5	Bristol Rvs	20	8	3	9	34:34	19
6	Millwall Ath	20	7	5	8	28:29	19
7	Portsmouth	20	6	7	7	26:29	19
8	West Ham	20	7	5	8	32:35	19
9	Reading	20	6	6	8	28:35	18
10	Fulham	20	5	5	10	23:32	15
11	Brentford	20	6	3	11	25:36	15

SEASON 1906/07

Date	Comp	H/A	Opponent	Result	Score
1 Sep	SLge	H	West Ham	L	1-2
3 Sep	WLge	H	Plymouth	D	0-0
5 Sep	SLge	A	Watford	D	1-1
8 Sep	SLge	A	Bristol Rvs	L	2-3
10 Sep	SLge	A	Southampton	L	2-3
13 Sep	F	H	London Cal	W	6-4
15 Sep	SLge	A	Swindon	D	0-0
17 Sep	F	H	Ilford	D	4-4
22 Sep	SLge	H	Norwich	D	2-2
24 Sep	SLge	H	Fulham	W	5-1
29 Sept	SLge	A	Luton	L	0-2
3 Oct	WLge	A	Southampton	L	0-2
6 Oct	SLge	H	C. Palace	W	3-0
8 Oct	SLge	A	West Ham	L	0-5
13 Oct	SLge	A	Brentford	D	2-2
20 Oct	WLge	H	Millwall	W	1-0
22 Oct	SCC	H	West Ham	W	2-0
27 Oct	SLge	A	Leyton	D	1-1
29 Oct	SLge	A	Fulham	L	1-2
3 Nov	SLge	H	Portsmouth	D	1-1
7 Nov	WLge	A	Portsmouth	L	0-1
10 Nov	SLge	H	N/Brompton	W	1-0
12 Nov	F	H	Camb Univ	W	4-2
14 Nov	F	A	Corinthians	L	1-6
19 Nov	F	H	Oxford Univ	W	2-1
24 Nov	SLge	A	Brighton	L	0-2
26 Nov	WLge	H	Portsmouth	W	4-2
1 Dec	SLge	H	Reading	W	2-0
8 Dec	F	H	Corinthians	W	5-0
12 Dec	WLge	A	Plymouth	D	2-2*
12 Dec	SLge	H	Plymouth	W	4-2*
15 Dec	SLge	H	Northampton	W	6-0
22 Dec	SLge	A	QPR	L	1-3
25 Dec	SLge	H	Millwall	W	3-1
26 Dec	SLge	A	Southampton	L	1-2
29 Dec	SLge	A	West Ham	L	2-4
5 Jan	SLge	H	Bristol Rvs	W	4-0
12 Jan	FC	H	Hull City	D	0-0
17 Jan	FCr	A	Hull City	D	0-0
19 Jan	SLge	H	Swindon	W	3-0
21 Jan	FCr	H	Hull City	W	1-0
26 Jan	SLge	A	Norwich	L	0-5
2 Feb	FC	H	Blackburn	D	1-1
7 Feb	FCr	H	Blackburn	D	1-1
9 Feb	FCr	A	C. Palace	W	1-0
11 Feb	FCr	§	Blackburn	W	1-0
16 Feb	SLge	H	Brentford	W	2-1
23 Feb	FC	A	Notts Co	L	0-4
2 Mar	SLge	H	Leyton	D	0-0
9 Mar	SLge	A	Portsmouth	L	1-3
16 Mar	SLge	H	N/Brompton	W	2-0
23 Mar	SLge	A	Plymouth	D	0-0
25 Mar	SLge	H	Luton	L	1-2
29 Mar	SLge	A	Southampton	W	2-0
30 Mar	SLge	H	Brighton	W	3-0
1 Apr	SLge	A	Millwall	W	1-0
2 Apr	F	H	Spurs 1901 XI	L	1-4†
3 Apr	SCC	H	QPR	W	4-0
6 Apr	SLge	A	Reading	L	0-2
8 Apr	WLge	H	West Ham	W	4-2
13 Apr	SLge	A	Watford	D	0-0
15 Apr	F	H	W.Browns XI	W	2-1
20 Apr	SLge	A	Northampton	L	0-2
22 Apr	WLge	A	Millwall	D	0-0
27 Apr	SLge	H	QPR	W	2-0
29 Apr	SCC	H	Southampton	W	2-0
26 May	F	A	Ostend Club	W	8-1‡
27 May	F	A	Fulham	W	2-1‡

* Spurs played Plymouth twice on the same day in both Southern and Western Leagues. The reserves played the Western League match
† Charity match: current Spurs side v 1901 side. Benefit for S. Mountford
‡ Played in Ostend, Belgium   § Played at Villa Park

Player	SL App	Goals
Badenoch	1	
Berry	1	
Bull W.	27	2
Burton O.	4	
Brearley H.	18	
Chaplin J.	34	
Chapman H.	11	3
Darnell	2	
Dow	9	3
Eames	7	2
Eggett	5	
Hewitt	31	11
Hughes E.	25	
Jones W.H.	9	
McDiarmid	7	
Morris T.	33	2
Pickett A.	15	4
Reid	26	16
Reilly C.H.	1	
Reilly G.	19	
Stansfield H.	10	2
Steel D.	6	
Tait A.	24	
Walker	9	
Walton J.	34	9
Watson J.	12	
Whitebourne J.	14	
Whyman A.	3	1
Wilkinson	2	
Woodward V.J.	19	8

Southern League 1906–07

1	Fulham	38	20 13 5	58:32	53
2	Portsmouth	38	22 7 9	63:36	51
3	Brighton	38	18 9 11	53:43	45
4	Luton	38	18 9 11	52:52	45
5	West Ham	38	15 14 9	60:41	44
6	TOTTENHAM	38	17 9 12	63:45	43
7	Millwall	38	18 6 14	71:50	42
8	Norwich	38	15 12 11	57:48	42
9	Watford	38	13 16 9	46:43	42
10	Brentford	38	17 8 13	57:56	42
11	Southampton	38	13 9 16	49:56	35
12	Reading	38	14 6 18	57:47	34
13	Leyton	38	11 12 15	36:60	34
14	Bristol Rvs	38	12 9 17	55:54	33
15	Plymouth	38	10 13 15	43:50	33
16	Swindon	38	11 11 16	43:54	33
17	N/Brompton	38	12 9 17	47:59	33
18	QPR	38	11 10 17	47:55	32
19	C. Palace	38	8 9 21	46:66	25
20	Northampton	38	5 9 24	29:87	19

Western League 'B' 1906–07

1	West Ham	10	7 1 2	25:14	15
2	Plymouth	10	5 3 2	16:10	13
3	Portsmouth	10	4 2 4	16:19	10
4	TOTTENHAM	10	3 3 4	13:15	9
5	Southampton	10	4 0 6	14:16	8
6	Millwall	10	1 3 6	5:15	5

SEASON 1907/08

Date	Comp	H/A	Opponent	Result	Score
2 Sep	SLge	A	QPR	D	3-3
7 Sep	SLge	A	West Ham	D	1-1
9 Sep	WLge	H	Bristol Rvs	W	10-0
14 Sep	SLge	H	QPR	W	3-2
18 Sep	WLge	A	Bristol Rvs	L	1-2
21 Sep	SLge	H	N/Brompton	W	2-1
23 Sep	WLge	A	Millwall	L	0-2
28 Sep	SLge	A	Swindon	L	0-1
30 Sep	SCC	H	Millwall	L	0-1
2 Oct	WLge	A	Reading	W	2-1
5 Oct	SLge	H	C. Palace	L	1-2
7 Oct	WLge	A	West Ham	W	2-1
12 Oct	SLge	A	Luton	L	1-3
14 Oct	WLge	H	Reading	L	0-2
19 Oct	SLge	A	Brighton	D	1-1
21 Oct	F	H	Ilford	W	10-0
23 Oct	WLge	A	C. Palace	L	0-2
26 Oct	SLge	A	Portsmouth	W	2-1
28 Oct	F	H	Clapton	W	2-0
2 Nov	SLge	H	Bradford PA	D	0-0
4 Nov	WLge	A	West Ham	W	3-1
9 Nov	SLge	A	Millwall	W	2-1
16 Nov	SLge	H	Brentford	W	1-0
18 Nov	SCC	A	Millwall	L	1-2
23 Nov	SLge	A	Bristol Rvs	D	0-0
25 Nov	WLge	H	Millwall	L	0-3
30 Nov	SLge	H	Leyton	W	1-0
2 Dec	WLge	H	C. Palace	W	1-0
7 Dec	SLge	A	Reading	L	1-3
9 Dec	WLge	A	Luton	W	5-1
14 Dec	SLge	H	Watford	W	5-0
16 Dec	WLge	H	Luton	W	2-0
21 Dec	SLge	H	Norwich	W	3-0
25 Dec	SLge	A	Northampton	W	2-0
26 Dec	SLge	A	Southampton	D	1-1
28 Dec	SLge	H	Northampton	L	1-2
4 Jan	SLge	H	West Ham	W	3-2
11 Jan	FC	A	Everton	L	0-1
18 Jan	SLge	A	N/Brompton	W	2-1
20 Jan	SLge	H	Plymouth	L	0-1
25 Jan	SLge	H	Swindon	W	1-0
1 Feb	F	H	Woolwich Asnl	L	0-1
8 Feb	SLge	H	Luton	L	1-2
12 Feb	SLge	A	C. Palace	W	2-0
15 Feb	SLge	A	Brighton	L	0-2
22 Feb	F	A	Chelsea	D	1-1
29 Feb	SLge	A	Bradford PA	W	2-1
7 Mar	SLge	H	Millwall	L	1-2
14 Mar	SLge	A	Brentford	L	0-3
21 Mar	SLge	H	Bristol Rvs	L	1-2
28 Mar	SLge	A	Leyton	W	5-2
4 Apr	SLge	H	Reading	W	2-0
6 Apr	SLge	A	Portsmouth	L	2-3
11 Apr	SLge	A	Watford	D	2-2
17 Apr	SLge	H	Southampton	W	3-0
18 Apr	SLge	A	Norwich	L	1-2
20 Apr	SLge	A	Plymouth	L	0-1
30 Apr	F	A	Clapton	L	0-2

Player	SL App	Goals		Player	SL App	Goals
Brewster	1			Payne G.	6	3
Bull W.	21	3		Pickett A.E.	13	2
Burton O.	31			Reid	11	2
Chaplin J.	30			Seeburg M.P.	15	4
Coquet E.	6			Stansfield H.	8	1
Cousins	2			Steel D.	25	1
Darnell J.	22			Tait A.	1	
Dixon A.	5			Walker R.H.	11	2
Gray	15			Walton J.	21	1
Hughes E.	1			Watson J.	3	
McNair W.	15	6		Whitbourne J.G.	5	
Manning G.	33			Whyman A.	8	
Middlemiss H.	25	8		Woodruff C.L.	5	3
Minter W.J.	9	4		Woodward V.J.	20	10
Morris T.	32			Own Goals		4
Pass J.E.	18	5				

Southern League 1907–08

1	QPR	38	21 9 8	82:57	51
2	Plymouth	38	19 11 8	50:31	49
3	Millwall Ath	38	19 8 11	49:32	46
4	C. Palace	38	17 10 11	54:51	44
5	Swindon	38	16 10 12	55:40	42
6	Bristol Rvs	38	16 10 12	59:56	42
7	TOTTENHAM	38	17 7 14	59:48	41
8	Northampton	38	15 11 12	50:41	41
9	Portsmouth	38	17 6 15	64:52	40
10	West Ham	38	15 10 13	47:48	40
11	Southampton	38	16 6 16	51:60	38
12	Reading	38	15 6 17	55:50	36
13	Bradford PA	38	12 12 14	53:54	36
14	Watford	38	12 10 16	47:59	34
15	Brentford	38	14 5 19	49:52	33
16	Norwich	38	12 9 17	46:49	33
17	Brighton	38	12 8 18	46:59	32
18	Luton	38	12 6 20	33:56	30
19	Leyton	38	8 11 19	51:74	27
20	N/Brompton	38	9 7 22	44:75	25

Western League 'B' 1907–08

1	Millwall	12	9 2 1	31:15	20
2	TOTTENHAM	12	7 0 5	26:13	14
3	Bristol Rvs	12	6 2 4	22:29	14
4	Luton	12	4 4 4	16:21	12
5	Reading	12	4 3 5	20:25	11
6	C. Palace	12	3 4 5	16:17	10
7	West Ham	12	1 1 10	16:27	3

238

SEASON 1908/09

1	Sep	Lge	H	Wolves	W	3-0
5	Sep	Lge	A	Leeds	L	0-1
12	Sep	Lge	H	Barnsley	W	4-0
19	Sep	Lge	H	Bolton	W	2-1
26	Sep	Lge	A	Hull	L	0-1
3	Oct	Lge	H	Derby	D	0-0
5	Oct	LCC	H	QPR	W	1-0
10	Oct	Lge	A	Blackpool	D	1-1
17	Oct	Lge	H	Chesterfield	W	4-0
24	Oct	Lge	A	Glossop	D	1-1
31	Oct	Lge	H	Stockport	D	0-0
2	Nov	LPCF	H	Clapton	D	1-1
7	Nov	Lge	A	WBA	L	0-3
14	Nov	Lge	H	Birmingham	W	4-0
21	Nov	Lge	A	Gainsbro'	W	2-0
28	Nov	Lge	H	Grimsby	W	2-0
30	Nov	LCC	A	West Ham	W	2-0
5	Dec	Lge	A	Fulham	W	3-2
12	Dec	Lge	H	Burnley	W	4-2
19	Dec	Lge	A	Bradford PA	W	2-0
25	Dec	Lge	A	Oldham	L	0-1
26	Dec	Lge	H	Oldham	W	3-0
28	Dec	Lge	A	Wolves	L	0-1
2	Jan	Lge	H	Leeds	W	3--0
9	Jan	Lge	A	Barnsley	D	1-1
16	Jan	FC	A	Man City	W	4-3
23	Jan	Lge	A	Bolton	W	1-0
30	Jan	Lge	H	Hull	D	0-0
6	Feb	FC	H	Fulham	W	1-0
13	Feb	Lge	H	Blackpool	W	4-1
20	Feb	FC	H	Burnley	D	0-0
24	Feb	FCr	A	Burnley	L	1-3
27	Feb	Lge	A	Glossop	D	3-3
6	Mar	Lge	A	Stockport	W	3-1
8	Mar	Lge	A	Chesterfield	W	3-1
13	Mar	Lge	H	WBA	L	1-3
20	Mar	Lge	A	Birmingham	D	3-3
22	Mar	LCC	A	Millwall	L	0-2
27	Mar	Lge	H	Gainsbro'	D	1-1
3	Apr	Lge	A	Grimsby	W	2-1
9	Apr	Lge	H	Clapton	L	0-1
10	Apr	Lge	H	Fulham	W	1-0
12	Apr	Lge	A	Clapton	D	0-0
17	Apr	Lge	A	Burnley	W	2-1
24	Apr	Lge	H	Bradford PA	W	3-0
28	Apr	Lge	A	Derby	D	1-1
29	Apr	F	A	Clapton	W	3-2
5	Jun	F	*	Everton	D	2-2
10	Jun	F	*	Uruguay Lge	W	8-0
13	Jun	F	*	Argentinos	W	1-0
16	Jun	F	*	Liga Argentina	W	4-1
19	Jun	F	*	Everton	L	0-4
20	Jun	F	*	Rosario	W	9-0
24	Jun	F	*	Alumini	W	5-0

* Tour of Uruguay and Argentina

Player	Lg App	Goals
Boreham F.	8	
Brough J.	1	
Bull W.	12	
Burton O.	33	
Coquet E.	37	
Curtis J.	2	1
Darnell J.	37	
Hewitson R.	30	
Leslie T.	2	
MacFarlane D.	16	2
Massey F.J.	1	
Middlemiss H.	38	14
Minter W.J.	34	14
Morris T.	24	1
Morton J.	2	
Seeburg M.P.	1	
Steel R.	37	12
Steel D.	38	1
Watson J.	24	2
Wilkes F.	6	
Woodruff C.L.	8	1
Woodward V.J.	27	19

Final table for Second Division

1	Bolton	38	24	4	10	59:28	52
2	**TOTTENHAM**	**38**	**20**	**11**	**7**	**67:32**	**51**
3	West Bromwich	38	19	13	6	56:27	51
4	Hull	38	19	6	13	63:39	44
5	Derby	38	16	11	11	55:41	43
6	Oldham	38	17	6	15	55:43	40
7	Wolverhampton	38	14	11	13	56:48	39
8	Glossop	38	15	8	15	57:53	38
9	Gainsbro'	38	15	8	15	49:70	38
10	Fulham	38	13	11	14	58:48	37
11	Birmingham	38	14	9	15	58:61	37
12	Leeds C.	38	14	7	17	43:53	35
13	Grimsby	38	14	7	17	41:54	35
14	Burnley	38	13	7	18	51:58	33
15	Clapton O.	38	12	9	17	37:49	33
16	Bradford PA	38	13	6	19	51:59	32
17	Barnsley	38	11	10	17	48:57	32
18	Stockport	38	14	3	21	39:71	31
19	Chesterfield T.	38	11	8	19	37:67	30
20	Blackpool	38	9	11	18	46:68	29

SEASON 1909/10

1	Sep	Lge	A	Sunderland	L	1-3
4	Sep	Lge	A	Everton	L	2-4
11	Sep	Lge	H	Man Utd	D	2-2
18	Sep	Lge	A	Brad City	L	1-5
20	Sep	LCC	A	Nunhead	W	9-0
25	Sep	Lge	H	Sheff Wed	W	3-0
29	Sep	F	A	Reading	W	3-2
2	Oct	Lge	A	Bristol C	D	0-0
9	Oct	Lge	H	Bury	W	1-0
11	Oct	LCC	H	Croydon	W	7-1
16	Oct	Lge	H	Middlesbro	L	1-3
30	Oct	Lge	H	Notts Co	L	1-3
1	Nov	LPCF	H	Arsenal	W	3-0
6	Nov	Lge	A	Newcastle	L	0-1
8	Nov	LCCsf	*	QPR	D	0-0
13	Nov	Lge	H	Liverpool	W	1-0
15	Nov	LCCsfr	†	QPR	W	4-1
20	Nov	Lge	A	Aston Villa	L	2-3
22	Nov	Lge	A	Preston	L	1-4
27	Nov	Lge	H	Sheff Utd	W	2-1
4	Dec	Lge	A	Arsenal	L	0-1
6	Dec	LCCf	*	Fulham	L	1-4
11	Dec	Lge	H	Bolton	D	1-1
18	Dec	Lge	A	Chelsea	L	1-2
25	Dec	Lge	H	Nottm For	D	2-2
27	Dec	Lge	A	Nottm For	D	2-2
1	Jan	Lge	A	Blackburn	L	0-2
8	Jan	Lge	H	Everton	W	3-0
15	Jan	FC	A	Plymouth	D	1-1
19	Jan	FCr	A	Plymouth	W	7-1
29	Jan	Lge	A	Man Utd	L	0-5
29	Jan	Lge	H	Bradford C	D	0-0
5	Feb	FC	A	Chelsea	W	1-0
12	Feb	Lge	H	Bristol C	W	3-2
19	Feb	FC	A	Swindon	L	2-3
26	Feb	Lge	A	Middlesbro	W	3-4
5	Mar	Lge	H	Preston	W	2-1
12	Mar	Lge	A	Notts Co	L	0-3
14	Mar	Lge	A	Sheff Utd	D	1-1
19	Mar	Lge	H	Newcastle	L	0-4
25	Mar	Lge	H	Sunderland	W	5-1
26	Mar	Lge	A	Liverpool	L	0-2
29	Mar	Lge	H	Blackburn	W	4-0
2	Apr	Lge	A	Aston Villa	D	1-1
9	Apr	Lge	A	Sheff Utd	D	1-1
16	Apr	Lge	H	Arsenal	D	1-1
20	Apr	Lge	A	Bury	L	1-3
23	Apr	Lge	A	Bolton	W	2-0
30	Apr	Lge	H	Chelsea	W	2-1

* Played at Chelsea
† Played at Fulham

Player	Lg App	Goals
Bentley F.W.	19	
Boreham F.	12	
Brown D.C.	1	
Brown I.	8	
Burton O.	4	
Coquet E.	27	
Curtis J.	37	3
Darnell J.	25	
Drabble F.	1	
Elkin R.H.	8	
Harris W.	7	
Humphreys P.	20	13
Joyce J.W.	23	
Kennedy J.J.	2	
Kerry A.H.G.	1	
Leslie T.	7	
Lunn T.H.	2	
Lyle A.	1	
MacFarlane D.	5	
Middlemiss H.	36	9
Minter W.J.	38	15
Morris T.	26	1
Newman E.	1	
Steel A.	1	
Steel D.	36	2
Steel R.	38	9
Tull W.D.	7	1
Wilkes F.	23	
Woodruff C.L.	2	

Final table for First Division

1	Aston Villa	38	23	7	8	84:42	53
2	Liverpool	38	21	6	11	78:57	48
3	Blackburn	38	18	9	11	73:55	45
4	Newcastle	38	19	7	12	70:56	45
5	Manchester U.	38	19	7	12	69:61	45
6	Sheffield U.	38	16	10	12	62:41	42
7	Bradford C.	38	17	8	13	64:47	42
8	Sunderland	38	18	5	15	66:51	41
9	Notts Co.	38	15	10	13	67:59	40
10	Everton	38	16	8	14	51:56	40
11	The Wednesday	38	15	9	14	60:63	39
12	Preston	38	15	5	18	52:58	35
13	Bury	38	12	9	17	62:66	33
14	Nottingham F.	38	11	11	16	54:72	33
15	**TOTTENHAM**	**38**	**11**	**10**	**17**	**53:69**	**32**
16	Bristol C.	38	12	8	18	45:60	32
17	Middlesbrough	38	11	9	18	56:73	31
18	Woolwich Asnl	38	11	9	18	37:67	31
19	Chelsea	38	11	7	20	47:70	29
20	Bolton	38	9	6	23	44:71	24

SEASON 1910/11

1 Sep	Lge	A	Everton	L	0-2		3 Jan	Lge	A	Man City	L	1-2
3 Sep	Lge	H	Sheff Wed	W	3-1		7 Jan	Lge	H	Bristol City	W	3-2
10 Sep	Lge	A	Bristol C	W	2-0		14 Jan	FC	H	Millwall	W	2-1
17 Sep	Lge	H	Newcastle	L	1-2		21 Jan	Lge	A	Newcastle	D	1-1
19 Sep	LCC	H	Clapton	W	1-0		4 Feb	FC	A	Blackburn	D	0-0
24 Sep	Lge	A	Oldham	L	0-2		9 Feb	FCr	H	Blackburn	L	0-2
1 Oct	Lge	A	Middlesbrough	L	0-2		11 Feb	Lge	A	Preston	L	0-2
3 Oct	LPCF	A	Chelsea	W	3-0		13 Feb	Lge	H	Middlesbrough	W	6-2
8 Oct	Lge	H	Preston	D	1-1		18 Feb	Lge	H	Notts Co	W	3-0
10 Oct	LCC	H	Chelsea	W	3-0		25 Feb	Lge	A	Aston Villa	L	0-4
15 Oct	Lge	A	Notts Co	L	0-1		4 Mar	Lge	H	Liverpool	W	1-0
22 Oct	Lge	H	Man Utd	D	2-2		11 Mar	Lge	A	Bury	L	1-2
29 Oct	Lge	A	Liverpool	L	1-2		15 Mar	Lge	A	Man Utd	L	2-3
5 Nov	Lge	H	Bury	W	5-0		18 Mar	Lge	H	Sheff Wed	W	2-1
7 Nov	LCCsf	A	Millwall	D	2-2*		27 Mar	Lge	H	Oldham	W	2-0
12 Nov	Lge	A	Sheff Utd	L	0-3		1 Apr	Lge	H	Sunderland	D	1-1
19 Nov	Lge	H	Aston Villa	L	1-2		8 Apr	Lge	A	Arsenal	L	0-2
21 Nov	LCCsfr	A	Millwall	W	2-0*		15 Apr	Lge	A	Brad City	W	2-0
26 Nov	Lge	A	Sunderland	L	0-4		17 Apr	Lge	H	Everton	L	0-1
3 Dec	Lge	H	Arsenal	W	3-1		22 Apr	Lge	A	Blackburn	L	0-3
5 Dec	LCCf	†	Fulham	W	2-1		7 May	F	‡	Nth German XI	W	4-1
10 Dec	Lge	A	Brad City	L	0-3		13 May	F	‡	Preussen	W	7-0
17 Dec	Lge	H	Blackburn	D	2-2		14 May	F	‡	Hertha	W	4-1
24 Dec	Lge	A	Nottm Forest	W	2-1		20 May	F	‡	Wacker	W	8-1
26 Dec	Lge	H	Nottm Forest	L	1-4		21 May	F	‡	Eintracht F.	W	4-1
27 Dec	Lge	H	Man City	D	1-1		25 May	F	‡	Kickers Vict	W	6-0
31 Dec	Lge	A	Sheff Wed	L	1-2							

* Played at Leyton
† Final played at Stamford Bridge
‡ German tour

Player	Lg App	Goals		Player	Lg App	Goals
Bentley F.W.	16			Kennedy J.J.	7	1
Birnie E.L.	4	1		Leslie T.	1	
Brown I.	4			Lunn T.H.	34	
Bulling E.	2			McTavish J.K.	7	
Collins T.	25			McTavish R.	11	2
Coquet E.	13			Middlemiss H.	30	4
Crompton E.	5			Minter W.J.	38	19
Curtis J.	30	1		Morris T.	11	
Darnell J.	38	2		Newman E.	2	1
Elkin R.H.	17			Rance C.S.	11	
Foreman T.	2	1		Steel D.	26	
Gosnell A.A.	5			Steel R.	29	9
Humphreys P.	24	10		Tull W.D.	3	1
Joyce J.W.	4			Wilkes F.	19	

Final table for First Division

1	Manchester U.	38	22	8	8	72:40	52
2	Aston Villa	38	22	7	9	69:41	51
3	Sunderland	38	15	15	8	67:48	45
4	Everton	38	19	7	12	50:36	45
5	Bradford C.	38	20	5	13	51:42	45
6	The Wednesday	38	17	8	13	47:48	42
7	Oldham	38	16	9	13	44:41	41
8	Newcastle	38	15	10	13	61:43	40
9	Sheffield U.	38	15	8	15	49:43	38
10	Woolwich Asnl	38	13	12	13	41:49	38
11	Notts Co.	38	14	10	14	37:45	38
12	Blackburn	38	13	11	14	62:54	37
13	Liverpool	38	15	7	16	53:53	37
14	Preston	38	12	11	15	40:49	35
15	**TOTTENHAM**	**38**	**13**	**6**	**19**	**52:63**	**32**
16	Middlesbrough	38	11	10	17	49:63	32
17	Manchester C.	38	9	13	16	43:58	31
18	Bury	38	9	11	18	43:71	29
19	Bristol C.	38	11	5	22	43:66	27
20	Nottingham F.	38	9	7	22	55:75	25

SEASON 1911/12

2 Sep	Lge	A	Everton	D	2-2		3 Feb	F	H	C. Orient	W	3-2
4 Sep	Lge	H	Sheff Wed	W	3-1		10 Feb	Lge	A	Bury	L	1-2
9 Sep	Lge	H	WBA	W	1-0		17 Feb	Lge	A	Middlesbro	W	2-1
16 Sep	Lge	A	Sunderland	D	1-1		24 Feb	Lge	A	Newcastle	D	2-2
18 Sep	LCC	A	Brentford	L	1-4		2 Mar	Lge	A	Preston	W	1-0
23 Sep	Lge	H	Blackburn	L	0-2		13 Mar	Lge	A	WBA	L	0-2
30 Sep	Lge	A	Sheff Wed	L	0-4		16 Mar	Lge	A	Liverpool	W	2-1
7 Oct	Lge	H	Bury	W	2-1		23 Mar	Lge	H	Aston Villa	W	2-1
14 Oct	Lge	A	Middlesbro	L	0-2		30 Mar	Lge	A	Newcastle	L	0-2
21 Oct	Lge	H	Notts Co	D	2-2		5 Apr	Lge	A	Man City	L	1-2
23 Oct	LPCF	H	Fulham	W	3-0		6 Apr	Lge	H	Sheff Utd	D	1-1
28 Oct	Lge	H	Preston	W	6-2		8 Apr	Lge	H	Man City	L	0-2
4 Nov	Lge	A	Man Utd	W	2-1		9 Apr	Lge	H	Man United	D	1-1
11 Nov	Lge	H	Liverpool	W	2-0		13 Apr	Lge	A	Oldham	L	1-2
18 Nov	Lge	A	Aston Villa	D	2-2		18 Apr	F	A	Northampton	L	0-2
25 Nov	Lge	H	Newcastle	L	1-2		20 Apr	Lge	H	Bolton	W	1-0
2 Dec	Lge	A	Sheff Utd	W	2-1		27 Apr	Lge	A	Bradford C	L	0-3
9 Dec	Lge	H	Oldham	W	4-0		29 Apr	F	*	Woolwich A.	L	0-3
16 Dec	Lge	A	Bolton	L	0-1		12 May	F	†	Hull City	L	0-2
23 Dec	Lge	H	Bradford C	L	2-3		16 May	F	‡	Bewegungs	W	3-1
25 Dec	Lge	H	Woolwich A.	W	5-0		20 May	F	‡	Sport Vienna	W	5-3
26 Dec	Lge	A	Woolwich A.	L	1-3		24 May	F	‡	Woolwich A.	L	0-4
30 Dec	Lge	H	Everton	L	0-1		27 May	F	‡	Varosi Torna	W	4-1
13 Jan	FC	A	WBA	L	0-3		28 May	F	‡	Olympic XI	D	2-2
20 Jan	Lge	H	Sunderland	D	0-0		30 May	F	‡	Olympic XI	W	4-3
27 Jan	Lge	A	Blackburn	D	0-0		2 Jun	F	‡	Olympic XI	L	0-3

* Titanic fund charity match at Shepherd's Bush (QPR ground)
† Bedekker Cup match in Brussels
‡ Tour of Leipzig (first game) and Vienna (remaining six games)

Player	Lg App	Goals		Player	Lg App	Goals
Bentley F.W.	1			Lunn T.H.	34	
Bliss H.	5	1		McTavish J.K.	30	3
Bowering G.	7			Mason T.L.	7	1
Brittan R.C.	26			Middlemiss H.	32	11
Collins T.	33			Minter W.J.	35	18
Crompton E.	3			Morris T.	2	
Curtis J.	9			Newman E.	19	6
Darnell J.	34	1		Rance C.S.	17	
Elliot J.	5	2		Steel D.	29	
Foreman T.	6			Steel R.	30	7
Grimsdell A.	2			Tattersall W.	2	
Humphreys P.	1			Webster F.	6	
Joyce J.W.	4			Wilkes F.	9	
Kennedy J.J.	4			Young A.	5	3
Lightfoot E.J.	21					

Final table for First Division

1	Blackburn	38	20	9	9	60:43	49
2	Everton	38	20	6	12	46:42	46
3	Newcastle	38	18	8	12	64:50	44
4	Bolton	38	20	3	15	54:43	43
5	The Wednesday	38	16	9	13	69:49	41
6	Aston Villa	38	17	7	14	76:63	41
7	Middlesbrough	38	16	8	14	56:45	40
8	Sunderland	38	14	11	13	58:51	39
9	West Bromwich	38	15	9	14	43:47	39
10	Woolwich Asnl	38	15	8	15	55:59	38
11	Bradford C.	38	15	8	15	46:50	38
12	**TOTTENHAM**	**38**	**14**	**9**	**15**	**53:53**	**37**
13	Manchester U.	38	13	11	14	45:60	37
14	Sheffield U.	38	13	10	15	63:56	36
15	Manchester C.	38	13	9	16	56:58	35
16	Notts Co.	38	14	7	17	46:63	35
17	Liverpool	38	12	10	16	49:55	34
18	Oldham	38	12	10	16	46:54	34
19	Preston	38	13	7	18	40:57	33
20	Bury	38	6	9	23	32:59	21

SEASON 1912/13

Date	Comp	H/A	Opponent	Result	Score
2 Sep	Lge	H	Everton	L	0-2
7 Sep	Lge	H	Sheff Wed	L	2-4
14 Sep	Lge	A	Blackburn	L	1-6
21 Sep	Lge	H	Derby	L	1-2
23 Sep	LCC	H	Bromley	W	3-0
28 Sep	Lge	A	Sunderland	D	2-2
5 Oct	Lge	A	Middlesbro	D	1-1
14 Oct	LPCF	A	Fulham	L	0-1
19 Oct	Lge	A	Man Utd	L	0-2
26 Oct	Lge	H	Aston Villa	D	3-3
28 Oct	LCC	H	C. Palace	D	3-3
2 Nov	Lge	A	Liverpool	L	1-4
4 Nov	Lge	H	Notts Co.	L	0-3
9 Nov	Lge	H	Bolton	L	0-1
11 Nov	LCC	A	C. Palace	L	1-4
16 Nov	Lge	A	Sheff Utd	L	0-4
23 Nov	Lge	H	Newcastle	W	1-0
30 Nov	Lge	A	Oldham	L	1-4
7 Dec	Lge	H	Chelsea	W	1-0
14 Dec	Lge	A	Woolwich A.	W	3-0
21 Dec	Lge	H	Bradford C.	W	2-1
25 Dec	Lge	A	Man City	D	2-2
26 Dec	Lge	H	Man City	W	4-0
28 Dec	Lge	A	Sheff Wed	L	1-2
1 Jan	Lge	A	Everton	W	2-1
4 Jan	Lge	H	Blackburn	L	0-1
11 Jan	FC	H	Blackpool	D	1-1
16 Jan	FCr	*	Blackpool	W	6-1
18 Jan	Lge	A	Derby	L	0-5
25 Jan	Lge	H	Sunderland	L	1-2
1 Feb	FC	A	Reading	L	0-1
8 Feb	Lge	H	Middlesbro	W	5-3
15 Feb	Lge	A	Notts Co.	W	1-0
22 Feb	Lge	H	Sheff Utd	W	1-0
1 Mar	Lge	A	Aston Villa	L	0-1
8 Mar	Lge	H	Liverpool	W	1-0
15 Mar	Lge	A	Bolton	L	0-2
21 Mar	Lge	H	WBA	W	3-1
24 Mar	Lge	A	WBA	L	1-4
29 Mar	Lge	A	Newcastle	L	0-3
31 Mar	Lge	H	Man Utd	D	1-1
5 Apr	Lge	H	Oldham	W	1-0
9 Apr	F	A	Watford	D	0-0
12 Apr	Lge	A	Chelsea	L	0-1
19 Apr	Lge	H	Woolwich A.	D	1-1
26 Apr	Lge	A	Bradford C.	L	1-3
1 Mar	F	‡	Red Star	W	4-1
4 May	F	‡	French XI	W	9-0

‡ Played in Paris
* Blackpool sold home advantage; game played at White Hart Lane

Player	Lg App	Goals	Player	Lg App	Goals
Bliss H.	18	7	Middlemiss H.	38	8
Brittan R.C.	14		Minter W.J.	37	11
Cantrell J.	25	12	Newman E.	3	
Collins T.	28	1	Rance C.S.	32	
Curtis J.	4		Steel R.	19	1
Darnell J.	4		Tate J.A.	2	
Elliott J.	6	1	Tattersall W.	30	3
Grimsdell A.	25		Upton S.	2	
Jones G.	7		Walden F.	1	
Joyce J.W.	20		Webster F.	34	
Lightfoot E.J.	15		Weir F.	34	1
Lunn T.H.	16		Young C.	4	

Final table for First Division

1	Sunderland	38	25	4	9	86:43	54
2	Aston Villa	38	19	12	7	86:52	50
3	The Wednesday	38	21	7	10	75:55	49
4	Manchester U.	38	19	8	11	69:43	46
5	Blackburn	38	16	13	9	79:43	45
6	Manchester C.	38	18	8	12	53:37	44
7	Derby	38	17	8	13	69:66	42
8	Bolton	38	16	10	12	62:63	42
9	Oldham	38	14	14	10	50:55	42
10	West Bromwich	38	13	12	13	57:50	38
11	Everton	38	15	7	16	48:54	37
12	Liverpool	38	16	5	17	61:71	37
13	Bradford C.	38	12	11	15	50:60	35
14	Newcastle	38	13	8	17	47:47	34
15	Sheffield U.	38	14	6	18	56:70	34
16	Middlesbrough	38	11	10	17	55:69	32
17	**TOTTENHAM**	**38**	**12**	**6**	**20**	**45:72**	**30**
18	Chelsea	38	11	6	21	51:73	28
19	Notts Co.	38	7	9	22	28:56	23
20	Woolwich Asnl	38	3	12	23	26:74	18

SEASON 1913/14

Date	Comp	H/A	Opponent	Result	Score
1 Sep	Lge	A	Sheff Utd	W	4-1
6 Sep	Lge	A	Chelsea	W	3-1
8 Sep	Lge	H	Sheff Utd	W	2-1
13 Sep	Lge	H	Derby	D	1-1
20 Sep	Lge	A	Oldham	L	0-3
22 Sep	LCC	H	Metrogas	W	11-2
27 Sep	Lge	H	Man City	W	3-1
4 Oct	Lge	A	Man Utd	L	1-3
11 Oct	Lge	H	Bradford C.	D	0-0
14 Oct	LCC	A	Fulham	W	2-0
18 Oct	Lge	A	Burnley	L	1-3
25 Oct	Lge	H	Blackburn	D	3-3
27 Oct	LPCF	H	C. Palace	L	1-2
1 Nov	Lge	A	Preston	W	2-1
8 Nov	Lge	H	Sunderland	L	1-4
10 Nov	LCCsf	*	Arsenal	W	2-1
15 Nov	Lge	A	Newcastle	L	0-2
22 Nov	Lge	H	Everton	W	4-1
29 Nov	Lge	A	Liverpool	L	1-2
6 Dec	Lge	H	WBA	W	3-0
8 Dec	LCCf	†	C. Palace	L	1-2
13 Dec	Lge	A	Aston Villa	D	3-3
20 Dec	Lge	H	Sheff Wed	D	1-1
26 Dec	Lge	H	Middlesbro	L	0-1
27 Dec	Lge	H	Chelsea	L	1-2
1 Jan	Lge	A	Bolton	L	0-3
3 Jan	Lge	A	Derby	L	0-4
10 Jan	FC	A	Leicester	D	5-5
15 Jan	FCr	H	Leicester	W	2-0
17 Jan	Lge	H	Oldham	W	3-1
24 Jan	Lge	A	Man City	L	1-2
31 Jan	FC	A	Man City	L	1-2
7 Feb	Lge	H	Man Utd	W	2-1
14 Feb	Lge	A	Bradford C.	L	1-2
21 Feb	Lge	H	Burnley	W	2-0
28 Feb	Lge	A	Blackburn	D	1-1
5 Mar	F		Mus. Hall Arts	W	3-0
7 Mar	Lge	H	Preston	W	1-0
14 Mar	Lge	A	Sunderland	L	0-2
21 Mar	Lge	H	Newcastle	D	0-0
28 Mar	Lge	A	Everton	D	1-1
4 Apr	Lge	H	Liverpool	D	0-0
10 Apr	Lge	H	Bolton	W	3-0
11 Apr	Lge	A	WBA	D	1-1
13 Apr	Lge	A	Middlesbro	L	0-6
18 Apr	Lge	H	Aston Villa	L	0-2
25 Apr	Lge	A	Sheff Wed	L	0-2
3 May	F	‡	Hanover	W	6-3
6 May	F	‡	Nuremburg	D	1-1
9 May	F	‡	Bayern FC	W	6-0
10 May	F	‡	Furth	D	2-2
13 May	F	‡	Milan	W	5-0
17 May	F	‡	Zurich	W	6-0
21 May	F	‡	St Gallen	W	3-0
23 May	F	‡	Pforzheim	W	5-0
24 May	F	‡	Stuttgart	W	1-0

* Played at Stamford Bridge
† Played at Highbury
‡ Tour of Germany and Switzerland

Player	Lg App	Goals	Player	Lg App	Goals
Banks J.A.	12		King A.	19	
Bauchop J.R.	10	6	Lightfoot E.J.	2	1
Bliss H.	29	6	Middlemiss H.	34	4
Bowler G.	3		Minter W.J.	16	5
Cantrell J.	33	15	Newman E.	5	
Cartwright W.	13		Oliver W.	2	
Clay T.	15		Sparrow H.	3	4
Collins T.	15		Steel R.	37	
Crowl S.R.	1		Tate J.A.	2	
Darnell J.	1		Tattersall W.	7	
Elliot J.E.	1		Walden F.	30	5
Fleming J.B.M.	8	1	Webster F.	33	
Grimsdell A.	37	1	Weir F.	33	
Joyce J.W.	17	1	Own Goal		1

Final table for First Division

1	Blackburn	38	20	11	7	78:42	51
2	Aston Villa	38	19	6	13	65:50	44
3	Middlesbrough	38	19	5	14	77:60	43
4	Oldham	38	17	9	12	55:45	43
5	West Bromwich	38	15	13	10	46:42	43
6	Bolton	38	16	10	12	65:52	42
7	Sunderland	38	17	6	15	63:52	40
8	Chelsea	38	16	7	15	46:55	39
9	Bradford C.	38	12	14	12	40:40	38
10	Sheffield U.	38	16	5	17	63:60	37
11	Newcastle	38	13	11	14	39:48	37
12	Burnley	38	12	12	14	61:53	36
13	Manchester C.	38	14	8	16	51:53	36
14	Manchester U.	38	15	6	17	52:62	36
15	Everton	38	12	11	15	46:55	35
16	Liverpool	38	14	7	17	46:62	35
17	**TOTTENHAM**	**38**	**12**	**10**	**16**	**50:62**	**34**
18	The Wednesday	38	13	8	17	53:70	34
19	Preston	38	12	6	20	52:69	30
20	Derby	38	8	11	19	55:71	27

SEASON 1914/15

22 Aug	WRF	H	Arsenal	L	1-5
2 Sep	Lge	H	Everton	L	1-3
5 Sep	Lge	H	Chelsea	D	1-1
12 Sep	Lge	A	Bradford C,	D	2-2
19 Sep	Lge	H	Burnley	L	1-3
21 Sep	LCC	A	Nunhead	W	2-1
26 Sep	Lge	A	Man City	L	1-2
28 Sep	Lge	H	WBA	W	2-0
3 Oct	Lge	A	Newcastle	L	0-4
10 Oct	Lge	H	Middlesbro	D	3-3
15 Oct	F	A	Chelsea	D	1-1
17 Oct	Lge	A	Sheff Utd	D	1-1
19 Oct	LCC	A	C. Palace	L	1-3
24 Oct	Lge	H	Aston Villa	L	0-2
28 Oct	LPCF	A	C. Palace	D	2-2
31 Oct	Lge	A	Liverpool	L	2-7
7 Nov	Lge	H	Bradford PA	W	3-0
14 Nov	Lge	A	Oldham	L	1-4
21 Nov	Lge	H	Man Utd	W	2-0
28 Nov	Lge	A	Bolton	L	2-4
5 Dec	Lge	H	Blackburn	L	0-4
12 Dec	Lge	A	Notts Co.	W	2-1
19 Dec	Lge	H	Sunderland	L	0-6
25 Dec	Lge	A	Sheff Wed	L	2-3
26 Dec	Lge	H	Sheff Wed	W	6-1
1 Jan	Lge	H	Everton	D	1-1
2 Jan	Lge	A	Chelsea	D	1-1
9 Jan	FC	H	Sunderland	W	2-1
16 Jan	Lge	H	Bradford C.	D	0-0
23 Jan	Lge	A	Burnley	L	1-3
30 Jan	FC	A	Norwich	L	2-3
6 Feb	F	H	Fulham	D	2-2
13 Feb	Lge	A	Middlesbro	L	5-7
20 Feb	Lge	H	Notts Co	W	2-0
27 Feb	Lge	A	Aston Villa	L	1-3
6 Mar	Lge	H	Liverpool	D	1-1
13 Mar	Lge	A	Bradford PA	L	1-5
15 Mar	Lge	H	Man City	D	2-2
20 Mar	Lge	H	Oldham	W	1-0
27 Mar	Lge	A	Man Utd	D	1-1
2 Apr	Lge	H	Newcastle	D	0-0
3 Apr	Lge	H	Bolton	W	4-2
6 Apr	Lge	A	WBA	L	2-3
10 Apr	Lge	A	Blackburn	L	1-4
17 Apr	F	H	Cameron High.	L	1-2
19 Apr	Lge	H	Sheff Utd	D	1-1
24 Apr	Lge	A	Sunderland	L	0-5

Player	Lg App	Goals	Player	Lg App	Goals
Banks J.A.	5		Lowe H.	2	
Bliss H.	33	21	Middlemiss H.	33	3
Cantrell J.	26	14	Minter W.J.	26	5
Clay T.	38	4	Pearson J.	17	
Collins T.	12		Rance C.S.	3	
Darnell J.	11		Sparrow H.	15	3
Eadon J.	5		Steel R.	36	2
Fleming J.B.M.	11	2	Tattersall W.	5	
Grimsdell A.	8		Walden F.	38	1
Jacques W.	28		Webster F.	9	
Joyce J.W.	5		Weir F.	29	1
Lightfoot E.J.	23	1			

Final table for First Division

1	Everton	38	19	8 11	76:47	46
2	Oldham	38	17	11 10	70:56	45
3	Blackburn	38	18	7 13	83:61	43
4	Burnley	38	18	7 13	61:47	43
5	Manchester C.	38	15	13 10	49:39	43
6	Sheffield U.	38	15	13 10	49:41	43
7	The Wednesday	38	15	13 10	61:54	43
8	Sunderland	38	18	5 15	81:72	41
9	Bradford P.A.	38	17	7 14	69:65	41
10	West Bromwich	38	15	10 13	51:43	40
11	Bradford C.	38	13	14 11	55:51	40
12	Middlesbrough	38	13	12 13	62:74	38
13	Liverpool	38	14	9 15	65:75	37
14	Aston Villa	38	13	11 14	62:72	37
15	Newcastle	38	11	10 17	46:48	32
16	Notts Co.	28	9	13 16	41:57	31
17	Bolton	38	11	8 19	68:84	30
18	Manchester U.	38	9	12 17	46:62	30
19	Chelsea	38	8	13 17	51:65	29
20	**TOTTENHAM**	**38**	**8**	**12 18**	**57:90**	**28**

SEASON 1915/16

4 Sep	Lge	A	Arsenal	L	0-2
11 Sep	Lge	H	Brentford	D	1-1
18 Sep	Lge	A	West Ham	D	1-1
25 Sep	Lge	H	Chelsea	L	1-3
2 Oct	Lge	H	C. Palace	L	2-4
9 Oct	Lge	A	QPR	W	4-0
16 Oct	Lge	H	Fulham	W	3-1
23 Oct	Lge	A	C. Orient	D	0-0
30 Oct	Lge	H	Watford	W	3-0
6 Nov	Lge	A	Millwall	L	2-3
13 Nov	Lge	H	Arsenal	D	3-3
20 Nov	Lge	A	Brentford	D	1-1
27 Nov	Lge	H	West Ham	W	3-0
4 Dec	Lge	A	Chelsea	L	1-8
11 Dec	Lge	A	C. Palace	L	2-4
18 Dec	Lge	H	QPR	W	2-1
25 Dec	Lge	H	Croydon Comm	W	3-0
27 Dec	Lge	A	Croydon Comm	D	0-0
1 Jan	Lge	A	Fulham	W	2-0
8 Jan	Lge	H	C. Orient	D	1-1
15 Jan	Lge	A	Watford	W	1-0
22 Jan	Lge	H	Millwall	D	2-2
29 Jan	F	H	C. Orient	L	0-1
5 Feb	LSupp	A	West Ham	L	0-2
12 Feb	LSupp	H	Croydon Comm	W	1-0
19 Feb	LSupp	A	Fulham	L	1-3
26 Feb	LSupp	H	Luton	W	7-4
4 Mar	LSupp	A	Arsenal	W	3-0
11 Mar	LSupp	H	QPR	D	0-0
18 Mar	LSupp	A	Croydon	D	3-3
25 Mar	LSupp	H	Fulham	W	4-0
1 Apr	LSupp	A	Luton	W	2-1
8 Apr	LSupp	H	Arsenal	W	3-2
15 Apr	LSupp	A	QPR	W	3-1
21 Apr	LSupp	H	C. Palace	W	3-1
24 Apr	LSupp	A	C. Palace	L	0-4
26 Apr	F	A	Norwich	D	1-1
29 Apr	LSupp	H	West Ham	D	1-1
6 May	F	A	C. Orient	L	2-3

Player	War Lg App	Goals	Player	War Lg App	Goals
Banks J.	17	7	Knighton T.	4	2
Barton P.	29	1	Lloyd H.	12	6
Bassett E.	28	9	Minter A.	3	1
Bliss H.	33	23	Morris J.	35	3
Chaplin A.	4		Page J.	1	
Clay T.	32	4	Page R.	3	
Darnell J.	15		Ralston A.	17	
Doyle J.	1		Rance C.	36	4
Elliott J.	33		Steel R.	29	6
Fricker F.	1		Thomas D.	9	1
Glen P.	1	1	Travers G.	3	
Hopkins T.	3	1	Watkins W.	1	
Jacques W.	18		Weir F.	1	
Joyce J.	17		Wilson A.	10	

London Combination 1915–16

1	Chelsea	22	17	3	2	71:18	37
2	Millwall	22	12	6	4	46:24	30
3	Arsenal	22	10	5	7	43:46	25
4	West Ham	22	10	4	8	47:35	24
5	Fulham	22	10	4	8	45:37	24
6	**TOTTENHAM**	**22**	**8**	**8**	**8**	**38:35**	**24**
7	Brentford	22	6	8	8	36:40	20
8	QPR	22	8	3	11	27:41	19
9	C. Palace	22	8	3	11	35:55	19
10	Watford	22	8	1	13	37:46	17
11	Clapton O.	22	4	6	12	22:44	14
12	Croydon Comm	22	3	5	14	24:50	11

Supplementary Tournament Group 1915–16

1	Chelsea	14	10	1	3	50:15	21
2	**TOTTENHAM**	**14**	**8**	**3**	**3**	**31:22**	**19**
3	Millwall	14	8	2	4	30:22	18
4	Watford	14	5	3	6	22:20	13
5	Brentford	14	5	2	7	29:33	12
6	Clapton O.	14	3	4	7	17:27	10
7	Reading	14	3	2	9	23:64	8

242

SEASON 1916/17

Date	Comp		Opponent		Result
2 Sep	Lge	H	Chelsea	L	0-2
9 Sep	Lge	A	Arsenal	D	1-1
16 Sep	Lge	*	Luton	L	2-3
23 Sep	Lge	A	Reading	W	4-2
30 Sep	Lge	†	Millwall	L	1-4
7 Oct	Lge	A	Watford	W	2-0
14 Oct	Lge	A	C. Orient	W	4-2
21 Oct	Lge	A	Fulham	L	1-2
28 Oct	Lge	†	QPR	L	4-5
4 Nov	Lge	A	West Ham	L	1-5
11 Nov	Lge	A	Southampton	L	0-1
18 Nov	Lge	*	C. Palace	W	3-1
25 Nov	Lge	A	Chelsea	W	4-2
2 Dec	Lge	*	Arsenal	W	4-1
9 Dec	Lge	A	Luton	W	3-1
16 Dec	Lge	*	Portsmouth	W	1-0‡
23 Dec	Lge	A	Millwall	D	3-3
25 Dec	Lge	A	Brentford	W	5-1
26 Dec	Lge	†	Brentford	W	5-2
30 Dec	Lge	*	Watford	W	3-0
6 Jan	Lge	A	C. Orient	W	2-1
13 Jan	Lge	†	Fulham	W	1-0
20 Jan	Lge	A	QPR	D	1-1
27 Jan	Lge	*	West Ham	W	
3 Feb	Lge	*	Southampton	W	3-1
10 Feb	Lge	A	C. Palace	W	1-0
17 Feb	Lge	A	Portsmouth	W	4-2
24 Feb	Lge	*	C. Palace	W	4-1
3 Mar	Lge	*	Luton	W	3-2
10 Mar	Lge	A	Southampton	W	4-2
17 Mar	Lge	*	C. Orient	W	5-2
24 Mar	Lge	A	West Ham	L	0-3
31 Mar	Lge	*	Portsmouth	W	10-0
6 Apr	Lge	†	Arsenal	D	0-0
7 Apr	Lge	A	C. Palace	W	3-0
9 Apr	Lge	A	Arsenal	L	2-3
10 Apr	Lge	*	Portsmouth	W	2-1
14 Apr	Lge	A	Luton	L	4-5
21 Apr	Lge	†	Southampton	W	4-0
28 Apr	Lge	A	C. Orient	W	8-0
5 May	F	A	West Ham	D	3-3

* White Hart Lane commissioned by War Office. Home games played at Highbury

† Home games played at Homerton, ground of Clapton Orient

‡ Abandoned

Player	War Lg App	Goals	Player	War Lg App	Goals
Banks J.	31	30	Jacques W.	38	
Barton P.	37	5	Lloyd H.	23	1
Bassett J.	36	26	McVey J.	2	
Bearman F.	1		Middlemiss H.	2	1
Bliss H.	26	19	Morris J.	4	1
Caldwell T.	1		Potter H.	13	4
Clay T.	30	3	Powell H.	1	
Clayton A.	1		Ralston A.	37	
Croft F.	2		Rance C.	23	1
Croft W.	2		Slade H.	1	
Crossley J.	1		Smith J.	1	
Crowl S.	12	1	Thwaites W.	9	3
Darnell J.	14	2	Travers G.	3	1
Elliott J.	36	3	Walden F.	30	6
Grimes W.	3	1	Watkin W.	1	
Hannaford C.	1	1	Weir F.	3	
Hawkins W.	9	2	Williamson E.	1	
Hoad S.	4		Own Goal		1
Hunt K.	1				

London Combination 1916–17

1	West Ham	40	30	5	5	110:45	65
2	Millwall	40	26	6	8	85:48	58
3	Chelsea	40	24	5	11	93:48	53
4	TOTTENHAM	40	24	5	11	112:62	53
5	Arsenal	40	19	10	11	62:47	48
6	Fulham	40	21	3	16	102:63	45
7	Luton	39	20	3	16	101:82	43
8	C. Palace	38	14	7	17	68:72	35
9	Southampton	39	13	8	18	57:80	34
10	QPR	39	10	9	20	48:86	29
11	Watford	39	8	9	22	69:115	25
12	Brentford	40	9	7	24	56:99	25
*13	Portsmouth	40	9	4	27	58:117	22
14	Clapton O.	40	6	7	27	49:104	19

* Took over record of Reading who had played and lost 7 games with 8 goals for and 34 against.
Note C. Palace v Luton, QPR v Watford, Southampton v C. Palace were never played. Each team played the others twice and then played *any* 7 of their rivals according to fixture availability.

SEASON 1917/18

Date	Comp		Opponent		Result
1 Sep	Lge	A	C. Palace	W	4-2
8 Sep	Lge	*	Chelsea	L	0-4
15 Sep	Lge	A	Brentford	L	2-5
22 Sep	Lge	*	Arsenal	L	1-2
29 Sep	Lge	A	West Ham	L	0-1
6 Oct	Lge	*	Fulham	W	1-0
13 Oct	Lge	A	QPR	W	3-2
20 Oct	Lge	†	C. Orient	W	2-1
27 Oct	Lge	*	C. Palace	W	1-0
3 Nov	Lge	A	Chelsea	D	0-0
10 Nov	Lge	*	Brentford	W	6-1
17 Nov	Lge	†	Arsenal	W	1-0
24 Nov	Lge	*	West Ham	W	2-0
1 Dec	Lge	A	Fulham	L	3-4
8 Dec	Lge	†	QPR	L	0-1
15 Dec	Lge	A	C. Orient	W	4-2
22 Dec	Lge	A	C. Palace	W	3-2
25 Dec	Lge	A	Millwall	W	5-0
26 Dec	Lge	†	Millwall	L	0-1
29 Dec	Lge	*	Chelsea	W	2-0
5 Jan	Lge	A	Brentford	W	3-2
12 Jan	Lge	A	Arsenal	W	4-1
19 Jan	Lge	A	West Ham	D	2-2
26 Jan	Lge	*	Fulham	L	0-1
2 Feb	Lge	A	QPR	W	7-2
9 Feb	Lge	†	Millwall	W	4-2
16 Feb	Lge	*	C. Palace	W	8-0
23 Feb	Lge	A	Chelsea	L	0-3
2 Mar	Lge	*	Brentford	W	3-0
9 Mar	Lge	A	Arsenal	L	1-4
16 Mar	Lge	*	West Ham	L	0-5
23 Mar	Lge	A	Fulham	W	3-0
29 Mar	Lge	A	C. Orient	W	3-2
30 Mar	Lge	†	QPR	L	1-2
1 Apr	Lge	†	C. Orient	W	5-2
6 Apr	Lge	A	Millwall	W	1-0
13 Apr	F	A	Chelsea	D	1-1
20 Apr	F	*	Chelsea	L	0-1
27 Apr	F	A	Fulham	L	0-3
4 May	F	‡	Fulham	L	2-3

* Home games played at Highbury

† Home games played at Homerton

‡ Played at Upton Park

Player	War Lg App	Goals	Player	War Lg App	Goals
Ayres	2		Jacques W.	29	
Baldwin	1		Laurence A.	5	1
Banks J.	33	21	Lightfoot E.	2	
Barnard	1	2	Lindsay A.	8	
Barton P.	4		Lindsay D.	5	2
Bassett E.	7	1	Lloyd H.	1	
Beaton	2		Middlemiss H.	6	2
Bird	1		Minter W.	3	4
Bliss H.	2		Nuttall J.	18	9
Brown R.	2		Peake	15	7
Clay T.	20		Potter H.	5	
Coomber G.	14	2	Ralston A.	36	
Crosswell T.	11		Rance C.	36	3
Crowl S.	1		Robinson	1	
Darnell J.	20		Saunders	1	1
Elliott J.	36	1	Spencer	1	1
Fleming J.	1		Thomas D.	7	1
Goldthorpe	7	5	Thwaites W.	2	
Halle W.	1		Tomkin	12	
Hawkins W.	36	10	Walden F.	33	7
Hill	2		Wren	1	
Hoffman	1		Own Goal		1
Jack	6	4			

London Combination 1917–18

1	Chelsea	36	21	8	7	82:39	50
2	West Ham	36	20	9	7	103:51	49
3	Fulham	36	20	7	9	75:60	47
4	TOTTENHAM	36	22	2	12	85:55	46
5	Arsenal	36	16	5	15	76:56	37
6	Brentford	36	16	3	17	81:95	35
7	C.Palace	36	13	4	19	54:83	30
8	QPR	36	14	2	20	48:73	30
9	Millwall	36	12	4	20	52:72	28
10	C. Orient	36	2	4	30	34:104	8

SEASON 1918/19

Date	Comp		Opponent	Res	Score
31 Aug	F	A	RAMC XI	D	1-1
7 Sep	Lge	A	Fulham	D	2-2
14 Sep	Lge	†	Brentford	D	1-1
21 Sep	Lge	A	West Ham	W	1-0
28 Sep	Lge	†	C. Orient	W	2-0
5 Oct	Lge	*	Chelsea	W	2-1
12 Oct	Lge	A	Arsenal	L	0-3
19 Oct	Lge	*	C. Palace	W	2-0
26 Oct	Lge	A	Millwall	W	2-0
2 Nov	Lge	†	Fulham	W	1-0
9 Nov	Lge	A	Brentford	L	1-7
16 Nov	Lge	†	West Ham	L	1-4
23 Nov	Lge	A	C. Orient	W	3-0
30 Nov	Lge	A	Chelsea	L	1-3
7 Dec	Lge	*	Arsenal	W	1-0
14 Dec	Lge	A	C. Palace	L	3-6
21 Dec	Lge	†	Millwall	L	0-3
25 Dec	Lge	A	QPR	D	1-1
26 Dec	Lge	†	QPR	D	0-0
28 Dec	Lge	A	Fulham	L	1-3
4 Jan	Lge	*	Brentford	D	1-1
11 Jan	Lge	A	West Ham	L	0-2
18 Jan	Lge	†	C. Orient	L	2-4
25 Jan	Lge	*	Chelsea	D	1-1
1 Feb	Lge	A	Arsenal	W	3-2
8 Feb	Lge	*	C. Palace	W	4-2
15 Feb	Lge	A	QPR	L	1-7
22 Feb	Lge	†	Fulham	L	0-2
1 Mar	Lge	A	Brentford	L	1-4
8 Mar	Lge	†	West Ham	L	0-1
15 Mar	Lge	A	C. Orient	W	2-1
22 Mar	Lge	A	Chelsea	W	2-1
29 Mar	Lge	*	Arsenal	L	0-1
5 Apr	Lge	A	C. Palace	D	2-2
12 Apr	Lge	*	QPR	L	2-3
18 Apr	Lge	*	Millwall	D	2-2
19 Apr	VC	‡	Fulham	L	0-2
21 Apr	Lge	A	Millwall	W	4-2
26 Apr	F	A	C. Orient	L	1-6

* Home games at Highbury
† Home games at Homerton
‡ Played at Stamford Bridge

Player	War Lg App	Goals	Player	War Lg App	Goals
Banks J.	27	5	Hoffman	1	
Barnard	7	2	Jack	13	3
Barton	14		Jacques W.	16	
Beaton S.	6		Jennings	1	
Bennett	4	1	Lindsay A.	16	
Blake H.	1		Lindsay C.	3	
Bliss H.	2	2	Lindsay D.	14	4
Bowlier	1		Lloyd	1	
Brown R.	1		McCalmont	1	1
Buley	1		McIver	3	
Cain	1	1	Middlemiss H.	4	3
Cantrell J.	2		Minter W.	9	9
Chester	2		Parsons	1	
Clay T.	24		Patterson	1	
Couchman	1		Peake	4	1
Darnell J.	21		Potter	2	
Dockray	11		Ralston A.	10	
Duncan	1		Rance C.	34	3
Eaden	1		Simmons	3	2
Elliott J.	18	1	Smith E.	4	
Fraser	1		Smith J.	5	1
Freeman	2		Thomas	8	4
Gee	2		Tomkins	21	
Goldthorpe	10	4	Walden F.	4	1
Grimsdell A.	9		Walters C.	1	
Hadyn-Price	9	3	Williams C.	3	1
Harbridge	2		Worral	11	
Hawkins	21				

London Combination 1918–19

1	Brentford	36	20	9	7	94:46	49
2	Arsenal	36	20	5	11	85:56	45
3	West Ham	36	17	7	12	65:51	41
4	Fulham	36	17	6	13	70:55	40
5	QPR	36	16	7	13	69:60	39
6	Chelsea	36	13	11	12	70:53	37
7	C. Palace	36	14	6	16	66:73	34
8	**TOTTENHAM**	36	13	8	15	52:72	34
9	Millwall	36	10	9	17	50:67	29
10	C. Orient	36	3	6	27	35:123	12

SEASON 1919/20

Date	Comp		Opponent	Res	Score
30 Aug	Lge	A	Coventry	W	5-0
1 Sep	Lge	H	Leicester	W	4-0
6 Sep	Lge	H	Coventry	W	4-1
11 Sep	Lge	A	Leicester	W	4-2
13 Sep	Lge	H	Sth Shields	W	2-0
20 Sep	Lge	H	Sth Shields	W	3-0
22 Sep	LnC	H	Millwall	W	6-0
27 Sep	Lge	H	Lincoln	W	6-1
29 Sep	F	A	Arsenal	W	1-0
4 Oct	Lge	A	Lincoln	D	1-1
6 Oct	LnC	A	C. Palace	L	2-3
11 Oct	Lge	H	C. Orient	W	2-1
18 Oct	Lge	A	C. Orient	W	4-0
27 Oct	Lge	A	Port Vale	W	1-0
1 Nov	Lge	H	Port Vale	W	1-0
8 Nov	Lge	A	Bury	L	1-2
15 Nov	Lge	H	Bury	W	2-1
22 Nov	Lge	A	Nottm Forest	D	1-1
29 Nov	Lge	H	Nottm Forest	W	5-2
6 Dec	Lge	A	Fulham	W	4-1
13 Dec	Lge	H	Fulham	W	4-0
15 Dec	F	H	Corinthians	W	4-1
20 Dec	Lge	A	Barnsley	L	0-3
25 Dec	Lge	H	Hull City	W	4-0
26 Dec	Lge	A	Hull City	W	3-1
27 Dec	Lge	H	Barnsley	W	4-0
3 Jan	Lge	A	Stockport	W	2-1
10 Jan	FC	A	Bristol Rvs	W	4-1
17 Jan	Lge	H	Stockport	W	2-0
24 Jan	Lge	A	Huddersfield	D	1-1
31 Jan	FC	H	West Stanley	W	4-0
7 Feb	Lge	A	Blackpool	W	1-0
14 Feb	Lge	H	Blackpool	D	2-2
16 Feb	Lge	H	Huddersfield	W	2-0
21 Feb	FC	H	West Ham	W	3-0
25 Feb	Lge	A	Bristol City	W	2-1
28 Feb	Lge	H	Bristol City	W	2-0
6 Mar	FC	H	Aston Villa	L	0-1
13 Mar	Lge	A	West Ham	L	1-2
20 Mar	Lge	H	Rotherham	W	2-0
22 Mar	Lge	H	West Ham	W	2-0
27 Mar	Lge	A	Rotherham	D	1-1
2 Apr	Lge	H	Wolves	W	4-2
3 Apr	Lge	H	Stoke	W	2-0
5 Apr	Lge	A	Wolves	W	3-1
10 Apr	Lge	A	Stoke	W	3-1
17 Apr	Lge	H	Grimsby	W	3-1
19 Apr	F	A	Mid Rhondda	D	0-0*
24 Apr	Lge	A	Grimsby	L	0-2
26 Apr	Lge	H	Birmingham	D	0-0
1 May	Lge	A	Birmingham	W	1-0
8 May	LCC	A	Norwich	W	4-0
15 May	CS	H	WBA	L	0-2

* Abandoned after 25 minutes

Player	Lg App	Goals	Player	Lg App	Goals
Archibald J.	13		Lorimer H.H.	4	
Banks J.A.	19	2	Lowe H.	1	
Bliss H.	42	31	McDonald R.J.	1	
Brown R.S.	20		Middlemiss H.	3	
Cantrell J.	30	19	Minter W.J.	19	7
Castle S.R.	2		Pearson J.	21	
Chipperfield J.	15	6	Rance C.S.	26	
Clay T.	27	2	Sage W.	1	
Dimmock J.H.	27	5	Seed J.M.	5	1
Elliott J.E.	1		Skinner J.F.	3	
Goodman A.A.	16	1	Smith B.	40	2
Grimsdell A.	37	14	Walden F.	32	4
Jacques W.	41		Walters C.	1	
Leese F.H.	1		Wilson C.	11	7
Lindsay A.F.	3		Own Goal		1

Final table for Second Division

1	**TOTTENHAM**	42	32	6	4	102:32	70
2	Huddersfield	42	28	8	6	97:38	64
3	Birmingham	42	24	8	10	85:34	56
4	Blackpool	42	21	10	11	65:47	52
5	Bury	42	20	8	14	60:44	48
6	Fulham	42	19	9	14	61:50	47
7	West Ham	42	19	9	14	47:40	47
8	Bristol C.	42	13	17	12	46:43	43
9	South Shields	42	15	12	15	58:48	42
10	Stoke	42	18	6	18	60:54	42
11	Hull	42	18	6	18	78:72	42
12	Barnsley	42	15	10	17	61:55	40
13	Port Vale	42	16	8	18	59:62	40
14	Leicester	42	15	10	17	41:61	40
15	Clapton Orient	42	16	6	20	51:59	38
16	Stockport	42	14	9	19	52:61	37
17	Rotherham Co.	42	13	8	21	51:83	34
18	Nottingham F.	42	11	9	22	43:73	31
19	Wolverhampton	42	10	10	22	55:80	30
20	Coventry	42	9	11	22	35:73	29
21	Lincoln	42	9	9	24	44:101	27
22	Grimsby	42	10	5	27	34:75	25

SEASON 1920/21

Date	Comp	H/A	Opponent	Result	Score
28 Aug	Lge	H	Blackburn	L	1-2
30 Aug	Lge	A	Derby	D	2-2
4 Sep	Lge	A	Blackburn	D	1-1
6 Sep	Lge	H	Derby	W	2-0
11 Sep	Lge	A	Aston Villa	L	2-4
18 Sep	Lge	H	Aston Villa	L	1-2
25 Sep	Lge	A	Man Utd	W	1-0
2 Oct	Lge	H	Man Utd	W	4-1
9 Oct	Lge	H	Chelsea	W	5-0
11 Oct	LCC	A	Barking	W	4-1
16 Oct	Lge	A	Chelsea	W	4-0
23 Oct	Lge	H	Burnley	L	1-2
25 Oct	LPCF	H	Arsenal	W	2-0
30 Oct	Lge	A	Burnley	L	0-2
1 Nov	LCC	H	Arsenal	W	3-1
6 Nov	Lge	H	Oldham	W	5-1
13 Nov	Lge	H	Oldham	W	5-2
18 Nov	F	A	Oxford Univ	L	0-1
20 Nov	Lge	H	Preston	L	1-2
27 Nov	Lge	A	Preston	L	1-4
4 Dec	Lge	H	Sheff Utd	W	4-1
11 Dec	Lge	A	Sheff Utd	D	1-1
18 Dec	Lge	H	Bolton	W	5-2
25 Dec	Lge	A	Newcastle	D	1-1
27 Dec	Lge	H	Newcastle	W	2-0
1 Jan	Lge	A	Bolton	L	0-1
8 Jan	FC	H	Bristol Rvs	W	6-2
15 Jan	Lge	H	Arsenal	W	2-1
22 Jan	Lge	A	Arsenal	L	2-3
29 Jan	FC	H	Bradford C	W	4-0
3 Feb	Lge	H	Bradford PA	W	2-0
5 Feb	Lge	A	Bradford PA	D	1-1
12 Feb	Lge	H	Man City	W	2-0
19 Feb	FC	A	Southend	W	4-1
23 Feb	Lge	A	West Brom	L	1-3
26 Feb	Lge	H	West Brom	W	1-0
5 Mar	FC	H	Aston Villa	W	1-0
9 Mar	Lge	A	Man City	L	0-2
12 Mar	Lge	H	Everton	W	2-0
19 Mar	FCsf	*	Preston	W	2-1
25 Mar	Lge	A	Liverpool	D	1-1
26 Mar	Lge	A	Sunderland	W	1-0
28 Mar	Lge	H	Liverpool	W	1-0
2 Apr	Lge	H	Sunderland	D	0-0
9 Apr	Lge	A	Bradford C	L	0-1
11 Apr	LCC	†	C. Orient	L	1-2
16 Apr	Lge	H	Bradford C	W	2-0
23 Apr	FCf	‡	Wolves	W	1-0
25 Apr	Lge	A	Huddersfield	L	0-2
27 Apr	Lge	A	Everton	D	0-0
30 Apr	Lge	H	Huddersfield	W	1-0
2 May	Lge	A	Middlesbrough	L	0-1
7 May	Lge	A	Middlesbrough	D	2-2
14 May	F	A	Fulham	W	4-0
16 May	CS	H	Burnley	W	2-0

* at Hillsborough
† at Highbury
‡ at Stamford Bridge

Player	Lg App	Goals	Player	Lg App	Goals
Archibald J.	6	1	Lindsay A.F.	5	
Banks J.A.	20	3	Lowe H.	5	
Bliss H.	36	17	McDonald R.J.	36	
Brown R.S.	2		Pearson J.	5	
Cantrell J.	23	7	Rance C.S.	14	
Castle S.R.	3		Seed J.M.	37	12
Clay T.	35	1	Skinner J.F.	2	
Dimmock J.H.	41	9	Smith B.	36	3
Forester M.	7		Thompson A.	3	
Grimsdell A.	38	3	Walden F.	22	5
Hunter A.C.	11		Walters C.	25	
Jacques W.	30		Wilson C.	20	9

Final table for First Division

1	Burnley	42	23 13 6	79:36	59
2	Manchester C.	42	24 6 12	70:50	54
3	Bolton	42	19 14 9	77:53	52
4	Liverpool	42	18 15 9	63:35	51
5	Newcastle	42	20 10 12	66:45	50
6	TOTTENHAM	42	19 9 14	70:48	47
7	Everton	42	17 13 12	66:55	47
8	Middlesbrough	42	17 12 13	53:53	46
9	The Arsenal	42	15 14 13	59:63	44
10	Aston Villa	42	18 7 17	63:70	43
11	Blackburn	42	13 15 14	57:59	41
12	Sunderland	42	14 13 15	57:60	41
13	Manchester U.	42	15 10 17	64:68	40
14	West Bromwich	42	13 14 15	54:58	40
15	Bradford C.	42	12 15 15	61:63	39
16	Preston	42	15 9 18	61:65	39
17	Huddersfield	42	15 9 18	42:49	39
18	Chelsea	42	13 13 16	48:58	39
19	Oldham	42	9 15 18	49:86	33
20	Sheffield U.	42	6 18 18	42:68	30
21	Derby	42	5 16 21	32:58	26
22	Bradford PA	42	8 8 26	43:76	24

SEASON 1921/22

Date	Comp	H/A	Opponent	Result	Score
27 Aug	Lge	A	Cardiff	W	1-0
29 Aug	Lge	H	Bolton	L	1-2
3 Sep	Lge	H	Cardiff	W	4-1
5 Sep	Lge	A	Bolton	L	0-1
10 Sep	Lge	H	Middlesbro	L	2-4
12 Sep	LPCF	A	West Ham	L	0-1
17 Sep	Lge	A	Middlesbro	D	0-0
19 Sep	F	A	Partick This.	L	1-3
22 Sep	F	A	Inverness Cale.	L	3-6
24 Sep	Lge	H	Aston Villa	W	3-1
1 Oct	Lge	A	Aston Villa	L	1-2
6 Oct	F	H	Corinthians	W	2-1
8 Oct	Lge	H	Man Utd	D	2-2
15 Oct	Lge	A	Man Utd	L	1-2
17 Oct	LCC	H	London Cal	W	5-0
22 Oct	Lge	H	Liverpool	L	0-1
29 Oct	Lge	A	Liverpool	D	1-1
31 Oct	LCC	H	Brentford	D	1-1
5 Nov	Lge	H	Newcastle	W	4-0
7 Nov	LCCr	A	Brentford	W	3-2
12 Nov	Lge	A	Newcastle	W	1-0
14 Nov	LCCsf	*	Arsenal	D	0-0
19 Nov	Lge	H	Burnley	D	1-1
21 Nov	LCCsfr	†	Arsenal	L	1-2
26 Nov	Lge	A	Burnley	L	0-1
1 Dec	F	A	Oxford Univ	W	1-0
3 Dec	Lge	H	Sheff Utd	W	2-1
10 Dec	Lge	A	Sheff Utd	L	0-1
17 Dec	Lge	H	Chelsea	D	0-0
24 Dec	Lge	A	Chelsea	W	2-1
26 Dec	Lge	H	Bradford C.	W	1-0
27 Dec	Lge	A	Bradford C.	W	4-0
31 Dec	Lge	H	Preston	W	5-0
7 Jan	FC	A	Brentford	W	2-0
14 Jan	Lge	A	Preston	W	2-1
21 Jan	Lge	A	WBA	L	0-3
28 Jan	FC	H	Watford	W	1-0
30 Jan	Lge	H	WBA	W	2-0
4 Feb	Lge	A	Man City	D	3-3
11 Feb	Lge	H	Man City	W	3-1
13 Feb	F	H	Oxford Univ	W	4-3
18 Feb	FC	H	Man City	W	2-1
25 Feb	Lge	H	Everton	W	2-0
4 Mar	FC	A	Cardiff	D	1-1
9 Mar	FCr	H	Cardiff	W	2-1
11 Mar	Lge	H	Sunderland	W	1-0
15 Mar	Lge	A	Everton	D	0-0
18 Mar	Lge	H	Huddersfield	W	1-0
25 Mar	FCsf	‡	Preston	L	1-2
27 Mar	Lge	A	Huddersfield	D	1-1
1 Apr	Lge	A	Birmingham	W	3-0
5 Apr	Lge	A	Sunderland	L	0-2
8 Apr	Lge	H	Birmingham	W	2-1
14 Apr	Lge	H	Oldham	W	3-1
15 Apr	Lge	H	Arsenal	W	2-0
17 Apr	Lge	A	Oldham	L	0-1
22 Apr	Lge	A	Arsenal	L	0-1
29 Apr	Lge	H	Blackburn	W	2-1
6 May	Lge	A	Blackburn	D	1-1

* at Stamford Bridge † at Homerton ‡ at Hillsborough

Player	Lg App	Goals	Player	Lg App	Goals
Archibald J.	5		Lorimer H.H.	1	
Banks J.A.	11	1	Lowe H.	12	
Blake H.E.	8		McDonald R.J.	40	
Bliss H.	23	7	Pearson J.	3	
Cantrell J.	13	3	Seed J.M.	36	10
Clay T.	37	8	Skinner J.F.	16	2
Dimmock J.H.	42	7	Smith B.	25	
Forster M.	4		Thompson A.	18	6
Grimsdell A.	35	3	Walden F.	28	2
Handley C.H.J.	1		Walters C.	33	
Hunter A.C.	12		Wilson C.	21	11
Jacques W.	22		Own Goals		2
Lindsay A.F.	16	3			

Final table for First Division

1	Liverpool	42	22 13 7	63:36	57
2	TOTTENHAM	42	21 9 12	65:39	51
3	Burnley	42	22 5 15	72:54	49
4	Cardiff	42	19 10 13	61:53	48
5	Aston Villa	42	22 3 17	74:55	47
6	Bolton	42	20 7 15	68:59	47
7	Newcastle	42	18 10 14	59:45	46
8	Middlesbrough	42	16 14 12	79:69	46
9	Chelsea	42	17 12 13	40:43	46
10	Manchester C.	42	18 9 15	65:70	45
11	Sheffield U.	42	15 10 17	59:54	40
12	Sunderland	42	16 8 18	60:62	40
13	West Bromwich	42	15 10 17	51:63	40
14	Huddersfield	42	15 9 18	53:54	39
15	Blackburn	42	13 12 17	54:57	38
16	Preston	42	13 12 17	42:65	38
17	The Arsenal	42	15 7 20	47:56	37
18	Birmingham	42	15 7 20	48:60	37
19	Oldham	42	13 11 18	38:50	37
20	Everton	42	12 12 18	57:55	36
21	Bradford C.	42	11 10 21	48:72	32
22	Manchester U.	42	8 12 22	41:73	28

SEASON 1922/23

26 Aug	Lge	H	Cardiff	D	1-1	1 Jan	Lge	A	Everton	L	1-3
2 Sep	Lge	A	Cardiff	W	3-2	6 Jan	Lge	H	Middlesbrough	W	2-0
4 Sep	Lge	H	Everton	W	2-0	13 Jan	FC	A	Worksop Town	D	0-0*
9 Sep	Lge	H	Burnley	L	1-3	15 Jan	FCr	H	Worksop Town	W	9-0
11 Sep	F	A	Corinthians	W	2-1	20 Jan	Lge	A	Oldham	W	3-0
16 Sep	Lge	A	Burnley	W	1-0	27 Jan	Lge	H	Oldham	W	3-0
23 Sep	Lge	H	Arsenal	L	1-2	3 Feb	FC	H	Man Utd	W	4-0
30 Sep	Lge	A	Arsenal	W	2-0	10 Feb	Lge	A	Blackburn	L	0-1
2 Oct	LPCF	H	West Ham	W	2-1	14 Feb	Lge	H	Blackburn	W	2-0
7 Oct	Lge	A	Aston Villa	L	0-2	17 Feb	Lge	H	Bolton	L	0-1
14 Oct	Lge	H	Aston Villa	L	1-2	19 Feb	F	H	Oxford Univ	L	1-2
16 Oct	F	A	Llanelli	L	1-2	24 Feb	FC	H	Cardiff	W	3-2
21 Oct	Lge	H	WBA	W	3-1	3 Mar	Lge	H	Man City	W	3-1
23 Oct	LCC	A	Arsenal	L	2-3	10 Mar	FC	H	Derby	L	0-1
28 Oct	Lge	A	WBA	L	1-5	14 Mar	Lge	A	Man City	L	0-3
4 Nov	Lge	H	Liverpool	L	2-4	17 Mar	Lge	A	Stoke	D	0-0
11 Nov	Lge	A	Liverpool	D	0-0	24 Mar	Lge	H	Stoke	W	3-1
16 Nov	F	H	Camb Univ	W	5-1	30 Mar	Lge	H	Preston	W	3-1
18 Nov	Lge	H	Newcastle	L	0-1	31 Mar	Lge	A	Sunderland	L	0-2
25 Nov	Lge	A	Newcastle	D	1-1	2 Apr	Lge	A	Preston	L	0-2
30 Nov	F	A	Oxford Univ	W	3-0	7 Apr	Lge	H	Sunderland	L	0-1
2 Dec	Lge	H	Nottm Forest	W	2-1	11 Apr	Lge	A	Bolton	W	2-0
9 Dec	Lge	A	Nottm Forest	W	1-0	14 Apr	Lge	A	Birmingham	L	1-2
16 Dec	Lge	A	Chelsea	D	0-0	21 Apr	Lge	H	Birmingham	W	2-0
23 Dec	Lge	H	Chelsea	W	3-1	28 Apr	Lge	A	Huddersfield	L	0-1
25 Dec	Lge	H	Sheff Utd	W	2-1	5 May	Lge	H	Huddersfield	D	0-0
26 Dec	Lge	A	Sheff Utd	L	0-2	7 May	F	H	West Ham	W	5-2
30 Dec	Lge	A	Middlesbrough	L	0-2						

* Worksop agreed to play first match at White Hart Lane

Player	Lg App	Goals	Player	Lg App	Goals
Banks J.A.	2		Lindsay A.F.	34	11
Barnett F.W.	2		Lowe H.	14	
Blake H.E.	36		McDonald R.J.	17	
Bliss H.	8	3	Maddison G.	5	
Brooks S.	7	1	Pearson J.	1	
Brown R.S.	12		Ross J.	6	
Cantrell J.	10	4	Seed J.M.	36	9
Clay T.	34	3	Sharp B.	2	
Dimmock J.H.	42	6	Skinner J.F.	15	1
Forster M.	12		Smith B.	32	2
Grimsdell A.	40	21	Thompson A.	2	
Handley C.H.J.	30	5	Walden F.	30	3
Hartley F.	1		Walters C.	29	
Jacques W.	1		Wilson C.	2	

Final table for First Division

1	Liverpool	42	26	8	8	70:31	60
2	Sunderland	42	22	10	10	72:54	54
3	Huddersfield	42	21	11	10	60:32	53
4	Newcastle	42	18	12	12	45:37	48
5	Everton	42	20	7	15	63:59	47
6	Aston Villa	42	18	10	14	64:51	46
7	West Bromwich	42	17	11	14	58:49	45
8	Manchester C.	42	17	11	14	50:49	45
9	Cardiff	42	18	7	17	73:59	43
10	Sheffield U.	42	16	10	16	68:64	42
11	The Arsenal	42	16	10	16	61:62	42
12	**TOTTENHAM**	**42**	**17**	**7**	**18**	**50:50**	**41**
13	Bolton	42	14	12	16	50:58	40
14	Blackburn	42	14	12	16	47:62	40
15	Burnley	42	16	6	20	58:59	38
16	Preston	42	13	11	18	60:64	37
17	Birmingham	42	13	11	18	41:57	37
18	Middlesbrough	42	13	10	19	57:63	36
19	Chelsea	42	9	18	15	45:53	36
20	Nottingham F.	42	13	8	21	41:70	34
21	Stoke	42	10	10	22	47:67	30
22	Oldham	42	10	10	22	35:65	30

SEASON 1923/24

25 Aug	Lge	H	Preston	W	2-0	25 Dec	Lge	H	Huddersfield	W	1-0
27 Aug	Lge	A	Chelsea	W	1-0	26 Dec	Lge	A	Huddersfield	L	1-2
1 Sep	Lge	A	Preston	D	2-2	29 Dec	Lge	H	Birmingham	D	1-1
3 Sep	Lge	H	Chelsea	L	0-1	1 Jan	Lge	A	Man City	L	0-1
8 Sep	Lge	H	Middlesbrough	W	2-1	5 Jan	Lge	A	Birmingham	L	2-3
15 Sep	Lge	A	Middlesbrough	W	1-0	12 Jan	FC	A	C. Palace	L	0-2
22 Sep	Lge	H	Bolton	D	0-0	19 Jan	Lge	H	Newcastle	W	2-0
29 Sep	Lge	A	Bolton	L	1-3	26 Jan	Lge	A	Newcastle	D	2-2
6 Oct	Lge	A	Notts Co	D	0-0	2 Feb	F	A	Chelsea	D	0-0
8 Oct	LPCF	H	Clapton O.	L	1-3	9 Feb	Lge	A	West Ham	D	0-0
13 Oct	Lge	H	Notts Co	L	1-3	16 Feb	Lge	H	Cardiff	D	1-1
20 Oct	Lge	A	Sunderland	L	0-1	18 Feb	F	H	Oxford Univ	W	8-1
22 Oct	LCC	A	C. Palace	D	1-1	1 Mar	Lge	H	Sheff Utd	L	1-2
25 Oct	F	A	Norwich	W	3-2	8 Mar	Lge	A	Sheff Utd	L	2-6
27 Oct	Lge	H	Sunderland	D	1-1	15 Mar	Lge	A	Aston Villa	D	0-0
29 Oct	LCC	H	C. Palace	W	2-1	22 Mar	Lge	H	Aston Villa	L	2-3
3 Nov	Lge	A	Nottm Forest	D	0-0	29 Mar	Lge	A	Liverpool	L	0-1
5 Nov	LCC	A	Clapton O.	L	0-2	5 Apr	Lge	H	Liverpool	D	1-1
10 Nov	Lge	H	Nottm Forest	W	3-0	7 Apr	Lge	A	Cardiff	L	1-2
15 Nov	F	A	Camb Univ	W	6-5	12 Apr	Lge	H	Everton	L	2-5
17 Nov	Lge	A	Arsenal	D	1-1	16 Apr	F	H	Inter Varsities	W	7-1
24 Nov	Lge	H	Arsenal	W	3-0	19 Apr	Lge	A	Everton	L	2-4
1 Dec	Lge	H	WBA	D	0-0	21 Apr	Lge	H	Man City	W	4-1
4 Dec	F	A	Oxford Univ	W	5-0	22 Apr	Lge	H	West Ham	L	0-1
8 Dec	Lge	A	WBA	L	1-4	26 Apr	Lge	A	Burnley	D	2-2
15 Dec	Lge	H	Blackburn	W	2-1	3 May	Lge	H	Burnley	W	1-0
22 Dec	Lge	A	Blackburn	W	1-0						

Player	Lg App	Goals	Player	Lg App	Goals
Barnett F.W.	2		Maddison G.	35	
Blake H.E.	7		Osborne F.R.	12	1
Brooks S.	3		Poynton C.	10	1
Brown R.S.	3		Ross J.	1	
Clay T.	40	1	Sage W.	7	
Dimmock J.H.	25	2	Seed J.M.	21	2
Elkes J.E.	37	11	Skinner J.F.	2	
Forster M.	35		Smith B.	41	1
Grimsdell A.	27	1	Thompson A.	7	1
Handley C.H.J.	22	5	Walden F.	34	1
Hargreaves H.	7	3	Walters C.	15	
Lindsay A.F.	39	19	White S.E.	5	
Lowe H.	22		Own Goal		1
McDonald R.J.	3				

Final table for First Division

1	Huddersfield	42	23	11	8	60:33	57
2	Cardiff	42	22	13	7	61:34	57
3	Sunderland	42	22	9	11	71:54	53
4	Bolton	42	18	14	10	68:34	50
5	Sheffield U.	42	19	12	11	69:49	50
6	Aston Villa	42	18	13	11	52:37	49
7	Everton	42	18	13	11	62:53	49
8	Blackburn	42	17	11	14	54:50	45
9	Newcastle	42	17	10	15	60:54	44
10	Notts Co.	42	14	14	14	44:49	42
11	Manchester C.	42	15	12	15	54:71	42
12	Liverpool	42	15	11	16	49:48	41
13	West Ham	42	13	15	14	40:43	41
14	Birmingham	42	13	13	16	41:49	39
15	**TOTTENHAM**	**42**	**12**	**14**	**16**	**50:56**	**38**
16	West Bromwich	42	12	14	16	51:62	38
17	Burnley	42	12	12	18	55:60	36
18	Preston	42	12	10	20	52:67	34
19	The Arsenal	42	12	9	21	40:63	33
20	Nottingham F.	42	10	12	20	42:64	32
21	Chelsea	42	9	14	19	31:53	32
22	Middlesbrough	42	7	8	27	37:60	22

SEASON 1924/25

Date	Comp	H/A	Opponent	Result	Score
30 Aug	Lge	H	Bolton	W	3-0
3 Sep	Lge	A	Birmingham	W	2-0
6 Sep	Lge	A	Notts Co.	D	0-0
8 Sep	Lge	A	WBA	L	0-2
13 Sep	Lge	H	Everton	D	0-0
20 Sep	Lge	A	Sunderland	L	1-4
22 Sep	Lge	H	WBA	L	0-1
27 Sep	Lge	H	Cardiff	D	1-1
4 Oct	Lge	A	Preston	W	3-0
11 Oct	Lge	H	Burnley	D	1-1
18 Oct	Lge	A	Leeds Utd	L	0-1
25 Oct	Lge	A	Arsenal	L	0-1
27 Oct	LCC	H	Fulham	W	5-1
1 Nov	Lge	H	Aston Villa	L	1-3
3 Nov	LPCF	A	C. Orient	L	1-2†
6 Nov	F	A	Oxford Univ	W	2-1
8 Nov	Lge	A	Huddersfield	W	2-1
10 Nov	Lge	H	Man City	D	1-1
15 Nov	Lge	H	Blackburn	W	5-0
17 Nov	LCC	H	Kingstonians	W	5-0
22 Nov	Lge	A	West Ham	D	1-1
24 Nov	LCC	*	C. Orient	L	1-2
29 Nov	Lge	H	Sheff Utd	W	4-1
6 Dec	Lge	A	Newcastle	D	1-1
13 Dec	Lge	H	Liverpool	D	1-1
20 Dec	Lge	A	Nottm Forest	L	0-1
25 Dec	Lge	H	Bury	D	1-1
27 Dec	Lge	A	Bolton	L	0-3
1 Jan	Lge	A	Bury	L	2-5
3 Jan	Lge	H	Notts Co.	D	1-1
10 Jan	FC	H	Northampton	W	3-0
17 Jan	Lge	A	Everton	L	0-1
24 Jan	Lge	H	Sunderland	W	1-0
31 Jan	FC	H	Bolton	D	1-1
3 Feb	FCr	A	Bolton	W	1-0
7 Feb	Lge	H	Preston	W	2-0
14 Feb	Lge	A	Burnley	W	4-1
21 Feb	FC	H	Blackburn	D	2-2
26 Feb	FCr	A	Blackburn	L	1-3
28 Feb	Lge	H	Arsenal	W	2-0
7 Mar	Lge	A	Aston Villa	W	1-0
9 Mar	Lge	H	Leeds Utd	W	2-1
14 Mar	Lge	H	Huddersfield	L	1-2
18 Mar	Lge	A	Cardiff	W	2-0
21 Mar	Lge	A	Blackburn	D	1-1
28 Mar	Lge	H	West Ham	D	1-1
4 Apr	Lge	A	Sheff Utd	L	0-2
10 Apr	Lge	A	Birmingham	L	0-1
11 Apr	Lge	H	Newcastle	W	3-0
18 Apr	Lge	A	Liverpool	L	0-1
25 Apr	Lge	H	Nottm Forest	W	1-0
2 May	Lge	A	Man City	L	0-1
9 May	F	A	Basel Old Boys	W	3-0
10 May	F	A	Zurich	W	2-0
17 May	F	A	Winterthur	W	4-0
18 May	F	A	Lausanne	W	6-1
20 May	F	A	La Chaux de Fonds	W	8-1
21 May	F	A	Bern	W	5-0
24 May	F	A	Basel	W	1-0

† abandoned after 70 minutes
* at Highbury

Player	Lg App	Goals	Player	Lg App	Goals
Clay T.	21	2	Osborne F.R.	23	
Dimmock J.H.	29	5	Poynton C.	24	
Elkes J.E.	33	10	Sage W.	1	
Forster M.	21		Seed J.M.	41	17
Grimsdell A.	14		Sharp B.	1	
Handley C.H.J.	14	3	Skinner J.F.	34	
Hargreaves H.	20	3	Skitt H.	27	
Hinton F.	42		Smith B.	37	1
Lane W.H.C.	17	6	Thompson A.	20	3
Lindsay A.F.	18	2	Walters C.	22	
Lowe H.	6		White S.E.	5	
McDonald R.J.	12				

Final table for First Division

1	Huddersfield	42	21	16	5	69:28	58
2	West Bromwich	42	23	10	9	58:34	56
3	Bolton	42	22	11	9	76:34	55
4	Liverpool	42	20	10	12	63:55	50
5	Bury	42	17	15	10	54:51	49
6	Newcastle	42	16	16	10	61:42	48
7	Sunderland	42	19	10	13	64:51	48
8	Birmingham	42	17	12	13	49:53	46
9	Notts Co.	42	16	13	13	42:31	45
10	Manchester C.	42	17	9	16	76:68	43
11	Cardiff	42	16	11	15	56:51	43
12	**TOTTENHAM**	**42**	**15**	**12**	**15**	**52:43**	**42**
13	West Ham	42	15	12	15	62:60	42
14	Sheffield U.	42	13	13	16	55:63	39
15	Aston Villa	42	13	13	16	58:71	39
16	Blackburn	42	11	13	18	53:66	35
17	Everton	42	12	11	19	40:60	35
18	Leeds	42	11	12	19	46:59	34
19	Burnley	42	11	12	19	46:75	34
20	The Arsenal	42	14	5	23	46:58	33
21	Preston	42	10	6	26	37:74	26
22	Nottingham F.	42	6	12	24	29:65	24

SEASON 1925/26

Date	Comp	H/A	Opponent	Result	Score
29 Aug	Lge	A	Arsenal	W	1-0
31 Aug	Lge	A	Sheff Utd	W	3-2
3 Sep	F	H	Real Madrid	W	4-0
5 Sep	Lge	H	Man City	W	1-0
7 Sep	Lge	H	Sheff Utd	W	3-2
12 Sep	Lge	A	Everton	D	1-1
14 Sep	Lge	A	Cardiff	L	1-2
15 Sep	LCC	A	Brentford	L	1-2
19 Sep	Lge	H	Huddersfield	D	5-5
21 Sep	Lge	A	Cardiff	W	1-0
26 Sep	Lge	A	Sunderland	L	0-3
3 Oct	Lge	H	Blackburn	W	4-2
10 Oct	Lge	A	Bury	L	0-3
17 Oct	Lge	A	Man Utd	D	0-0
22 Oct	F	A	Norwich	L	2-3*
24 Oct	Lge	H	Liverpool	W	3-1
31 Oct	Lge	A	Leicester	L	3-5
7 Nov	Lge	H	West Ham	W	4-2
12 Nov	F	A	Camb Univ	L	1-2
14 Nov	Lge	A	Newcastle	L	1-3
16 Nov	LPCF	H	QPR	W	1-0
21 Nov	Lge	H	Bolton	L	2-3
26 Nov	F	A	Oxford Univ	W	4-1
28 Nov	Lge	A	Notts Co	L	2-4
5 Dec	Lge	A	Aston Villa	D	2-2
12 Dec	Lge	A	Burnley	W	2-1
19 Dec	Lge	H	Leeds	W	3-2
25 Dec	Lge	A	Birmingham	L	1-3
26 Dec	Lge	H	Birmingham	W	2-1
2 Jan	Lge	H	Arsenal	D	1-1
9 Jan	FC	H	West Ham	W	5-0
16 Jan	Lge	A	Man City	D	0-0
23 Jan	Lge	H	Everton	D	1-1
30 Jan	FC	H	Man Utd	D	2-2
3 Feb	FCr	A	Man Utd	L	0-2
6 Feb	Lge	H	Sunderland	L	0-2
13 Feb	Lge	A	Blackburn	L	2-4
20 Feb	Lge	H	Bury	W	4-2
27 Feb	Lge	H	Man Utd	L	0-1
3 Mar	Lge	A	Huddersfield	L	1-2
6 Mar	Lge	A	Liverpool	D	0-0
13 Mar	Lge	H	Leicester	L	1-3
20 Mar	Lge	A	West Ham	L	1-3
25 Mar	Lge	H	Newcastle	W	1-0
27 Mar	F	A	Hull	L	0-5
2 Apr	Lge	H	WBA	W	3-2
3 Apr	Lge	A	Bolton	D	1-1
5 Apr	Lge	A	WBA	L	0-1
10 Apr	Lge	H	Notts Co	W	4-0
17 Apr	Lge	A	Aston Villa	L	0-3
24 Apr	Lge	H	Burnley	L	0-2
1 May	Lge	A	Leeds	L	1-4
3 May	F	A	West Ham	D	1-1

* Played at Bury St Edmunds

Player	Lg App	Goals	Player	Lg App	Goals
Bann W.	8		Lowe H.	2	
Britton J.	9		Osborne F.R.	39	25
Clay T.	34	2	Roe T.W.	4	1
Dimmock J.H.	40	14	Sage W.	3	
Elkes J.E.	31	11	Seed J.M.	30	6
Forster M.	42		Skinner J.F.	17	
Grimsdell A.	13		Skitt H.	35	
Handley C.H.J.	2		Smith B.	38	
Hargreaves H.	8	1	Smith J.	7	
Hinton I.F.	15		Thompson A.	35	4
Kaine W.E.	11		Walters C.	1	
Lane W.H.C.	5		White S.E.	10	
Lindsay A.F.	23	2			

Final table for First Division

1	Huddersfield	42	23	11	8	92:60	57
2	The Arsenal	42	22	8	12	87:63	52
3	Sunderland	42	21	6	15	96:80	48
4	Bury	42	20	7	15	85:77	47
5	Sheffield U.	42	19	8	15	102:82	46
6	Aston Villa	42	16	12	14	86:76	44
7	Liverpool	42	14	16	12	70:63	44
8	Bolton	42	17	10	15	75:76	44
9	Manchester U.	42	19	6	17	66:73	44
10	Newcastle	42	16	10	16	84:75	42
11	Everton	42	12	18	12	72:70	42
12	Blackburn	42	15	11	16	91:80	41
13	West Bromwich	42	16	8	18	79:78	40
14	Birmingham	42	16	8	18	66:81	40
15	**TOTTENHAM**	**42**	**15**	**9**	**18**	**66:79**	**39**
16	Cardiff	42	16	7	19	61:76	39
17	Leicester	42	14	10	18	70:80	38
18	West Ham	42	15	7	20	63:76	37
19	Leeds	42	14	8	20	64:76	36
20	Burnley	42	13	10	19	85:108	36
21	Manchester C.	42	12	11	19	89:100	35
22	Notts Co.	42	13	7	22	54:74	33

Date	Comp	H/A	Opponent	Result	Score
28 Aug	Lge	H	Everton	W	2-1
30 Aug	Lge	H	Sheff Wed	W	7-3
4 Sep	Lge	A	Blackburn	L	0-1
6 Sep	Lge	H	Leicester	D	2-2
11 Sep	Lge	H	Huddersfield	D	3-3
13 Sep	Lge	A	Leicester	D	2-2
18 Sep	Lge	A	Sunderland	L	2-3
20 Sep	F	H	Bohemians	W	1-0
25 Sep	Lge	H	WBA	W	3-0
27 Sep	LCC	A	Millwall	L	2-5
2 Oct	Lge	A	Bury	D	0-0
9 Oct	Lge	H	Birmingham	W	6-1
16 Oct	Lge	H	Sheff Utd	W	3-1
23 Oct	Lge	A	Derby	L	1-4
30 Oct	Lge	H	Bolton	W	1-0
4 Nov	F	A	Camb Univ	W	3-2
6 Nov	Lge	A	Aston Villa	W	3-2
8 Nov	LPCF	H	C. Orient	W	3-1
11 Nov	F	A	Oxford Univ	W	7-0
13 Nov	Lge	H	Cardiff	W	4-1
20 Nov	Lge	A	Burnley	L	0-5
27 Nov	Lge	H	Newcastle	L	1-3
29 Nov	F	A	Corinthians	W	2-0
4 Dec	Lge	A	Leeds	D	1-1
11 Dec	Lge	H	Liverpool	L	1-2
18 Dec	Lge	A	Arsenal	W	4-2
25 Dec	Lge	H	Man Utd	D	1-1
27 Dec	Lge	A	Man Utd	L	1-2
28 Dec	Lge	A	Sheff Wed	L	1-3
8 Jan	FC	A	West Ham	L	2-3
15 Jan	Lge	A	Everton	W	2-1
22 Jan	Lge	H	Blackburn	D	1-1
29 Jan	Lge	A	Huddersfield	L	0-2
5 Feb	Lge	H	Sunderland	L	0-2
12 Feb	Lge	A	WBA	L	0-5
19 Feb	Lge	H	Bury	W	1-0
26 Feb	Lge	A	Birmingham	L	0-1
5 Mar	Lge	A	Sheff Utd	D	3-3
12 Mar	Lge	H	Derby	W	3-2
19 Mar	Lge	A	Bolton	D	2-2
26 Mar	Lge	A	Aston Villa	L	0-1
2 Apr	Lge	A	Cardiff	W	2-1
9 Apr	Lge	H	Burnley	W	4-1
15 Apr	Lge	H	West Ham	L	1-3
16 Apr	Lge	A	Newcastle	L	2-3
18 Apr	Lge	A	West Ham	W	2-1
23 Apr	Lge	H	Leeds	W	4-1
30 Apr	Lge	A	Liverpool	L	0-1
7 May	Lge	H	Arsenal	L	0-4

Player	Lg App	Goals
Barnett F.W.	1	
Bellamy W.R.	1	
Blair J.G.	24	10
Britton J.	18	
Clay T.	16	
Dimmock J.H.	41	19
Elkes J.E.	40	2
Forster M.	35	
Grimsdell A.	2	
Handley C.H.J.	24	10
Lane W.H.C.	4	1
Lindsay A.F.	37	
Lowe H.	1	
Nicholls J.H.	1	
O'Callaghan E.	13	5
Osborne F.R.	34	9
Poynton C.	31	
Richardson J.	2	
Roe T.W.	3	3
Sanders A.W.	12	7
Seed J.M.	23	7
Skitt H.	22	
Smith B.	24	
Smith J.	23	
Thompson A.	30	3

Final table for First Division

1	Newcastle	42	25	6	11	96:58	56
2	Huddersfield	42	17	17	8	76:60	51
3	Sunderland	42	21	7	14	98:70	49
4	Bolton	42	19	10	13	84:62	48
5	Burnley	42	19	9	14	91:80	47
6	West Ham	42	19	8	15	86:70	46
7	Leicester	42	17	12	13	85:70	46
8	Sheffield U.	42	17	10	15	74:86	44
9	Liverpool	42	18	7	17	69:61	43
10	Aston Villa	42	18	7	17	81:83	43
11	The Arsenal	42	17	9	16	77:86	43
12	Derby	42	17	7	18	86:73	41
13	**TOTTENHAM**	42	16	9	17	76:78	41
14	Cardiff	42	16	9	17	55:65	41
15	Manchester U.	42	13	14	15	52:64	40
16	The Wednesday	42	15	9	18	75:92	39
17	Birmingham	42	17	4	21	64:73	38
18	Blackburn	42	15	8	19	77:96	38
19	Bury	42	12	12	18	68:77	36
20	Everton	42	12	10	20	64:90	34
21	Leeds	42	11	8	23	69:88	30
22	West Bromwich	42	11	8	23	65:86	30

Date	Comp	H/A	Opponent	Result	Score
27 Aug	Lge	H	Birmingham	W	1-0
31 Aug	Lge	A	Middlesbrough	L	1-3
3 Sep	Lge	A	Newcastle	L	1-4
10 Sep	Lge	H	Huddersfield	D	2-2
12 Sep	Lge	H	Middlesbrough	W	4-2
17 Sep	Lge	A	Portsmouth	L	0-3
22 Sep	Lge	H	Leicester	W	2-1
24 Sep	Lge	A	Man Utd	L	0-3
1 Oct	Lge	H	Everton	L	1-3
8 Oct	Lge	A	Cardiff	L	1-2
13 Oct	F	A	Norwich	D	1-1
15 Oct	Lge	H	Blackburn	D	1-1
17 Oct	LCC	A	Fulham	L	2-5
22 Oct	Lge	H	Sunderland	W	3-1
26 Oct	F	A	Reading	W	5-2
29 Oct	Lge	A	Derby	D	1-1
3 Nov	F	A	Camb Univ	L	1-2
5 Nov	Lge	H	West Ham	W	5-3
7 Nov	LPCF	H	Clapton O.	W	4-3
10 Nov	F	H	Oxford Univ	W	5-2
12 Nov	Lge	A	Aston Villa	W	2-1
19 Nov	Lge	H	Sheff Utd	D	2-2
3 Dec	Lge	H	Burnley	W	5-0
5 Dec	F	H	West Ham	D	1-1
10 Dec	Lge	A	Bury	W	2-1
17 Dec	Lge	H	Liverpool	W	3-1
24 Dec	Lge	A	Leicester	L	1-6
26 Dec	Lge	A	Bolton	L	1-4
31 Dec	Lge	A	Birmingham	L	2-3
2 Jan	Lge	A	Arsenal	D	1-1
7 Jan	Lge	H	Newcastle	W	5-2
14 Jan	FC	A	Bristol C.	W	2-1
21 Jan	Lge	A	Huddersfield	L	2-4
28 Jan	FC	H	Oldham	W	3-0
4 Feb	Lge	H	Man Utd	W	4-1
6 Feb	Lge	H	Bolton	L	1-2
11 Feb	Lge	H	Everton	W	5-2
18 Feb	FC	A	Leicester	W	3-0
25 Feb	Lge	A	Blackburn	L	1-2
3 Mar	FC	A	Huddersfield	L	1-6
5 Mar	Lge	H	Cardiff	W	1-0
10 Mar	Lge	H	Derby	L	1-2
17 Mar	Lge	A	West Ham	D	1-1
19 Mar	Lge	H	Portsmouth	L	0-3
26 Mar	Lge	H	Aston Villa	W	2-1
28 Mar	Lge	A	Sunderland	D	0-0
31 Mar	Lge	A	Sheff Utd	L	1-3
6 Apr	Lge	H	Sheff Wed	L	1-3
7 Apr	Lge	H	Arsenal	W	2-0
10 Apr	Lge	A	Sheff Wed	L	2-4
14 Apr	Lge	A	Burnley	D	2-2
21 Apr	Lge	H	Bury	L	1-4
23 Apr	F	A	Norwich	L	0-3
25 Apr	F	A	Ebbw Vale	W	7-3
28 Apr	Lge	A	Liverpool	L	0-2
6 May	F	A	Olympic XI	W	5-2
9 May	F	A	Den Haag	W	6-2
13 May	F	A	All Holland XI	W	3-0
16 May	F	A	Rotterdam	W	3-0

Player	Lg App	Goals
Armstrong J.W.	11	4
Austin P.	1	
Barnett F.W.	5	
Bellamy W.R.	4	
Blair J.G.	5	4
Britton J.	13	
Clay T.	16	
Dimmock J.H.	38	12
Elkes J.E.	22	5
Evans A.A.	3	
Forster M.	32	
Grimsdell A.	35	2
Handley C.H.J.	27	4
Hartley F.	2	
Helliwell S.	2	
Lowdell A.	34	
Lindsay A.F.	18	3
Nicholls J.H.	3	
O'Callaghan E.	42	19
Osborne F.R.	31	18
Poynton C.	14	
Richardson J.	24	
Sanders A.W.	1	
Skitt H.	38	
Smith B.	8	
Spiers C.H.	26	
Thompson A.	4	
Townley J.C.	3	2
Own Goal		1

Final table for First Division

1	Everton	42	20	13	9	102:66	53
2	Huddersfield	42	22	7	13	91:68	51
3	Leicester	42	18	12	12	96:72	48
4	Derby	42	17	10	15	96:83	44
5	Bury	42	20	4	18	80:80	44
6	Cardiff	42	17	10	15	70:80	44
7	Bolton	42	16	11	15	81:66	43
8	Aston Villa	42	17	9	16	78:73	43
9	Newcastle	42	15	13	14	79:81	43
10	Arsenal	42	13	15	14	82:86	41
11	Birmingham	42	13	15	14	70:75	41
12	Blackburn	42	16	9	17	66:78	41
13	Sheffield U.	42	15	10	17	79:86	40
14	The Wednesday	42	13	13	16	81:78	39
15	Sunderland	42	15	9	18	74:76	39
16	Liverpool	42	13	13	16	84:87	39
17	West Ham	42	14	11	17	81:88	39
18	Manchester U.	42	16	7	19	72:80	39
19	Burnley	42	16	7	19	82:98	39
20	Portsmouth	42	16	7	19	66:90	39
21	**TOTTENHAM**	42	15	8	19	74:86	38
22	Middlesbrough	42	11	15	16	81:88	37

SEASON 1928/29

Date	Comp		Opponent		Score
25 Aug	Lge	H	Oldham	W	4-1
27 Aug	Lge	H	Middlesbrough	L	2-5
1 Sept	Lge	A	Southampton	D	1-1
8 Sep	Lge	H	Wolves	W	3-2
15 Sep	Lge	A	Notts Co	L	0-2
22 Sep	Lge	H	Millwall	W	2-1
29 Sep	Lge	A	Port Vale	L	1-2
4 Oct	F	A	Norwich	W	4-2
6 Oct	Lge	H	Hull	W	4-1
13 Oct	Lge	A	Bradford	L	1-4
15 Oct	LCC	H	London Cal	W	2-1
20 Oct	Lge	H	Grimsby	W	2-1
27 Oct	Lge	A	Stoke	L	0-2
29 Oct	LCC	A	QPR	D	1-1
3 Nov	Lge	H	Clapton O.	W	2-1
5 Nov	LCC	H	QPR	W	3-1
10 Nov	Lge	A'	Swansea	L	0-4
15 Nov	F	H	Camb Univ	W	12-3
17 Nov	Lge	H	Nottm Forest	W	2-1
21 Nov	F	A	Oxford Univ	W	4-2
24 Nov	Lge	A	Bristol City	L	1-2
26 Nov	LCCsf	*	Charlton	W	5-3
1 Dec	Lge	H	Barnsley	W	2-0
3 Dec	LPCF	A	Clapton O.	W	4-2
8 Dec	Lge	A	Chelsea	D	1-1
15 Dec	Lge	H	Blackpool	L	1-2
22 Dec	Lge	A	West Brom	L	2-3
25 Dec	Lge	H	Reading	D	2-2
26 Dec	Lge	A	Reading	L	3-4
29 Dec	Lge	A	Oldham	L	1-3
1 Jan	Lge	A	Middlesbrough	L	0-3
5 Jan	Lge	H	Southampton	W	3-2
12 Jan	FC	A	Reading	L	0-2
19 Jan	Lge	A	Wolves	L	2-4
26 Jan	Lge	H	Notts Co	W	3-0
2 Feb	Lge	A	Millwall	L	1-5
9 Feb	Lge	H	Port Vale	W	4-2
23 Feb	Lge	H	Bradford	W	3-2
2 Mar	Lge	A	Grimsby	L	0-2
9 Mar	Lge	H	Stoke	W	1-0
16 Mar	Lge	A	C. Orient	W	3-2
23 Mar	Lge	H	Swansea	D	1-1
29 Mar	Lge	A	Preston	D	2-2
30 Mar	Lge	A	Nottm Forest	D	2-2
1 Apr	Lge	H	Preston	W	2-0
6 Apr	Lge	H	Bristol City	D	1-1
13 Apr	Lge	A	Barnsley	L	1-4
15 Apr	Lge	A	Hull City	D	1-1
20 Apr	Lge	H	Chelsea	W	4-1
27 Apr	Lge	A	Blackpool	D	2-2
4 May	Lge	H	WBA	W	2-0
6 May	LCCf	†	Millwall	W	5-1
11 May	F	A	Sliema	W	7-1
12 May	F	A	Valletta	W	2-1
16 May	F	A	British Army	W	5-0
18 May	F	A	British Navy	W	1-0
19 May	F	A	Floriana	W	2-1
21 May	F	A	Pick/Malta XI	W	5-1

* at Upton Park   † at Highbury

Player	Lg App	Goals	Player	Lg App	Goals
Armstrong J.W.	12	3	Herod E.R.B.	13	
Bann W.E.	4		Knight J.G.	1	
Barnett F.W.	6	1	Lindsay A.F.	6	
Bellamy W.R.	9		Lowdell A.	39	
Cable T.H.	2		Nicholls J.	11	
Clay T.	5		O'Callaghan E.	36	10
Crompton A.	8	1	Osborne F.R.	33	16
Dimmock J.H.	30	11	Poynton C.	23	1
Elkes J.E.	27	10	Richardson J.	12	
Evans A.A.	2		Roberts W.T.	4	2
Forster M.	33		Scott J.	12	4
Galloway R.	3	2	Skitt H.	29	
Grimsdell A.	11		Smith B.	10	
Handley C.H.J.	1		Smy J.	4	
Harper E.C.	11	11	Spiers C.H.	31	
Hartley F.	3	1	Thompson A.	13	1
Helliwell S.	6		Wilding H.T.	12	1

Final table for Second Division

1	Middlesbrough	42	22	11	9	92:57	55
2	Grimsby	42	24	5	13	82:61	53
3	Bradford PA	42	22	4	16	88:70	48
4	Southampton	42	17	14	11	74:60	48
5	Notts Co.	42	19	9	14	78:65	47
6	Stoke	42	17	12	13	74:51	46
7	West Bromwich	42	19	8	15	80:79	46
8	Blackpool	42	19	7	16	92:76	45
9	Chelsea	42	17	10	15	64:65	44
10	TOTTENHAM	42	17	9	16	75:81	43
11	Nottingham F.	42	15	12	15	71:70	42
12	Hull	42	13	14	15	58:63	40
13	Preston	42	15	9	18	78:79	39
14	Millwall	42	16	7	19	71:86	39
15	Reading	42	15	9	18	63:86	39
16	Barnsley	42	16	6	20	69:66	38
17	Wolverhampton	42	15	7	20	77:81	37
18	Oldham	42	16	5	21	54:75	37
19	Swansea	42	13	10	19	62:75	36
20	Bristol C.	42	13	10	19	58:72	36
21	Port Vale	42	15	4	23	71:86	34
22	Clapton O.	42	12	8	22	45:72	32

SEASON 1929/30

Date	Comp		Opponent		Score
31 Aug	Lge	A	Bradford PA	L	1-2
2 Sep	Lge	A	Millwall	W	5-2
7 Sep	Lge	H	Barnsley	W	2-1
14 Sep	Lge	A	Blackpool	L	2-3
21 Sep	Lge	H	Bury	D	2-2
23 Sep	Lge	H	Millwall	D	1-1
28 Sep	Lge	A	Chelsea	L	0-3
5 Oct	Lge	H	Nottm Forest	D	1-1
9 Oct	Lge	H	Stoke	W	3-1
10 Oct	F	A	Norwich	L	0-1
12 Oct	Lge	A	Oldham	L	0-2
13 Oct	LCC	A	C. Orient	L	1-2
19 Oct	Lge	A	Wolves	L	0-3
26 Oct	Lge	H	Bradford C	D	1-1
2 Nov	Lge	A	Swansea	W	1-0
4 Nov	LPCF	H	Crystal P.	W	5-0
9 Nov	Lge	H	Cardiff	L	1-2
16 Nov	Lge	H	Preston	L	0-4
23 Nov	Lge	A	Bristol C.	W	2-1
30 Nov	Lge	A	Notts Co.	W	1-0
7 Dec	Lge	H	Reading	D	0-0
14 Dec	Lge	A	Charlton	L	0-1
21 Dec	Lge	H	Hull City	D	2-2
25 Dec	Lge	H	Southampton	W	3-2
26 Dec	Lge	A	Southampton	L	0-1
28 Dec	Lge	A	Bradford PA	D	1-1
4 Jan	Lge	A	Barnsley	L	0-2
11 Jan	FC	H	Man City	D	2-2
14 Jan	FCr	A	Man City	L	1-4
18 Jan	Lge	H	Blackpool	W	6-1
25 Jan	Lge	A	Bury	L	1-2
1 Feb	Lge	H	Chelsea	D	3-3
8 Feb	Lge	A	Nottm Forest	D	0-0
15 Feb	Lge	H	Oldham	W	2-1
22 Feb	Lge	H	Wolves	W	4-2
1 Mar	Lge	A	Bradford C	W	2-0
8 Mar	Lge	H	Swansea	W	3-0
15 Mar	Lge	A	Cardiff	L	0-1
22 Mar	Lge	H	Preston	W	1-0
29 Mar	Lge	A	Bristol C	L	0-1
5 Apr	Lge	H	Notts Co	W	2-0
12 Apr	Lge	A	Reading	L	0-3
18 Apr	Lge	H	WBA	L	0-2
19 Apr	Lge	H	Charlton	W	3-0
21 Apr	Lge	A	WBA	L	3-4
26 Apr	Lge	A	Hull City	L	0-2
3 May	Lge	A	Stoke City	L	0-1

Player	Lg App	Goals	Player	Lg App	Goals
Armstrong J.W.	5		Lowdell A.	13	
Bellamy W.R.	12	2	Meads T.	33	2
Cable T.H.	34		O'Callaghan E.	10	4
Cook G.W.	32	9	Osborne F.R.	32	9
Crompton A.	7	1	Poynton C.	16	1
Davies W.	14	2	Reddish J.	3	
Dimmock J.H.	32	6	Rowley R.W.M.	9	4
Evans T.	3		Scott J.	5	
Harper E.C.	19	14	Skitt H.	37	
Hartley F.	1		Smy J.	7	2
Forster M.	15		Spiers C.H.	42	
Herod E.R.B.	41		Thompson A.	21	2
Illingworth J.	9		Own Goal		1
Lindsay A.F.	10				

Final table for Second Division

1	Blackpool	42	27	4	11	98:67	58
2	Chelsea	42	22	11	9	74:46	55
3	Oldham	42	21	11	10	90:51	53
4	Bradford PA	42	19	12	11	91:70	50
5	Bury	42	22	5	15	78:67	49
6	West Bromwich	42	21	5	16	105:73	47
7	Southampton	42	17	11	14	77:76	45
8	Cardiff	42	18	8	16	61:59	44
9	Wolverhampton	42	16	9	17	77:79	41
10	Nottingham F.	42	13	15	14	55:69	41
11	Stoke	42	16	8	18	74:72	40
12	TOTTENHAM	42	15	9	18	59:61	39
13	Charlton	42	14	11	17	59:63	39
14	Millwall	42	12	15	15	57:73	39
15	Swansea	42	14	9	19	57:61	37
16	Preston	42	13	11	18	65:80	37
17	Barnsley	42	14	8	20	56:71	36
18	Bradford C.	42	12	12	18	60:77	36
19	Reading	42	12	11	19	54:67	35
20	Bristol C.	42	13	9	20	61:83	35
21	Hull	42	14	7	21	51:78	35
22	Notts Co.	42	9	15	18	54:70	33

30 Aug	Lge	H	Reading	W	7-1			
1 Sep	Lge	H	Burnley	W	8-1			
6 Sep	Lge	A	Wolves	L	1-3			
8 Sep	Lge	A	Preston	L	1-2			
13 Sep	Lge	H	Bradford PA	W	3-2			
15 Sep	Lge	H	Preston	D	0-0			
20 Sep	Lge	A	Stoke	L	1-2			
27 Sep	Lge	H	Millwall	W	4-1			
4 Oct	Lge	A	Oldham	W	2-1			
11 Oct	Lge	H	Nottm Forest	W	2-1			
13 Oct	LCC	H	Charlton	W	6-0			
18 Oct	Lge	H	Bury	W	3-1			
25 Oct	Lge	A	Everton	L	2-4			
27 Oct	LCC	A	Chelsea	W	2-1			
30 Oct	F	A	Oxford Univ	W	3-0			
1 Nov	Lge	H	Charlton	W	5-0			
3 Nov	LPCF	A	C. Palace	D	2-2			
8 Nov	Lge	A	Bradford C	L	0-2			
13 Nov	F	H	Camb Univ	W	8-0			
15 Nov	Lge	H	Swansea	D	1-1			
17 Nov	LCCsf	*	Ilford	W	8-1			
22 Nov	Lge	A	WBA	W	2-0			
29 Nov	Lge	H	Port Vale	W	5-0			
6 Dec	Lge	A	Plymouth	L	0-2			
8 Dec	F	A	West Ham	W	2-1			
13 Dec	Lge	H	Bristol C	W	4-1			
20 Dec	Lge	A	Barnsley	W	1-0			
25 Dec	Lge	H	Southampton	L	1-3			
26 Dec	Lge	A	Southampton	W	3-0			
27 Dec	Lge	A	Reading	W	2-1			
3 Jan	Lge	H	Wolves	W	1-0			
10 Jan	FC	H	Preston	W	3-1			
17 Jan	Lge	A	Bradford PA	L	1-4			
24 Jan	FC	A	WBA	L	0-1			
26 Jan	Lge	H	Stoke City	W	3-0			
31 Jan	Lge	A	Millwall	W	3-2			
7 Feb	Lge	H	Oldham	W	4-0			
14 Feb	Lge	A	Nottm Forest	D	2-2			
21 Feb	Lge	A	Bury	L	0-2			
28 Feb	F	H	Huddersfield	L	2-4			
7 Mar	Lge	A	Charlton	L	0-1			
14 Mar	Lge	H	Bradford C	W	3-1			
16 Mar	Lge	H	Everton	W	1-0			
21 Mar	Lge	A	Swansea	W	2-1			
28 Mar	Lge	A	WBA	D	2-2			
3 Apr	Lge	H	Cardiff	D	2-2			
4 Apr	Lge	A	Port Vale	L	0-3			
6 Apr	Lge	A	Cardiff	D	0-0			
11 Apr	Lge	H	Plymouth	D	1-1			
18 Apr	Lge	A	Bristol C	L	1-2			
25 Apr	Lge	H	Barnsley	W	4-2			
2 May	Lge	A	Burnley	L	0-1			
4 May	LCCf	†	Arsenal	L	1-2			

* at Upton Park   † at Stamford Bridge

Player	Lg App	Goals	Player	Lg App	Goals
Ashford W.J.	14		Meads T.	41	
Bellamy W.R.	17	4	Messer A.T.	39	2
Cable T.H.	4		O'Callaghan E.	37	10
Cook G.W.	31	12	Osborne F.R.	6	
Davies W.	42	4	Poynton C.	5	
Dimmock J.H.	13	4	Rowley R.W.M.	8	3
Harper E.C.	30	36	Scott J.	1	
Herod E.R.B.	3		Skitt H.	24	
Hodgkinson H.	39		Smailes J.	11	3
Howe L.	3		Smy J.	6	4
Hunt G.S.	9	4	Spiers C.H.	42	
Lyons A.	37	2			

Final table for Second Division

1	Everton	42	28	5	9	121:66	61
2	West Bromwich	42	22	10	10	83:49	54
3	**TOTTENHAM**	**42**	**22**	**7**	**13**	**88:55**	**51**
4	Wolverhampton	42	21	5	16	84:67	47
5	Port Vale	42	21	5	16	67:61	47
6	Bradford PA	42	18	10	14	97:66	46
7	Preston	42	17	11	14	83:64	45
8	Burnley	42	17	11	14	81:77	45
9	Southampton	42	19	6	17	74:62	44
10	Bradford C.	42	17	10	15	61:63	44
11	Stoke	42	17	10	15	64:71	44
12	Oldham	42	16	10	16	61:72	42
13	Bury	42	19	3	20	75:82	41
14	Millwall	42	16	7	19	71:80	39
15	Charlton	42	15	9	18	59:86	39
16	Bristol C.	42	15	8	19	54:82	38
17	Nottingham F.	42	14	9	19	80:85	37
18	Plymouth	42	14	8	20	76:84	36
19	Barnsley	42	13	9	20	59:79	35
20	Swansea	42	12	10	20	51:74	34
21	Reading	42	12	6	24	72:96	30
22	Cardiff	42	8	9	25	47:87	25

29 Aug	Lge	A	Wolves	L	0-4			
31 Aug	Lge	H	Preston	W	4-0			
5 Sep	Lge	H	Bradford PA	D	3-3			
7 Sep	Lge	A	Southampton	L	1-2			
12 Sep	Lge	A	Man Utd	D	1-1			
14 Sep	Lge	H	Southampton	W	5-2			
19 Sep	Lge	H	Barnsley	W	4-2			
26 Sep	Lge	H	Nottm Forest	L	1-3			
3 Oct	Lge	A	Chesterfield	L	2-4			
10 Oct	Lge	A	Burnley	D	1-1			
11 Oct	LCC	H	Brentford	W	4-1			
17 Oct	Lge	A	Notts Co	L	1-3			
24 Oct	Lge	H	Plymouth	L	0-1			
28 Oct	LCC	A	Kingstonian	W	3-1			
31 Oct	Lge	A	Bristol C	D	1-1			
5 Nov	F	A	Camb Univ	W	9-3			
7 Nov	Lge	H	Swansea	W	6-2			
14 Nov	Lge	A	Bury	D	1-1			
16 Nov	LCCsf	‡	C. Palace	L	0-2			
19 Nov	F	A	Oxford Univ	D	5-5			
21 Nov	Lge	H	Port Vale	W	9-3			
28 Nov	Lge	A	Millwall	W	2-1			
5 Dec	Lge	H	Bradford C	L	1-5			
12 Dec	Lge	A	Leeds	L	0-1			
19 Dec	Lge	H	Oldham	W	3-2			
25 Dec	Lge	H	Charlton	L	0-1			
26 Dec	Lge	A	Charlton	W	5-2			
2 Jan	Lge	H	Wolves	D	3-3			
9 Jan	FC	D	Sheff Wed	D	2-2			
13 Jan	FCr	A	Sheff Wed	L	1-3			
16 Jan	Lge	A	Bradford PA	L	1-2			
23 Jan	Lge	H	Man Utd	W	4-1			
30 Jan	Lge	A	Barnsley	L	2-3			
6 Feb	Lge	A	Nottm Forest	W	3-1			
13 Feb	Lge	H	Chesterfield	D	3-3			
20 Feb	Lge	A	Burnley	L	0-2			
27 Feb	Lge	H	Notts Co	W	2-0			
5 Mar	Lge	A	Plymouth	L	1-4			
12 Mar	Lge	H	Bristol C	W	2-1			
19 Mar	Lge	A	Swansea	D	1-1			
25 Mar	Lge	H	Stoke	D	3-3			
26 Mar	Lge	H	Bury	D	0-0			
28 Mar	Lge	A	Stoke	D	2-2			
2 Apr	Lge	A	Port Vale	W	3-1			
9 Apr	Lge	A	Millwall	W	1-0			
16 Apr	Lge	A	Bradford C	L	0-2			
23 Apr	Lge	H	Leeds	W	3-1			
30 Apr	Lge	A	Oldham	W	2-1			
7 May	Lge	A	Preston	L	0-2			
12 May	F	A	Guernsey XI	W	2-1			
16 May	F	A	Jersey XI	W	9-0			

‡ Played at Upton Park. After this date, Tottenham no longer put out their first team in London Challenge Cup matches

Player	Lg App	Goals	Player	Lg App	Goals
Alsford W.J.	10		Marshall W.H.	1	
Bellamy W.R.	12	3	Meads T.	27	3
Brain J.	32	8	Messer A.T.	11	
Cable T.H.	2		Moran J.	12	
Colquhoun D.M.	36	1	Nicholls J.H.	2	
Davies W.	38	12	O'Callaghan E.	34	16
Evans T.	12	3	Poynton C.	25	
Evans W.	28	5	Reddish J.	3	
Felton W.	10		Rowe A.S.	29	
Greenfield G.	12	5	Rowley R.W.M.	7	3
Harper E.C.	3	1	Smailes J.	5	
Hodgkinson H.	17		Spiers C.H.	17	
Hunt G.S.	37	25	Taylor A.	23	
Lyons A.	17	1	Own Goal		1

Final table for Second Division

1	Wolverhampton	42	24	8	10	115:49	56
2	Leeds	42	22	10	10	78:54	54
3	Stoke	42	19	14	9	69:48	52
4	Plymouth	42	20	9	13	100:66	49
5	Bury	42	21	7	14	70:58	49
6	Bradford PA	42	21	7	14	72:63	49
7	Bradford C.	42	16	13	13	80:61	45
8	**TOTTENHAM**	**42**	**16**	**11**	**15**	**87:78**	**43**
9	Millwall	42	17	9	16	61:61	43
10	Charlton	42	17	9	16	61:66	43
11	Nottingham F.	42	16	10	16	77:72	42
12	Manchester U.	42	17	8	17	71:72	42
13	Preston	42	16	10	16	75:77	42
14	Southampton	42	17	7	18	66:77	41
15	Swansea	42	16	7	19	73:75	39
16	Notts Co.	42	13	12	17	75:75	38
17	Chesterfield	42	13	11	18	64:86	37
18	Oldham	42	13	10	19	62:84	36
19	Burnley	42	13	9	20	59:87	35
20	Port Vale	42	13	7	22	58:89	33
21	Barnsley	42	12	9	21	55:91	33
22	Bristol C.	42	6	11	25	39:78	23

SEASON 1932/33

Date	Comp	H/A	Opponent	Result
27 Aug	Lge	H	Charlton	W 4-1
29 Aug	Lge	A	Nottm Forest	L 1-3
3 Sep	Lge	A	Stoke	L 0-2
5 Sep	Lge	H	Nottm Forest	W 0-0
10 Sep	Lge	H	Man Utd	W 6-1
17 Sep	Lge	A	Bury	L 0-1
24 Sep	Lge	A	Grimsby	L 2-3
1 Oct	Lge	H	Oldham	D 1-1
8 Oct	Lge	A	Preston	W 6-2
15 Oct	Lge	H	Burnley	W 4-1
22 Oct	Lge	H	Southampton	W 5-0
27 Oct	F	A	Oxford Univ	W 6-0
29 Oct	Lge	A	Millwall	W 4-1
3 Nov	F	A	Camb Univ	D 3-3
5 Nov	Lge	H	Port Vale	W 4-0
12 Nov	Lge	A	Lincoln	D 2-2
19 Nov	Lge	H	Chesterfield	W 4-1
26 Nov	Lge	A	Bradford C.	W 1-0
3 Dec	Lge	H	Swansea	W 7-0
10 Dec	Lge	A	Fulham	D 2-2
17 Dec	Lge	H	West Ham	D 2-2
24 Dec	Lge	A	Notts Co.	L 0-3
26 Dec	Lge	A	Bradford PA	D 3-3
27 Dec	Lge	H	Bradford PA	W 2-0
31 Dec	Lge	A	Charlton	W 3-0
7 Jan	Lge	H	Stoke City	W 3-2
14 Jan	FC	A	Oldham	W 6-0
21 Jan	Lge	A	Man Utd	L 1-2
28 Jan	FC	A	Luton	L 0-2
1 Feb	Lge	H	Bury	W 2-1
4 Feb	Lge	H	Grimsby	W 4-3
11 Feb	Lge	A	Oldham	W 5-1
18 Feb	Lge	H	Preston	D 1-1
4 Mar	Lge	A	Southampton	D 1-1
11 Mar	Lge	H	Millwall	W 2-1
18 Mar	Lge	A	Port Vale	D 1-1
25 Mar	Lge	H	Lincoln	W 3-2
1 Apr	Lge	A	Chesterfield	D 1-1
8 Apr	Lge	H	Bradford C	D 1-1
14 Apr	Lge	H	Plymouth	D 0-0
15 Apr	Lge	A	Swansea	W 2-0
17 Apr	Lge	A	Plymouth	D 2-2
22 Apr	Lge	H	Fulham	D 0-0
24 Apr	Lge	A	Burnley	D 1-1
29 Apr	Lge	A	West Ham	L 0-1
6 May	Lge	H	Notts Co	W 3-1
11 May	F	A	Chanl Isle XI	W 6-0
13 May	F	A	Guernsey XI	W 8-0
18 May	F	A	Jersey XI	W 5-1

Player	Lg App	Goals
Allen A.	1	1
Alsford W.J.	2	
Bellamy W.R.	3	
Brain J.	12	2
Colquhoun D.	29	1
Davies W.	15	1
Evans T.	16	1
Evans W.	42	28
Felton W.	41	
Greenfield G.	13	6
Hall G.W.	21	1
Lowe L.	18	7
Hunt G.S.	41	32
Levene D.	5	
McCormick J.	9	
Meads T.	35	
Morrison J.A.	1	1
Nicholls J.H.	37	
O'Callaghan E.	32	15
Poynton C.	4	
Rowe A.S.	41	
Taylor A.	5	
Whatley W.J.	39	

Final table for Second Division

1	Stoke	42	25	6 11	78:39	56
2	**TOTTENHAM**	**42**	**20**	**15 7**	**96:51**	**55**
3	Fulham	42	20	10 12	78:65	50
4	Bury	42	20	9 13	84:59	49
5	Nottingham F.	42	17	15 10	67:59	49
6	Manchester U.	42	15	13 14	71:68	43
7	Millwall	42	16	11 15	59:57	43
8	Bradford PA	42	17	8 17	77:71	42
9	Preston	42	16	10 16	74:70	42
10	Swansea	42	19	4 19	50:54	42
11	Bradford C.	42	14	13 15	65:61	41
12	Southampton	42	18	5 19	66:66	41
13	Grimsby	42	14	13 15	79:84	41
14	Plymouth	42	16	9 17	63:67	41
15	Notts Co.	42	15	10 17	67:78	40
16	Oldham	42	15	8 19	67:80	38
17	Port Vale	42	14	10 18	66:79	38
18	Lincoln	42	12	13 17	72:87	37
19	Burnley	42	11	14 17	67:79	36
20	West Ham	42	13	9 20	75:93	35
21	Chesterfield	42	12	10 20	61:84	34
22	Charlton	42	12	7 23	60:91	31

SEASON 1933/34

Date	Comp	H/A	Opponent	Result
26 Aug	Lge	A	Sheff Utd	D 0-0
28 Aug	Lge	H	Wolves	W 4-0
2 Sep	Lge	H	Aston Villa	W 3-2
4 Sep	Lge	A	Wolves	L 0-1
9 Sep	Lge	A	Leicester	W 3-1
16 Sep	Lge	H	Arsenal	D 1-1
23 Sep	Lge	H	Liverpool	L 0-3
30 Sep	Lge	A	Chelsea	W 4-0
7 Oct	Lge	H	Sunderland	W 3-1
14 Oct	Lge	A	Portsmouth	W 1-0
21 Oct	Lge	A	Everton	D 1-1
28 Oct	Lge	H	Middlesbrough	W 2-0
2 Nov	F	H	Oxford Univ	W 3-1
4 Nov	Lge	A	WBA	W 2-1
11 Nov	Lge	A	Newcastle	W 4-0
18 Nov	Lge	A	Leeds	D 0-0
23 Nov	F	A	Camb Univ	W 6-0
25 Nov	Lge	H	Derby	L 1-2
2 Dec	Lge	A	Man City	L 0-2
9 Dec	Lge	H	Birmingham	W 3-2
16 Dec	Lge	A	Sheff Wed	L 1-2
23 Dec	Lge	H	Blackburn	W 4-1
25 Dec	Lge	H	Huddersfield	L 1-3
26 Dec	Lge	A	Huddersfield	L 0-2
30 Dec	Lge	H	Sheff Utd	W 4-1
1 Jan	Lge	A	Blackburn	L 0-1
6 Jan	Lge	A	Aston Villa	W 5-1
13 Jan	FC	H	Everton	W 3-0
20 Jan	Lge	H	Leicester	L 0-1
27 Jan	FC	H	West Ham	W 4-1
31 Jan	Lge	A	Arsenal	W 3-1
3 Feb	Lge	A	Liverpool	L 1-3
10 Feb	Lge	H	Chelsea	W 2-1
17 Feb	FC	H	Aston Villa	L 0-1
21 Feb	Lge	A	Sunderland	L 0-6
24 Feb	Lge	H	Portsmouth	D 0-0
3 Mar	Lge	H	Everton	W 3-0
5 Mar	F	H	The Army	W 4-1
10 Mar	Lge	A	Middlesbrough	D 1-1
17 Mar	Lge	H	WBA	W 2-1
24 Mar	Lge	A	Newcastle	W 3-1
30 Mar	Lge	H	Stoke	D 0-0
31 Mar	Lge	H	Leeds	W 5-1
2 Apr	Lge	A	Stoke	L 0-2
7 Apr	Lge	A	Derby	L 3-4
14 Apr	Lge	H	Man City	W 5-1
21 Apr	Lge	A	Birmingham	L 0-2
28 Apr	Lge	H	Sheff Wed	W 4-3
30 Apr	F	A	Luton	D 2-2
2 May	SLS	H	Corinthians	W 7-4

Player	Lg App	Goals
Alsford W.J.	13	
Bellamy W.R.	5	
Bolan L.A.	1	
Channell F.C.	22	
Colquhoun D.M.	13	
Day A.	3	
Evans T.	26	
Evans W.	36	16
Hall B.A.C.	2	
Hall G.W.	42	3
Hedley F.	1	
Howe L.	10	6
Hunt G.S.	40	32
Felton W.	22	1
McCormick J.	40	9
Meads T.	30	1
Nicholls J.H.	42	
O'Callaghan E.	32	11
Rowe A.S.	42	
Whatley W.J.	40	

Final table for First Division

1	Arsenal	42	25	9 8	75:47	59
2	Huddersfield	42	23	10 9	90:61	56
3	**TOTTENHAM**	**42**	**21**	**7 14**	**79:56**	**49**
4	Derby	42	17	11 14	68:54	45
5	Manchester C.	42	17	11 14	65:72	45
6	Sunderland	42	16	12 14	81:56	44
7	West Bromwich	42	17	10 15	78:70	44
8	Blackburn	42	18	7 17	74:81	43
9	Leeds	42	17	8 17	75:66	42
10	Portsmouth	42	15	12 15	52:55	42
11	Sheffield W.	42	16	9 17	62:67	41
12	Stoke	42	15	11 16	58:71	41
13	Aston Villa	42	14	12 16	78:75	40
14	Everton	42	12	16 14	62:63	40
15	Wolverhampton	42	14	12 16	74:86	40
16	Middlesbrough	42	16	7 19	68:80	39
17	Leicester	42	14	11 17	59:74	39
18	Liverpool	42	14	10 18	79:87	38
19	Chelsea	42	14	8 20	67:69	36
20	Birmingham	42	12	12 18	54:56	36
21	Newcastle	42	10	14 18	68:77	34
22	Sheffield U.	42	12	7 23	58:101	31

SEASON 1934/35

Date	Comp		Opponent		Result
25 Aug	Lge	H	Everton	D	1-1
27 Aug	Lge	H	Preston	L	1-2
1 Sep	Lge	A	Huddersfield	D	0-0
3 Sep	Lge	A	Preston	L	0-1
8 Sep	Lge	H	Wolves	W	3-1
15 Sep	Lge	A	Chelsea	W	3-1
22 Sep	Lge	H	Aston Villa	L	0-2
29 Sep	Lge	A	Derby	L	1-2
6 Oct	Lge	H	Leicester	D	2-2
13 Oct	Lge	A	Sunderland	W	2-1
20 Oct	Lge	A	Arsenal	L	1-5
27 Oct	Lge	H	Portsmouth	W	4-1
1 Nov	F	A	Oxford Univ	W	4-3
5 Nov	Lge	A	Man City	L	1-3
7 Nov	SLS	H	Corinthians	W	7-2
10 Nov	Lge	H	Middlesbrough	W	3-1
14 Nov	Lge	H	Camb Univ	W	4-0
17 Nov	Lge	A	WBA	L	0-4
24 Nov	Lge	H	Sheff Wed	W	3-2
1 Dec	Lge	A	Birmingham	L	1-2
8 Dec	Lge	H	Stoke	W	3-2
15 Dec	Lge	H	Liverpool	L	1-4
22 Dec	Lge	H	Leeds	D	1-1
25 Dec	Lge	A	Grimsby	L	0-3
26 Dec	Lge	H	Grimsby	W	2-1
29 Dec	Lge	A	Everton	L	2-5
1 Jan	Lge	A	Blackburn	L	0-2
5 Jan	Lge	H	Huddersfield	D	0-0
12 Jan	FC	H	Man City	W	1-0
19 Jan	Lge	A	Wolves	L	2-6
26 Jan	FC	H	Newcastle	W	2-0
30 Jan	Lge	H	Chelsea	L	1-3
2 Feb	Lge	A	Aston Villa	L	0-1
9 Feb	Lge	H	Derby	D	2-2
16 Feb	FC	H	Bolton	D	1-1
20 Feb	FCr	A	Bolton	D	1-1
23 Feb	Lge	H	Sunderland	D	1-1
25 Feb	FCr	*	Bolton	L	0-2
6 Mar	Lge	H	Arsenal	L	0-6
9 Mar	Lge	A	Portsmouth	D	1-1
16 Mar	Lge	H	Man City	D	0-0
23 Mar	Lge	A	Middlesbrough	L	1-3
28 Mar	Lge	A	Leicester	L	0-6
30 Mar	Lge	H	WBA	L	0-1
6 Apr	Lge	A	Sheff Wed	L	0-4
13 Apr	Lge	H	Birmingham	D	1-1
19 Apr	Lge	H	Blackburn	W	1-0
20 Apr	Lge	A	Stoke	L	1-4
24 Apr	F	A	Burton Town	D	2-2
27 Apr	Lge	H	Liverpool	W	5-1
4 May	Lge	A	Leeds	L	3-4
16 May	F	A	Chanl Isle XI	W	5-0
18 May	F	A	Guernsey XI	W	5-0

* Played at Villa Park

Player	Lg App	Goals	Player	Lg App	Goals
Alsford W.J.	21		Howe L.F.	32	2
Bell S.	8	2	Hunt D.A.	12	4
Bellamy W.R.	7	1	Hunt G.S.	30	10
Bolan L.A.	9	3	Illingworth J.	1	
Brain J.	1		Jones C.	8	
Burgon A.	4		King	1	
Channell F.C.	41	1	Levene D.	3	
Colquhoun D.M.	3		Meads T.	18	
Day A.	9		McCormick J.	28	6
Duncan A.	6		Morrison J.A.	2	1
Evans T.	28		Nicholls J.H.	21	
Evans W.	32	12	O'Callaghan E.	16	4
Fullwood J.	2		Phypers E.	2	
Goldsmith G.	1		Rowe A.S.	18	
Greenfield G.	6		Sargent F.A.	1	
Hall A.G.	12	3	Taylor A.	18	
Hall G.W.	18	3	Whatley W.J.	37	
Hedley F.	3	1	Own Goal		1
Hooper P.G.	3				

Final table for First Division

1	Arsenal	42	23	12	7	115:46	58
2	Sunderland	42	19	16	7	90:51	54
3	Sheffield W.	42	18	13	11	70:64	49
4	Manchester C.	42	20	8	14	82:67	48
5	Grimsby	42	17	11	14	78:60	45
6	Derby	42	18	9	15	81:66	45
7	Liverpool	42	19	7	16	85:88	45
8	Everton	42	16	12	14	89:88	44
9	West Bromwich	42	17	10	15	83:83	44
10	Stoke	42	18	6	18	71:70	42
11	Preston	42	15	12	15	62:67	42
12	Chelsea	42	16	9	17	73:82	41
13	Aston Villa	42	14	13	15	74:88	41
14	Portsmouth	42	15	10	17	71:72	40
15	Blackburn	42	14	11	17	66:78	39
16	Huddersfield	42	14	10	18	76:71	38
17	Wolverhampton	42	15	8	19	88:94	38
18	Leeds	42	13	12	17	75:92	38
19	Birmingham	42	13	10	19	63:81	36
20	Middlesbrough	42	10	14	18	70:90	34
21	Leicester	42	12	9	21	61:86	33
22	**TOTTENHAM**	**42**	**10**	**10**	**22**	**54:93**	**30**

SEASON 1935/36

Date	Comp		Opponent		Result
31 Aug	Lge	A	Bradford C.	W	1-0
2 Sep	Lge	H	Hull	W	3-1
7 Sep	Lge	H	Newcastle	L	1-2
9 Sep	Lge	A	Hull	L	0-1
14 Sep	Lge	A	Sheff Utd	D	1-1
16 Sep	Lge	H	Barnsley	W	3-0
21 Sep	Lge	A	Man Utd	D	0-0
28 Sep	Lge	H	Port Vale	W	5-2
5 Oct	Lge	A	Fulham	W	2-1
12 Oct	Lge	H	Burnley	W	5-1
19 Oct	Lge	H	Bradford	W	4-0
26 Oct	Lge	A	Leicester	L	1-4
2 Nov	Lge	H	Swansea	W	7-2
9 Nov	Lge	A	West Ham	D	2-2
16 Nov	Lge	H	Bury	W	4-3
21 Nov	F	H	Oxford Univ	W	4-2
23 Nov	Lge	A	Southampton	L	0-2
28 Nov	F	A	Camb Univ	L	0-1
30 Nov	Lge	H	Blackpool	W	3-1
7 Dec	Lge	A	Nottm Forest	L	1-4
14 Dec	Lge	H	Norwich	W	2-1
21 Dec	Lge	A	Doncaster	L	1-4
25 Dec	Lge	H	Plymouth	L	1-2
26 Dec	Lge	A	Plymouth	L	1-2
28 Dec	Lge	H	Bradford C	W	4-0
4 Jan	Lge	A	Newcastle	W	4-1
11 Jan	FC	H	Southend	D	4-4
15 Jan	FCr	A	Southend	W	2-1
18 Jan	FC	A	Sheff Utd	D	1-1
25 Jan	FC	A	Huddersfield	W	1-0
1 Feb	Lge	A	Port Vale	W	5-1
5 Feb	Lge	H	Man Utd	D	0-0
8 Feb	Lge	H	Fulham	D	2-2
15 Feb	FC	A	Bradford PA	D	0-0
17 Feb	FCr	H	Bradford PA	W	2-1
22 Feb	Lge	A	Bradford PA	W	5-2
29 Feb	FC	A	Sheff Utd	L	1-3
4 Mar	Lge	H	Nottm Forest	D	1-1
7 Mar	Lge	A	Bury	D	1-1
14 Mar	Lge	H	West Ham	L	1-3
21 Mar	Lge	A	Swansea	D	1-1
28 Mar	Lge	H	Southampton	W	8-0
4 Apr	Lge	A	Blackpool	W	4-2
10 Apr	Lge	H	Charlton	D	1-1
11 Apr	Lge	H	Leicester	D	1-1
13 Apr	Lge	A	Charlton	L	1-2
18 Apr	Lge	A	Newcastle	L	0-1
20 Apr	Lge	A	Burnley	D	0-0
25 Apr	Lge	A	Doncaster	W	3-1
2 May	Lge	A	Barnsley	D	0-0

Player	Lg App	Goals	Player	Lg App	Goals
Alsford W.J.	14		Howe L.	33	6
Bell S.	5	3	Hunt D.A.	4	2
Buckingham V.F.	16		Hunt G.S.	15	11
Channell F.C.	32		Jones C.	10	
Day A.	1		McCormick J.	21	3
Duncan A.	24	6	Meek J.	10	5
Edrich W.J.	9	1	Morrison J.A.	32	25
Evans T.	8		Nicholls J.H.	7	
Evans W.	33	15	Phypers E.	26	
Fullwood J.	12	1	Rowe A.S.	28	
Grice F.	7		Sargent F.A.	16	5
Hall A.E.	1		Taylor A.	14	
Hall A.G.	4		Ward R.A.	8	
Hall G.W.	32	6	Whatley W.J.	19	
Hooper P.G.	21		Own Goals		2

Final table for Second Division

1	Manchester U.	42	22	12	8	85:43	56
2	Charlton	42	22	11	9	85:58	55
3	Sheffield U.	42	20	12	10	79:50	52
4	West Ham	42	22	8	12	90:68	52
5	**TOTTENHAM**	**42**	**18**	**13**	**11**	**91:55**	**49**
6	Leicester	42	19	10	13	79:57	48
7	Plymouth	42	20	8	14	71:57	48
8	Newcastle	42	20	6	16	88:79	46
9	Fulham	42	15	14	13	76:52	44
10	Blackpool	42	18	7	17	93:72	43
11	Norwich	42	17	9	16	72:65	43
12	Bradford C.	42	15	13	14	55:65	43
13	Swansea	42	15	9	18	67:76	39
14	Bury	42	13	12	17	66:84	38
15	Burnley	42	12	13	17	50:59	37
16	Bradford PA	42	14	9	19	62:84	37
17	Southampton	42	14	9	19	47:65	37
18	Doncaster	42	14	9	19	51:71	37
19	Nottingham F.	42	12	11	19	69:76	35
20	Barnsley	42	12	9	21	54:80	33
21	Port Vale	42	12	8	22	56:106	32
22	Hull	42	5	10	27	47:111	20

SEASON 1936/37

Date	Comp		Opponent	Res	Score		Date	Comp		Opponent	Res	Score
29 Aug	Lge	A	West Ham	L	1-2		2 Jan	Lge	A	Norwich	W	3-2
31 Aug	Lge	A	Blackpool	D	0-0		9 Jan	Lge	H	Newcastle	L	0-1
5 Sep	Lge	H	Norwich	L	2-3		16 Jan	FC	A	Portsmouth	W	5-0
12 Sep	Lge	A	Newcastle	W	1-0		23 Jan	Lge	A	Bradford	L	2-3
14 Sep	Lge	H	Leicester	W	4-2		30 Jan	FC	H	Plymouth	W	1-0
19 Sep	Lge	H	Bradford	W	5-1		3 Feb	Lge	H	Barnsley	W	3-0
21 Sep	Lge	H	Blackpool	L	1-2		6 Feb	Lge	A	Sheff Utd	L	2-3
26 Sep	Lge	A	Barnsley	L	0-1		13 Feb	Lge	H	Burnley	W	3-0
3 Oct	Lge	H	Sheff Utd	D	2-2		20 Feb	FC	A	Everton	D	1-1
10 Oct	Lge	A	Burnley	L	1-3		22 Feb	FCr	H	Everton	W	4-3
17 Oct	Lge	H	Southampton	W	4-0		24 Feb	Lge	A	Southampton	L	0-1
24 Oct	Lge	A	Swansea	L	1-2		27 Feb	Lge	H	Swansea	W	3-1
31 Oct	Lge	H	Bradford C	W	5-1		6 Mar	FC	H	Preston	L	1-3
7 Nov	Lge	A	Aston Villa	D	1-1		10 Mar	Lge	A	Bradford C	D	2-2
14 Nov	Lge	H	Chesterfield	W	5-1		13 Mar	Lge	H	Aston Villa	D	2-2
16 Nov	F	H	Corinthians	W	5-1		20 Mar	Lge	A	Chesterfield	W	3-1
19 Nov	F	A	Oxford Univ	W	2-0		26 Mar	Lge	A	Bury	L	3-5
26 Nov	F	A	Camb Univ	W	6-2		27 Mar	Lge	H	Nottm Forest	W	2-1
28 Nov	Lge	H	Plymouth	L	1-3		29 Mar	Lge	H	Bury	W	2-0
5 Dec	Lge	A	Coventry	L	0-1		3 Apr	Lge	A	Plymouth	D	2-2
12 Dec	Lge	H	Doncaster	W	2-0		10 Apr	Lge	A	Coventry	W	3-1
19 Dec	Lge	A	Fulham	D	3-3		17 Apr	Lge	A	Doncaster	D	1-1
25 Dec	Lge	A	Blackburn	W	4-0		21 Apr	Lge	A	Nottm Forest	L	0-3
26 Dec	Lge	H	West Ham	L	2-3		24 Apr	Lge	H	Fulham	D	1-1
28 Dec	Lge	H	Blackburn	W	5-1		1 May	Lge	A	Leicester	L	1-4

Player	Lg App	Goals		Player	Lg App	Goals
Alexander S.	9	1		Cooper P.G.	3	
Alsford W.J.	7			Howe L.	28	
Bell S.	2	1		Hunt D.A.	1	
Blyth J.	11			Hunt G.S.	13	10
Brown J.	4			Ludford G.A.	1	
Buckingham V.F.	25			McCormick J.	35	8
Duncan A.	29	9		Meek J.	28	9
Edrich W.J.	11	3		Miller L.	23	12
Evans T.	1			Morrison J.A.	32	29
Evans W.	7	2		Page A.E.	15	
Fullwood J.	5			Phypers E.	2	
Grice F.	22			Ringrose A.	10	
Hall A.E.	1			Rowe A.S.	15	
Hall G.W.	19	1		Ward R.A.	32	3
Hall J.	39			Whatley W.J.	32	

Final table for Second Division

1	Leicester	42	24	8 10	89:57	56
2	Blackpool	42	24	7 11	88:53	55
3	Bury	42	22	8 12	74:55	52
4	Newcastle	42	22	5 15	80:56	49
5	Plymouth	42	18	13 11	71:53	49
6	West Ham	42	19	11 12	73:55	49
7	Sheffield U.	42	18	10 14	66:54	46
8	Coventry	42	17	11 14	66:54	45
9	Aston Villa	42	16	12 14	82:70	44
10	TOTTENHAM	42	17	9 16	88:66	43
11	Fulham	42	15	13 14	71:61	43
12	Blackburn	42	16	10 16	70:62	42
13	Burnley	42	16	10 16	57:61	42
14	Barnsley	42	16	9 17	50:64	41
15	Chesterfield	42	16	8 18	84:89	40
16	Swansea	42	15	7 20	50:65	37
17	Norwich	42	14	8 20	63:71	36
18	Nottingham F.	42	12	10 20	68:90	34
19	Southampton	42	11	12 19	53:77	34
20	Bradford PA	42	12	9 21	52:88	33
21	Bradford C.	42	9	12 21	54:94	30
22	Doncaster	42	7	10 25	30:84	24

SEASON 1937/38

Date	Comp		Opponent	Res	Score		Date	Comp		Opponent	Res	Score
28 Aug	Lge	H	Coventry	D	0-0		8 Jan	FC	H	Blackburn	W	3-2
30 Aug	Lge	H	Burnley	W	4-0		15 Jan	Lge	H	Nottm Forest	W	3-0
4 Sep	Lge	A	Nottm Forest	L	1-3		22 Jan	FC	A	N/Brighton	D	0-0
6 Sep	Lge	A	Burnley	L	1-2		26 Jan	FCr	H	N/Brighton	W	5-2
11 Sep	Lge	H	Newcastle	D	2-2		29 Jan	Lge	H	Luton	W	3-0
16 Sep	Lge	A	Sheff Wed	W	3-0		2 Feb	Lge	A	Newcastle	L	0-1
18 Sep	Lge	A	Luton	W	4-2		5 Feb	Lge	A	Barnsley	D	1-1
25 Sep	Lge	H	Barnsley	W	3-0		12 Feb	FC	A	Chesterfield	D	2-2
2 Oct	Lge	A	Stockport	L	2-3		16 Feb	FCr	H	Chesterfield	W	2-1
9 Oct	Lge	A	Man Utd	L	0-1		19 Feb	Lge	A	Man Utd	W	1-0
16 Oct	Lge	A	Fulham	L	1-3		23 Feb	Lge	H	Stockport	W	2-0
23 Oct	Lge	H	Plymouth	W	3-2		26 Feb	Lge	H	Fulham	D	1-1
30 Oct	Lge	A	Chesterfield	D	2-2		7 Mar	FC	H	Sunderland	L	0-1*
6 Nov	Lge	H	Swansea	W	2-0		9 Mar	Lge	A	Plymouth	D	2-2
13 Nov	Lge	A	Norwich	L	1-2		12 Mar	Lge	H	Chesterfield	W	2-0
18 Nov	F	H	Oxford Univ	W	3-2		19 Mar	Lge	A	Swansea	L	2-3
20 Nov	Lge	H	West Ham	W	2-0		26 Mar	Lge	H	Norwich	W	4-0
25 Nov	F	A	Camb Univ	L	2-3		2 Apr	Lge	A	West Ham	W	3-1
27 Nov	Lge	A	Bradford PA	L	1-3		9 Apr	Lge	H	Bradford PA	W	2-1
4 Dec	Lge	H	Aston Villa	W	2-1		15 Apr	Lge	H	Sheff Utd	L	1-2
11 Dec	Lge	A	Southampton	L	1-2		16 Apr	Lge	A	Aston Villa	L	0-2
18 Dec	Lge	H	Blackburn	W	3-1		18 Apr	Lge	A	Sheff Utd	L	0-1
25 Dec	Lge	A	Bury	W	2-1		23 Apr	Lge	H	Southampton	W	5-0
26 Dec	Lge	H	Bury	L	1-3		30 Apr	Lge	A	Blackburn	L	1-2
1 Jan	Lge	A	Coventry	L	1-2		7 May	Lge	H	Sheff Wed	L	1-2

* Tottenham's record attendance (75,038)

Player	Lg App	Goals		Player	Lg App	Goals
Buckingham V.F.	29			Ludford G.A.	1	
Duncan A.	13	2		Lyman C.C.	24	4
Fullwood J.	15			McCormick J.	3	
Gibbons A.H.	27	13		Meek J.	7	1
Grice F.	17	1		Miller L.	16	5
Hall A.E.	6			Morrison J.A.	39	23
Hall G.W.	30	4		Page A.E.	23	
Hall J.	12			Rowe A.S.	9	
Hitchins A.W.	10			Sargent F.A.	42	14
Hooper P.G.	30			Spelman I.	8	
Howe L.	33	4		Ward R.A.	42	4
Jeffrey G.	1	1		Whatley W.J.	25	

Final table for Second Division

1	Aston Villa	42	25	7 10	73:35	57
2	Manchester U.	42	22	9 11	82:50	53
3	Sheffield U.	42	22	9 11	73:56	53
4	Coventry	42	20	12 10	66:45	52
5	TOTTENHAM	42	19	6 17	76:54	44
6	Burnley	42	17	10 15	54:54	44
7	Bradford PA	42	17	9 16	69:56	43
8	Fulham	42	16	11 15	61:57	43
9	West Ham	42	14	14 14	53:52	42
10	Bury	42	18	5 19	63:60	41
11	Chesterfield	42	16	9 17	63:63	41
12	Luton	42	15	10 17	89:86	40
13	Plymouth	42	14	12 16	57:65	40
14	Norwich	42	14	11 17	56:75	39
15	Southampton	42	15	9 18	55:77	39
16	Blackburn	42	14	10 18	71:80	38
17	Sheffield W.	42	14	10 18	48:56	38
18	Swansea	42	13	12 17	45:73	38
19	Newcastle	42	14	8 20	51:58	36
20	Nottingham F.	42	14	8 20	47:60	36
21	Barnsley	42	11	14 17	50:64	36
22	Stockport	42	11	9 22	43:70	31

Season 1938/39 fixtures

20 Aug	Jt	A	Arsenal	W	2-0		7 Jan	FC	H	Watford	W	7-1
27 Aug	Lge	A	Southampton	W	2-1		14 Jan	Lge	H	Nottm Forest	W	4-1
29 Aug	Lge	H	Sheff Wed	D	3-3		21 Jan	FC	A	West Ham	D	3-3
3 Sep	Lge	H	Coventry	W	2-1		28 Jan	Lge	H	WBA	D	2-2
10 Sep	Lge	A	Nottm Forest	L	1-2		30 Jan	FCr	H	West Ham	D	1-1
12 Sep	Lge	H	Sheff Utd	D	2-2		2 Feb	FCr	*	West Ham	L	1-2
17 Sep	Lge	H	Newcastle	W	1-0		4 Feb	Lge	A	Norwich	W	2-1
24 Sep	Lge	A	WBA	L	3-4		11 Feb	Lge	H	Luton	L	0-1
1 Oct	Lge	H	Norwich	W	4-1		18 Feb	Lge	A	Fulham	L	0-1
8 Oct	Lge	A	Luton	D	0-0		25 Feb	Lge	H	Blackburn	W	4-3
15 Oct	Lge	H	Fulham	W	1-0		1 Mar	Lge	A	Newcastle	W	1-0
22 Oct	Lge	A	Blackburn	L	1-3		4 Mar	Lge	A	West Ham	W	2-0
29 Oct	Lge	H	West Ham	W	2-1		11 Mar	Lge	H	Man City	L	2-3
5 Nov	Lge	A	Man City	L	0-2		18 Mar	Lge	A	Bradford PA	D	0-0
12 Nov	Lge	H	Bradford PA	D	2-2		25 Mar	Lge	H	Swansea	W	3-0
19 Nov	Lge	A	Swansea	D	1-1		1 Apr	Lge	A	Chesterfield	L	1-3
26 Nov	Lge	H	Chesterfield	D	2-2		7 Apr	Lge	H	Plymouth	W	1-0
3 Dec	Lge	A	Tranmere	W	2-0		8 Apr	Lge	H	Tranmere	W	3-1
10 Dec	Lge	H	Millwall	W	4-0		10 Apr	Lge	A	Plymouth	W	1-0
17 Dec	Lge	A	Bury	L	1-3		15 Apr	Lge	A	Millwall	L	0-2
24 Dec	Lge	H	Southampton	D	1-1		22 Apr	Lge	H	Bury	W	4-3
26 Dec	Lge	A	Burnley	L	0-1		29 Apr	Lge	A	Sheff Wed	W	0-1
27 Dec	Lge	H	Burnley	W	1-0		6 May	Lge	A	Sheff Utd	L	1-6
31 Dec	Lge	A	Coventry	L	0-4							

*Played at Highbury
Jt Jubilee Trust Fund

Player	Lg App	Goals		Player	Lg App	Goals
Buckingham V.F.	41	1		Lyman C.C.	22	6
Burgess W.A.R.	17	1		McCormick J.	1	
Cox F.J.A.	9	2		Miller L.	17	5
Duncan A.	21	5		Morrison J.A.	27	9
Grice F.	1			Nicholson W.E.	8	
Hall A.E.	24	10		Page A.E.	17	
Hall G.W.	40	9		Sargent F.A.	34	4
Hall J.	2			Spelman I.	20	2
Hitchins A.W.	25	1		Sproston B.	9	
Cooper P.G.	40			Tomkin A.H.	2	
Howe L.	8	1		Ward R.A.	33	3
Ludford G.A.	10	6		Whatley W.J.	34	2

Second Division 1938–39

1	Blackburn	42	25	5	12	94:60	55
2	Sheffield U.	42	20	14	8	69:41	54
3	Sheffield W.	42	21	11	10	88:59	53
4	Coventry	42	21	8	13	62:45	50
5	Manchester C.	42	21	7	14	96:72	49
6	Chesterfield	42	20	9	13	69:52	49
7	Luton	42	22	5	15	82:66	49
8	TOTTENHAM	42	19	9	14	67:62	47
9	Newcastle	42	18	10	14	61:48	46
10	West Bromwich	42	18	9	15	89:72	45
11	West Ham	42	17	10	15	70:52	44
12	Fulham	42	17	10	15	61:55	44
13	Millwall	42	14	14	14	64:53	42
14	Burnley	42	15	9	18	50:56	39
15	Plymouth	42	15	9	18	49:55	38
16	Bury	42	12	13	17	65:74	37
17	Bradford PA	42	12	11	19	61:82	35
18	Southampton	42	13	9	20	56:82	35
19	Swansea	42	11	12	19	50:83	34
20	Nottingham F.	42	10	11	21	49:82	31
21	Norwich	42	13	5	24	50:91	31
22	Tranmere	42	6	5	31	39:99	17

Season 1939/40 fixtures

19 Aug	Jt	H	Arsenal	L	0-1		25 Jan	Lge	H	Arsenal	L	0-1
26 Aug	Lge*	H	Birmingham	D	1-1		10 Feb	Lge	A	West Ham	L	0-2
31 Aug	Lge*	A	Newport	D	1-1		17 Feb	Lge	H	Charlton	W	2-0
2 Sep	Lge*	A	WBA	W	4-3		24 Feb	Lge	A	Chelsea	W	2-0
23 Sep	F	A	Chelmsford	L	2-4		28 Feb	Lge	A	C. Palace	D	1-1
30 Sep	F	A	Chelsea	L	2-4		2 Mar	Lge	H	Southampton	W	4-1
7 Oct	F	H	West Ham	L	0-2		9 Mar	Lge	H	Brentford	D	1-1
21 Oct	Lge	A	Southend	W	2-0		16 Mar	Lge	A	Portsmouth	W	2-1
28 Oct	Lge	H	Millwall	W	3-0		23 Mar	Lge	A	Millwall	L	1-2
4 Nov	Lge	H	West Ham	L	1-2		23 Mar	Lge	A	Fulham	W	3-2
11 Nov	Lge	H	Watford	W	8-2		25 Mar	Lge	A	Millwall	D	1-1
18 Nov	Lge	H	Arsenal	L	1-2		30 Mar	Lge	A	Arsenal	D	1-1
25 Dec	Lge	H	Charlton	W	4-2		6 Apr	Lge	H	West Ham	L	2-6
2 Dec	Lge	A	C. Orient	L	1-2		10 Apr	Lge	H	Fulham	W	3-1
9 Dec	Lge	H	C. Palace	L	1-3		13 Apr	Lge	A	Charlton	W	4-2
16 Dec	Lge	A	Norwich	L	2-5		20 Apr	CUP	A	C. Palace	L	1-4
23 Dec	Lge	H	Southend	L	3-4‡		24 Apr	Lge	A	Arsenal	W	4-2
25 Dec	Lge	A	Millwall	L	1-5		27 Apr	CUP	H	C. Palace	W	2-1
26 Dec	Lge	H	West Ham	L	0-1		4 May	Lge	A	Brentford	W	3-2
30 Jan	Lge	A	Watford	L	1-6		11 May	Lge	H	Portsmouth	W	4-1
13 Jan	Lge	A	Charlton	W	5-1		18 May	Lge	A	Southampton	D	3-3
17 Jan	Lge	H	Southend	L	2-4		25 May	Lge	H	Chelsea	W	3-2
20 Jan	Lge	H	C. Orient	L	2-3		27 May	Lge	H	Norwich	D	2-2

Jt Football League Jubilee match
* Three Football League fixtures which were played before the season was abandoned. Other League matches this season were in the two Regional Leagues South.   ‡ Match abandoned and replayed on 17 Jan.

Player	Lg App	Goals		Player	Lg App	Goals
Buckingham V.F.	3			Lyman C.C.	1	
Burgess W.A.R.	3	1		Morrison J.A.	1	3
Dix R.W.	3	1		Nicholson W.E.	3	
Hall G.W.	3			Page A.E.	1	
Hitchins A.W.	2			Sargent F.A.	3	1
Hooper P.G.	3			Tomkin A.H.	2	
Ludford G.A.	2			Ward R.A.	3	

Player	War Lg App	Goals		Player	War Lg App	Goals
Bennett L.	11	6		Ludford G.	11	7
Buckingham V.	14			Lyman C.	6	1
Burchell	1			McCormick J.	6	
Burgess R.	14	2		McEwan	3	
Cox F.	10	1		Medley L.	23	10
Ditchburn E.	2			Morrison J.	29	21
Dorling	12			Ottewell*	1	
Dowers	2			Page A.	7	
Duncan A.	16	4		Piper	1	
Evans	1			Sargent F.	15	5
Hall A.E.	4	2		Spelman I.	11	
Hall G.W.	26	4		Stephens		
Hitchins	32			Tomkin A.	1	2
Hooper P.	33			Ward R.	21	2
Howe L.	31	5		Whatley G.	33	
Hunt D.	2	2		Wilbert G.	1	

* Guest

Second Division 1939–40

1	Luton	3	2	1	0	7:1	5
2	Birmingham	3	2	1	0	5:1	5
3	Coventry	3	1	2	0	8:6	4
4	Plymouth	3	2	0	1	4:3	4
5	West Ham	3	2	0	1	5:4	4
6	Leicester	3	2	0	1	6:5	4
7	TOTTENHAM	3	1	2	0	6:5	4
8	Nottingham F.	3	2	0	1	5:5	4
9	Millwall	3	1	1	1	5:4	3
10	Newport	3	1	1	1	5:4	3
11	Manchester C.	3	1	1	1	6:5	3
12	WBA	3	1	1	1	8:8	3
13	Bury	3	1	1	1	4:5	3
14	Newcastle	3	1	0	2	8:6	2
15	Chesterfield	2	1	0	1	2:2	2
16	Barnsley	3	1	0	2	7:8	2
17	Southampton	3	1	0	2	5:6	2
18	Sheffield W.	3	1	0	2	3:5	2
19	Swansea	3	1	0	2	5:11	2
20	Fulham	3	0	1	2	3:6	1
21	Burnley	2	0	1	1	1:3	1
22	Bradford	3	0	1	2	2:7	1

These were the Football League standings at the point the competition was abandoned.

Regional League South 'A' 1939–40

1	Arsenal	18	13	4	1	62:22	30
2	West Ham	18	12	1	5	57:33	25
3	Millwall	18	8	5	5	46:38	21
4	Watford	18	9	3	6	44:38	21
5	Norwich	18	7	6	5	41:36	20
6	Charlton	18	8	1	9	61:58	17
7	C. Palace	18	5	3	10	39:56	13
8	C. Orient	18	5	3	10	28:60	13
9	TOTTENHAM	18	5	2	11	37:43	12
10	Southend	18	4	0	14	30:61	8

Regional League South 'C' 1939–40

1	TOTTENHAM	18	11	4	3	43:30	26
2	West Ham	18	10	4	4	53:28	24
3	Arsenal	18	9	5	4	41:26	23
4	Brentford	18	8	4	6	42:34	20
5	Millwall	18	7	5	6	36:30	19
6	Charlton	18	7	4	7	39:36	18
7	Fulham	18	8	1	9	38:42	17
8	Southampton	18	5	3	10	28:55	13
9	Chelsea	18	4	3	11	33:53	11
10	Portsmouth	18	3	3	12	26:45	9

SEASON 1940/41

Date	Comp	H/A	Opponent	Res	Score
31 Aug	Lge	H	West Ham	L	2-3
7 Sep	Lge	A	West Ham	W	4-1*
14 Sep	Lge	H	Chelsea	W	3-2*
21 Sep	Lge	A	Chelsea	L	1-4
28 Sep	Lge	H	Charlton	L	1-3
5 Oct	Lge	A	QPR	D	1-1
12 Oct	Lge	H	QPR	L	2-3*
19 Oct	Lge	A	Charlton	L	0-4
26 Oct	Lge	H	Portsmouth	L	1-2
2 Nov	Lge	A	Luton	D	1-1
16 Nov	Lge	A	Arsenal	D	1-1
23 Nov	Lge	H	Luton	W	2-1*
30 Nov	Lge	A	Southend	L	2-3†
7 Dec	Lge	H	QPR	L	2-3
21 Dec	Lge	H	C. Orient	W	9-0
25 Dec	Lge	H	Millwall	D	3-3
28 Dec	Lge	H	C. Orient	W	7-0
4 Jan	LCup	H	C. Orient	W	3-0
11 Jan	LCup	A	C. Orient	W	9-1
18 Jan	LCup	A	Millwall	W	3-1
25 Jan	LCup	H	Millwall	W	4-0
1 Feb	LCup	H	West Ham	L	1-2
8 Feb	LCup	A	West Ham	L	2-3
15 Feb	LGC	H	Bournemouth	W	4-1
22 Feb	LGC	A	Bournemouth	W	6-1
1 Mar	LGC	H	Northampton	W	4-0
8 Mar	LGC	A	Northampton	W	3-1
15 Mar	Lge	H	Millwall	L	0-1
22 Mar	LGC	H	Cardiff	D	3-3
29 Mar	LGC	A	Cardiff	W	3-2
5 Apr	LGC	A	Arsenal	L	1-2
12 Apr	LGC	H	Arsenal	D	1-1
14 Apr	LCup	H	Reading	D	2-2
19 Apr	LCup	A	Reading	D	2-2
26 Apr	Lge	A	Aldershot	W	3-2
3 May	LCup	H	Arsenal	D	3-3
10 May	Lge	H	C. Palace	D	1-1
17 May	Lge	A	Leicester	W	2-1
21 May	LCup	A	Arsenal	W	3-0
24 May	Lge	H	Leicester	W	3-0
31 May	LCupsf	H	Brentford	L	0-2
7 Jun	Lge	H	Fulham	W	2-1

* Matches abandoned
† Played at Chelmsford

Player	War Lg App	Goals
Arnold*	1	
Bennett L.	5	
Broadis I.	4	2
Brown J.	1	
Buckingham V.	14	
Burdett	1	
Burgess R.	9	8
Duncan A.	17	5
Flack*	5	
Gibbons A.	8	9
Goodman*	1	
Hall G.W.	15	3
Henley*	1	
Hitchens	22	
Hooper P.	14	
Howe L.	4	2
Ludford G.	23	11
McCarthy	1	
McCormick J.	2	
Medley L.	6	2
Newman A.	1	
O'Callaghan F.	8	1
Paton*	4	
Piper	3	
Sainsbury	1	
Sargent F.	6	1
Saunders*	3	
Skinner	3	1
Sperrin J.	4	2
Sperrin W.	8	3
Wallace J.	1	
Wallis J.	2	
Ward R.	22	2
Whartley W.	20	
White R.	13	
Own Goal		1

* Guest

Regional League South 1940–41

1	C. Palace	27	16	4	7	86:44	1.954
2	West Ham	25	14	6	5	70:39	1.794
3	Coventry	10	5	3	2	28:16	1.750
4	Arsenal	19	10	5	4	66:38	1.736
5	Cardiff	24	12	5	7	75:50	1.500
6	Reading	26	14	5	7	73:51	1.431
7	Norwich	19	9	2	8	73:55	1.327
8	Watford	35	15	6	14	96:73	1.315
9	Portsmouth	31	16	2	13	92:71	1.296
10	TOTTENHAM	23	9	5	9	53:41	1.292
11	Millwall	31	16	5	10	73:57	1.280
12	Walsall	32	14	7	11	100:80	1.250
13	WBA	28	13	5	10	83:69	1.202
14	Leicester	33	17	5	11	87:73	1.191
15	Northampton	30	14	3	13	84:71	1.183
16	Bristol C.	20	10	2	8	55:48	1.145
17	Mansfield	29	12	6	11	77:68	1.132
18	Charlton	19	7	4	8	37:34	1.088
19	Aldershot	24	14	2	8	73:68	1.073
20	Brentford	23	9	3	11	51:51	1.000
21	Chelsea	23	10	4	9	57:58	0.981
22	Birmingham	16	7	1	8	38:43	0.883
23	Fulham	30	10	7	13	62:73	0.849
24	Luton	35	11	7	17	82:100	0.820
25	Stoke	36	9	9	18	76:96	0.791
26	QPR	23	8	3	12	47:60	0.783
22	Brighton	25	8	7	10	51:75	0.680
28	Nottingham F.	25	7	3	15	50:77	0.649
29	Bournemouth	27	9	3	15	59:92	0.641
30	Notts Co.	21	8	3	10	42:66	0.636
31	Southend	29	12	4	13	64:101	0.633
32	Southampton	31	4	4	23	53:111	0.477
33	Swansea	10	2	1	7	12:33	0.363
34	C. Orient	15	1	3	11	19:66	0.287

Final placings were decided solely on goal average.

SEASON 1941/42

Date	Comp	H/A	Opponent	Res	Score
30 Aug	Lge	H	Watford	W	5-0
6 Sep	Lge	A	Aldershot	L	2-3
13 Sep	Lge	H	Millwall	W	3-0
20 Sep	Lge	A	Arsenal	L	0-3
27 Sep	Lge	H	QPR	W	3-1
4 Oct	Lge	A	Reading	D	1-1
11 Oct	Lge	H	Brighton	L	1-2
18 Oct	Lge	A	Brentford	W	4-1
25 Oct	Lge	H	C. Palace	D	1-1
1 Nov	Lge	H	Fulham	D	2-2
8 Nov	Lge	H	C. Orient	W	2-0
15 Nov	Lge	A	Portsmouth	W	2-1
22 Nov	Lge	A	Chelsea	D	1-1
29 Nov	Lge	A	Charlton	L	1-2
6 Dec	Lge	H	West Ham	D	1-1
13 Dec	Lge	A	Watford	W	2-1
20 Dec	Lge	H	Aldershot	D	1-1
25 Dec	Lge	A	Millwall	W	2-1
27 Dec	Lge	H	Arsenal	L	1-2
3 Jan	Lge	A	QPR	L	0-1
10 Jan	Lge	H	Reading	W	2-1
17 Jan	Lge	A	Brighton	L	2-5
31 Jan	Lge	A	C. Palace	D	2-2
14 Feb	Lge	A	C. Orient	W	3-2
21 Feb	Lge	H	Portsmouth	D	1-1
28 Feb	Lge	H	Chelsea	W	2-0
7 Mar	Lge	H	Charlton	W	2-0
14 Mar	Lge	A	West Ham	W	3-2
21 Mar	CUP	H	Reading	W	2-1
28 Mar	CUP	H	Watford	W	5-2
4 Apr	CUP	H	Reading	W	2-1
6 Apr	CUP	A	Watford	D	0-0
11 Apr	CUP	H	Charlton	L	0-3
18 Apr	CUP	A	Charlton	L	0-4
25 Apr	Lge	H	Brentford	W	2-1
2 May	Lge	H	Fulham	W	7-1
25 Mar	F	A	C. Palace	W	5-3

Player	War Lg App	Goals	Player	War Lg App	Goals
Bennett F.	4		Ludford G.	24	15
Bennett L.	1	1	Mannion W.*	4	
Broadis I.	29	11	McCormick J.	1	
Buckingham V.	1		Noble*	6	3
Burgess R.	5	2	Pearson*	2	
Cox F.	2		Revell*	1	1
Ditchburn E.	10		Sainsbury	3	
Duncan A.	24	3	Sibley	3	1
Edwards R.	1		Sperrin J.	3	
Finch*	1		Sperrin W.	8	
Fitzgerald*	1		Stevens	1	2
Gibbons A.	23	18	Tickridge	30	
Gilberg H.	2		Trailer	1	
Hall G.W.	29	1	Ward R.	30	
Hitchens	26		Whatley W.	5	
Hooper P.	16		White R.	24	2
Howe L.	4	1	Williams*	3	
Joliffe	1		Woodward	1	

* Guest

London League 1941–42

1	Arsenal	30	23	2	5	108:43	48
2	Portsmouth	30	20	2	8	105:59	42
3	West Ham	30	17	5	8	81:44	39
4	Aldershot	30	17	5	8	85:56	39
5	TOTTENHAM	30	15	8	7	61:41	38
6	C. Palace	30	14	6	10	70:53	34
7	Reading	30	13	8	9	76:58	34
8	Charlton	30	14	5	11	72:64	33
9	Brentford	30	14	2	14	80:76	30
10	QPR	30	11	3	16	52:59	25
11	Fulham	30	10	4	16	79:99	24
12	Brighton	30	9	4	17	71:108	22
13	Chelsea	30	8	4	18	56:88	20
14	Millwall	30	7	5	18	53:82	19
15	C. Orient	30	5	7	18	42:94	17
16	Watford	30	6	4	20	47:114	16

SEASON 1942/43

Date	Comp		Opponent	Res	Score
29 Aug	Lge	H	C. Palace	L	1-3
5 Sep	Lge	A	QPR	W	1-0
12 Sep	Lge	H	Charlton	W	6-1
19 Sep	Lge	A	West Ham	L	1-3
26 Sep	Lge	H	Southampton	D	1-1
3 Oct	Lge	H	Aldershot	W	4-0
10 Oct	Lge	H	Millwall	W	2-1
17 Oct	Lge	A	Reading	W	6-2
24 Oct	Lge	A	Portsmouth	L	0-1
31 Oct	Lge	H	Chelsea	D	1-1
7 Nov	Lge	H	Arsenal	W	1-0
14 Nov	Lge	A	Luton	D	3-3
21 Nov	Lge	H	Watford	W	6-0
28 Nov	Lge	A	C. Palace	D	0-0
5 Dec	Lge	H	QPR	W	6-0
12 Dec	Lge	A	Charlton	W	3-0
19 Dec	Lge	H	West Ham	W	2-0
25 Dec	Lge	H	Brentford	D	1-1
26 Dec	Lge	A	Brentford	L	1-2
2 Jan	Lge	A	Southampton	L	1-2
9 Jan	Lge	A	Aldershot	W	3-1
16 Jan	Lge	A	Millwall	W	3-0
23 Jan	Lge	H	Reading	D	2-2
30 Jan	Lge	H	Portsmouth	W	5-2
6 Feb	Lge	A	Chelsea	W	1-0
13 Feb	Lge	A	Arsenal	L	0-1
20 Feb	Lge	H	Luton	W	4-1
27 Feb	Lge	A	Watford	W	3-0
6 Mar	CUP	H	Chelsea	W	2-0
13 Mar	CUP	A	Reading	D	1-1
20 Mar	CUP	H	Millwall	W	5-0
27 Mar	CUP	A	Chelsea	W	2-0
3 Apr	CUP	H	Reading	L	1-2
10 Apr	CUP	A	Millwall	W	1-0
17 Apr	F	A	QPR	D	1-1
24 Apr	F	H	Charlton	W	2-1
26 Apr	F	H	Fulham	W	3-0
1 May	F	H	C. Orient	W	4-3
8 May	F	H	Arsenal	L	1-2

SEASON 1943/44

Date	Comp		Opponent	Res	Score
28 Aug	Lge	H	C. Palace	D	1-1
4 Sep	Lge	A	QPR	L	0-1
11 Sep	Lge	H	Charlton	W	4-2
18 Sep	Lge	A	West Ham	D	3-3
25 Sep	Lge	H	Southampton	D	2-2
2 Oct	Lge	H	Aldershot	W	5-2
9 Oct	Lge	H	Brighton	W	2-0
16 Oct	Lge	A	Reading	W	3-2
23 Oct	Lge	A	Luton	L	2-4
30 Oct	Lge	H	Chelsea	W	5-1
6 Nov	Lge	H	Brentford	W	2-0
13 Nov	Lge	A	C. Orient	W	4-0
20 Nov	Lge	H	Watford	W	4-2
27 Nov	Lge	A	C. Palace	L	0-3
4 Dec	Lge	H	QPR	D	2-2
11 Dec	Lge	A	Charlton	W	2-0
18 Dec	Lge	H	Arsenal	W	2-1
25 Dec	Lge	H	Fulham	W	2-0
27 Dec	Lge	A	Fulham	W	2-0
1 Jan	Lge	H	West Ham	W	1-0
8 Jan	Lge	H	Brentford	W	1-0
15 Jan	Lge	A	Southampton	W	3-2
22 Jan	Lge	A	Aldershot	W	1-0
29 Jan	Lge	A	Brighton	W	2-0
5 Feb	Lge	H	Reading	D	2-2
12 Feb	Lge	H	Luton	W	8-1
19 Feb	CUP	*	Millwall	W	1-0
26 Feb	CUP	H	Portsmouth	W	1-0
4 Mar	CUP	A	Aldershot	L	1-2
11 Mar	CUP	H	Millwall	W	1-0
18 Mar	CUP	A	Portsmouth	W	2-1
25 Mar	CUP	H	Aldershot	W	2-0
1 Apr	CUPsf	†	Charlton	L	0-3
8 Apr	Lge	A	Chelsea	D	1-1
10 Apr	F	A	Millwall	D	0-0
22 Apr	Lge	A	Arsenal	D	3-3
29 Apr	Lge	H	C. Orient	W	1-0
6 May	Lge	A	Watford	D	1-1

* Played at Selhurst Park
† Played at Stamford Bridge

Players 1942/43

Player	War Lg App	Goals	Player	War Lg App	Goals
Barron	1		Hares*	1	
Beasley*	21	10	Hooper P.	16	
Bennett L.	1		Howe L.	16	
Briggs*	2		Jackson*	2	
Broadis I.	9	2	Ludford G.	23	15
Browne	3		Marshall*	1	
Burgess R.	4		Martin*	19	6
Chapman*	1		McCormick J.*	2	
Chisholm	28		Muir	1	
Cox F.	3	2	Nicholson W.	1	
Ditchburn E.	9		O'Callaghan E.	6	2
Dix R.	1		Pattison*	12	3
Duncan A.	1		Sainsbury	1	
Eastham*	1		Sargent	1	1
Edwards R.	3	1	Sperrin W.	3	2
Finlay	3		Staley*	1	
Gibbons A.	23	17	Ward R.	26	1
Gurr	1		Whatley W.	11	
Hall G.W.	25	6	White R.	25	

* Guest

Players 1943/44

Player	War Lg App	Goals	Player	War Lg App	Goals
Adams	4		Howe L.	5	1
Beasley	28	11	Jones*	16	7
Bennett L.	1	1	Ludford G.	13	1
Briggs*	1		Manley*	1	
Browne	2		Martin*	14	3
Bryant	3	1	Mogford*	4	
Buckingham V.	6		Mosley	3	1
Burgess R.	19	7	O'Callaghan E.	2	
Chisholm	24		O'Donnell*	11	7
Clayton*	2	1	Page	2	
Cox F.	9	1	Rowley*	18	19
Davie*	1		Sainsbury	1	
Ditchburn E.	21		Smith T.*	2	1
Dix R.	2		Walters	9	4
Downer*	1		Ward R.	30	1
Edwards R.	2		Whatley W.	21	
Flack*	2		Whent	2	1
Gibbins	1		White R.	22	1
Gilberg H.	1		Willis	6	
Hall G.W.	6		Wilson*	1	
Harris*	1	·	Young*	2	
Hooper P.	8		Own Goals		2

* Guest

Football League South 1942-43

1	Arsenal	28	21	1	6	102:40	43
2	TOTTENHAM	28	16	6	6	68:28	38
3	QPR	28	18	2	8	64:49	38
4	Portsmouth	28	16	3	9	66:52	35
5	Southampton	28	14	5	9	86:58	33
6	West Ham	28	14	5	9	80:66	33
7	Chelsea	28	14	4	10	52:45	32
8	Aldershot	28	14	2	12	87:77	30
9	Brentford	28	12	5	11	64:63	29
10	Charlton	28	13	3	12	68:75	29
11	C. Orient	28	11	5	12	54:72	27
12	Brighton	28	10	5	13	64:72	25
13	Reading	28	9	6	13	67:74	24
14	Fulham	28	10	2	16	69:78	22
15	C. Palace	28	7	5	16	49:75	19
16	Millwall	28	6	5	17	66:88	17
17	Watford	28	7	2	19	51:88	16
18	Luton	28	4	6	18	48:100	14

Football League South 1943-44

1	TOTTENHAM	30	19	8	3	71:36	46
2	West Ham	30	17	7	6	76:39	41
3	QPR	30	14	12	4	69:54	40
4	Arsenal	30	14	10	6	72:42	38
5	C. Palace	30	16	5	9	75:53	37
6	Portsmouth	30	16	5	9	68:59	37
7	Brentford	30	14	7	9	71:51	35
8	Chelsea	30	16	2	12	79:55	34
9	Fulham	30	11	9	10	80:73	31
10	Millwall	30	13	4	13	70:66	30
11	Aldershot	30	12	6	12	64:73	30
12	Reading	30	12	3	15	73:62	27
13	Southampton	30	10	7	13	67:88	27
14	Charlton	30	9	7	14	57:73	25
15	Watford	30	6	8	16	58:80	20
16	Brighton	30	9	2	19	55:82	20
17	C. Orient	30	4	3	23	32:87	11
18	Luton	30	3	5	22	42:104	11

SEASON 1944/45

Date	Comp	H/A	Opponent	Res	Score
19 Aug	F	A	Coventry	L	1-3
26 Aug	Lge	H	West Ham	D	2-2
2 Sep	Lge	H	Arsenal	W	4-0
9 Sep	Lge	A	Reading	D	0-0
16 Sep	Lge	H	Portsmouth	D	1-1
23 Sep	Lge	A	Southampton	W	3-1
30 Sep	Lge	H	Charlton	W	2-1
7 Oct	Lge	A	C. Palace	W	3-1
14 Oct	Lge	H	Chelsea	L	1-5
21 Oct	Lge	A	Luton	W	9-1
28 Oct	Lge	H	Brentford	D	2-2
4 Nov	Lge	H	Aldershot	W	7-0
11 Nov	Lge	A	Millwall	W	4-3
18 Nov	Lge	A	C. Orient	W	2-0
25 Nov	Lge	H	Fulham	W	2-1
2 Dec	Lge	A	West Ham	W	1-0
9 Dec	Lge	A	Arsenal	W	3-2
16 Dec	Lge	H	Reading	W	3-2
23 Dec	Lge	A	QPR	D	0-0
25 Dec	Lge	H	QPR	W	4-2
30 Dec	Lge	A	Portsmouth	D	0-0
6 Jan	Lge	H	Southampton	W	4-0
13 Jan	Lge	A	Charlton	W	2-1
20 Jan	Lge	H	C. Palace	W	3-1
27 Jan	Lge	A	Chelsea	W	2-1
3 Feb	CUP	H	QPR	D	1-1
10 Feb	CUP	A	West Ham	L	0-1
17 Feb	CUP	H	Aldershot	W	6-1
24 Feb	CUP	A	QPR	L	0-1
3 Mar	CUP	H	West Ham	W	4-0
10 Mar	CUP	A	Aldershot	W	2-0
24 Mar	Lge	A	Brentford	W	2-0
1 Apr	Lge	A	Aldershot	W	2-1
7 Apr	F	A	C. Palace	L	1-3
14 Apr	Lge	H	Millwall	W	4-0
21 Apr	Lge	H	C. Orient	W	4-0
28 Apr	Lge	A	Fulham	W	4-2
5 May	Lge	H	Luton	W	1-0
19 May	F	H	Arsenal	W	4-0
26 May	F	H	Fulham	D	2-2

Player	War Lg App	Goals	Player	War Lg App	Goals
Adams	4		Jackson*	2	
Anderson*	1		Ludford G.	12	5
Beasley*	24	9	Martin*	1	
Boulton*	1		Medley L.	7	1
Broadis	6	2	Mogford	3	
Brown*	3		Muir*	1	
Burgess R.	23	10	Oakes*	1	
Burke*	10		O'Donnell*	2	1
Burnett*	1	2	Page	3	
Chisholm	6		Pryde*	1	
Dix	1		Rowley*	2	2
Duke*	2		Smith K.*	1	
Dunn*	1		Stevens	11	5
Flavell*	11		Swift	1	
Foreman*	5	8	Wallis	4	
Gibbons A.	11	10	Walters	30	8
Gilberg H.	8	6	Ward R.	30	5
Goodman	1		Whatley W.	1	
Hall A.E.	5	2	White R.	24	
Hall F.*	14		Whittingham*	1	1
Henley*	1	1	Willis	27	
Howe L.	5	1	Own Goals		2
Hughes*	21				

* Guest

Football League South 1944–45

1	TOTTENHAM	30	23	6	1	81:30	52
2	West Ham	30	22	3	5	96:47	47
3	Brentford	30	17	4	9	87:57	38
4	Chelsea	30	16	5	9	100:55	37
5	Southampton	30	17	3	10	96:69	37
6	C. Palace	30	15	5	10	74:70	35
7	Reading	30	14	6	10	78:68	34
8	Arsenal	30	14	3	13	77:67	31
9	QPR	30	10	10	10	70:61	30
10	Watford	30	11	6	13	66:84	28
11	Fulham	30	11	4	15	79:83	26
12	Portsmouth	30	11	4	15	56:61	26
13	Charlton	30	12	2	16	72:81	26
14	Brighton	30	10	2	18	66:95	22
15	Luton	30	6	7	17	56:104	19
16	Aldershot	30	7	4	19	44:85	18
17	Millwall	30	5	7	18	50:84	17
18	Clapton O.	30	5	7	18	39:86	17

SEASON 1945/46

Date	Comp	H/A	Opponent	Res	Score
25 Aug	Lge	H	Wolves	L	1-4
1 Sep	Lge	A	Wolves	L	2-4
8 Sep	Lge	A	West Ham	D	1-1
12 Sep	Lge	H	Leicester	W	6-2
15 Sep	Lge	H	West Ham	L	2-3
22 Sep	Lge	A	West Brom	L	0-5
29 Sep	Lge	H	West Brom	W	4-2
6 Oct	Lge	A	Birmingham C.	L	0-8
13 Oct	Lge	A	Birmingham C.	L	0-1
20 Oct	Lge	A	Swansea	L	2-4
27 Oct	Lge	H	Swansea	W	3-1
3 Nov	Lge	H	Brentford	W	1-0
10 Nov	Lge	A	Brentford	W	3-1
17 Nov	Lge	A	Chelsea	W	2-1
24 Nov	Lge	H	Chelsea	W	3-2
1 Dec	Lge	H	Millwall	W	5-1
8 Dec	Lge	A	Millwall	L	2-3
15 Dec	Lge	A	Southampton	L	2-3
22 Dec	Lge	H	Southampton	W	4-3
25 Dec	Lge	H	Derby	L	2-5
26 Dec	Lge	A	Derby	L	0-2
29 Dec	Lge	A	Leicester	L	0-4
5 Jan	FC	H	Brentford	D	2-2
10 Jan	FC	A	Brentford	L	0-2*
12 Jan	Lge	A	Luton	L	1-3
19 Jan	Lge	A	Luton	L	2-3
26 Jan	Lge	H	Coventry	W	2-0
2 Feb	Lge	A	Aston Villa	L	1-5
9 Feb	Lge	A	Arsenal	D	1-1
16 Feb	Lge	H	Arsenal	W	2-0
20 Feb	Lge	H	Aston Villa	W	3-0
23 Feb	Lge	H	Charlton	W	2-1
2 Mar	F	H	Chelsea	W	4-2
9 Mar	Lge	A	Fulham	D	1-1
16 Mar	Lge	H	Fulham	L	1-3
23 Mar	Lge	H	Plymouth	W	2-0
30 Mar	Lge	A	Plymouth	W	1-0
6 Apr	Lge	A	Portsmouth	W	1-0
13 Apr	Lge	H	Portsmouth	W	2-0
17 Apr	Lge	A	Charlton	L	0-1
19 Apr	Lge	H	Nottm Forest	W	3-2
20 Apr	Lge	A	Newport	W	4-1
22 Apr	Lge	A	Nottm Forest	W	2-0
27 Apr	Lge	H	Newport	W	2-0
4 May	Lge	A	Coventry	W	1-0
7 May	F	H	FA XI	W	4-1†

* Second leg, not a replay   † Willie Hall testimonial

Player	War Lg App	Goals	Player	War Lg App	Goals
Acquroff J.*	2	2	Howe L.	1	
Adams	1		Howshall*	1	
Baily E.	1		Hughes W.	27	
Beasley	2		Jinks J.*	1	2
Bennett L.	11		Joslin*	4	
Blair J.	2	1	Ludford G.	30	3
Broadis I.	9	5	Lyman G.	21	7
Buckingham V.	19		McCormick J.	3	1
Burgess R.	37	7	Medley L.	17	3
Chisholm	1		Morrison J.	1	
Cox F.	1		Nicholson W.	11	
Ditchburn E.	2		Page	16	
Dix R.	26	4	Rundle C.	4	
Duquemin L.	1		Sargent	2	
Ferrier*	1		Skinner G.	11	2
Fletcher	1		Smith*	4	
Ford*	3		Stevens L.	13	1
Foreman G.	10	13	Walters W.	2	
Garwood L.	1		Ward R.	26	4
Gibbons A.	21	14	Whitchurch C.	17	4
Gilberg H.	1		White A.	1	
Hall A.E.	24	5	White R.	24	
Hall F.	6		Willis A.	32	
Hall J.	9		Young*	1	

* Guest

Football League South 1945–46

1	Birmingham	42	28	5	9	96:45	61
2	Aston Villa	42	25	11	6	106:58	61
3	Charlton	42	25	10	7	92:45	60
4	Derby	42	24	7	11	101:62	55
5	WBA	42	22	8	12	104:69	52
6	Wolves	42	20	11	11	75:48	51
7	West Ham	42	20	11	11	94:76	51
8	Fulham	42	20	10	12	93:73	50
9	TOTTENHAM	42	22	3	17	78:81	47
10	Chelsea	42	19	6	17	92:80	44
11	Arsenal	42	16	11	15	76:73	43
12	Millwall	42	17	8	17	79:105	42
13	Coventry	42	15	10	17	70:69	40
14	Brentford	42	14	10	18	82:72	38
15	Nottingham F.	42	12	13	17	72:73	37
16	Southampton	42	14	9	19	97:105	37
17	Swansea	42	15	7	20	90:112	37
18	Luton	42	13	7	22	60:92	33
19	Portsmouth	42	11	6	25	66:87	28
20	Leicester	42	8	7	27	57:101	23
21	Newport	42	9	2	31	52:125	20
22	Plymouth	42	3	8	31	39:120	14

SEASON 1946/47

Date	Comp	H/A	Opponent	Result		Date	Comp	H/A	Opponent	Result	
31 Aug	Lge	H	Birmingham	L	1-2	11 Jan	FC	H	Stoke	D	2-2
7 Sep	Lge	A	WBA	L	2-3	15 Jan	FCr	A	Stoke	L	0-1
9 Sep	Lge	H	Southampton	W	2-1	18 Jan	Lge	A	Newcastle	L	0-1
14 Sep	Lge	H	Newcastle	D	1-1	25 Jan	F	H	Arsenal	W	2-0
19 Sep	Lge	A	Newport	W	4-2	27 Jan	Lge	H	Swansea	W	3-1
21 Sep	Lge	A	Swansea	W	2-0	1 Feb	Lge	A	Man City	L	0-1
28 Sep	Lge	H	Man City	D	0-0	18 Feb	Lge	A	Burnley	D	0-0
5 Oct	Lge	H	Burnley	D	1-1	1 Mar	Lge	A	Sheff Wed	L	1-5
7 Oct	Lge	H	Newport	W	3-1	8 Mar	Lge	H	Fulham	D	1-1
12 Oct	Lge	A	Barnsley	W	3-1	22 Mar	Lge	H	Luton	W	2-1
19 Oct	Lge	A	West Ham	D	2-2	29 Mar	Lge	A	Plymouth	W	4-3
26 Oct	Lge	H	Sheff Wed	W	2-0	4 Apr	Lge	H	Nottm Forest	W	2-0
31 Oct	F	A	Oxford Univ	W	2-0	5 Apr	Lge	A	Leicester	W	2-1
2 Nov	Lge	A	Fulham	D	1-1	7 Apr	Lge	A	Nottm Forest	D	1-1
9 Nov	Lge	H	Bury	W	2-1	12 Apr	Lge	A	Chesterfield	D	0-0
16 Nov	Lge	A	Luton	L	2-3	19 Apr	Lge	H	Millwall	W	2-1
20 Nov	F	A	Camb Univ	L	3-4	26 Apr	Lge	A	Bradford PA	L	1-2
23 Nov	Lge	H	Plymouth	W	2-1	3 May	Lge	A	Bury	W	2-1
30 Nov	Lge	A	Leicester	D	1-1	10 May	Lge	A	Southampton	L	0-1
7 Dec	Lge	H	Chesterfield	L	3-4	12 May	F	A	Norwich	W	2-0
14 Dec	Lge	A	Millwall	W	3-0	17 May	Lge	H	West Ham	D	0-0
21 Dec	Lge	H	Bradford PA	D	3-3	7 Jun	Lge	H	Barnsley	D	1-1
25 Dec	Lge	A	Coventry	L	1-3	13 Jun	F	A	Marseille	L	1-2
26 Dec	Lge	H	Coventry	D	0-0	15 Jun	F	A	Toulouse	L	1-2
28 Dec	Lge	A	Birmingham	L	0-1	19 Jun	F	A	Montpelier	W	1-0
4 Jan	Lge	H	WBA	W	2-0	21 Jun	F	A	St Etienne	W	2-0

Player	Lg App	Goals	Player	Lg App	Goals
Baily E.F.	1		Medley L.D.	10	4
Bennett L.D.	38	14	Nicholson W.E.	39	
Buckingham V.F.	27		Rundle C.R.	18	10
Burgess W.A.R.	40	5	Skinner G.	1	
Cox F.J.A.	25	5	Stevens L.W.J.	30	1
Ditchburn E.G.	41		Ludford G.A.	41	2
Dix R.W.	31	5	Tickeridge S.	14	
Foreman G.A.	36	15	Trailor C.H.	1	
Gilberg H.	1		Walters W.E.	1	1
Hall A.E.	8		Whitchurch C.H.	8	2
Hughes W.A.	1		Willis A.	37	
Jones W.E.A.	1		Woodward H.J.	11	
Joseph L.	1		Own Goal		1

Final table for Second Division

1	Manchester C.	42	26	10	6	78:35	62
2	Burnley	42	22	14	6	65:29	58
3	Birmingham	42	25	5	12	74:33	55
4	Chesterfield	42	18	14	10	58:44	50
5	Newcastle	42	19	10	13	95:62	48
6	**TOTTENHAM**	**42**	**17**	**14**	**11**	**65:53**	**48**
7	West Bromwich	42	20	8	14	88:75	48
8	Coventry	42	16	13	13	66:59	45
9	Leicester	42	18	7	17	69:64	43
10	Barnsley	42	17	8	17	84:86	42
11	Nottingham F.	42	15	10	17	69:74	40
12	West Ham	42	16	8	18	70:76	40
13	Luton	42	16	7	19	71:73	39
14	Southampton	42	15	9	18	69:76	39
15	Fulham	42	15	9	18	63:74	39
16	Bradford PA	42	14	11	17	65:77	39
17	Bury	42	12	12	18	80:78	36
18	Millwall	42	14	8	20	56:79	36
19	Plymouth	42	14	5	23	79:96	33
20	Sheffield W.	42	12	8	22	67:88	32
21	Swansea	42	11	7	24	55:83	29
22	Newport	42	10	3	29	61:133	23

SEASON 1947/48

Date	Comp	H/A	Opponent	Result		Date	Comp	H/A	Opponent	Result	
23 Aug	Lge	A	WBA	L	0-1	3 Jan	Lge	A	Sheff Wed	L	0-1
27 Aug	Lge	A	Bury	L	0-2	10 Jan	FC	A	Bolton	W	2-0
30 Aug	Lge	H	Sheff Wed	W	5-1	17 Jan	Lge	H	Cardiff	W	2-1
1 Sep	Lge	H	Bury	D	2-2	24 Jan	FC	H	WBA	W	3-1
6 Sep	Lge	A	Cardiff	W	3-0	31 Jan	Lge	A	Bradford	W	2-0
8 Sep	Lge	A	West Ham	D	1-1	7 Feb	FC	H	Leicester	W	5-2
13 Sep	Lge	H	Bradford PA	W	3-1	14 Feb	Lge	A	Doncaster	D	1-1
15 Sep	Lge	H	West Ham	W	2-2	21 Feb	Lge	H	Southampton	D	0-0
20 Sep	Lge	A	Nottm Forest	L	0-1	28 Feb	FC	A	Southampton	W	1-0
27 Sep	Lge	H	Doncaster	W	2-0	6 Mar	Lge	A	Plymouth	D	1-1
4 Oct	Lge	A	Southampton	D	1-1	13 Mar	FCsf	*	Blackpool	L	1-3
11 Oct	Lge	A	Barnsley	L	1-2	15 Mar	Lge	H	Barnsley	L	0-3
18 Oct	Lge	H	Plymouth	W	2-0	20 Mar	Lge	A	Brentford	L	0-2
25 Oct	Lge	A	Luton	D	0-0	26 Mar	Lge	A	Millwall	D	0-0
30 Oct	F	A	Oxford Univ	W	4-1	27 Mar	Lge	H	Leicester	D	0-0
1 Nov	Lge	H	Brentford	W	4-0	29 Mar	Lge	H	Millwall	W	3-2
8 Nov	Lge	A	Leicester	W	3-0	3 Apr	Lge	A	Leeds	W	3-1
15 Nov	Lge	H	Leeds	W	3-1	5 Apr	Lge	H	Luton	L	0-1
22 Nov	Lge	A	Fulham	W	2-0	10 Apr	Lge	H	Fulham	L	0-2
29 Nov	Lge	H	Coventry	W	2-1	12 Apr	Lge	H	Nottm Forest	L	0-3
6 Dec	Lge	A	Newcastle	L	0-1	17 Apr	Lge	A	Coventry	D	1-1
13 Dec	Lge	A	Birmingham	L	1-2	24 Apr	Lge	H	Newcastle	D	1-1
20 Dec	Lge	H	WBA	D	1-1	1 May	Lge	A	Birmingham	D	0-0
25 Dec	Lge	H	Chesterfield	W	3-0	12 May	F	A	Jersey	W	3-0
27 Dec	Lge	A	Chesterfield	L	1-3	15 May	F	A	Guernsey	W	7-0

* Semi-final played at Villa Park

Player	Lg App	Goals	Player	Lg App	Goals
Baily E.F.	22	5	Jordan J.W.	23	10
Bennett L.D.	36	8	Ludford G.A.	8	
Buckingham V.F.	42		Medley L.D.	2	
Burgess W.A.R.	31	2	Nicholson W.E.	38	
Chisholm J.R.	2		Rundle C.R.	6	1
Cox F.J.A.	34	4	Stevens L.W.J.	22	4
Ditchburn E.G.	41		Tickridge S.	39	
Dix R.W.	5		Trailor C.H.	9	
Duquemin L.S.	36	16	Walters W.E.	1	
Flint K.	5	1	Willis A.	3	
Gilberg H.	1		Withers C.F.	1	
Hughes W.A.	1		Woodward H.J.	35	1
Jones W.E.A.	19	3	Own Goal		1

Final table for Second Division

1	Birmingham	42	22	15	5	55:24	59
2	Newcastle	42	24	8	10	72:41	56
3	Southampton	42	21	10	11	71:53	52
4	Sheffield W.	42	20	11	11	66:53	51
5	Cardiff	42	18	11	13	61:58	47
6	West Ham	42	16	14	12	55:53	46
7	West Bromwich	42	18	9	15	63:58	45
8	**TOTTENHAM**	**42**	**15**	**14**	**13**	**56:43**	**44**
9	Leicester	42	16	11	15	60:57	43
10	Coventry	42	14	13	15	59:52	41
11	Fulham	42	15	10	17	47:46	40
12	Barnsley	42	15	10	17	62:64	40
13	Luton	42	14	12	16	56:59	40
14	Bradford PA	42	16	8	18	68:72	40
15	Brentford	42	13	14	15	44:61	40
16	Chesterfield	42	16	7	19	54:55	39
17	Plymouth	42	9	20	13	40:58	38
18	Leeds	42	14	8	20	62:72	36
19	Nottingham F.	42	14	7	21	54:60	35
20	Bury	42	9	16	17	58:68	34
21	Doncaster	42	9	11	22	40:66	29
22	Millwall	42	9	11	22	44:74	29

SEASON 1948/49

Date	Comp	H/A	Opponent	Result	Score
21 Aug	Lge	H	Sheff Wed	W	3-2
23 Aug	Lge	A	Coventry	L	0-2
28 Aug	Lge	A	Lincoln	D	0-0
30 Aug	Lge	H	Coventry	W	4-0
4 Sep	Lge	H	Chesterfield	W	4-0
8 Sep	Lge	A	Leeds	D	0-0
11 Sep	Lge	A	WBA	D	2-2
13 Sep	Lge	H	Leeds	D	2-2
18 Sep	Lge	H	Bury	W	3-1
20 Sep	F	A	Chelmsford	W	5-1
25 Sep	Lge	A	West Ham	L	0-1
2 Oct	Lge	H	Blackburn	W	4-0
9 Oct	Lge	A	Cardiff	W	1-0
16 Oct	Lge	H	QPR	W	1-0
23 Oct	Lge	A	Luton	D	1-1
28 Oct	F	A	Oxford Univ	W	7-0
30 Oct	Lge	H	Bradford PA	W	5-1
6 Nov	Lge	A	Southampton	L	1-3
13 Nov	Lge	H	Barnsley	W	4-1
20 Nov	Lge	A	Grimsby	D	1-1
25 Nov	F	A	Camb Univ	W	4-1
4 Dec	Lge	A	Fulham	D	1-1
11 Dec	Lge	H	Plymouth	W	3-0
18 Dec	Lge	A	Sheff Wed	L	1-3
25 Dec	Lge	A	Leicester	W	2-1
27 Dec	Lge	H	Leicester	D	1-1
1 Jan	Lge	H	Lincoln	L	1-2
8 Jan	FC	A	Arsenal	L	0-3
15 Jan	Lge	A	Chesterfield	L	0-1
22 Jan	Lge	H	WBA	W	2-0
29 Jan	F	H	Middlesbrough	W	4-1
5 Feb	Lge	A	Bury	D	1-1
12 Feb	Lge	H	Nottm Forest	W	2-1
19 Feb	Lge	H	West Ham	D	1-1
26 Feb	Lge	A	Blackburn	D	1-1
5 Mar	Lge	H	Cardiff	L	0-1
12 Mar	Lge	A	QPR	D	0-0
19 Mar	Lge	H	Luton	W	2-1
26 Mar	Lge	A	Bradford PA	D	1-1
2 Apr	Lge	H	Southampton	L	0-1
9 Apr	Lge	A	Barnsley	L	1-4
15 Apr	Lge	H	Brentford	W	2-0
16 Apr	Lge	H	Grimsby	W	5-2
18 Apr	Lge	A	Brentford	D	1-1
23 Apr	Lge	A	Nottm Forest	D	2-2
25 Apr	F	H	Hibernian	L	2-5
30 Apr	Lge	H	Fulham	D	1-1
7 May	Lge	A	Plymouth	W	5-0
9 May	F	A	Crnwall Co XI	W	2-0

Player	Lg App	Goals	Player	Lg App	Goals
Baily E.F.	41	11	Medley L.D.	6	3
Bennett L.D.	42	19	Nicholson W.E.	41	2
Buckingham V.F.	25		Rundle C.R.	4	1
Burgess W.A.R.	40	3	Stevens L.W.J.	2	
Clarke H.A.	10		Tickridge S.	41	
Cox F.J.A.	31	4	Toulouse C.H.	2	
Ditchburn E.G.	42		Walters W.E.	12	1
Duquemin L.S.	37	15	Willis A.	10	
Garwood L.F.	2		Withers C.F.	12	
Jones W.E.A.	35	12	Woodward H.J.	17	
Ludford G.A.	10		Own Goal		1

Final table for Second Division

1	Fulham	42	24	9	9	77:37	57
2	West Bromwich	42	24	8	10	69:39	56
3	Southampton	42	23	9	10	69:36	55
4	Cardiff	42	19	13	10	62:47	51
5	TOTTENHAM	42	17	16	9	72:44	50
6	Chesterfield	42	15	17	10	51:45	47
7	West Ham	42	18	10	14	56:58	46
8	Sheffield W.	42	15	13	14	63:56	43
9	Barnsley	42	14	12	16	62:61	40
10	Luton	42	14	12	16	55:57	40
11	Grimsby	42	15	10	17	72:76	40
12	Bury	42	17	6	19	67:76	40
13	QPR	42	14	11	17	44:62	39
14	Blackburn	42	15	8	19	53:63	38
15	Leeds	42	12	13	17	55:63	37
16	Coventry	42	15	7	20	55:64	37
17	Bradford PA	42	13	11	18	65:78	37
18	Brentford	42	11	14	17	42:53	36
19	Leicester	42	10	16	16	62:79	36
20	Plymouth	42	12	12	18	49:64	36
21	Nottingham F.	42	14	7	21	50:54	35
22	Lincoln	42	8	12	22	53:91	28

SEASON 1949/50

Date	Comp	H/A	Opponent	Result	Score
20 Aug	Lge	A	Brentford	W	4-1
22 Aug	Lge	H	Plymouth	W	4-1
27 Aug	Lge	H	Blackburn	L	2-3
31 Aug	Lge	A	Plymouth	W	2-0
3 Sep	Lge	A	Cardiff	W	1-0
5 Sep	Lge	H	Sheff Wed	W	1-0
10 Sep	Lge	H	Leeds	W	2-0
17 Sep	Lge	H	Bury	W	3-1
24 Sep	Lge	A	Leicester	W	2-1
1 Oct	Lge	H	Bradford	W	5-0
8 Oct	Lge	A	Southampton	D	1-1
15 Oct	Lge	H	Coventry	W	3-1
22 Oct	Lge	A	Luton	D	1-1
27 Oct	F	A	Camb Univ	L	2-3
29 Oct	Lge	H	Barnsley	W	2-0
5 Nov	Lge	A	West Ham	W	1-0
10 Nov	F	A	Oxford Univ	W	3-1
12 Nov	Lge	H	Sheff Utd	W	7-0
19 Nov	Lge	A	Grimsby	W	3-2
26 Nov	Lge	H	QPR	W	3-0
3 Dec	Lge	A	Preston	W	3-1
10 Dec	Lge	H	Swansea	W	3-1
17 Dec	Lge	H	Brentford	D	1-1
24 Dec	Lge	A	Blackburn	W	2-1
26 Dec	Lge	H	Chesterfield	W	1-0
27 Dec	Lge	A	Chesterfield	D	1-1
31 Dec	Lge	H	Cardiff	W	2-0
7 Jan	FC	A	Stoke	W	1-0
14 Jan	Lge	A	Leeds	L	0-3
21 Jan	Lge	A	Bury	W	2-1
28 Jan	FC	H	Sunderland	W	5-1
4 Feb	Lge	H	Leicester	L	0-2
11 Feb	FC	A	Everton	L	0-1
18 Feb	Lge	A	Bradford	W	3-1
25 Feb	Lge	H	Southampton	W	4-0
4 Mar	Lge	A	Coventry	W	1-0
11 Mar	Lge	H	Luton	D	0-0
18 Mar	Lge	A	Barnsley	L	0-2
25 Mar	Lge	H	West Ham	W	4-1
1 Apr	Lge	A	QPR	W	2-0
7 Apr	Lge	H	Hull	D	0-0
8 Apr	Lge	H	Preston	W	3-2
10 Apr	Lge	A	Hull	L	0-1
15 Apr	Lge	A	Sheff Utd	L	1-2
22 Apr	Lge	H	Grimsby	L	1-2
24 Apr	F	A	Chelmsford	W	4-1
29 Apr	Lge	A	Swansea	L	0-1
1 May	F	H	Hibernian	L	0-1
6 May	Lge	A	Sheff Wed	D	0-0
8 May	F	A	Norwich	D	2-2
14 May	F	A	Hanover	W	3-0
18 May	F	A	Tennis-Borussia	W	2-0
21 May	F	A	Wacker Innsbruck	W	5-2
24 May	F	A	Borussia-Dortmund	W	4-0
27 May	F	A	Ryl Beerschot	L	1-2

Player	Lg App	Goals	Player	Lg App	Goals
Baily E.F.	40	8	Medley L.D.	42	18
Bennett L.D.	35	14	Nicholson W.E.	39	2
Burgess W.A.R.	39		Ramsey A.E.	41	4
Clarke H.A.	42		Rees W.	11	3
Cook R.	3		Scarth J.	4	2
Ditchburn E.G.	42		Tickridge S.	1	
Duquemin L.S.	40	16	Walters W.E.	35	14
Ludford G.A.	4		Willis A.	2	
Marchi A.V.	2		Withers C.F.	40	

Final table for Second Division

1	TOTTENHAM	42	27	7	8	81:35	61
2	Sheffield W.	42	18	16	8	67:48	52
3	Sheffield U.	42	19	14	9	68:49	52
4	Southampton	42	19	14	9	64:48	52
5	Leeds	42	17	13	12	54:45	47
6	Preston	42	18	9	15	60:49	45
7	Hull	42	17	11	14	64:72	45
8	Swansea	42	17	9	16	53:49	43
9	Brentford	42	15	13	14	44:49	43
10	Cardiff	42	16	10	16	41:44	42
11	Grimsby	42	16	8	18	74:73	40
12	Coventry	42	13	13	16	55:55	39
13	Barnsley	42	13	13	16	64:67	39
14	Chesterfield	42	15	9	18	43:47	39
15	Leicester	42	12	15	15	55:65	39
16	Blackburn	42	14	10	18	55:60	38
17	Luton	42	10	18	14	41:51	38
18	Bury	42	14	9	19	60:65	37
19	West Ham	42	12	12	18	53:61	36
20	QPR	42	11	12	19	40:57	34
21	Plymouth	42	8	16	18	44:65	32
22	Bradford PA	42	10	11	21	51:77	31

Date	Comp	H/A	Opponent	Res	Score		Date	Comp	H/A	Opponent	Res	Score
19 Aug	Lge	H	Blackpool	L	1-4		20 Jan	Lge	H	Wolves	W	2-1
23 Aug	Lge	A	Bolton	W	4-1		27 Jan	F	A	Cardiff	W	3-2
26 Aug	Lge	A	Arsenal	D	2-2		3 Feb	Lge	A	Sunderland	D	0-0
28 Aug	Lge	H	Bolton	W	4-2		6 Feb	F	A	Standard Liege	W	4-1
2 Sep	Lge	A	Charlton	D	1-1		17 Feb	Lge	H	Aston Villa	W	3-2
6 Sep	Lge	A	Liverpool	L	1-2		24 Feb	Lge	A	Burnley	L	0-2
9 Sep	Lge	H	Man Utd	W	1-0		3 Mar	Lge	H	Chelsea	W	2-1
16 Sep	Lge	A	Wolves	L	1-2		10 Mar	Lge	A	Stoke	D	0-0
18 Sep	F	H	Lovells Ath.	W	8-0		17 Mar	Lge	H	WBA	W	5-0
23 Sep	Lge	H	Sunderland	D	1-1		23 Mar	Lge	A	Fulham	W	1-0
30 Sep	Lge	A	Aston Villa	W	3-2		24 Mar	Lge	A	Portsmouth	D	1-1
7 Oct	Lge	H	Burnley	W	1-0		26 Mar	Lge	H	Fulham	W	2-1
14 Oct	Lge	A	Chelsea	W	2-0		31 Mar	Lge	H	Everton	W	3-0
21 Oct	Lge	H	Stoke	W	6-1		7 Apr	Lge	A	Newcastle	W	1-0
28 Oct	Lge	A	WBA	W	2-1		14 Apr	Lge	H	Huddersfield	L	0-2
4 Nov	Lge	H	Portsmouth	W	5-1		21 Apr	Lge	A	Middlesbro	D	1-1
9 Nov	F	A	Camb Univ	W	2-1*		23 Apr	F	A	Hibernian	D	0-1
9 Nov	F	A	Oxford Univ	D	1-1*		28 Apr	Lge	H	Sheff Wed	D	1-0
11 Nov	Lge	A	Everton	W	2-1		30 Apr	F	A	Chelmsford	W	7-3
18 Nov	Lge	H	Newcastle	W	7-0		5 May	Lge	H	Liverpool	W	3-1
25 Nov	Lge	A	Huddersfield	L	2-3		7 May	F	H	FC Austria	L	0-1
2 Dec	Lge	H	Middlesbro	D	3-3		10 May	F	A	Scunthorpe	D	0-0
9 Dec	Lge	A	Sheff Wed	D	1-1		12 May	F	H	Bor. Dortmund	W	2-1
16 Dec	Lge	A	Blackpool	W	1-0		14 May	F	†	Arsenal	D	0-0
23 Dec	Lge	H	Arsenal	W	1-0		16 May	F	A	Racing Club Paris	W	4-2
25 Dec	Lge	A	Derby	D	1-1		29 May	F	A	Danish XI	W	4-2
26 Dec	Lge	H	Derby	W	2-1		30 May	F	A	Danish XI	D	2-2
30 Dec	Lge	H	Charlton	W	1-0		31 May	F	A	Danish XI	W	2-0
6 Jan	FC	A	Huddersfield	L	0-2							
13 Jan	Lge	A	Man Utd	L	1-2							

* Half first team played at Oxford, half at Cambridge. At the time Oxford were being coached by Vic Buckingham and Cambridge by Bill Nicholson. † Festival of Britain match played at Selhurst P.

Player	Lg App	Goals	Player	Lg App	Goals
Baily E.F.	40	12	Nicholson W.E.	41	1
Brittan C.	8		Ramsey A.E.	40	4
Bennett L.D.	25	7	Scarth J.	1	
Burgess W.A.R.	35	2	Tickridge S.	1	
Clarke H.A.	42		Uphill D.E.	2	1
Ditchburn E.G.	42		Walters W.E.	40	15
Duquemin L.S.	33	14	Willis A.	39	
McClellan S.B.	7	3	Withers C.F.	4	
Medley L.D.	35	11	Wright A.M.	2	1
Murphy P.	25	9	Own Goals		2

Final table for First Division

1	**TOTTENHAM**	42	25	10	7	82:44 60
2	Manchester U.	42	24	8	10	74:40 56
3	Blackpool	42	20	10	12	79:53 50
4	Newcastle	42	18	13	11	62:53 49
5	Arsenal	42	19	9	14	73:56 47
6	Middlesbrough	42	18	11	13	76:65 47
7	Portsmouth	42	16	15	11	71:68 47
8	Bolton	42	19	7	16	64:61 45
9	Liverpool	42	16	11	15	53:59 43
10	Burnley	42	14	14	14	48:43 42
11	Derby	42	16	8	18	81:75 40
12	Sunderland	42	12	16	14	63:73 40
13	Stoke	42	13	14	15	50:59 40
14	Wolverhampton	42	15	8	19	74:61 38
15	Aston Villa	42	12	13	17	66:68 37
16	West Bromwich	42	13	11	18	53:61 37
17	Charlton	42	14	9	19	63:80 37
18	Fulham	42	13	11	18	52:68 37
19	Huddersfield	42	15	6	21	64:92 36
20	Chelsea	42	12	8	22	53:65 32
21	Sheffield W.	42	12	8	22	64:83 32
22	Everton	42	12	8	22	48:86 32

Date	Comp	H/A	Opponent	Res	Score		Date	Comp	H/A	Opponent	Res	Score
18 Aug	Lge	A	Middlesbro'	L	1-2		26 Jan	Lge	A	Man Utd	L	0-2
20 Aug	Lge	H	Fulham	W	1-0		2 Feb	FC	H	Newcastle	L	0-3
25 Aug	Lge	H	WBA	W	3-1		9 Feb	Lge	H	Arsenal	L	1-2
29 Aug	Lge	A	Fulham	W	2-1		16 Feb	Lge	A	Man City	D	1-1
1 Sep	Lge	A	Newcastle	L	2-7		23 Feb	Lge	H	Preston	W	1-0
3 Sep	Lge	A	Burnley	D	1-1		1 Mar	Lge	H	Derby	W	5-0
8 Sep	Lge	H	Bolton	W	2-1		8 Mar	Lge	A	Aston Villa	W	3-0
10 Sep	Lge	H	Burnley	D	1-1		15 Mar	Lge	H	Sunderland	W	2-0
15 Sep	Lge	A	Stoke C.	W	6-1		22 Mar	Lge	A	Wolves	D	1-1
22 Sep	Lge	H	Man Utd	W	2-0		26 Mar	F	A	FC Austria	D	2-2
24 Sep	CS	H	Newcastle	W	2-1		2 Apr	Lge	H	Huddersfield	W	1-0
29 Sep	Lge	A	Arsenal	D	1-1		12 Apr	Lge	H	Portsmouth	W	3-1
6 Oct	Lge	H	Man City	W	1-2		14 Apr	Lge	A	Preston	D	1-1
10 Oct	F	H	Copenhagen XI	W	2-1		19 Apr	Lge	A	Liverpool	D	1-1
13 Oct	Lge	A	Derby	L	2-4		23 Apr	F	H	Hibernian	L	1-2
20 Oct	Lge	H	Aston Villa	W	2-0		26 Apr	Lge	H	Blackpool	W	2-0
27 Oct	Lge	A	Sunderland	W	1-0		30 Apr	Lge	A	Chelsea	W	2-0
3 Nov	Lge	H	Wolves	W	4-2		3 May	F	A	Racing, Paris	W	2-1
10 Nov	Lge	A	Huddersfield	D	1-1		5 May	F	A	Ipswich	D	2-2
17 Nov	Lge	H	Chelsea	W	3-2		11 May	F	A	Crittalls Ath.	W	8-1
24 Nov	Lge	A	Portsmouth	L	0-2		22 May	F		Toronto	W	7-0*
1 Dec	Lge	H	Liverpool	L	2-3		26 May	F		Saskatchewan	W	18-1*
8 Dec	Lge	A	Blackpool	L	0-1		31 May	F		British Col.	W	9-2*
15 Dec	Lge	H	Middlesbro'	W	3-1		2 Jun	F		Victoria	W	7-0*
22 Dec	Lge	A	WBA	L	1-3		4 Jun	F		British Col.	W	8-2*
25 Dec	Lge	A	Charlton	W	3-0		7 Jun	F		Alberta	W	11-0*
26 Dec	Lge	H	Charlton	L	2-3		9 Jun	F		Manitoba	W	5-0*
29 Dec	Lge	H	Newcastle	W	2-1		14 Jun	F		Man Utd	W	5-0*
5 Jan	Lge	A	Bolton	D	1-1		15 Jun	F		Man Utd	W	7-1*
12 Jan	FC	A	Scunthorpe	W	3-0		18 Jun	F		Quebec	W	8-0*
19 Jan	Lge	H	Stoke	W	2-0							

* End of season tour to Canada

Player	Lg App	Goals	Player	Lg App	Goals
Adams C.J.	5	1	Murphy P.	13	5
Baily E.F.	30	4	Nicholson W.E.	37	1
Bennett L.D.	35	19	Ramsey A.E.	38	5
Brittan C.	6		Robb G.W.	1	1
Burgess W.A.R.	40		Robshaw H.K.	1	
Clarke H.A.	33		Scarth J.W.	2	1
Ditchburn E.G.	42		Uphill D.E.	2	
Duquemin L.S.	25	12	Walters W.E.	37	11
Farley B.R.	1		Wetton R.	7	
Harmer T.C.	13	3	Willis A.	17	
King D.A.	2		Withers C.F.	29	
McClellan S.B.	12	3	Own Goals		2
Medley L.D.	34	8			

Final table for First Division

1	Manchester U.	42	23	11	8	95:52 57
2	**TOTTENHAM**	42	22	9	11	76:51 53
3	Arsenal	42	21	11	10	80:61 53
4	Portsmouth	42	20	8	14	68:58 48
5	Bolton	42	19	10	13	65:61 48
6	Aston Villa	42	19	9	14	79:70 47
7	Preston	42	17	12	13	74:54 46
8	Newcastle	42	18	9	15	98:73 45
9	Blackpool	42	18	9	15	64:64 45
10	Charlton	42	17	10	15	68:63 44
11	Liverpool	42	12	19	11	57:61 43
12	Sunderland	42	15	12	15	70:61 42
13	West Bromwich	42	14	13	15	74:77 41
14	Burnley	42	15	10	17	56:63 40
15	Manchester C.	42	13	13	16	58:61 39
16	Wolverhampton	42	12	14	16	73:73 38
17	Derby	42	15	7	20	63:80 37
18	Middlesbrough	42	15	6	21	64:88 36
19	Chelsea	42	14	8	20	52:72 36
20	Stoke	42	12	7	23	49:88 31
21	Huddersfield	42	10	8	24	49:82 28
22	Fulham	42	8	11	23	58:77 27

SEASON 1952/53

Date	Comp	H/A	Opponent	Res	Score
23 Aug	Lge	H	WBA	L	3-4
27 Aug	Lge	A	Man City	W	1-0
30 Aug	Lge	A	Newcastle	D	1-1
1 Sep	Lge	H	Man City	D	3-3
6 Sep	Lge	H	Cardiff	W	2-1
10 Sep	Lge	A	Liverpool	L	1-2
13 Sep	Lge	A	Sheff Wed	L	0-2
15 Sep	Lge	H	Liverpool	W	3-1
20 Sep	Lge	H	Arsenal	L	1-3
27 Sep	Lge	H	Burnley	W	2-1
4 Oct	Lge	A	Preston	L	0-1
11 Oct	Lge	A	Derby	D	0-0
18 Oct	Lge	H	Blackpool	W	4-0
25 Oct	Lge	A	Chelsea	L	1-2
27 Oct	F	A	Gloucester	L	1-2
1 Nov	Lge	H	Man Utd	L	1-2
5 Nov	F	A	Oxford Univ	W	3-0
6 Nov	F	A	Camb Univ	D	2-2
8 Nov	Lge	A	Portsmouth	L	1-2
15 Nov	Lge	H	Bolton	D	1-1
22 Nov	Lge	A	Aston Villa	W	3-0
29 Nov	Lge	H	Sunderland	D	2-2
6 Dec	Lge	A	Wolves	D	0-0
13 Dec	Lge	H	Charlton	W	2-0
20 Dec	Lge	A	WBA	L	1-2
25 Dec	Lge	H	Middlesbro'	W	7-1
27 Dec	Lge	A	Middlesbro'	W	4-0
3 Jan	Lge	H	Newcastle	W	3-2
10 Jan	FC	A	Tranmere	D	1-1
12 Jan	FCr	H	Tranmere	W	9-1
17 Jan	Lge	A	Cardiff	D	0-0
24 Jan	Lge	H	Sheff Wed	W	2-1
31 Jan	FC	A	Preston	D	2-2
4 Feb	FCr	H	Preston	W	1-0
7 Feb	Lge	A	Arsenal	L	0-4
14 Feb	FC	A	Halifax	W	3-0
17 Feb	Lge	H	Burnley	L	2-3
21 Feb	Lge	H	Preston	D	4-4
28 Feb	FC	A	Birmingham	D	1-1
4 Mar	FCr	H	Birmingham	D	2-2
7 Mar	Lge	A	Blackpool	L	0-2
9 Mar	FCr	*	Birmingham	W	1-0
12 Mar	Lge	H	Derby	W	5-2
14 Mar	Lge	H	Chelsea	L	2-3
21 Mar	FCsf	†	Blackpool	L	1-2
25 Mar	Lge	A	Man Utd	L	2-3
28 Mar	Lge	H	Portsmouth	D	3-3
3 Apr	Lge	H	Stoke	W	1-0
4 Apr	Lge	A	Bolton	W	3-2
6 Apr	Lge	A	Stoke	L	0-2
11 Apr	Lge	H	Aston Villa	D	1-1
15 Apr	F	A	West Ham	L	1-2
18 Apr	Lge	A	Sunderland	D	1-1
20 Apr	F	A	Reading	W	4-0
25 Apr	Lge	H	Wolves	W	3-2
30 Apr	Lge	A	Charlton	L	2-3
4 May	F	A	Arsenal	W	2-0
11 May	‡	A	Hibernian	D	1-1
12 May	‡	A	Hibernian	L	1-2
15 May	F	A	Hearts	L	0-2
30 May	F	A	Racing, Paris	D	1-1

* Second replay at Molineux † Semi-final at Villa Park ‡ Coronation Cup

Player	Lg App	Goals
Adams C.J.	1	
Baily E.F.	30	6
Baker P.R.B.	1	
Bennett L.D.	30	14
Brittan C.	9	
Brooks J.	1	
Burgess W.A.R.	30	2
Clarke H.A.	31	
Ditchburn E.G.	42	
Duquemin L.S.	38	18
Dicker L.R.	10	2
Gibbins E.	1	
Groves V.G.	3	2
Grubb A.J.	2	
Harmer T.C.	17	4
Hollis R.W.	3	1
Hopkins M.	2	
King P.A.	10	
McClellan S.B.	17	8
Marchi A.V.	5	
Medley L.D.	21	1
Nicholson W.E.	31	
Ramsey A.E.	37	6
Robb G.W.	6	2
Stokes A.F.	2	1
Uphill D.E.	2	1
Walters W.E.	26	8
Wetton R.	12	
Willis A.	27	1
Own Goal		1

Final table for First Division

1	Arsenal	42	21	12	9	97:64	54
2	Preston	42	21	12	9	85:60	54
3	Wolverhampton	42	19	13	10	86:63	51
4	West Bromwich	42	21	8	13	66:60	50
5	Charlton	42	19	11	12	77:63	49
6	Burnley	42	18	12	12	67:52	48
7	Blackpool	42	19	9	14	71:70	47
8	Manchester U.	42	18	10	14	69:72	46
9	Sunderland	42	15	13	14	68:82	43
10	TOTTENHAM	42	15	11	16	78:69	41
11	Aston Villa	42	14	13	15	63:61	41
12	Cardiff	42	14	12	16	54:46	40
13	Middlesbrough	42	14	11	17	70:77	39
14	Bolton	42	15	9	18	61:69	39
15	Portsmouth	42	14	10	18	74:83	38
16	Newcastle	42	14	9	19	59:70	37
17	Liverpool	42	14	8	20	61:82	36
18	Sheffield W.	42	12	11	19	62:72	35
19	Chelsea	42	12	11	19	56:66	35
20	Manchester C.	42	14	7	21	72:87	35
21	Stoke	42	12	10	20	53:66	34
22	Derby	42	11	10	21	59:74	32

SEASON 1953/54

Date	Comp	H/A	Opponent	Res	Score
19 Aug	Lge	H	Aston Villa	W	1-0
22 Aug	Lge	A	Sheff Wed	L	1-2
26 Aug	Lge	H	Charlton	W	3-1
29 Aug	Lge	H	Middlesbrough	W	4-1
3 Sep	Lge	A	Charlton	W	1-0
5 Sep	Lge	A	WBA	L	0-3
7 Sep	Lge	A	Burnley	L	2-4
12 Sep	Lge	H	Liverpool	W	2-1
16 Sep	Lge	H	Burnley	L	2-3
19 Sep	Lge	A	Newcastle	W	3-1
21 Sep	F	A	Hibernian	W	1-0
26 Sep	Lge	H	Man Utd	D	1-1
29 Sep	F	A	Racing Club	W	5-3
3 Oct	Lge	A	Bolton	L	0-2
10 Oct	Lge	H	Arsenal	L	1-4
17 Oct	Lge	A	Cardiff	L	0-1
19 Oct	F	A	Millwall	W	2-0
24 Oct	Lge	H	Man City	W	3-0
28 Oct	F	H	FC Austria	W	3-2
31 Oct	Lge	A	Sunderland	L	3-4
7 Nov	Lge	H	Chelsea	W	2-1
14 Nov	Lge	A	Blackpool	L	0-1
21 Nov	Lge	H	Huddersfield	W	1-0
28 Nov	Lge	A	Sheff Utd	L	2-5
5 Dec	Lge	A	Wolves	L	2-3
12 Dec	Lge	H	Aston Villa	W	2-1
19 Dec	Lge	H	Sheff Wed	W	3-1
25 Dec	Lge	A	Portsmouth	D	1-1
26 Dec	Lge	A	Portsmouth	D	1-1
2 Jan	Lge	A	Middlesbrough	L	0-3
9 Jan	FC	A	Leeds	D	3-3
13 Jan	FCr	A	Leeds	W	1-0
16 Jan	Lge	H	WBA	L	0-1
23 Jan	Lge	A	Liverpool	D	2-2
30 Jan	FC	A	Man City	W	1-0
6 Feb	Lge	H	Newcastle	W	3-0
13 Feb	Lge	A	Man Utd	L	0-2
20 Feb	FC	H	Hull	D	1-1
24 Feb	FCr	H	Hull	W	2-0
27 Feb	Lge	A	Arsenal	W	3-0
3 Mar	Lge	H	Bolton	W	3-2
6 Mar	Lge	H	Cardiff	L	0-1
13 Mar	FC	A	WBA	L	0-3
17 Mar	Lge	A	Man City	L	1-4
20 Mar	Lge	H	Sunderland	L	0-3
27 Mar	Lge	A	Chelsea	L	0-1
3 Apr	Lge	H	Blackpool	D	2-2
5 Apr	F	H	Hibernian	W	3-2
10 Apr	Lge	A	Huddersfield	W	5-2
16 Apr	Lge	A	Preston	L	1-2
17 Apr	Lge	H	Sheff Utd	W	2-1
19 Apr	Lge	H	Preston	L	2-6
24 Apr	Lge	A	Wolves	L	0-2
28 Apr	F	A	Austria Select	L	0-2
1 May	F	A	Stuttgart	L	1-3
5 May	F	A	Eintracht	L	0-1
7 May	F	A	Hamburg SV	D	2-2

Player	Lg App	Goals
Baily E.F.	33	5
Baker P.R.B.	4	1
Bennett L.D.	26	4
Brittan C.	3	1
Brooks J.	18	2
Burgess W.A.R.	24	
Clarke H.A.	41	
Ditchburn E.G.	39	
Dunmore D.G.I.	10	2
Duquemin L.S.	27	9
Groves V.G.	1	1
Harmer T.C.	6	2
Hopkins M.	2	
Hutchinson G.H.	5	1
King D.A.	2	
Marchi A.V.	8	1
McClellan S.B.	5	
Nicholson W.E.	30	
Owen A.W.	1	
Ramsey A.E.	37	2
Reynolds R.S.M.	3	
Robb G.W.	37	16
Stokes A.F.	2	1
Walters W.E.	37	14
Wetton R.	21	
Willis A.	9	
Withers C.F.	31	
Own Goals		3

Final table for First Division

1	Wolverhampton	42	25	7	10	96:56	57
2	West Bromwich	42	22	9	11	86:63	53
3	Huddersfield	42	20	11	11	78:61	51
4	Manchester U.	42	18	12	12	73:58	48
5	Bolton	42	18	12	12	75:60	48
6	Blackpool	42	19	10	13	80:69	48
7	Burnley	42	21	4	17	78:67	46
8	Chelsea	42	16	12	14	74:68	44
9	Charlton	42	19	6	17	75:77	44
10	Cardiff	42	18	8	16	51:71	44
11	Preston	42	19	5	18	87:58	43
12	Arsenal	42	15	13	14	75:73	43
13	Aston Villa	42	16	9	17	70:68	41
14	Portsmouth	42	14	11	17	81:89	39
15	Newcastle	42	14	10	18	72:77	38
16	TOTTENHAM	42	16	5	21	65:76	37
17	Manchester C.	42	14	9	19	62:77	37
18	Sunderland	42	14	8	20	80:89	36
19	Sheffield W.	42	15	6	21	70:91	36
20	Sheffield U.	42	11	11	20	69:90	33
21	Middlesbrough	42	10	10	22	60:91	30
22	Liverpool	42	9	10	23	68:97	28

SEASON 1954/55

Date		Venue	Opponent	Res	Score
14 Aug	F	A	Lille Olym	D	1-1
21 Aug	Lge	A	Aston Villa	W	4-2
25 Aug	Lge	H	Wolves	W	3-2
28 Aug	Lge	H	Sunderland	L	0-1
30 Aug	Lge	A	Wolves	L	2-4
4 Sep	Lge	A	Arsenal	L	0-2
8 Sep	Lge	H	Man Utd	L	0-2
11 Sep	Lge	A	Sheff Wed	D	2-2
15 Sep	Lge	A	Man Utd	L	1-2
18 Sep	Lge	H	Portsmouth	D	1-1
25 Sep	Lge	A	Blackpool	L	1-5
2 Oct	Lge	H	Charlton	L	1-4
9 Oct	Lge	H	WBA	W	3-1
11 Oct	F	A	QPR	L	1-2
16 Oct	F	A	Newcastle	D	4-4
18 Oct	F	H	Sptklub Vienna	L	1-2
23 Oct	Lge	A	Preston	W	3-1
30 Oct	Lge	A	Sheff Utd	L	1-4
2 Nov	F	H	Essen Rot Weiss	W	4-2
6 Nov	Lge	H	Cardiff	L	0-2
13 Nov	Lge	A	Chelsea	L	1-2
15 Nov	F	H	Finchley	D	2-2
20 Nov	Lge	H	Leicester	W	5-1
27 Nov	Lge	A	Burnley	W	2-1
29 Nov	F	A	Accrington St.	D	0-0
4 Dec	Lge	H	Everton	L	1-3
11 Dec	Lge	A	Man City	D	0-0
18 Dec	Lge	H	Aston Villa	D	1-1
25 Dec	Lge	A	Bolton	W	2-1
27 Dec	Lge	H	Bolton	W	2-0
1 Jan	Lge	A	Sunderland	D	1-1
8 Jan	FC	A	Gateshead	W	2-0
15 Jan	Lge	H	Arsenal	L	0-1
22 Jan	Lge	H	Sheff Wed	W	7-2
29 Jan	FC	H	Port Vale	W	4-2
5 Feb	Lge	A	Portsmouth	W	3-0
12 Feb	Lge	H	Blackpool	W	3-2
19 Feb	FC	A	York	L	1-3
2 Mar	F	H	Arsenal	L	1-4
5 Mar	Lge	H	Man City	D	2-2
9 Mar	F	H	Racing, Paris	W	6-0
12 Mar	Lge	A	Preston	L	0-1
14 Mar	F	A	Hibernian	D	1-1
19 Mar	Lge	H	Sheff Utd	W	5-0
26 Mar	Lge	A	Cardiff	W	2-1
30 Mar	F	H	FC Servette	W	5-1
2 Apr	Lge	H	Chelsea	L	2-4
9 Apr	Lge	A	Everton	W	2-1
11 Apr	Lge	H	Huddersfield	D	1-1
12 Apr	Lge	A	Huddersfield	L	0-1
16 Apr	Lge	H	Burnley	L	0-3
23 Apr	Lge	A	Leicester	L	0-2
27 Apr	Lge	A	WBA	W	2-1
30 Apr	Lge	H	Newcastle	W	2-1
5 May	Lge	A	Charlton	W	2-1
11 May	F	A	FC Austria	L	2-6
15 May	F	A	Kinizi, Hungary	L	1-4
18 May	F	A	Vegas, Hun.	L	2-4
19 May	F	A	Pecs Doza	W	1-0
25 May	F	A	Racing, Paris	D	0-0

Player	Lg App	Goals	Player	Lg App	Goals
Baily E.F.	41	12	Henry R.P.	1	
Baker P.R.B.	8		Hopkins M.	32	
Bennett L.D.	6	2	King D.A.	5	
Blanchflower R.D.	22		McClellan S.B.	11	8
Brittan C.	10	7	Marchi A.V.	32	
Brooks J.	31		Nicholson W.E.	10	
Clarke H.A.	36		Ramsey A.E.	33	3
Ditchburn E.G.	16	1	Reynolds R.S.M.	26	
Dowsett G.J.	1	7	Robb G.W.	36	8
Dunmore D.G.I.	22	8	Walters W.E.	7	2
Duquemin L.S.	19		Wetton R.	5	
Dyson T.K.	1	13	Withers C.F.	11	
Gavin J.T.	29		Woods A.E.	6	
Harmer T.C.	5		Own Goal		1

Final table for First Division

1	Chelsea	42 20 12 10	81:57	52
2	Wolverhampton	42 19 10 13	89:70	48
3	Portsmouth	42 18 12 12	74:62	48
4	Sunderland	42 15 18 9	64:54	48
5	Manchester U.	42 20 7 15	84:74	47
6	Aston Villa	42 20 7 15	72:73	47
7	Manchester C.	42 18 10 14	76:69	46
8	Newcastle	42 17 9 16	89:77	43
9	Arsenal	42 17 9 16	69:63	43
10	Burnley	42 17 9 16	51:48	43
11	Everton	42 16 10 16	62:68	42
12	Huddersfield	42 14 13 15	63:68	41
13	Sheffield U.	42 17 7 18	70:86	41
14	Preston	42 16 8 18	83:64	40
15	Charlton	42 15 10 18	76:75	40
16	**TOTTENHAM**	**42 16 8 18**	**72:73**	**40**
17	West Bromwich	42 16 8 18	76:96	40
18	Bolton	42 13 13 16	62:69	39
19	Blackpool	42 14 10 18	60:64	38
20	Cardiff	42 13 11 18	62:76	37
21	Leicester	42 12 11 19	74:86	35
22	Sheffield W.	42 8 10 24	63:100	26

SEASON 1955/56

Date		Venue	Opponent	Res	Score
20 Aug	Lge	H	Burnley	L	0-1
24 Aug	Lge	A	Man Utd	D	2-2
27 Aug	Lge	A	Luton	L	1-2
31 Aug	Lge	H	Man Utd	L	1-2
3 Sep	Lge	H	Charlton	L	2-3
5 Sep	Lge	A	Sheff Utd	L	0-2
10 Sep	Lge	H	Arsenal	W	3-1
17 Sep	Lge	A	Everton	L	1-2
24 Sep	Lge	H	Newcastle	W	3-1
25 Sep	F	A	Aarhus	W	4-3
1 Oct	Lge	A	Birmingham	L	0-3
8 Oct	Lge	A	Bolton	L	0-3
12 Oct	F	H	FC Vasas	L	1-2
15 Oct	Lge	A	Chelsea	L	0-2
22 Oct	Lge	A	Sunderland	L	2-3
24 Oct	F	H	Plymouth	D	0-0
29 Oct	Lge	A	Portsmouth	L	1-4
5 Nov	Lge	H	Cardiff	D	1-1
12 Nov	Lge	A	Man City	W	2-1
14 Nov	F	A	Partick Thistle	L	0-1
19 Nov	Lge	H	Wolves	W	2-1
26 Nov	Lge	A	Aston Villa	W	2-0
3 Dec	Lge	H	Blackpool	D	1-1
6 Dec	F	H	Swansea	W	4-1
10 Dec	Lge	A	Huddersfield	L	0-1
17 Dec	Lge	H	Burnley	L	0-2
24 Dec	Lge	H	Luton	W	2-1
26 Dec	Lge	H	WBA	W	4-1
27 Dec	Lge	A	WBA	L	0-1
31 Dec	Lge	A	Charlton	W	2-1
7 Jan	FC	H	Boston Utd	W	4-0
14 Jan	Lge	A	Arsenal	W	1-0
21 Jan	Lge	H	Everton	D	1-1
28 Jan	FC	H	Middlesbrough	W	3-1
4 Feb	Lge	A	Newcastle	W	2-1
11 Feb	Lge	H.	Birmingham	L	0-1
18 Feb	FC	A	Doncaster	W	2-0
25 Feb	Lge	H	Chelsea	W	4-0
3 Mar	FC	H	West Ham	D	3-3
8 Mar	FCr	A	West Ham	W	2-1
10 Mar	Lge	H	Portsmouth	D	1-1
17 Mar	FCsf	†	Man City	L	0-1
21 Mar	Lge	A	Bolton	L	2-3
24 Mar	Lge	H	Man City	W	2-1
30 Mar	Lge	H	Preston	L	0-4
31 Mar	Lge	A	Sunderland	L	2-3
2 Apr	Lge	A	Preston	D	3-3
7 Apr	Lge	H	Aston Villa	W	4-3
14 Apr	Lge	A	Blackpool	W	2-0
18 Apr	Lge	A	Wolves	L	1-5
21 Apr	Lge	H	Huddersfield	L	1-2
23 Apr	Lge	A	Cardiff	D	0-0
28 Apr	Lge	H	Sheff Utd	W	3-1

† at Villa Park

Player	Lg App	Goals	Player	Lg App	Goals
Baily E.F.	18	1	Henry R.P.	1	
Baker P.R.B.	5		Hopkins M.	41	
Blanchflower R.D.	40		McClellan S.B.	16	7
Brittan C.	1		Marchi A.V.	42	1
Brooks J.	39	10	Norman M.	27	1
Clarke H.A.	39	4	Reynolds R.S.M.	28	
Ditchburn E.G.	14		Robb G.W.	41	7
Dulin M.C.	6		Ryden J.J.	3	1
Dunmore D.G.I.	10	1	Smith R.A.	21	10
Duquemin L.S.	17	5	Stokes A.F.	11	5
Dyston T.K.	3		Whalley E.	2	
Gavin J.T.	3	2	Walters W.E.	14	1
Harmer T.C.	10	5	Withers C.F.	10	

Final table for First Division

1	Manchester U.	42 25 10 7	83:51	60
2	Blackpool	42 20 9 13	86:62	49
3	Wolverhampton	42 20 9 13	89:65	49
4	Manchester C.	42 18 10 14	82:69	46
5	Arsenal	42 18 10 14	60:61	46
6	Birmingham	42 18 9 15	75:57	45
7	Burnley	42 18 8 16	64:54	44
8	Bolton	42 18 7 17	71:58	43
9	Sunderland	42 17 9 16	80:95	43
10	Luton	42 17 8 17	66:64	42
11	Newcastle	42 17 7 18	85:70	41
12	Portsmouth	42 16 7 19	78:85	41
13	West Bromwich	42 18 5 19	58:70	41
14	Charlton	42 17 6 19	75:81	40
15	Everton	42 15 10 17	55:69	40
16	Chelsea	42 14 11 17	64:77	39
17	Cardiff	42 15 9 18	55:69	39
18	**TOTTENHAM**	**42 15 7 20**	**61:71**	**37**
19	Preston	42 14 8 20	73:72	36
20	Aston Villa	42 11 13 18	52:69	35
21	Huddersfield	42 14 7 21	54:83	35
22	Sheffield U.	42 12 9 21	63:77	33

SEASON 1956/57

Date	Comp	H/A	Opponent	Result	Score
18 Aug	Lge	A	Preston	W	4-1
22 Aug	Lge	A	Man City	D	2-2
25 Aug	Lge	H	Leeds	W	5-1
29 Aug	Lge	H	Man City	W	3-2
1 Sep	Lge	A	Bolton	L	0-1
3 Sep	Lge	A	Blackpool	L	1-4
8 Sep	Lge	A	Wolves	W	4-1
11 Sep	F	H	Racing, Paris	W	2-0
15 Sep	Lge	A	Aston Villa	W	4-2
17 Sep	F	A	Hibernian	W	5-1
22 Sep	Lge	H	Luton	W	5-0
26 Sep	F	H	Partick Thistle	W	4-1
29 Sep	Lge	A	Sunderland	W	2-0
6 Oct	Lge	A	Chelsea	W	4-2
13 Oct	Lge	H	Cardiff	W	5-0
15 Oct	F	A	Hearts	L	2-3
20 Oct	Lge	A	Arsenal	L	1-3
27 Oct	Lge	H	Burnley	W	2-0
31 Oct	F	H	Hibernian	D	3-3
3 Nov	Lge	A	Portsmouth	W	3-2
10 Nov	Lge	H	Newcastle	W	3-1
12 Nov	F	H	Hearts	W	4-2
17 Nov	Lge	A	Sheff Wed	L	1-4
24 Nov	Lge	H	Man Utd	D	2-2
26 Nov	F	A	Partick Thistle	L	0-2
1 Dec	Lge	A	Birmingham	D	0-0
3 Dec	F	H	Red Banner	W	7-1
8 Dec	Lge	H	WBA	D	2-2
15 Dec	Lge	H	Preston	D	1-1
25 Dec	Lge	H	Everton	W	6-0
26 Dec	Lge	A	Everton	D	1-1
29 Dec	Lge	H	Bolton	W	4-0
5 Jan	FC	H	Leicester	W	2-0
12 Jan	Lge	A	Wolves	L	0-3
19 Jan	Lge	H	Aston Villa	W	3-0
26 Jan	FC	H	Chelsea	W	4-0
2 Feb	Lge	A	Luton	W	3-1
9 Feb	Lge	H	Sunderland	W	5-2
16 Feb	FC	A	Bournemouth	L	1-3
20 Feb	Lge	H	Chelsea	L	3-4
2 Mar	Lge	A	Leeds Utd	D	1-1
9 Mar	Lge	A	WBA	D	1-1
13 Mar	Lge	H	Arsenal	L	1-3
16 Mar	Lge	H	Portsmouth	W	2-0
19 Mar	F	A	Comb. Antwerp	W	2-1
23 Mar	Lge	A	Newcastle	D	2-2
30 Mar	Lge	H	Sheff Wed	D	1-1
6 Apr	Lge	A	Man Utd	D	0-0
13 Apr	Lge	H	Birmingham	W	5-1
19 Apr	Lge	A	Charlton	D	1-1
20 Apr	Lge	A	Cardiff	W	3-0
22 Apr	Lge	H	Charlton	W	6-2
27 Apr	Lge	H	Blackpool	W	2-1
29 Apr	Lge	A	Burnley	L	0-1
19 May	F		Celtic	W	4-3*
22 May	F		Essex Co. XI	W	8-1*
25 May	F		Ontario All Stars	W	7-0*
29 May	F		Alberta	W	6-1*
1 Jun	F		Celtic	W	6-3*
3 Jun	F		British Col.	L	0-2*
4 Jun	F		Manitoba All Stars	W	12-0*
8 Jun	F		Celtic	W	3-1*
9 Jun	F		Celtic	L	0-1*

* Canadian tour

Player	Lg App	Goals	Player	Lg App	Goals
Baker P.R.B.	38		Hopkins M.	35	
Blanchflower R.D.	39	1	Marchi A.V.	42	
Brittan C.	1		Medwin T.C.	37	14
Brooks J.	23	11	Norman M.	16	
Clarke H.A.	21		Reynolds R.S.M.	13	
Ditchburn E.G.	29		Robb G.W.	37	14
Dulin M.C.	1		Ryden J.J.	15	
Dunmore D.G.I.	5	3	Stokes A.F.	21	18
Duquemin L.S.	2	1	Smith R.A.	33	18
Dyson T.K.	8	3	Whalley E.	2	
Harmer T.C.	42	17	Wilkie R.M.	1	
Henry R.P.	1		Own Goals		4

Final table for First Division

	Team	P	W	D	L	F:A	Pts
1	Manchester U.	42	28	8	6	103:54	64
2	TOTTENHAM	42	22	12	8	104:56	56
3	Preston	42	23	10	9	84:56	56
4	Blackpool	42	22	9	11	93:65	53
5	Arsenal	42	21	8	13	85:69	50
6	Wolverhampton	42	20	8	14	94:70	48
7	Burnley	42	18	10	14	56:50	46
8	Leeds	42	15	14	13	72:63	44
9	Bolton	42	16	12	14	65:65	44
10	Aston Villa	42	14	15	13	65:55	43
11	West Bromwich	42	14	14	14	59:61	42
=12	Birmingham	42	15	9	18	69:69	39
=12	Chelsea	42	13	13	16	73:73	39
14	Sheffield W.	42	16	6	20	82:88	38
15	Everton	42	14	10	18	61:79	38
16	Luton	42	14	9	19	58:76	37
17	Newcastle	42	14	8	20	67:87	36
18	Manchester C.	42	13	9	20	78:88	35
19	Portsmouth	42	10	13	19	62:92	33
20	Sunderland	42	12	8	22	67:88	32
21	Cardiff	42	10	9	23	53:88	29
22	Charlton	42	9	4	29	62:120	22

SEASON 1957/58

Date	Comp	H/A	Opponent	Result	Score
3 Aug	F	A	IFB Stuttgart	D	2-2
24 Aug	Lge	H	Chelsea	D	1-1
28 Aug	Lge	A	Portsmouth	L	1-5
31 Aug	Lge	H	Newcastle	L	1-3
4 Sep	Lge	H	Portsmouth	L	3-5
7 Sep	Lge	H	Burnley	W	3-1
11 Sep	Lge	A	Birmingham	D	0-0
14 Sep	Lge	A	Preston	L	1-3
18 Sep	Lge	H	Birmingham	W	7-1
21 Sep	Lge	H	Sheff Wed	W	4-2
28 Sep	Lge	A	Man City	L	1-5
2 Oct	Lge	A	Wolves	L	0-4
5 Oct	Lge	H	Nottm Forest	L	3-4
12 Oct	Lge	A	Arsenal	W	3-1
14 Oct	F	A	Hibernian	L	2-5
19 Oct	Lge	A	Bolton	L	2-3
23 Oct	F	A	Swiss Nat. XI	W	5-4
26 Oct	Lge	H	Leeds	W	2-0
2 Nov	Lge	A	Sunderland	D	1-1
6 Nov	F	A	Bristol C.	L	3-4
9 Nov	Lge	H	Everton	W	3-1
11 Nov	F	H	IFB Stuttgart	W	3-2
16 Nov	Lge	A	Aston Villa	D	1-1
23 Nov	Lge	H	Luton	W	3-1
30 Nov	Lge	A	Man Utd	W	4-3
7 Dec	Lge	H	Leicester	L	1-4
14 Dec	Lge	A	Blackpool	W	2-0
21 Dec	Lge	A	Chelsea	W	4-2
26 Dec	Lge	H	Wolves	W	1-0
28 Dec	Lge	H	Newcastle	D	3-3
4 Jan	FC	H	Leicester	W	4-0
11 Jan	Lge	A	Burnley	L	0-2
18 Jan	Lge	H	Preston	D	3-3
25 Jan	FC	H	Sheff Utd	L	0-3
1 Feb	Lge	A	Sheff Wed	L	0-2
8 Feb	Lge	H	Man City	W	5-1
15 Feb	Lge	A	Nottm Forest	W	2-1
22 Feb	Lge	A	Arsenal	D	4-4
1 Mar	F	H	Partick Thistle	W	4-1
8 Mar	Lge	A	Leeds U.	W	2-1
12 Mar	Lge	H	Bolton	W	4-1
15 Mar	Lge	H	Sunderland	L	0-1
22 Mar	Lge	A	Luton	D	0-0
27 Mar	F	A	Rotterdam XI	W	4-1
29 Mar	Lge	H	Aston Villa	W	6-2
4 Apr	Lge	H	WBA	D	0-0
5 Apr	Lge	A	Everton	W	4-3
7 Apr	Lge	A	WBA	W	2-0
12 Apr	Lge	H	Man Utd	W	1-0
14 Apr	F	H	Hibernian	W	4-0
19 Apr	Lge	A	Leicester	W	3-1
24 Apr	F	H	Canto de Rio	W	4-1
26 Apr	Lge	H	Blackpool	W	2-1

Player	Lg App	Goals	Player	Lg App	Goals
Baker P.R.B.	18		Hopkins M.	26	
Bing T.E.	1		Iley J.	19	
Blanchflower R.D.	40		Ireland J.J.C.	1	
Brittan C.	3		Jones C.W.	10	1
Brooks J.	25	10	Medwin T.C.	39	14
Clayton E.	5	3	Norman M.	33	1
Ditchburn E.G.	26		Reynolds R.S.M.	16	
Dulin M.C.	3	2	Robb G.W.	15	3
Dunmore D.G.I.	5	2	Ryden J.J.	35	
Dyson T.K.	12	2	Smith R.A.	38	36
Harmer T.C.	40	9	Stokes A.F.	15	8
Henry R.P.	15		Walley E.	1	
Hills J.R.	21		Own Goals		2

Final table for First Division

	Team	P	W	D	L	F:A	Pts
1	Wolverhampton	42	28	8	6	103:47	64
2	Preston	42	26	7	9	100:51	59
3	TOTTENHAM	42	21	9	12	93:77	51
4	West Bromwich	42	18	14	10	92:70	50
5	Manchester C.	42	22	5	15	104:100	49
6	Burnley	42	21	5	16	80:74	47
7	Blackpool	42	19	6	17	80:67	44
8	Luton	42	19	6	17	69:63	44
9	Manchester U.	42	16	11	15	85:75	43
10	Nottingham F.	42	16	10	16	69:63	42
11	Chelsea	42	15	12	15	83:79	42
12	Arsenal	42	16	7	19	73:85	39
13	Birmingham	42	14	11	17	76:89	39
14	Aston Villa	42	16	7	19	73:86	39
15	Bolton	42	14	10	18	65:87	38
16	Everton	42	13	11	18	65:75	37
17	Leeds	42	14	9	19	51:63	37
18	Leicester	42	14	5	23	91:112	33
19	Newcastle	42	12	8	22	73:81	32
20	Portsmouth	42	12	8	22	73:88	32
21	Sunderland	42	10	12	20	54:97	32
22	Sheffield W.	42	12	7	23	69:92	31

SEASON 1958/59

Date	Comp	H/A	Opponent	Result	Score
23 Aug	Lge	H	Blackpool	L	2-3
27 Aug	Lge	A	Chelsea	L	2-4
30 Aug	Lge	A	Blackburn	L	0-5
3 Sep	Lge	H	Chelsea	W	4-0
6 Sep	Lge	H	Newcastle	L	1-3
10 Sep	Lge	A	Nottm Forest	D	1-1
13 Sep	Lge	A	Arsenal	L	1-3
17 Sep	Lge	H	Nottm Forest	W	1-0
20 Sep	Lge	A	Man Utd	D	2-2
27 Sep	Lge	H	Wolves	W	2-1
4 Oct	Lge	A	Portsmouth	D	1-1
11 Oct	Lge	H	Everton	W	10-4
14 Oct	F	H	Bella Vista	W	3-1
18 Oct	Lge	A	Leicester	W	4-3
25 Oct	Lge	H	Leeds Utd	L	2-3
1 Nov	Lge	A	Man City	L	1-5
8 Nov	Lge	H	Bolton	D	1-1
10 Nov	F	H	Hibernian	W	5-2
15 Nov	Lge	A	Luton	W	2-1
22 Nov	Lge	A	Birmingham	L	0-4
29 Nov	Lge	A	WBA	L	3-4
6 Dec	Lge	H	Preston	L	1-2
8 Dec	F	H	Bucharest Sel.	W	4-2
13 Dec	Lge	A	Burnley	L	1-3
20 Dec	Lge	A	Blackpool	D	0-0
25 Dec	Lge	A	West Ham	L	1-2
26 Dec	Lge	H	West Ham	L	1-4
3 Jan	Lge	H	Blackburn	W	3-1
10 Jan	FC	H	West Ham	W	2-0
17 Jan	Lge	A	Newcastle	W	2-1
24 Jan	FC	H	Newport	W	4-1
31 Jan	Lge	A	Arsenal	L	1-4
7 Feb	Lge	H	Man Utd	L	1-3
14 Feb	FC	H	Norwich	D	1-1
18 Feb	FCr	A	Norwich	L	0-1
21 Feb	Lge	H	Portsmouth	D	4-4
28 Feb	Lge	A	Everton	L	1-2
2 Mar	Lge	A	Wolves	D	1-1
7 Mar	Lge	H	Leicester	W	6-0
14 Mar	Lge	A	Leeds	L	1-3
21 Mar	Lge	H	Man City	W	3-1
27 Mar	Lge	H	Aston Villa	W	3-2
28 Mar	Lge	A	Bolton	L	1-4
30 Mar	Lge	A	Aston Villa	D	1-1
4 Apr	Lge	H	Luton	W	3-0
8 Apr	Lge	H	Burnley	D	2-2
11 Apr	Lge	A	Birmingham	L	1-5
18 Apr	Lge	H	WBA	W	5-0
25 Apr	Lge	A	Preston	D	2-2
27 May	F	A	Moscow Torpedo	W	1-0
1 Jun	F	A	Dynamo Kiev	W	2-1
4 Jun	F	A	Com Russian XI	L	1-3

Player	Lg App	Goals	Player	Lg App	Goals
Baker P.R.B.	36		Hopkins M.	34	
Blanchflower R.D.	36	1	Iley J.	34	1
Brooks J.	25	3	Ireland J.J.C.	2	
Clayton E.	11	4	Jones C.W.	22	5
Ditchburn E.G.	2		Mackay D.C.	4	1
Dodge W.C.	5		Medwin T.C.	35	14
Dunmore D.G.I.	13	6	Norman M.	35	3
Dyson T.K.	7		Ryden J.J.	10	1
Harmer T.C.	35	4	Robb G.W.	9	2
Henry R.P.	8		Sharpe F.C.	2	1
Hills J.R.	7		Smith R.A.	36	32
Hollowbread J.F.	40		Stokes A.F.	14	7

Final table for First Division

1	Wolverhampton	42	28	5	9	110:49	61
2	Manchester U.	42	24	7	11	103:66	55
3	Arsenal	42	21	8	13	88:68	50
4	Bolton	42	20	10	12	79:66	50
5	West Bromwich	42	18	13	11	88:68	49
6	West Ham	42	21	6	15	85:70	48
7	Burnley	42	19	10	13	81:70	48
8	Blackpool	42	18	11	13	66:49	47
9	Birmingham	42	20	6	16	84:68	46
10	Blackburn	42	17	10	15	76:70	44
11	Newcastle	42	17	7	18	80:80	41
12	Preston	42	17	7	18	70:77	41
13	Nottingham F.	42	17	6	19	71:74	40
14	Chelsea	42	18	4	20	77:98	40
15	Leeds	42	15	9	18	57:74	39
16	Everton	42	17	4	21	71:87	38
17	Luton	42	12	13	17	68:71	37
18	**TOTTENHAM**	**42**	**13**	**10**	**19**	**85:95**	**36**
19	Leicester	42	11	10	21	67:98	32
20	Manchester C.	42	11	9	22	64:95	31
21	Aston Villa	42	11	8	23	58:87	30
22	Portsmouth	42	6	9	27	64:112	21

SEASON 1959/60

Date	Comp	H/A	Opponent	Result	Score
22 Aug	Lge	A	Newcastle	W	5-1
26 Aug	Lge	H	WBA	D	2-2
29 Aug	Lge	H	Birmingham	D	0-0
2 Sep	Lge	A	WBA	W	2-1
5 Sep	Lge	A	Arsenal	D	1-1
9 Sep	Lge	A	West Ham	D	2-2
12 Sep	Lge	A	Man Utd	W	5-1
14 Sep	Lge	A	West Ham	W	2-1
19 Sep	Lge	H	Preston	W	5-1
26 Sep	Lge	A	Leicester	D	1-1
3 Oct	Lge	H	Burnley	D	1-1
10 Oct	Lge	H	Wolves	W	5-1
17 Oct	Lge	A	Sheff Wed	L	1-2
21 Oct	F	A	Reading	W	5-2
24 Oct	Lge	H	Nottm Forest	W	2-1
31 Oct	Lge	A	Man City	W	2-1
7 Nov	Lge	H	Bolton	L	0-2
14 Nov	Lge	A	Luton	L	0-1
16 Nov	F	H	Moscow Torpedo	W	3-2
21 Nov	Lge	H	Everton	W	3-0
28 Nov	Lge	A	Blackpool	D	2-2
5 Dec	Lge	A	Blackburn	W	2-1
12 Dec	Lge	A	Fulham	D	1-1
19 Dec	Lge	H	Newcastle	W	4-0
26 Dec	Lge	A	Leeds	W	4-2
28 Dec	Lge	H	Leeds	L	1-4
2 Jan	Lge	A	Birmingham	W	1-0
9 Jan	FC	A	Newport	W	4-0
16 Jan	Lge	H	Arsenal	W	3-0
23 Jan	Lge	H	Man Utd	W	2-1
30 Jan	FC	A	Crewe	D	2-2
3 Feb	FCr	H	Crewe	W	13-2
6 Feb	Lge	A	Preston	D	1-1
13 Feb	Lge	H	Leicester	L	1-2
20 Feb	FC	H	Blackburn	L	1-3
27 Feb	Lge	A	Blackburn	W	4-1
1 Mar	Lge	A	Burnley	L	0-2
5 Mar	Lge	H	Sheff Wed	W	4-1
12 Mar	Lge	A	Nottm Forest	W	3-1
19 Mar	Lge	H	Fulham	D	1-1
26 Mar	Lge	A	Bolton	L	1-2
2 Apr	Lge	H	Luton	D	1-1
9 Apr	Lge	A	Everton	L	1-2
15 Apr	Lge	A	Chelsea	W	3-1
16 Apr	Lge	H	Man City	L	0-1
18 Apr	Lge	H	Chelsea	L	0-1
23 Apr	Lge	A	Wolves	W	3-1
30 Apr	Lge	H	Blackpool	W	4-1
2 May	F	A	C. Palace	D	2-2
25 May	F	A	Juventus	L	0-2

Player	Lg App	Goals	Player	Lg App	Goals
Allen L.W.	15	7	Hopkins M.	14	
Baker R.P.B.	41		Harmer T.C.	37	3
Blanchflower R.D.	40	2	Jones C.W.	38	20
Brooks J.	4	2	Mackay D.C.	38	11
Brown W.D.F.	40		Marchi A.V.	14	1
Clayton E.	1		Medwin T.C.	26	4
Dodge W.C.	1		Norman M.	39	
Dunmore D.G.I.	10	2	Smith J.	1	
Dyson T.K.	6		Smith R.A.	40	25
Henry R.P.	25		White J.A.	28	5
Hills J.R.	1		Worley L.F.	1	
Hollowbread J.F.	2		Own Goals		4

Final table for First Division

1	Burnley	42	24	7	11	85:61	55
2	Wolverhampton	42	24	6	12	106:67	54
3	**TOTTENHAM**	**42**	**21**	**11**	**10**	**86:50**	**53**
4	West Bromwich	42	19	11	12	83:57	49
5	Sheffield W.	42	19	11	12	80:59	49
6	Bolton	42	20	8	14	59:51	48
7	Manchester U.	42	19	7	16	102:80	45
8	Newcastle	42	18	8	16	82:78	44
9	Preston	42	16	12	14	79:76	44
10	Fulham	42	17	10	15	73:80	44
11	Blackpool	42	15	10	17	59:71	40
12	Leicester	42	13	13	16	66:75	39
13	Arsenal	42	15	9	18	68:80	39
14	West Ham	42	16	6	20	75:91	38
15	Everton	42	13	11	18	73:78	37
16	Manchester C.	42	17	3	22	78:84	37
17	Blackburn	42	16	5	21	60:70	37
18	Chelsea	42	14	9	19	76:91	37
19	Birmingham	42	13	10	19	63:80	36
20	Nottingham F.	42	13	9	20	50:74	35
21	Leeds	42	12	10	20	65:92	34
22	Luton	42	9	12	21	50:73	30

THE DOUBLE SEASON—1960/61

Date		Res	Score	Comp	Opponent	Att	BROWN	BAKER	HENRY	BL'FLOWER	NORMAN	MACKAY	JONES	WHITE	R. SMITH	ALLEN	DYSON	MEDWIN	SAUL	MARCHI	DODGE	ATKINSON	COLLINS	HOLLOWB'D	BARTON	J. SMITH
Aug 20	H	W	2-0	Lge	Everton	47,440	1	2	3	4	5	6	7	8	9[1]	10[1]	11									
Aug 22	A	W	3-1	Lge	Blackpool	27,656	1	2	3	4	5	6		8	9	10	11[2]	7[1]								
Aug 27	A	W	4-1	Lge	Blackburn	26,700	1	2	3	4	5	6		8	9[2]	10[1]	11[1]	7								
Aug 31	H	W	3-1	Lge	Blackpool	45,684	1	2	3	4	5	6		8	9[3]	10	11	7								
Sep 3	H	W	4-1	Lge	Man Utd	55,445	1	2	3	4	5	6		8	9[2]	10[2]	11	7								
Sep 7	A	W	2-1	Lge	Bolton	41,151	1	2	3	4	5	6		8[1]		10[1]	11	7	9							
Sep 10	A	W	3-2	Lge	Arsenal	60,088	1	2	3	4	5	6		8		10[1]	11[1]	7	9[1]							
Sep 14	H	W	3-1	Lge	Bolton	43,559	1	2	3	4[1]	5	6	7	8	9[2]	10	11									
Sep 17	A	W	2-1	Lge	Leicester	30,129	1	2	3	4	5	6	7	8	9[2]	10	11									
Sep 24	H	W	6-2	Lge	Aston Villa	61,356	1	2	3	4	5	6[1]	7	8[2]	9[1]	10[1]	11[1]									
Oct 1	A	W	4-0	Lge	Wolves	55,000	1	2	3	4[1]	5		7[1]	8	9	10[1]	11[1]			6						
Oct 10	H	D	1-1	Lge	Man City	58,916	1	2	3	4	5	6	7	8	9[1]	10	11									
Oct 15	A	W	4-0	Lge	Nottm Forest	37,198	1	2	3	4	5	6[1]	7[2]	8[1]	9	10	11									
Oct 24	H	L	3-5	F	Army XI	5,947	1	2	3		5					10[1]	11		9	6	4	7[1]	8			
Oct 29	A	W	4-3	Lge	Newcastle	51,369	1	2	3	4	5[1]	6	7[1]	8[1]	9[1]	10	11									
Nov 2	H	W	3-2	Lge	Cardiff	47,605	1	2	3	4[1]	5	6		8	9	10	11[1]	7[1]								
Nov 5	H	W	5-1	Lge	Fulham	56,270	1	2	3	4	5	6	7[2]	8[1]	9	10[2]	11									
Nov 12	A	L	1-2	Lge	Sheffield Wed	56,363	1	2	3	4	5[1]	6	7	8	9	10	11									
Nov 14	H	W	5-2	F	Dinamo Tbilisi	38,649	1	2	3	4	5	6[2]		8	9	10	11[1]	7[2]								
Nov 19	H	W	6-0	Lge	Birmingham	46,010	1	2	3	4	5	6	7[2]	8[1]	9[1]	10	11[2]									
Nov 26	A	W	3-1	Lge	WBA	37,800	1	2	3	4	5	6	7	8	9[2]	10	11									
Dec 3	H	D	4-4	Lge	Burnley	58,737	1	2	3	4	5[1]	6[1]	7[2]	8	9	10	11									
Dec 10	A	W	1-0	Lge	Preston	21,657	1	2	3	4	5	6	7	8[1]		10	11		9							
Dec 17	A	W	3-1	Lge	Everton	61,052	1	2	3	4	5	6[1]	7	8[1]	9	10[1]	11									
Dec 24	H	W	2-0	Lge	West Ham	54,930	1	2	3	4	5	6	7	8[1]	9	10	11[1]									
Dec 26	A	W	3-0	Lge	West Ham	34,481		2	3	4	5	6		8[1]	9	10[1]	11	7						1		
Dec 31	H	W	5-2	Lge	Blackburn	48,742	1	2	3	4[1]	5			8	9[2]	10[2]	11	7		6						
Jan 7	H	W	3-2	FC	Charlton	54,969	1	2	3	4	5	6		8	9	10[2]	11[1]	7								
Jan 16	A	L	0-2	Lge	Man Utd	65,295	1		3	4	5	6		8	9	10	11								2	7
Jan 21	H	W	4-2	Lge	Arsenal	65,251	1	2	3	4[1]	5	6	7	8	9[1]	10[2]	11									
Jan 28	H	W	5-1	FC	Crewe	53,721	1	2	3	4	5	6[1]	7[1]	8	9[1]	10[1]	11[1]									
Feb 4	H	L	2-3	Lge	Leicester	53,627	1	2	3	4[1]	5	6	7	8		10[1]	11									
Feb 11	A	W	2-1	Lge	Aston Villa	50,810	1	2	3	4	5	6	7	8	9[1]	10	11[1]									
Feb 18	A	W	2-0	FC	Aston Villa	69,000	1	2	3	4	5	6	7[2]	8	9	10	11									
Feb 22	H	D	1-1	Lge	Wolves	62,261	1	2	3	4	5	6	7	8	9[1]	10	11									
Feb 25	A	W	1-0	Lge	Man City	40,278	1	2	3	4		6		8	9	10	11	7[1]		5						
Mar 4	A	D	1-1	FC	Sunderland	63,000	1	2	3	4	5	6	7[1]	8	9	10	11									
Mar 8	H	W	5-0	FCr	Sunderland	64,797	1	2	3	4	5	6[1]	7	8	9[2]	10[1]	11[2]									
Mar 11	A	L	2-3	Lge	Cardiff	58,000	1	2	3	4	5	6	7	8	9	10[1]	11[1]									
Mar 18		W	3-0	FCsf	Burnley (Villa Park)	69,968	1	2	3	4	5	6	7[1]	8	9[2]	10	11									
Mar 22	H	L	1-2	Lge	Newcastle	46,470	1	2	3	4	5	6	7	8	9	10[1]	11									
Mar 25	A	D	0-0	Lge	Fulham	38,536	1	2	3	4	5		7	8		10	11			9	6					
Mar 31	H	W	4-2	Lge	Chelsea	65,032	1	2	3	4	5		7[2]	8		10	11			9[1]	6					
Apr 1	H	W	5-0	Lge	Preston	46,325	1	2	3	4	5	6	7[3]	8[1]		10		11	9[1]							
Apr 3	A	W	3-2	Lge	Chelsea	57,103	1	2	3	4	5[1]	6	7	8	9[1]	10		11[1]								
Apr 8	A	W	3-2	Lge	Birmingham	40,960	1	2	3	4	5	6	7	8[1]	9[1]	10[1]	11									
Apr 17	H	W	2-1	Lge	Sheffield Wed	62,000	1	2	3	4	5	6	7	8	9[1]	10[1]	11									
Apr 22	A	L	2-4	Lge	Burnley	28,397	1	2[1]	3	4	5	6		8	9[1]	10	11	7								
Apr 26	H	W	1-0	Lge	Nottm Forest	35,743	1	2	3	4	5			8	9	10	11	7[1]		6						
Apr 29	H	L	1-2	Lge	WBA	51,880	1	2	3	4	5	6	7	8	9[1]	10	11									
May 6		W	2-0	FCf	Leicester (Wembley)	100,000	1	2	3	4	5	6	7	8	9[1]	10	11[1]									
May 15	A	W	2-1	F	Feijenoord	40,000	1	2	3	4	5	6		8	9	10[1]	11	7[1]								
May 17	A	W	3-0	F	Amsterdam XI	30,000	1	2	3	4	5	6		8[1]	9	10[1]	11[1]	7								
Total League App							41	41	42	42	41	37	29	42	36	42	40	14	6	6				1	1	1
Total League Goals								1		6	4	4	15	13	28	22	12	5	3							

(one own goal)

265

SEASON 1961/62

12	Aug	CS	H	England Sel. XI	W	3-2
19	Aug	Lge	A	Blackpool	W	2-1
23	Aug	Lge	H	West Ham	D	2-2
26	Aug	Lge	H	Arsenal	W	4-3
28	Aug	Lge	A	West Ham	L	1-2
2	Sep	Lge	H	Cardiff	W	3-2
4	Sep	Lge	H	Sheff Utd	D	1-1
9	Sep	Lge	A	Man Utd	L	0-1
13	Sep	EC	A	Gornik	L	2-4
16	Sep	Lge	H	Wolves	W	1-0
20	Sep	EC	H	Gornik	W	8-1
23	Sep	Lge	A	Nottm Forest	L	0-2
30	Sep	Lge	H	Aston Villa	W	1-0
9	Oct	Lge	A	Bolton	W	2-1
14	Oct	Lge	H	Man City	W	2-0
21	Oct	Lge	A	Ipswich	L	2-3
28	Oct	Lge	H	Burnley	W	4-2
1	Nov	EC	A	Feijenoord	W	3-1
4	Nov	Lge	A	Everton	L	0-3
11	Nov	Lge	H	Fulham	W	4-2
15	Nov	EC	H	Feijenoord	D	1-1
18	Nov	Lge	A	Sheff Wed	D	0-0
25	Nov	Lge	H	Leicester	L	1-2
2	Dec	Lge	A	WBA	W	4-2
9	Dec	Lge	H	Birmingham	W	3-1
16	Dec	Lge	H	Blackpool	L	1-2
23	Dec	Lge	A	Arsenal	L	1-2
26	Dec	Lge	H	Chelsea	W	2-0
30	Dec	Lge	A	Chelsea	W	5-2
6	Jan	FC	A	Birmingham	D	3-3
10	Jan	FCr	H	Birmingham	W	4-2
13	Jan	Lge	A	Cardiff	D	1-1
20	Jan	Lge	H	Man Utd	D	2-2
27	Jan	FC	A	Plymouth	W	5-1
3	Feb	Lge	A	Wolves	L	1-3
10	Feb	Lge	H	Nottm Forest	W	4-2
14	Feb	EC	A	Dukla Prague	L	0-1
17	Feb	FC	A	WBA	W	4-2
21	Feb	Lge	A	Aston Villa	D	0-0
24	Feb	Lge	H	Bolton	D	2-2
26	Feb	EC	H	Dukla Prague	W	4-2
3	Mar	Lge	A	Man City	L	2-6
10	Mar	FC	H	Aston Villa	W	2-0
14	Mar	Lge	A	Ipswich	L	1-3
17	Mar	Lge	A	Burnley	D	2-2
21	Mar	ECsf	A	Benfica	L	1-3
24	Mar	Lge	H	Everton	W	3-1
31	Mar	FCsf	*	Man Utd	W	3-1
5	Apr	ECsf	H	Benfica	W	2-1
7	Apr	Lge	H	Sheff Wed	W	4-0
9	Apr	Lge	A	Sheff Utd	D	3-3
17	Apr	Lge	A	Fulham	D	1-1
20	Apr	Lge	H	Blackburn	W	4-1
21	Apr	Lge	A	WBA	L	1-2
23	Apr	Lge	A	Blackburn	W	1-0
28	Apr	Lge	A	Birmingham	W	3-2
30	Apr	Lge	A	Leicester	W	3-2
5	May	FCf	†	Burnley	W	3-1
26	May	F	A	Tel Aviv Select	W	2-1
30	May	F	A	Haifa Select	W	5-0

* Semi-final at Hillsborough   † Final at Wembley

Player	Lg App	Goals	Player	Lg App	Goals
Allen L.W.	23	9	Hopkins M.	5	
Baker P.R.B.	36		Jones C.W.	38	16
Barton K.R.	2		Mackay D.C.	26	8
Blanchflower R.D.	39	2	Marchi A.V.	21	
Clayton E.	7	3	Medwin T.C.	20	5
Brown W.D.F.	35		Norman M.	40	
Collins J.	2		Saul F.L.	8	3
Dyson T.K.	23	6	Smith J.	5	
Greaves J.P.	22	21	Smith R.A.	26	6
Henry R.P.	41		White J.A.	36	8
Hollowbread J.F.	7		Own Goal		1

Final table for First Division

1	Ipswich	42	24	8	10	93:67	56
2	Burnley	42	21	11	10	101:67	53
3	**TOTTENHAM**	**42**	**21**	**10**	**11**	**88:69**	**52**
4	Everton	42	20	11	11	88:54	51
5	Sheffield U.	42	19	9	14	61:69	47
6	Sheffield W.	42	20	6	16	72:58	46
7	Aston Villa	42	18	8	16	65:56	44
8	West Ham	42	17	10	15	76:82	44
9	West Bromwich	42	15	13	14	83:67	43
10	Arsenal	42	16	11	15	71:72	43
11	Bolton	42	16	10	16	62:66	42
12	Manchester C.	42	17	7	18	78:81	41
13	Blackpool	42	15	11	16	70:75	41
14	Leicester	42	17	6	19	72:71	40
15	Manchester U.	42	15	9	18	72:75	39
16	Blackburn	42	14	11	17	50:58	39
17	Birmingham	42	14	10	18	65:81	38
18	Wolverhampton	42	13	10	19	73:86	36
19	Nottingham F.	42	13	10	19	63:79	36
20	Fulham	42	13	7	22	66:74	33
21	Cardiff	42	9	14	19	50:81	32
22	Chelsea	42	9	10	23	63:94	28

SEASON 1962/63

11	Aug	CS	A	Ipswich	W	5-1
18	Aug	Lge	H	Birmingham	W	3-0
20	Aug	Lge	A	Aston Villa	L	1-2
25	Aug	Lge	A	West Ham	W	6-1
29	Aug	Lge	H	Aston Villa	W	4-2
1	Sep	Lge	H	Man City	W	4-2
8	Sep	Lge	A	Blackpool	W	2-1
12	Sep	Lge	H	Wolves	L	1-2
15	Sep	Lge	H	Blackburn	W	4-1
19	Sep	Lge	A	Wolves	D	2-2
22	Sep	Lge	A	Sheff Utd	L	1-3
29	Sep	Lge	H	Nottm Forest	W	9-2
6	Oct	Lge	A	Arsenal	D	4-4
13	Oct	Lge	A	WBA	W	2-1
20	Oct	Lge	H	Man Utd	W	6-2
27	Oct	Lge	A	Leyton Orient	W	5-1
31	Oct	ECWC	H	Rangers	W	5-2
3	Nov	Lge	H	Leicester	W	4-0
10	Nov	Lge	A	Fulham	W	2-0
14	Nov	F	A	Zamalek	W	7-3
17	Nov	Lge	H	Sheff Wed	D	1-1
24	Nov	Lge	A	Burnley	L	1-2
1	Dec	Lge	H	Everton	D	0-0
8	Dec	Lge	A	Bolton	L	0-1
11	Dec	ECWC	A	Rangers	W	3-2
15	Dec	Lge	A	Birmingham	W	2-0
22	Dec	Lge	H	West Ham	D	4-4
26	Dec	Lge	H	Ipswich	W	5-0
16	Jan	FC	H	Burnley	L	0-3
19	Jan	Lge	H	Blackpool	W	2-0
26	Jan	F	H	Arsenal	W	2-0
2	Feb	F	A	Portsmouth	W	3-2
23	Feb	Lge	A	Arsenal	W	3-2
2	Mar	Lge	H	WBA	W	2-1
5	Mar	ECWC	A	Slovan Bratislava	L	0-2
9	Mar	Lge	A	Man Utd	W	2-0
14	Mar	ECWC	H	Slovan Bratislava	W	6-0
16	Mar	Lge	A	Ipswich	W	4-2
23	Mar	Lge	A	Leicester	D	2-2
27	Mar	Lge	H	Leyton Orient	W	2-0
30	Mar	Lge	H	Burnley	D	1-1
8	Apr	Lge	A	Sheff Wed	L	1-3
12	Apr	Lge	A	Liverpool	L	2-5
13	Apr	Lge	H	Fulham	D	1-1
15	Apr	Lge	H	Liverpool	W	7-2
20	Apr	Lge	A	Everton	L	0-1
24	Apr	ECWCsf	A	OFK Belgrade	W	2-1
27	Apr	Lge	H	Bolton	W	4-1
1	May	ECWCsf	H	OFK Belgrade	W	3-1
4	May	Lge	H	Sheff Utd	W	4-2
11	May	Lge	A	Man City	L	0-1
15	May	ECWCf	†	Atletico Madrid	W	5-1
18	May	Lge	A	Nottm Forest	D	1-1
20	May	Lge	A	Blackburn Rvs	L	0-3
31	May	F	*	NSAFL XI	W	5-1
5	Jun	F	*	NFL XI	W	5-2
8	Jun	F	*	S Africa XI	W	3-1

† European Cup Winners Cup final played in Rotterdam
* Tour of S Africa

Player	Lg App	Goals	Player	Lg App	Goals
Allen L.W.	25	5	Mackay D.C.	37	6
Baker P.R.B.	33		Marchi A.V.	22	3
Blanchflower R.D.	24	3	Medwin T.C.	26	9
Brown W.D.F.	40		Norman M.	38	1
Clayton E.	3		Piper R.D.	1	
Dyson T.K.	13	2	Saul F.P.	10	4
Greaves J.P.	41	37	Smith J.	7	1
Henry R.P.	42		Smith R.A.	15	8
Hollowbread J.F.	2		White J.A.	37	8
Hopkins M.	9		Own Goals		4
Jones C.W.	37	20			

Final table for First Division

1	Everton	42	25	11	6	84:42	61
2	**TOTTENHAM**	**42**	**23**	**9**	**10**	**111:62**	**55**
3	Burnley	42	22	10	10	78:57	54
4	Leicester	42	20	12	10	79:53	52
5	Wolverhampton	42	20	10	12	93:65	50
6	Sheffield W.	42	19	10	13	77:63	48
7	Arsenal	42	18	10	14	86:77	46
8	Liverpool	42	17	10	15	71:59	44
9	Nottingham F.	42	17	10	15	67:69	44
10	Sheffield U.	42	16	12	14	58:60	44
11	Blackburn	42	15	12	15	79:71	42
12	West Ham	42	14	12	16	73:69	40
13	Blackpool	42	13	14	15	58:64	40
14	West Bromwich	42	16	7	19	71:79	39
15	Aston Villa	42	15	8	19	62:68	38
16	Fulham	42	14	10	18	50:71	38
17	Ipswich	42	12	11	19	59:78	35
18	Bolton	42	15	5	22	55:75	35
19	Manchester U.	42	12	10	20	67:81	34
20	Birmingham	42	10	13	19	63:90	33
21	Manchester C.	42	10	11	21	58:102	31
22	Leyton Orient	42	6	9	27	37:81	21

SEASON 1963/64

Date	Comp	H/A	Opponent	Result	Score		Date	Comp	H/A	Opponent	Result	Score
24 Aug	Lge	A	Stoke City	L	1-2		26 Dec	Lge	A	WBA	D	4-4
28 Aug	Lge	A	Wolves	W	4-1		28 Dec	Lge	H	WBA	L	0-2
31 Aug	Lge	H	Nottm Forest	W	4-1		5 Jan	FC	H	Chelsea	D	1-1
4 Sep	Lge	H	Wolves	W	4-3		8 Jan	FCr	A	Chelsea	L	0-2
7 Sep	Lge	A	Blackburn	L	2-7		11 Jan	Lge	H	Blackburn	W	4-1
14 Sep	Lge	H	Blackpool	W	6-1		18 Jan	Lge	A	Blackpool	W	2-0
16 Sep	Lge	A	Aston Villa	W	4-2		25 Jan	Lge	H	Aston Villa	W	3-1
21 Sep	Lge	A	Chelsea	W	3-0		1 Feb	Lge	H	Chelsea	L	1-2
28 Sep	Lge	H	West Ham	W	3-0		8 Feb	Lge	A	West Ham	L	0-4
2 Oct	Lge	H	Birmingham	W	6-1		15 Feb	Lge	H	Sheff Utd	D	0-0
5 Oct	Lge	A	Sheff Utd	D	3-3		22 Feb	Lge	H	Arsenal	W	3-1
15 Oct	Lge	A	Arsenal	D	4-4		29 Feb	Lge	A	Birmingham	W	2-1
19 Oct	Lge	H	Leicester	D	1-1		7 Mar	Lge	H	Everton	L	2-4
26 Oct	Lge	A	Everton	L	0-1		21 Mar	Lge	H	Man Utd	L	2-3
2 Nov	Lge	H	Fulham	W	1-0		27 Mar	Lge	H	Liverpool	L	1-3
9 Nov	Lge	A	Man Utd	L	1-4		28 Mar	Lge	A	Fulham	D	1-1
16 Nov	Lge	H	Burnley	W	3-2		30 Mar	Lge	A	Liverpool	L	1-3
23 Nov	Lge	A	Ipswich	W	3-2		4 Apr	Lge	H	Ipswich	W	6-3
30 Nov	Lge	H	Sheff Wed	D	1-1		13 Apr	Lge	A	Sheff Wed	L	0-2
3 Dec	ECWC	H	Man Utd	W	2-0		18 Apr	Lge	H	Bolton	W	1-0
7 Dec	Lge	A	Bolton	W	3-1		21 Apr	Lge	A	Burnley	L	2-7
10 Dec	ECWC	A	Man Utd	L	1-4		25 Apr	Lge	A	Leicester	W	1-0
14 Dec	Lge	H	Stoke	W	2-1		28 Apr	F	A	Coventry	W	6-5
21 Dec	Lge	A	Nottm Forest	W	2-1							

SEASON 1964/65

Date	Comp	H/A	Opponent	Result	Score		Date	Comp	H/A	Opponent	Result	Score
5 Aug	F	A	Glasgow Sel	L	2-4		28 Dec	Lge	H	Nottm Forest	W	4-0
8 Aug	F	A	Feijenoord	L	3-4		2 Jan	Lge	A	Birmingham	L	0-1
22 Aug	Lge	H	Sheff Utd	W	2-0		9 Jan	FC	A	Torquay Utd	D	3-3
25 Aug	Lge	A	Burnley	D	2-2		16 Jan	Lge	H	West Ham	W	3-2
29 Aug	Lge	H	Everton	L	1-4		18 Jan	FCr	H	Torquay Utd	W	5-1
2 Sep	Lge	H	Burnley	W	4-1		23 Jan	Lge	A	WBA	L	0-2
5 Sep	Lge	H	Birmingham	W	4-1		30 Jan	FC	A	Ipswich	W	5-0
9 Sep	Lge	A	Stoke	L	0-2		6 Feb	Lge	H	Man Utd	W	1-0
12 Sep	Lge	A	West Ham	L	2-3		13 Feb	Lge	H	Fulham	L	1-4
17 Sep	Lge	H	Stoke	W	2-1		20 Feb	FC	A	Chelsea	L	0-1
19 Sep	Lge	H	WBA	W	1-0		23 Feb	Lge	A	Arsenal	L	1-3
23 Sep	F	A	Copenhagen XI	L	1-2		27 Feb	Lge	H	Leeds Utd	D	0-0
26 Sep	Lge	A	Man Utd	L	1-4		10 Mar	Lge	A	Chelsea	L	1-3
28 Sep	Lge	A	Blackpool	D	1-1		13 Mar	Lge	H	Blackpool	W	4-1
5 Oct	Lge	H	Fulham	W	3-0		20 Mar	Lge	A	Sunderland	L	1-2
10 Oct	Lge	H	Arsenal	W	3-1		27 Mar	Lge	H	Wolves	W	7-4
17 Oct	Lge	A	Leeds	L	1-3		3 Apr	Lge	A	Aston Villa	L	0-1
24 Oct	Lge	H	Chelsea	D	1-1		9 Apr	Lge	H	Liverpool	W	3-0
31 Oct	Lge	H	Leicester	L	2-4		16 Apr	Lge	H	Blackburn	W	5-2
7 Nov	Lge	A	Sunderland	W	3-0		17 Apr	Lge	A	Sheff Wed	L	0-1
11 Nov	*	H	Scotland XI	L	2-6		19 Apr	Lge	A	Blackburn	L	1-3
14 Nov	Lge	A	Wolves	L	1-3		24 Apr	Lge	H	Leicester	W	6-2
21 Nov	Lge	H	Aston Villa	W	4-0		27 Apr	F	A	Anderlecht	L	2-4
28 Oct	Lge	A	Liverpool	D	1-1		29 Apr	F	A	Coventry	W	3-0
5 Dec	Lge	H	Sheff Wed	W	3-2		18 May	F	A	DWS Amsterdam	L	0-1
8 Dec	F	A	Leytonstone	W	5-0		22 May	F	A	Telstar	W	3-2
12 Dec	Lge	A	Sheff Utd	D	3-3		21 Jun	F	A	Hakoah	W	3-1†
19 Dec	Lge	A	Everton	D	2-2		24 Jun	F	A	Maccabi Sel	W	3-2†
26 Dec	Lge	A	Nottm Forest	W	2-1							

* John White testimonial match   † Tour of Israel

1963/64 Players

Player	Lg App	Goals	Player	Lg App	Goals
Allen L.W.	8	1	Jones C.W.	39	14
Beal P.	16		Mackay D.C.	17	3
Baker P.R.B.	35	1	Marchi A.V.	21	1
Barton K.R.	1		Mullery A.P.	9	1
Blanchflower R.D.	15		Norman M.	42	3
Brown L.	9	1	Possee D.J.	1	1
Brown W.D.F.	27		Robertson J.	3	1
Clayton E.	1		Saul F.L.	2	
Dyson T.K.	39	11	Smith J.	7	
Greaves J.P.	41	35	Smith R.A.	26	13
Henry R.P.	29		White J.A.	40	6
Hollowbread J.F.	15		Own Goals		5
Hopkins M.	19				

1964/65 Players

Player	Lg App	Goals	Player	Lg App	Goals
Allen L.W.	6	2	Jones C.W.	39	13
Baker P.	3		Knowles C.B.	38	
Beal P.	8		Low A.R.	6	1
Brown L.	16	1	Marchi A.V.	17	
Brown W.D.F.	19		Mullery A.P.	42	2
Clayton E.	15	1	Norman M.	30	1
Dyson T.K.	32	5	Possee D.J.	1	
Gilzean A.J.	20	11	Robertson J.G.	36	7
Greaves J.P.	41	29	Saul F.L.	23	11
Henry R.P.	41	1	Weller K.	6	
Jennings P.A.	23		Own Goals		2

Final table for First Division (1963/64)

		P	W	D	L	F:A	Pts
1	Liverpool	42	26	5	11	92:45	57
2	Manchester U.	42	23	7	12	90:62	53
3	Everton	42	21	10	11	84:64	52
4	**TOTTENHAM**	**42**	**22**	**7**	**13**	**97:81**	**51**
5	Chelsea	42	20	10	12	72:56	50
6	Sheffield W.	42	19	11	12	84:67	49
7	Blackburn	42	18	10	14	89:65	46
8	Arsenal	42	17	11	14	90:82	45
9	Burnley	42	17	10	15	71:64	44
10	West Bromwich	42	16	11	15	70:61	43
11	Leicester	42	16	11	15	61:58	43
12	Sheffield U.	42	16	11	15	61:64	43
13	Nottingham F.	42	16	9	17	64:68	41
14	West Ham	42	14	12	16	69:74	40
15	Fulham	42	13	13	16	58:65	39
16	Wolverhampton	42	12	15	15	70:80	39
17	Stoke	42	14	10	18	77:78	38
18	Blackpool	42	13	9	20	52:73	35
19	Aston Villa	42	11	12	19	62:71	34
20	Birmingham	42	11	7	24	54:92	29
21	Bolton	42	10	8	24	48:80	28
22	Ipswich	42	9	7	26	56:121	25

Final table for First Division (1964/65)

		P	W	D	L	F:A	Pts
1	Manchester U.	42	26	9	7	89:39	61
2	Leeds	42	26	9	7	83:52	61
3	Chelsea	42	24	8	10	89:54	56
4	Everton	42	17	15	10	69:60	49
5	Nottingham F.	42	17	13	12	71:67	47
6	**TOTTENHAM**	**42**	**19**	**7**	**16**	**87:71**	**45**
7	Liverpool	42	17	10	15	67:73	44
8	Sheffield W.	42	16	11	15	57:55	43
9	West Ham	42	19	4	19	82:71	42
10	Blackburn	42	16	10	16	83:79	42
11	Stoke	42	16	10	16	67:66	42
12	Burnley	42	16	10	16	70:70	42
13	Arsenal	42	17	7	18	69:75	41
14	West Bromwich	42	13	13	16	70:65	39
15	Sunderland	42	14	9	19	64:74	37
16	Aston Villa	42	16	5	21	57:82	37
17	Blackpool	42	12	11	19	67:78	35
18	Leicester	42	11	13	18	69:85	35
19	Sheffield U.	42	12	11	19	50:64	35
20	Fulham	42	11	12	19	60:78	34
21	Wolverhampton	42	13	4	25	59:89	30
22	Birmingham	42	8	11	23	64:96	27

SEASON 1965/66

Date	Comp	H/A	Opponent	Result	Score
14 Aug	F	A	Valencia	W	2-1
15 Aug	F	A	Standard Liege	W	1-0
25 Aug	Lge	H	Leicester	W	4-2
27 Aug	Lge	H	Blackpool	W	4-0
1 Sep	Lge	A	Leicester	D	2-2
4 Sep	Lge	A	Fulham	W	2-0
8 Sep	Lge	H	Leeds	W	3-2
11 Sep	Lge	H	Arsenal	D	2-2
15 Sep	Lge	A	Leeds	L	0-2
18 Sep	Lge	H	Liverpool	W	2-1
22 Sep	F	A	Walton & Hersham	W	8-1
25 Sep	Lge	A	Aston Villa	L	2-3
6 Oct	Lge	H	Sunderland	W	3-0
9 Oct	Lge	A	Everton	L	1-3
16 Oct	Lge	H	Man Utd	W	5-1
23 Oct	Lge	A	Newcastle	D	0-0
30 Oct	Lge	H	WBA	W	2-1
6 Nov	Lge	A	Nottm Forest	L	0-1
13 Nov	Lge	H	Sheff Wed	L	2-3
18 Nov	F	H	Hungarian Sel	W	4-0
20 Nov	Lge	A	Northampton	W	2-0
27 Nov	Lge	H	Stoke	D	2-2
4 Dec	Lge	A	Burnley	D	1-1
11 Dec	Lge	H	Chelsea	W	4-2
18 Dec	Lge	A	Man Utd	L	1-5
27 Dec	Lge	H	Sheff Utd	W	1-0
28 Dec	Lge	A	Sheff Utd	W	3-1
1 Jan	Lge	H	Everton	D	2-2
8 Jan	Lge	A	Chelsea	L	1-2
15 Jan	Lge	H	Newcastle	D	2-2
22 Jan	FC	H	Middlesbrough	W	4-0
29 Jan	Lge	H	Blackburn	W	4-0
5 Feb	Lge	A	Blackpool	D	0-0
12 Feb	FC	H	Burnley	W	4-3
19 Feb	Lge	H	Fulham	W	4-3
5 Mar	FC	A	Preston	L	1-2
8 Mar	Lge	A	Arsenal	D	1-1
12 Mar	Lge	A	Liverpool	L	0-1
19 Mar	Lge	H	Aston Villa	D	5-5
26 Mar	Lge	A	Sunderland	L	0-2
2 Apr	Lge	H	Nottm Forest	L	2-3
8 Apr	Lge	H	West Ham	L	1-4
9 Apr	Lge	A	Sheff Wed	D	1-1
16 Apr	Lge	H	Northampton	D	1-1
23 Apr	Lge	A	Stoke City	W	1-0
25 Apr	Lge	A	West Ham	L	0-2
30 Apr	Lge	H	Burnley	L	0-1
3 May	F	A	Legia Warsaw	L	0-2
7 May	Lge	A	WBA	L	1-2
9 May	Lge	A	Blackburn	W	1-0
15 May	F	A	Sarpsborg	W	3-0*
19 May	F	A	Bermuda Sel	W	3-2*
21 May	F	A	Celtic	L	0-1*
25 May	F	A	Hartford USA XI	W	3-0*
29 May	F	A	Bologna	L	0-1*
1 Jun	F	A	Celtic	L	1-2*
4 Jun	F	A	Celtic	D	1-1*
5 Jun	F	A	Vancouver Sel	W	3-0*
12 Jun	F	A	Mexico Sel	W	1-0*
15 Jun	F	A	Mexico Americano	W	2-0*
17 Jun	F	A	Bayern Munich	W	3-0*
19 Jun	F	A	Bayern Munich	D	1-1*

* North American tour matches

Player	Lg App	Goals	Player	Lg App	Goals
Beal P.	21		Kinnear J.P.	8	
Brown L.	37	1	Knowles C.B.	41	3
Brown W.D.F.	20		Low A.R.	1	(1)
Clayton E.	38	9	Mackay D.C.	41	6
Collins J.L.	2		Mullery A.P.	40	1
Gilzean A.J.	40	12	Norman M.	16	1
Greaves J.P.	29	15	Pitt S.W.	1	
Henry R.P.	1		Possee D.J.	17	3
Hoy R.E.	5		Robertson J.G.	33	6
Jennings P.A.	22		Saul F.L.	26	8
Johnson N.	10	(1)	1	Venables T.	1	
Jones C.W.	9	8	Weller K.	5	1

Note: first season using substitutes, with appearances as sub in brackets. League appearances include full appearances **plus** occasions when player came on as sub. Sub not leaving bench is not recorded.

Final table for First Division

1	Liverpool	42	26 9 7	79:34	61
2	Leeds	42	23 9 10	79:38	55
3	Burnley	42	24 7 11	79:47	55
4	Manchester U.	42	18 15 9	84:59	51
5	Chelsea	42	22 7 13	65:53	51
6	West Bromwich	42	19 12 11	91:69	50
7	Leicester	42	21 7 14	80:65	49
8	**TOTTENHAM**	**42**	**16 12 14**	**75:66**	**44**
9	Sheffield U.	42	16 11 15	56:59	43
10	Stoke	42	15 12 15	65:64	42
11	Everton	42	15 11 16	56:62	41
12	West Ham	42	15 9 18	70:83	39
13	Blackpool	42	14 9 19	55:65	37
14	Arsenal	42	12 13 17	62:75	37
15	Newcastle	42	14 9 19	50:63	37
16	Aston Villa	42	15 6 21	69:80	36
17	Sheffield W.	42	14 8 20	56:66	36
18	Nottingham F.	42	14 8 20	56:72	36
19	Sunderland	42	14 8 20	51:72	36
20	Fulham	42	14 7 21	67:85	35
21	Northampton	42	10 13 19	55:92	33
22	Blackburn	42	8 4 30	57:88	20

SEASON 1966/67

Date	Comp	H/A	Opponent	Result	Score
14 Aug	F	A	Malaga	W	2-1
15 Aug	F	A	Benfica	W	2-1
20 Aug	Lge	H	Leeds	W	3-1
24 Aug	Lge	A	Stoke	L	0-2
27 Aug	Lge	A	Newcastle	W	2-0
31 Aug	Lge	H	Stoke	W	2-0
3 Sep	Lge	H	Arsenal	W	3-1
6 Sep	Lge	A	Sheff Utd	L	1-2
10 Sep	Lge	H	Man Utd	W	2-1
14 Sep	FLC	A	West Ham	L	0-1
17 Sep	Lge	A	Burnley	D	2-2
24 Sep	Lge	H	Nottm Forest	W	2-1
1 Oct	Lge	A	Fulham	W	4-3
8 Oct	Lge	A	Man City	W	2-1
10 Oct	F	A	Dundee	W	3-2
15 Oct	Lge	H	Blackpool	L	1-3
26 Oct	Lge	A	Chelsea	L	0-3
29 Oct	Lge	H	Aston Villa	L	0-1
5 Nov	Lge	A	Blackpool	D	2-2
12 Nov	Lge	H	West Ham	L	3-4
19 Nov	Lge	A	Sheff Wed	L	0-1
23 Nov	F	H	Polish Sel XI	W	2-1
26 Nov	Lge	H	Southampton	W	3-0
3 Dec	Lge	A	Sunderland	W	1-0
10 Dec	Lge	H	Leicester	W	2-0
17 Dec	Lge	A	Leeds	L	2-3
26 Dec	Lge	A	WBA	L	0-3
27 Dec	Lge	H	WBA	D	0-0
31 Dec	Lge	H	Newcastle	W	4-0
7 Jan	Lge	A	Arsenal	W	2-0
14 Jan	Lge	A	Man Utd	L	0-1
21 Jan	Lge	H	Burnley	W	2-0
28 Jan	FC	A	Millwall	D	0-0
1 Feb	FCr	H	Millwall	W	1-0
4 Feb	FC	A	Nottm Forest	D	1-1
11 Feb	Lge	H	Fulham	W	4-2
18 Feb	FC	H	Portsmouth	W	3-1
25 Feb	Lge	H	Man City	D	1-1
4 Mar	Lge	H	Aston Villa	D	3-3
11 Mar	FC	H	Bristol City	W	2-0
18 Mar	Lge	H	Chelsea	D	1-1
22 Mar	Lge	A	Everton	W	1-0
25 Mar	Lge	A	Leicester	W	1-0
27 Mar	Lge	H	Everton	W	2-0
1 Apr	Lge	H	Liverpool	W	2-1
8 Apr	FC	A	Birmingham	D	0-0
12 Apr	FCr	H	Birmingham	W	6-0
15 Apr	Lge	H	Sheff Wed	W	2-1
22 Apr	Lge	A	Southampton	W	1-0
29 Apr	FCsf	*	Nottm Forest	W	2-1
3 May	Lge	H	Sunderland	W	1-0
6 May	Lge	A	Liverpool	D	0-0
9 May	Lge	A	West Ham	W	2-0
13 May	Lge	H	Sheff Utd	W	2-0
20 May	FCf	†	Chelsea	W	2-1
30 May	F	A	FC Zurich	W	2-0
1 Jun	F	A	Yng Boys Bern	W	3-2
7 Jun	F	A	Servette	W	4-1

* Semi-final played at Hillsborough   † Final played at Wembley

Player	Lg App	Goals	Player	Lg App	Goals
Beal P.	26		Knowles C.B.	42	1
Bond D.	1	(1)	Low A.R.	1	(1)
Brown W.D.F.	1		Mackay D.C.	39	3
Clayton E.	9	(3)	Mullery A.P.	39	5
England M.	42	1	Robertson J.G.	40	6
Gilzean A.J.	40	18	Saul F.L.	22	(2)	4
Greaves J.P.	38	23	Venables T.	41	3
Jennings P.A.	41		Weller K.	10	(2)	
Jones C.W.	20	6	Own Goal		1
Kinnear J.P.	20	(1)			

Final table for First Division

1	Manchester U.	42	24 12 6	84:45	60
2	Nottingham F.	42	23 10 9	64:41	56
3	**TOTTENHAM**	**42**	**24 8 10**	**71:48**	**56**
4	Leeds	42	22 11 9	62:42	55
5	Liverpool	42	19 13 10	64:47	51
6	Everton	42	19 10 13	65:46	48
7	Arsenal	42	16 14 12	58:47	46
8	Leicester	42	18 8 16	78:71	44
9	Chelsea	42	15 14 13	67:62	44
10	Sheffield U.	42	16 10 16	52:59	42
11	Sheffield W.	42	14 13 15	56:47	41
12	Stoke	42	17 7 18	63:58	41
13	West Bromwich	42	16 7 19	77:73	39
14	Burnley	42	15 9 18	66:76	39
15	Manchester C.	42	12 15 15	43:52	39
16	West Ham	42	14 8 20	80:84	36
17	Sunderland	42	14 8 20	58:72	36
18	Fulham	42	11 12 19	71:83	34
19	Southampton	42	14 6 22	74:92	34
20	Newcastle	42	12 9 21	39:81	33
21	Aston Villa	42	11 7 24	54:85	29
22	Blackpool	42	6 9 27	41:76	21

SEASON 1967/68

Date	Comp	H/A	Opponent	Result	Score
5 Aug	F	A	Celtic	D	3-3
12 Aug	CS	A	Man Utd	D	3-3
19 Aug	Lge	A	Leicester	W	3-2
23 Aug	Lge	H	Everton	D	1-1
26 Aug	Lge	H	West Ham	W	5-1
29 Aug	Lge	A	Everton	W	1-0
2 Sep	Lge	A	Burnley	L	1-5
6 Sep	Lge	H	Wolves	W	2-1
9 Sep	Lge	H	Sheff Wed	W	2-1
16 Sep	Lge	A	Arsenal	L	0-4
20 Sep	ECWC	A	Hajduk Split	W	2-0
23 Sep	Lge	A	Man Utd	L	1-3
27 Sep	ECWC	A	Hajduk Split	W	4-3
30 Sep	Lge	H	Sunderland	W	3-0
7 Oct	Lge	H	Sheff Utd	D	1-1
14 Oct	Lge	A	Coventry	W	3-2
25 Oct	Lge	H	Nottm Forest	D	1-1
28 Oct	Lge	A	Stoke	L	1-2
4 Nov	Lge	H	Liverpool	D	1-1
11 Nov	Lge	A	Southampton	W	2-1
18 Nov	Lge	H	Chelsea	W	2-0
25 Nov	Lge	A	WBA	L	0-2
29 Nov	ECWC	A	Olymp. Lyon	L	0-1
2 Dec	Lge	H	Newcastle	D	1-1
9 Dec	Lge	A	Man City	L	1-4
13 Dec	ECWC	H	Olymp. Lyon	W	4-3
16 Dec	Lge	H	Leicester	L	0-1
23 Dec	Lge	A	West Ham	L	1-2
26 Dec	Lge	H	Fulham	D	2-2
30 Dec	Lge	A	Fulham	W	2-1
17 Jan	Lge	A	Sheff Wed	W	2-1
20 Jan	Lge	H	Arsenal	W	1-0
28 Jan	FC	A	Man Utd	D	2-2
31 Jan	FCr	H	Man Utd	W	1-0
3 Feb	Lge	H	Man Utd	L	1-2
10 Feb	Lge	A	Sunderland	W	1-0
17 Feb	FC	H	Preston	W	3-1
26 Feb	Lge	A	Sheff Utd	L	2-3
1 Mar	Lge	H	WBA	D	0-0
9 Mar	FC	H	Liverpool	D	1-1
12 Mar	FCr	A	Liverpool	L	1-2
16 Mar	Lge	A	Nottm Forest	D	0-0
23 Mar	Lge	H	Stoke	W	3-0
30 Mar	Lge	H	Burnley	W	5-0
6 Apr	Lge	H	Southampton	W	6-1
12 Apr	Lge	H	Leeds	W	2-1
13 Apr	Lge	A	Chelsea	L	0-2
17 Apr	Lge	A	Leeds	L	0-1
20 Apr	Lge	H	Coventry	W	4-2
27 Apr	Lge	A	Newcastle	W	3-1
29 Apr	Lge	A	Liverpool	D	1-1
4 May	Lge	H	Man City	L	1-3
11 May	Lge	A	Wolves	L	1-2
15 May	F	A	Panathinaikos	D	2-2
19 May	F	A	Anorthosis	W	5-0
22 May	F	A	AEL	W	7-1
25 May	F	A	Cyprus XI	W	3-0
29 May	F	A	Apoel	W	3-0

Player	Lg App		Goals	Player	Lg App		Goals
Beal P.	35	(1)		Kinnear J.P.	30	(1)	1
Bond D.	6	(1)		Knowles C.B.	42		
Chivers M.	18		7	Mackay D.C.	29		1
Clayton E.	2	(1)		Mullery A.P.	41		2
England M.	31		3	Robertson J.G.	34	(1)	5
Gilzean A.J.	34	(2)	8	Saul F.L.	19	(2)	4
Greaves J.P.	39		23	Venables T.	36	(1)	2
Hoy R.E.	5			Want A.G.	2		
Jennings P.A.	42			Own Goals			2
Jones C.W.	30	(3)	12				

Final table for First Division

1	Manchester C.	42	26	6	10	86:43	58
2	Manchester U.	42	24	8	10	89:55	56
3	Liverpool	42	22	11	9	71:40	55
4	Leeds	42	22	9	11	71:41	53
5	Everton	42	23	6	13	67:40	52
6	Chelsea	42	18	12	12	62:68	48
7	**TOTTENHAM**	**42**	**19**	**9**	**14**	**70:59**	**47**
8	West Bromwich	42	17	12	13	75:62	46
9	Arsenal	42	17	10	15	60:56	44
10	Newcastle	42	13	15	14	54:67	41
11	Nottingham F.	42	14	11	17	52:64	39
12	West Ham	42	14	10	18	73:69	38
13	Leicester	42	13	12	17	64:69	38
14	Burnley	42	14	10	18	64:71	38
15	Sunderland	42	13	11	18	51:61	37
16	Southampton	42	13	11	18	66:83	37
17	Wolverhampton	42	14	8	20	66:75	36
18	Stoke	42	14	7	21	50:73	35
19	Sheffield W.	42	11	12	19	51:63	34
20	Coventry	42	9	15	18	51:71	33
21	Sheffield U.	42	11	10	21	49:70	32
22	Fulham	42	10	7	25	56:98	27

SEASON 1968/69

Date	Comp	H/A	Opponent	Result	Score
31 Jul	F	H	Rangers	W	3-1
3 Aug	F	A	FK Austria	D	2-2
10 Aug	Lge	H	Arsenal	L	1-2
17 Aug	Lge	A	Everton	W	2-0
21 Aug	Lge	H	WBA	D	1-1
24 Aug	Lge	H	Sheff Wed	L	1-2
28 Aug	Lge	H	Man Utd	L	1-3
31 Aug	Lge	A	Chelsea	D	2-2
4 Sep	FLC	A	Aston Villa	W	4-1
7 Sep	Lge	H	Burnley	W	7-0
14 Sep	Lge	A	West Ham	D	2-2
17 Sep	Lge	A	Coventry	W	2-1
21 Sep	Lge	H	Nottm Forest	W	2-1
25 Sep	FLC	H	Exeter	W	6-3
28 Sep	Lge	A	Newcastle	D	2-2
5 Oct	Lge	H	Leicester	W	3-2
9 Oct	Lge	H	Man Utd	D	2-2
12 Oct	Lge	A	Man City	L	0-4
16 Oct	FLC	H	Peterborough	W	1-0
19 Oct	Lge	H	Liverpool	W	2-1
26 Oct	Lge	A	Ipswich	W	1-0
30 Oct	FLC	H	Southampton	W	1-0
2 Nov	Lge	H	Stoke	D	1-1
9 Nov	Lge	A	Leeds	D	0-0
16 Nov	Lge	H	Sunderland	W	5-1
20 Nov	FLCsf	A	Arsenal	L	0-1
23 Nov	Lge	A	Southampton	L	1-2
4 Dec	FLCsf	H	Arsenal	D	1-1
7 Dec	Lge	A	Wolves	L	0-2
14 Dec	Lge	H	Man City	D	1-1
21 Dec	Lge	A	Liverpool	L	0-1
4 Jan	FC	A	Walsall	W	1-0
11 Jan	Lge	A	Stoke	D	1-1
18 Jan	Lge	H	Leeds	D	0-0
25 Jan	FC	H	Wolves	W	2-1
29 Jan	Lge	H	QPR	W	3-2
1 Feb	Lge	A	Sunderland	D	0-0
12 Feb	FC	H	Aston Villa	W	3-2
15 Feb	Lge	A	QPR	D	1-1
22 Feb	Lge	H	Wolves	D	1-1
1 Mar	FC	A	Man City	L	0-1
8 Mar	Lge	H	Everton	D	1-1
18 Mar	Lge	H	Ipswich	D	2-2
22 Mar	Lge	H	Chelsea	W	1-0
24 Mar	Lge	A	Arsenal	L	0-1
29 Mar	Lge	A	Burnley	D	2-2
2 Apr	Lge	H	Newcastle	L	0-1
4 Apr	Lge	H	Coventry	W	2-0
7 Apr	Lge	A	WBA	L	3-4
12 Apr	Lge	A	Nottm Forest	W	2-0
19 Apr	Lge	H	West Ham	W	1-0
22 Apr	Lge	H	Southampton	W	2-1
29 Apr	Lge	A	Leicester	L	0-1
12 May	Lge	A	Sheff Wed	D	0-0
15 May	F	A	West Ham	W	4-3*
17 May	F	A	Aston Villa	D	2-2*
28 May	F	A	Fiorentina	L	0-3*
1 Jun	F	A	Rangers	W	4-3*

* Games played on tour of North America; West Ham in Baltimore, Villa in Atlanta, Fiorentina and Rangers in Toronto

Player	Lg App		Goals	Player	Lg App		Goals
Beal P.	39		1	Johnson N.	16	(3)	3
Bond D.	2			Jones C.W.	7	(1)	5
Chivers M.	10		3	Kinnear J.P.	24		
Collins J.L.	1			Knowles C.B.	37	(1)	2
Collins P.	24	(3)		Morgan R.	13		3
England M.	36		3	Mullery A.P.	41		1
Evans R.	6	(1)		Pearce J.	27	(3)	3
Gilzean A.J.	37		7	Pratt J.	9	(1)	
Greaves J.P.	42		27	Robertson J.G.	11	(3)	1
Jenkins D.	11	(1)	2	Venables T.	37		
Jennings P.A.	42			Want A.G.	8	(1)	

Final table for First Division

1	Leeds	42	27	13	2	66:26	67
2	Liverpool	42	25	11	6	63:24	61
3	Everton	42	21	15	6	77:36	57
4	Arsenal	42	22	12	8	56:27	56
5	Chelsea	42	20	10	12	73:53	50
6	**TOTTENHAM**	**42**	**14**	**17**	**11**	**61:51**	**45**
7	Southampton	42	16	13	13	57:48	45
8	West Ham	42	13	18	11	66:50	44
9	Newcastle	42	15	14	13	61:55	44
10	West Bromwich	42	16	11	15	64:67	43
11	Manchester U.	42	15	12	15	57:53	42
12	Ipswich	42	15	11	16	59:60	41
13	Manchester C.	42	15	10	17	64:55	40
14	Burnley	42	15	9	18	55:82	39
15	Sheffield W.	42	10	16	16	41:54	36
16	Wolverhampton	42	10	15	17	41:58	35
17	Sunderland	42	11	12	19	43:67	34
18	Nottingham F.	42	10	13	19	45:57	33
19	Stoke	42	9	15	18	40:63	33
20	Coventry	42	10	11	21	46:64	31
21	Leicester	42	9	12	21	39:68	30
22	QPR	42	4	10	28	39:95	18

SEASON 1969/70

Date	Comp	H/A	Opponent	Result	Score
2 Aug	F	A	Hearts	D	1-1
4 Aug	F	A	Rangers	W	1-0
9 Aug	Lge	A	Leeds	L	1-3
13 Aug	Lge	H	Burnley	W	4-0
16 Aug	Lge	H	Liverpool	L	0-2
19 Aug	Lge	A	Burnley	W	2-0
23 Aug	Lge	A	Crystal P.	W	2-0
27 Aug	Lge	H	Chelsea	D	1-1
30 Aug	Lge	H	Ipswich	W	3-2
3 Sep	FLC	A	Wolves	L	0-1
6 Sep	Lge	A	West Ham	W	1-0
13 Sep	Lge	H	Man City	L	0-3
16 Sep	Lge	A	Arsenal	W	3-2
20 Sep	Lge	A	Derby	L	0-5
27 Sep	Lge	H	Sunderland	L	0-1
4 Oct	Lge	A	Southampton	D	2-2
7 Oct	Lge	A	Liverpool	D	0-0
11 Oct	Lge	H	Wolves	L	0-1
18 Oct	Lge	H	Newcastle	W	2-1
25 Oct	Lge	A	Stoke	D	1-1
1 Nov	Lge	H	Sheff Wed	W	1-0
8 Nov	Lge	A	Nottm Forest	D	2-2
15 Nov	Lge	H	WBA	W	2-0
22 Nov	Lge	A	Man Utd	L	1-3
6 Dec	Lge	A	Coventry	L	2-3
13 Dec	Lge	A	Man City	D	1-1
17 Dec	Lge	H	Everton	D	0-0
20 Dec	Lge	H	West Ham	L	0-2
26 Dec	Lge	H	Crystal P.	W	2-0
27 Dec	Lge	A	Ipswich	L	0-2
3 Jan	FC	A	Bradford C	D	2-2
7 Jan	FCr	H	Bradford C	W	5-0
10 Jan	Lge	H	Derby	W	2-1
17 Jan	Lge	A	Sunderland	L	1-2
24 Jan	FC	H	Crystal P.	D	0-0
28 Jan	FCr	A	Crystal P.	L	0-1
31 Jan	Lge	H	Southampton	L	0-1
7 Feb	Lge	A	Wolves	D	2-2
14 Feb	Lge	H	Leeds	D	1-1
21 Feb	Lge	H	Stoke	W	1-0
28 Feb	Lge	A	Newcastle	W	2-1
11 Mar	Lge	H	Everton	L	0-1
14 Mar	Lge	A	Everton	L	2-3
21 Mar	Lge	H	Coventry	L	1-2
27 Mar	Lge	H	Nottm Forest	W	4-1
28 Mar	Lge	A	WBA	D	1-1
30 Mar	Lge	H	Sheff Wed	W	1-0
4 Apr	Lge	A	Chelsea	L	0-1
13 Apr	Lge	H	Man Utd	W	2-1
2 May	Lge	A	Arsenal	W	1-0
13 May	F	A	Valletta	W	3-0
16 May	F	A	Sliema Wand	W	2-1
17 May	F	A	Malta Sel	L	0-1

Player	Lg App		Goals	Player	Lg App		Goals
Beal P.	31	(2)		Kinnear J.P.	9		
Bond D.	12		1	Knowles C.B.	33		
Chivers M.	31	(4)	11	Morgan R.	37		4
Collins P.	18	(2)	2	Mullery A.P.	41		4
England M.	36		1	Naylor T.	3		
Evans R.	16	(1)		Pearce J.	31	(6)	7
Gilzean A.J.	36	(2)	10	Perryman S.	23		1
Greaves J.P.	28		8	Peters M.	7		2
Hancock K.	1			Pratt J.	12		1
Jenkins D.	3	(2)		Want A.G.	29	(3)	
Jennings P.A.	41			Woolcott R.	1		
Johnson N.	5		1	Own Goal			1

Final table for First Division

1	Everton	42	29	8	5	72:34	66
2	Leeds	42	21	15	6	84:49	57
3	Chelsea	42	21	13	8	70:50	55
4	Derby	42	22	9	11	64:37	53
5	Liverpool	42	20	11	11	65:42	51
6	Coventry	42	19	11	12	58:48	49
7	Newcastle	42	17	13	12	57:35	47
8	Manchester U.	42	14	17	11	66:61	45
9	Stoke	42	15	15	12	56:52	45
10	Manchester C.	42	16	11	15	55:48	43
11	**TOTTENHAM**	**42**	**17**	**9**	**16**	**54:55**	**43**
12	Arsenal	42	12	18	12	51:49	42
13	Wolverhampton	42	12	16	14	55:57	40
14	Burnley	42	12	15	15	56:61	39
15	Nottingham F.	42	10	18	14	50:71	38
16	West Bromwich	42	14	9	19	58:66	37
17	West Ham	42	12	12	18	51:60	36
18	Ipswich	42	10	11	21	40:63	31
19	Southampton	42	6	17	19	46:67	29
20	Crystal Palace	42	6	15	21	34:68	27
21	Sunderland	42	6	14	22	30:68	26
22	Sheffield W.	42	8	9	25	40:71	25

SEASON 1970/71

Date	Comp	H/A	Opponent	Result	Score
3 Aug	F	H	Rangers	W	2-0
7 Aug	F	A	IFC Koln	L	0-1
8 Aug	F	A	Atletico Mad.	L	0-1
15 Aug	Lge	H	West Ham	D	2-2
19 Aug	Lge	A	Leeds	L	0-2
22 Aug	Lge	A	Wolves	W	3-0
25 Aug	Lge	A	Southampton	D	0-0
29 Aug	Lge	H	Coventry	W	1-0
1 Sep	Lge	A	Huddersfield	D	1-1
5 Sep	Lge	A	Arsenal	L	0-2
9 Sep	FLC	H	Swansea	W	3-0
12 Sep	Lge	H	Blackpool	W	3-0
16 Sep	TEX	H	Dunfermline	W	4-0
19 Sep	Lge	A	Crystal P.	W	3-0
26 Sep	Lge	H	Man City	W	2-0
29 Sep	TEX	A	Dunfermline	W	3-0
3 Oct	Lge	A	Derby	D	1-1
7 Oct	FLC	H	Sheff Utd	W	2-1
10 Oct	Lge	H	Liverpool	W	1-0
17 Oct	Lge	A	West Ham	D	2-2
21 Oct	TEX	H	Motherwell	W	3-2
24 Oct	Lge	H	Stoke	W	3-0
28 Oct	FLC	H	WBA	W	5-0
31 Oct	Lge	A	Nottm Forest	W	1-0
3 Nov	TEX	A	Motherwell	L	1-3
7 Nov	Lge	H	Burnley	W	4-0
14 Nov	Lge	A	Chelsea	W	2-0
18 Nov	FLC	H	Coventry	W	4-1
21 Nov	Lge	H	Newcastle	L	1-2
28 Nov	Lge	A	Everton	D	0-0
5 Dec	Lge	H	Man Utd	D	2-2
12 Dec	Lge	A	WBA	L	1-3
16 Dec	FLCsf	A	Bristol City	D	1-1
19 Dec	Lge	H	Wolves	D	0-0
23 Dec	FLCsf	H	Bristol City	W	2-0
2 Jan	FC	H	Sheff Wed	W	4-1
9 Jan	Lge	A	Leeds	W	2-1
16 Jan	Lge	H	Southampton	L	1-3
23 Jan	FC	A	Carlisle	W	3-2
30 Jan	Lge	H	Everton	W	2-1
6 Feb	Lge	A	Man Utd	L	1-2
13 Feb	FC	H	Nottm Forest	W	2-1
17 Feb	Lge	H	WBA	D	2-2
20 Feb	Lge	A	Newcastle	L	0-1
27 Feb	FLCf	*	Aston Villa	W	2-0
6 Mar	FC	A	Liverpool	D	0-0
10 Mar	Lge	H	Nottm Forest	L	0-1
13 Mar	Lge	H	Chelsea	W	2-1
16 Mar	FCr	H	Liverpool	L	0-1
20 Mar	Lge	A	Burnley	D	0-0
23 Mar	Lge	A	Ipswich	W	2-1
3 Apr	Lge	A	Coventry	D	0-0
7 Apr	Lge	H	Derby	W	2-1
10 Apr	Lge	H	Ipswich	W	2-0
12 Apr	Lge	A	Blackpool	D	0-0
17 Apr	Lge	A	Liverpool	D	0-0
24 Apr	Lge	H	C. Palace	W	2-0
28 Apr	Lge	H	Huddersfield	D	1-1
1 May	Lge	A	Man City	W	1-0
3 May	Lge	H	Arsenal	L	0-1
5 May	Lge	A	Stoke	W	1-0
29 May	F	A	All Japan XI	W	6-0
3 Jun	F	A	All Japan XI	W	7-2
9 Jun	F	A	All Japan XI	W	3-0

* Played at Wembley

Player	Lg App		Goals	Player	Lg App		Goals
Beal P.	32			Knowles C.B.	38		
Bond D.	2	(1)		Morgan R.	8		1
Chivers M.	42		21	Mullery A.P.	41		6
Collins P.	26			Naylor T.	4	(1)	
England M.	22		1	Neighbour J.	17	(5)	
Evans R.	7			Pearce J.	32	(10)	2
Gilzean A.J.	38		9	Perryman S.	42		3
Hancock K.	2			Peters M.	42		9
Jennings P.A.	40			Pratt J.	7	(2)	
Johnson N.	3	(3)		Want A.G.	4		
Kinnear J.P.	35			Own Goals			2

Final table for First Division

1	Arsenal	42	29	7	6	71:29	65
2	Leeds	42	27	10	5	72:30	64
3	**TOTTENHAM**	**42**	**19**	**14**	**9**	**54:33**	**52**
4	Wolverhampton	42	22	8	12	64:54	52
5	Liverpool	42	17	17	8	42:24	51
6	Chelsea	42	18	15	9	52:42	51
7	Southampton	42	17	12	13	56:44	46
8	Manchester U.	42	16	11	15	65:66	43
9	Derby	42	16	10	16	56:54	42
10	Coventry	42	16	10	16	37:38	42
11	Manchester C.	42	12	17	13	47:42	41
12	Newcastle	42	14	13	15	44:46	41
13	Stoke	42	12	13	17	44:48	37
14	Everton	42	12	13	17	54:60	37
15	Huddersfield	42	11	14	17	40:49	36
16	Nottingham F.	42	14	8	20	42:61	36
17	West Bromwich	42	10	15	17	58:75	35
18	Crystal Palace	42	12	11	19	38:57	35
19	Ipswich	42	12	10	20	42:48	34
20	West Ham	42	10	14	18	47:60	34
21	Burnley	42	7	13	22	29:63	27
22	Blackpool	42	4	15	23	34:66	23

SEASON 1971/72

Date	Comp	H/A	Opponent	Result	Score
7 Aug	F	A	Hearts	L	1-2
9 Aug	F	A	Rangers	L	0-1
14 Aug	Lge	A	Wolves	D	2-2
18 Aug	Lge	H	Newcastle	D	0-0
21 Aug	Lge	H	Huddersfield	W	4-1
25 Aug	Lge	A†	Leeds	D	1-1
28 Aug	Lge	A	Man City	L	0-4
1 Sep	*	A	Torino	W	1-0
4 Sep	Lge	H	Liverpool	W	2-0
8 Sep	FLC	A	WBA	W	1-0
11 Sep	Lge	A	Sheff Utd	D	2-2
14 Sep	UEFA	A	Keflavik	W	6-1
18 Sep	Lge	H	C. Palace	W	3-0
22 Sep	*	H	Torino	W	2-0
25 Sep	Lge	A	Coventry	L	0-1
28 Sep	UEFA	H	Keflavik	W	9-0
2 Oct	Lge	H	Ipswich	W	2-1
6 Oct	FLC	A	Torquay	W	4-1
9 Oct	Lge	A	Derby	D	2-2
16 Oct	Lge	H	Wolves	W	4-1
20 Oct	UEFA	A	Nantes	D	0-0
23 Oct	Lge	H	Nottm Forest	W	6-1
27 Oct	FLC	H	Preston	D	1-1
30 Oct	Lge	A	Stoke	L	0-2
2 Nov	UEFA	H	Nantes	W	1-0
6 Nov	Lge	H	Everton	W	3-0
8 Nov	FLCr	A	Preston	W	2-1
13 Nov	Lge	A	Man Utd	L	1-3
17 Nov	FLC	H	Blackpool	W	2-0
20 Nov	Lge	H	WBA	W	3-2
24 Nov	Lge	H	Arsenal	D	1-1
27 Nov	Lge	A	Chelsea	L	0-1
4 Dec	Lge	H	Southampton	W	1-0
8 Dec	UEFA	H	Rapid Bucarest	W	3-0
11 Dec	Lge	A	Leicester	W	1-0
15 Dec	UEFA	A	Rapid Bucarest	W	2-0
18 Dec	Lge	A	Liverpool	D	0-0
22 Dec	FLCsf	A	Chelsea	L	2-3
27 Dec	Lge	H	West Ham	L	0-1
1 Jan	Lge	A	Crystal P.	D	1-1
5 Jan	FLCsf	H	Chelsea	D	2-2
8 Jan	Lge	H	Man City	D	1-1
15 Jan	FC	H	Carlisle	D	1-1
18 Jan	FCr	A	Carlisle	W	3-1
22 Jan	Lge	A	Newcastle	L	1-3
29 Jan	Lge	H	Leeds U.	W	1-0
5 Feb	FC	H	Rotherham	W	2-0
12 Feb	Lge	A	Nottm Forest	W	1-0
19 Feb	Lge	H	Stoke	W	2-0
26 Feb	FC	A	Everton	W	2-0
1 Mar	Lge	A	Everton	D	1-1
4 Mar	Lge	H	Man Utd	W	2-0
7 Mar	UEFA	A	UT Arad	W	2-0
11 Mar	Lge	H	Derby	L	0-1
18 Mar	FC	A	Leeds	L	1-2
21 Mar	UEFA	H	UT Arad	D	1-1
25 Mar	Lge	H	Sheff Utd	W	2-0
28 Mar	Lge	A	Huddersfield	D	1-1
31 Mar	Lge	H	Coventry	W	1-0
1 Apr	Lge	A	West Ham	L	0-2
3 Apr	Lge	A	Ipswich	L	1-2
5 Apr	UEFAsf	H	AC Milan	W	2-1
8 Apr	Lge	A	WBA	D	1-1
15 Apr	Lge	H	Chelsea	W	3-0
19 Apr	UEFAsf	A	AC Milan	D	1-1
22 Apr	Lge	A	Southampton	D	0-0
29 Apr	Lge	H	Leicester	W	4-3
3 May	UEFAf	A	Wolves	W	2-1
11 May	Lge	A	Arsenal	W	2-0
17 May	UEFAf	H	Wolves	D	1-1
7 Jun	F	A	Maccabi	W	3-2

* Anglo-Italian League Cup Winners Cup (two legs) † Played at Boothferry Park

Player	Lg App	Goals	Player	Lg App	Goals
Beal P.	32		Knowles C.B.	34	2
Chivers M.	39	25	Morgan R.	10 (2)	
Coates R.	32	2	Mullery A.	18	3
Collins P.	7 (1)		Naylor T.	12	
Daines B.	1		Neighbour J.	14 (2)	1
England M.	38	2	Pearce J.	15 (6)	5
Evans R.	22		Perryman S.	40 (1)	
Gilzean A.	38	11	Peters M.	35	10
Holder P.	6 (2)		Pratt J.	23 (8)	1
Jennings P.A.	41		Want A.G.	7	
Kinnear J.P.	21 (1)		Own Goal		1

Final table for First Division

1	Derby	42	24	10	8	69:33	58
2	Leeds	42	24	9	9	73:31	57
3	Liverpool	42	24	9	9	64:30	57
4	Manchester C.	42	23	11	8	77:45	57
5	Arsenal	42	22	8	12	58:40	52
6	**TOTTENHAM**	**42**	**19**	**13**	**10**	**63:42**	**51**
7	Chelsea	42	18	12	12	58:49	48
8	Manchester U.	42	19	10	13	69:61	48
9	Wolverhampton	42	18	11	13	65:57	47
10	Sheffield U.	42	17	12	13	61:60	46
11	Newcastle	42	15	11	16	49:52	41
12	Leicester	42	13	13	16	41:46	39
13	Ipswich	42	11	16	15	39:53	38
14	West Ham	42	12	12	18	47:51	36
15	Everton	42	9	18	15	37:48	36
16	West Bromwich	42	12	11	19	42:54	35
17	Stoke	42	10	15	17	39:56	35
18	Coventry	42	9	15	18	44:67	33
19	Southampton	42	12	7	23	52:80	31
20	Crystal Palace	42	8	13	21	39:65	29
21	Nottingham F.	42	8	9	25	47:81	25
22	Huddersfield	42	6	13	23	27:59	25

SEASON 1972/73

Date	Comp	H/A	Opponent	Result	Score
29 Jul	F	A	Bournemouth	W	4-2
2 Aug	F	A	Aston Villa	D	0-0
7 Aug	F	A	Celtic	L	0-1
12 Aug	Lge	H	Coventry	W	2-1
16 Aug	Lge	A	WBA	W	1-0
19 Aug	Lge	A	Wolves	L	2-3
23 Aug	Lge	H	Birmingham	W	2-0
26 Aug	Lge	H	Leeds Utd	D	0-0
30 Aug	Lge	A	Newcastle	W	1-0
2 Sep	Lge	A	Ipswich	D	1-1
6 Sep	FLC	H	Huddersfield	W	2-1
9 Sep	Lge	H	C. Palace	W	2-1
13 Sep	UEFA	A	Lyn Oslo	W	6-3
16 Sep	Lge	A	Man City	L	1-2
23 Sep	Lge	H	West Ham	W	1-0
27 Sep	UEFA	H	Lyn Oslo	W	6-0
30 Sep	Lge	A	Derby	L	1-2
3 Oct	FLC	A	Middlesbrough	D	1-1
7 Oct	Lge	H	Stoke	W	4-3
11 Oct	FLCr	H	Middlesbrough	D	0-0
14 Oct	Lge	A	Norwich	L	1-2
17 Oct	*	H	Feijenoord	W	2-1
21 Oct	Lge	H	Chelsea	L	0-1
25 Oct	UEFA	H	Olympiakos	W	4-0
28 Oct	Lge	A	Man Utd	W	4-1
30 Oct	FLCr	H	Middlesbrough	W	2-1
1 Nov	FLC	H	Millwall	W	2-0
4 Nov	Lge	A	Birmingham	D	0-0
8 Nov	UEFA	A	Olympiakos	L	0-1
11 Nov	Lge	H	WBA	D	1-1
18 Nov	Lge	A	Leicester	W	1-0
25 Nov	Lge	H	Liverpool	L	1-2
29 Nov	UEFA	H	Red Star	W	2-0
2 Dec	Lge	A	Southampton	D	1-1
4 Dec	FLC	A	Liverpool	D	1-1
6 Dec	FLCr	H	Liverpool	W	3-1
9 Dec	Lge	H	Arsenal	L	1-2
13 Dec	UEFA	A	Red Star	L	0-1
16 Dec	Lge	A	Everton	L	1-3
20 Dec	FLCsf	A	Wolves	W	2-1
23 Dec	Lge	H	Sheff Utd	W	2-0
26 Dec	Lge	A	West Ham	D	2-2
30 Dec	FLCsf	H	Wolves	D	2-2
6 Jan	Lge	A	Leeds	L	1-2
13 Jan	FC	A	Margate	W	6-0
20 Jan	Lge	H	Ipswich	L	0-1
27 Jan	Lge	A	C. Palace	D	0-0
3 Feb	FC	A	Derby	D	1-1
7 Feb	FCr	H	Derby	L	3-5
10 Feb	Lge	H	Man City	L	2-3
17 Feb	Lge	A	Coventry	W	1-0
24 Feb	Lge	H	Everton	W	3-0
3 Mar	FLCf	†	Norwich	W	1-0
7 Mar	UEFA	H	Vitoria Setubal	W	1-0
10 Mar	Lge	H	Norwich	W	3-0
14 Mar	Lge	A	Stoke	D	1-1
21 Mar	UEFA	A	Vitoria Setubal	L	1-2
24 Mar	Lge	H	Man Utd	D	1-1
31 Mar	Lge	A	Liverpool	D	1-1
3 Apr	Lge	A	Chelsea	W	1-0
7 Apr	Lge	H	Southampton	L	1-2
10 Apr	UEFAsf	A	Liverpool	L	0-1
14 Apr	Lge	A	Arsenal	D	1-1
18 Apr	Lge	H	Derby	W	1-0
21 Apr	Lge	H	Leicester	D	1-1
25 Apr	UEFAsf	H	Liverpool	W	2-1
28 Apr	Lge	H	Newcastle	W	3-2
30 Apr	Lge	H	Wolves	D	2-2
2 May	Lge	A	Sheff Utd	L	2-3

* Jimmy Greaves testimonial † Played at Wembley

Player	Lg App	Goals	Player	Lg App	Goals
Beal P.	24		Jennings P.	40	
Chivers M.	38	17	Kinnear J.	24	1
Clarke R.	1 (1)		Knowles C.	35	
Coates R.	32 (3)	2	Naylor T.	16 (2)	
Collins P.	7	2	Neighbour J.	7 (1)	1
Daines B.	2		Pearce J.	35 (8)	4
Dillon M.	8		Perryman S.	41	2
England M.	31	1	Peters M.	41	15
Evans R.	24 (1)		Pratt J.	38 (1)	5
Gilzean A.	35	5	Own Goals		3

Final table for First Division

1	Liverpool	42	25	10	7	72:42	60
2	Arsenal	42	23	11	8	57:43	57
3	Leeds	42	21	11	10	71:45	53
4	Ipswich	42	17	14	11	55:45	48
5	Wolverhampton	42	18	11	13	66:54	47
6	West Ham	42	17	12	13	67:53	46
7	Derby	42	19	8	15	56:54	46
8	**TOTTENHAM**	**42**	**16**	**13**	**13**	**58:48**	**45**
9	Newcastle	42	16	13	13	60:51	45
10	Birmingham	42	15	12	15	53:54	42
11	Manchester C.	42	15	11	16	57:60	41
12	Chelsea	42	13	14	15	49:51	40
13	Southampton	42	11	18	13	47:52	40
14	Sheffield U.	42	15	10	17	51:59	40
15	Stoke	42	14	10	18	61:56	38
16	Leicester	42	10	17	15	40:46	37
17	Everton	42	13	11	18	41:49	37
18	Manchester U.	42	12	13	17	44:60	37
19	Coventry	42	13	9	20	40:55	35
20	Norwich	42	11	10	21	36:63	32
21	C. Palace	42	9	12	21	41:58	30
22	West Bromwich	42	9	10	23	38:62	28

SEASON 1973/74

8 Aug	F	A	Ajax	L	1-4
11 Aug	F	A	Cardiff	W	3-1
18 Aug	F	A	Sunderland	W	1-0
25 Aug	Lge	A	Coventry	L	0-1
28 Aug	Lge	A	Birmingham	W	2-1
1 Sep	Lge	H	Leeds	L	0-3
5 Sep	Lge	H	Burnley	L	2-3
8 Sep	Lge	A	West Ham	W	1-0
11 Sep	Lge	A	Burnley	D	2-2
15 Sep	Lge	H	Sheff Utd	L	1-2
19 Sep	UEFA	A	Grasshoppers	W	5-1
22 Sep	Lge	A	Liverpool	L	2-3
29 Sep	Lge	H	Derby	W	1-0
3 Oct	UEFA	H	Grasshoppers	W	4-1
6 Oct	Lge	A	Ipswich	D	0-0
8 Oct	FLC	A	QPR	L	0-1
13 Oct	Lge	H	Arsenal	W	2-0
20 Oct	Lge	A	Norwich	D	1-1
24 Oct	UEFA	A	Aberdeen	D	1-1
27 Oct	Lge	H	Newcastle	L	0-2
3 Nov	Lge	A	Everton	D	1-1
7 Nov	UEFA	H	Aberdeen	W	4-1
10 Nov	Lge	H	Man Utd	W	2-1
17 Nov	Lge	A	Southampton	D	1-1
24 Nov	Lge	H	Wolves	L	1-3
28 Nov	UEFA	A	Dinamo Tbilisi	D	1-1
1 Dec	Lge	A	Leicester	L	0-3
3 Dec	*	H	Bayern Munich	D	2-2
8 Dec	Lge	H	Stoke	W	2-1
12 Dec	UEFA	H	Dinamo Tbilisi	W	5-1
15 Dec	Lge	H	Man City	L	0-2
22 Dec	Lge	A	Derby	L	0-2
26 Dec	Lge	H	QPR	D	0-0
29 Dec	Lge	H	West Ham	W	2-0
1 Jan	Lge	A	Leeds	D	1-1
5 Jan	FC	A	Leicester	L	0-1
12 Jan	Lge	A	Sheff Utd	D	2-2
19 Jan	Lge	H	Coventry	W	2-1
2 Feb	Lge	A	Man City	D	0-0
6 Feb	Lge	H	Birmingham	W	4-2
16 Feb	Lge	A	Arsenal	W	1-0
23 Feb	Lge	H	Ipswich	D	1-1
2 Mar	Lge	A	QPR	L	1-3
6 Mar	UEFA	A	IFC Koln	W	2-1
16 Mar	Lge	H	Norwich	D	0-0
20 Mar	UEFA	H	IFC Koln	W	3-0
23 Mar	Lge	A	Man Utd	W	1-0
30 Mar	Lge	H	Everton	L	0-2
3 Apr	Lge	H	Chelsea	L	1-2
6 Apr	Lge	A	Wolves	D	1-1
10 Apr	UEFAsf	A	Locomotiv Leipzig	W	2-1
13 Apr	Lge	H	Southampton	W	3-1
15 Apr	Lge	A	Chelsea	D	0-0
20 Apr	Lge	A	Stoke	L	0-1
24 Apr	UEFAsf	H	Lokomotiv Leipzig	W	2-0
27 Apr	Lge	H	Leicester	W	1-0
8 May	Lge	H	Liverpool	D	1-1
11 May	Lge	A	Newcastle	W	2-0
21 May	UEFAf	H	Feyenoord	D	2-2
29 May	UEFAf	A	Feyenoord	L	0-2
8 Jun	F	A	Mauritius XI	W	5-0
13 Jun	F	A	Mauritius XI	W	6-3
16 Jun	F	A	Mauritius XI	W	6-0

* Testimonial for Phil Beal

Player	Lg App		Goals
Beal P.	41		
Chivers M.	40	(1)	17
Coats R.	36		3
Daines B.	5		
Dillon M.	16	(3)	1
England M.	33		
Evans R.	40		2
Gilzean A.	25	(4)	3
Holder P.	7	(2)	1
Jennings P.	36		
Kinnear J.	7	(4)	
Knowles C.	20		2
Lee T.	1		
McGrath C.	25	(3)	5
McNab N.	1	(1)	
Naylor T.	28	(1)	
Neighbour J.	14	(3)	
Osgood K.	1	(1)	
Perryman S.	39		1
Peters M.	35		6
Pratt J.	35		4

Final table for First Division

1	Leeds	42	24	14	4	66:31	62
2	Liverpool	42	22	13	7	52:31	57
3	Derby	42	17	14	11	52:42	48
4	Ipswich	42	18	11	13	67:58	47
5	Stoke	42	15	16	11	54:42	46
6	Burnley	42	16	14	12	56:53	46
7	Everton	42	16	12	14	50:48	44
8	QPR	42	13	17	12	56:52	43
9	Leicester	42	13	16	13	51:41	42
10	Arsenal	42	14	14	14	49:51	42
11	**TOTTENHAM**	**42**	**14**	**14**	**14**	**45:50**	**42**
12	Wolverhampton	42	13	15	14	49:49	41
13	Sheffield U.	42	14	12	16	44:49	40
14	Manchester C.	42	14	12	16	39:46	40
15	Newcastle	42	13	13	17	49:48	38
16	Coventry	42	14	10	18	43:54	38
17	Chelsea	42	12	13	17	56:60	37
18	West Ham	42	11	15	16	55:60	37
19	Birmingham	42	12	13	17	52:64	37
20	Southampton	42	11	14	17	47:68	36
21	Manchester U.	42	10	12	20	38:48	32
22	Norwich	42	7	15	20	37:62	29

SEASON 1974/75

3 Aug	F	A	Hearts	D	1-1
7 Aug	F	A	Portsmouth	W	2-0
10 Aug	F	A	Fulham	W	1-0
17 Aug	Lge	H	Ipswich	L	0-1
21 Aug	Lge	A	Man City	L	0-1
24 Aug	Lge	A	Carlisle	L	0-1
28 Aug	Lge	H	Man City	L	1-2
31 Aug	Lge	H	Derby	W	2-0
7 Sep	Lge	A	Liverpool	L	2-5
11 Sep	FLC	H	Middlesbrough	L	0-4
14 Sep	Lge	H	West Ham	W	2-1
21 Sep	Lge	A	Wolves	W	3-2
28 Sep	Lge	A	Middlesbrough	L	1-2
5 Oct	Lge	H	Burnley	L	2-3
12 Oct	Lge	A	Chelsea	L	0-1
16 Oct	Lge	A	Carlisle	D	1-1
19 Oct	Lge	H	Arsenal	W	2-0
26 Oct	Lge	A	Luton	D	1-1
2 Nov	Lge	A	Stoke	D	2-2
9 Nov	Lge	H	Everton	D	1-1
16 Nov	Lge	A	Leicester	W	2-1
23 Nov	Lge	H	Birmingham	D	0-0
27 Nov	*	H	Red Star	W	2-0
30 Nov	Lge	A	Sheff Utd	W	1-0
4 Dec	Lge	A	Leeds	L	1-2
7 Dec	Lge	H	Newcastle	W	3-0
14 Dec	Lge	A	Ipswich	L	0-4
21 Dec	Lge	H	QPR	L	1-2
26 Dec	Lge	A	West Ham	D	1-1
28 Dec	Lge	H	Coventry	D	1-1
4 Jan	FC	A	Nottm Forest	D	1-1
8 Jan	FCr	H	Nottm Forest	L	0-1
11 Jan	Lge	A	Newcastle	W	5-2
18 Jan	Lge	H	Sheff Utd	L	1-3
24 Jan	F	A	Watford	W	3-2
27 Jan	F	A	Enfield	W	2-1
1 Feb	Lge	A	Everton	L	0-1
8 Feb	Lge	H	Stoke	L	0-2
15 Feb	Lge	A	Coventry	D	1-1
18 Feb	Lge	A	Birmingham	L	0-1
22 Feb	Lge	H	Leicester	L	0-3
26 Feb	F	A	Red Star	W	1-0
1 Mar	Lge	A	Derby	L	1-3
15 Mar	Lge	A	Middlesbrough	L	0-3
22 Mar	Lge	H	Liverpool	L	0-2
28 Mar	Lge	H	Wolves	W	3-0
29 Mar	Lge	A	QPR	W	1-0
5 Apr	Lge	H	Luton	W	2-1
12 Apr	Lge	A	Burnley	L	2-3
19 Apr	Lge	H	Chelsea	W	2-0
26 Apr	Lge	A	Arsenal	L	0-1
28 Apr	Lge	H	Leeds	W	4-2

* Testimonial for Alan Gilzean

Player	Lg App		Goals
Beal P.	28		
Chivers M.	28	(1)	10
Coates R.	30	(4)	1
Conn A.	17	(1)	6
Daines B.	1		
Duncan J.	28		12
England M.	31		2
Evans R.	21	(1)	
Jennings P.	41		
Jones C.	16		1
Kinnear J.	17		
Knowles C.	31		4
McAllister D.	8	(1)	
McGrath C.	9	(4)	
McNab N.	2		
Naylor T.	38	(1)	
Neighbour T.	25	(4)	3
Osgood K.	10		
Perryman S.	42		6
Peters M.	29		4
Pratt J.	29	(2)	1
Own Goals			2

Final table for First Division

1	Derby	42	21	11	10	67:49	53
2	Liverpool	42	20	11	11	60:39	51
3	Ipswich	42	23	5	14	66:44	51
4	Everton	42	16	18	8	56:42	50
5	Stoke	42	17	15	10	64:48	49
6	Sheffield U.	42	18	13	11	58:51	49
7	Middlesbrough	42	18	12	12	54:40	48
8	Manchester C.	42	18	10	14	54:54	46
9	Leeds	42	16	13	13	57:49	45
10	Burnley	42	17	11	14	68:67	45
11	QPR	42	16	10	16	54:54	42
12	Wolverhampton	42	14	11	17	57:54	39
13	West Ham	42	13	13	16	58:59	39
14	Coventry	42	12	15	15	51:62	39
15	Newcastle	42	15	9	18	59:72	39
16	Arsenal	42	13	11	18	47:49	37
17	Birmingham	42	14	9	19	53:61	37
18	Leicester	42	12	12	18	46:60	36
19	**TOTTENHAM**	**42**	**13**	**8**	**21**	**52:63**	**34**
20	Luton	42	11	11	20	47:65	33
21	Chelsea	42	9	15	18	42:72	33
22	Carlisle	42	12	5	25	43:59	29

SEASON 1975/76

Date		Comp		Opponent		Result	Date		Comp		Opponent		Result
23 Jul	F		A	Rot Weiss	D	1-1	26 Dec	Lge		H	Birmingham	L	1-3
25 Jul	F		A	Karlsruhe	L	1-2	27 Dec	Lge		A	Coventry	D	2-2
29 Jul	F		A	Hanover	D	1-1	3 Jan	FC		H	Stoke	D	1-1
3 Aug	F		A	NAC Breda	W	1-0	10 Jan	Lge		A	Derby	W	3-2
8 Aug	F		A	Bristol Rvs	W	4-1	14 Jan	FLCsf		H	Newcastle	W	1-0
16 Aug	Lge		H	Middlesbrough	W	1-0	17 Jan	Lge		H	Man Utd	D	1-1
20 Aug	Lge		H	Ipswich	D	1-1	21 Jan	FLCsf		A	Newcastle	L	1-3
23 Aug	Lge		A	Liverpool	L	2-3	24 Jan	FCr		A	Stoke	L	1-2
25 Aug	Lge		A	West Ham	L	0-1	31 Jan	Lge		A	Ipswich	W	2-1
30 Aug	Lge		H	Norwich	D	2-2	7 Feb	Lge		H	West Ham	D	1-1
6 Sep	Lge		A	Man Utd	L	2-3	14 Feb	Lge		H	QPR	L	0-3
9 Sep	FLC		A	Watford	W	1-0	21 Feb	Lge		H	Stoke	W	2-1
13 Sep	Lge		H	Derby	L	2-3	24 Feb	Lge		A	Everton	L	0-1
20 Sep	Lge		A	Leeds	D	1-1	28 Feb	Lge		H	Leicester	D	1-1
27 Sep	Lge		H	Arsenal	D	0-0	6 Mar	Lge		A	Norwich	L	1-3
29 Sep	F		A	Le Stade			13 Mar	Lge		H	Aston Villa	W	5-2
				Rennais	D	1-1	16 Mar	Lge		A	Wolves	W	1-0
4 Oct	Lge		A	Newcastle	D	0-0	20 Mar	Lge		A	Burnley	W	2-1
8 Oct	FLC		A	Crewe	W	2-0	23 Mar	†		A	Brighton	W	6-1
11 Oct	Lge		A	Aston Villa	D	1-1	27 Mar	Lge		H	Sheff Utd	W	5-0
18 Oct	Lge		H	Man City	D	2-2	3 Apr	Lge		A	Arsenal	W	2-0
22 Oct	*		H	Arsenal	D	2-2	10 Apr	Lge		H	Leeds	D	0-0
25 Oct	Lge		A	Leicester	W	3-2	17 Apr	Lge		A	Birmingham	L	1-3
27 Oct	Lge		A	Millwall	L	1-3	19 Apr	Lge		H	Coventry	W	4-1
1 Nov	Lge		H	Wolves	W	2-1	21 Apr	F		A	Nrth Herts XI	L	1-2
8 Nov	FLC		A	QPR	D	0-0	24 Apr	Lge		H	Newcastle	L	0-3
12 Nov	Lge		H	West Ham	D	0-0	27 Apr	F		A	Toronto		
15 Nov	Lge		H	Stoke	D	1-1					Metros	W	1-0
22 Nov	FLCr		H	Man City	L	1-2	1 May	F		A	Fiji Select	W	4-0
24 Nov	Lge		A	West Ham	W	2-0	3 May	F		A	Auckland XI	W	5-3
29 Nov	FLC		H	Burnley	W	2-1	5 May	F		A	Wellington XI	W	3-2
3 Dec	Lge		H	Doncaster	W	7-2	9 May	F		A	Victoria	W	3-1
6 Dec	Lge		A	Sheff Utd	W	2-1	12 May	F		A	N. Sth Wales	W	5-1
10 Dec	Lge		H	Everton	D	2-2	16 May	F		A	Australian XI	W	3-2
13 Dec	Lge		H	Liverpool	L	0-4	18 May	F		A	South Aust.	W	5-2
20 Dec	Lge		A	Middlesbrough	L	0-1	23 May	F		A	Western Aust.	W	4-0

* Testimonial for Cyril Knowles   † Testimonial for Joe Kinnear

Player	Lg App		Goals	Player	Lg App		Goals
Brotherston N.	1			McGrath C.	4	(1)	
Chivers M.	35	(4)	7	McNab N.	15	(4)	
Coates R.	24	(3)	2	Naylor T.	36		
Conn A.	8	(1)		Neighbour J.	35		3
Daines B.	2			Osgood K.	42		3
Duncan J.	37	(2)	20	Perryman S.	40		6
Hoddle G.	7	(1)	1	Pratt T.	41		10
Jennings P.	40			Robinson M.	2	(1)	1
Jones C.	34	(9)	5	Smith I.	2		
Kinnear J.	1			Stead M.	4		
Knowles C.	10			Walford S.	2	(1)	
McAllister D.	35		2	Young W.	35		3

Final table for First Division

1	Liverpool	42	23	14	5	66:31	60
2	QPR	42	24	11	7	67:33	59
3	Manchester U.	42	23	10	10	68:42	56
4	Derby	42	21	11	10	75:58	53
5	Leeds	42	21	9	12	65:46	51
6	Ipswich	42	16	14	12	54:48	46
7	Leicester	42	13	19	10	48:51	45
8	Manchester C.	42	16	12	15	64:46	43
9	**TOTTENHAM**	**42**	**14**	**15**	**13**	**63:63**	**43**
10	Norwich	42	16	10	16	58:58	42
11	Everton	42	15	12	15	60:66	42
12	Stoke	42	15	11	16	48:50	41
13	Middlesbrough	42	15	10	17	46:45	40
14	Coventry	42	13	14	15	47:57	40
15	Newcastle	42	15	9	18	71:62	39
16	Aston Villa	42	11	17	14	51:59	39
17	Arsenal	42	13	10	19	47:53	36
18	West Ham	42	13	10	19	48:71	36
19	Birmingham	42	13	7	22	57:75	33
20	Wolverhampton	42	10	10	22	51:68	30
21	Burnley	42	9	10	23	43:66	28
22	Sheffield U.	42	6	10	26	33:82	22

SEASON 1976/77

Date		Comp		Opponent		Result	Date		Comp		Opponent		Result
24 Jul	F		A	Osnabruck	W	3-1	18 Dec	Lge		A	Leicester	L	1-2
28 Jul	F		A	Eintracht	L	1-4	27 Dec	Lge		H	Arsenal	D	2-2
31 Jul	F		A	IFC Koln	L	1-3	1 Jan	Lge		H	West Ham	W	2-1
4 Aug	F		A	Baunatal	W	2-1	8 Jan	FC		A	Cardiff	L	0-1
6 Aug	F		A	Bad Honnef	W	2-0	11 Jan	Lge		A	QPR	L	1-2
10 Aug	F		A	Swindon	L	1-3	22 Jan	Lge		H	Ipswich	W	1-0
16 Aug	F		H	Ryl Antwerp	D	1-1	5 Feb	Lge		A	Middlesbrough	L	0-2
21 Aug	Lge		A	Ipswich	L	1-3	12 Feb	Lge		H	Man Utd	L	1-3
25 Aug	Lge		H	Newcastle	L	0-2	19 Feb	Lge		A	Leeds	L	1-2
28 Aug	Lge		H	Middlesbrough	D	0-0	26 Feb	Lge		A	Newcastle	L	0-2
31 Aug	FLC		A	Middlesbrough	W	2-1	5 Mar	Lge		A	Norwich	W	3-1
4 Sep	Lge		A	Man Utd	W	3-2	9 Mar	Lge		H	Liverpool	W	1-0
11 Sep	Lge		H	Leeds Utd	W	1-0	12 Mar	Lge		H	WBA	L	0-2
18 Sep	Lge		A	Liverpool	L	0-2	19 Mar	Lge		A	Birmingham	W	2-1
22 Sep	FLC		H	Wrexham	W	2-3	23 Mar	Lge		H	Derby	D	0-0
25 Sep	Lge		H	Norwich	D	1-1	26 Mar	Lge		A	Everton	L	0-4
2 Oct	Lge		A	WBA	L	2-4	2 Apr	Lge		A	Coventry	D	1-1
9 Oct	F†		A	Arsenal	W	2-1	9 Apr	Lge		H	QPR	W	3-0
12 Oct	F		A	Napredac	L	0-4	11 Apr	Lge		A	Arsenal	L	0-1
16 Oct	Lge		A	Derby	L	2-8	12 Apr	Lge		A	Bristol City	L	0-1
20 Oct	Lge		H	Birmingham	W	1-0	16 Apr	Lge		H	Sunderland	D	1-1
23 Oct	Lge		H	Coventry	L	0-1	20 Apr	Lge		A	Aston Villa	L	1-2
30 Oct	Lge		H	Everton	D	3-3	23 Apr	Lge		A	Stoke	D	0-0
6 Nov	Lge		A	West Ham	L	3-5	30 Apr	Lge		H	Aston Villa	W	3-1
13 Nov	Lge		H	Bristol City	L	0-1	7 May	Lge		A	Man City	L	0-5
20 Nov	Lge		A	Sunderland	L	1-2	14 May	Lge		H	Leicester	W	2-0
23 Nov	F*		H	Arsenal	W	3-2	17 May	F		A	Stord	W	5-0
27 Nov	Lge		H	Stoke	W	2-0	19 May	F		A	Sogndal	W	6-0
11 Dec	Lge		H	Man City	D	2-2							

* Pat Jennings Testimonial   † Peter Simpson Testimonial

Player	Lg App		Goals	Player	Lg App		Goals
Armstrong G.	21	(1)	3	McAllister D.	12	(2)	1
Coates R.	31	(3)	3	McNab N.	10	(4)	
Conn A.	13	(1)		Moores I.	17	(1)	2
Daines B.	19			Naylor T.	40		
Duncan J.	9		4	Neighbour J.	7		
Gorman J.	15			Osgood K.	42		7
Hoddle G.	39		4	Perryman S.	42		1
Holmes J.	10		1	Pratt J.	34	(4)	4
Jennings P.	23			Stead M.	8		
Jones C.	31		9	Taylor P.	32	(1)	8
Keeley G.	6	(1)		Young W.	19		1

Final Table for First Division

1	Liverpool	42	23	11	8	62:33	57
2	Manchester C.	42	21	14	7	60:34	56
3	Ipswich	42	22	8	12	66:39	56
4	Aston Villa	42	22	7	13	76:50	51
5	Newcastle	42	18	13	11	64:49	49
6	Manchester U.	42	18	11	13	71:62	47
7	West Bromwich	42	16	13	13	62:56	45
8	Arsenal	42	16	11	15	64:59	43
9	Everton	42	14	14	14	62:64	42
10	Leeds	42	15	12	15	48:51	42
11	Leicester	42	12	18	12	47:60	42
12	Middlesbrough	42	14	13	15	40:45	41
13	Birmingham	42	13	12	17	63:61	38
14	QPR	42	13	12	17	47:52	38
15	Derby	42	9	19	14	50:55	37
16	Norwich	42	14	9	19	47:64	37
17	West Ham	42	11	14	17	46:65	36
18	Bristol C.	42	11	13	18	38:48	35
19	Coventry	42	10	15	17	48:59	35
20	Sunderland	42	11	12	19	46:54	34
21	Stoke	42	10	14	18	28:51	34
22	**TOTTENHAM**	**42**	**12**	**9**	**21**	**48:72**	**33**

SEASON 1977/78

7 Aug	A	Royale Union	W	2-0*	2 Jan	Lge	A	Sheff Utd	D	2-2
10 Aug	A	Leicester	W	2-1*	7 Jan	FC	H	Bolton	D	2-2
12 Aug	A	Norsjo	W	3-2*	10 Jan	FCr	A	Bolton	L	1-2
20 Aug	Lge	H	Sheff Utd	W	4-2	14 Jan	Lge	A	Notts Co.	D	3-3
24 Aug	Lge	A	Blackburn	D	0-0	21 Jan	Lge	H	Cardiff	W	2-1
27 Aug	Lge	H	Notts Co.	W	2-1	4 Feb	Lge	A	Fulham	D	1-1
31 Aug	FLC	H	Wimbledon	W	4-0	11 Feb	Lge	H	Blackpool	D	2-2
3 Sep	Lge	A	Cardiff	D	0-0	22 Feb	Lge	A	Luton	W	4-1
10 Sep	Lge	H	Fulham	W	1-0	25 Feb	Lge	H	Orient	D	1-1
17 Sep	Lge	A	Blackpool	W	2-0	4 Mar	Lge	A	Oldham	D	1-1
24 Sep	Lge	H	Luton	W	2-0	11 Mar	Lge	H	Charlton	W	2-1
1 Oct	Lge	A	Orient	D	1-1	18 Mar	Lge	A	Bristol Rvs	W	3-2
4 Oct	Lge	A	Hull	W	2-0	22 Mar	Lge	H	Stoke	W	3-1
8 Oct	Lge	H	Oldham	W	5-1	25 Mar	Lge	A	Mansfield	D	3-3
15 Oct	Lge	A	Charlton	L	1-4	27 Mar	Lge	H	Millwall	D	3-3
22 Oct	FLC	H	Coventry	L	2-3	1 Apr	Lge	A	Burnley	L	1-2
26 Oct	Lge	H	Bristol Rvs	W	9-0	8 Apr	Lge	H	Bolton	W	1-0
29 Oct	Lge	A	Stoke	W	3-1	15 Apr	Lge	A	Brighton	L	1-3
5 Nov	Lge	H	Burnley	W	3-0	22 Apr	Lge	H	Sunderland	L	2-3
12 Nov	Lge	A	Crystal P.	W	2-1	26 Apr	Lge	H	Hull	W	1-0
19 Nov	Lge	H	Brighton	D	0-0	29 Apr	Lge	A	Southampton	D	0-0
22 Nov	F	A	Arsenal	W	3-1	3 May	F	A	Truro City	W	8-2
26 Nov	Lge	A	Bolton	L	0-1	5 May	F	A	Orient	W	3-1
3 Dec	Lge	H	Southampton	D	0-0	8 May	F	A	Aleppo Select	W	1-0
10 Dec	Lge	A	Sunderland	W	2-1	10 May	F	A	Syrian Select	W	4-0
17 Dec	Lge	H	Crystal P.	D	2-2	12 May	†	H	Arsenal	L	3-5
26 Dec	Lge	A	Millwall	W	3-1	15 May	F	A	Hamark'tene	L	0-3
27 Dec	Lge	H	Mansfield	D	1-1	17 May	F	A	FC Kvik	W	2-0
31 Dec	Lge	H	Blackburn	W	4-0	19 May	F	A	Karlstad BK	W	4-1

* Scandinavian tour
† Testimonial for John Pratt

Player	Lg App		Goals	Player	Lg App		Goals
Armstrong G.	19	(9)	2	McNab N.	42		3
Coates R.	3	(2)		Moores I.	10	(3)	4
Daines B.	42			Naylor T.	37		
Duncan J.	27		16	Osgood K.	18		3
Hoddle G.	41		12	Perryman S.	42		1
Holmes J.	38			Pratt J.	42		7
Jones C.	20		8	Robinson M.	4		1
Lee C.	25	(2)	11	Stead M.	3	(1)	
McAllister D.	25		4	Taylor P.	41		11

Final table for Second Division

1	Bolton	42	24	10	8	63:33	58
2	Southampton	42	22	13	7	70:39	57
3	**TOTTENHAM**	**42**	**20**	**16**	**6**	**83:49**	**56**
4	Brighton	42	22	12	8	63:38	56
5	Blackburn	42	16	13	13	56:60	45
6	Sunderland	42	14	16	12	67:59	44
7	Stoke	42	16	10	16	53:49	42
8	Oldham	42	13	16	13	54:58	42
9	Crystal P.	42	13	15	14	50:47	41
10	Fulham	42	14	13	15	49:49	41
11	Burnley	42	15	10	17	56:64	40
12	Sheffield U.	42	16	8	18	62:73	40
13	Luton	42	14	10	18	54:52	38
14	Orient	42	10	18	14	43:49	38
15	Notts Co.	42	11	16	15	54:62	38
16	Millwall	42	12	14	16	49:57	38
17	Charlton	42	13	12	17	55:68	38
18	Bristol R.	42	13	12	17	61:77	38
19	Cardiff	42	13	12	17	51:71	38
20	Blackpool	42	12	13	17	59:60	37
21	Mansfield	42	10	11	21	49:69	31
22	Hull	42	8	12	22	34:52	28

SEASON 1978/79

5 Aug	F	A	Aberdeen	L	1-3	16 Jan	FCr	A	Altrincham	W	3-0*
8 Aug	F	A	Ryl Antwerp	W	3-1	20 Jan	Lge	H	Leeds	L	1-2
10 Aug	F	A	Venlo	L	0-1	3 Feb	Lge	H	Man City	L	0-3
12 Aug	F	A	Bohemians	W	4-0	10 Feb	Lge	A	Coventry	W	3-1
19 Aug	Lge	A	Nottm Forest	D	1-1	12 Feb	FC	H	Wrexham	D	3-3
23 Aug	Lge	H	Aston Villa	L	1-4	21 Feb	FCr	A	Wrexham	W	3-2
26 Aug	Lge	H	Chelsea	D	2-2	24 Feb	Lge	A	Birmingham	L	0-1
29 Aug	FLC	A	Swansea	D	2-2	28 Feb	FC	A	Oldham	W	1-0
2 Sep	Lge	A	Liverpool	L	0-7	3 Mar	FCr	H	Derby	W	2-0
6 Sep	FLCr	H	Swansea	L	1-3	10 Mar	Lge	A	Man Utd	D	1-1
9 Sep	Lge	A	Bristol C.	W	1-0	14 Mar	Lge	A	Man Utd	L	0-2
16 Sep	Lge	A	Leeds	W	2-1	17 Mar	Lge	H	Norwich	D	0-0
19 Sep	F	A	Aldershot	D	1-1	24 Mar	Lge	A	Aston Villa	W	3-2
23 Sep	Lge	A	Man City	L	0-2	28 Mar	Lge	H	Southampton	D	0-0
26 Sep	F	A	IFK Gothnburg	L	0-1	31 Mar	Lge	A	Middlesbrough	L	0-1
30 Sep	Lge	H	Coventry	D	1-1	3 Apr	Lge	A	Wolves	L	2-3
7 Oct	Lge	A	WBA	W	1-0	7 Apr	Lge	H	Middlesbrough	L	1-2
9 Oct	F	A	Saudi Arab XI	W	4-2	10 Apr	Lge	A	Arsenal	L	0-1
14 Oct	Lge	H	Birmingham	W	1-0	14 Apr	Lge	H	QPR	D	1-1
16 Oct	F	A	Wolves	L	1-2	16 Apr	F	A	Southampton	D	3-3
21 Oct	Lge	A	Derby	D	2-2	21 Apr	Lge	H	Man Utd	D	1-1
28 Oct	Lge	H	Bolton	W	2-1	24 Apr	F	A	QPR	W	3-1
4 Nov	Lge	A	Norwich	D	2-2	28 Apr	Lge	A	Ipswich	L	1-2
11 Nov	Lge	H	Nottm Forest	L	1-3	30 Apr	†	H	West Ham	D	2-2
18 Nov	Lge	A	Chelsea	W	3-1	5 May	Lge	H	Everton	D	1-1
22 Nov	Lge	H	Liverpool	D	0-0	8 May	Lge	A	Bolton	W	3-1
25 Nov	Lge	H	Wolves	W	1-0	11 May	F	A	Gillingham	W	3-2
4 Dec	F	A	West Ham	L	2-4	14 May	Lge	H	WBA	W	1-0
9 Dec	Lge	H	Ipswich	W	1-0	16 May	F	A	Kuwait Army	W	2-1
16 Dec	Lge	A	Man Utd	L	0-2	23 May	F	A	Selangor Sel	W	4-0
18 Dec	F	A	El Nasr	L	0-3	27 May	F	A	Indonesia	W	6-0‡
23 Dec	Lge	H	Arsenal	L	0-5	29 May	F	A	Japan XI	W	2-0‡
26 Dec	Lge	A	QPR	D	2-2	31 May	F	A	Fiorentina	D	1-1‡
30 Dec	Lge	A	Everton	D	1-1	2 Jun	F	A	San Lorenzo	W	5-3‡
10 Jan	FC	H	Altrincham	D	1-1	5 Jun	F	A	Dundee Utd	W	2-0‡
13 Jan	Lge	A	Bristol C.	D	0-0	6 Jun	F	A	Bermuda Sel	W	3-1

* Played at Maine Road † Testimonial for Steve Perryman
‡ Games played during 'Japan Cup' tournament

Player	Lg App		Goals
Aleksic M.	5		
Ardiles O.	38		3
Armstrong G.	10	(3)	1
Beavon S.	1		
Daines B.	14		
Duncan J.	2		1
Falco M.	1		1
Galvin T.	1		
Gorman J.	15		
Hoddle G.	35	(1)	7
Holmes J.	33		1
Jones C.	19	(1)	5
Kendall M.	23		
Lacy J.	35		
Lee C.	27	(1)	8
McAllister D.	38		
McNab N.	2		
Miller P.	7		
Moores I.	2		
Naylor T.	22		
Perryman S.	42		
Pratt J.	38	(1)	4
Smith G.	2	(1)	
Taylor P.	33	(1)	10
Villa R.	32	(6)	2
Own Goals			3

Final table for First Division

1	Liverpool	42	30	8	4	85:16	68
2	Nottingham F.	42	21	18	3	61:26	60
3	West Bromwich	42	24	11	7	72:35	59
4	Everton	42	17	17	8	52:40	51
5	Leeds	42	18	14	10	70:52	50
6	Ipswich	42	20	9	13	63:49	49
7	Arsenal	42	17	14	11	61:48	48
8	Aston Villa	42	15	16	11	59:49	46
9	Manchester U.	42	15	15	12	60:63	45
10	Coventry	42	14	16	12	58:68	44
11	**TOTTENHAM**	**42**	**13**	**15**	**14**	**48:61**	**41**
12	Middlesbrough	42	15	10	17	57:50	40
13	Bristol C.	42	15	10	17	47:51	40
14	Southampton	42	12	16	14	47:53	40
15	Manchester C.	42	13	13	16	58:56	39
16	Norwich	42	7	23	12	51:57	37
17	Bolton	42	12	11	19	54:75	35
18	Wolverhampton	42	13	8	21	44:68	34
19	Derby	42	10	11	21	44:71	31
20	QPR	42	6	13	23	45:73	25
21	Birmingham	42	6	10	26	37:64	22
22	Chelsea	42	5	10	27	44:92	20

SEASON 1979/80

Date	Comp	H/A	Opponent	Result	Score
2 Aug	F	A	Gillingham	D	1-1
4 Aug	F	A	Oxford	L	1-2
7 Aug	F	A	Dundee Utd	L	2-3
8 Aug	F	A	Aberdeen	L	0-2
11 Aug	F	A	Orient	D	1-1
18 Aug	Lge	H	Middlesbrough	L	1-3
22 Aug	Lge	A	Norwich	L	0-4
25 Aug	Lge	A	Stoke	L	1-3
29 Aug	FLC	H	Man Utd	W	2-1
1 Sep	Lge	H	Man City	W	2-1
5 Sep	FLC	A	Man Utd	L	1-3
8 Sep	Lge	H	Brighton	W	2-1
15 Sep	Lge	A	Southampton	L	2-5
22 Sep	Lge	H	WBA	D	1-1
29 Sep	Lge	A	Coventry	D	1-1
6 Oct	Lge	A	Crystal P.	D	1-1
10 Oct	Lge	H	Norwich	W	3-2
13 Oct	Lge	H	Derby	W	1-0
20 Oct	Lge	A	Leeds	W	2-1
27 Oct	Lge	H	Nottm Forest	W	1-0
3 Nov	Lge	A	Middlesbrough	D	0-0
6 Nov	F	A	Widad Maroc	W	4-2
10 Nov	Lge	H	Bolton	W	2-0
17 Nov	Lge	A	Liverpool	L	1-2
24 Nov	Lge	A	Everton	D	1-1
1 Dec	Lge	H	Man Utd	L	1-2
8 Dec	Lge	A	Bristol C.	W	3-1
15 Dec	Lge	H	Aston Villa	L	1-2
21 Dec	Lge	A	Ipswich	L	1-3
26 Dec	Lge	A	Arsenal	L	0-1
29 Dec	Lge	H	Stoke	W	1-0
5 Jan	FC	H	Man Utd	D	1-1
9 Jan	FCr	A	Man Utd	W	1-0
12 Jan	Lge	A	Man City	D	1-1
19 Jan	Lge	A	Brighton	W	2-0
26 Jan	FC	A	Swindon	D	0-0
30 Jan	FCr	H	Swindon	W	2-1
2 Feb	Lge	H	Southampton	D	0-0
9 Feb	Lge	A	WBA	L	1-2
16 Feb	FC	H	Birmingham	W	3-1
23 Feb	Lge	A	Derby	L	1-2
27 Feb	Lge	H	Coventry	W	4-3
1 Mar	Lge	H	Leeds	W	2-1
8 Mar	FC	H	Liverpool	L	0-1
11 Mar	Lge	A	Nottm Forest	L	0-4
15 Mar	Lge	H	Crystal P.	L	1-2
22 Mar	Lge	A	Bolton	L	1-2
29 Mar	Lge	H	Liverpool	W	2-0
2 Apr	Lge	A	Ipswich	L	0-2
5 Apr	Lge	A	Wolves	W	2-1
7 Apr	Lge	H	Arsenal	L	1-2
12 Apr	Lge	A	Man Utd	L	1-4
15 Apr	F	A	Crystal P.	W	3-2
19 Apr	Lge	H	Everton	W	3-0
23 Apr	Lge	H	Wolves	D	2-2
26 Apr	Lge	A	Aston Villa	L	0-1
29 Apr	*	H	Crystal P.	L	0-2
3 May	Lge	H	Bristol C.	D	0-0
5 May	F	A	Bournemouth	W	2-1
7 May	F	A	Hertford Town	W	4-0
11 May	F	A	Vienna Select	L	0-3
13 May	F	A	Sturm Graz	L	0-2

* Testimonial for Terry Naylor

Player	Lg App		Goals
Aleksic M.	8		
Armstrong G.	30	(2)	4
Ardiles O.	40		3
Beavon S.	3	(1)	
Daines B.	32		
Falco M.	9	(2)	2
Galvin T.	10	(3)	4
Gibson T.	1		
Hazard M.	3		
Hoddle G.	41		19
Hughton C.	39		1
Jones C.	37	(1)	9
Kendall M.	2		
Lacy J.	4		
Lee C.	10	(2)	
McAllister D.	36	(1)	1
Miller P.	27		2
Naylor T.	7	(1)	
Perryman S.	40		1
Pratt J.	24	(5)	2
Smith G.	14		
Southey P.	1		
Taylor P.	9	(2)	
Villa R.	22		3
Yorath T.	33		1

Final table for First Division

1	Liverpool	42	25 10 7	81:30	60
2	Manchester U.	42	24 10 8	65:35	58
3	Ipswich	42	22 9 11	68:39	53
4	Arsenal	42	18 16 8	52:36	52
5	Nottingham F.	42	20 8 14	63:43	48
6	Wolverhampton	42	19 9 14	58:47	47
7	Aston Villa	42	16 14 12	51:50	46
8	Southampton	42	18 9 15	65:53	45
9	Middlesbrough	42	16 12 14	50:44	44
10	West Bromwich	42	11 19 12	54:50	41
11	Leeds	42	13 14 15	46:50	40
12	Norwich	42	13 14 15	58:66	40
13	Crystal P.	42	12 16 14	41:50	40
14	**TOTTENHAM**	**42**	**15 10 17**	**52:62**	**40**
15	Coventry	42	16 7 19	56:66	39
16	Brighton	42	11 15 16	47:57	37
17	Manchester C.	42	12 13 17	43:66	37
18	Stoke	42	13 10 19	44:58	36
19	Everton	42	9 17 16	43:51	35
20	Bristol C.	42	9 13 20	37:66	31
21	Derby	42	11 8 23	47:67	30
22	Bolton	42	5 15 22	38:73	25

SEASON 1980/81

Date	Comp	H/A	Opponent	Result	Score
28 Jul	F	A	Southend	D	1-1
30 Jul	F	A	Portsmouth	W	2-1
2 Aug	F	A	PSV Eindhoven	L	2-4
4 Aug	F	A	Rangers	L	1-2
5 Aug	F	A	Dundee Utd	L	1-4
8 Aug	F	A	Swansea	L	0-1
16 Aug	Lge	H	Nottm Forest	W	2-0
19 Aug	Lge	A	C. Palace	W	4-3
23 Aug	Lge	H	Brighton	D	2-2
27 Aug	FLC	A	Orient	W	1-0
30 Aug	Lge	A	Arsenal	L	0-2
3 Sep	FLC	H	Orient	W	3-1
6 Sep	Lge	H	Man Utd	D	0-0
13 Sep	Lge	A	Leeds	D	0-0
20 Sep	Lge	H	Sunderland	D	0-0
24 Sep	FLC	H	C. Palace	D	0-0
27 Sep	Lge	A	Leicester	L	1-2
30 Sep	FLCr	A	C. Palace	W	3-1
4 Oct	Lge	A	Stoke	W	3-2
11 Oct	Lge	H	Middlesbrough	W	3-2
18 Oct	Lge	A	Aston Villa	L	0-3
22 Oct	Lge	A	Man City	L	1-3
25 Oct	Lge	H	Coventry	W	4-1
1 Nov	Lge	A	Everton	D	2-2
4 Nov	FLC	H	Arsenal	W	1-0
8 Nov	Lge	H	Wolves	D	2-2
12 Nov	Lge	H	C. Palace	W	4-2
15 Nov	Lge	A	Nottm Forest	W	3-0
17 Nov	F	A	Weymouth	W	6-1
22 Nov	Lge	A	Birmingham	L	1-2
29 Nov	Lge	H	WBA	L	2-3
2 Dec	FLC	A	West Ham	L	0-1
6 Dec	Lge	A	Liverpool	L	1-2
13 Dec	Lge	H	Man City	W	2-1
17 Dec	Lge	H	Ipswich	W	5-3
20 Dec	Lge	A	Middlesbrough	L	1-4
26 Dec	Lge	H	Southampton	D	4-4
27 Dec	Lge	A	Norwich	D	2-2
3 Jan	FC	A	QPR	D	0-0
7 Jan	FCr	H	QPR	W	3-1
10 Jan	Lge	H	Birmingham	W	1-0
17 Jan	Lge	H	Arsenal	W	2-0
24 Jan	FC	H	Hull City	W	2-0
31 Jan	Lge	A	Brighton	W	2-0
2 Feb	F	A	Jersey Sel XI	W	5-0
7 Feb	Lge	H	Leeds	D	1-1
14 Feb	FC	H	Coventry	W	3-1
17 Feb	Lge	A	Man Utd	D	0-0
21 Feb	Lge	H	Leicester	L	1-2
28 Feb	Lge	A	Sunderland	D	1-1
7 Mar	FC	H	Exeter	W	2-0
11 Mar	Lge	H	Stoke	D	2-2
14 Mar	Lge	A	Ipswich	L	0-3
21 Mar	Lge	H	Aston Villa	W	2-0
28 Mar	Lge	A	Coventry	W	1-0
4 Apr	Lge	H	Everton	D	2-2
11 Apr	FCsf	*	Wolves	D	2-2
15 Apr	FCsfr	*	Wolves	W	3-0
18 Apr	Lge	H	Norwich	L	2-3
20 Apr	Lge	A	Southampton	D	1-1
25 Apr	Lge	H	Liverpool	D	1-1
30 Apr	Lge	A	Wolves	L	0-1
2 May	Lge	A	WBA	L	2-4
9 May	FCf	†	Man City	D	1-1
11 May	‡	H	West Ham	D	0-0
14 May	FCfr	†	Man City	W	3-2
24 May	F	A	Bahrain XI	W	3-0
26 May	F	A	Kuwait Army XI	W	2-1
28 May	F	A	Bahrain XI	W	5-3
10 Jun	F	A	Trabzonspor	W	4-0
13 Jun	F	A	Fenerbahce	W	5-1

* First semi-final at Hillsborough, replay at Highbury
† Cup final and replay at Wembley   ‡ Testimonial for Barry Daines

Player	Lg App		Goals
Aleksic M.	10		
Archibald S.	41	(1)	20
Ardiles O.	36		5
Armstrong G.	4	(4)	
Brooke G.	18	(8)	3
Crooks G.	40		16
Daines B.	28		
Falco M.	3		1
Galvin T.	18	(1)	1
Hazard M.	4	(2)	
Hoddle G.	38		12
Hughton C.	34		1
Kendall M.	4		
Lacy J.	31		2
Mazzon G.	2	(1)	
McAllister D.	18		
Miller P.	25	(1)	2
O'Reilly G.	2	(1)	
Perryman S.	42		2
Roberts G.	24	(3)	
Smith G.	20	(2)	1
Taylor P.	8	(3)	1
Villa R.	29	(1)	2
Yorath T.	15	(4)	
Own Goal			1

Final table for First Division

1	Aston Villa	42	26 8 8	72:40	60
2	Ipswich	42	23 10 9	77:43	56
3	Arsenal	42	19 15 8	61:45	53
4	West Bromwich	42	20 12 10	60:42	52
5	Liverpool	42	17 17 8	62:46	51
6	Southampton	42	20 10 12	76:56	50
7	Nottingham F.	42	19 12 11	62:45	50
8	Manchester U.	42	15 18 9	51:36	48
9	Leeds	42	17 10 15	39:47	44
10	**TOTTENHAM**	**42**	**14 15 13**	**70:68**	**43**
11	Stoke	42	12 18 12	51:60	42
12	Manchester C.	42	14 11 17	56:59	39
13	Birmingham	42	13 12 17	50:61	38
14	Middlesbrough	42	16 5 21	53:61	37
15	Everton	42	13 10 19	55:58	36
16	Coventry	42	13 10 19	48:68	36
17	Sunderland	42	14 7 21	58:53	35
18	Wolverhampton	42	13 9 20	47:55	35
19	Brighton	42	14 7 21	54:67	35
20	Norwich	42	13 7 22	49:73	33
21	Leicester	42	13 6 23	40:67	32
22	C. Palace	42	6 7 29	47:83	19

SEASON 1981/82

Date	Comp		Opponent	Res	Score
8 Aug	F	A	Glentoran	D	3-3
10 Aug	F	A	Limerick	W	6-2
12 Aug	F	A	Norwich	D	2-2
16 Aug	F	A	Aberdeen	W	1-0
22 Aug	CS	*	Aston Villa	D	2-2
29 Aug	Lge	A	Middlesbrough	W	3-1
2 Sep	Lge	H	West Ham	L	0-4
5 Sep	Lge	H	Aston Villa	L	1-3
12 Sep	Lge	A	Wolves	W	1-0
16 Sep	ECWC	A	Ajax	W	3-1
19 Sep	Lge	H	Everton	W	3-0
22 Sep	Lge	A	Swansea	L	1-2
26 Sep	Lge	A	Man City	W	1-0
29 Sep	ECWC	H	Ajax	W	3-0
3 Oct	Lge	H	Nottm Forest	W	3-0
7 Oct	FLC	H	Man Utd	W	1-0
10 Oct	Lge	H	Stoke	W	2-0
12 Oct	F	A	Luton	D	2-2
17 Oct	Lge	A	Sunderland	W	2-0
21 Oct	ECWC	A	Dundalk	D	1-1
24 Oct	Lge	H	Brighton	L	0-1
28 Oct	FLC	A	Man Utd	W	1-0
31 Oct	Lge	A	Southampton	W	2-1
4 Nov	ECWC	H	Dundalk	W	1-0
7 Nov	Lge	H	WBA	L	1-2
11 Nov	FLC	H	Wrexham	W	2-0
14 Nov	F	A	Israeli Sel	W	3-2
21 Nov	Lge	H	Man Utd	W	3-1
28 Nov	Lge	A	Notts C	D	2-2
2 Dec	FLC	H	Fulham	W	1-0
5 Dec	Lge	H	Coventry	L	1-2
12 Dec	Lge	A	Leeds	D	0-0
22 Dec	F	A	Plymouth	D	1-1
29 Dec	F	A	Sp Lisbon	L	2-3
2 Jan	FC	H	Arsenal	W	1-0
18 Jan	FLC	H	Nottm Forest	W	1-0
23 Jan	FC	H	Leeds	W	1-0
27 Jan	Lge	H	Middlesbrough	W	1-0
30 Jan	Lge	A	Everton	D	1-1
3 Feb	FLCsf	A	WBA	D	0-0
6 Feb	Lge	H	Wolves	W	6-1
10 Feb	FLCsf	H	WBA	W	1-0
13 Feb	FC	H	Aston Villa	W	1-0
17 Feb	Lge	A	Aston Villa	D	1-1
20 Feb	Lge	H	Man City	W	2-0
22 Feb	F	A	Jersey Sel	W	8-3
27 Feb	Lge	A	Stoke	W	2-0
3 Mar	ECWC	H	Eintrach Fr.	W	2-0
6 Mar	FC	A	Chelsea	W	3-2
9 Mar	Lge	A	Brighton	W	3-1
13 Mar	FLCf	*	Liverpool	L	1-3
17 Mar	ECWC	A	Eintracht Fr.	L	1-2
20 Mar	Lge	H	Southampton	W	3-2
23 Mar	Lge	A	Birmingham	D	0-0
27 Mar	Lge	A	WBA	L	0-1
29 Mar	Lge	H	Arsenal	D	2-2
3 Apr	FCsf	†	Leicester	W	2-0
7 Apr	ECWCsf	H	Barcelona	D	1-1
10 Apr	Lge	H	Ipswich	W	1-0
12 Apr	Lge	A	Arsenal	W	3-1
14 Apr	Lge	H	Sunderland	D	2-2
17 Apr	Lge	A	Man Utd	L	0-2
21 Apr	ECWCsf	A	Barcelona	L	0-1
24 Apr	Lge	H	Notts C	W	3-1
28 Apr	Lge	H	Birmingham	D	1-1
1 May	Lge	A	Coventry	D	0-0
3 May	Lge	H	Liverpool	D	2-2
5 May	Lge	H	Swansea	W	2-1
8 May	Lge	H	Leeds	W	2-1
10 May	Lge	A	West Ham	D	2-2
12 May	Lge	A	Nottm Forest	L	0-2
15 May	Lge	H	Liverpool	L	1-3
17 May	Lge	A	Ipswich	L	1-2
22 May	FCf	*	QPR	D	1-1
27 May	FCfr	*	QPR	W	1-0

* at Wembley   † at Villa Park

SEASON 1982/83

Date	Comp		Opponent	Res	Score
3 Aug	F	A	Scunthorpe	W	5-0
6 Aug	F	A	Lausanne	L	0-3
8 Aug	F	A	Rangers	W	1-0
13 Aug	F	A	Ajax	L	2-3[1]
18 Aug	F	A	Cologne	D	0-0[1]
21 Aug	CS	*	Liverpool	L	0-1
28 Aug	Lge	H	Luton	D	2-2
31 Aug	Lge	A	Ipswich	W	2-1
4 Sep	Lge	A	Everton	L	1-3
8 Sep	Lge	H	Southampton	W	6-0
11 Sep	Lge	H	Man City	L	1-2
15 Sep	ECWC	A	Coleraine	W	3-0
18 Sep	Lge	A	Sunderland	W	1-0
20 Sep	F	A	Barnet	L	1-2[2]
25 Sep	Lge	H	Nottm Forest	W	4-1
29 Sep	ECWC	H	Coleraine	W	4-0
2 Oct	Lge	A	Swansea	L	0-2
6 Oct	FLC	H	Brighton	D	1-1
9 Oct	Lge	H	Coventry	W	4-0
16 Oct	Lge	H	Norwich	D	0-0
20 Oct	ECWC	H	Bayern Munich	D	1-1
23 Oct	Lge	H	Notts County	W	4-2
26 Oct	FLC	H	Brighton	W	1-0
30 Oct	Lge	A	Aston Villa	L	0-4
3 Nov	ECWC	A	Bayern Munich	L	1-4
6 Nov	Lge	H	Watford	L	0-1
9 Nov	FLC	A	Gillingham	W	4-2
13 Nov	Lge	A	Man Utd	L	0-1
20 Nov	Lge	H	West Ham	W	2-1
27 Nov	Lge	A	Liverpool	L	0-3
1 Dec	FLC	H	Luton	W	1-0
4 Dec	Lge	H	WBA	D	1-1
11 Dec	Lge	A	Stoke	L	0-2
18 Dec	Lge	H	Birmingham	W	2-1
20 Dec	F	A	Borussia Moen	L	0-2[3]
22 Dec	F	A	Israel Nat. Team	D	2-2[3]
27 Dec	Lge	A	Arsenal	L	0-2
28 Dec	Lge	H	Brighton	W	2-0
1 Jan	Lge	A	West Ham	L	0-3
3 Jan	Lge	H	Everton	W	2-1
8 Jan	FC	A	Southampton	W	1-0
15 Jan	Lge	A	Luton	D	1-1
19 Jan	FLC	H	Burnley	L	1-4
22 Jan	Lge	H	Sunderland	D	1-1
29 Jan	FC	H	WBA	W	2-1
5 Feb	Lge	A	Man City	D	2-2
12 Feb	Lge	H	Swansea	W	1-0
19 Feb	FC	A	Everton	L	0-2
26 Feb	Lge	H	Norwich	D	0-0
5 Mar	Lge	A	Notts County	L	0-3
12 Mar	Lge	A	Coventry	D	1-1
19 Mar	Lge	A	Watford	W	1-0
23 Mar	Lge	H	Aston Villa	W	2-0
25 Mar	F	A	Northerners(G.)	W	6-1
2 Apr	Lge	A	Brighton	L	1-2
4 Apr	Lge	H	Arsenal	W	5-0
9 Apr	Lge	A	Nottm Forest	D	2-2
16 Apr	Lge	A	Ipswich	W	3-1
19 Apr	F	A	Bristol Rovers	W	3-2[4]
23 Apr	Lge	A	WBA	W	1-0
30 Apr	Lge	H	Liverpool	W	2-0
3 May	Lge	A	Southampton	W	2-1
7 May	Lge	A	Birmingham	L	0-2
11 May	Lge	H	Man Utd	W	2-0
14 May	Lge	H	Stoke	W	4-1
17 May	F	A	Trinidad Nat. XI	D	2-2
20 May	F	A	A.S.L. Trinidad		2-1
23 May	F	A	Charlton	D	4-4[5]
30 May	F	A	Aalesund	W	3-2
4 Jun	F	A	Man Utd	L	1-2[6]
11 Jun	F	A	Man Utd	W	2-0[6]

1. Amsterdam 707 tournament.   2. Brinkman testimonail.   3. In Tel Aviv.   4. Bristol Rovers centenary match.   5. Powell testimonial.   6. Sun international challenge trophy tournament in Swaziland.   *at Wembley.

Season 1981/82 Players

Player	Lg App		Goals
Aleksic M.	2		
Archibald S.	27	(1)	6
Ardiles O.	26		2
Brooke G.	16	(4)	4
Clemence R.	38		
Corbett P.	4	(1)	1
Crook I.	4	(1)	
Crooks G.	27		13
Dick A.	1		
Falco M.	21		5
Galvin A.	32		3
Gibson T.	1		
Hazard M.	28	(2)	5
Hoddle G.	34		10
Hughton C.	37		2
Jones C.	7	(4)	
Lacy J.	12	(5)	
Miller P.	35		
O'Reilly G.	4		
Parks A.	2		
Perryman S.	42		1
Price P.	21	(3)	
Roberts G.	37	(2)	6
Smith G.	2	(1)	
Villa R.	27	(1)	8
Own Goal			1

Final table for First Division

1	Liverpool	42	26	9	7	80:32	87
2	Ipswich	42	26	5	11	75:53	83
3	Manchester U.	42	22	12	8	59:29	78
4	**TOTTENHAM**	42	20	11	11	67:48	71
5	Arsenal	42	20	11	11	48:37	71
6	Swansea	42	21	6	15	58:51	69
7	Southampton	42	19	9	14	72:67	66
8	Everton	42	17	13	12	56:50	64
9	West Ham	42	14	16	12	66:57	58
10	Manchester C.	42	15	13	14	49:50	58
11	Aston Villa	42	15	12	15	55:53	57
12	Nottm Forest	42	15	12	15	42:48	57
13	Brighton	42	13	13	16	43:52	52
14	Coventry	42	13	11	18	56:62	50
15	Notts Co.	42	13	8	21	61:69	47
16	Birmingham	42	10	14	18	53:61	44
17	WBA	42	11	11	20	46:57	44
18	Stoke	42	12	8	22	44:63	44
19	Sunderland	42	11	11	20	38:58	44
20	Leeds	42	10	12	20	39:61	42
21	Wolverhampton	42	10	10	22	32:63	40
22	Middlesbrough	42	8	15	19	34:52	39

Season 1982/83 Players

Player	Lg App		Goals
Archibald S	31		11
Ardiles O.	2		
Brazil A.	12		6
Brooke G.	23	(4)	7
Clemence R.	41		
Corbett P.	1	(1)	
Crook I.	4	(3)	
Crooks G.	26		8
Dick A.	2		
Falco M.	16	(5)	5
Galvin A.	26		2
Gibson T.	16	(2)	4
Hazard M.	18	(3)	1
Hoddle G.	24	(2)	1
Hughton C.	38		3
Lacy J.	22		
Mabbut G.	38		10
Mazzon G.	2		
Miller P.	23		1
O'Reilly G.	26	(1)	
Parks A.	1		
Perryman S.	33	(1)	1
Price P.	16		
Roberts G.	24	(4)	2
Villa R.	23	(1)	2
Webster S.	2	(1)	
Own Goal			1

Final table for First Division

1	Liverpool	42	24	10	8	87:37	82
2	Watford	42	22	5	15	74:57	71
3	Manchester U.	42	19	13	10	56:38	70
4	**TOTTENHAM**	42	20	9	13	65:50	69
5	Nottm Forest	42	20	9	13	62:50	69
6	Aston Villa	42	21	5	16	62:50	68
7	Everton	42	18	10	14	66:48	64
8	West Ham	42	20	4	18	68:62	64
9	Ipswich	42	15	13	14	64:50	58
10	Arsenal	42	16	10	16	58:56	58
11	W.B.A.	42	15	12	15	51:49	57
12	Southampton	42	15	12	15	54:58	57
13	Stoke	42	16	9	17	53:64	57
14	Norwich	42	14	12	16	52:58	54
15	Notts Co	42	15	7	20	55:71	52
16	Sunderland	42	12	14	16	48:61	50
17	Birmingham	42	12	14	16	40:55	50
18	Luton	42	12	13	17	65:84	49
19	Coventry	42	13	9	20	48:59	48
20	Manchester C.	42	13	8	21	47:70	47
21	Swansea	42	10	11	21	51:69	41
22	Brighton	42	9	13	20	38:68	40

SEASON 1983/84

Date	Comp	Venue	Opponent	Result
2 Aug	F	A	Hertford Town	W 2-1
3 Aug	F	A	Southall	W 8-0
4 Aug	F	A	Enfield	W 4-1
6 Aug	F	A	Brentford	W 4-2[1]
6 Aug	F	A	Aylesbury	W 4-0[1]
9 Aug	F	A	Portsmouth	W 3-1
10 Aug	F	A	Aldershot	L 0-1
12 Aug	F	A	Brighton	D 0-0
13 Aug	F	A	Lewes	W 6-0
16 Aug	F	A	Celtic	D 1-1
17 Aug	F	A	Dundee Utd	D 1-1[2]
21 Aug	F	H	West Ham	D 1-1[3]
27 Aug	Lge	A	Ipswich	L 1-3
29 Aug	Lge	H	Coventry	D 1-1
3 Sep	Lge	H	West Ham	L 0-2
7 Sep	Lge	A	WBA	D 1-1
10 Sep	Lge	A	Leicester	W 3-0
14 Sep	UEFA	A	Drogheda	W 6-0
17 Sep	Lge	H	Everton	L 1-2
24 Sep	Lge	A	Watford	W 3-2
28 Sep	UEFA	H	Drogheda	W 8-0
2 Oct	Lge	H	Nottm Forest	W 2-1
5 Oct	FLC	H	Lincoln	W 3-1
8 Oct	F	A	Vale Recreation	W 7-2
15 Oct	Lge	A	Wolves	W 3-2
19 Oct	UEFA	H	Feyenoord	W 4-2
22 Oct	Lge	A	Birmingham	W 1-0
26 Oct	FLC	A	Lincoln	L 1-2
29 Oct	Lge	H	Notts County	W 1-0
2 Nov	UEFA	A	Feyenoord	W 2-0
5 Nov	Lge	A	Stoke	D 1-1
9 Nov	FLC	H	Arsenal	L 1-2
12 Nov	Lge	H	Liverpool	D 2-2
19 Nov	Lge	A	Luton	W 4-2
23 Nov	UEEA	A	Bayern Munich	L 0-1
26 Nov	Lge	H	QP.R.	W 3-2
3 Dec	Lge	A	Norwich	L 1-2
7 Dec	UEFA	H	Bayern Munich	W 2-0
10 Dec	Lge	H	Southampton	D 0-0
16 Dec	Lge	A	Man Utd	L 2-4
26 Dec	Lge	H	Arsenal	L 2-4
27 Dec	Lge	A	Aston Villa	D 0-0
31 Dec	Lge	A	West Ham	L 1-4
2 Jan	Lge	H	Watford	L 2-3
7 Jan	FC	A	Fulham	D 0-0
11 Jan	FCr	H	Fulham	W 2-0
14 Jan	Lge	A	Ipswich	W 2-0
21 Jan	Lge	A	Everton	L 1-2
28 Jan	FC	H	Norwich	D 0-0
1 Feb	FCr	A	Norwich	L 1-2
24 Feb	Lge	A	Nottm Forest	D 2-2
8 Feb	Lge	H	Sunderland	W 3-0
11 Feb	Lge	H	Leicester	W 3-2
21 Feb	Lge	A	Notts County	D 0-0
25 Feb	Lge	H	Birmingham	L 0-t
3 Mar	Lge	H	Stoke	W 1-0
7 Mar	UEFA	H	F.K. Austria	W 2-0
10 Mar	Lge	A	Liverpool	L 1-3
17 Mar	Lge	H	WBA	L 0-1
21 Mar	UEFA	A	F.K. Austria	D 2-2
24 Mar	Lge	A	Coventry	W 4-2
26 Mar	F	A	Wimbledon	W 5-0[4]
31 Mar	Lge	H	Wolves	W 1-0
7 Apr	Lge	A	Sunderland	D 1-1
11 Apr	UEFAsf	A	Hajduk Split	L 1-2
14 Apr	Lge	H	Luton	W 2-1
18 Apr	Lge	H	Aston Villa	W 2-1
21 Apr	Lge	A	Arsenal	L 2-3
25 Apr	UEFAsf	A	Hajduk Split	W 1-0
28 Apr	Lge	A	Q.P.R.	L 1-2
5 May	Lge	H	Norwich	W 2-0
7 May	Lge	A	Southampton	L 0-5
9 May	UEFAf	A	Anderlecht	D 1-1
12 May	Lge	H	Man Utd	D 1-1
18 May	F	A	West Ham	L 1-4[5]
23 May	UEFAf	H	Anderlecht	D 1-1[6]
29 May	F	H	England XI	D 2-2[7]
2 Jun	F	A	Liverpool	L 2-5[8]
9 Jun	F	A	Liverpool	D 1-1[8]

1. Half the first team played in each match. 2 McAlpine testimonial. 3. Nicholson testimonial 4. Bassett testimonial. 5. Holland testimonial. 6. Spurs won 4-3 on penalties 7. Burkinshaw testimonial. 8. Sun international challenge trophy tournament in Swaziland.

Player	LgApp		Goals
Archibald S.	32	(1)	21
Ardiles O.	9	(1)	
Bowen M.	7	(1)	
Brace R.	1	(1)	
Brazil A.	19	(2)	3
Brooke G.	12	(5)	
Clemence R.	26		
Cockram A.	2		
Cooke R.	9		(1)
Crook I.	3		
Crooks G.	10	(4)	1
Culverhouse	2	(1)	
Dick A.	11	(1)	2
Falco M	36	(4)	13
Galvin A.	30		1
Hazard M.	11	(2)	2
Hoddle G.	24		4
Hughton C.	34		3
Mabbutt G.	21		2
Millar P.	21	(1)	
O'Reilly G.	12	(3)	
Parks A.	16		
Perryman S.	41		1
Price P.	2	(1)	
Roberts G.	35		6
Stevens G.	40	(3)	4
Thomas D.	27	(1)	
Webster S.	1		

Final table for First Division

1	Liverpool	42	22	14	6	73:32	80
2	Southampton	42	22	11	9	66:38	77
3	Nottm Forest	42	22	8	12	76:45	74
4	Manchester U	42	20	14	8	71:41	74
5	Q.P.R.	42	22	7	13	67:37	73
6	Arsenal	42	18	9	15	74:60	63
7	Everton	42	16	14	12	44:42	62
8	**tottenham**	42	17	10	15	64:65	61
9	West Ham	42	17	9	16	60:55	60
10	Aston Villa	42	17	9	16	59:61	60
11	Watford	42	16	9	17	68:77	57
12	Ipswich	42	15	8	19	55:57	53
13	Sunderland	42	13	13	16	42:53	52
14	Norwich	42	12	15	15	48:49	51
15	Leicester	42	13	12	17	65:68	51
16	Luton	42	14	9	19	53:66	51
17	WBA	42	14	9	19	48:62	51
18	Stoke	42	13	11	18	44:63	50
19	Coventry	42	13	11	18	57:77	50
20	Birmingham	42	12	12	18	39:50	48
21	Notts Co	42	10	11	21	50:72	41
22	Wolverhampton	42	6	11	25	27:80	29

SEASON 1984/85

Date	Comp	Venue	Opponent	Result
27 Jul	F	A	St. Jordal Blink	W 9-0
29 Jul	F	A	Ostersund	W 4-0
31 Ju1	F	A	Viking	W 1-0
4 Aug	F	A	Enfield	W 7-0
6 Aug	F	A	OGC Nice	D 2-2
11 Aug	F	A	Brentford	W 3-0
16 Aug	F	A	Man City	W 2-0
18 Aug	F	A	Sheff Utd	W 3-0
20 Aug	F	H	Fulham	W 3-1[1]
25 Aug	Lge	A	Everton	W 4-1
27 Aug	Lge	H	Leicester	D 2-2
1 Sep	Lge	H	Norwich	W 1-0
4 Sep	Lge	A	Sunderland	L 0-1
8 Sep	Lge	A	Sheff Wed	L 1-2
12 Sep	F	A	Real Madrid	L 0-1[2]
15 Sep	Lge	H	QPR	W 5-0
19 Sep	UEFA	A	SC Braga	W 3-0
22 Sep	Lge	A	Aston Villa	W 1-0
26 Sep	FLC	A	Halifax	W 5-1
29 Sep	Lge	H	Luton	W 4-2
3 Oct	UEFA	H	SC Braga	W 6-0
6 Oct	Lge	A	Southampton	L 0-1
9 Oct	FLC	H	Halifax	W 4-0
12 Oct	Lge	H	Liverpool	W 1-0
14 Oct	F	A	Malta Natl XI	W 1-0
20 Oct	Lge	A	Man Utd	L 0-1
24 Oct	UEFA	A	FC Bruges	L 1-2
27 Oct	Lge	H	Stoke	W 4-0
31 Oct	FLC	A	Liverpool	W 1-0
3 Nov	Lge	A	WBA	L 2-3
7 Nov	UEFA	H	FC Bruges	H 3-0
10 Nov	Lge	A	Nottm Forest	A 2-1
13 Nov	F	A	Sutton Utd	W 5-3[3]
17 Nov	Lge	A	Ipswich	A 3-0
21 Nov	FLC	A	Sunderland	D 0-0
24 Nov	Lge	H	Chelsea	D 1-1
28 Nov	UEFA	H	Bohemians	W 2-0
1 Dec	Lge	A	Coventry	D 1-1
5 Dec	FLC	H	Sunderland	L 1-2
8 Dec	Lge	H	Newcastle	W 3-1
12 Dec	UEFA	A	Bohemians	D 1-1
15 Dec	Lge	A	Watford	W 2-1
22 Dec	Lpe	A	Norwich	W 2-1
26 Dec	Lge	H	West Ham	D 2-2
29 Dec	Lge	H	Sunderland	W 2-0
1 Jan	Lge	A	Arsenal	W 2-1
5 Jan	FC	H	Charlton	D 1-1
12 Jan	Lge	A	QPR	D 2-2
23 Jan	FC	A	Charlton	W 1-0
27 Jan	FC	A	Liverpool	L 0-1
2 Feb	Lge	A	Luton	D 2-2
23 Feb	Lge	A	WBA	W 1-0
2 Mar	Lge	A	Stoke	W 1-0
6 Mar	UEFA	H	Real Madrid	L 0-1
8 Mar	F	+	Kuwait Natl XI	W 1-0
12 Mar	Lge	H	Man Utd	L 1-2
16 Mar	Lge	A	Liverpool	W 1-0
20 Mar	UEFA	A	Real Madrid	D 0-0
23 Mar	Lge	H	Southampton	W 5-1
30 Mar	Lge	A	Aston Villa	L 0-2
3 Apr	Lge	H	Everton	L 1-2
6 Apr	Lge	A	West Ham	D 1-1
8 Apr	F	A	Guernsey XI	W 5-0
13 Apr	Lge	A	Leicester	W 2-1
17 Apr	Lge	H	Arsenal	L 0-2
20 Apr	Lge	H	Ipswich	L 2-3
27 Apr	Lge	A	Chelsea	D 1-1
29 Apr	F	A	Bristol Rovers	W 6-2[4]
4 May	Lge	H	Coventry	W 4-2
6 May	Lge	A	Newcastle	W 3-2
8 May	F	A	Arsenal	W 3-2[5]
11 May	Lge	H	Watford	L 1-5
14 May	Lge	H	Sheff Wed	W 2-0
17 May	Lge	H	Nottm Forest	W 1-0
23 May	F	A	Seiko	W 4-0
29 May	F		Australia Natl XI	L 0-1[6]
1 Jun	F		Udinese	L 0-2[8]
5 Jun	F		Vasco da Gama	D 1-1[6]
9 Jun	F		Udinese	W 4-1[6]

+ At Amman, Jordan 1.Peter Southey Memorial 2. Benito testimonial 3. Pritchard testimonial 4. Bristol Cancer Fund Match 5. Pat Jennings farewell 6. Australian international tournament at Melbourne, Sydney and Adelaide.

Player	LgApp		Goals
Allen C.	13	(1)	7
Ardiles O.	11	(1)	2
Bowen M.	6		
Brooke G.	4	(3)	1
Chiedozie J.	34	(3)	5
Clemence R.	42		
Crook I.	5	(3)	1
Crooks G.	22		10
Dick A.	2		
Falco M.	42		22
Galvin A.	38		4
Hazard M.	23	(8)	4
Hoddle G.	28	(2)	8
Hughton C.	31	(2)	1
Leworthy D.	6		3
Mabbutt G.	25	(10)	2
Miler P.	39		
Perryman S.	42		1
Roberts G.	40		7
Stevens G.	28		
Thomas D.	16	(2)	

Final table for First Division

1	Everton	42	28	6	8	88:43	90
2	Liverpool	42	22	11	9	66:35	77
3	**tottenham**	42	23	8	11	78:51	77
4	Man Utd	42	22	10	10	77:47	76
5	Southampton	42	19	11	12	56:47	68
6	Chelsea	42	18	12	12	63:48	66
7	Arsenal	42	19	9	14	61:49	66
8	Sheff Wed	42	17	14	11	58:45	65
9	Nottm Forest	42	19	7	16	56:48	64
10	Aston Villa	42	15	11	16	60:60	56
11	Watford	42	14	13	15	81:71	55
12	West Brom	42	16	7	19	58:62	55
13	Luton	42	15	9	18	57:61	54
14	Newcastle	42	13	13	16	55:70	52
15	Leicester	42	15	6	21	66:73	51
16	West Ham	42	13	12	17	51:68	51
17	Ipswich	42	13	11	18	46:47	50
18	Coventry	42	15	5	22	47:64	50
19	QPR	42	13	11	18	53:72	50
20	Norwich	42	13	10	19	46:64	49
21	Sunderland	42	10	10	22	40:62	40
22	Stoke	42	3	8	31	24:91	17

SEASON 1985/86

24 Jul	F	A	Chesterfield	W	4-2
27 Jul	F	A	Bournemouth	W	3-0
31 Jul	F	A	Plymouth	L	0-1
3 Aug	F	A	Exeter	D	2-2
4 Aug	F	H	Arsenal	D	1-1[1]
10 Aug	F	A	Norwich	D	1-1
17 Aug	Lge	H	Watford	W	4-0
21 Aug	Lge	A	Oxford	D	1-1
24 Aug	Lge	A	Ipswich	L	0-1
26 Aug	Lge	H	Everton	L	0-1
31 Aug	Lge	A	Man City	L	1-2
4 Sep	Lge	H	Chelsea	W	4-1
7 Sep	Lge	H	Newcastle	W	5-1
10 Sep	F	A	Fareham Town	W	6-3
14 Sep	Lge	A	Nottm Forest	W	1-0
21 Sep	Lge	H	Sheff Wed	W	5-1
23 Sep	FLC	A	Orient	L	0-2
28 Sep	Lge	A	Liverpool	L	1-4
2 Oct	SSSC	H	Southampton	W	2-1
5 Oct	Lge	A	WBA	D	1-1
14 Oct	F	A	Maidstone Utd	W	2-1[2]
20 Oct	Lge	A	Coventry	W	3-2
26 Oct	Lge	H	Leicester	L	1-3
30 Oct	FLC	H	Orient	W	4-0
2 Nov	Lge	A	Southampton	L	0-1
6 Nov	FLC	H	Wimbledon	W	2-0
9 Nov	Lge	H	Luton	L	1-3
16 Nov	Lge	A	Man Utd	D	0-0
20 Nov	FLC	H	Portsmouth	D	0-0
23 Nov	Lge	H	QPR	D	1-1
27 Nov	FLC	A	Portsmouth	D	0-0
30 Nov	Lge	A	Aston Villa	W	2-1
3 Dec	SSSC	A	Liverpool	L	0-2
7 Dec	Lge	H	Oxford	W	5-1
10 Dec	FLC	A	Portsmouth	L	0-1
14 Dec	Lge	A	Watford	L	0-1
17 Dec	SSSC	A	Southampton	W	3-1
21 Dec	Lge	H	Ipswich	W	2-0
26 Dec	Lge	H	West Ham	W	1-0
28 Dec	Lge	A	Chelsea	L	0-2
1 Jan	Lge	A	Arsenal	D	0-0
4 Jan	FC	A	Oxford	D	1-1
8 Jan	FC	H	Oxford	W	2-1
11 Jan	Lge	H	Nottm Forest	L	0-3
14 Jan	SSSC	H	Liverpool	L	0-3
18 Jan	Lge	H	Man City	L	0-2
25 Jan	FC	A	Notts County	D	1-1
29 Jan	FC	A	Notts County	W	5-0
1 Feb	Lge	A	Everton	L	0-1
5 Feb	SSSC	H	Everton	D	0-0
8 Feb	Lge	H	Coventry	L	0-1
10 Feb	F	A	Jersey FAXI	W	7-0
22 Feb	Lge	A	Sheff Wed	W	2-1
2 Mar	Lge	H	Liverpool	L	1-2
4 Mar	FC	H	Everton	L	1-2
8 Mar	Lge	H	WBA	W	5-0
15 Mar	Lge	A	Birmingham	W	2-1
19 Mar	SSSC	A	Everton	L	1-3
22 Mar	Lge	A	Newcastle	D	2-2
29 Mar	Lge	H	Arsenal	W	1-0
31 Mar	Lge	A	West Ham	L	1-2
5 Apr	Lge	A	Leicester	W	4-1
6 Apr	F	A	Rangers	W	2-0
12 Apr	Lge	A	Luton	D	1-1
16 Apr	Lge	H	Birmingham	W	2-0
19 Apr	Lge	H	Man Utd	D	0-0
22 Apr	F	A	Chelmsford	W	8-2[3]
26 Apr	Lge	A	QPR	W	5-2
1 May	F	H	Inter Milan	W	2-1[4]
3 May	Lge	H	Aston Villa	W	4-2
5 May	Lge	H	Southampton	W	5-3
9 May	F	A	Brentford	L	3-4[5]
12 May	F	A	West Ham	L	1-5[6]

1. Glenn Hoddle testimonial 2. Thompson testimonial 3. Johnson testimonial 4. Ossie Ardiles benefit 5. Salman testimonial 6. Ampofo benefit

Player	LgApp		Goals
Allen C.	19	(3)	9
Allen P	33	(4)	1
Ardiles O.	23	(3)	1
Bowen M.	2	(1)	1
Chiedozie J.	18	(5)	7
Clemence R.	42		
Cooke R.	2	(2)	2
Crook I.	4	(3)	
Dick A.	1		
Falco M.	40		19
Galvin A.	23		4
Hazard M.	4	(1)	1
Hoddle G.	31		7
Howells D	1		1
Hughton C.	33		1
Leworthy D	5	(3)	
Mabbutt G.	32	(3)	3
Miller P.	29		2
Perryman S.	23	(1)	1
Roberts G.	32		1
Stevens G.	29	(1)	2
Thomas D.	27		1
Waddle C.	39		11

Final table for First Division

1	Liverpool	42	26	10	6	89:37	88
2	Everton	42	26	8	8	87:41	86
3	West Ham	42	26	6	10	74:40	84
4	Manchester U.	42	22	10	10	70:36	76
5	Sheffield W.	42	21	10	11	63:54	73
6	Chelsea	42	20	11	11	57:56	71
7	Arsenal	42	20	9	13	49:47	69
8	Nottingham F	42	19	11	12	69:53	68
9	Luton	42	18	12	12	61:44	66
10	**tottenham**	42	19	8	15	74:52	65
11	Newcastle	42	17	12	13	67:72	63
12	Watford	42	16	11	15	69:62	59
13	Q.P.R.	42	15	7	20	53:64	52
14	Southampton	42	12	10	20	51:62	46
15	Manchester C.	42	11	12	19	43:57	45
16	Aston Villa	42	10	14	18	51:67	44
17	Coventry	42	11	10	21	48:71	43
18	Oxford	42	10	12	20	62:80	42
19	Leicester	42	10	12	20	54:76	42
20	Ipswich	42	11	8	23	32:55	41
21	Birmingham	42	8	5	29	30:73	29
22	West Bromwich	42	4	12	26	35:89	24

SEASON 1986/87

2 Aug	F	H	Rangers	D	1-1[1]
4 Aug	F	A	Aldershot	W	3-2
8 Aug	F	A	Brighton	W	4-0[2]
12 Aug	F	A	Gillingham	D	1-1[3]
19 Aug	F	A	PSV Eindhoven	D	1-1[4]
20 Aug	F	A	AC Milan	W	2-1[5]
23 Aug	Lge	A	Aston Villa	W	3-0
25 Aug	Lge	H	Newcastle	D	1-1
30 Aug	Lge	H	Manchester C.	W	1-0
2 Sep	Lge	A	Southampton	L	0-2
6 Sep	Lge	A	Arsenal	D	0-0
13 Sep	Lge	H	Chelsea	L	1-3
20 Sep	Lge	A	Leicester	W	2-1
23 Sep	FLC	A	Barnsley	W	3-2
27 Sep	Lge	H	Everton	W	2-0
4 Oct	Lge	H	Luton	D	0-0
8 Oct	FLC	H	Barnsley	W	5-3
11 Oct	Lge	A	Liverpool	W	1-0
18 Oct	Lge	H	Sheff Wed	D	1-1
25 Oct	Lge	A	QPR	L	0-2
29 Oct	FLC	H	Birmingham	W	5-0
1 Nov	Lge	H	Wimbledon	L	1-2
4 Nov	F	H	SV Hamburg	W	5-1
8 Nov	Lge	A	Norwich	L	1-2
15 Nov	Lge	H	Coventry	W	1-0
22 Nov	Lge	A	Oxford	W	4-2
26 Nov	FLC	A	Cambridge Utd	W	3-1
29 Nov	Lge	H	Nottm Forest	L	2-3
7 Dec	Lge	A	Man Utd	D	3-3
13 Dec	Lge	H	Watford	W	2-1
16 Dec	F	A	Bermuda Natl XI	W	3-1
20 Dec	Lge	A	Chelsea	W	2-0
26 Dec	Lge	H	West Ham	W	4-0
27 Dec	Lge	A	Coventry	L	3-4
1 Jan	Lge	A	Charlton	W	2-0
4 Jan	Lge	H	Arsenal	L	1-2
10 Jan	FC	H	Scunthorpe	W	3-2
20 Jan	F	A	Linfield	W	3-2[6]
24 Jan	Lge	H	Aston Villa	W	3-0
27 Jan	FLC	A	West Ham	D	1-1
31 Jan	FC	H	Crystal P	W	4-0
2 Feb	FLC	H	West Ham	W	5-0
8 Feb	FLC	A	Arsenal	W	1-0
14 Feb	Lge	H	Southampton	W	2-0
21 Feb	FC	H	Newcastle	W	1-0
25 Feb	Lge	H	Leicester	W	5-0
1 Mar	FLCsf	A	Arsenal	L	1-2
4 Mar	FLCsfr	H	Arsenal	L	1-2
7 Mar	Lge	H	QPR	W	1-0
15 Mar	FC	A	Wimbledon	W	2-0
22 Mar	Lge	H	Liverpool	W	1-0
25 Mar	Lge	A	Newcastle	D	1-1
28 Mar	Lge	A	Luton	L	1-3
4 Apr	Lge	H	Norwich	W	3-0
7 Apr	Lge	A	Sheff Wed	W	1-0
11 Apr	FCsf	*	Watford	W	4-1
15 Apr	Lge	A	Man City	D	1-1
18 Apr	Lge	H	Charlton	W	1-0
20 Apr	Lge	A	West Ham	L	1-2
22 Apr	Lge	A	Wimbledon	D	2-2
25 Apr	Lge	H	Oxford	W	3-1
2 May	Lge	A	Nottm Forest	L	0-2
4 May	Lge	H	Man Utd	W	4-0
9 May	Lge	A	Watford	L	0-1
11 May	Lge	A	Everton	L	0-1
16 May	FCf	+	Coventry	L	2-3
29 May	F	A	Millonarios	L	0-1[7]

* at Villa Park + at Wembley 1. Paul Miller testimonial 2. Ryan testimonial 3. Weatherley testimonial 4. Gamper Tournament, Barcelona lost 3-4 on pens 5. Gamper Tournament, Barcelona 6. Coyle testimonial 7. at Miami

Player	LgApp		Goals
Allen C	39	(1)	33
Allen P	37	(3)	3
Ardiles O	25	(9)	
Bowen M	2	(1)	1
Chiedozie J.	1		
Claesen N.	26	(8)	8
Close S.	2	(1)	
Clemence R.	40		
Falco M.	6	(1)	
Galvin A.	24	(4)	1
Gough R	40		2
Gray P.	1		
Hoddle G.	35	(1)	3
Hodge S.	19		4
Howells D.	1		
Hughton C.	9		
Mabbutt G.	37		1
Miller P	2		
Moncur J.	1		
Moran P.	1		
O'Shea T.	2	(1)	
Parks A.	2		
Polston J.	6		
Roberts G.	17		1
Ruddock N.	4		
Samways V.	2	(1)	
Stevens G.	20		
Stimson M.	1		
Thomas D.	17	(4)	
Thomas M.	39		4
Waddle C.	39		6
Own Goal			1

Final table for First Division

1	Everton	42	26	8	8	76:31	86
2	Liverpool	42	23	8	11	72:42	77
3	**tottenham**	42	21	8	13	68:43	71
4	Arsenal	42	20	10	12	58:35	70
5	Norwich	42	17	17	8	53:51	68
6	Wimbledon	42	19	9	14	57:50	66
7	Luton	42	18	12	12	47:45	66
8	Nottingham F.	42	18	11	13	64:51	65
9	Watford	42	18	9	15	67:54	63
10	Coventry	42	17	12	13	50:45	63
11	Manchester U.	42	14	14	14	52:45	56
12	Southampton	42	14	10	18	69:68	52
13	Sheffield W.	42	13	13	16	58:59	52
14	Chelsea	42	13	13	16	53:64	52
15	West Ham	42	14	10	18	52:67	52
16	Q.P.R.	42	13	11	18	48:64	50
17	Newcastle	42	12	11	19	47:65	47
18	Oxford	42	11	13	18	44:69	46
19	Charlton	42	11	11	20	45:55	44
20	Leicester	42	11	9	22	54:76	42
21	Manchester C.	42	8	15	19	36:57	39
22	Aston Villa	42	8	12	22	45:79	36

SEASON 1987/88

Date		Comp		Opponent		Result
23 Jul	F	A	Exeter	W	1-0
25 Jul	F	A	Bournemouth	H D	4-4
30 Jul	F	A	Orebro SK	L	1-3
1 Aug	F	A	Lansi Uudenmaan XI	W	7-2
3 Aug	F	A	Vasteras XI	W	4-2
5 Aug	F	A	Marsta IK	W	5-0
6 Aug	F	A	Div 1 North XI	L	0-1
10 Aug	F	H	Arsenal	W	3-1[1]
15 Aug	Lge	A	Coventry	L	1-2
19 Aug	Lge	H	Newcastle	W	3-1
22 Aug	Lge	H	Chelsea	W	1-0
29 Aug	Lge	A	Watford	D	1-1
1 Sep	Lge	H	Oxford	W	3-0
5 Sep	Lge	A	Everton	D	0-0
12 Sep	Lge	H	Southampton	W	2-1
19 Sep	Lge	A	West Ham	W	1-0
23 Sep	FLC	A	Torquay	L	0-1
26 Sep	Lge	A	Man Utd	L	0-1
3 Oct	Lge	H	Sheff Wed	W	2-0
7 Oct	FLC	H	Torquay	W	3-0
10 Oct	Lge	A	Norwich	L	1-2
18 Oct	Lge	H	Arsenal	L	1-2
20 Oct	F	H	West Ham	D	2-2[2]
24 Oct	Lge	A	Nottm Forest	L	0-3
28 Oct	FLC	A	Aston Villa	L	1-2
31 Oct	Lge	H	Wimbledon	L	0-3
4 Nov	Lge	A	Portsmouth	D	0-0
10 Nov	F	A	St. Albans	W	6-0
14 Nov	Lge	H	QPR	D	1-1
21 Nov	Lge	A	Luton	L	0-2
28 Nov	Lge	H	Liverpool	L	0-2
5 Dec	F	A	Brentford	D	0-0
13 Dec	Lge	H	Charlton	L	0-1
20 Dec	Lge	A	Derby	W	2-1
26 Dec	Lge	A	Southampton	L	1-2
28 Dec	Lge	H	West Ham	W	2-1
1 Jan	Lge	H	Watford	W	2-1
2 Jan	Lge	A	Chelsea	D	0-0
9 Jan	FC	A	Oldham	W	4-2
16 Jan	Lge	H	Coventry	D	2-2
23 Jan	Lge	A	Newcastle	L	0-2
30 Jan	FC	A	Port Vale	L	1-2
13 Feb	Lge	A	Oxford	D	0-0
15 Feb	F	H	AS Monaco	L	0-4
19 Feb	F	A	WBA	L	1-4[3]
23 Feb	Lge	H	Man Utd	D	1-1
27 Feb	Lge	H	Sheff Wed	W	3-0
1 Mar	Lge	H	Derby	D	0-0
6 Mar	Lge	A	Arsenal	L	1-2
9 Mar	Lge	H	Everton	W	2-1
12 Mar	Lge	H	Norwich	L	1-3
19 Mar	Lge	A	Wimbledon	L	0-3
26 Mar	Lge	H	Nottm Forest	D	1-1
28 Mar	F	H	Man Utd	L	2-3[4]
2 Apr	Lge	H	Portsmouth	L	0-1
4 Apr	Lge	A	QPR	L	0-2
15 Apr	F	A	Hull	L	1-2[5]
23 Apr	Lge	A	Liverpool	L	0-1
26 Apr	F	A	Crystal P.	D	3-3[6]
2 May	Lge	A	Charlton	D	1-1
4 May	Lge	H	Luton	W	2-1
6 May	F	A	Barnet	W	2-1[7]
10 May	F	A	Euskadi	L	0-4[8]

1. Chris Hughton testimonial 2. Tony Galvin testimonial 3. Brown benefit 4. Danny Thomas benefit 5. Radcliff testimonial 6. Cannon testimonial 7. Millett testimonial 8. at Bilbao

Player	LgApp		Goals
Allen C.	34	(3)	11
Allen P.	39		3
Ardiles O.	28	(2)	
Claesen N.	24	(5)	10
Clemence R.	11		
Close S.	7	(5)	
Fairclough C.	40		4
Fenwick T.	17		
Gough R.	9		
Gray P.	1	(1)	
Hodge S.	26	(1)	3
Howells D.	11	(8)	
Hughton C.	13	(1)	
Mabbutt G.	37		2
Metgod J.	12	(7)	
Mimms R.	13		
Moncur J.	5	(2)	
Moran P.	13	(4)	1
O'Shea T.	1	(1)	
Parks A.	16		
Polston J.	2	(2)	
Ruddock N.	5	(2)	
Samways V.	26	(5)	
Statham B.	18	(4)	
Stevens G.	18		
Thomas M.	36	(1)	
Waddle C.	22	(1)	2
Walsh P.	11		1
Own Goal			1

Final table for First Division

1	Liverpool	40	26	12	2	87:24	90
2	Manchester U.	40	23	12	5	71:38	81
3	Nottingham F.	40	20	13	7	67:39	73
4	Everton	40	19	13	8	53:27	70
5	Q.P.R.	40	19	10	11	48:38	67
6	Arsenal	40	18	12	10	58:39	66
7	Wimbledon	40	14	15	11	58:47	57
8	Newcastle	40	14	14	12	55:53	56
9	Luton	40	14	11	15	57:58	53
10	Coventry	40	13	14	13	46:53	53
11	Sheffield W.	40	15	8	17	52:66	53
12	Southampton	40	12	14	14	49:53	50
13	**tottenham**	40	12	11	17	38:48	47
14	Norwich	40	12	9	19	40:52	45
15	Derby	40	10	13	17	35:45	43
16	West Ham	40	9	15	16	40:52	42
17	Charlton	40	9	15	16	38:52	42
18	Chelsea	40	9	15	16	50:68	42
19	Portsmouth	40	7	14	19	36:66	35
20	Watford	40	7	11	22	27:51	32
21	Oxford	40	6	13	21	44:80	31

SEASON 1988/89

Date		Comp		Opponent		Result
26 Jul	F	A	Vederslov & D IF	W	4-1
28 Jul	F	A	Trelleborgs FF	W	3-0
31 Jul	F	A	GAIS	D	1-1
2 Aug	F	A	Jonkopings Sodra	D	1-1
7 Aug	F	A	Dundee Utd	D	1-1[1]
10 Aug	F	A	Reading	L	1-2[2]
13 Aug	F	*	Arsenal	L	0-4
14 Aug	F	*	AC Milan	L	1-2
16 Aug	F	A	Chelsea	D	0-0[3]
21 Aug	F	A	West Ham	L	0-2[4]
3 Sep	Lge	A	Newcastle	D	2-2
6 Sep	F	A	Swansea	W	3-0[5]
10 Sep	Lge	H	Arsenal	L	2-3
17 Sep	Lge	A	Liverpool	D	1-1
24 Sep	Lge	H	Middlesbrough	W	3-2
27 Sep	FLC	A	Notts Co.	D	1-1
1 Oct	Lge	H	Man Utd	D	2-2
8 Oct	Lge	A	Charlton	D	2-2
11 Oct	FLC	H	Notts Co.	W	2-1
18 Oct	F	A	Home Farm	W	4-0
22 Oct	Lge	A	Norwich	L	1-3
25 Oct	Lge	H	Southampton	L	1-2
29 Oct	Lge	A	Aston Villa	L	1-2
1 Nov	FLC	H	Blackburn	D	0-0
5 Nov	Lge	H	Derby	L	1-3
9 Nov	FLC	A	Blackburn	W	2-1
12 Nov	Lge	H	Wimbledon	W	3-2
20 Nov	Lge	A	Sheff Wed	W	2-0
23 Nov	Lge	A	Coventry	D	1-1
26 Nov	Lge	H	QPR	D	2-2
30 Nov	FLC	A	Southampton	L	1-2
3 Dec	Lge	A	Everton	L	0-1
10 Dec	Lge	H	Millwall	W	2-0
17 Dec	Lge	A	West Ham	W	2-0
26 Dec	Lge	H	Luton	D	0-0
31 Dec	Lge	H	Newcastle	W	2-0
2 Jan	Lge	A	Arsenal	L	0-2
7 Jan	FC	A	Bradford City	D	0-1
15 Jan	FC	H	Nottm Forest	L	1-2
17 Jan	F	H	AS Monaco	L	1-3
21 Jan	Lge	A	Middlesbrough	D	2-2
5 Feb	Lge	A	Man Utd	L	0-1
11 Feb	Lge	H	Charlton	D	1-1
21 Feb	Lge	H	Norwich	W	2-1
25 Feb	Lge	A	Southampton	W	2-0
1 Mar	Lge	H	Aston Villa	W	2-0
4 Mar	F	H	Bordeaux	L	1-2
11 Mar	Lge	A	Derby	D	1-1
18 Mar	Lge	A	Coventry	D	1-1
22 Mar	Lge	A	Nottm Forest	W	2-1
26 Mar	Lge	H	Liverpool	L	1-2
28 Mar	Lge	A	Luton	W	3-1
1 Apr	Lge	H	West Ham	W	3-0
4 Apr	F	A	Charlton	L	3-4[6]
12 Apr	Lge	H	Sheff Wed	D	0-0
15 Apr	Lge	A	Wimbledon	W	2-1
22 Apr	Lge	H	Everton	W	2-1
29 Apr	Lge	A	Millwall	W	5-0
13 May	Lge	A	QPR	L	0-1

* Wembley International Tournament

1. Narey testimonial 2. Hicks testimonial 3. Pates testimonial 4. Martin testimonial 5. Hughes benefit 6. Gritt testimonial

Player	LgApp		Goals
Allen P.	37	(2)	1
Bergsson G.	8		
Butters G.	28	(1)	1
Fairclough C.	20		1
Fenwick T.	34		8
Gascoigne P.	32	(1)	6
Gray P.	1	(1)	
Howells D.	27	(15)	3
Hughton C.	21	(1)	
Mabbutt G.	38		1
Mimms R.	20		
Moncur J.	1	(1)	
Moran P.	8	(4)	
Nayim	11	(3)	2
Polston J.	3	(3)	
Robson M.	5	(2)	
Samways V.	19	(7)	3
Statham B.	6		
Stevens G.	5		
Stewart P.	30	(1)	12
Stimson M.	1	(1)	
Thomas M.	25	(3)	1
Thorstvedt E.	18		
Waddle C.	38		14
Walsh P.	33	(5)	6
Own Goal			1

Final table for First Division

1	Arsenal	38	22	10	6	73:36	76
2	Liverpool	38	22	10	6	65:28	76
3	Nottingham F.	38	17	13	8	64:43	64
4	Norwich	38	17	11	10	48:45	62
5	Derby	38	17	7	14	40:38	58
6	**tottenham**	38	15	12	11	60:46	57
7	Coventry	38	14	13	11	47:42	55
8	Everton	38	14	12	12	50:45	54
9	Q.P.R.	38	14	11	13	43:37	53
10	Millwall	38	14	11	13	47:52	53
11	Manchester U.	38	13	12	13	45:35	51
12	Wimbledon	38	14	9	15	50:46	51
13	Southampton	38	10	15	13	52:66	45
14	Charlton	38	10	12	16	44:58	42
15	Sheffield W.	38	10	12	16	34:51	42
16	Luton	38	10	11	17	42:53	41
17	Aston Villa	38	9	13	16	45:56	40
18	Middlesbrough	38	9	12	17	44:61	39
19	West Ham	38	10	8	20	37:62	38
20	Newcastle	38	7	10	21	32:63	31

SEASON 1989/90

Date	Comp	H/A	Opponent	Result	Score
19 Jul	F	H*	Fulham	W	3-1
23 Jul	F	A	Bohemians	W	2-0
25 Jul	F	A	Cork City	W	3-0
28 Jul	F	H*	Bournemouth	W	6-0
1 Aug	F	H*	Swindon	L	0-1
6 Aug	F	A	Rangers	L	0-1
8 Aug	F	A	Viking	W	5-1
10 Aug	F	A	Brann	W	2-0
11 Aug	F	+	Dinamo Bucharest	L	1-3
13 Aug	F	+	Atletico Madrid	L	0-1
19 Aug	Lge	H	Luton	W	2-1
22 Aug	Lge	A	Everton	L	1-2
26 Aug	Lge	A	Man City	D	1-1
9 Sep	Lge	A	Aston Villa	L	0-2
16 Sep	Lge	H	Chelsea	L	1-4
20 Sep	FLC	H	Southend	W	1-0
23 Sep	Lge	A	Norwich	D	2-2
30 Sep	Lge	H	QPR	W	3-2
4 Oct	FLC	A	Southend	L	2-3
14 Oct	Lge	A	Charlton	W	3-1
18 Oct	Lge	H	Arsenal	W	2-1
21 Oct	Lge	H	Sheff Wed	W	3-0
25 Oct	FLC	A	Man Utd	W	3-0
29 Oct	Lge	A	Liverpool	L	0-1
31 Oct	F	A*	SM Caen	W	2-1
4 Nov	Lge	A	Southampton	D	1-1
6 Nov	F	A	Leicester	W	5-2[1]
11 Nov	Lge	H	Wimbledon	L	0-1
18 Nov	Lge	A	Crystal P.	W	3-2
22 Nov	FLC	A	Tranmere	D	2-2
2 Dec	Lge	A	Luton	D	0-0
9 Dec	Lge	H	Everton	W	2-1
16 Dec	Lge	A	Man Utd	W	1-0
26 Dec	Lge	H	Millwall	W	3-1
30 Dec	Lge	H	Nottm Forest	L	2-3
1 Jan	Lge	A	Coventry	D	0-0
6 Jan	FC	H	Southampton	L	1-3
13 Jan	Lge	H	Man City	D	1-1
17 Jan	FLC	A	Nottm Forest	D	2-2
20 Jan	Lge	A	Arsenal	L	0-1
24 Jan	FLC	H	Nottm Forest	L	2-3
26 Jan	F	A	Plymouth	W	3-0[2]
4 Feb	Lge	H	Norwich	W	4-0
10 Feb	Lge	A	Chelsea	W	2-1
21 Feb	Lge	H	Aston Villa	L	0-2
24 Feb	Lge	A	Derby	L	1-2
3 Mar	Lge	H	Crystal P.	L	0-1
10 Mar	Lge	H	Charlton	W	3-0
17 Mar	Lge	A	QPR	L	1-3
21 Mar	Lge	H	Liverpool	W	1-0
31 Mar	Lge	A	Sheff Weds	W	4-2
3 Apr	F	A	Brighton	W	3-0[3]
7 Apr	Lge	A	Nottm Forest	W	3-1
14 Apr	Lge	A	Coventry	W	3-2
16 Apr	Lge	A	Millwall	W	1-0
21 Apr	Lge	H	Man Utd	W	2-1
23 Apr	F	A	Valerengen	D	1-1
28 Apr	Lge	A	Wimbledon	L	0-1
1 May	F	H	N. Ireland XI	W	2-1[4]
5 May	Lge	H	Southampton	W	2-1

H* At Chase Lodge + Villa Tournament, Madrid   A* At Cherborg

1. Ramsey testimonial 2. Crudgington testimonial 3. Moseley testimonial
4. Danny Blanchflower benefit

Player	LgApp		Goals
Allen P	32	(3)	6
Bergsson G.	18	(1)	
Butters G.	7		
Fenwick T.	10		
Gascoigne P.	34		6
Howells D.	34	(1)	5
Hughton C.	8		
Lineker G.	38		24
Mabbutt G.	36		
Mimms R.	4		
Moncur J.	5	(3)	1
Moran P.	5	(5)	1
Nayim	19	(1)	
Polston A.	1	(1)	
Polston J.	13	(2)	1
Robson M.	3	(3)	
Samways V.	23	(5)	3
Sedgley S.	32	(1)	
Stevens G.	7	(3)	
Stewart P.	28	(4)	8
Thomas M.	26	(9)	1
Thorstvedt E.	34		
Van den Hauwe P.	31		
Walsh P.	26	(14)	2
Own Goal			1

Final table for First Division

1	Liverpool	38	23	10	5	78:40	79
2	Aston Villa	38	21	7	10	57:38	70
3	**tottenham**	38	19	6	13	60:47	63
4	Arsenal	38	18	8	12	54:38	62
5	Chelsea	38	16	12	10	58:50	60
6	Everton	38	17	8	13	57:46	59
7	Southampton	38	15	10	13	71:63	55
8	Wimbledon	38	13	16	9	47:40	55
9	Nottingham F.	38	15	9	14	55:47	54
10	Norwich	38	13	14	11	44:42	53
11	Q.P.R.	38	13	11	14	45:44	50
12	Coventry	38	14	7	17	40:59	49
13	Manchester U.	38	13	9	16	46:47	48
14	Manchester C.	38	12	12	14	43:52	48
15	Crystal P.	38	13	9	16	42:66	48
16	Derby	38	13	7	18	43:40	46
17	Luton	38	10	13	15	43:57	43
18	Sheffield W.	38	11	10	17	35:51	43
19	Charlton	38	7	9	22	31:57	30
20	Millwall	38	5	11	22	39:65	26

SEASON 1990/91

Date	Comp	H/A	Opponent	Result	Score
27 Jul	F	H*	Ipswich	W	3-0
30 Jul	F	H*	Maidstone	L	0-1
1 Aug	F	A	Shelbourne	W	3-0
3 Aug	F	A	Derry City	W	3-0
7 Aug	F	A	Brann	W	1-0
9 Aug	F	A	Viking	D	1-1
11 Aug	F	A	Sogndal	W	1-0
13 Aug	F	A	Hearts	D	1-1
17 Aug	F	H	West Ham	W	4-1[1]
20 Aug	F	A	Southend	W	4-1
25 Aug	Lge	H	Man City	W	3-1
28 Aug	Lge	A	Sunderland	D	0-0
1 Sep	Lge	A	Arsenal	D	0-0
8 Sep	Lge	H	Derby	W	3-0
15 Sep	Lge	A	Leeds	W	2-0
22 Sep	Lge	H	Crystal P.	D	1-1
26 Sep	FLC	H	Hartlepool	W	5-0
29 Sep	Lge	H	Aston Villa	W	2-1
6 Oct	Lge	A	QPR	D	0-0
9 Oct	FLC	A	Hartlepool	W	2-1
13 Oct	F	A	Arsenal	W	5-2[2]
20 Oct	Lge	H	Sheff Utd	W	4-0
27 Oct	Lge	A	Nottm Forest	W	2-1
30 Oct	FLC	H	Bradford City	W	2-1
4 Nov	Lge	A	Liverpool	L	1-3
10 Nov	Lge	H	Wimbledon	W	4-2
12 Nov	F	A	West Ham	L	3-4[3]
18 Nov	Lge	A	Everton	D	1-1
24 Nov	Lge	H	Norwich	W	2-1
27 Nov	FLC	A	Sheff Utd	W	2-0
1 Dec	Lge	A	Chelsea	L	2-3
8 Dec	Lge	H	Sunderland	D	3-3
15 Dec	Lge	A	Man City	L	1-2
22 Dec	Lge	H	Luton	W	2-1
26 Dec	Lge	A	Coventry	L	0-2
29 Dec	Lge	A	Southampton	L	0-3
1 Jan	Lge	H	Man Utd	L	1-2
5 Jan	FC	A	Blackpool	W	1-0
12 Jan	FC	H	Arsenal	D	0-0
16 Jan	FLC	A	Chelsea	D	0-0
20 Jan	Lge	A	Derby	W	1-0
23 Jan	FLC	A	Chelsea	L	0-3
26 Jan	FC	H	Oxford	W	4-2
2 Feb	Lge	H	Leeds	D	0-0
16 Feb	FC	A	Portsmouth	W	2-1
23 Feb	Lge	A	Wimbledon	L	1-5
2 Mar	Lge	H	Chelsea	D	1-1
10 Mar	FC	H	Notts Co.	W	2-1
16 Mar	Lge	A	Aston Villa	L	2-3
23 Mar	Lge	H	QPR	D	0-0
30 Mar	Lge	H	Coventry	D	2-2
1 Apr	Lge	A	Luton	D	0-0
6 Apr	Lge	H	Southampton	W	2-0
10 Apr	Lge	A	Norwich	L	1-2
14 Apr	FCsf	*	Arsenal	W	3-1
17 Apr	Lge	A	Crystal P.	L	0-1
20 Apr	Lge	A	Sheff Utd	D	2-2
24 Apr	Lge	H	Everton	D	3-3
4 May	Lge	H	Nottm Forest	D	1-1
11 May	Lge	A	Liverpool	L	0-2
18 May	FCf	*	Nottm Forest	W	2-1
20 May	Lge	A	Man Utd	D	1-1
2 Jun	F	A*	Vasco Da Gama	D	0-0
5 Jun	F	A*	Thailand Natl XI	W	2-1
9 Jun	F	A*	Japan Natl XI	L	0-4

* At Wembley   A* Kirin Cup at Kobe, Nagoya & Tokyo   H* at Chase Lodge

1. Ray Clemence benefit 2. Rix testimonial 3. Bonds testimonial

Player	LgApp		Goals
Allen P.	36	(2)	3
Bergsson G.	12	(3)	1
Edinburgh J.	16	(2)	1
Fenwick T.	4		
Garland P.	1	(1)	
Gascoigne P.	26		7
Gray P.	6	(3)	
Hendon I.	2	(2)	
Hendry J.	4	(2)	2
Howells D.	29		4
Lineker G.	32		15
Mabbutt G.	35		2
Moncur J.	9	(5)	
Moran P.	1	(1)	
Nayim	33	(1)	5
Samways V.	23	(9)	1
Sedgley S.	34	(1)	
Stewart P.	35		3
Thomas M.	31	(8)	
Thorstvedt E.	37		
Tuttle D.	6	(2)	
Van den Hauwe P.	32	(1)	
Walker I.	1		
Walsh P.	29	(13)	7

Final table for First Division

1	Arsenal	38	24	13	1	74:18	83	*2
2	Liverpool	38	23	7	8	77:40	76	
3	Crystal P.	38	20	9	9	50:41	69	
4	Leeds	38	19	7	12	65:47	64	
5	Manchester C.	38	17	11	10	64:53	62	
6	Manchester U.	38	16	12	10	58:45	59	*1
7	Wimbledon	38	14	14	10	53:46	56	
8	Nottingham F.	38	14	12	12	65:50	54	
9	Everton	38	13	12	13	50:46	51	
10	**tottenham**	38	11	16	11	51:50	49	
11	Chelsea	38	13	10	15	58:69	49	
12	Q.P.R.	38	12	10	16	44:53	46	
13	Sheffied U.	38	13	7	18	36:55	46	
14	Southampton	38	12	9	17	58:69	45	
15	Norwich	38	13	6	19	41:64	45	
16	Coventry	38	11	11	16	42:49	44	
17	Aston Villa	38	9	14	15	46:58	41	
18	Luton	38	10	7	21	42:61	37	
19	Sunderland	38	8	10	20	38:60	34	
20	Derby	38	5	9	24	37:75	24	

*2 Two Points deducted
*1 One point deducted

SEASON 1991/92

Date	Comp		Opponent	Res	Score
23 Jul	F	A	Sligo Rovers	W	4-0
25 Jul	F	A	Drogheda Utd	W	2-0
27 Jul	F	A	Shelbourne	W	3-1
30 Jul	F	A	Brann	D	1-1
1 Aug	F	A	Bryne	L	0-4
4 Aug	F	A	Celtic	L	0-1
10 Aug	CS	*	Arsenal	D	0-0
11 Aug	F	A*	AC Messina	L	0-2
13 AUR	F	A*	US Catanzaro	W	1-0
17 Aug	Lge	A	Southampton	W	3-2
21 Aug	ECWC	A	SV Stockerau	W	1-0
24 Aug	Lge	A	Chelsea	L	1-3
28 Aug	Lge	A	Nottm Forest	W	3-1
31 Aug	Lge	A	Norwich	W	1-0
4 Sep	ECWC	H	SV Stockerau	W	1-0
7 Sep	Lge	A	Aston Villa	D	0-0
14 Sep	Lge	H	QPR	W	2-0
17 Sep	ECWC	A	Hajduk Split	L	0-1[1]
21 Sep	Lge	A	Wimbledon	W	5-3
25 Sep	FLC	A	Swansea	L	0-1
28 Sep	Lge	H	Man Utd	L	1-2
2 Oct	ECWC	H	Hajduk Split	W	2-0
5 Oct	Lge	A	Everton	L	1-3
9 Oct	FLC	H	Swansea	W	5-1
19 Oct	Lge	H	Man City	L	0-1
23 Oct	ECWC	H	FC Porto	W	3-1
26 Oct	Lge	A	West Ham	L	1-2
29 Oct	FLC	A	Grimsby	W	3-0
2 Nov	Lge	A	Sheff Wed	D	0-0
7 Nov	ECWC	A	FC Porto	D	0-0
10 Nov	F	H	Spurs	D	2-2[2]
16 Nov	Lge	H	Luton	W	4-1
23 Nov	Lge	H	Sheff Utd	L	0-1
1 Dec	Lge	A	Arsenal	L	0-2
4 Dec	FLC	A	Coventry	W	2-1
7 Dec	Lge	H	Notts Co.	W	2-1
14 Dec	Lge	A	Leeds	D	1-1
18 Dec	Lge	H	Liverpool	L	1-2
22 Dec	Lge	A	Crystal P.	W	2-1
26 Dec	Lge	H	Nottm Forest	L	1-2
28 Dec	Lge	H	Norwich	W	3-0
1 Jan	Lge	A	Coventry	W	2-1
5 Jan	FC	A	Aston Villa	D	0-0
8 Jan	FLC	H	Norwich	W	2-1
11 Jan	Lge	A	Chelsea	L	0-2
14 Jan	FC	H	Aston Villa	L	0-1
18 Jan	Lge	H	Southampton	L	1-2
25 Jan	Lge	A	Oldham	D	0-0
1 Feb	Lge	A	Man City	L	0-1
9 Feb	FLCsf	A	Nottm Forest	D	1-1
16 Feb	Lge	H	Crystal P.	D	1-1
22 Feb	Lge	H	Arsenal	D	1-1
1 Mar	FLCsf	H	Nottm Forest	L	1-2
4 Mar	ECWC	A	Feyenoord	L	0-1
7 Mar	Lge	H	Leeds	L	1-3
11 Mar	Lge	A	Luton	D	0-0
14 Mar	Lge	H	Sheff Wed	L	0-2
18 Mar	ECWC	H	Feyenoord	D	0-0
21 Mar	LRe	A	Liverpool	L	1-2
28 Mar	Lge	H	Coventry	W	4-3
1 Apr	Lge	H	West Ham	W	3-0
4 Apr	Lge	H	Aston Villa	L	2-5
7 Apr	LRe	A	Notts County	W	2-0
11 Apr	Lge	A	QPR	W	2-1
14 Apr	Lge	A	Sheff Utd	L	0-2
18 Apr	Lge	H	Wimbledon	W	3-2
20 Apr	Lge	A	Oldham	L	0-1
25 Apr	Lge	H	Everton	D	3-3
2 May	Lge	A	Man Utd	L	1-3
5 May	F	A	Cardiff	W	2-0[3]
8 May	F	A	Hull City	W	6-2[4]

* At Wembley   A* Ceravolo Tournament at Catanzaro

1. At Linz 2. Cyril Knowles Memorial 3. Parsons testimonial 4. Roberts testimonial

Player	LgApp		Goals
Allen P.	39	(1)	3
Bergsson G.	28	(11)	1
Cundy J.	10		
Durie G.	31		7
Edinburgh J.	23	(1)	
Fenwick T.	23	(1)	
Gray A.	14		1
Hendon I.	2	(2)	
Hendry J.	5	(4)	1
Houghton S.	10	(10)	2
Howells D.	31	(4)	1
Lineker G.	35		28
Mabbutt G.	40		2
Minton J.	2		1
Nayim	31	(9)	1
Samways V.	27	(1)	1
Sedgley S.	34	(13)	
Stewart P.	38		5
Thorstvedt E.	24		
Tuttle D.	2		
Van den Hauwe P.	18	(5)	
Walker I.	18		
Walsh P.	29	(12)	3
Own Goal			1

Final table for First Division

		P	W	D	L	F:A	Pts
1	Leeds	42	22	16	4	74:37	82
2	Manchester U.	42	21	15	6	63:33	78
3	Sheffield W.	42	21	12	9	62:49	75
4	Arsenal	42	19	15	8	81:46	72
5	Manchester C.	42	20	10	12	61:4B	70
6	Liverpool	42	16	16	10	47:40	64
7	Aston Villa	42	17	9	16	48:44	60
8	Nottingham F.	42	16	13	15	60:58	59
9	Sheffield U.	42	16	9	17	65:63	57
10	Crystal P.	42	14	15	13	53:61	57
11	Q.P.R.	42	12	18	12	48:47	54
12	Everton	42	13	14	15	52:51	53
13	Wimbledon	42	13	14	15	53:53	53
14	Chelsea	42	13	14	15	50:60	53
15	tottenham	42	15	7	20	58:63	52
16	Southampton	42	14	10	18	39:55	52
17	Oldham	42	14	9	19	63:67	51
18	Norwich	42	11	12	19	47:63	45
19	Coventry	42	11	11	20	35:44	44
20	Luton	42	10	12	20	38:71	42
21	Notts Co.	42	10	10	22	40:62	40
22	West Ham	42	9	11	22	37:59	38

SEASON 1992/93

Date	Comp		Opponent	Res	Score
20 Jul	F	H*Reading		W	3-1
21 Jul	F	H*Gillingham		W	2-0
25 Jul	F	A	Hearts	W	2-1
29 Jul	F	A	Brighton	D	1-1
1 Aug	F	A	Glenavon	W	1-0
3 Aug	F	A	WBA	W	2-0
5 Aug	F	A	Sunderland	W	3-0[1]
8 Aug	F	A	Watford	W	2-0
10 Aug	F	A	Portsmouth	L	2-4
15 Aug	Lge	A	Southampton	D	0-0
19 Aug	Lge	H	Coventry	L	0-2
22 Aug	Lge	H	Crystal P.	D	2-2
25 Aug	Lge	A	Leeds	L	0-5
30 Aug	Lge	A	Ipswich	D	1-1
2 Sep	Lge	H	Sheff Utd	W	2-0
5 Sep	Lge	H	Everton	W	2-1
14 Sep	Lge	A	Coventry	L	0-1
19 Sep	Lge	H	Man Utd	D	1-1
21 Sep	FLC	H	Brentford	W	3-1
23 Sep	F	A	SS Lazio	L	0-3[2]
27 Sep	Lge	A	Sheff Wed	L	0-2
3 Oct	Lge	A	QPR	L	1-4
7 Oct	FLC	A	Brentford	W	4-2
17 Oct	Lge	H	Middlesbrough	D	2-2
20 Oct	F	H	SS Lazio	L	0-2[2]
25 Oct	Lge	A	Wimbledon	D	1-1
28 Oct	FLC	A	Man City	W	1-0
31 Oct	Lge	H	Liverpool	W	2-0
7 Nov	Lge	A	Blackburn	W	2-0
10 Nov	F	A	Swansea	D	3-3[3]
21 Nov	Lge	H	Aston Villa	D	0-0
28 Nov	Lge	A	Man City	W	1-0
2 Dec	FLC	A	Nottm Forest	L	0-2
5 Dec	Lge	H	Chelsea	L	1-2
12 Dec	Lge	H	Arsenal	W	1-0
19 Dec	Lge	A	Oldham	L	1-2
26 Dec	Lge	A	Norwich	D	0-0
28 Dec	Lge	H	Nottm Forest	W	2-1
2 Jan	FC	A+Marlow		W	5-1
9 Jan	Lge	A	Man Utd	L	1-4
16 Jan	Lge	H	Sheff Wed	L	0-2
24 Jan	FC	A	Norwich	W	2-0
27 Jan	Lge	H	Ipswich	L	0-2
30 Jan	Lge	A	Crystal P.	W	3-1
7 Feb	Lge	H	Southampton	W	4-3
10 Feb	Lge	A	Everton	W	2-1
14 Feb	FC	H	Wimbledon	W	3-2
20 Feb	Lge	H	Leeds	W	4-0
27 Feb	Lge	H	QPR	W	3-2
2 Mar	Lge	A	Sheff Utd	L	0-6
7 Mar	FC	A	Man City	W	4-2
10 Mar	Lge	A	Aston Villa	D	0-0
20 Mar	Lge	A	Chelsea	D	1-1
24 Mar	Lge	H	Man City	W	3-1
28 Mar	F	A	Crystal P.	D	3-3[4]
4 Apr	FCsf	*	Arsenal	L	0-1
9 Apr	Lge	H	Norwich	W	5-1
12 Apr	Lge	A	Nottm Forest	L	1-2
17 Apr	Lge	H	Oldham	W	4-1
20 Apr	Lge	A	Middlesbrough	L	0-3
23 Apr	F	A	Real Zaragoza	L	0-2
27 Apr	F	H	Real Madrid	L	0-1[5]
27 Apr	F	H	Inter Milan	D	0-0[5]+
1 May	Lge	H	Wimbledon	D	1-1
5 May	Lge	H	Blackburn	L	1-2
8 May	Lge	A	Liverpool	L	2-6
11 May	Lge	H	Arsenal	W	3-1
14 May	F	A	Enfield	W	5-1[6]

H* At Chase Lodge   * At Wembley   A+ Played at White Hart Lane

1. City Celebration match 2. Capital Cup 3. Woolacott testimonial 4. Allison testimonial
5. Fiorucci Cup Tournament 5+ Lost 6-5 on penalties 6. Eddie Baily testimonial

Player	LgApp		Goals
Allen P.	38		3
Anderton D.	34	(2)	6
Austin D.	34	(1)	
Barmby N.	22	(5)	6
Bergsson G.	5	(5)	
Campbell S.	1	(1)	1
Cundy J.	15	(2)	1
Dearden K.	1	(1)	
Durie G.	17		3
Edinburgh J.	32	(1)	
Fenwick T.	5	(2)	
Gray A.	17	(8)	1
Hendry J.	5	(2)	2
Hill D.	4	(2)	
Hodges L.	4	(4)	
Howells D.	18	(2)	1
Mabbutt G.	29		2
McDonald D.	2		
Moran P.	3	(3)	
Nayim	18	(3)	3
Nethercott S.	5	(2)	
Ruddock N.	38		3
Samways V.	34		
Sedgley S.	22	(2)	3
Sheringham E.	38		21
Thorstvedt E.	27	(2)	
Turner A.	18	(11)	3
Tuttle D.	5	(1)	
Van den Hauwe P.	18	(5)	
Walker I.	17		
Watson K.	5	(1)	
Own Goal			1

Final table for FA Premier League

		P	W	D	L	F:A	Pts
1	Manchester U.	42	24	12	6	66:31	84
2	Aston Villa	42	21	11	10	57:40	74
3	Norwich	42	21	9	12	61:65	72
4	Blackburn	42	20	11	11	68:46	71
5	Q.P.R.	42	17	12	13	63:55	63
6	Liverpool	42	16	11	15	62:55	59
7	Sheffield W.	42	15	14	13	55:51	59
8	tottenham	42	16	11	15	60:66	59
9	Manchester C.	42	15	12	15	56:51	57
10	Arsenal	42	15	11	16	40:38	56
11	Chelsea	42	14	14	14	51:54	56
12	Wimbledon	42	14	12	16	56:55	54
13	Everton	42	15	8	19	53:55	53
14	Sheffield U.	42	14	10	18	54:53	52
15	Coventry	42	13	13	16	52:57	52
16	Ipswich	42	12	16	14	50:55	52
17	Leeds	42	12	15	15	57:62	51
18	Southampton	42	13	11	18	54:61	50
19	Oldham	42	13	10	19	63:74	49
20	Crystal P.	42	11	16	15	48:61	49
21	Middlesbrough	42	11	11	20	54:75	44
22	Nottingham F.	42	10	10	22	41:62	40

SEASON 1993/94

16 Jul	F	A	Shelbourne	W	4-2	
18 Jul	F	A	Drogheda Utd	W	3-1	
23 Jul	F	A	Team Nord Trond.	W	1-0	
25 Jul	F	A	Lyn Oslo	D	0-0[1]	
27 Jul	F	A	Team Porsgrunn	W	5-4	
31 Jul	F	H	SS Lazio	W	3-2[2]	
1 Aug	F	H	Chelsea	L	0-4[2]	
6 Aug	F	A	Brentford	D	0-0[3]	
9 Aug	F	A	Peterborough	W	2-1	
14 Aug	Lge	A	Newcastle	W	1-0	
16 Aug	Lge	H	Arsenal	L	0-1	
21 Aug	Lge	H	Man City	W	1-0	
25 Aug	Lge	A	Liverpool	W	2-1	
28 Aug	Lge	A	Aston Villa	L	0-1	
1 Sep	Lge	H	Chelsea	D	1-1	
11 Sep	Lge	A	Sheff Utd	D	2-2	
18 Sep	Lge	H	Oldham	W	5-0	
22 Sep	FLC	A	Burnley	D	0-0	
26 Sep	Lge	A	Ipswich	D	2-2	
3 Oct	Lge	H	Everton	W	3-2	
6 Oct	FLC	H	Burnley	W	3-1	
11 Oct	F	A	Brann	L	0-2	
16 Oct	Lge	A	Man Utd	L	1-2	
19 Oct	F	A	Hartlepool	W	3-1[4]	
23 Oct	Lge	H	Swindon	D	1-1	
27 Oct	FLC	A	Derby	W	1-0	
30 Oct	Lge	A	Blackburn	L	0-1	
6 Nov	Lge	A	Southampton	L	0-1	
20 Nov	Lge	H	Leeds	D	1-1	
24 Nov	Lge	H	Wimbledon	D	1-1	
27 Nov	Lge	A	QPR	D	1-1	
1 Dec	FLC	H	Blackburn	W	1-0	
4 Dec	Lge	H	Newcastle	L	1-2	
6 Dec	Lge	A	Arsenal	D	1-1	
11 Dec	Lge	A	Man City	W	2-0	
18 Dec	Lge	H	Liverpool	D	3-3	
27 Dec	Lge	H	Norwich	L	1-3	
28 Dec	Lge	A	West Ham	W	3-1	
1 Jan	Lge	H	Coventry	L	1-2	
3 Jan	Lge	A	Sheff Wed	L	0-1	
8 Jan	FC	A	Peterborough	D	1-1	
12 Jan	FLC	H	Aston Villa	L	1-2	
15 Jan	Lge	H	Man Utd	L	0-1	
19 Jan	FC	H	Peterborough	D	1-1[5]	
22 Jan	Lge	A	Swindon	L	1-2	
29 Jan	FC	A	Ipswich	L	0-3	
5 Feb	Lge	H	Sheff Wed	L	1-3	
12 Feb	Lge	H	Blackburn	L	0-2	
15 Feb	F	A+	Atletico Madrid	W	2-1	
27 Feb	Lge	A	Chelsea	L	3-4	
2 Mar	Lge	A	Aston Villa	D	1-1	
5 Mar	Lge	H	Sheff Utd	D	2-2	
19 Mar	Lge	A	Ipswich	D	1-1	
26 Mar	Lge	A	Everton	W	1-0	
2 Apr	Lge	A	Norwich	W	2-1	
4 Apr	Lge	H	West Ham	L	1-4	
9 Apr	Lge	A	Coventry	L	0-1	
17 Apr	Lge	A	Leeds	L	0-2	
23 Apr	L8e	H	Southampton	W	3-0	
30 Apr	Lge	A	Wimbledon	L	1-2	
5 May	Lge	A	Oldham	W	2-0	
7 May	Lge	H	QPR	L	1-2	

A+ Played at Jerez

1. Sundby testimonial 2. Makita International Tournament 3. Millen testimonial 4. Cyril Knowles Tribute 5. Won 5-4 on penalties

SEASON 1994/95

22 Jul	F	A	Bournemouth	W	5-0	
25 Jul	F	A	Cambridge	W	3-0	
29 Jul	F	A	Bristol City	W	3-0	
2 Aug	F	A	Brighton	W	3-0	
6 Aug	F	A	Watford	D	1-1	
9 Aug	F	A	Shelbourne	W	1-0	
20 Aug	Lge	A	Sheff Wed	W	4-3	
24 Aug	Lge	H	Everton	W	2-1	
27 Aug	Lge	H	Man Utd	L	0-1	
30 Aug	Lge	A	Ipswich	W	3-1	
12 Sep	Lge	H	Southampton	L	1-2	
17 Sep	Lge	A	Leicester	L	1-3	
21 Sep	FLC	A	Watford	W	6-3	
24 Sep	Lge	H	Nottm Forest	L	1-4	
1 Oct	Lge	A	Wimbledon	W	2-1	
4 Oct	FLC	H	Watford	L	2-3	
8 Oct	Lge	H	QPR	D	1-1	
15 Oct	Lge	A	Leeds	D	1-1	
22 Oct	Lge	A	Man City	L	2-5	
26 Oct	FLC	A	Notts County	L	0-3	
29 Oct	Lge	H	West Ham	W	3-1	
5 Nov	Lge	A	Blackburn	L	0-2	
11 Nov	F	A	Reading	D	1-1	
19 Nov	Lge	H	Aston Villa	L	3-4	
23 Nov	Lge	A	Chelsea	D	0-0	
26 Nov	Lge	A	Liverpool	D	1-1	
3 Dec	Lge	H	Newcastle	W	4-2	
10 Dec	Lge	H	Sheff Wed	W	3-1	
17 Dec	Lge	A	Everton	D	0-0	
26 Dec	Lge	A	Norwich	W	2-0	
27 Dec	Lge	H	Crystal P.	D	0-0	
31 Dec	Lge	A	Coventry	W	4-0	
2 Jan	Lge	H	Arsenal	W	1-0	
7 Jan	FC	H	Altrincham	W	3-0	
14 Jan	Lge	A	West Ham	W	2-1	
25 Jan	Lge	A	Aston Villa	L	0-1	
29 Jan	FC	A	Sunderland	W	4-1	
5 Feb	Lge	H	Blackburn	W	3-1	
11 Feb	Lge	A	Chelsea	D	1-1	
18 Feb	FC	H	Southampton	D	1-1	
25 Feb	Lge	H	Wimbledon	L	1-2	
1 Mar	FC	A	Southampton	W	6-2	
4 Mar	Lge	H	Nottm Forest	D	2-2	
8 Mar	Lge	H	Ipswich	W	3-0	
11 Mar	FC	A	Liverpool	W	2-1	
15 Mar	Lge	A	Man Utd	D	0-0	
18 Mar	Lge	H	Leicester	W	1-0	
22 Mar	Lge	H	Liverpool	D	0-0	
2 Apr	Lge	A	Southampton	L	3-4	
9 Apr	FCsf		*Everton	L	1-4	
11 Apr	Lge	H	Man City	W	2-1	
14 Apr	Lge	A	Crystal P.	D	1-1	
17 Apr	Lge	H	Norwich	W	1-0	
29 Apr	Lge	A	Arsenal	D	1-1	
3 May	Lge	A	Newcastle	D	3-3	
6 May	Lge	A	QPR	L	1-2	
9 May	Lge	H	Coventry	L	1-3	
14 May	Lge	H	Leeds	D	1-1	
21 May	F	A	Kitchee/Eastern	W	7-2[2]	
24 May	F	A	Guangzhou	W	2-1[2]	
26 May	F	A	Singapore Lions	D	1-1[2]	

* at Elland Road

1. Richard Cooke testimonial 2. Tour to Hong Kong, China and Singapore

Player	LgApp		Goals
Allen P.	1	(1)	
Anderton D.	37	(2)	6
Austin D.	23	(3)	
Barmby N.	27		5
Calderwood C.	26		
Campbell S.	34	(7)	
Carr S.	1		
Caskey D.	25	(9)	4
Dozzell J.	32	(4)	8
Durie G.	10		1
Edinburgh J.	25	(1)	
Gray A.	2	(2)	1
Hazard M.	17	(4)	2
Hendry J.	3	(3)	
Hill D.	3	(2)	
Howells D.	18	(3)	1
Kerslake D.	17	(1)	
Mabbutt G.	29		
Mahorn P.	1		
Moran S.	5	(5)	
Nethercott S.	10	(1)	
Robinson S.	2	(1)	
Rosenthal R.	15	(4)	2
Samways V.	39		3
Scott K.	12		1
Sedgley S.	42		6
Sheringham E.	19	(2)	13
Thorstvedt E.	32		
Turner A.	1	(1)	
Walker I.	11	(1)	
Own Goal			1

Final table for FA Premier League

1	Manchester U.	42	27	11	4	80:38	92
2	Blackburn	42	25	9	8	63:36	84
3	Newcastle	42	23	8	11	82:41	77
4	Arsenal	42	18	17	7	53:28	71
5	Leeds	42	18	16	8	65:39	70
6	Wimbledon	42	18	11	13	56:53	65
7	Sheffield W.	42	16	16	10	76:54	64
8	Liverpool	42	17	9	16	59:55	60
9	Q.P.R.	42	16	12	14	62:61	60
10	Aston Villa	42	15	12	15	46:50	57
11	Coventry	42	14	14	14	43:45	56
12	Norwich	42	12	17	13	65:61	53
13	West Ham	42	13	13	16	47:58	52
14	Chelsea	42	13	12	17	49:53	51
15	**tottenham**	42	11	12	19	54:59	45
16	Manchester C.	42	9	18	15	38:49	45
17	Everton	42	12	8	22	42:63	44
18	Southampton	42	12	7	23	49:65	43
19	Ipswich	42	9	16	17	35:58	43
20	Sheffield U.	42	8	18	16	42:60	42
21	Oldham	42	9	13	20	42:68	40
22	Swindon	42	5	15	22	47:100	30

Player	LgApp		Goals
Anderton D.	37		5
Austin D.	24	(1)	
Barmby N.	38	(1)	9
Calderwood C.	36	(1)	2
Campbell S.	30	(1)	
Caskey D.	4	(3)	
Dozzell J.	7	(1)	
Dumitrescu I.	13	(2)	4
Edinburgh J.	31	(2)	
Hazard M.	11	(9)	
Hill D.	3	(2)	
Howells D.	26		1
Kerslake D.	18	(2)	
Klinsmann J.	41		20
Mabbutt G.	36	(3)	
McMahon G.	2		
Nethercott S.	17	(9)	
Popescu G.	23		3
Rosenthal R.	20	(6)	
Scott K.	4		
Sheringham E.	42	(1)	18
Thorstvedt E.	1		
Turner A.	1		
Walker I.	41		
Own goals			4

Final table for FA Premier League

1	Blackburn	42	27	8	7	80:39	89
2	Manchester U.	42	26	10	6	77:28	88
3	Nottingham F.	42	22	11	9	72:43	77
4	Liverpool	42	21	11	10	65:37	74
5	Leeds	42	20	13	9	59:38	73
6	Newcastle	42	20	12	10	67:47	72
7	**tottenham**	42	16	14	12	66:58	62
8	Q.P.R.	42	17	9	16	61:59	60
9	Wimbledon	42	15	11	16	48:65	56
10	Southampton	42	12	18	12	61:63	54
11	Chelsea	42	13	15	14	50:55	54
12	Arsenal	42	13	12	17	52:49	51
13	Sheffield W.	42	13	12	17	49:57	51
14	West Ham	42	13	11	18	44:48	50
15	Everton	42	11	17	14	44:51	50
16	Coventry	42	12	14	16	44:62	50
17	Manchester C.	42	12	13	17	53:64	49
18	Aston Villa	42	11	15	16	51:56	48
19	Crystal P.	42	11	12	19	34:49	45
20	Norwich	42	10	13	19	37:54	43
21	Leicester	42	6	11	25	45:80	29
22	Ipswich	42	7	6	29	36:93	27

International Appearances by Tottenham Players

For England

Player	Caps won to 13 May 1995	Goals scored	International debut while at Tottenham		Opponents
Allen C.D.	2	0	29 Apr	87	Turkey
Alsford W.J.	1	0	6 Apr	35	Scotland
Anderton D.R.	6	1	9 Mar	94	Denmark
Baily E.F.	9	5	2 Jul	50	Spain
Barmby N.J.	1	0	29 Apr	95	Uruguay
Bliss H.	1	0	9 Apr	21	Scotland
Brooks J.	3	2	14 Nov	56	Wales
Chivers M.H.	24	13	3 Feb	71	Malta
Clarke H.A.	1	0	3 Apr	54	Scotland
Clay T.	4	0	15 Mar	20	Wales
Clemence R.N.	5	0	9 Sep	81	Norway
Coates R.	2	0	12 May	71	Malta
Dimmock J.H.	3	0	9 Apr	21	Scotland
Ditchburn E.G.	6	0	2 Dec	48	Switzerland
Fenwick T.W.	1	0	17 Feb	88	Israel
Gascoigne P.J.	20	2	14 Sep	88	Denmark
Greaves J.P.	42	28	14 Apr	62	Scotland
Grimsdell A.	6	0	15 Mar	20	Wales
Hall G.W.	10	9	16 Dec	33	France
Henry R.P.	1	0	27 Feb	63	France
Hoddle G.	44	8	22 Nov	79	Bulgaria
Hodge S.B.	4	0	18 Feb	87	Spain
Hunt G.S.	3	1	1 Apr	33	Scotland
Knowles C.B.	4	0	6 Dec	67	USSR
Lineker G.W.	38	18	6 Sep	89	Sweden
Mabbutt G.V.	16	1	13 Oct	82	West Germany
Medley L.D.	6	1	15 Nov	50	Wales
Mullery A.P.	35	1	9 Dec	64	Holland
Nicholson W.E.	1	1	19 May	51	Portugal
Norman M.	23	0	20 May	62	Peru
Osborne F.R.	2	3	8 Dec	24	Belgium
Perryman S.J.	1	0	2 Jun	82	Iceland
Peters M.S.	34	9	18 Apr	70	Wales
Ramsey A.E.	31	3	30 Nov	49	Italy
Robb G.W.	1	0	25 Nov	53	Hungary
Roberts G.P.	6	0	28 May	83	N. Ireland
Rowe A.S.	1	0	16 Dec	33	France
Seed J.M.	5	1	21 May	21	Belgium
Sheringham E.P.	6	0	29 May	93	Poland
Smith B.	2	0	9 Apr	21	Scotland
Smith R.A.	15	13	8 Oct	60	N. Ireland
Sproston B.	2	0	22 Oct	38	Wales
Stevens G.A.	7	0	17 Oct	84	Finland
Stewart P.A.	3	0	11 Sep	91	Germany
Waddle C.R.	36	6	11 Sep	85	Romania
Walden F.I.	2	0	4 Apr	14	Scotland
Willis A.	1	0	3 Oct	51	France
Woodward V.J.	21	27	14 Feb	03	Ireland

For Ireland/Northern Ireland

Player	Caps won to 13 May 1995	Goals scored	International debut while at Tottenham		Opponents
Armstrong G.J.	27	5	27 Apr	77	West Germany
Blanchflower R.D.	43	2	2 Oct	54	England
Jennings P.A.	75	0	3 Oct	64	England
Kirwan J.F.	12	2	24 Feb	00	Wales
McGrath R.C.	6	1	11 May	74	Scotland
O'Hagan C.	5	1	18 Mar	05	Scotland
Rowley R.W.M.	2	1	22 Apr	31	Wales

For Republic of Ireland

Player	Caps won to 13 May 1995	Goals scored	International debut while at Tottenham		Opponents
Galvin A.	19	1	22 Sep	82	Holland
Gavin J.T.	2	0	1 May	55	Holland
Holmes J.P.	12	0	30 Mar	77	France
Hughton C.W.G.	51	1	29 Oct	79	USA
Kinnear J.P.	24	0	22 Feb	67	Turkey

For Scotland

Player	Caps won to 13 May 1995	Goals scored	International debut while at Tottenham		Opponents
Archibald S.	22	3	16 May	80	N. Ireland
Brazil A.B.	2	1	28 May	83	Wales
Brown A.	1	1	5 Apr	02	England *
Brown W.D.F.	24	0	3 Oct	59	N. Ireland
Calderwood C.	2	1	29 Mar	95	Russia
Conn A.J.	2	0	20 May	75	N. Ireland
Durie G.S.	13	2	11 Sep	91	Switzerland
Gilzean A.J.	17	8	8 May	65	Spain
Gough C.R.	8	0	10 Sep	86	Bulgaria
Mackay D.C.	18	4	11 Apr	59	England
Robertson J.G.	1	0	. 3 Oct	64	Wales
White J.A.	18	1	14 Nov	59	Wales

* Match completed but later declared unofficial due to Ibrox Disaster.

For Wales

Player	Caps won to 13 May 1995	Goals scored	International debut while at Tottenham		Opponents
Bowen R.M.	2	0	10 May	86	Canada
Burgess W.A.R.	32	1	19 Oct	46	Scotland
Day A.	1	0	4 Nov	33	N. Ireland
England H.M.	24	2	22 Oct	66	Scotland
Evans W.	6	1	7 Dec	32	N. Ireland
Hopkins M.	34	0	11 Apr	56	N. Ireland
Hughes E.	12	0	2 Mar	01	Scotland
Jones C.W.	41	12	16 Apr	58	N. Ireland
Jones J.L.	12	0	19 Feb	98	N. Ireland
Jones W.E.A.	2	0	23 Oct	48	Scotland
Medwin T.C.	27	6	20 Oct	56	Scotland
O'Callaghan	11	3	2 Feb	29	N. Ireland
Price P.T.	14	0	18 Nov	81	USSR
Rees W.	1	0	8 Mar	50	N. Ireland
Whatley W.J.	2	0	22 Oct	38	England
Yorath T.C.	8	0	11 Sep	79	Rep. Ireland

For Argentina

Player	Caps won to 13 May 1995	Goals scored	International debut while at Tottenham		Opponents
Ardiles O.C.	8	1	22 May	79	Holland

For Belgium

Player	Caps won to 13 May 1995	Goals scored	International debut while at Tottenham		Opponents
Claesen N.P.J.	9	6	14 Oct	86	Luxembourg

For Germany

Player	Caps won to 13 May 1995	Goals scored	International debut while at Tottenham		Opponents
Klinsmann J.	8	5	7 Sep	94	Russia

For Iceland

Player	Caps won to 13 May 1995	Goals scored	International debut while at Tottenham		Opponents
Bergsson G.	30	0	19 May	89	England 'B'

For Israel

Player	Caps won to 13 May 1995	Goals scored	International debut while at Tottenham		Opponents
Rosenthal R.	9	4	31 May	94	Argentina

For Nigeria

Player	Caps won to 13 May 1995	Goals scored	International debut while at Tottenham		Opponents
Chiedozie J.O.	3	0	20 Oct	84	Liberia

For Norway

Player	Caps won to 13 May 1995	Goals scored	International debut while at Tottenham		Opponents
Thorstvedt E.	39	0	2 May	89	Poland

For Romania

Player	Caps won to 13 May 1995	Goals scored	International debut while at Tottenham		Opponents
Dumitrescu I.	5	1	7 Sep	94	Azerbaijan
Popescu G.	6	1	8 Oct	94	France

Note: Peacetime Full Internationals only of players on Tottenham's books. All details as at 13 May 1995.

Football League Appearances September 1908-July 1995

Player	Total Apps	Came on as sub	Gls	Player	Total Apps	Came on as sub	Gls	Player	Total Apps	Came on as sub	Gls
Adams C.J.	6		1	Clayton E.	92	4	20	Gray A.A.	33	10	3
Aleksic II.A.	25			Clemence R.N.	240			Gray P.	95		
Alexander S.	9		1	Close S.C.	9	6		Greaves J.P.	321		220
Allen C.D.	105	8	60	Coates R.	188	15	13	Greenfield G.W.	31		11
Allen J.	1		1	Cockram A.	2			Grice F.	47		1
Allen L.W.	119		47	Collins J.	2			Grimsdell A.	324		26
Allen P.K.	292	16	23	Collins J.L.	2			Groves V.G.	4		3
Alsford W.J.	81		9	Collins P.J.	83	6	4	Grubb A.J.	2		
Anderton D.R.	108	4	17	Collins T.	113		1	Hall A.E.B.	40		10
Archibald J.	24		1	Colquhoun D.W.	81		2	Hall A.G.	16	3	
Archibald S.	131	3	58	Conn A.J.	38	3	6	Hall B.A.C.	2		
Ardiles O.C.	238	16	16	Cook G.W.	63		21	Hall G.W.	202		27
Armstrong G.J.	84	19	10	Cook R.K.	3			Hall J.	53		
Armstrong J.W.	28		7	Cooke R.E.	11	2	2	Hancock K.P.	3		
Austin D.B.	81	5		Coquet E.	77			Handley C.H.J.	121		27
Austin P.C.	1			Corbett P.A.	5	2	1	Hargreaves H.	35		7
Baily E.F.	296		64	Cox F.J.A.	99	.	15	Harmer T.C.	205	47	
Baker P.R.B.	299		3	Crompton A.	15		2	Harper E.C.	63		63
Banks J.A.	69		6	Crompton G.E.	8			Harris W.	7		
Bann W.E.	12			Crook I.S.	20	10	1	Hartley F.	7		1
Barmby N.J.	87	6	20	Crooks G.A.	125	4	48	Hazard M.	119	31	15
Barnett F.W.	16			Crowl S.R.	1			Hedley F.	4		1
Barton K.R.	4			Culverhouse I.B.	2	1		Helliwell S.	8		
Bauchop J.R.	10		6	Cundy J.V.	25	2	1	Hendon I.M.	44		
Beal P.	333	3	1	Curtis J.J.	82		5	Hendry J.M.	17	12	5
Beavon M.S.	4	1		Daines B.R.	146			Henry R.P.	247		
Bell S.	15		6	Darnell J.	150		3	Herod E.R.B.	57		
Bellamy W.R.	70		10	Davies W.	109		19	Hewitson R.	30		
Bennett L.D.	272		102	Day A.	13			Hill D.R.L.	106		
Bentley F.W.	36		5	Dearden K.C.	1	1		Hiills J.R.	29		
Bergsson G.	71	20	2	Dick A.J.	17	1	2	Hinton W.F.W.	57		
Bing T.E.	1			Dicker L.R.	102			Hitchins A.W.	35		1
Birnie E.L.	4		1	Dillon M.L.	24	3	1	Hoddle G.	377	7	88
Blair J.G.	29		14	Dimmock J.H.	400		100	Hodge S.B.	45	1	7
Blake H.E.	51			Ditchburn E.G.	418			Hodges L.L.	4	4	
Blanchflower R.D.	337		15	Dix R.W.	36		5	Hodgkinson H.	56		
Bliss H.	194		93	Dodge W.C.	6			Holder P.	13	4	1
Blyth J.	11			Dowsett G.J.	1		1	Hollis R.W.	3		1
Bolan L.A.	10		3	Dozzell J.A.W.	39	5	8	Hollowbread J.F.	67		
Bond D.J.T.	23	3	1	Drabble F.	1			Holmes J.P.	81	2	
Boreham F.	20			Dulin M.C.	10		2	Hooper P.G.W.	97		
Bowen R.	17	3	22	Dumitrescu I.	13	2	4	Hopkins M.	219		
Bowering E.G.	7			Duncan A.	93		22	Houghton S.A.	10	10	2
Bowler G.H.	3			Duncan J.P.	103	2	53	Howe L.F.	16	5	26
Brace R.L.	1	1		Dunmore D.G.I.	75		23	Howells D.G.	196	33	17
Brain J.	45		10	Duquemin L.S.	274		114	Hoy R.E.	10		
Brazil A.B.	31	2	9	Durie G.S.	58		11	Hughes W.A.	2		
Brittain R.C.	40			Dyson T.K.	184		41	Hughton C.W.G.	297	4	12
Brittan C.	41		1	Eadon J.P.	5			Humphreys P.	45		23
Britton J.	40			Edinburgh J.C.	127	7	1	Hunt D.A	17		6
Brooke G.J.	73	24	15	Edrich W.J.	20		4	Hunt G.S.	185		124
Brooks J.	166	46		Elkes A.J.	190		49	Hunter A.C.	23		
Brooks S.	10		1	Elkin B.H.W.	25			Hutchinson G.H.	5		1
Brotherston N.	1			Elliott J.E.	13		3	Iley J.	53		1
Brough J.	1			England H.M.	300		14	Illingworth J.W.	10		
Brown D.C.	1			Evans A.	5			Ireland J.J.C.	3		
Brown I.R.J	12			Evans R.L.	136	4	2	Jaques W.	123		
Brown J.	4			Evans T.	94		4	Jeffrey G.	1		
Brown L.	62		3	Evans W.	178		78	Jenkins D.J.	14	3	2
Brown R.E.	1			Fairclough C.H.	60		5	Jennings P.A.	472		
Brown R.S.	37			Falco M.P.	174	12	68	Johnson N. J.	34	7	5
Brown W.D.F.	222			Farley B.H.	1			Jones C.	18		
Buckingham V.F.	204		1	Felton W.	73			Jones C.H.	164	15	37
Bull W.	12			Fenwick T.W.	93	3	8	Jones C.W.	318	4	135
Bulling E.	2			Fleming J.B.M.	19		3	Jones G.	7		
Burgess W.W.R.	297		15	Flint K.	5		1	Jones W.E.A.	55		14
Burgon F.A.	4			Foreman A.G.	36		14	Jordan J.W.	24		10
Burton O.	37			Forman T.	8		1	Joseph L.	1		
Butters G.	35	1	1	Forster M.	236			Joyce J.W.	73		
Cable T.H.	42			Fullwood J.	34		1	Kaine W.E.J.C.	11		
Calderwood C.	62	1	2	Galloway S.R.	3		2	Keeley A.J.	6	1	
Campbell S.J.	65		9	Galvin A.	201	7	20	Kendall M.	29		
Cantrell J.	160		74	Garland P.J.	1	1		Kennedy J.J.	13		
Carr S.	1			Garwood L.F.	2			Kerry A.H.G.	1		
Cartwright W.	13			Gascoigne P.J.	92	1	19	Kerslake D.	35	3	
Caskey D.	29	12	4	Gavin J.T.	32		15	King A.	19		
Castle S.E.R.	5			Gibbins E.	1			King D.A.	19		
Channell F.C.	95		1	Gibbons A.H.	27		13	King E.F.	1		
Chiedozie J.O.	53	8	12	Gibson T.B	18	2	4	Kinnear J.P.	196	7	2
Chipperfield J.J.	15		6	Gilberg	2			Klinsmann J.	41		20
Chisholm J.R.	2			Gilzean A.J.	343	8	93	Knight J.G.	1		
Chivers M.H.	278	10	118	Goldsrnitn G.	1			Knowles C.B.	401	1	15
Claesen N.P.J.	50	13	18	Goodman A.A.	16		1	Lacy J.	104	5	2
Clarke H.A.	295		4	Gorman J.	30			Lane J.H.C.	26		7
Clarke R.C.	1	1		Gosnell A.A.	5			Lee C.	62	5	18
Clay T.	318		23	Gough C.R.	49		2	Lee T.W.G.	1		

Football League Appearances September 1908-July 1995

Player	Total Apps	Came on as sub	Gls
Leslie T.S.	10		
Levene D.J.	8		
Leworthy D.J.	11	3	3
Lightfoot E.J.	61		2
Lindsay A.E.	209		40
Lineker G.W.	105		67
Lorimer H.H.	5		
Low A.R.	8	2	1
Lowdell A.E.	86		
Lowe H.	65		
Ludford G.A.	75		8
Lunn T.H.	86		
Lyle A.	1		
Lyman C.C.	46		10
Lyons A.T.	54		3
Mabbutt G.V.	433	16	27
MacFarlane D.	21		2
Mackay D.C.	268		42
Maddison G.	40		
Mahorn P.G.	1		
Marchi A.V.	232		7
Marshall W.H.	1		
Mason T.L.	7		1
Massey F.J.	1		
Mazzon G.	4	1	
McAllister D.	172	4	9
McClellan S.B.	68		29
McCormick J.	137		26
McDonald D.H.	2		
McDonald R.J.	109		
McGrath R.C.	38	8	5
McMahon G.	2		
McNab N.	72	9	3
McTavish J.K.	37		3
McTavish R.	11		2
Meads T.	184		6
Medley L.D.	150		45
Medwin T.C.	197		65
Meek J.	45		15
Messer A.T.	50		2
Metgod J.A.B.	12	7	
Middlemiss H.	244		52
Miller L.R.	56		22
Miller P.R.	208	2	7
Mimms R.A.	37		
Minter W.J.	243		95
Minton J.S.T.	2		1
Moncur J.F.	21	11	1
Moores I.R.	29	4	6
Moran J.	12		
Moran P.	36	22	2
Morgan R.E.	68	2	8
Morris T.H.	63		2
Morrison J.A.	133		88
Morton J.C.	2		
Mullery A.P.	312		25
Murphy P.	38		14
Nayim	112	17	11
Naylor T.M.P.	243	6	
Neighbour J.E.	119	15	8
Nethercott S.D.	32	12	
Newman E.H.	30		7
Nicholls J.M.	124		
Nicholson W.E.	314		6
Norman M.	357		16
O'Callaghan E.	252		93
Oliver W.	2		
O'Reilly G.M.	45	6	
Osborne F.R.	210		78
Osgood K.	113	1	13
O'Shea T.J.	3	2	
Owen A.W.	1		
Page A.E.	55		
Parks A.	37		
Pearce J.W.	141	33	21
Pearson J.	47		
Perryman S.J.	655	2	31
Peters M.S.	189		46
Phypers E.	30		
Piper R.D.	1		
Pitt S.W.	1		
Polston A.	1	1	
Polston J.D.	24	7	1
Popescu G.	23		3
Possee D.J.	19		4
Poynton C.	152		3
Pratt J.A.	331	24	39
Price P.T.	39	4	
Ramsey A.E.	226		24
Rance C.S.	103		
Reddish J.	6		
Rees W.	11		3
Reynolds R.S.M.	86		
Richardson J.	38		
Ringrose A.A.	10		
Robb G.W.	182		53
Roberts G.P.	209	9	23
Roberts W.T.	4		2
Robertson J.G.	157	4	25
Robinson M.J.	6	1	2
Robinson S.	1	1	
Robshaw H.W.	1		
Robson M.A.	8	5	
Roe T.W.	7		4
Rosenthal R.	35	10	2
Ross J.D.	7		
Rowe A.S.	182		
Rowley R.W.M.	24		10
Ruddock N.	47	2	3
Rundle C.R.	28		12
Ryden J.J.	63		2
Sage W.	12		
Samways V.	193	28	11
Sanders A.W.	13		7
Sargent F.A.	93		23
Saul F.L.	116	4	37
Scarth J.W.	7		3
Scott J.	18		4
Scott K.W.	16		1
Sedgley S.P.	164	17	9
Seeburg M.P.	1		
Seed J.M.	229		64
Sharp B.	3		
Sharpe F.C.	2		1
Sheringham E.P.	99	3	52
Skinner G.E.H.	1		
Skinner J.F.	89		3
Skitt H.	212		
Smailes J.	16		3
Smith B.	291		9
Smith G.M.	38	4	1
Smith I.R.	2		
Smith J.	21		1
Smith J.M.A.	30		
Smith R.A.	271		176
Smy J.	17		6
Southey P.C.	1		
Sparrow H.	18		7
Spelman I.	28		2
Spiers C.H.	158		
Sproston B.	9		
Statham B.	24	4	
Stead M.J.	15	1	
Steel A.	1		
Steel D.	129		3
Steel R.L.	226		41
Stevens G.A.	147	7	6
Stevens L.W.G.	54		5
Stewart P.A.	131	5	28
Stimson M.	2	1	
Stokes A.E.	65		40
Tate J.A.	4		
Tattersall W.S.	44		3
Taylor A.	60		
Taylor P.J.	123	7	31
Thomas D.J.	87	7	1
Thomas M.A.	157	21	6
Thompson A.	153		20
Thorstvedt E.	173	2	
Tickridge S.	95		
Tomkin A.H.	2		
Toulouse C.H.	2		
Townley J.C.	3		2
Trailor C.H.	11		
Tull W.D.J.	10		2
Turner A.P.	20	12	3
Tuttle D.P.	13	3	
Uphill D.E.	6		2
Upton S.	2		
Van den Hauwe P.W.R.	116	6	
Venables T.F.	115	1	5
Villa R.J.	133	9	18
Waddle C.R.	138	1	33
Walden F.I.	215		21
Walford S.J.	2	1	
Walker I.M.	88	1	
Walley E.	5		
Walsh P.A.	128	44	19
Walters C.	106		
Walters W.E.	210		66
Walton J.	24		2
Want A.G.	50	4	
Ward R.A.	115		10
Watson K.E.	5		1
Webster F.J.	82		
Webster S.P.	3	1	
Weir W.F.	96		2
Weller K.	21	2	1
Wetton R.	45		
Whatley W.J.	226		2
Whitchurch C.H.	8		2
White J.A.	183		40
White S.E.	20		
Wilding H.T.O.	12		1
Wilkes F.	57		
Wilkie R.M.	1		
Willis A.	144	1	
Wilson C.	54		27
Withers C.F.	153		
Woodruff C.L.	10		1
Woods A.E.	6		
Woodward H.J.	63		1
Woodward V.J.	27		18
Woolcott R.A.	1		
Worley L.F.	1		
Wright A.M.	2		1
Yorath T.C.	48	4	1
Young A.S.	5		3
Young C.	4		
Young W.D.	54		3
Own goals			74

Note: Details relate to Football League/Premier League peacetime seasons from 1908-09 to 1994-95 inclusive. Total appearances column includes those as a used substitute shown in the second column.

Index

(Page numbers in italics refer to captions and illustrations)